Venice Reconsidered

Venice Reconsidered

The History and Civilization of an Italian City-State, 1297–1797

EDITED BY

John Martin and Dennis Romano

The Johns Hopkins University Press
BALTIMORE AND LONDON

© 2000 The Johns Hopkins University Press
All rights reserved. Published 2000
Printed in the United States of America on acid-free paper

Johns Hopkins Paperbacks edition, 2002
2 4 6 8 9 7 5 3 1

The Johns Hopkins University Press
2715 North Charles Street
Baltimore, Maryland 21218-4363
www.press.jhu.edu

Library of Congress Cataloging-in-Publication Data
will be found at the end of this book.
A catalog record for this book is available from the British Library.

ISBN 0-8018-7308-8 (pbk.)

In Memoriam

FELIX GILBERT
(1905–1991)

FREDERIC C. LANE
(1900–1984)

Contents

Preface   ix
List of Contributors   xv

Reconsidering Venice   I
JOHN MARTIN AND DENNIS ROMANO

Part I. The Setting

1 Toward an Ecological Understanding of the Myth of Venice   39
ELISABETH CROUZET-PAVAN

Part II. Politics and Culture

2 The *Serrata* of the Great Council and Venetian Society, 1286–1323   67
GERHARD RÖSCH

3 Hard Times and Ducal Radiance: Andrea Dandolo and the
   Construction of the Ruler in Fourteenth-Century Venice   89
DEBRA PINCUS

4 Was There Republicanism in the Renaissance Republics?
   Venice after Agnadello   137
EDWARD MUIR

5 Confronting New Realities: Venice and the Peace of Bologna, 1530 168
ELISABETH G. GLEASON

6 "A Plot Discover'd?" Myth, Legend, and the "Spanish"
   Conspiracy against Venice in 1618   185
RICHARD MACKENNEY

7　Opera, Festivity, and Spectacle in "Revolutionary" Venice:
　　Phantasms of Time and History　　　　　　　　　　　　　217
　　MARTHA FELDMAN

Part III. Society and Culture

8　Identity and Ideology in Renaissance Venice: The Third *Serrata*　　263
　　STANLEY CHOJNACKI

9　Behind the Walls: The Material Culture of Venetian Elites　　295
　　PATRICIA FORTINI BROWN

10　Elite Citizens　　　　　　　　　　　　　　　　　　　339
　　JAMES S. GRUBB

11　Veronese's High Altarpiece for San Sebastiano: A Patrician
　　Commission for a Counter Reformation Church　　　　　365
　　PETER HUMFREY

12　Early Modern Venice as a Center of Information and
　　Communication　　　　　　　　　　　　　　　　　389
　　PETER BURKE

13　Toward a Social History of Women in Venice: From the
　　Renaissance to the Enlightenment　　　　　　　　　　420
　　FEDERICA AMBROSINI

14　Slave Redemption in Venice, 1585–1797　　　　　　　454
　　ROBERT C. DAVIS

Part IV. After the Fall

15　The Creation of Venetian Historiography　　　　　　491
　　CLAUDIO POVOLO

Index　521

Preface

THE CONJUNCTION IN 1997 of two anniversaries—one associated with the birth, the other with the death, of the Venetian Republic—provided the inspiration for this volume. The year 1297 is the date traditionally associated with the establishment of the city's republican regime. According to some accounts, it was in that year that membership in the city's supreme legislative body was first legally defined in an act known as the *Serrata* (Closing of the Great Council). Ever since, historians have looked upon this effort to limit membership in the city's ruling class to a select set of nearly two hundred families as the inaugural event in the creation of the Venetian constitution. The year 1797, by contrast, marked the collapse of the Republic. On 12 May of that year, with Napoleon Bonaparte's troops positioned at the edge of the lagoon, the Great Council, which was filled with legislators many of whom were direct descendants of the men who had established the Republic at the end of the thirteenth century, hastily voted itself out of existence. The Republic had endured for five hundred years—half a millennium.

Taking these anniversaries as our point of departure, we invited leading scholars from across the disciplines to reflect upon the city's history and civilization, to question old verities and pose new questions. In particular, we asked them to take John R. Hale's volume of a quarter-century ago, *Renaissance Venice*—a book that defined Venetian studies for a generation—as a model. The result was a three-day conference at Syracuse University in September 1997 at which approximately one hundred seventy scholars and students, most of them from Europe and North America, came together to explore the significance of Venice and its past. Many of the papers presented at the conference have been revised and recast and are presented here.

The picture of Venice that emerges from these essays is, we believe, strikingly different from earlier portrayals of the Republic's history. First, the traditional chronology of Venetian history, including the significance of the years

1297 and 1797, is itself being rethought. The Serrata, the act that gave republican Venice its form, is now seen, not as a moment of legislative definition, but rather as an ongoing political and social process that would inform Venetian politics throughout the Republic's history. Similarly, while the fall of Venice to Napoleon signaled the end of the Republic, it simultaneously marked the beginning of debate about a new kind of Venetian society under foreign aegis and sparked renewed commentary on Venice's republican past. It is no longer possible to isolate the history of the Republic between the dates 1297 and 1797. At the same time, scholars continue to debate the significance of other turning points in Venetian history, although consensus seems to be building around the view, first presented in essays by Gaetano Cozzi and Felix Gilbert in the Hale volume, that the first half of the sixteenth century marked a particularly crucial moment of reorientation and redefinition.

That volume also contained, in essays by Stanley Chojnacki on the composition of the patriciate and David Herlihy on the population of Verona, some of the first products of what was then called the "new" social history. That trickle has turned into a river, resulting in an almost complete change in our perceptions of Venetian society. The old vision of Venetian society as rigidly defined, tripartite, and hierarchical, with the patricians maintaining a particular monopoly over political and cultural power, is collapsing under a mountain of evidence demonstrating that social categories, such as patrician and *cittadino* (citizen), were ever changing and evolving. The study of women, gender, and nonelites has had a particularly salutary effect, encouraging scholars to question images of Venetian society derived from legal texts and theoretical treatises and present a more nuanced picture alert to contestation as well as to consensus.

The study of culture is also bearing rich fruit as scholars of art, music, and literature bring their expertise to questions long associated with social and political history, and vice versa. In particular, through their studies of patronage they have illuminated the mechanisms and processes by which patricians and *popolani* alike created a vision of society and themselves. And through their analyses of the meanings and functions of art, music, and architecture they have begun to explore variants of the myth of Venice—that nearly inexhaustible repertoire of stories the Venetians told themselves about themselves. Perhaps the most significant development in Venetian studies signaled by this volume is its truly interdisciplinary nature today.

Indeed, it is the value of an interdisciplinary approach for a grasp of Venetian history that this volume emphasizes. We have long been aware of the multiplicity of angles or perspectives from which Venice is studied. In 1979–80, for example, when we were both first in Venice for our doctoral research, we found ourselves surrounded by fellow scholars of the most diverse interests. Then, as now, the Venetian archives were an interdisciplinary site of the first order where scholars from art history, musicology, and literature took their places next to students of politics, society, and the economy. Conversations over coffee were intellectually stimulating. It was clear at once that scholars of Venice, despite the diversity of their fields, inevitably share an interest in one another's work. Accordingly, our goal in bringing together the varied contributions to this volume was never to offer a comprehensive overview of Venice's past. Rather we have sought to convey to readers the dynamism of the field and the ways in which scholars from different disciplines might enter into dialogue with one another. The themes found in this volume—the collapse of the old chronological boundaries of Venetian history, the emphasis on fluidity and process in the study of Venetian politics and society, the intrinsic role of art, music, and literature in fashioning the way Venetians understood and viewed themselves—and the willingness of scholars in many different fields of expertise to engage one another suggest that the future of Venetian studies is bright indeed. It is our hope that the essays we present here will inspire a new generation of students in a variety of fields to continue to raise new questions about the history of this Republic—in short, to reconsider Venice yet again.

THE MAKING OF THIS BOOK has been a pleasure, and it is a privilege now to express our appreciation to the people who helped make it possible. Our first debt of gratitude must go to the Gladys Krieble Delmas Foundation. This institution, which has long been a friend to Venetian studies, offered a significant grant that underwrote a major portion of the expenses for the 1997 conference at Syracuse University from which the essays in this volume developed. We also received substantial funding and support from the Ray Smith Symposium Series of the Humanities Council of the College of Arts and Sciences of Syracuse University, the President's Office at Trinity University, the Syracuse University Library Associates, the dean of the Maxwell School of Citizenship and Public Affairs at Syracuse, and the departments of history at both institutions. As a complement to our meeting, Four Seasons Baroque performed a concert of Venetian music, the Lowe Art Gallery mounted an exhibit of Venetian prints and paintings, and the Special Collections Department of the Syracuse University Library provided a display of *venetiana* from the Leopold von Ranke Collection—each reminding us how very much Venetian culture continues to fascinate and delight us. For the latter, we are especially grateful for the curatorial efforts of Mark Weimer, Peter Verheyen, and Holly Hurlburt. Moreover, it was a special pleasure to benefit from the experience and assistance of the Office of Conference Planning at Syracuse University. There both Peggy Van Arnam and Christine Adams went out of their way to help us pin down the myriad details that planners of international conferences inevitably confront. We also thank David Stam, university librarian emeritus and a trustee of the Delmas Foundation, whose counsel and support ensured that the conference would be an occasion not only for scholarship but also for conviviality.

Several distinguished scholars gave of their energy and expertise to serve as chairs and commentators at the 1997 meeting. This group included Benjamin Kohl, Marion Leathers Kuntz, Patricia Labalme, Brian Pullan, Ellen Rosand, and Juergen Schulz. Marino Berengo, though he was unable to attend the conference, sent his commentary, and Stanley Chojnacki graciously filled in on his panel at the last minute. The insights and comments of these scholars not only enriched the discussions at our gathering but enhanced each of the essays that follow as well. Indeed, we are grateful to all who attended the conference and whose conversation and participation helped shape our collective reflections on Venetian history and culture. We were very saddened, however, to learn of the untimely death of Professor Gerhard Rösch, whose contribution to this volume, based largely on his important book on the Serrata, appears below. Many others have also played important roles. Chief among them has been Eunice Herrington, of the history department at Trinity. Given the many complexities of a project of this kind, she was indispensable in the production of this text. Not only did she provide crucial support as an editor and manage with humor a frequently revised manuscript but she supported this project with her interest, insight, and intelligence—we are sincerely appreciative for all she has done. We also thank Frances Bockus, Patricia Bohrer, Wendy Edler, and Evelyn Luce for their crucial support along the way.

Henry Tom, our editor at the Johns Hopkins University Press, has played a key role. An active partner since the inception of the idea for this volume, he attended the conference, gave us early feedback about the papers, and has maintained an active interest in the project ever since. To him and to Joanne Allen, our copyeditor, we are most grateful, as we are to the readers for the press, whose comments have served in several important ways to strengthen this book.

From their very different perspectives Felix Gilbert and Frederic C. Lane, both of whom were born at the beginning of the last century, illuminated the history of Venice with clarity and passion. Their writings and teaching continue to play an important role in the nurturing of the study of Venice as a new century begins. We dedicate this volume to their memory.

Contributors

Federica Ambrosini is a professor of Venetian history at the University of Padua.

Patricia Fortini Brown is a professor of art and archaeology at Princeton University.

Peter Burke is a professor of cultural history at the University of Cambridge and a fellow of Emmanuel College.

Stanley Chojnacki is a professor of history at the University of North Carolina, Chapel Hill.

Elisabeth Crouzet-Pavan is a professor of medieval history at the University of Paris IV Sorbonne.

Robert C. Davis is an associate professor of history at Ohio State University.

Martha Feldman is an associate professor of music at the University of Chicago.

Elisabeth G. Gleason is a professor emeritus of the University of San Francisco.

James S. Grubb is a professor of history at the University of Maryland—Baltimore County.

Peter Humfrey is a professor of art history at the University of St Andrews.

Richard Mackenney is a reader in history at the University of Edinburgh.

John Martin is a professor of history at Trinity University.

Edward Muir is the Clarence L. Ver Steeg Professor in the Arts and Sciences at Northwestern University.

Debra Pincus is a professor emeritus of the University of British Columbia and guest curator at the National Gallery of Art, Washington, D.C.

Claudio Povolo is professor of the history of political institutions at the University of Venice.

Dennis Romano is a professor of history at Syracuse University.

Gerhard Rösch was a professor of history at the Westfälische Wilhelms-Universität Münster before his death in 1999.

Venice Reconsidered

Reconsidering Venice

JOHN MARTIN AND DENNIS ROMANO

VENICE was not only one of the greatest cities of medieval and early modern Europe, it was also one of Europe's most enduring republics, an expansive empire and, from the fifteenth century on, an imposing regional state. At the height of its power in the sixteenth century, the city of Venice counted nearly 170,000 souls, with a population of more than two million in its subject territories. Its republican constitution, which took shape in the late thirteenth century, when the formidable Edward I was the king of England and the pope was Boniface VIII, stood for five hundred years, until its fall to Napoleon on 12 May 1797. Its empire reached from the Alps, through the cities, towns, and villages of northeastern Italy, across the Adriatic to Istria, Dalmatia, Corfu, Crete, and Cyprus. A maritime power, Venice served as an entrepôt for trade between Europe and the Middle East, and as early as the thirteenth century its merchants (possibly including Marco Polo) traveled as far as India and China. Crucially, the wealth derived at first from trade and then from industry (primarily textiles) helped Venice remain independent from foreign control down to the end of the eighteenth century.

Medieval and early modern Venice was also one of the great cultural capitals of Europe. It was home to scores of artists, musicians, and writers of international stature. Indeed, it is difficult to think of Venice without also thinking of Giovanni Bellini, Andrea Palladio, Veronica Franco, Giovanni Gabrieli, Paolo Sarpi, Carlo Goldoni, Antonio Vivaldi, and Giambattista Tiepolo, to name only some of Venice's major creative figures. Nearby Padua, which had been under Venetian control since 1405, was the site of one of the most influential universities of the Renaissance, and from the late fifteenth to the mid-seventeenth century Venice was one of the leading centers of printing in the world. That the city of Venice was itself, as a man-made island, an ecological improbability—a frail construction in the center of a coastal enclave protected from the sea by a string of thin barrier islands (the *lidi*)—has had the inevitable result of making Venice one of the most fascinating and thus one of the most intensively studied societies in history.[1]

Not surprisingly, scholars have traveled to Venice for the most varied reasons. Some have sought in the shimmering mosaics of its churches echoes of the city's Byzantine past and especially of the role Venice played as the link between Europe and Asia. Others have pored over fading account books and maritime contracts and explored the canteens of its decaying Arsenal, the state shipyard, in search of the origins of modern capitalism. Still others have conjured up—in Titian's sumptuous Venuses, in the autobiographical writings of Giacomo Casanova, and in the drawing rooms of eighteenth-century palaces—an erotic past seemingly alien to the modern spirit. But Venetian history and civilization are inevitably far greater than any one narrative can encompass. There are simply too many Venices, too many unknown dimensions. Just when one believes one is beginning to follow the story line, Venice transmogrifies and, both in spite of and because of the richness of its archives and artistic treasures, is again a mystery, an enigma, an indecipherable maze of interweaving stories, false and true.

Nonetheless, Venice does offer a central story, one that acts as a constant in the ever-changing complexity of its history. It is the story of Venetian stability. Other states, whether in Italy or north of the Alps, were subject to frequent change in the nature of their rule. Venice's longevity as a republic made it an exception. Indeed, this aspect of Venetian exceptionalism, combined with many other of its remarkable elements, came together in the writings of humanists and other panegyrists to develop what would come to be known as the "myth" of Venice. The myth, which first emerged as a coherent and influential representation of the city in the late Middle Ages, portrays Venice as an ideal republic, a strong maritime empire, and an independent state in which the Venetian nobles were devoted to the ideals of civic humanism and the commercial virtues of sobriety, hard work, and self-sacrifice. Venice, that is, appeared to be a city like no other. Moreover, whereas other towns were torn by internal discord, Venice, as Petrarch observed as early as the fourteenth century, was stable, ruled by wise laws. It was a new Sparta. It was the Serenissima, the most serene republic.[2]

Yet Venice has not always been represented in a positive light. Alongside the view that Venice was an open, just, tolerant, and benevolent republic, a countermyth portrayed Venice as a repressive state, harshly governed by a decadent and secretive oligarchy. According to this antimyth, which first took shape as Venice began to expand its power over the *terraferma,* or the mainland towns and villages, of northeastern Italy in the early fifteenth century, a small circle of aristocrats not only controlled the levers of political power in Venice itself but also sought to place the rest of Italy under its dominion.[3] "One sees here a universal hatred against them," Machiavelli wrote of the Venetians in a dispatch to the Florentine government in 1503, alluding to what he and many of his contemporaries saw as a Venetian campaign to place all of Italy under its rule.[4] By the early seventeenth century, as Richard Mackenney's contribution to this volume makes clear, the antimyth had struck a different key. Venice was represented not as hungry for domination but rather as an oppressive and secretive tyranny. It was, however, in the eighteenth century that the countermyth assumed a coherent form. For by then Enlightenment republicanism had made the Venetian Republic, with its franchise restricted to a well-defined nobility of birth (at that time limited to approximately 2 percent of the city's population), seem an anachronism in an age of more democratic aspirations. Several critics, notably Jean-Jacques Rousseau, who spent the year 1743–44 as secretary to the French ambassador to Venice, found the Venetian government secretive and repressive. In *The Social Contract* (1762) Rousseau characterized the Republic as a "simulacrum" of the real thing and went so far as to condemn the Council of Ten as "a tribunal of blood." In his *Confessions* (1770) Rousseau underscored the decadence of Venetian society, which he famously connected to the "defects in that Republic's highly vaunted constitution." He did, however, admire Venetian music, not only the exquisite performances of its operas and conservatories but also the popular songs sung in the city's taverns and in its streets.[5]

These two powerful representations—one a myth that idealizes Venice, the other an antimyth that vilifies it—have played a decisive role in shaping the way scholars approach Venice, its history, and its civilization. As Claudio Povolo's essay in this volume shows, the first major modern history of the Republic, Pierre Antoine Noël Daru's *Histoire de la République de Venise,* published in eight volumes (1815–19), portrays Venice as decadent, oligarchic, and incapable of reform. Given his loyalty to Napoleon, whom he served both during and after the Italian campaign, Daru's harsh historical treatment of Venice can be read in part as a partisan attack on a political system he himself had helped to destroy. Nonetheless, in the early nineteenth century, despite occasional protestations from Venetian scholars who maintained (correctly) that his documentary evidence was largely unreliable, Daru's interpretation of the Republic was widely shared, as such literary works as Lord Byron's *Marino Faliero, Doge of Venice* (1823) and James Fenimore Cooper's *The Bravo: A Venetian Story* (1834) illustrate.[6] Indeed, in a recent book Povolo has even made the tantalizing suggestion that the masterpiece of modern Italian literature, Alessandro Manzoni's *The Betrothed,* published in three volumes in 1825–27, which portrays the repressive rule of aristocrats over their peasants in seventeenth-century Lombardy, was based on the record of a trial from the early-seventeenth-century Veneto.[7] And the countermyth exercised a considerable hold over John Ruskin as well, whose *Stones of Venice* (1851–53), while celebrating the creativity and individualism of the medieval craftsman, deplored the decline in artistic talent and vitality in the period beginning with the Renaissance, when, in Ruskin's view, medieval liberties were suffocated by an increasingly repressive state.[8]

It was not until the mid-nineteenth century, with the publication of Samuele Romanin's *Storia documentata di Venezia,* that modern historians effectively resurrected the positive myth of the Republic.[9] Romanin's work owed its documentary rigor largely to the example of Leopold von Ranke, who not only mined the Venetian archives for his studies of early modern European politics but himself contributed three well-researched essays to Venetian history.[10] But Romanin's project was also shaped by the climate of the time, which encouraged scholars to view the Venetian Republic in the context of Italian unity.[11] Indeed, much of the scholarship of the late nineteenth and early twentieth centuries focused on constitutional and legal developments as historians sought to uncover the medieval roots of the modern nation-state. Thus, like historians of England and France who looked back to the early development of monarchic power and parliamentary rule, historians of Venice sought to reconstruct the city's constitutional development as the Byzantine protectorate with its quasi-monarchic doge slowly evolved into a republican commune with a ducal head of state. For many of these historians, moreover, the Venetian polity reached a state of constitutional perfection around 1310, in the wake of the Querini-Tiepolo conspiracy, with the creation of the Council of Ten, a golden age that not coincidentally corresponded with the period of Venetian commercial greatness.[12] Many of these same historians considered the later centuries, when Venice, like the other Italian medieval city-states, fell under foreign domination, less worthy of consideration, especially as these were the years when Italy failed to make a smooth transition to nationhood.[13]

Indeed, from the mid-nineteenth to the mid-twentieth century the Venetian myth would continue to find its proponents both among scholars who turned to the Republic as a model for their own times and among those who saw in the secretiveness and the repressiveness of the Venetian state an example of a political system to be avoided. Both the myth and the antimyth, that is, have enjoyed an extraordinary afterlife in which scholars have, whether consciously or unconsciously, molded their interpretations of Venetian history in order to further their own political or cultural agendas. Remarkably, this interpretative dialectic between myth and countermyth continued to define Venetian studies in the first three decades after the Second World War. In the scholarship of that generation it is possible to distinguish two relatively clearly delineated interpretations of Venetian history. Some historians tended to celebrate Venice's significance as a model republic. In Italy the most significant contribution to this perspective was Gaetano Cozzi's *Il doge Niccolò Contarini* (1958), which analyzed an entire generation of Venetian nobles who, beginning at the end of the sixteenth century, emerged both as reformers of the Venetian constitution, seeking to limit the power of the Council of Ten, and as articulate critics of the papacy's efforts in the early seventeenth century to curtail Venice's independence.[14] Indeed, for Cozzi—as for several scholars—the Interdict Controversy of 1606–7 became the emblematic struggle that defined the Venetian Republic as tolerant and open, free from the tyranny of the Counter Reformation Church, animated by an aristocracy steeped in the values of civic humanism and evangelism, and committed to commerce and an irenic diplomacy.

But it was American scholars who developed the theme of Renaissance republicanism most fully. In its most exaggerated form this historiography sought in the Renaissance republics of Venice and Florence the origins of an unbroken and transatlantic republican tradition, a tradition reborn in new lands through the transmission of a few central concepts and texts. While the fundamental work in this historiography was Hans Baron's *Crisis of the Early Italian Renaissance,* which focused on Florentine developments, Venetian historians were quick to follow suit, with Baron himself leading the way with his studies of Venetian humanist traditions.[15] In the United States the theme of Renaissance republicanism was most fully adopted by Frederic C. Lane and William Bouwsma, both of whom served as president of the American Historical Association. In his 1965 presidential address Lane, the founder of Venetian studies in the United States, placed Venice within the tradition of Western republicanism. Lane's specialties were economic and maritime history, but he did not hesitate to put Venice to ideological use. In the address he praised late medieval Venetian capitalism as a precondition for Renaissance republicanism—"the most distinctive and significant aspect of . . . the Italian city-states"—and offered in the guise of history what was in fact a late-twentieth-century version of the myth of Venice:

> The Venetian Republic gained a high reputation for the success with which it solved many problems in state building that were to confront European governments during the next few centuries, namely, upholding public law over private privilege and vengeance, curbing the Church's political influence, and inventing mercantilist measures to increase wealth. Byzantine traditions and the relative weakness of professional organizations at Venice made it easier to establish there a coordination of social life under the sovereignty of the Republic.[16]

Three years later, in his *Venice and the Defense of Republican Liberty,* Bouwsma argued that Paolo Sarpi and others in Venice revived the Florentine humanist discourse of republican liberty during Venice's struggle with the papacy in the Interdict Crisis. As the heroic wording of its title suggests, this book was a further elaboration of Cozzi's study.[17] As a corollary to their civic humanist emphasis, American scholars, with very few exceptions, have been concerned, at least until recently, with the capital city only, viewing the Renaissance from a decidedly urban perspective.

Other scholars, by contrast, have stressed the Venice of the antimyth. From their perspective, the central problem was not Venice's role as an Exemplary Republic but rather its decadence. To Fernand Braudel—Venice stood at the center of his celebrated study *The Mediterranean and the Mediterranean World in the Age of Philip II*—Venetian economic history was largely the story of the Republic's inability to adjust to the shifting economic structures of the long sixteenth century.[18] Intellectual historians have also stressed Venice's decadence, especially in the eighteenth century, when Enlightenment ideas, though known in the Veneto, had little impact on the way the Venetian aristocracy shaped either its political or its economic policies.[19] But the antimyth has found its most articulate expression in political history. The two most influential works on the Venetian state have been Marino Berengo's *La società veneta alla fine del Settecento* (1956) and Angelo Ventura's *Nobiltà e popolo nella società veneta del '400 e '500* (1964), both of which explored especially the relationship between the capital city (the *dominante*) and its mainland territories (the *dominio*). Berengo viewed the decadence of the Venetian state as a consequence of the aristocracy's inability to share power and its abuse of justice, its twisting the courts to serve its own interests. Ventura concentrated on the dominante's exploitation of the dominio, especially its high-handed techniques, which undercut the autonomy and authority of local notables. For him the Venetian territorial state was feudal, backward, and an inevitable target of Napoleon.[20] To oversimplify, one might say that alongside the rather triumphalist history of the Venetian Republic celebrated primarily by American scholars, Italian scholars in the postwar period have looked harder at the realities of Venice as a regional state, stressing the degree to which its political and legal institutions varied from city to city and place to place.

But what is the status of the myth and the antimyth today, especially among scholars who were born after 1945, many of whom are represented in this volume? In a provocative and important essay published in 1986 James S. Grubb maintained that there were reasons to believe that the myth of Venice, while it would never be discarded entirely, had lost its power for this "younger" generation, for whom, in Grubb's words, "neither myth nor antimyth seems compelling." And Grubb's explanation, at least with respect to the evident decline of the positive, celebratory myth of the Venetian Republic, is largely one of generational experience. "As memory of Nazism, Fascism, and the Cold War fades in a generation of historians born since 1945," Grubb observed, "the urgency for a model of a free society's resistance to tyranny has been blunted."[21] In another lucid survey of Venetian historiography Nicholas S. Davidson has made much the same point. The immediate postwar generation, preoccupied with the problem of building strong democratic states in the wake of fascism and war, Davidson argues, naturally turned to Venice as a model republic. But the intellectual outlook of the more recent generation of Venetian scholars has been shaped by an entirely different set of experiences, above all by upheavals in the social and political structures of the Western democracies in the late 1960s. As Grubb trenchantly writes, "The logical implications of an exemplary Venetian Republic, with blue-blood paternalism on the one hand and happily powerless masses on the other, are dubious lessons for our own day—especially if we take seriously Ventura's demonstration of the patriciate's systematic abuses of justice, tax evasion, fiscal corruption, abuse of office, and in general thorough exploitation of class privilege at the expense of underlings."[22]

Although it is certainly true that the celebratory myth of Venice has witnessed an eclipse in the historical writing of the most recent generation of Venetianists, it is by no means clear that Venetian studies have escaped entirely the interpretative framework of these competing representations of Venetian society. For whereas the preceding generation found Venice a model of an ordered, well-regulated society, the more recent scholarship on Venice, as Davidson eloquently argues, has tended to highlight fissures, tensions, contradictions, and elements of disorder in Venice. "What we see in recent Venetian historiography," he observes, "is a shift in interest from order to disorder, from orthodoxy to dissent, from the center of power to the broader social context."[23] Thus, in the current scholarship Venice is no longer represented as the Exemplary Republic. On the contrary, much recent scholarship has highlighted Venetian domination of the terraferma and, in particular, the institutional and legal framework within which Venice ruled its subject territories. Perhaps the most significant work in this respect has been Claudio Povolo's *L'intrigo dell'onore: Poteri e istituzioni nella Repubblica di Venezia tra Cinque e Seicento,* though the field has been crowded with both Italian and non-Italian scholars.[24] But the shift in emphasis has also been true of studies of the dominante, with recent scholarship underscoring social and cultural tensions.[25] However, this generation has been interested not only in tensions, approaching Venetian history in the spirit of what Paul Ricoeur calls "a hermeneutics of suspicion," but also in inclusion. Thus there is a profusion of new works on women, Jews, workers, vagabonds, and other long-neglected groups.[26] Indeed, because it was so profoundly multicultural and diverse, Venice seems especially suited to current sensitivities and concerns, though precisely which version of the myth lives on is less evident. Perhaps it is the myth of Venice as a multicultural metropolis—with its diverse ethnic subcultures of Greeks, Germans, Jews, Turks, and Armenians living in relative harmony—that resonates most strongly with the concerns of scholars today.

But even if in certain respects the dialectic between myth and antimyth perdures, Grubb was likely right that the power and appeal of the myth have been attenuated. This is largely the result of a number of studies that began in the late 1950s and continued into the seventies and even eighties, in which—for the first time—the myth itself became the object of interest, an interest that continues to animate current scholarship. Indeed, beginning with Gina Fasoli's and Franco Gaeta's seminal articles on this subject in 1958 and 1961, finding support in art historical studies such as Staale Sinding-Larsen's *Christ in the Council Hall* (1974), and continuing to Grubb's essay itself, myriad scholars have helped to make clear that, although it should not be viewed as a representation of Venetian realities, the myth of Venice has nonetheless played an important role in shaping Venetian society, politics, and culture.[27] They have, in short, not only specified the fundamental attributes of the myth but also shown how the myth served particular functions and interests. In Fasoli's view, the central elements of the myth were the beauty of the city, the stability of its government, the greatness of its empire, the piety of its citizens, and, finally, its *libertà,* its exceptional ability to preserve its independence from foreign power. On the most basic level, the work of Fasoli, Gaeta, and others has made it possible to analyze the myth itself as a kind of constitutive discourse. This discourse functioned not only within Venetian society itself, where it served to legitimate the power of certain ruling groups and to provide people with a means of making sense of their social order, but also abroad, where—in late-fifteenth-century Florence, in seventeenth-century England and Holland, and in eighteenth-century America—Venice became a model for republicans, a central element in what William Bouwsma has called "the political education of Europe."[28] The identification of the power of the myth as a discourse also had a tremendously important effect on the study of Venetian art and music, whose portrayal of the city's history, legends, and, yes, myth could now be fruitfully analyzed. From the mosaics and the music of San Marco to the rich and variegated cultural life of the city's churches, monasteries, guilds, and confraternities, art, music, literature, and theater have come to be seen as vehicles that celebrated and reproduced Venetian culture.[29]

But the analysis of the myth as discourse also has significant implications for our approach to Venetian history. It suggests that scholars do not have to analyze the history of Venice from within the framework of Venice either as Exemplary Republic or as Repressive State. In short, we are no longer obligated to rehash old battles. This does not mean that our studies of Venice will be more objective than those of an earlier generation, but it has led to a set of decidedly new questions and, more significantly, to a new set of assumptions or a new paradigm in Venetian studies. In the history of Venetian politics it is now possible to view the legal and governing institutions not merely as the expression of classical models but as rooted in the complex social and economic structures of the city and its territories. In social and economic history it is now possible to discover beneath the images and representations of Venetian constitutional stability and social harmony an almost incessant fluidity of status groups and tradesmen. Finally, in cultural history this shift in perspective has made culture itself an integral part of history, facilitating the tying of such fields as intellectual history, art history, music history, and even the study of ritual more closely than ever to the concerns of political and social historians.

THE STUDY of Italian political history has been shaped by a tendency, evident at least since Machiavelli, to classify states as either republics or principalities. "All the states, all the dominions that have held sway over men, have been either republics or principalities," Machiavelli wrote in the first sentence of the first chapter of *The Prince,* a distinction he reinforced by devoting this famous book to a discussion of principalities (seignorial regimes or monarchies) and his longer, less well known but nonetheless influential *Discourses* to an analysis of republics.[30]

To a large degree this dichotomy has also shaped the traditional understanding of Venetian political history. As the preceding discussion of the myth of Venice makes clear, the republican history of Venice is well known. But if there is general agreement that the city of Venice should be characterized as a republic, there is no consensus about how to characterize Venice's rule over both the terraferma and the *stato da mar* (its far-flung dependencies and colonies in the eastern Mediterranean). For the Venetian government acted not as a republic but rather as a kind of collective prince over its diverse subject territories, whether the smaller cities and towns of the terraferma, the powerful feudal families, whose power the Venetian government contained but was never able to break, or the various merchant colonies of its maritime empire. From the vantage point of traditional scholarship Venice was somehow both a republic and a principality. Accordingly, one early-twentieth-century scholar described the Venetian political system as a diarchy; others have thought of it as a kind of federation.[31] Yet while both these terms help conceptualize the apparent contradictions in the Venetian polity, neither succeeds in elucidating how the Venetian state worked in practice.

Recent work on Venice, however, has moved away from these rather abstract formulations and concentrated on the distribution of power. Thus scholars, formerly intent on explicating the constitutional and institutional history of the Republic, have grown increasingly conscious of numerous subtle shifts in the distribution of power among the Venetian elite, alert to fissures within the nobility, and suspicious of the motives of various patrician groups. For example, in their contributions to this volume Gerhard Rösch and Stanley Chojnacki make clear that the development of both the patriciate and the governing institutions of the state was an ongoing process. In a similar fashion, Debra Pincus enriches our understanding of the doge's role in the late medieval period. Using art—in this case ducal tomb monuments of the fourteenth century—she demonstrates, among other things, that there was no constitutional fixity with regard to the doge, that ducal power was renegotiated during each ducal reign and that as the doge's legal power was circumscribed his sacred and ritual power increased. And Elisabeth Crouzet-Pavan suggests here, as she does in her magisterial study *"Sopra le acque salse": Espaces, pouvoir et société à Venise,* a dynamic interaction between the physical environment and human action in the development of the Venetian state. In her view, it was the need, evident from the later fifteenth century on, to contain the now menacing waters of the lagoon that promoted new bureaucracies and new powers of the state.[32] Although they differ in emphasis and in focus, these studies resonate with the later work of Cozzi and others whose analyses of Venetian political magistracies, especially those devoted to law, have demonstrated how certain institutions, most notably the Council of Ten, became ascendant in the sixteenth century in the wake of the war against the League of Cambrai.[33] Several other scholars, among them the German historians Volker Hunecke and Oliver Thomas Domzalski, as well as the Italian scholars Piero Del Negro and Giovanni Scarabello, have highlighted comparable shifts in the institutional and political histories of Venice in the seventeenth and eighteenth centuries.[34]

Just as scholars have tended to move away from an overidealized image of the Venetian Republic and learned to examine its history with closer attention to actual institutional, legal, and fiscal practices, historians have also developed a far more nuanced view of the Venetian state. As noted above, the works of Angelo Ventura and Marino Berengo served a generation ago to place the study of Venetian rule of the terraferma on a par with the analysis of the political history of the city. But it is doubtful that anyone could have predicted the enormous energy that would be devoted to this theme over the next thirty years—down to the present. In these analyses the study of institutions has remained central. Scholars have explored the role of the patrician administrators *(rettori, podestà, capitani)* that the Venetian government dispatched to the terraferma to protect its interests. In general the Venetians found it advantageous to undercut the authority of the local oligarchies while granting a certain formal recognition to the continuation of their institutions, legal and legislative. The process required a complicated balancing act. The Venetians, whose own outlook had been shaped largely by life in a commercial, cosmopolitan city, confronted a political mosaic on the terraferma of petty tyrants, local grandees, feudal lords, patrician elites, and peasant communes.[35] In addition to these secular powers, moreover, historians have also explored, though inadequately, the role of Venetian ecclesiastical administrators in the countryside, for virtually all of the bishops and most of the abbots of the greater houses were themselves members of important Venetian families, and they too exercised considerable authority in the Venetian state.[36] But it has become clear that a purely institutional approach does not cut deeply enough. Scholars have now begun to emphasize the importance of understanding the social, economic, and cultural matrices in which these institutions operated; they have been particularly successful in illuminating the development of agriculture and protoindustrialization on the terraferma, the interpenetration of city and countryside in such phenomena as *villegiatura,* and the image of the peasant in Venetian literature.[37] Much more attention is now given to the study of social practices and to microhistorical analyses. Not surprisingly, the picture that is emerging neither celebrates the expansion of Venetian power onto the terraferma nor condemns it as a simple act of repression of peripheral territories by a centralizing power.

On the contrary, scholars now approach the Venetian state as a complex mosaic of diverse political structures. In such cities as Brescia and Vicenza local oligarchies still clung to power, though their spheres of influence were often restricted by their Venetian lords. And in the countryside peasants often continued to enjoy a measure of freedom in their communal institutions. Indeed, recent scholarship has made clear that Ventura's celebrated thesis emphasizing the aristocratization of the landed elites and the erosion of traditional communal freedoms, while of enormous heuristic value, undoubtedly exaggerated the degree to which these traditional institutions and freedoms atrophied from the sixteenth century on. But Venetian administrators not only found it necessary to mediate between diverse councils and legal institutions in both the subject cities and the countryside; they also confronted the entrenched landed interests of great feudal families such as the Savorgnan in the Friuli. Accordingly, the early modern Venetian state can now be seen as a *regional state,* a phrase used by the eminent Italian political historian Giorgio Chittolini to describe the Italian political systems of this period not in terms of the traditional Machiavellian or classical vocabulary but rather in relation to their fundamental realities, namely, a significant concern for the security of their borders, an acceptance of the coexistence of multiple, even contradictory forms of political organization; a new appreciation of the perdurance and functionality of apparently irrational social practices such as feuds or clientalism; and, at least from the perspective of Enlightenment theories of the state, a complex blurring of the boundaries between public and private forms of power.[38]

Among Italian scholars, the more recent works of Cozzi and Povolo have been especially valuable in explicating the interplay of the varied institutions of the Venetian state as a mosaic of varied forms of political domination and subjugation.[39] Within American scholarship the work of Edward Muir has been especially compelling. In the essay he offers here Muir invites a dialogue with Italian scholarship by attempting to decipher the role republican ideology and republican practices played in binding together the Venetian regional state. As he does in his book *Mad Blood Stirring,* Muir presents a dizzyingly complex picture of Venetian and terraferma political culture in which currents of medieval republicanism (the *ben comune*), classically inspired Renaissance republicanism, and feudal and courtly traditions competed and intertwined all the way from the halls of the ducal palace in Venice to the rural communes of the Friuli. The connection Muir makes between these two traditions of scholarship, largely because of the degree to which it is based on the careful analysis of particular practices and discourses in well-defined contexts, opens an especially promising avenue for further research into Venetian political history.

What Muir and the other scholars who have begun work on these and related political themes have made clear is the need to go beyond purely legal and institutional perspectives. Future considerations of the development of the Venetian government will have to take into account the interaction of many factors, including the control of resources and the environment, bureaucratic infighting, patterns of feuding, patron-client relations, and evolving social and cultural practices. Even more urgent is the need to integrate or at least confront the American historiographical concern with republicanism and the Italian concern with the development of the regional state. While Muir's essay represents a promising beginning and there is already much work—for example, on the consequences of terraferma expansion for the distribution of power within the Venetian bureaucracy, which illustrates the impact of expansion on republican practice—scholars working in each tradition need to ask how their work might shed light on the concerns of scholars working in the other tradition. To give but one example, historians might explore the ways in which ducal imagery was reshaped by the acquisition of the mainland territory and what consequences, if any, this had for the distribution of power between the doge and the councils of government. Such a dialogue might also help scholars rethink the periodization of the republican traditions and of the regional state, both of which suffer in the existing literature either from a lack of diachronic refinement or from lingering dependence on a narrative of rise and decline.

Indeed, the fall of the Venetian Republic to Napoleon in 1797, when the Great Council voted itself out of existence, was a determining moment in the creation of that narrative—what we might call the organic model of Venetian history—for now Venice, like ancient Rome, could be understood to have had a rise to grandeur, a golden or imperial age, and a slow but inevitable decline, and the city could serve as another proof of the theory that the polity is analogous to the human body. Venice's organic history was most easily read through its imperial and economic fortunes. The fate of empire, from the first tentative efforts to control the northern Adriatic in the ninth and tenth centuries to the final attempts to resist the advance of the Turks in the seventeenth and eighteenth centuries, along with the story of Venice's rise to riches, including the dramatic turning point with the news in 1499 of a Portuguese fleet's arrival in India, seemed to confirm this theory and allowed historians to make sense of Venice's past. Other aspects of the Venetian experience, including society and art, were reinterpreted to accord with this model as well. Emblematic of efforts to trace a congruence between the cultural, political, and economic fortunes of the city and its underlying social structures is Pompeo Molmenti's monumental *Storia di Venezia nella vita privata,* first published in 1880 and now in its seventh edition, whose three chronologically arranged volumes bear the subtitles, *La Grandezza, Lo Splendore,* and *Il Decadimento.* The power of the model is such that it has continued to shape scholarship down to the late twentieth century, as a rapid survey of titles in the field makes clear.[40]

A model of the rise, splendor, and decline of Venetian civilization is no longer tenable. This is not to say that time and its charting did not play a central role in Venetian history. But Venetian notions of historical time were to some degree the product, as Patricia Fortini Brown has emphasized in her recent book *Venice and Antiquity,* of the city's lack of a Roman past.[41] Having no direct link to the classical and Christian chronologies that shaped the histories of other places and peoples, Venetians were free to create and shape their own past. As they rewrote their history, especially the story of the city's foundation, they identified particular moments of import: the *praedestinatio* of Saint Mark, the flight from Attila, the city's foundation on the Feast of the Annunciation, and the move from Malamocco to Rialto. Venetians were no less inventive at the time of the fall of the Republic. Indeed, as Martha Feldman makes clear in her contribution to this volume, one of the great moments in the rewriting of the past (as well as opera) occurred during the summer of 1797, after the Republic fell to Napoleon. In those revolutionary days the Venetians annihilated their own history as they attempted to turn the clock back to 1297 and the days before aristocratic "tyranny" began. In the long run, however, their efforts to define 1797 as a moment of rebirth and renewal collapsed beneath an alternative reading of that year as one of decline and death. Indeed, throughout the centuries, Venetians rewrote their history to tell again who they were. From the perspective of the lived experience of Venetians, that is, the temporal dimension was malleable; and the particular ways in which they described the origins of their city or their republic or their state tell us much about how they saw themselves.

IN HIS CELEBRATED HISTORY of the Renaissance, first published in 1860, the Swiss historian Jacob Burckhardt paid especial attention to two Italian cities, Venice and Florence. "Among the cities which maintained their independence are two of deep significance for the history of the human race," Burckhardt wrote, "Florence, the city of incessant movement, which has left us a record of the thoughts and aspirations of each and all who, for three centuries, took part in this movement, and Venice, the city of apparent stagnation and of political secrecy."[42] Burckhardt was wise to include the term *apparent* in this characterization, for recent work on Venice has radically transformed our understanding of the social and economic history of both the city and its subject territories. Indeed, we believe it fruitful to appropriate Burckhardt's phrase "the city of incessant movement," which he used to describe Florence, and apply it to Venice, for Venice, despite its appearance of stability, was a city of constant change in both its internal social arrangements and its relations with the outside world.

It has not always been easy to see beyond the facade of stability that has mesmerized observers of Venice from the Renaissance to Burckhardt and beyond. The most familiar representation of Venice, after all, has been that of a society of orders. This model, which placed the nobility at the summit of a hierarchy and the *popolani* at its base, originated with theorists of Venetian republicanism, who set about the task of explaining both the longevity of Venetian political institutions and the relative absence of social conflict in the city and its subject territories. Powerfully influenced by their knowledge of classical models and Roman history, these writers found the explanation for Venetian success in the Aristotelian and Polybian ideals of mixed government. Gasparo Contarini, the best known of these authors, argued in his *De magistratibus et republica Venetorum,* for example, that the classical forms of government—monarchy, aristocracy, and democracy—were institutionalized in Venice in the doge, the Senate, and the Great Council and that the city's social harmony was the result of a commitment on the part of the nobles to justice and the welfare of the populace.[43]

One consequence of this theorizing by Contarini and other contributors to the myth of Venice has been the canonization of the vision of Venetian society as consisting of well-defined orders arranged hierarchically. And, indeed it is useful to know that from the time of the Serrata to its fall to Napoleon five hundred years later the ruling class of the city—male nobles and their families— generally made up less than 4–5 percent of the population.[44] Only adult noble males had the right to sit in the Great Council and to participate in the political life of the Republic. Next in prestige were the *cittadini* (citizens), a diverse group comprising some 5–8 percent of the population whose privileges granted them entry into the state bureaucracy (to act, for example, as secretaries in the Ducal Chancery) or special commercial privileges as merchants. Many cittadini were among the wealthiest and most influential members of Venetian society.[45] Finally, at the base of this "hierarchy" were the artisans, shopkeepers, and workers, who accounted for the remaining 90 percent of the city's inhabitants. However, recent scholarship, much of it found in the essays included here, suggests that the received model of Venetian society as a rigidly hierarchical and tripartite one in which legal definitions of status were central, is collapsing under the weight of several trends—new readings by intellectual historians of the works of such political theorists as Contarini; a growing emphasis by historians of painting, sculpture, architecture, and music on the social and political functions of the arts in Venetian cultural life; and novel approaches by the practitioners of the "new" social history to previously neglected groups in Venetian society, especially women, artisans, and workers.

First, scholars are increasingly aware of the degree to which late medieval and early modern writers offered idealized images of Venice. While these representations had important cultural functions, they also often masked social and political realities. In this light, treatises such as Contarini's are now read less as roadmaps to Venetian society and more as artifacts of sixteenth- and seventeenth-century struggles for position, power, and place both within Venice and beyond. On this front Elisabeth Gleason's recent studies of Contarini, including her essay presented in this volume, and Margaret King's survey of humanism in the fifteenth century, in which she argues that the humanist writers sought to inculcate the value of *unanimitas* within the patriciate, are exemplary.[46]

A second, related development has been the introduction into the debate about society and social structure of a whole body of research, most of it carried out by historians of art, music, and literature, on a vast array of evidence from the realm of culture, traditionally defined. Much of this work, such as Peter Humfrey's examination of Soranzo family commissions at San Sebastiano, involves issues of patronage, including the ways elite families in particular used conspicuous acts of patronage and display to assert, establish, or maintain social prominence. But another body of work, represented here in the contributions of Patricia Brown and Martha Feldman, explores ways in which acts of patronage, consumption, and performance were themselves moments of contestation and negotiation over ever-shifting social boundaries.

Both the growing skepticism about the reliability of Venetian treatises and a new interest in the political and cultural uses of art for an understanding of Venetian society have been matched by a veritable explosion of work by social historians. One of the most promising lines of inquiry has been prosopographical, and its origins can be traced in large measure to Stanley Chojnacki's article in John Hale's *Renaissance Venice,* "In Search of the Venetian Patriciate." As Chojnacki noted in that piece, the lively and often contentious debates about the Serrata and its significance were waged largely in ignorance of the players involved; it was, and to some extent remains, unclear exactly who the nobles were at any particular moment in time.[47] The identification of large groups of individual actors or at least the construction of collective biographies is now proceeding on many fronts.[48] Another broad line of investigation among social historians entails examining practice, especially rites of passage, when critical choices (about marriage partners, sponsors and godparents, executors, etc.) needed to be made. Again Chojnacki's work is illustrative.[49] Many of these rites involved an individual's or a kin network's reaching beyond itself to establish links to other individuals, kinship groups, or even institutions. Hence, they allow historians to trace the constant re-creation of social structures and attitudes at moments of high-stakes decision making.

For example, in their essays included here Gerhard Rösch and Chojnacki demonstrate quite clearly that there was not one moment, the Serrata, when the qualifications for noble status and the qualifiers for that status were definitively established. Rather, during the course of the Republic's history nobility was continuously redefined (although there was a remarkable continuity among most of the constituent families). As Rösch's essay demonstrates, the Serrata should be viewed not as a legislative act but rather as a social and political evolution that began in the 1280s and took decades to accomplish. Reinforcing Rösch's findings, Chojnacki's study makes a convincing case that it is possible to discern a second and a third Serrata.[50] But even this third moment of definition, at the beginning of the sixteenth century, should not be considered conclusive, since additional adjustments were made in the seventeenth century, when entry into the nobility was put up for sale, and after the fall of the Republic, when the status of the Venetian nobility was redefined again, this time by the Austrian Habsburgs.[51] However, the nobility was not the only group whose status underwent constant redefinition. James Grubb's search for the cittadini suggests a similar lack of definition among that social group, and almost certainly a close study of various professions and a prosopography of guild leaders would yield similar results among the *popolo*.[52]

In fact, in recent years many social historians have turned their attention to the experience of the popolo. This constitutes a major shift in historiographical interest, for even a survey as recent as Frederic Lane's *Venice: A Maritime Republic* (1973) portrayed the working classes as playing almost no role in the story of Venetian development between the tumultuous decade of the 1260s, when the guilds were subordinated to the patriciate under the jurisdiction of the Giustizieri Vecchi, and the later sixteenth and seventeenth centuries, when manpower shortages in the navy once again brought guildsmen to the fore of the government's interest.[53] Moreover, traditionally, when the history of these groups has been given consideration, it has been largely in the context of noble- and cittadino-based charitable efforts and public-assistance programs or at the margins in studies of immigrant, minority, or heretical groups. But this scholarship has undergone significant shifts in the 1980s and 1990s as students of Venice, like their counterparts in other fields, have begun to examine the history of nonelite groups from new angles. In Venetian studies, Carlo Ginzburg's studies of popular beliefs among the peasants of the Friuli played an especially pivotal role. Ginzburg's preface to his now classic work *The Cheese and the Worms: The Cosmos of a Sixteenth-Century Miller,* first published in 1976, raised a number of enticing theoretical issues about the nature of the study of popular culture that have inspired an entire generation of scholars whose work explores groups such as the shipwrights and other workers of the Arsenal, fishermen from the parish of San Niccolò dei Mendicoli, household servants, witches, vagabonds and others long beyond the purview of historians.[54] Women too have become the subject of analysis. In addition to the researches of Chojnacki, which are by and large restricted to the lives of patrician women, such scholars as Federica Ambrosini, Monica Chojnacka, Joanne Ferraro, and Linda Guzzetti have begun to pull back the veil on the experience of popolano women as well.[55] Consequently, it is no longer possible to imagine the popolani as an unvariegated and inert mass passively dominated by the cittadini and the nobles. On the contrary, the term *popolani* covered a broad spectrum of individuals, from wealthy artisans and merchants (whose experience often paralleled that of the cittadini) to poor day laborers, washerwomen, and peasants.

From the essays included in this volume, questioning old verities and applying new methods, a picture of Venetian society emerges that is infinitely more complex than the one previously presented.[56] One of the most striking features of this new vision, as all these new research trends suggest, is the growing recognition on the part of scholars of social status and position as an ongoing process of definition and self- or group-assertion. Clearly, the earlier model of Venetian society as neatly tripartite is eroding. It is now evident that legal status was only one of several factors determining social position in Venice. Many of the essays included here suggest that cultural factors (including lifestyle, cultural patronage, religion, and gender) must be considered along with birth, wealth, and officeholding in thinking about how Venetians assessed their own (and others') place in society. The essays by Brown and Grubb both point to fluidity and lack of legal fixity. Brown's essay raises the issue of individual or family self-presentation through domestic space, problematizes the meaning of sumptuary laws, and underscores the importance of style of life in defining status. Grubb finds that at least one group among the cittadini appear to have asserted their status not through regular officeholding in the chancery but rather by their inclusion in chronicle lists of cittadino families. Nothing better illustrates just how complicated our picture of Venetian society has become than Federica Ambrosini's portrayal of a changing social and cultural climate in which women were often able to create and sustain certain options and freedoms despite the enormous restraints they confronted in a patriarchal setting.

Economic historians have also fundamentally altered our understanding of late medieval and early modern Venice. If an earlier generation celebrated Venice as an example, if not *the* example, of an emerging capitalism, more recent studies have moved away from an emphasis on the city itself as a center of trade and commerce to stress instead the variety of economic forms that co-existed throughout the Republic as a whole. This tendency was already present in the work of Frederic Lane. While most of his scholarship focused on aspects of maritime trade, capital accumulation, business practices, and banking—all aspects closely connected to the development of commercial capitalism—he was also one of the first to underscore the central role that industry and manufacturing came to play in the Venetian economy in the sixteenth century, as the city's privileged trading position as an entrepôt between Europe and the Middle East was threatened in the wake of the Portuguese circumnavigation of Africa.[57] To be sure, trade remains an important theme, as one might expect, but the history of industry both in the city itself and throughout the mainland has become a major area of investigation. Economic historians no longer emphasize the problem of the origins of capitalism but examine instead the complex ways in which the Venetian economy both shaped and was shaped by social and political realities.

This has been especially true in three areas. First, like their counterparts in political history, economic historians have substituted an analytical framework of transformation and adjustment for the more traditional narratives of growth and decay.[58] Second, and again the parallels to recent trends in political history are striking, they have moved away from an emphasis on the dominante and begun to explore the economy of both the terraferma and the Venetian colonies in the eastern Mediterranean, highlighting the place of both trade and industry in the creation of regional economies. This work has been especially important in the analysis of cottage industry and related problems of proto-industrialization in the Venetian hinterland.[59] But scholars have also cast new light on the history of agriculture and land management, which are important dimensions in the history of the regional state, though more needs to be done on the interplay of economic and political developments in both the late medieval and early modern periods.[60] Finally, economic historians, often in close alliance with social historians, have begun to explicate the history of such aspects of the Venetian economy as the roles of work and wealth in shaping the experience of Venetians rich and poor. These new initiatives have already done much to illuminate the history of labor, of the guilds, and of immigration.[61] But they also promise a better sense of the ways in which trade, manufacturing, wealth, and property ownership defined status in both city and countryside as well as methods for understanding the levers that lifted certain families into prominence as others fell from power. Particularly through analyses of familial wealth, economic historians seem poised to fill in many gaps in the new vision of Venetian society as fluid, porous, flexible, and ever-changing.

Indeed, one of the most productive areas of recent Venetian scholarship, one that has benefited in significant ways from interdisciplinary perspectives, which draw not only on social and economic history but on institutional and cultural history as well, has been the study of foreign communities in Venice. Indeed, as several generations of economic historians in particular have taught us, Venice, perhaps more than any other city in Western Europe, was a cosmopolitan center where merchants from throughout the European and Mediterranean worlds gathered to exchange goods and to learn news of foreign markets. At the end of the fifteenth century, for example, the French diplomat Philippe de Commynes observed that in Venice "most of the people are foreigners." Not long afterwards, the Venetian patrician and banker Girolamo Priuli made a similar observation about his native city: "With the exception of the patricians and some cittadini, all the rest are foreigners and very few are Venetians." Two generations later, in 1581, Francesco Sansovino underscored the striking presence of foreigners in the city in his compendious *Venetia città nobilissima et singolare,* a kind of guidebook to the monuments and the history of the Republic. "Peoples from the most distant parts of the world gather here," he wrote, "to trade and to conduct business. And though these peoples differ among themselves in appearance, in customs, and in languages, they all agree in praising such an admirable city."[62] These writers exaggerated only a little. The commercial importance of the city, its wealth, and its reputation for cultural freedom had attracted men and women from all corners of the European and Mediterranean worlds. At various points in its history Venice hosted colonies of Greeks, Germans, and Turks. The Greeks lived in a well-defined community in Castello; the Germans, most of them merchants, resided at Rialto in the Fondaco dei Tedeschi; and Turks lived in a somewhat more loosely knit community in the parish of San Giacomo dall'Orio. The Jews, themselves a multi-ethnic community of German, Italian, Iberian, and Levantine origins, were confined to the Ghetto from 1516 on.[63] There were other neighborhoods in which particular ethnic groups were concentrated. The Slavs and the Armenians, for example, tended to live in the *sestiere* (district) of Santa Croce, and the Florentines and the Lucchesi both chose to reside in the parishes nearest the Rialto.[64]

Venice found numerous ways to negotiate its interests with foreigners, including, as Robert Davis shows in his essay here, the freeing and ritual reintegration into society of ransomed slaves. Many wealthy merchants from other lands were granted citizenship; certain trading communities were recognized; persons passing through were accommodated; and at times guilds were open to immigrants. We might imagine Venice, therefore, as a city that not only allowed for a certain degree of social mobility up and down the status hierarchies but also was characterized by remarkable geographical mobility. Indeed, in our view, the central paradox in Venetian history lies in the sharp contrast between the tendency of Venetians both to represent and to think about themselves in terms of fixed categories and the underlying reality of economic, social, and geographic fluidity.[65] The relation between the social and commercial world of Venice, which was constantly in motion, and the representation of Venice as a stable society needs further study and elaboration.

Moreover, as Chojnacki's and Ambrosini's essays make clear, much more attention needs to be paid to issues of gender. In some fundamental ways the older vision of Venetian society was inextricably tied to a patriarchal order and male categories of status. When gender is figured into the equation, several questions emerge that are only beginning to be answered. First, did women and girls, both noble and non-noble, have a significantly different understanding of social structure and place than men and boys (as some of Chojnacki's research suggests), and if so, what were its effects?[66] Second, can gender questions be located as central to the fluidity of Venetian society? Some of the material presented here indicates that it was persons who did not fit conventional gender and family roles—spinsters, prostitutes, bastards, bachelors—whose status was least defined and who bridged or fell between status groups.[67] The role of the religious (both women and men, secular and regular) in reinforcing, mediating, or modifying conceptions of social rank also needs to be explored.

Finally, much work remains to be done on Venetian social structure in the nineteenth and twentieth centuries and on the role nineteenth- and twentieth-century historiography has played in shaping our view of Venetian society during the Republic. As Brian Pullan observed in reference to the events of the summer of 1797, within the space of a few weeks everyone became a cittadino—a citizen of a new revolutionary government.[68] The long-term significance of that moment of democratization needs to be unpacked, as does the role that scholars, several of them scions of noble families, have played in shaping our view of Venice's social past. Just as nineteenth-century political agendas shaped the writing of Venice's political history, so struggles for social position framed the vision of Venetian society.[69] Historians need to consider those agendas in shaping and reshaping the Venetian past.

IN THE REALM of Venetian culture no less than in those of political and social history, scholars have begun to push back boundaries and to offer a more inclusive and more dynamic history. No longer content with merely formal questions of style, influence, and composition, they have embraced a broad range of perspectives and adopted a truly interdisciplinary approach. What is more, the study of culture has expanded beyond the fine arts. Inspired in large part by work in social and cultural anthropology, many Venetianists have participated in remapping the boundaries of cultural studies in medieval and early modern Venice, reconsidering in their work topics as diverse as the occult sciences, magic, and sexuality.

The result has been a profusion of new studies of Venetian art, architecture, music, and intellectual life, the best of which seek to explore the relation of ideas and art to the context(s) in which works were produced. Several of the contributions in this volume point to this trend. Elisabeth Gleason's reading of Gasparo Contarini's *De magistratibus et republica Venetorum* shows how the political climate in Venice in the years immediately following the Peace of Bologna in 1530 shaped Contarini's work. Peter Humfrey's study of Veronese's painting for the high altar at the parish church of San Sebastiano demonstrates the value of exploring the religious and familial contexts in which art was embedded. Moreover, in keeping with the interest of many recent studies of Renaissance art, Humfrey places particular emphasis on the dynamics of patronage and raises important questions about the role of noblewomen as patrons.[70] Patricia Brown's essay on interior spaces shows how aesthetic objects were charged with social meanings. And Peter Burke's synthetic study of early modern Venice as "a center of communication and information," especially in its attention to the diverse aspects of publishing in Venice in the sixteenth and seventeenth centuries, illuminates intellectual and cultural trends over the long term. In particular, Burke underscores the polyglot and culturally varied production of books in the city and challenges overly simple notions of cultural decline as a salient characteristic of seventeenth-century Venice. One of the most important results of work like Burke's has been an uncoupling of cultural studies from narratives of rise and decline and their replacement by a vision of Venetian cultural life from the thirteenth century through the eighteenth as particularly rich and dynamic. Understanding the sources of that creativity and dynamism remains a central concern of Venetian scholars, as does the effort to identify what was essentially "Venetian" about them.

Most scholars agree that one of the primary sources of Venetian cultural dynamism was the large number and wide-ranging character of patrons, both institutional and individual, who commissioned works of art, employed musicians, subscribed to opera and theater seasons, and provided support for poets and other intellectuals.[71] Given its vast resources and the number of magistracies and courts that it comprised, the state was almost certainly the leading patron in terms of the number of commissions it undertook and in the dominant cultural narrative it created. The everyday business of running the state, as well as extraordinary moments of celebration and crisis, provided numerous opportunities for the government—through individual doges, the procurators of San Marco, and councils and magistracies—to employ artists, architects, and musicians. What is more, the works they produced, especially the mosaics and decorations of the basilica of San Marco and the architecture and paintings of the ducal palace, became touchstones and reference points for everyone, from patricians trying to embellish their private palaces, to *scuole* (confraternities) attempting to outdo their competitors, to heretics seeking confirmation of their prophetic visions.[72]

Yet what distinguished Venice from many of the smaller princely cities of Italy (and even from its republican counterparts, such as Florence and Genoa) was the vast number of alternatives to state-sponsored patronage. Thanks to the pioneering work of Brian Pullan the *scuole grandi,* the five largest and most prestigious confraternities in the city, are the best known of these patrons.[73] These institutions were controlled in large part by cittadino administrators who not only competed with one another in the construction and decoration of magnificent meeting halls—competition that led to condemnation by men such as Alessandro Caravia in the mid-sixteenth century—but used these organizations and the patronage opportunities they afforded to assert their prominence alongside that of the patricians.[74] As Patricia Brown has shown, the scuole especially favored narrative painting cycles that had their counterpart (and prototype) in works in the ducal palace.[75]

But the scuole grandi were only one of many kinds of religious institutions that served as sources of artistic patronage. In addition, the city was home to numerous monasteries, convents, and hospitals, as well as approximately seventy parish churches. Furthermore, there were scores, if not hundreds, of *scuole piccole,* smaller confraternities that served the religious and social needs of neighborhoods, occupational groups, and ethnic minorities and were important patrons in their own right, commissioning everything from meeting halls to altarpieces and banners.[76] Guilds, as Peter Humfrey and Richard Mackenney have shown, provided yet another form of corporate patronage, as did the even more modest *traghetti,* or unions of ferryboat operators.[77] The thick web of religious, charitable, and occupational institutions that were part of the Venetian social order provided an essential foundation for the cultivation of the arts.

Complicating the picture even further are the large number of wealthy families who defied the much-vaunted republican ethos of *mediocritas* and commissioned works of art, architecture, music, and literature to glorify themselves. Every century is filled with examples of patrons, both patrician and nonpatrician—Marino Contarini and Giovanni Dario in the fifteenth century, Zorzi Corner in the sixteenth, the Pesaro in the seventeenth, and the Labia in the eighteenth century—who used domestic architecture in particular to assert their individual and familial status. Indeed, Francis Haskell has suggested, one reason for Venice's continuing cultural dynamism was that in the seventeenth and eighteenth centuries families, especially newly rich families, took the lead in commissions as state patronage declined.[78]

If the rich variety of patrons accounts in part for the dynamism of Venetian cultural production throughout the centuries, it does not explain the particular Venetian qualities of the art and music of the Republic. Here too, older, more formal definitions of *venezianità,* such as Giorgio Vasari's well-worn contrast between Florentine *disegno* and Venetian *colore,* are giving way to a more complex understanding of the ideological meanings and uses of Venetian culture. No longer are the arts reduced to epiphenomena. On the contrary, the work of historians of art and music has made clear that the arts played a constitutive role in the shaping and preservation of Venetian identity, especially its identity as a republic. As Ellen Rosand has observed, "The achievements of artists, musicians, poets, and printers not only contributed to the evolving myth of Venice, they gave it shape, made it legible."[79]

The visual arts and in particular the complex of buildings around piazza San Marco have long been recognized by scholars as vehicles by which the Venetian Republic authenticated its past, inculcated republican values, and created allusions to Rome, Constantinople, and Jerusalem.[80] Even Canaletto's panoramic city views, which scholars for a long time considered little more than "postcard" souvenirs of the grand tour, are now understood as purveyors of the myth of Venice as the Exemplary Republic.[81] But this celebration was no less apparent in music, as recent studies of madrigal, opera, and the choral groups of the *ospedali grandi,* whose highly skilled female musicians Rousseau greatly admired, have shown.[82] These studies indicate a concern not only with context but also with how the myth of Venice was represented and functioned in Venetian culture.

But the study of Venetian culture is no longer linked only to the study of the fine arts, nor does it take as its goal the deciphering of a single message in that culture. Many Venetianists have redrawn the boundaries of cultural studies in Venice by incorporating the insights of social and cultural anthropology. In this context, the breakthrough book was Edward Muir's *Civic Ritual in Renaissance Venice* (1981). In this work several long-debated issues in Venetian history, from the myth of Venice and the function of Venetian parishes to the nature of Venetian republicanism, were cast in a new light. Rather than conceiving of republicanism, for example, as exclusively a matter of either political institutions or intellectual history, Muir made a convincing case that it was necessary to explore the ways in which the Venetian government both expressed and reinforced its power through legends, ceremonies, and rituals. Moreover, in Muir's analysis neither the myth of Venice nor the legends and rituals that gave it expression were mere *instrumenta regni*. As Muir wrote, "The myth's function, then, if it can ever be reduced to anything so simple, is not just to reinforce status discriminations, such as keeping the lower classes in their place, nor is it just to maintain group loyalties; its function is to make a 'meta-social commentary' on the whole matter of organizing people around certain institutions."[83] Muir's argument, by demonstrating that facile distinctions between myth and reality were ultimately unproductive, went a long way in recasting Venetian historiography and also opened the door for those wishing to explore alternative commentaries on the myth. These new approaches include Robert Davis's analysis of popular violence in the late Renaissance city, Guido Ruggiero's explorations of witchcraft, magic, and illicit sexuality, and Manfredo Tafuri's decoding through architectural programs of fractures within the ruling elite itself.[84] The most recent development, then, here best represented by Martha Feldman's essay on opera at the time of the fall of the Republic, is that scholars can now approach symbolic and signifying systems as themselves constituent forms of social and political action. Here, opera, a genre that was perfected in Venice, becomes not only a vehicle through which Venetians imagined their society but also an instrument through which revolutionary and Jacobin Venetians attempted to reshape the Venetian imagination by redefining time and space.

Thus, the dynamism of Venetian culture was the result of two interconnected phenomena: on the one hand, artists, writers, and musicians benefited from a multiplicity of patrons, both institutional and individual, who wished to memorialize and honor themselves; on the other, these artists were able to join in a common and especially rich dialogue about the significance of Venice itself. They created works of art that appropriated, elaborated, modified, and challenged the mythic meaning of the city. As they did in the councils of the government, so also through their art and music Venetians debated what it meant to be Venetian and to live in a republic.

In spite of all this, many issues remain unexplored. Scholars have only begun to appreciate the complexities of Venetian popular culture and its relation to the culture of the elites. At times, as in many of the city's festivals and religious events, these cultural spheres appear to have overlapped and to have been mutually influential. At other times, however, fissures opened up. Issues of resistance and opposition among both patricians in council and the lower classes in the streets and workshops and peasants in the fields need further examination as well.[85] Tafuri's emphasis on contestation, which he saw made manifest in differing architectural styles, needs to be taken up by scholars interested in other arts as well. Indeed, formal studies may take on new life if they are pursued along these lines.

Closely related to these concerns is the issue of the reception of the messages posed by art, music, and ritual. Given the paucity of sources containing observers' reactions to works of art and other events, scholars will need to find new ways to recover how people thought about what they saw and heard. In the visual arts, for example, further investigation of the marketplace's role in the production of works of both high art and everyday objects, as well as the ways in which those objects were recycled across generations and for different uses, may reveal changes in what it meant to be Venetian.[86] Music, dance, and costume, in which imitation, repetition, and borrowing can sometimes be detected, should also provide particularly rich fields for such approaches.

CONTEMPORARY SCHOLARSHIP has largely abandoned the paradigms that for so long shaped the understanding of the Venetian past. Today Venice does not appear, as it did to the panegyrists of the fifteenth and sixteenth centuries, as uniformly triumphant, just, and free; nor does it appear as it did to its critics, especially those of the eighteenth and nineteenth centuries, as secretive, repressive, even ossified. As the myth and antimyth have themselves become objects of analysis, scholars in a variety of disciplines have found new ways to integrate the cultural history of the Republic—from its representations in art and in humanist literature, for example, to the rituals that shaped the lives of Venetians themselves—into the larger social and cultural history of the Serenissima. But recent work has also modified this larger history in important ways. Notions of rise and decline have yielded to a more variegated set of narratives in which scholars examine the subtle ways Venice adjusted, often quite dynamically, to the larger transformations around it. Thus, while great events—from the Serrata, to the battle of Agnadello, to the fall— remain useful starting points for reflections on the history of Venice, each period is now read less as a prologue to the next and more as an integral part of the particular economic, political, and cultural contexts of the time. This scholarship, in short, has done away with a unilinear reading of Venice's past, a reading that was perhaps too uncritically linked to a traditional narrative of Western development. Thus, in this sense too we note a significant break from earlier assumptions that structured the study of Venetian history and civilization.

NOTES

1. Several recent surveys offer comprehensive overviews of Venetian history and culture: Girolamo Arnaldi and Manlio Pastore Stocchi, eds., *Storia della cultura veneta*, 6 vols. (Vicenza, 1976–86); the new *Storia di Venezia: Dalle origini alla caduta della Serenissima*, 12 vols. (Rome, 1992–98); and the books dedicated to Venice in the Storia d'Italia series under the general direction of Giuseppe Galasso and published by UTET: Giorgio Cracco, *Un "altro mondo": Venezia nel medioevo dal secolo XI al secolo XIV* (Turin, 1986); Gaetano Cozzi and Michael Knapton, *La Repubblica di Venezia nell'età moderna: Dalla guerra di Chioggia al 1517* (Turin, 1986); Gaetano Cozzi, Michael Knapton, and Giovanni Scarabello, *La Repubblica di Venezia nell'età moderna: Dal 1517 alla fine della Repubblica* (Turin, 1992). For a recent guide to Venetian historiography, see Giorgio Zordan, *Repertorio di storiografia veneziana: Testi e studi* (Padua, 1998).

2. The literature on the myth of Venice is extensive; James S. Grubb, "When Myths Lose Power: Four Decades of Venetian Historiography," *Journal of Modern History* 58 (1986): 43–94, remains the best introduction, though for an important perspective that stresses the intrinsic and dynamic role of the myth in the making of Venetian history and politics, see Elisabeth Crouzet-Pavan, *Venise triomphante: Les horizons d'un mythe* (Paris, 1999).

3. Nicolai Rubinstein, "Italian Reactions to Terraferma Expansion in the Fifteenth Century," in *Renaissance Venice*, ed. J. R. Hale (London, 1973), 197–217.

4. Machiavelli, *Legazioni e commissarie*, ed. Sergio Bertelli, 3 vols. (Milan, 1964), 2:676.

5. Jean-Jacques Rousseau, *The Social Contract*, trans. Maurice Cranston (London, 1968), 167, 170; idem, *The Confessions*, trans. J. M. Cohen (London, 1953), 294–95, 377 (quotation).

6. On the representation of Venice in early nineteenth-century literature, see John Pemble, *Venice Rediscovered* (Oxford, 1995), 88–92.

7. Claudio Povolo, *Il romanziere e l'archivista: Da un processo veneziano del '600 all'anonimo manoscritto dei Promessi Sposi* (Venice, 1993).

8. John Ruskin, *The Stones of Venice*, 3 vols. (London, 1851–53).

9. Samuele Romanin, *Storia documentata di Venezia*, 10 vols. (Venice, 1853–61).

10. Ranke's three essays are *Über die Verschwörung gegen Venedig im Jahre 1618* (Berlin, 1831); "Die Venezianer in Morea: 1685–1715," *Historisch-Politische Zeitschrift* 2 (1835): 405–502; and "Venedig im sechzehnten Jahrhundert und im Anfang des siebzehnten," in Ranke, *Zur venezianischen Geschichte*, vol. 42 of *Sämmtliche Werke* (Leipzig, 1878), 1–133. On Ranke's contribution to Venetian historiography, see Ranke, *Venezia nel Cinquecento con un saggio introduttivo di Ugo Tucci*, trans. Ingeborg Zapperi Walter (Rome, 1974), 1–69; Edward Muir, ed., *The Leopold von Ranke Manuscript Collection of Syracuse University: The Complete Catalogue* (Syracuse, 1983); and Gino Benzoni, "Ranke's Favorite Source: The Venetian Relazioni: Impressions with Allusions to Later Historiography," in *Leopold von Ranke and the Shaping of the Historical Discipline*, ed. Georg G. Iggers and James M. Powell (Syracuse, 1990), 45–57.

11. See Gino Benzoni, "La storiografia," in Arnaldi and Stocchi, *Storia della cultura veneta*, 6:597–623, esp. 605–9.

12. See, e.g., Giuseppe Maranini's *La costituzione di Venezia*, 2 vols. (Venice, 1927–31); and Enrico Besta, *Il senato veneziano (origine, costituzione, attribuzioni e riti)*, in Miscellanea di storia veneta, 2d ser., 5 (1899): 1–290.

13. At the same time, a major effort was made to publish the capitularies and earliest deliberations of government bodies. See, e.g., Roberto Cessi, ed., *Deliberazioni del Maggior Consiglio di Venezia*, 3 vols. (Bologna, 1931–50).

14. Gaetano Cozzi, *Il doge Niccolò Contarini: Ricerche sul patriziato veneziano agli inizi del Seicento* (Venice, 1958), now reprinted in Cozzi, *Venezia barocca: Conflitti di uomini e idee nella crisi del Seicento veneziano* (Venice, 1995), 1–246.

15. Hans Baron, *The Crisis of the Early Italian Renaissance: Civic Humanism and Republican Liberty in an Age of Classicism and Tyranny*, 2 vols. (Princeton, 1955); idem, *Humanistic and Political Literature in Florence and Venice at the Beginning of the Quattrocento: Studies in Criticism and Chronology* (Cambridge, Mass., 1955).

16. Frederic C. Lane, "At the Roots of Republicanism," *American Historical Review* 71 (1966): 403–20, quotations on 404 and 409.

17. William J. Bouwsma, *Venice and the Defense of Republican Liberty: Renaissance Values in the Age of the Counter Reformation* (Berkeley, 1968). (Bouwsma served as president of the American Historical Association in 1978.) See also Giovanni Silvano, *La "Republica de' Viniziani": Ricerche sul repubblicanesimo veneziano in età moderna* (Florence, 1993).

18. Fernand Braudel, *The Mediterranean and the Mediterranean World in the Age of Philip II,* trans. Siân Reynolds, 2 vols. (New York, 1972–73); originally published as *La Méditerranée et le monde méditerranéen à l'époque de Philippe II,* 2d ed. (Paris, 1966).

19. Georges Georgelin, *Venise au siècle des lumières* (Paris, 1978); Franco Venturi, *Venezia nel secondo Settecento* (Turin, 1980); and Piero Del Negro, ed., *Giammaria Ortes: Un 'filosofo' veneziano del Settecento* (Florence, 1993).

20. Marino Berengo, *La società veneta alla fine del Settecento: Ricerche storiche* (Florence, 1956); Angelo Ventura, *Nobiltà e popolo nella società veneta del '400 e '500,* 2d ed. (Milan, 1993).

21. Grubb, "When Myths Lose Power," 86, 60.

22. Ibid., 60. For an excellent overview of the shifting perspectives on Venetian history, see Nicholas S. Davidson, "'In Dialogue with the Past': Venetian Research from the 1960s to the 1990s," *Bulletin of the Society for Renaissance Studies* 15 (1997): 13–24.

23. Davidson, "In Dialogue with the Past," 22.

24. Claudio Povolo, *L'intrigo dell'onore: Poteri e istituzioni nella Repubblica di Venezia tra Cinque e Seicento* (Verona, 1997). For a survey of other recent studies of the relationship of Venice and the terraferma, see Michael Knapton, "'Nobiltà e popolo' e un trentennio di storiografia veneta," *Nuova Rivista Storica* 82 (1998): 167–92.

25. See Guido Ruggiero, *Violence in Early Renaissance Venice* (New Brunswick, N.J., 1980); and John Martin, *Venice's Hidden Enemies: Italian Heretics in a Renaissance City* (Berkeley, 1993).

26. Several examples of these works are given in nn. 54 and 55 below. For Ricoeur's "hermeneutics of suspicion," see esp. his *Freud and Philosophy: An Essay on Interpretation,* trans. Denise Savage (New Haven, 1970), 32–36.

27. Gina Fasoli, "Nascità di un mito," in *Studi storici in onore di Gioacchino Volpe,* 2 vols. (Florence, 1958), 1:445–79; Franco Gaeta, "Alcune considerazioni sul mito di Venezia," *Bibliothèque d'Humanisme et Renaissance* 23 (1961): 58–75; Staale Sinding-Larsen, *Christ in the Council Hall: Studies in the Religious Iconography of the Venetian Republic,* Acta ad Archaeologiam et Artium Historiam Pertinentia, 5 (Rome, 1974); Edward Muir, *Civic Ritual in Renaissance Venice* (Princeton, 1981).

28. William Bouwsma, "Venice and the Political Education of Europe," in Hale, *Renaissance Venice,* 445–66. See also Felix Gilbert, "The Venetian Constitution in Florentine Political Thought," in *History: Choice and Commitment* (Cambridge, Mass., 1977), 179–214; Eco O. G. Haitsma Mulier, *The Myth of Venice and Dutch Republican Thought in the Seventeenth Century* (Assen, The Netherlands, 1980); James Harrington, *The Commonwealth of Oceana and a System of Politics* (1656), ed. J. G. A. Pocock (Cambridge, 1992); Piero Del Negro, *Il mito americano nella Venezia del '700* (Padua, 1986); and, for a fascinating effort at a grand narrative of republican theory from the Renaissance through the French and American Revolutions, J. G. A. Pocock, *The Machiavellian Moment: Florentine Political Thought and the Atlantic Republican Tradition* (Princeton, 1975).

29. See Ellen Rosand, "Music and the Myth of Venice," *Renaissance Quarterly* 30 (1977): 511–37; and David Rosand, "*Venetia Figurata:* The Iconography of a Myth," in *Interpretazioni veneziane: Studi di storia dell'arte in onore di Michelangelo Muraro,* ed. David Rosand (Venice, 1984), 177–96.

30. Machiavelli, *The Prince,* trans. George Bull (Harmondsworth, 1961); idem, *The Discourses,* ed. and trans. Bernard Crick (Harmondsworth, 1970). On the relation between these two works, along with an important critique of the Crick edition of *The Discourses,* see Gilbert, *History,* 91–176.

31. Francesco Ercole, "Comuni e signori nel Veneto (Scaligeri, Caminesi, Carraresi)," *Nuovo Archivio Veneto* 19 (1910): 255–337, reprinted in idem, *Dal comune al principato: Saggi sulla storia del diritto pubblico del Rinascimento italiano* (Florence, 1929).

32. Elisabeth Crouzet-Pavan, *"Sopra le acque salse": Espaces, pouvoir, et société à Venise à la fin du Moyen Age,* 2 vols. (Rome, 1992).

33. See Felix Gilbert, "Venice in the Crisis of the League of Cambrai," in Hale, *Renaissance Venice,* 274–92; and Gaetano Cozzi, "Authority and the Law in Renaissance Venice," ibid., 293–345.

34. Volker Hunecke, *Der venezianische Adel am Ende der Republik, 1646–1797: Demographie, Familie, Haushalt* (Tübingen, 1995); Oliver Thomas Domzalski, *Politische Karrieren und Machtverteilung im venezianischen Adel, 1646–1797* (Sigmaringen, 1996); Piero Del Negro, "La distribuzione del potere all'interno del patriziato veneziano del Settecento," in *I ceti dirigenti in Italia in età moderna e contemporanea,* ed. Amelio Tagliaferri (Udine, 1984); Giovanni Scarabello, "Una casata di governanti del '700 riformatore veneziano," in *I Querini Stampalia,* ed. Giorgio Busatto and Madile Gambino (Venice, 1987).

35. Joanne M. Ferraro, *Family and Public Life in Brescia, 1580–1650: The Foundations of Power in the Venetian State* (Cambridge, 1993); James S. Grubb, *Firstborn of Venice: Vicenza in the Early Renaissance State* (Baltimore, 1988); Edward Muir, *Mad Blood Stirring: Vendetta and Factions in Friuli during the Renaissance* (Baltimore, 1993); Giorgio Cracco and Michael Knapton, eds., *Dentro lo "Stado italiano": Venezia e la terraferma fra Quattro e Seicento* (Trent, 1984); Giuseppe del Torre, *Venezia e la terraferma dopo la guerra di Cambrai: Fiscalità e amministrazione (1515–1530)* (Milan, 1986).

36 On ecclesiastical institutions and the Venetian terraferma, see Giuseppe Trebbi, *Francesco Barbaro: Patrizio veneto e Patriarca d'Aquileia* (Udine, 1984); and Giorgio Chittolini, "Stati regionali e istituzioni ecclesiastiche nell'Italia centrosettentrionale del Quattrocento," in the Einaudi, *Storia d'Italia: Annali,* ed. Ruggiero Romano and Corrado Vivanti, vol. 9, ed. Giorgio Chittolini and Giovanni Miccoli (Turin, 1986), 147–93.

37. See, e.g., the studies by Salvatore Ciriacono, including "Venise et ses villes: Structuration et déstructuration d'un marché régional XVIe–XVIIIe siècle," *Revue Historique* 276 (1986): 287–307, and "Mass Consumption Goods and Luxury Goods: The De-Industrialization of the Republic of Venice from the Sixteenth to the Seventeenth Century," in *The Rise and Decline of Urban Industries in Italy and the Low Countries (Late Middle Ages—Early Modern Times),* ed. Herman Van der Wee (Leuven, 1988). For images of peasants in literature, see Giorgio Padoan, "Angelo Beolco, detto il Ruzante," in Arnaldi and Stocchi, *Storia della cultura veneta,* 3, pt. 3: 343–75. See also James S. Ackerman, "The Geopolitics of Venetan Architecture in the Time of Titian," in *Titian: His World and His Legacy,* ed. David Rosand (New York, 1982), 41–71, in which Ackerman uses the term *Venetan* to mean "'of Veneto' (including Venice)" (41).

38. Giorgio Chittolini, *La formazione dello stato regionale e le istituzioni del contado: Secoli XIV e XV* (Turin, 1979); idem, *Città, comunità e feudi negli stati dell'Italia centrosettentrionale: Secoli XIV–XVI* (Milan, 1996). For a useful introduction to the recent scholarship on the state in late medieval and early modern Italy, see Julius Kirshner, ed., *The Origins of the State in Italy* (Chicago, 1995).

39. See Gaetano Cozzi, ed., *Stato, società e giustizia nella Repubblica veneta (sec. XV–XVIII),* vol. 1 (Rome, 1980); idem, *Repubblica di Venezia e stati italiani: Politica e giustizia del secolo XVI al secolo XVIII* (Turin, 1982); and Povolo, *L'intrigo dell'onore.*

40. Pompeo Molmenti, *La storia di Venezia nella vita privata: Dalle origini alla caduta della Repubblica,* 3 vols., 7th ed. (1927–29; reprint, Trieste, 1973). On the continuing influence of the organic model, see, e.g., James C. Davis, *The Decline of the Venetian Nobility as a Ruling Class* (Baltimore, 1962); Richard Tilden Rapp, *Industry and Economic Decline in Seventeenth-Century Venice* (Cambridge, Mass., 1976); Alberto Tenenti, *Piracy and the Decline of Venice, 1580–1618* (Berkeley, 1967), originally published as *Venezia e i corsari, 1580–1615* (Bari, 1961); and Terisio Pignatti, *The Golden Age of Venetian Painting* (Los Angeles, 1979).

41. Patricia Fortini Brown, *Venice and Antiquity: The Venetian Sense of the Past* (New Haven, 1996).

42. Jacob Burckhardt, *The Civilization of the Renaissance in Italy,* trans. S. G. C. Middlemore, 2 vols. (New York, 1958), 1:82.

43. Elizabeth G. Gleason, *Gasparo Contarini: Venice, Rome, and Reform* (Berkeley, 1993); Silvano, *La "Republica de' Viniziani,"* 117.

44. For the population figures, see Daniele Beltrami, *Storia della popolazione di Venezia dalla fine del secolo XVI alla caduta della Repubblica* (Padua, 1954), 72.

45. Ibid.

46. In addition to Gleason's *Gasparo Contarini*, see her "Reading between the Lines of Gasparo Contarini's Treatise on the Venetian State," *Historical Reflections / Réflexions Historiques* 15 (1988): 3–25; see also Margaret L. King, *Venetian Humanism in an Age of Patrician Dominance* (Princeton, 1986).

47. Stanley Chojnacki, "In Search of the Venetian Patriciate: Families and Factions in the Fourteenth Century," in Hale, *Renaissance Venice*, 47–90.

48. Hunecke, *Der venezianische Adel am Ende der Republik;* Alexander Francis Cowan, *The Urban Patriciate: Lübeck and Venice, 1580–1700* (Cologne, 1986).

49. See, e.g., Chojnacki's study of registration for the *Balla d'Oro*, a male patrician rite of adulthood, "Political Adulthood in Fifteenth-Century Venice," *American Historical Review* 91 (1986): 791–810. See also Victor Crescenzi, *"Esse de maiori consilio": Legittimità civile e legittimazione politica nella Repubblica di Venezia (secc. XIII–XVI)* (Rome, 1996).

50. Stanley Chojnacki, "Social Identity in Renaissance Venice: The Second *Serrata,*" *Renaissance Studies* 8 (1994): 341–58, as well as his contribution to this volume: "Identity and Ideology in Renaissance Venice: The Third *Serrata.*"

51. For the sale of titles of nobility, see Davis, *Decline of the Venetian Nobility;* for the Habsburg period, Paul Ginsborg, *Daniele Manin and the Venetian Revolution of 1848–49* (Cambridge, 1979), 18–19, 32–33, 45.

52. For the popolo, see Ugo Tucci, "Carriere popolane e dinastie di mestiere a Venezia," in *Gerarchie economiche e gerarchie sociali: Secoli XII–XVIII* (Florence, 1990), 817–51.

53. Frederic C. Lane, *Venice: A Maritime Republic* (Baltimore, 1973).

54. Carlo Ginzburg, *The Cheese and the Worms: The Cosmos of a Sixteenth-Century Miller,* trans. John Tedeschi and Anne C. Tedeschi (Baltimore, 1980). For workers in the Arsenal, see Robert C. Davis, *Shipbuilders of the Venetian Arsenal: Workers and Workplace in the Preindustrial City* (Baltimore, 1991); for fishermen, Roberto Zago, *I Nicolotti: Storia di una comunità di pescatori a Venezia nell'età moderna* (Padua, 1982); for servants, Dennis Romano, *Housecraft and Statecraft: Domestic Service in Renaissance Venice, 1400–1600* (Baltimore, 1996); for witches, Ruth Martin, *Witchcraft and the Inquisition in Venice, 1550–1650* (Oxford, 1989); and for vagabonds, Francesca Meneghetti Casarin, *I vagabondi, la società e lo stato nella Repubblica veneta alla fine del '700* (Rome, 1984).

55. For studies on women, see Federica Ambrosini, "'Da mia manu propria': Donna, scrittura e prassi testamentaria nella Venezia del Cinquecento," in *Non uno itinere: Studi storici offerti dagli allievi a Federico Seneca* (Venice, 1993), 33–54; Monica Chojnacka, "Women, Charity, and Community in Early Modern Venice: The Casa delle Zitelle," *Renaissance Quarterly* 51 (1998): 68–91; Stanley Chojnacki, "Dowries and Kinsmen in Early Renaissance Venice," *Journal of Interdisciplinary History* 4 (1975): 571–600; idem, "Patrician Women in Early Renaissance Venice," *Studies in the Renaissance* 21 (1974): 176–203; Joanne Ferraro, "The Power to Decide: Battered Wives in Early

Modern Venice," *Renaissance Quarterly* 48 (1995): 492–512; Linda Guzzetti, "Separations and Separated Couples in Fourteenth-Century Venice," in *Marriage in Italy, 1300–1650,* ed. Trevor Dean and K. J. P. Lowe (Cambridge, 1998), 249–74; and idem, "Le donne a Venezia nel XIV secolo: Uno studio sulla loro presenza nella società e nella famiglia," *Studi Veneziani,* n.s., 35 (1998): 15–88.

56. For another recent collection of essays that point in these new directions, see Ellen E. Kittell and Thomas Madden, eds., *Medieval and Renaissance Venice* (Urbana, 1999).

57. See the following works by Lane: *Venetian Ships and Shipbuilders of the Renaissance* (Baltimore, 1936); *Andrea Barbarigo: Merchant of Venice* (Baltimore, 1944); *Venice and History: The Collected Papers of Frederic C. Lane* (Baltimore, 1966); *Studies in Venetian Social and Economic History* (London, 1987); and, with Reinhold C. Mueller, *Money and Banking in Medieval and Renaissance Venice,* vol. 1, *Coins and Moneys of Account* (Baltimore, 1985) (see also vol. 2, *The Venetian Money Market: Banks, Panics, and the Public Debt, 1200–1500* [Baltimore, 1997], by Reinhold C. Mueller). For an overview of Lane's contributions, see Hermann Kellenbenz, "Frederic C. Lane," *Journal of European Economic History* 17 (1988): 159–84.

58. See Brian Pullan, ed., *Crisis and Change in the Venetian Economy in the Sixteenth and Seventeenth Centuries* (London, 1968); Rapp, *Industry and Economic Decline;* and James C. Davis, *A Venetian Family and Its Fortune, 1500–1900: The Donà and the Conservation of Their Wealth* (Philadelphia, 1975).

59. On Venetian trading communities abroad, see esp. Benjamin Arbel, *Trading Nations: Jews and Venetians in the Early Modern Eastern Mediterranean* (New York, 1995), as well as David Jacoby's important articles, many of which appear in his *Recherches sur la Méditerranée orientale du XIIe au XVIe siècle: Peuples, sociétés, économies* (London, 1979). On problems of industry the literature is enormous, but see esp. Salvatore Ciriacono, "Venise et la Vénétie dans la transition vers l'industrialisation: A propos des théories de Franklin Mendels," in *Etudes en memoire de Franklin Mendels,* ed. René Leboutte (Geneva, 1996), 291–318.

60. On agriculture and land management, see Gigi Corazzol, *Fitti e livelli a grano: Un aspetto del credito rurale nel Veneto del '500* (Milan, 1979); Salvatore Ciriacono, *Acque e agricoltura: Venezia, l'Olanda e la bonifica europea in età moderna* (Milan, 1994); and, more generally, Giuseppe Gullino, "Venezia e le campagne," in *Storia di Venezia,* 8:651–702. On the relation of the Venetian economy to the development of the state, see the discussion of war and finance by Michael Knapton in Cozzi and Knapton, *La Repubblica di Venezia nell'età moderna: Dalla guerra de Chioggia al 1517,* 275–345; and Jean Claude Hocquet, "The Middle Ages, Developments and Continuities: City State and Market Economy," in *The Origins of the Modern State in Europe: Economic Systems and State Finance,* ed. Richard Bonney (Oxford, 1995), 81–100.

61. Luca Molà, *La comunità dei Lucchesi a Venezia: Immigrazione e industria della seta nel tardo medioevo* (Venice, 1994); Richard Mackenney, *Tradesmen and Traders: The World of the Guilds in Venice and Europe, c. 1250–c. 1650* (Totowa, N.J., 1987); Francesca Trivellato, "Salaires et justice dans les corporations vénitiennes au 17e siècle: Le cas des manufactures de verre," *Annales: Histoire, Sciences Sociales* 54 (1999): 245–73.

62. Philippe de Commynes, *Mémoires,* ed. Joseph Calmette, 3 vols. (Paris, 1965–81), 3:114; Girolamo Priuli, *I diari di Girolamo Priuli [AA. 1499–1512],* ed. Roberto Cessi, Rerum Italicarum Scriptores, 24, pt. 3, tome 4 (Bologna, 1938), 101; Francesco Sansovino, *Venetia città nobilissima et singolare, con aggiunta da Giustiniano Martinioni,* 2 vols. (1663; reprint, Venice, 1968), 1:4.

63. The literature on the Jews in Venice is immense. For an orientation, see Cecil Roth, *The History of the Jews in Venice* (Philadelphia, 1930); and David Malkiel, *A Separate Republic: The Mechanics and Dynamics of Jewish Self-Government* (Jerusalem, 1991). On the Turks, see Paolo Preto, *Venezia e i Turchi* (Venice, 1975); on the Germans, Henry Simonsfeld, *Der Fondaco dei Tedeschi in Venedig und die deutsch-venetianischen Handelsbeziehungen,* 2 vols. (1887; reprint, Stuttgart, 1987).

64. Two recent works on immigrants are Molà, *La comunità dei Lucchesi a Venezia;* and Brunehilde Imhaus, *Le minoranze orientali a Venezia, 1300–1510* (Rome, 1997).

65. In an interesting parallel, Angelo Ventura has noted a tendency of the Venetian government to mask innovation in the guise of tradition (see "Scrittori politici e scritture di governo," in Arnaldi and Stocchi, *Storia della cultura veneta,* 3, pt. 3: 546–48).

66. Stanley Chojnacki, "The Power of Love: Wives and Husbands in Late Medieval Venice," in *Women and Power in the Middle Ages,* ed. Mary Erler and Maryanne Kowaleski (Athens, Ga., 1988), 126–48; idem, "'The Most Serious Duty': Motherhood, Gender, and Patrician Culture in Renaissance Venice," in *Refiguring Women: Perspectives on Gender and the Italian Renaissance,* ed. Marilyn Migiel and Juliana Schiesari (Ithaca, 1991), 133–54.

67. Stanley Chojnacki, "Subaltern Patriarchs: Patrician Bachelors in Renaissance Venice," in *Medieval Masculinities: Regarding Men in the Middle Ages,* ed. Clare A. Lees (Minneapolis, 1994), 73–90.

68. Brian Pullan, comment on session "Society: Inclusions and Exclusions" at the conference "Venice Reconsidered," Syracuse, N.Y., 20 September 1997.

69. For a general introduction, see Benzoni, "La storiografia," esp. 597–612.

70. Among the studies dealing with female patronage, see Rona Goffen, *Piety and Patronage in Renaissance Venice: Bellini, Titian, and the Franciscans* (New Haven, 1986), esp. ch. 2; and Douglas Lewis, "Patterns of Preference: Patronage of Sixteenth-Century Architects by the Venetian Patriciate," in *Patronage in the Renaissance,* ed. Guy Fitch Lytle and Stephen Orgel (Princeton, 1981), 354–80.

71. See esp. H. G. Koenigsberger, "Republics and Courts in Italian and European Culture," *Past and Present,* no. 83 (1979): 32–56. See also Michel Hochmann, *Peintres et commanditaires à Venise (1540–1628)* (Rome, 1992).

72. For references to the ducal palace in domestic architecture, see Richard J. Goy, *The House of Gold: Building a Palace in Medieval Venice* (Cambridge, 1992), 164–67; to San Marco in the scuole, Norbert Huse and Wolfgang Wolters, *The Art of Renaissance Venice: Architecture, Sculpture, and Painting, 1460–1590,* trans. Edmund Jephcott (Chicago, 1990), 106–8; and to heretics and the mosaics of San Marco, Martin, *Venice's Hidden Enemies,* 198–201.

73. Brian Pullan, *Rich and Poor in Renaissance Venice: The Social Institutions of a*

Catholic State, to 1620 (Cambridge, Mass., 1971). In 1552 the number of scuole grandi grew to six when the confraternity of San Teodoro was raised to that dignity.

74. Patricia Fortini Brown, "Honor and Necessity: The Dynamics of Patronage in the Confraternities of Renaissance Venice," *Studi Veneziani*, n.s., 14 (1987): 179–212.

75. Patricia Fortini Brown, *Venetian Narrative Painting in the Age of Carpaccio* (New Haven, 1988).

76. Peter Humfrey, *The Altarpiece in Renaissance Venice* (New Haven, 1993), 110–21.

77. Peter Humfrey and Richard Mackenney, "The Venetian Trade Guilds as Patrons of Art in the Renaissance," *Burlington Magazine* 128 (1986): 317–30; for *traghetti*, see Romano, *Housecraft and Statecraft*, 169.

78. Francis Haskell, *Patrons and Painters: A Study in the Relations between Italian Art and Society in the Age of the Baroque* (New York, 1963), 247–67.

79. Ellen Rosand, comment on session "Politics and Culture in the Late Republic" at the conference "Venice Reconsidered," Syracuse, N.Y., 21 September 1997.

80. For the use of paintings to authenticate the past, see Brown, *Venetian Narrative Painting*, 79–86; for the employment of sculpture to inculcate republican values, see Edward Muir, "Art and Pageantry in Renaissance Venice," *American Historical Review* 84 (1979), esp. 34–35; for architectural allusions to Rome, Constantinople, and Jerusalem in piazza San Marco, see Juergen Schulz, "La piazza medievale di San Marco," *Annali di Architettura* 4–5 (1992–93): 134–56; Debra Pincus, "Venice and the Two Romes: Byzantium and Rome as a Double Heritage in Venetian Cultural Politics," *Artibus et Historiae* 26 (1992): 101–14; and Lionello Puppi, "Venezia come Gerusalemme nella cultura figurativa del Rinascimento," in *La città italiana del Rinascimento fra utopia e realtà*, ed. August Buck and Bodo Guthmüller (Venice, 1984), 117–36.

81. Bruce Redford, *Venice and the Grand Tour* (New Haven, 1996), ch. 3, esp. 76–80.

82. Martha Feldman, *City Culture and the Madrigal at Venice* (Berkeley, 1995); Ellen Rosand, *Opera in Seventeenth-Century Venice: The Creation of a Genre* (Berkeley, 1991); Jane L. Baldauf-Berdes, *Women Musicians of Venice: Musical Foundations, 1525–1855* (Oxford, 1993).

83. Muir, *Civic Ritual in Renaissance Venice*, quotation on 56.

84. Robert C. Davis, *The War of the Fists: Popular Culture and Popular Violence in Late Renaissance Venice* (New York, 1994); Guido Ruggiero, *Binding Passions: Tales of Magic, Marriage, and Power at the End of the Renaissance* (New York, 1993); Manfredo Tafuri, *Venezia e il Rinascimento* (Turin, 1985).

85. See Linda L. Carroll, "Carnival Rites as Vehicles of Protest in Renaissance Venice," *Sixteenth Century Journal* 16 (1985): 487–502.

86. Two studies that suggest these possibilities are Patricia Allerston, "Wedding Finery in Sixteenth-Century Venice," in Dean and Lowe, *Marriage in Italy*, 25–40; and Dennis Romano, "Aspects of Patronage in Fifteenth- and Sixteenth-Century Venice," *Renaissance Quarterly* 46 (1993): 712–33.

I

The Setting

I

Toward an Ecological Understanding of the Myth of Venice

ELISABETH CROUZET-PAVAN

Perhaps no city on earth has a more striking relationship with its environment than Venice, a thriving human community improbably built upon water and nestled in the lagoons of the northern Adriatic. In the first written account of Venetian life, dating from the sixth century, when the islands of the lagoon were first settled, Cassiodorus described an amphibious people who made their living off salt and fish. And later commentators have never ceased remarking on the city's extraordinary locale, to which they have attributed aspects of its life as diverse as its apparent social harmony and the use of shimmering colors by its celebrated artists. In this essay, which reprises some of the themes of her path-breaking study "Sopra le acque salse": Espaces, pouvoir et société à Venise à la fin du Moyen Age, *Elisabeth Crouzet-Pavan offers a more complex picture of Venice's environmental development, one in which the relationship between the Venetians and their surroundings is portrayed as reciprocal. She argues that the Republic's social and political structures developed in a complex reciprocal relation to the environmental history of the city, as efforts to wrest land from the waters of the lagoon both shaped and were shaped by the city's magistracies and ideals. Over time, the myth of Venice's providential founding on beneficent waters gave way to a discourse about nature's dangers. In Crouzet-Pavan's formulation, the natural environment, human action, and ideology together gave form to the Venetian experience.*

VENICE—a harmonious structure of stone, wood, and brick, a composition of fullness and emptiness, a bold and successful artifact—reigns over a series of lagoons. The unique urban mass of Venice stands out against a watery background. Arrayed around this center, which is more symbolic than geographic, is a series of islets.[1] In the distance looms a shoreline marking the frontiers of another world, which, however, the *dominante* little by little subdued: it is a rural landscape, symbolized by a field or two and a couple of trees.[2] Not quite so far away, just beyond the taut cordon of beaches, begins another expanse, of a sea that replenishes the lagoon just as it replenishes the city. This aquatic region seems naturally to amplify the inner circle of Venetian waters, offering an escape from finitude and bestowing life and depth.[3]

Such is the way Venice is described in fifteenth-century travelers' accounts and above all in maps and plans that were continually reproduced throughout the early modern period.[4] Moreover, as is so often true with regard to Venice, reality cannot be separated from its *mise en scène*. Historian-onlookers have long been impressed by this *mise en scène*. According to this persistent representation, the city, a triumph of human industry, dominates the elements of an ordered, pacified nature. The Venetian community, we are told, subjugated the waters of the lagoons as it established its dominance, amassed its wealth, and secured its maritime dominion before conquering an empire on the *terraferma,* the Venetian term for the mainland. As a result, the water, the environment, and its constraints have long been ignored by historians of Venice. To be sure, numerous monographs have been written about the geography of the lagoons and the gradual mastery of this difficult environment. But these have been in a traditional vein, and until recently they constituted a distinct historiographic sector whose potential contributions were not incorporated into a more general account.[5] Of course the peculiarities of the site and of the geographical situation of a city built between two worlds and fully engaged in the maritime environment were included among the factors invoked to explain the success of Venice's commercial adventure. And descriptions of the lagoons were always provided as background for discussions of how the city was populated, how people settled the various islands and shores and began to exploit local resources. But once the ineluctable growth of Rialto-Venice begins, it tends to monopolize historical attention. In many prominent works of history the water, tamed and reduced to a mere element of the marvelous Venetian décor, figures only in discussions of the urban aesthetic and theatricality or in meditations on the city's magic. Thus the lagoons have been relegated to oblivion: emptied of their people and activity on behalf of the capital, they were simultaneously stripped of their history.[6]

Images, in other words, have once again shaped historical thinking, ensnaring it in redundant representations. In seeking to understand the waters of Venice and the relation between its people and their environment, I therefore begin by examining the unavoidable image that has long stood as an impenetrable screen, namely, that Venice is built upon the sea and that its environment is a positive space, a sort of protective cocoon that sustains and defends its very existence.

Our story begins with Giovanni Diacono's reconstruction of the Venetian past, the first account of how the site by the lagoon was settled.[7] On the mainland the Lombard invasion marked a veritable turning point, the end of an era. People unwilling to submit to barbarian domination fled into the lagoons with relics and treasures from their churches. They were free men, and they fled in order to preserve their freedom in a watery realm not subject to anyone's rule. Being religious, they also fled to protect the Christian religion from the Lombard invaders. This account of the original migration, which established once and for all the basic outlines of the city's history—antiquity, liberty, faith in God[8]—also established an image of the waters around Venice that for centuries remained equally inviolable. Because the inhospitable marshes and mud flats of the lagoon basin were never described, the area came to be seen as an auspicious shelter, a tranquil setting wherein a blessed history was free to begin, or, rather, begin again. In this connection the fact that some versions of the *Origo* gave incompatible accounts of the original situation makes no difference, for all dramatized the refugees' march toward the lagoon and thus hinted at a miraculous aspect to the founding of a city amid marshes where heavenly signs and apparitions were already numerous.[9]

Giovanni Diacono chose to keep silent about the difficulties of settlement, the precarious beginnings, in order to portray a lagoon subsequently dotted with fortifications and cities, as if churches and houses, which already composed an admirable ensemble, had sprung up spontaneously.[10] The repeated use of words such as *urbs* and *civitas* was intended to create an image of a landscape that from the beginning looked like a city. We are a long way from the earliest description of the lagoons, left by Cassiodorus, as a place where shelter was cobbled together out of reeds and the land was perpetually in danger of inundation by rivers and tides.[11] By contrast, certain fragments of the *Origo* depict a more laborious inception, a progressive colonization of the territory. Still, the first history of Venice demonstrated that from the beginning the city was constructed as a place of order, beauty, and urbanity. And all subsequent histories—histories of the miracle in stone that is Venice—were shaped by the nature of the city's origins. In later texts, however, what was extraordinary about the urbanization of the lagoons was dramatized by contrasting it with the fragility of the early settlements. This rhetorical device soon became a standard feature of the local narrative tradition. In the fifteenth century, Bernardo

Giustinian invoked it once more when he portrayed the ancient lagoon as a place populated by a race of sailors who owed their very lives to the water.[12]

Whatever differences separate these various accounts of early Venetian life, the same assumption underlies them all: that the lagoons, where God entered into a pact with the community, had been designated by Providence as the place where the destiny of Venice would be fulfilled. This theme of Venetian predestination found its ultimate expression, of course, in Saint Mark's dream as preserved in the chronicles of the thirteenth and fourteenth centuries.[13] But even before the embrace of this legend marked the final reconstruction of the city's early history, other fictions, less polished yet no less rich in symbolism, were composed to demonstrate the divine election of the lagoons and Rialto. In a territory designated by God began a history willed by God, according to both the legend of San Magno and the forged document that supposedly was the city's founding charter.[14] Furthermore, even though the legend of Saint Mark was jettisoned at the end of the Middle Ages, the history of Venice continued to be interpreted in providentialist terms. Echoes of the providentialist conception still reverberate through the major political texts of the fifteenth century, following a pattern allegedly laid down in speeches by Doge Tommaso Mocenigo as well as in the most routine legislative pronouncements of the councils.[15] Venice was a city from which God had never withdrawn his protection; his benevolence could not be forfeited. The pact concluded with God could not be broken.

Symbolism of this sort had profound implications for the writing of history. To begin with, the history that began, once the *duplicatio* was complete, within the protective embrace of the lagoons was said to be an absolutely new history, totally without precedent (even if the chronicles stated this as a mere postulate). All the texts agree that refugees from Altino, Padua, Treviso, and Oderzo fled to the islands and barrier beaches and thereafter ceased further communication with the cities of the terraferma, soon to be leveled by the new conquerors. What came into being then was a new society of the lagoons, a sovereign society not beholden to any of the forces contending for power on the peninsula.[16] A mission was thus ascribed to the waters: that of putting distance between the settlers and the vagaries of Continental affairs. Thanks to this barrier, to this supposedly impenetrable frontier, the fate of the lagoon was totally divorced from that of the Continent. Out of this came the fundamental axiom that Venetians by their very nature shunned the mainland. The divorce between the two worlds was supposed to be ontological, and of course it had to be maintained if Venetian history was to preserve its coherence and deeper meaning. These notions proved durable, as we have seen, to the point that they became veritable stereotypes. They explain the inveterate orientations of Venetian historiography and tell us why the links between Venice and the terraferma were ignored for so long. Because the myth, which came into being even as the history was being formulated, celebrated the lagoons as a sanctuary, it necessarily denied the existence of countless essential exchanges between the city on the water and a vast hinterland, just as it denied the economic penetration of the mainland that began centuries before the territorial conquest. It wiped out all memory of the way Venetian land acquisitions had very early given rise to a *contado invisibile* and of how people, goods, and capital had circulated almost constantly.[17] It was even responsible for distorting the realities of the lagoon's morphology, for it said nothing about the existence, in the ambiguous extremities of the basin near Torcello to the north and the Brenta delta to the south, of an amphibious world in which water, land, and marsh merged and people came and went.[18]

In the mythology of Venice the lagoons were thus the cornerstone of the city's independence and future power. The protective waters opened onto other spaces, which were soon explored and tamed: the shelter of the lagoons permitted the adventure on the high seas. If the people of Venice naturally ignored the mainland, the sea was their legacy. It was their duty to cultivate that heritage for the sake of their wealth and glory. And when they were not sailing on the waters of the lagoon or the sea, they expanded the horizons of their early commerce simply by sailing up the rivers that emptied into their basin.[19] To be sure, the community on the lagoon, lacking any agricultural base of its own, had no choice but to take to the sea and rivers in search of what it needed to survive. As the chronicles told the tale, however, this imperious necessity became the fulfillment of a destiny, if not the realization of a design. These early analytic choices have proved to be remarkably tenacious.

In short, for the Venetians as well as for their historians of the distant and not so distant past, the prefect Cassiodorus had said it all. Here men worked not with scythes and other tools for cultivating the earth but with ships and the cylinders that were used in the beginning to exploit the salt marshes. The Venetians did not wield the swing plow, and from the first they were sailors. Within a few centuries their flimsy reed dwellings were transformed into a city of stone. The Venetians became rich, but still they shunned the plow; they went to sea instead. The myth, in other words, continued to be a source of fiction for many, many years.

The perennially refurbished myth of Venice's origins transformed a harsh, hostile environment of mud and water into the most promising and admirable of sites for founding a city. From the first, Venice was insular, that is, free and unique, and soon she became rich and powerful as well. Her insularity enabled her to deny the possibility of decline while maintaining her strength and independence. Listen to Girolamo Priuli in June 1509. With "ultramontane" troops camped nearby, Venice was in the grip of fear, and the memoirist described the preparations for the city's defense. What did he see? The storing of provisions, of course, as well as the construction of bastions at river mouths and gaps in the barrier beaches. But above all he saw that the city was protected by its waters, which were abundant and deep and could not be crossed by any enemy, according to experts on the lagoon's hydraulics. This gave Priuli hope: the turmoil of the outside world would end on the *ripe salse*. As always, the community took refuge in its *aque maritime et salse* in order to survive. The war made the lagoon's ancient boundaries valid once again. The Venetians would make their stand at Santa Marta, Lizzafusina, or Chioggia.[20]

Subsequent events would gratify Prilui's hopes and reinforce what historians were writing before Agnadello and even more assertively afterward, namely, that Venice, protected by water as impregnable as any wall, would always remain safe. But for anyone who knows the texts, the ripe salse so lavishly praised by the chronicler are more evocative than the aphorism about the "holy walls of the fatherland."[21] In the shelter of its lagoon the Venetian community matured until it was ready to fulfill its unique destiny. In time of peril, delivered from the terraferma, the city rediscovered the uniqueness of its past. Thus the much-vaunted isolation of Venice was more than just geographical: it was the source of all of the city's other distinctive traits.

EVEN AS MAJOR REVISIONS were being made in virtually every area of Venetian historiography, the city—buildings and their arrangment, the site wherein groups, networks, and activities flourished, the theater that served as an essential setting for action both routine and extraordinary, the framework within which the community elaborated its system of signs—tended to remain, as in the images described above, miraculously suspended between earth and water, as if the *forma urbis* constituted a neutral and invariable datum. Yet the history of this city was that of a living organism. Its planning and construction were arduous; its parts were not all built, inhabited, or embellished simultaneously. The lengthy construction process involved work on any number of difficult, intractable sites. And how can one reconstitute the life of this urban community—the lives of its people and of the places where they built and rebuilt—without touching on a wider area, one that includes the lagoons? The Venetians did not sever the ties between the built-up areas and the surrounding waters.[22] They knew that the very survival of their city depended heavily on the natural environment, whose history we propose to reconstruct precisely because that environment was no more static than the city itself. By the fifteenth century the problems of the environment had become central and exerted a powerful influence on Venetian actions as well as representations.

Any scholar who wishes to do justice to the early centuries of Venetian history, which for want of sources remain shrouded in darkness, must try to imagine an endless series of public and private works. In order to survive, people had to shore up banks, drain swamps, and build, at first with flimsy materials but later with brick and stone brought from the terraferma. The settlement at Rialto marked the beginning of a long period during which a city was created where before there had been nothing but fetid marshes. In Venice, time became space: as the city took shape, grew, and made itself beautiful, it also extended the very ground on which it stood. At first, apart from a few rocky outcroppings, such as Dorsoduro, and a few more solid islands on which people settled and built homes and churches, the land itself did not exist. This in itself is a strikingly singular fact about Venice. In the absence of any preexisting ancient site, any organizing central kernel, any inherited plan, the urban fabric was gradually knitted together out of scraps, scarce bits of land that loomed up out of the water. Then, little by little, as the city began to take control of space, as each islet drained and parceled out its land, the fabric grew. As a result, the relation between land and water was constantly changing. The boundary between these two elements defined the city's limits. This brings us to another distinctive fact about Venice. Everywhere else in the Middle Ages, cities built and vigilantly defended walls, enclosures that were repeatedly enlarged. In most places the building of new walls largely determined the pace of urbanization. In the lagoon the only confining obstacle was water. Venice erected its only defenses at the outer limits of its territory, a tower in Mestre in the days before Venetian forces sallied forth to conquer the terraferma and some small bastions at San Nicolò on the *lido* to defend the major inlets on the barrier beaches that protected Venice from the sea.

The indispensable first step in expanding the city was therefore to create land on which to build. Forays were made into the lagoon and interior ponds; new territory was conquered by dredging, draining, driving pilings, making various other improvements, and linking isolated bits of land.[23] These activities coincided with continuing settlement. Over the years the wave of improvements swelled and became a formidable tide; settlement sites proliferated, and new islands emerged. As for the network of canals, if one excepts the Grand Canal, which defined the overall shape of the city, and the broad channel of the Giudecca, canals were no more stable a part of the landscape than was land. In other words, the canal network was not a fixed feature of the environment as a river might have been in another place. Many old canals were drained eventually, while new ones were created by dredging. The entire system was continually reshaped.

Elsewhere, the city, in order to grow, eliminated vegetation and swallowed up fields and gardens. We should bear in mind that what was being colonized was water and mud.[24] Terms such as *rio terrà* and *piscina* remind anyone who strolls through Venice today of these landfilling operations of the past. And many of the few straight streets that cut through the maze of byways follow the traces of drained canals whose memory would otherwise be lost.

Of course this brief essay cannot possibly bring to life all the projects, great and small, that were undertaken over the centuries, interrupted only by outbreaks of plague and periods of demographic or economic recession.[25] Initially expansion was spearheaded by large secular and, above all, ecclesiastical landowners, who led improvement projects in individual parishes. In this continuous process of creation the religious orders actually played a leading role for many years. The Benedictines, for example, were very active in the Dorsoduro district. In the thirteenth century they launched a major improvement project around the monastery of San Gregorio, between the Grand Canal and the Giudecca. By the end of the century the entire area was divided into lots. Houses were built of brick and often roofed with tile. New land-communication routes *(calli)* were added to the existing aquatic network, which was reorganized. Later the founding of the mendicant orders had a major impact on urban development. The Franciscans lent support to developments already under way in the vicinity of San Tomà by building their first church there. A noble family from the district, the Badoers, had already launched an attack on the extensive swamps and backwaters that were limiting the city's growth. On the north side, at Santi Giovanni e Paolo, the Dominicans moved into veritable frontier territory. The pioneering efforts of the Carmelites and the Augustinians also deserve mention. On the city's shifting fringes, subject to perpetual redefinition, the role of the religious orders persisted for many years.[26]

In the last decades of the thirteenth century, however, things began to change. The political authorities began to take control of and even organize the collective project of urban development. The government reasserted its dominion over water and marshland. In exchange for a "water rent," it granted concessions on pools and ponds, marshes and putrid wastelands—on any expanse or enclave that disrupted the urban fabric and inhibited progress. The commune even commissioned certain major improvement projects directly. Of these the most spectacular was the plan to create a new island, the Giudecca Nuova, between San Giorgio Maggiore and the Giudecca; this goal was achieved when a new island did indeed emerge from the water and mud in the first decades of the fourteenth century.[27] More often, however, the communal authorities acted through magistracies (primarily the Piovego) to oversee drainage projects in the various parishes.[28] Landowners large and small, together with their neighbors in the *contrade,* set out to conquer new land. They attacked the interior swamps and ponds as well as the fringes of the lagoon. As swamp after swamp was drained and land and buildings slowly but steadily took the place of water, a city began to emerge.

Growth accelerated throughout the thirteenth century and continued at a particularly rapid pace until the early 1340s.[29] The first demographic reverses, attested for the years 1307 and 1320, still had little effect on this remarkable growth despite the undoubted number of victims; the head of steam already built up was simply too great. We must therefore imagine this as a period of intense activity. On the fringes of Venice, on the outer edges of hundreds of gardens on the Giudecca, in Santa Croce, and in Cannaregio, stakes were driven into the ground every day and a few square yards of spongy earth were enclosed with boards. Here landlords dumped waste matter along with a little earth and mud. Slowly the swamp was chipped away. Meanwhile, flotillas of boats circulated from one quarter to another. Mud dredged from the canals, construction rubble, and garbage swept up from markets and streets all served as fill. Anything was good enough to fill in yet another pond, to consolidate yet another parcel of land. Construction did not begin to slow until just before the shock of the Black Plague. By 1343 the slowdown in communal concessions was noticeable. Then the plague hit, and it was not until 1385 that the conquest of new land showed signs of resuming. Although the worst plague years in the fifteenth century also witnessed a slowing of construction, expansion resumed on several fronts, albeit without the formidable strength and vitality of the early fourteenth century.

Meanwhile, other changes, similarly encouraged or guided by the government through its designated magistrates, also affected the shape of the emerging city.[30] New streets were created and existing ones enlarged. Space was cleared for a few major thoroughfares that linked the various sections of the city. These streets, the first to be paved with stones, carried traffic from the welter of secondary streets that fanned out into individual parishes.[31] Quays were built, shored up, and repaired when the water eroded them. Bridges were built and rebuilt, at first of wood and then, in the fifteenth century, of stone. Now traffic could flow from quarter to quarter. Indeed, in the last centuries of the Middle Ages the original network of canals was already backed up by a network of land routes. The result was a veritable revolution that transformed the traffic flow in Venice.[32] Different functions were assigned to the two systems of communication. People were now inclined to follow the calli unless forced by the absence of a bridge over a waterway to take a ferry. Merchandise and other heavier cargoes went by canal from port to marketplace, from the Arsenal to the basin of San Marco, or from one warehouse to another.

Locating one of the largest cities in the Medieval West in the middle of a lagoon thus required unremitting labor, organization, and imaginative use of technology. For centuries the history of Venice, a city perpetually under construction, was one of energetic activity. Here I am not allowing myself to be misled by the reconstructions of the chronicles, which boldly assert that from the moment the duchy moved its seat to Rialto in 810 the government assumed responsibility for all hydraulic improvements and never relinquished it thereafter. The facts speak for themselves. Countless cartons full of documents—Great Council deliberations, notarized acts, court documents, monastic charters—tell us how day after day the city increased and organized its space. Further evidence of Venetian energy can be found in speeches, which tirelessly detailed and celebrated the city's irrepressible progress. The vocabulary of public documents up to the fourteenth century is one of a young, active, conquering city. Despite the technical difficulties, the occasional failures, and the financial burden, which was onerous for public and private treasuries alike, the texts that governed urban policy remained optimistic. Expressing faith in steady progress, they describe a formidable spirit: the swamps were receding, the lakes were shrinking, and the territorial gains in every area of improvement were considerable. *Pallificare et allevare, facere palos, serrare de tolle, proicere, ampliare, atterare, elongare, extendere, fabricare, aptare, levare, hedificare, domos facere*—whether in Latin or the vernacular, all of these verbs refer to the drainage and apportionment of new land. Repeated in hundreds of documents, they mark the successive phases of lengthy projects. They report on the mobilization of forces. For centuries the people of the city gave unstintingly of their creative energy. Indeed, as the sources make clear, even if improvement did provoke conflict, encourage speculation, and make some people rich, there was nevertheless strong solidarity in the face of a hostile environment. The *vicini* of the parish societies led an effort that, if not always collective, was at least concerted.[33] The community came together in a perpetual battle against the water, a battle in which the city's very survival was at stake. From council decisions alluding to what was extraordinary about the city the people of Venice had created in the midst of the salt marshes one gets the impression that the pride expressed by the council members was shared not just by the ruling elite but by large numbers of ordinary people as well.[34]

In the fifteenth century, however, this optimism evidently faltered. Since the first settlement at Rialto the land had been all-conquering; now the water began to threaten. The vocabulary changed, and Venice began to describe itself as imperiled by water, by the very environment in which it had grown up. Its history became that of a place that people had providentially built for themselves to live in but that now found itself under attack by a deadly force. Defending the city from this new danger required unrelenting effort. One by one, the rhetorical mechanisms of an endangered city were put into place.

One reflection of the new thinking about hydraulics and the growing awareness of the problems of the site is the first treatise on the lagoon, written in the second half of the century.[35] It was a product of the elite who had taken charge of the most important offices in the Venetian state's new bureaucracy. Its author, Marco Corner, the man who for a time was in charge of wood procurement for the city, in his official capacity had made a systematic inspection of the rivers by which wood arrived either floating on the surface of the water or carried as cargo by various vessels. Later he was twice elected *savio alle acque,* and as such it was his duty to oversee a new project that had just recently gotten under way, the diversion of the Brenta.[36] In other words, here was a man whose official responsibilities had led him to develop a certain technical competence.

This noble, who became a specialist in hydrographic affairs, then wrote a history of the lagoon in which he proposed a series of emergency measures to deal with what he saw as a grave threat to the lagoon's well-being. Knowledge of the past, Corner observed, helps us to understand the future. His treatise begins with a description of the Adriatic coast as it looked many centuries earlier. He describes a sort of lost paradise, a vast, primitive lagoon that stretched from Ravenna to Aquileia. In those halcyon days, Concordia, Altino, and Oderzo were touched by the sea. But as the land expanded, the sea receded. At this point in his narrative Corner links historical time to recent events and deplores the fact that even as he writes the same phenomena can be observed in the marshes of the Venetian basin. The ancient sites of Cittanova and Jesolo, surrounded by marshland that had become unhealthy, were abandoned. Only a handful of survivors remained on the barrier beaches of Lio Maggiore, which could boast of as many as seven churches.[37] Ruin after ruin, abandoned settlement after abandoned settlement, dereliction after dereliction, he charts the progress of an ecological disaster. In each case Corner explicitly points a finger of guilt at the Sile and Piave Rivers. All of the woes that he describes can be traced to a single cause: the discharge of fresh water into the lagoon and the consequent deposit of silt.

Everywhere in the basin, according to Corner, the same destructive process was at work: the lagoons were shrinking irreversibly. This posed a direct threat to the city of Venice, since even there a shortage of water threatened the very artery on which the life and prosperity of the city depended: the Grand Canal. In the face of all these threats something had to be done about the rivers.[38] Despite this dramatic presentation, however, Corner's rescue plan was not adopted. One of his central proposals—to divert the Brenta in the vicinity of Stra and channel it by way of the Canal delle Bebbe to the port of Brondolo, far from Venice—is known to have been rejected. In order to maintain navigation on the river and protect various industries situated along its banks, a less radical diversion was chosen instead. The water from the Brenta was redirected toward Malamocco. This did nothing to halt the flow of fresh water into the Venice basin and simply shifted the sedimentation problem to a new location. Corner's second proposal—to divert the Sile from the lagoon toward Lio Maggiore—was also dismissed.[39]

For all its qualities, Corner's treatise was a polemical text that needs to be placed in its original context if it is to be fully understood. The conquest of the terraferma and the constitution of a Venetian territorial state changed the dimensions of the problem of the lagoon. In the first place, it was finally possible for the Venetians to take direct action to alter the course of the rivers that emptied into their lagoon. In the fifteenth and sixteenth centuries, therefore, many of the Senate's debates and on-the-spot inspections, as well as much of the hydrographic literature, were taken up with the question of diverting rivers. And some of the major projects that were adopted attacked this very problem with varying degrees of success.

In addition, terraferma expansion had an impact on the economic equilibrium of Venice. To the Signoria now fell the difficult task of reconciling the interests of a city whose fortunes rested on commerce with those of a mainland state dependent on agriculture and crafts.[40] Diverting rivers gave rise to difficulties and conflicts precisely because it was impossible to satisfy the contradictory demands of these two constituencies. The hydrographic question thus became a durable bone of contention between, broadly speaking, a party of the port and the lagoon and a party of the land. Not surprisingly, governmental action was hindered, slowed, and at times subverted as a result of the many pressures to which it was subject and frequent changes of course. As for Corner, it hardly needs stating that he was in the lagoon camp.

Nevertheless, his passion is not the end of the story. The public record contains a rather bleak picture. Corner deplored the silting of the lido inlets and the steady expansion of salt marsh and stagnant water. Official councils and magistrates described the same dangers. We know now, of course, that the fragile, unstable lagoon environment was and is being transformed by contrary forces all but impossible for human beings to control. Attentive care and unremitting effort are required. The record of fifteenth-century public deliberations shows that people at that time were aware of the growing dangers.

Take the situation of the port, for example. The environment of the estuary closest to Venice, that of San Nicolò, had always been harsh. As early as the fourteenth century a number of projects had attempted to increase the depth and flow rate of the port channel, but the methods selected were at cross-purposes with one another.[41] By the second half of the fifteenth century project followed project without interruption. By limiting the width of the inlet at Malamocco and submerging a number of wooden caissons and rafts, the experts hoped to increase the flow of water into San Nicolò. But the work accomplished nothing. "To the great peril of ships and galleys, the port is filling with sand, and water is lacking."[42] "Over the past few years the sand bar not only has moved closer to the shore but has progressed to the point where, when the winds are unfavorable, ships must wait in order to enter the port."[43] "The situation of our port is getting worse because the water now is too low virtually around the clock."[44] In these circumstances the usual remedies, such as using lighters to load and unload ships riding at anchor, were no longer sufficient. High-tonnage ships were often diverted toward the Malamocco inlet, a little farther down the coast.

Silted beds also threatened the system of urban canals. There was not enough water. The muddy canals gave off a fetid, unhealthy stench. Corruption stalked the city. The danger, according to the sources, was twofold. Swamps and reeds laid siege to Venice, eating away at the lagoon and moving toward populated areas. But within the city proper, grass was growing in the canals, and Venice was in great danger of drying up. The same words occur over and over: *mud, sludge, filth, foulness, corruption.*[45] Yet the canals were indispensable to the life of

Venice. They constituted a communications network, and they still provided water for many household and workshop needs. Above all, they kept the city clean and pure.

At this point the basin began to shrink and tidal flows diminished. Senators proclaimed that not only the canals but the city itself was at risk.[46] Venice began flushing its whole system of canals at regular intervals.[47] Most of this work was still done by hand, with shovels, after each canal was blocked off and drained. On the Grand Canal, however, machines were used. The justification for all this work and for the use of innovative technology was simple: the rate of silt accumulation was rising inexorably. Judging by the countless inspections carried out by commissions responsible for rivers, beaches, and lagoons, the degradation of the ecosystem must have been serious and widespread. The commissions' notes and reports invariably stress the inadequacy of the work being done and the growing magnitude of the problems faced.

Corner's description of changes in the northern lagoon is also confirmed by a number of other sources. Indeed, an abundance of documents enables us to follow almost step by step the changes in the aspect of the northern basin, especially the terrible devastation around Torcello. Until the fourteenth century the muddy area extending out from the terraferma was limited in size. The silt deposited by the Sile to the north and the Zero and Dese to the south had had only a limited impact. Then something happened that changed things dramatically: the Dese altered its course.[48] Its sedimentation rate increased. With the influx of fresh water and mud, the number of halophilic plants also increased. Little by little, swamps invaded the northern lagoon, and with them came anopheles mosquitoes. Death cut a swathe through the region. The archipelago of Costanziaca was the first to feel its effects: life there was wiped out in the early fifteenth century. Then the Amiana Islands were affected. Mud swallowed up ancient pastures and orchards. Campaniles collapsed, and a landscape of only ruins and a few huts remained amid the swamps. Next it was the turn of the islets of Torcello, already devastated by an earlier demographic depression and various structural economic difficulties.[49]

It thus appears that the lagoon became a fragile place during these decades. No doubt it had always been so. But the environment was transformed, and the changes, as the sources agree with unmistakable unanimity, caused unstable equilibria to break down and made the situation more precarious than ever. The triumphant community of Venice, which for centuries had been caught up in the process of conquering territory and creating an urban order, was candid about its fears. Behind the image of a beautiful city protected by its lovely aquatic setting we find problems and anxieties. The aquatic equilibria had to be maintained. And yet, as we know from repeated declarations by councils and magistrates, countless obstacles stood in the way of this essential project.

H O W   A R E   W E to interpret these dramatic changes? One must begin, of course, by taking note of the very real ecological factors affecting the type of environment in which Venice developed. Even today it is not easy to maintain the equilibrium of the lagoon.[50] The environment evolves according to a vast chronology of its own, upon which the humans who live there impose their shorter-term chronology.[51] Although we still know far too little about the history of the environment, in order to understand the history of Venice we also need to understand the history of the site, and in the case of Venice that history was one of constant change. Some scholars argue that the very geography of the basin underwent a major transformation during the Middle Ages.[52] But that hypothetical possibility aside, it remains true that the lagoons were and are in constant flux. Nature is unusually active here, and to enumerate all the changes that frequently conflicting natural forces have wrought in the region would be an endless task; land has been submerged, sediment has been deposited, bays have been reshaped, and the boundary between flowing and stagnant water has shifted constantly. In the fifteenth century, as we have seen, the basin shrank and became unhealthy. Even if some public documents of the time overstated the problem, surviving engineering reports confirm that for ten or twenty years the expansion of mud flats and silting of channels were important issues.[53]

Of course the Venetians soon tried to control the complex environmental factors involved. Their efforts to channel currents and rivers and protect beaches were not without effect, but every attempt to dam or divert a stream or to close or reopen one of the inlets through the barrier beaches affected a whole range of equilibria of whose very existence the people involved had only the vaguest inkling. In the long history of managing the environment some things were more important than others. The hydrographic problem was surely paramount. And until Venice actually conquered an empire on the terrraferma Venetians could do nothing about river silt and were at the mercy of various decisions taken by their neighbors.[54]

The state of technology also imposed limits on what could be attempted. Take the reinforcement of the beaches, for example. Until the great sea walls, the *murazzi,* were completed in 1782, this was an ongoing struggle, and the whole project is indicative of the willingness of governments from the fourteenth to the eighteenth century to persevere in a monumental undertaking as well as to spend substantial sums of money. The archives of the magistracy in charge of this project in the fifteenth century yield a virtually unbroken record of what the effort entailed. A storm had opened a breach in the coastal defenses, which had to be repaired at once. The long-term goal was to build up, restore, and reinforce the beach. To that end, an earthen embankment was put in place, and over time its height was increased. Later, a stone causeway was erected in front of this earthen embankment to absorb the brunt of the waves. In a carefully orchestrated ballet vessels laden with blocks of stone for this defensive wall were dispatched from the Dalmatian coast. Elsewhere, palisades built upon a double or triple row of pilings were used to stabilize the sandbar. In the second half of the century a series of contracts were awarded; these tell us a great deal about the steady flow of cash from public coffers into the pockets of entrepreneurs and skilled workers to pay for the construction of this defensive bulwark.[55] Yet the same records also prove that however dogged the government was in carrying on the fight, it was also obliged, at least until the murazzi were completed, to repair sea walls, which succumbed with troubling regularity to the battering waves.

It should also be noted that when it came time to make decisions, many factors that had nothing to do with preserving the environment naturally came into play. I have already alluded to the debates that arose over the issue of hydrographic regulation.[56] The authorities were repeatedly obliged to accept compromises, take half-measures, and make choices. How could the needs of a populous and industrious city be reconciled with the protection of the lagoon? Decision makers often were torn between laxity and severity. The management of the urban canals illustrates these dilemmas to perfection. Filth from the sewers, pollution from tanneries and dye shops, debris from construction sites, trimmings from the marketplace, waste from lime and brick ovens—all of this ended up in the canals, just as, in other cities, it ended up in the river. The canals were not stagnant, to be sure, and the tides helped to clean them out and sweep pollution out of the basin. But the silting of channels was compounded by the abundance of waste. The excess of human and artisanal discharge made it necessary to flush the canals with increasing frequency. Countless ordinances were adopted to protect the water. Yet violators often avoided paying the price or received pardons because commerce and production still took precedence.

Furthermore, knowledge of the environment and its many problems came slowly. It was not until the fifteenth century that people began to investigate the issues in any systematic way. The authorities began to call upon the experience and expertise of pilots, fishermen, and elderly men.[57] Interest in the problems of the lagoon was awakened in some of the nobles who were called upon to fill various positions and to take part in commissions to inspect dikes, ports, and canals or to conduct investigations and write reports. A substantial amount of information was gathered. Reports, notes, and drawings were preserved. Archives were created to store records of earlier measures for dealing with hydrographic matters and problems of the lagoon.[58] And in the last third of the fifteenth century, as elections of savii alle acque became more regular, a staff of technical experts began to be assembled, men upon whose services the magistrates could call as needed. The new office in charge of the environment had a budget from which it could pay its own staff of engineers.[59]

This was how things stood at the end of the fifteenth century. The Signoria by this point had the means to act. It could call on the services of a stable of competent engineers as well as on a group of entrepreneurs with experience in hydraulic projects. A pragmatic culture had developed. Yet debate remained bitter, and the proposed solutions were contradictory. Worst of all were the repeated assertions that the environment was steadily going downhill. Does this mean that all the efforts came to naught, that public action was of no avail, and that the new technology was a waste? Do the failures imply that man is incapable of dominating his environment and must submit to its vicissitudes? And does man's feeling of helplessness explain why the fear of seeing the elements destroy the Venetian creation recurs in the texts with such plaintive regularity? The challenge of Venice—to build a city in a swamp—was of course extreme. It could succeed, or so the texts insisted again and again, only with the blessing of Providence. And for a long time it had succeeded, but now man's triumph over the environment seemed about to turn to defeat. The rebellious environment could no longer be subjugated, the authorities maintained. The image of the chosen city hung in the balance. The most powerful city-state in the West thus discovered that its relation to the ecosystem clearly limited its ability to launch and succeed at new undertakings. Behind the myth of the lagoon as protector lay certain inescapable obsessions and a complex relationship between the community and its environment.

How are we to make sense of this? There can be no doubt that Venice's problems were real and that they became more severe than ever in the fifteenth century. As we have seen, the history of the lagoon environment followed its own chronology, and our knowledge of its evolution remains imperfect. Furthermore, human intervention was in some cases ineffective or even counterproductive. Finally, the population had a major impact on the site. A number of indicators suggest that when demographic growth resumed, this impact continued to be felt. Coastal farmland was dearly coveted. Excessive exploitation of the lagoon's resources unbalanced the environment. Within the city, people became more acutely aware of noxious pollution and other problems. But there can also be no doubt that the crisis and the anxiety began to be dramatized in the fifteenth century in the ideological discourse of the Venetian state. The relation between words and things is not determined solely by changes in the way people look at their world. Semantic evolution, I want to argue, was also used by the Venetian state, which, because it wanted to be the unique arbiter of meaning for those who inhabited its territory, seized upon the lagoon as a way of declaring itself to be the sole sovereign power. To be sure, according to the texts of decisions that dealt with highly technical problems in highly technical terms, the community always maintained its trust in Providence. The city continued to believe that it had been chosen by God to carry out his designs. Nevertheless, the new discourse of danger, which coexisted with this older rhetoric, marked a crucial change in both the political history and the mythology of Venice. It helped to desacralize the Venetian mentality by presenting the state, its magistrates, and their courses of action as capable of preserving the city and ensuring the survival of its inhabitants.

The discourse of danger served a number of purposes at once. It legitimated increased governmental intervention in resource management and preservation of the ecosystem and justified the resulting costs and encroachments on private initiative. It legitimated the establishment of a new bureaucracy as new offices were created to replace the medieval magistrates, whose role diminished. It also sought to strengthen solidarity among the members of the lagoon community at a time when, owing to the completion of urban construction, it might otherwise have declined. Finally, and most important, it bestowed upon the political authorities of Venice the supreme responsibility of ensuring the city's survival. In the face of innumerable perils, of countless new dangers, it was up to the state to triumph over adversity and deal with whatever hazards arose. By turning the environment and its problems into a target of instrumental action by the state, the state affirmed its own role as the indispensable ruler of time and space.

Thus began a new phase of Venetian history. To be sure, fifteenth-century hydraulic projects had their ups and downs. Firmness often gave way to declarations of helplessness and half-measures that were either contradictory, useless, or ill-advised. State action had many weaknesses. In the first half of the sixteenth century, however, more clearly defined principles of hydraulic policy began to emerge. Finally, in the seventeenth century various "macro-hydraulic" projects put an end to the threat from the rivers and made it possible to devise a rational policy for saving the basin, whose present-day contours are a result of that effort.[60]

Throughout the history of Venice, then, there have been periods when community spirit was focused and utilized in the name of what was presented as the common good. In this way, moreover, the political authorities defused various tensions and conflicts for their own benefit. First, there was the heroic age of progress during which a city was built on land reclaimed from the swamps. Later, from the fifteenth century on, came what I want to call the age of water, during which active measures were required to save the city. As projects multiplied, as the need for action was described as ever more urgent and imperative, state control increased.[61]

The community's own interpretations of its history thus mesh nicely. If we forget about the original image of a Venice protected by the sanctuary of its lagoon, we discover an image of more recent origin but no less tenacious: that of a marvelous city determined to survive in an impossible location. As Venetians describe the fragility of the site and the crisis of the ecosystem, they make the very existence of their city seem that much more miraculous. Seen in this light, the history of Venice is supposed to be a microcosm of man's relation to the environment. It exemplifies, we are told, the slow, arduous process of learning to deal with the elements of nature. But we are also told that because Venice overcame all obstacles and survived, the battle was on the whole victorious. Once again the city is seen as miraculously suspended between land and water. Inevitably, whoever writes the history of Venice seems condemned to write the history of its myths.

Translation by Arthur Goldhammer

NOTES

1. This is the way the geography of the lagoon was represented in 1500 by Jacopo de' Barbari, whose great map depicts some of the land masses around the Rialto archipelago. However, because of its extensive development and density, as well as its central position, the city of Venice dominates the map and is without doubt the focus of attention. The lagoon's islets, including those in the northern part of the basin, are clearly portrayed as modest satellites of the imposing Venetian ensemble. It has been shown that Barbari's model influenced how Venice was seen for a very long time

afterward. Take, for instance, the map by Ignazio Danti (1536–86), which can be seen in the Vatican's Gallerie delle Carte Geografiche (see J. Schulz, "Jacopo de' Barbari's View of Venice: Map Making, City Views, and Moralized Geography before the Year 1500," *Art Bulletin* 60, no. 3 [1978]: 425–74. See also G. Mazzariol and T. Pignatti, *La pianta prospettica di Venezia del 1500 disegnata da Jacopo de Barbari* [Venice, 1962]; T. Pignatti, "La pianta di Venezia de Jacopo de Barbari," *Bolletino dei Musei Civici Veneziani* 1–2 [1954]: 9–49; and G. Cassini, *Piante e vedute prospettiche di Venezia (1479–1855)* [Venice, 1971]. For an analysis of various cartographic representations, see also G. D. Romanelli, "Venezia tra l'oscurità degl'inchiostri: Cinque secoli de cartografia," introduction to the catalog *Venezia, piante e vedute,* ed. S. Biadene [Venice, 1982]; and J. Schulz, "Maps As Metaphors: Mural Map Cycles in the Italian Renaissance," in *Art and Cartography: Six Historical Essays,* ed. D. Woodward [Chicago, 1987], 97–122, 223–29. Finally, one other work that is indispensable for the history of iconographic representation is D. Rosand, "*Venezia Figurata:* The Iconography of a Myth," in *Interpretazioni veneziane: Studi di storia dell'arte in onore di Michelangelo Muraro,* ed. D. Rosand [Venice, 1984], 177–96).

2. This representation underscores what a number of recent historical works have finally shown, namely, that the Venetian basin was strongly linked to both the sea and the mainland. Hence it bears comparison with the more explicit representations of the lion, the symbol of Venice's patron saint, showing the well-known lion in the "andante" position—in profile, with one front paw resting on the Gospel, the other on the ground, while the two hind paws are in the water. The lion is looking toward the land, however. In 1516 Carpaccio was commissioned to do a painting with this theme. But as early as 1415, in the years following Venice's expansion into the *terraferma,* Jacobello del Fiore was the first to paint an "andante" lion (see M. Pozza, "I proprietari fondiari in Terraferma," in *Storia di Venezia: Dalle origini alla caduta della Serenissima,* 12 vols. [Rome, 1992–98], vol. 2, *L'età del Comune,* ed. G. Cracco and G. Ortalli, 661–80).

3. For the Venetians' complex and ambivalent attitude toward the sea, see A. Tenenti, "Il senso del mare," in *Storia di Venezia,* vol. 12, *Il Mare,* ed. A. Tenenti and U. Tucci; and idem, "The Sense of Space and Time in the Venetian World of the Fifteenth and Sixteenth Centuries," in *Renaissance Venice,* ed. J. R. Hale (London, 1973).

4. See E. Crouzet-Pavan, "Récits, images et mythes: Venise dans l'iter hierosolymitain," *Mélanges de l'Ecole française de Rome* 96, no. 1 (1984): 489–535, reprinted in idem, *Venise: Une invention de la ville, XIIIe–XVe siècle* (Seyssel, France, 1997), 256–72. Note, however, that some early modern maps depict both the city and its lagoons, whereas others depict the city alone. Over time maps of the second type became increasingly common.

5. The bibliography is impressive but uneven in quality. Among the earliest works are G. Rompiasio, *Metodo in pratica di sommario o sua compilazione delle leggi, terminazioni ed ordini appartenenti agli Ill. ed Ecc. Collegio e Magistrato alle Acque* (1771; reprint, Venice, 1988); C. Tentori, *Della legislazione veneziana sulla preservazione della laguna, Dissertazione storico-filosofico-critica* (Venice, 1792); B. Zendrini, *Memorie storiche dello stato antico e moderno delle lagune di Venezia e de quei fiumi che restarono divertiti per la conservazione delle medesime* (Padua, 1811); C. Vacani di Forteolivolo, *Della laguna di Venezia e dei fiumi nelle*

attigue provincie: Memorie (Florence, 1867); and A. Averone, *Saggio sull'antica idrografia veneta* (Mantua, 1911). Various historiographic approaches are illustrated by several more recent works, including *Mostra storica della laguna veneta* (Venice, 1970), in particular in that work B. Lanfranchi and L. Lanfranchi, "La laguna dal secolo VI al XIV" (74–84), M. F. Tiepolo, "Difesa a mare" (133–38), P. Selmi, "Politica lagunare della Veneta Reppublica dal secolo XIV al secolo XVIII" (105–15), and G. A. Ravalli Modoni, "Scrittori tecnici di problemi lagunari" (169–73); Ministero dei Lavori Pubblici, Magistrato alle acque, Venezia, Convegno di studi, *Laguna, fiumi, lidi: Cinque secoli di gestione delle acque nelle Venezie* (Venice, 1983); Archivio di Stato, Venice (ASV), *Laguna, lidi, fiumi: Cinque secoli di gestione delle acque* (Venice, 1983): S. Ciriacono, "Scrittori d'idraulica e politica delle acque," in *Storia della cultura veneta,* ed. Girolamo Arnaldi and Manlio Pastore Stocchi, 6 vols. (Vicenza, 1976–86), 3, pt. 2: 491–512; and finally, culminating recent methodological developments, the monumental and stimulating study by W. Dorigo, *Venezia: Origini: Fondamenti, ipotesi, metodi,* 2 vols. (Milan, 1983). The following works are still quite useful: G. Pavanello, "Di un'antica laguna scomparsa (La laguna eracliana)," *Archivio Veneto-Tridentino* 3 (1923): 263–307; idem, *La Laguna veneta (Note illustrative e breve sommario storico)* (Rome, 1931); idem, "Della caduta dell'Impero romano alla costituzione de nuovi centri politici e della laguna veneta propriamente detta," in G. Brunelli, G. Magrini, et al., eds., *La laguna di Venezia,* pt. 3, *La storia della laguna fino al 1140* (Venice, 1935), 53–73; R. Cessi, "Il problema della Brenta dal secolo XII al secolo XV," in ibid., vol. 2, pt. 4, tome 7 (Venice, 1943), 81–100; idem, "Evoluzione storica del problema lagunare," in *Atti del convegno per la conservazione e difesa della laguna e città di Venezia* (Venice, 1960), 23–64.

    6. On the causes of this forgetfulness, see E. Crouzet-Pavan, *La mort lente de Torcello: Histoire d'une cité disparue* (Paris, 1995). A number of more recent works representing a variety of approaches attest to a new interest in the history of the lagoon's communities, among them E. Concina, *Chioggia, saggio di storia urbanistica dalla formazione al 1870* (Treviso, 1977); J. C. Hocquet, *Le sel et la fortune de Venise: Production et monopole,* 2d ed., 2 vols. (Lille, 1982), and, by the same author, several articles reprinted in his *Chioggia capitale del sale nel Medioevo* (Sottomarina, Italy, 1991); and R. J. Goy, *Chioggia and the Villages of the Venetian Lagoon* (Cambridge, 1985).

    7. See G. B. Monticolo, ed., *Cronache veneziane antichissime* (Rome, 1890); and Giovanni Diacono, *La cronaca veneziana,* ed. M. de Biasi, 2 vols. (Venice, 1988). Scholars now believe that the *Chronica de singulis patriarchis Novae Aquileiae,* published in *Cronache veneziane antichissime,* was written between 1045 and 1053. The earliest Venetian narrative source is therefore Diacono's chronicle.

    8. Owing to the *duplicatio,* the Venice of the lagoon was, according to the narrative, basically a repetition of the first, mainland Venice and therefore already endowed with a lengthy history. This theme not only compensated for the newness of the island societies, however; it also invented a past, which became Venice's. The chronicler laid claim to a heritage because, he said, the Lombard invasion had introduced a discontinuity into the history of the terraferma. A civilization ended on the mainland and survived only in the lagoon, where Venice was at the same time called upon to forge a new history (see A. Carile, "Le origini di Venezia nella tradizione storiografica," in Arnaldi

and Stocchi, *Storia della cultura veneta*, 1:135–66; and A. Carile and G. Fedalto, *Le origini di Venezia* [Bologna, 1978]).

9. R. Cessi, ed., *Origo civitatum Italiae seu Venetiarum* (Rome, 1933), 30–35.

10. G. Fasoli, "I fondamenti della storiografia veneziana," in *La storiografia veneziana fino al secolo XVI: Aspetti e problemi*, ed. A. Pertusi (Florence, 1970), 11–44, reprinted in Fasoli, *Scritti di storia medievale*, ed. F. Bocchi, A. Carile, and A. I. Pini (Bologna, 1974); Crouzet-Pavan, *La mort lente de Torcello*, 36–41.

11. Magnus Aurelius Cassiodorus, *Variarum libri XII*, ed. A. J. Fridh, Corpus Christianorum, Latin Series, 96 (Turnhout, Belgium, 1973), 492.

12. Bernardo Giustinian, *De origine urbis Venetiarum*, in J. G. Graevius, *Thesaurus antiquitatum et historiarum Italiae*, vol. 5, pt. 1 (Leiden, 1722).

13. Carile and Fedalto, *Le origini di Venezia*, 32–33. The vast bibliography on Saint Mark's dream is cited in Crouzet-Pavan, *La mort lente de Torcello*, 69–71.

14. On the composition of the legend of San Magno and its analysis and use by certain Venetian chroniclers, see Crouzet-Pavan, *La mort lente de Torcello*, 61–65. The basic reference on the supposed charter is still V. Lazzarini, "Il preteso documento della fondazione di Venezia e la cronaca del medico Jacopo Dondi," *Atti dell'Istituto Veneto di Scienze, Lettere ed Arti* 75, pt. 2 (1915–16): 1263–81. For an analysis of minor forgeries that added complexity to the principal founding myth of 421, see Crouzet-Pavan, *La mort lente de Torcello*, 65–69.

15. The providentialist theme is particularly clear in Mocenigo's speech of 1421 (see Marin Sanuto, *Vitae ducum venetorum*, ed. Ludovico A. Muratori, Rerum Italicarum Scriptores, 22 [Milan, 1733], cols. 949–58). Regarding legislative pronouncements, I am thinking in particular of repressive legislation in regard to morals (see, e.g., E. Crouzet-Pavan, *"Sopra le acque salse": Espaces, pouvoir, et société à Venise à la fin du Moyen Age*, 2 vols. [Rome, 1992], 2:845–46; and idem, "Une fleur du mal? Les jeunes dans l'Italie médiévale (XIIIe–XVe siècle)," in *Histoire des jeunes en occident de l'antiquité à l'époque moderne*, ed. G. Levi and J.-C. Schmitt [Paris, 1996], 209–11).

16. To a large extent the independence of Venice from ties with the mainland explains the surprisingly durable legend according to which new episcopal sees were established in the lagoon at the time of the great migration, as the bishops of the terraferma one by one abandoned their old sees in favor of new ones. In reality, it took some time for the duchy to establish a stable religious system.

17. On the *contado invisibile*, see S. Bortolami, "L'agricoltura," in *Storia di Venezia*, vol. 2, *L'età del Comune*, 461–90.

18. The myth implied that the territorial state was at best a useless appendage to the Republic, at worst a damaging one, and in any case of little interest to historians because unconnected with its political and economic realities. As a result, knowledge about the Venetian terraferma for a long time remained superficial and vague. Distant traffic and convoys were analyzed; Romagna and the constitution of the Empire were scrutinized; and the effects of the Turkish incursion and, later, of the presumably catastrophic (for Venice) era of discovery were described. Apart from the study of military exploits associated with the conquest and reconquest of the mainland territory, the *stato di terra* was neglected. Over the past three or four decades, however, the

perspective has shifted dramatically. A vast inquiry is under way, begun by two pioneering works, M. Berengo's *La società veneta alla fine del Settecento: Ricerche storiche* (Florence, 1956) and A. Ventura's *Nobiltà e popolo nella società veneta del '400 e '500,* 2d ed. (Milan, 1993). Many subsequent monographs reflecting various points of view have deepened our knowledge.

19. Interestingly, according to the official historiography, from the beginning Venetians clashed with Paduans for control of the mouths of these rivers (see P. Morosini, *Historia della città e repubblica di Venezia* [Venice, 1637], 3–4).

20. Girolamo Priuli, *I diarii di Girolamo Priuli [AA. 1499–1512],* ed. Roberto Cessi, Rerum Italicarum Scriptores, 24, pt. 3, vol. 4 (Bologna, 1938), 19–24, 30–31.

21. The humanist Giovanni Battista Egnazio wrote the following very explicit verses for the *magistrato alle acque:*

> Venetorum urbs divina disponente
> Providentia aquis fundata
> Aquarum abitu circumsepta
> Aquis pro muro munitur
> Quisquis igitur quoquo modo
> Publicis aquis inferre detrimentum
> Ausus fuerit Hostis Patriae judicetur

(quoted in P. Selmi, "Politica lagunare della veneta Repubblica," 108–9). The formula, repeated endlessly, occurs in countless treatises on the lagoon, official histories of the Republic, and many compilations. To cite a few other references from a wealth of similar ones, see the dedication to Antonio Piscina in ASV, Archivio Proprio Giovanni Poleni, reg. 27; ASV, Archivio Proprio Trevisan, reg. 4, bk. 1; Luigi Cornaro, *Trattato di acque* (Padua, 1560), 1–3; and Bernardo Trevisan, *Trattato della laguna* (Venice, 1715).

22. Here we touch on the whole complex and evolving problem of the political, legal, economic, and cultural relations between the capital city and the duchy, with its land, water, and people living in a space that was more than just an occupied territory. For more on this view of the matter, see Crouzet-Pavan, *La mort lente de Torcello.*

23. Here I am briefly summarizing the findings of Crouzet-Pavan, *"Sopra le acque salse,"* 1:57–139. For a brief overview, see G. Bellavitis and G. D. Romanelli, *Le città nella storia d'Italia: Venezia* (Rome, 1985).

24. See the suggestive remarks in B. Cecchetti, "La vita dei veneziani nel 1300: Parte 1, La città, la laguna," *Archivio Veneto* 27 (1884): 5–54, 321–37; 28 (1884): 5–29, 267–96; and 29 (1885): 9–48, reprinted in Cecchetti, *La vita dei Veneziani nel 1300* (Bologna, 1980).

25. Crouzet-Pavan, *"Sopra le acque salse,"* 1:116–25.

26. Ibid., 97–116.

27. Ibid., 72–96.

28. On the various bodies of magistrates that successively ran the city and their respective jurisdictions, see ibid., 267–87.

29. The growth of Venice, despite some characteristics that make it unique, needs to be seen in a wider context and compared with that of other Italian cities expanding at

about the same time. For examples, see F. Sznura, *L'espansione urbana di Firenze nel Dugento* (Florence, 1975); M. Fanti, "Le lottizzazioni monastiche e lo sviluppo urbano di Bologna nel Duecento," *Atti e memorie della Deputazione di Storia Patria per la Romagna,* n.s., no. 27 (1976): 121–43; F. Bocchi, "Suburbi e fasce suburbane nella città dell'Italia medievale," *Storia della Città,* no. 4 (1977): 1–33; E. Hubert, *Espace urbain et habitat à Rome du Xe siècle à la fin du XIIIe siècle* (Rome, 1990), 134–40; G. Andenna, "Il monastero e l'evoluzione urbanistica di Brescia tra XI e XII secolo," in *S. Giulia di Brescia: Archeologia, arte, storia di un monastero regio dai Longobardi al Barbarossa,* ed. C. Stella and G. Brentegani (Brescia, 1992), 93–118; E. Guidoni, "Un monumento della tecnica urbanistica duecentesca: L'espansione di Brescia del 1237," in *La Lombardia: Il territorio, l'ambiente, il paesaggio,* ed. C. Pirovano, vol. 1 (Milan, 1981), 127–36; and G. M. Varanini, "L'espansione urbana di Verona in età comunale: Dati e problemi," in *Spazio, società, potere dell'Italia dei Comuni,* ed. G. Rossetti (Naples, 1986), 1–26. And for a brief overview of public and private initiatives in the construction of medieval cities, see E. Crouzet-Pavan, "Entre collaboration et affrontement: Le public et le privé dans les grands travaux urbains," in *Tecnologia y sociedad: Las grandes obras publicas en la Europa medieval* (Pamplona, 1996), 363–80.

30. Crouzet-Pavan, *"Sopra le acque salse,"* 1:265–85.

31. Ibid., 212–14. See also G. Mazzi, "Note per una definizione della funzione viaria a Venezia," *Archivio Veneto,* 5th ser., 99 (1973): 6–29.

32. Crouzet-Pavan, *"Sopra le acque salse,"* 1:194–214.

33. Venetian statutes define a *vicinus* as one who owns land in the parish in which he resides: "vicini qui possessiones habent in parochia ubicunque habitarent" (*Volumen Statutorum legium ac iurium de venetorum . . . Statuta veneta cum correctionibus et additionibus novissimis,* ed. D. Rizzardo Griffo [Venice, 1681], bk. 6, ch. 3, fols. 87v–88r). Broadly speaking, the *vicini* bore much of the burden of urban policy. Whatever the project— widening, paving, or repairing a road, constructing or repairing a bridge, dredging a canal—the commune relied on landowners to pay for the work, and *estimi* of real-estate values, regularly updated, determined each property owner's share. In most cases only those who owned adjacent land were concerned. For larger projects the entire neighborhood bore the financial burden collectively. When a project benefited two parishes, they divided the cost. The commune itself participated financially only when it had a direct interest in the project, which was rare.

34. In the brief space available here I cannot take up the question of the doubtless disparate attitudes of the poorest citizens and recent immigrants. Spatial cultures and practices vary widely; they reveal differences of chronology, resistances, and contradictions. For some hints on these matters, see Crouzet-Pavan, *"Sopra le acque salse,"* 2:739–98; and idem, *Venise,* 160–86.

35. M. Cornaro, *Scritture sulla laguna,* in *Antichi scrittori d'idraulica veneta,* ed. G. Pavanello, vol. 1 (Venice, 1919).

36. Giuseppe Gullino, "Marco Cornaro," in *Dizionario biografico degli italiani,* vol. 29 (Rome, 1983), 254–55.

37. Cornaro, *Scritture sulla laguna,* 75–78.

38. After Marco Corner, Paolo Sabbadino in the late fifteenth century suggested a

similar program of radical diversion of rivers, but it was his son, Cristoforo, whose discussion of the problems of the lagoon thoroughly explored the issues.

39. There was also a suggestion to divert the Piave so that "tra Lio Mazor e porto de Brondolo havesse a capitar tute aque" (see Cornaro, *Scritture sulla laguna,* 150).

40. Ciriacono, "Scrittori d'idraulica e politica delle acque."

41. Currents of sea water that enter the lagoon through one of the inlets in the barrier beaches do not mix with currents that enter through the other inlets. The lagoon is divided into basins of unequal size, and each inlet feeds its own basin. When the tide ebbs, the current reverses and water flows out through the same passage by which it entered. As a result, the volumetric ratio between the basins is not fixed. The flow rate of each current depends on the relationship between the size of the basin and the location of the mouth. The greater the surface area of the basin, the greater the flow rate (see Crouzet-Pavan, *"Sopra le acque salse,"* 1:355–57).

42. ASV, Senato, Terra, reg. 5, fol. 81v.

43. Ibid., reg. 7, fol. 37v.

44. Ibid., reg. 9, fol. 151v.

45. ASV, Savi ed esecutori alle acque, busta 330, fols. 61v, 66r; ASV, Senato, Terra, reg. 9, fol. 121v., reg. 10, fol. 152r, and reg. 11, fol. 8r.

46. ASV, Senato, Terra, reg. 12, fol. 69r.

47. For further details, see Crouzet-Pavan, *"Sopra le acque salse,"* 1:319–33.

48. R. Cessi, "Lo sviluppo dell'interramento nella laguna settentrionale e il problema della Piave e del Sile fino al secolo XV," in Brunelli, Magrini, et al., *La laguna di Venezia,* vol. 2, pt. 4, tome 7, pp. 81–100.

49. Crouzet-Pavan, *La mort lente de Torcello,* 326–35.

50. The Venetian basin is the largest series of lagoons on the northern Adriatic coast. Extensive stretches of salt or brackish water, the remains of a vast complex that once stretched from the Po to the Isonzo, are protected from the sea by a virtually unbroken series of sandy barrier beaches. But they are also fed by tidal flows, which enter through shifting channels or inlets. It was not until relatively late in the evolution of this system that the number of inlets was reduced to three: one at Chioggia, which opens to the south, and, closer to Venice, the Malamocco and Lido inlets. Various flat bits of land punctuate this almost unbroken seascape. The *barene* (shoals), which are covered with a distinctive vegetation, sit just a few inches above the water and are submerged only by the highest tides. There are also many islets and small archipelagos, probably formed by alluvial deposits from the rivers that empty into the basin; over time these have been shored up and expanded by human effort. This whole ecosystem was and is subject to continual transformation owing to the combined action of the sea, the rivers, and man. The Venetian lagoon today looks quite different from the way it looked at the end of the Middle Ages.

51. On the long-term evolution of the environment in contrast to the shorter time scale of human history, see E. Crouzet-Pavan and J. P. Poussou, "L'histoire de l'environnement: Un retour à la macrohistoire (Economie et écologie: ennemies ou alliées?)," in *XVIIIe Congrès des sciences historiques: Actes* (Montreal, 1995), 369–96.

52. In fact, according to one recent hypothesis, the lagoons did not exist in their

current form until the eleventh or twelfth century. W. Dorigo argues that the area around Venice was at first a series of *stagna,* areas periodically covered by water when the rivers flooded or, to a lesser extent, during very high tides. According to Dorigo, despite the hydrographic disorder caused by the deluges of the seventh century, and despite the first exceptional *acque alte* of the eighth century, the lagoon still had not formed by the end of the eighth century. Land, water, and marsh still coexisted in an unstable environment. In the late sixth century, however, in the northern part of the region, between Altino, Lio Piccolo, and Lio Maggiore, the diversion of the branch of the Piave that used to join with the Sile near Altino slowed the rate of alluvial deposit, which had ensured that the land would remain above the water. This led to an increase in the number of marshes and stagna. In the ninth century the old equilibrium between land and water, already disrupted by the earlier subsidence, was further compromised, initiating a series of changes that ultimately resulted in the formation of a virtually unbroken lagoon in the eleventh and twelfth centuries (see Dorigo, *Venezia: Origini,* 1:14–18, 76–205).

53. In 1505 the engineer Piero Sambo tried, for example, to measure the frightening progression of the *canneto* in sections where his father had earlier directed various hydraulic projects (primarily work on the course of the Brenta, which had been shifted from Lizzafusina to the Corbola canal) (see *La difesa idraulica della laguna veneta nel secolo XVI: Relazioni dei periti,* ed. R. Cessi and N. Spada, Antichi Scrittori d'Idraulica Veneta, 3 [Venice, 1952], 5–8). The *canneto* was a crucial element in the equilibrium of the lagoon environment. It was an area in which a dense vegetation of reeds and other marsh plants grew on a muddy bottom. The tidal flow had ceased to enter these built-up areas of mud; thus, the *canneto* was a precursor of the dead lagoon.

54. The Brenta issue therefore exacerbated conflict with Padua (see Cessi, "Il problema della Brenta dal secolo XII al secolo XV"). In particular, the Paduan effort to divert the river in 1142 increased the risk of sand buildup for the Venetians.

55. Crouzet-Pavan, "*Sopra le acque salse,*" 1:344–57.

56. Other important issues included the central problem of river navigation, securing a supply of fresh water for Venice, and pressure from mill owners and other industrial operators.

57. For examples of such inspections, see Crouzet-Pavan, "*Sopra le acque salse,*" 1:362–63.

58. The Senate decided to compile chancellery documents in 1405. Additional steps were taken in 1489. A notary was assigned to research legislation pertaining to the lagoon in the archives of the Great Council, the Senate, the Council of Forty, and the books of the Commemoriali.

59. See A. Favaro, "Notizie storiche sul magistrato veneto alle acque," *Nuovo Archivio Veneto,* n.s., no. 9 (1905): 179–99.

60. S. Ciriacono, *Acque e agricoltura: Venezia, l'Olanda e la bonifica europea in età moderna* (Milan, 1994), 162–70.

61. Other phases, related to other projects and goals, also need to be identified. One key moment was obviously connected with the *renovatio urbis* instigated by Doge Andrea Gritti.

II

Politics and Culture

2

The Serrata of the Great Council and Venetian Society, 1286–1323

GERHARD RÖSCH

Around the turn of the fourteenth century many of the communes of north and central Italy reached political and constitutional settlements after decades of conflict between the old nobility, new merchants, and artisans. In 1293, for example, Florence passed the Ordinances of Justice, establishing the city's guild-based republican regime. Other cities, such as Padua and Ferrara, opted for princely rule. Venice too saw the conclusion of decades of social and political unrest. According to the traditional interpretation, the Venetian crisis was resolved with the passage in 1297 of a law known as the Serrata, *or Closing, of the Great Council, a constitutional act that firmly established the city's republican regime on the basis of family membership and hereditary right and in so doing defined the ruling class of nobles. The* Serrata *has assumed a central place in Venetian historiography, and some of the most eminent scholars of the Venetian Middle Ages, including Roberto Cessi, Frederic Lane, and Giorgio Cracco, have debated its significance. In this essay, which draws on his important 1989 study* Der venezianische Adel bis zur Schließung des Großen Rats, *Gerhard Rösch tests the findings of these earlier historians and concludes that the* Serrata *was in actuality an extended process of social, legal, and political adjustment lasting more than three decades. Although the* Serrata *no longer stands as a discrete historical event, scholars nonetheless continue to explore the effect it had on the way Venetians thought about themselves, about their history, and, in particular, about questions of social privilege down to the end of the Republic.*

FOR NEARLY A CENTURY following the fall of Venice in 1797, historians, enchanted by the ideal of a polity that had endured for five hundred years, imagined the *Serrata,* or the Closing, of the Great Council in 1297 as the legislative act that gave birth to the Republic. In more recent scholarship this nineteenth-century "myth" of the Serrata has given way to an increasingly nuanced understanding of the establishment of the Venetian state. Rather than viewing the Venetian constitution as the product of one decisive event that can be dated to 1297, historians have come to see it as the outgrowth of a protracted process.

Yet twentieth-century scholarship on the Serrata has been marked by its own debates. Several scholars have held that legislative action in 1297 did in fact constitute a closing of the Great Council, restricting its membership to an elite group of Venetian patricians, while others have interpreted the Serrata primarily as an enlargement of the Great Council, an effort to extend membership to a larger number of distinguished families. The Italian historian Gherardo Ortalli has attempted to mediate between these two positions. As he writes in the most recent article on this subject, "In 1297 the so-called Serrata of the Great Council was achieved under Doge Pietro Gradenigo. On the one hand, it extended participation in the highest offices by accepting distinguished families of popular origin, while on the other, it prevented the acceptance of new groups of families."[1] Was the Great Council enlarged or closed at the end of the thirteenth century? The answer is crucial for understanding the constitutional as well as the social history of the Republic.[2]

Recent research has demonstrated the presence in Venetian society of a relatively well defined group of families who viewed themselves as noble long before the so-called Serrata. At the same time, it has shown that late medieval Venetian society was not as rigidly hierarchical as earlier historians assumed. After the conquest of Constantinople in 1204 and the extension of the Venetian colonial empire, for instance, many families were admitted to the leading ranks in the city. Most of these families had actively participated in the communal government of the twelfth century, but in the thirteenth century they merged with the old and noble families. So whereas in the first half of the thirteenth century we can distinguish between nobles *(nobiles)* and distinguished commoners *(populares veteres),* by the second half contemporary chronicles no longer made this distinction, but described all members of the ruling group in Venice as nobles. Indeed, an analysis of the membership of the Great Council from this period indicates that it represented the body of Venetian aristocracy long before the Serrata. The fifteen most distinguished families of the city provided 40 percent of the council members.[3] Thus, well before 1297 descent, age, and family reputation all determined eligibility for membership in the Great Council.[4] The families that had led the city for generations ruled it, and the sources consistently refer to them as nobles.[5]

This elite also managed to quash the political stirrings of the *popolo*.[6] When riots broke out in 1266 and in 1275 they were quickly quelled.[7] The guilds, the institutional expression of the popolo's aspirations, were granted certain rights of self-administration but were subject to oversight by the Giustizieri Vecchi, a magistracy whose members were drawn exclusively from the nobility.[8] When a prohibition on arming the guilds was included in the *promissione* (oath) of Doge Jacopo Contarini in 1275 the victory of the nobles over the popolo was complete.[9] Thus, some decades before the legislative acts that have come to be known as the Serrata, the amalgamation of the noble class and the subordination of the popolo had created the structures that many scholars have attributed to the Serrata itself.

If past research questioned the significance of the Serrata by demonstrating that social and constitutional arrangements once attributed to it had emerged before 1297, then recent scholarship has done so by emphasizing that Venetian society continued to evolve in significant ways after 1297.[10] Stanley Chojnacki, for example, has detected what he calls a second and a third Serrata in Renaissance Venice; he locates the second in a series of reforms in the early fifteenth century and the third in a similar process of constitutional and social adjustment at the start of the sixteenth century.[11] In light of the emergence of a new paradigm that sees the development of the politically enfranchised nobility of Venice as the result of a more protracted, more dynamic process, it is clearly time to reconsider the Serrata of the Great Council and its role in the development of Venetian politics and government.

Such a reconsideration is no easy task.[12] No law establishing the electoral procedures now known as the Serrata has come down to us, and in fact, it is probable that no such legislation ever existed. Instead, various resolutions concerning the election of Great Council members can be found from 1286 to 1323. Only in 1323 was the stage reached that historians writing in the fifteenth century would call the "closing," a development they placed in 1296–97. In the sixteenth century the genealogist Marco Barbaro described it as follows:

> From 1296 [*sic*] to the present, the dignity of noble citizens and members of the Great Council was and is one and the same, because there is no one in the Great Council who is not one of our noble citizens, nor is there any one of our nobly born citizens who is not either a member or eligible to be a member of the Great Council. And even if there are citizens of noble and gentle blood, nonetheless, when we speak of or write simply about a Venetian citizen [*semplicemente cittadino Veneto*], we mean and intend a citizen who is not, and is not eligible to be, a

member of the Great Council even if his father had been the emperor. And when we speak or write about a noble citizen [*nobile cittadino*], we mean and intend by it a citizen who is, or is eligible to be, in the Great Council even if his father, before he was raised to the dignity, had been of the most vile lineage; and after the closing [*Serrata*] of the Great Council, the chancery was prohibited from writing in its public records the title of nobility for those who were not, or are not eligible to be, members of the Great Council.[13]

According to Barbaro, in 1296–97 the Venetian aristocracy had defined itself and had become a virtual caste whose composition had changed only with the addition of a small number of new members.[14]

In this essay, by contrast, I intend to show that the Serrata of the Great Council was the product of a debate that lasted from 1286 to 1323 and that it resulted in a complete change in the procedures for admission to the council that clearly defined who was eligible for the council and thus who belonged to the Venetian nobility.

C U R I O U S L Y , the Serrata of the Great Council, often seen as the decisive turning point in Venetian constitutional and social history, is not mentioned in nearly contemporary Venetian sources.[15] The great chronicle of Andrea Dandolo only covers the period up to 1280, but his *Chronica brevis* also includes the dogeship of Pietro Gradenigo (1289–1311). Dandolo, who had intimate knowledge of the Venetian state, reports: "This Doge with his councils ordered that some commoners be admitted to the Great Council."[16] Dandolo makes no mention of a closing. The Giustinian chronicle, which is also relatively contemporary to the events, makes this same point more precisely. It states that in January 1303 the doge ordered that numerous refugees from Acre and the surrounding area, as well as an equal number of Venetian commoners who had distinguished themselves in the Second Genoese War (1294–99), be admitted to the Great Council.[17] Thus, while both chronicles describe the process that Frederic Lane calls the "enlargement of the Great Council," neither mentions a closing.

The same is true of Nicolò Trevisan's *Cronica di Venezia,* Lane's principal guide for his understanding of the Serrata. Under the heading "Come fu istituito l'ordine del Maggior Consiglio de Venetia" it describes how until the year 1296 two nobles from each of the city's six *sestieri* (administrative districts) elected 450 to 470 members to the Great Council every September.[18] They chose three or four members from each noble family and as many as possible (but not more than 15) from their own families. A short but correct summary of the resolution from 1297 (which I consider below) follows this entry. The chronicler then lists the names of 215 men who were admitted to the council at that time and emphasizes that he copied this list from the originals in the chancery, where not all the names were legible. Since the author emphasizes that the process of approbation continued until the dogeship of Francesco Foscari (1423–57), we have a *terminus ante quem*. The fifteenth-century chronicler drew his knowledge from the records of the chancery and the minutes of the council, but his information about the period before 1297 is demonstrably incorrect. Nevertheless, two points should be stressed: first, there is no mention of a serrata; and second, when writing about the period before the passage of the law, the chronicler wrote explicitly, even naturally, about a Venetian nobility.

A second account of the Serrata appears a little later in the chronicle; it is evidently the work of a different author.[19] We cannot be certain that this was Nicolò Trevisan, as Lane supposed, for the entire chronicle, as it comes down to us in a manuscript of the late sixteenth century, has been heavily reworked. The author gives a general evaluation of the politics of Doge Pietro Gradenigo:

> He [Gradenigo] wished to reform the Great Council, into which he wished to admit a larger number of families so that they might be recognized as noble and equal to the others, and not that a few families (only) should be the chief and most revered of the city, taking away (at the same time, however) from the citizens and the common people the way that they used to have of being admitted to the Great Council. And the root of this innovation was the hatred which he had towards the common people who before his election had acclaimed Doge Messer Jacomo Tiepolo . . . and continued after his election to show their preference for the house of Tiepolo.[20]

This description contains a contradiction. First, the author mentions a point we already know from the Dandolo and Giustinian chronicles, namely, that Doge Gradenigo wished to admit new members. But he then goes on to claim that Gradenigo prevented the admission of nonnobles in the future because of his hatred for the followers of Tiepolo. Whether or not the story about Tiepolo is true—for it is likely constructed from events surrounding Gradenigo's election as doge and the Querini-Tiepolo conspiracy of 1310—the assertion that admission to the council was blocked for citizens is clearly wrong, as we will see, for under this doge in particular various ways of electing *novi homines* (new men) were discussed repeatedly.

If this account indeed dates from the second half of the fourteenth century, then it is unique in its depiction of events and not very credible. It is more likely a product of the fifteenth century, when reports of popular opposition

to Doge Pietro Gradenigo became more frequent and the events were portrayed—as in Marcantonio Sabellico's classically inspired *Rerum venetarum ab
urbe condita* (1487)—as a fight on the Roman model between patricians and
plebians.[21] It is in these fifteenth-century accounts that we find the first mention of the closure. What fifteenth-century Venetian chroniclers described was
the state of society in their time, for after the first two decades of the fourteenth
century only thirty families were admitted to the council (during the turbulent
years of the War of Chioggia).[22] Subsequently a policy of keeping the classes
apart was pursued, and the nobility became a closed, hereditary aristocracy.
Fifteenth-century chroniclers dated this state of affairs back to the end of the
thirteenth century and interpreted a resolution of the council as a closing,
although we now know that there is no evidence to support such an interpretation. Indeed, already in the sixteenth century the Florentine Donato Giannotti
was skeptical about the idea of a serrata. In his dialogue on the government of
Venice he wrote: "I never read or understood what caused and brought about
the closing of the council."[23] The Venetian chronicles are of little help here.

IN ORDER to understand the changes in the electoral system as they evolved
after 1297, we need first to consider electoral procedures before that date.[24]
Elections had two parts: nomination *(electio)* by a set of electors and a subsequent vote *(approbatio)* in the Great Council. Before elections, those whose
terms were expiring selected the electors and established the voting procedures. In this way the sitting council directly influenced the selection of the
new one, and because the number of members in the Great Council had grown
smaller and smaller over the preceding decades, the danger existed that through
the clever manipulation of the electoral process a party might succeed in excluding the opposition from the newly elected council.

There were, moreover, two distinct categories of council members: regularly elected members and ex-officio members. The latter included the doge
and members of the Signoria, the Quarantia (the Forty), and the Senate, as well
as other high officials of the state. When a regularly elected member of the
Great Council was appointed to a high political office, he did not withdraw
from the council but rather represented his office within it. Of course, the seat
that he had held up to that time, which was an elected seat, had to be filled by a
successor, and for this reason by-elections were held. Electors (actually nomi-
nators) with terms of six months were designated to handle these by-elections.
As a consequence of all this, the membership and the composition of the Great
Council changed constantly throughout the year.

Changes in these electoral procedures were first instituted eleven years before the so-called Serrata of 1297. On 3 October 1286 a proposal was put forward that all regularly elected members of the Senate and the Great Council be confirmed by a majority of the Forty beforehand, a motion that apparently did not pass. Two days later, on 5 October, an attempt was made to confine membership in the councils to those whose fathers and grandfathers had already been members. For a *novus homo* to be elected, he would have to receive a majority first in the Ducal Council and then in the Great Council.[25] Doge Giovanni Dandolo (1280–89) opposed this proposal, and it failed to pass. A proposal of 17 October suggesting that the electors' nominations be approved by the Forty, the Senate, and the Ducal Council in a joint meeting failed as well.[26] Thus, attempts were made to limit the ability of the electors to admit lesser families to the political bodies and to make them dependent on larger majorities. But these did not constitute a "closing" since the procedures explicitly provided for the admission of the newly rich. Ten years later, on 6 March 1296, these proposals were again brought forward, and again they failed to pass.[27] Finally, on 28 February 1297, when elections were due, admission was organized in a new way, with three different procedures or categories of membership and a trial period of one and a half years for the new procedures.[28] The first category comprised those who had been members of the council in the last four years. They had to be confirmed with twelve votes in the Forty. The second category included those who had been in the council but had given up their seats because they were absent from the city; they could ask the Forty to reconfirm them with twelve votes. The third category was made up of persons who had not been members of the council in the preceding four years; they could be nominated to the council by the electors following the rules laid down for them by the doge and his councilors. Given the existence of an option for admitting new men, these procedures should not be considered a closing of the Great Council.

Two points should be made here. First, the primary intention of these new electoral procedures was to elect members who had political experience. This was advisable since at the time Venice was fighting a war against its major maritime rival, Genoa, and was involved in a war against Padua as well. Therefore, it seemed prudent first to hold a vote on those men who had been members of the council in the preceding years, which would ensure political continuity. Only then would further members be nominated, although they would only need the same number of votes (12) in the Forty as the other members.[29] A secondary intention, as Roberto Cessi suggested, was to resolve a structural problem within the Great Council itself.[30] Given officeholders' right to sit in the council as ex-officio members, the one hundred regularly elected members could at any time have been outvoted by officeholding members, who in this way could have completely taken over the leadership of the state. The new procedure, however, allowed the overall number of members to increase indefinitely, avoiding this dilemma, although the inner circle's power was still preserved, since the doge and his council determined the number of members, the *electores* drew up the lists of candidates, and the Forty approved them.

The records of the Great Council for the next few years are fragmentary. But some resolutions have survived indicating that the electoral procedure was not changed again. However, in December 1298 a resolution was put forward in an attempt to bring about the closing of the Forty. It stated that in the future only men whose fathers and grandfathers had been members of the Great Council should qualify for election to the Forty.[31] Clearly the old families wanted to control this body, which had never before claimed a leading role in the state. It is important to remember that the Forty had to vote on new members of the Great Council. Thus, by attempting to limit the Forty to established families, the old families were seeking to retain for themselves the right to select new members. For the first time, then, an attempt was made to link admission to a council explicitly to qualification for council membership in the third generation.

On 22 March 1300 yet another step was taken toward the closing of the political elite. A law was passed prohibiting the doge and his council from nominating *novi homines* for election to the Great Council without the prior approval of a majority in the Forty.[32] Margarete Merores was probably correct in identifying this procedure for admission as the same one that, for the first time in 1317, was called *per gratiam*.[33] Now men who did not belong to the established families of the ruling class had to find a requisite majority in the Forty. But in the ensuing years it became more and more difficult to achieve the necessary majorities through this procedure. In 1307 the rule was changed; now twenty-five votes were needed in the Forty and six in the Ducal Council.[34] By 1311 this had been changed to thirty votes in the Forty and a majority in the Great Council.[35] That same year the necessary percentage of votes in the Great Council was raised to two-thirds. These changes indicate that a group of patricians favored closing the Great Council.

At the beginning of the fourteenth century, then, there were three possible means of acquiring membership in the Great Council.[36] First, those who were already members could ask the Forty to approve their further participation. Since only twelve votes were needed, this was generally easy to achieve. As Frederic Lane noted, these men were for all intents and purposes members for life. If they left Venice for the East or elsewhere, they lost their privilege, but it could be revived by a single vote of the Forty. Second, the doge and his council could decide on the election of new members who had not yet been active in the council. The electors nominated the new members, and the Forty approved them. The consensus was that only members of certain families, that is, men whose ancestors had already qualified for council membership, could be elected in this way. Without a formal resolution of any kind a cluster of elite families effectively cut themselves off from the rest of the population. Third, the Signoria could announce a citizen eligible per gratiam, although approval of the Forty and of the Great Council was needed. As noted above, the number of votes required in this procedure increased constantly. Again a tendency of the higher ranks to distinguish themselves from the rest of the populace is clearly detectable.

Other minor changes followed. In 1315 the minimum age for a seat in the council was set at eighteen years. At the same time, it was decided that everyone who was eligible should be registered with the Forty.[37] Registration was necessary because the electors were no longer able to keep track of who was eligible for admission. This book of registrants, now lost, represents the beginning of the registry of noble births, which from the sixteenth century on was known as the *Libro d'Oro,* or Golden Book.[38]

Yet this procedure must have been misused, for on 8 January 1317 Tommaso Dandolo, former head of the Forty, proposed a motion demanding investigation of doubtful claims to noble status. Moreover, those who had gained unauthorized entry were threatened with the enormous fine of three hundred pounds. The motion was approved, and its enforcement entrusted to the Avogadori di Comun (state attorneys).[39] Men who had entered the council per gratiam (and thus had not registered) were explicitly exempted from the fines. However, only in 1323 was it explicitly stated that only those men whose ancestors had been in the council were eligible for admission by this procedure.[40] In 1321 the system of electors itself was abolished, and every member of the Venetian aristocracy twenty-five years of age and older was granted a seat and a vote in the Great Council; some eighteen-year-olds chosen by lot also could gain early admission.[41] With the exception of a few offices, such as that of the chancellor of the Republic, the right to vote was now connected solely to membership in the Great Council.[42] All in all, it had taken a whole generation of changes and modifications before what has been described in the historiography as the closing of the Great Council was achieved.

Reviewing the developments, we see that in the years after 1297 the Great Council was not yet closed since the per gratiam procedure remained.[43] In the third book of his genealogies of the Venetian nobility Marco Barbaro lists a large number of families who were admitted per gratiam between 1298 and 1310. Only later, under the influence of new social and political developments, would Venetians come to read the events of these years as a "closing." For the first few years, however, the exact opposite was the case. Doge Pietro Gradenigo not only admitted families expelled from Acre and the Holy Land but also, according to the chronicle of Doge Andrea Dandolo, admitted some commoners to the council with the consent of the officials in charge. Gradenigo pursued a policy of opening the council and enlarging the Venetian upper class. It is likely that it was the opponents of this policy who made it more and more difficult for novi homines to meet the requirements for admission. What is clear is that after 1310 things changed, although we cannot be certain whether the Querini-Tiepolo conspiracy led to this development.

While some Venetians were admitted to the Great Council per gratiam after 1310, it is nonetheless true that a more restrictive policy was pursued. No commoners were among the newly admitted members. Instead two groups were dominant: foreigners and bearers of well-known family names. Considering the state of foreign affairs, it made sense to admit important foreign nobles as honorary members of the Great Council. After all, it cost little, since these individuals did not take part in the sessions in Venice. Among those admitted were Enrico Scrovegni of Padua (1301), the marquis Azzo of Ferrara, of the house of Este (1304), the count of Treviso, Rambaldo di Colalto (1309), Rinaldo de' Pucci of Florence (1311), Cangrande della Scala of Verona (1329), and Lodovico Gonzaga of Mantua (1332).[44]

There were also discussions about marriage, since legitimate birth was a prerequisite for noble status. The marriage registers of the Venetian nobility, the second part of the Libro d'Oro, originated from this prerequisite. A resolution excluding men of illegitimate birth had been strictly enforced since 1277.[45] In fact, the records of the Republic were originally meant to serve as a basis for proving legitimacy. Such a procedure, however, proved difficult in practice, and officials were forced again and again to refer to fama publica. Once an ancestor with the same name was found in the registers, direct descent still had to be proven. Illustrative is the case of Candio, Donato, and Barbaro Abrami, who had emigrated to Crete. In 1345, to support their claim for admission, they presented a genealogy to the Forty and the Ducal Council and provided the testimony of some Greeks that it was public opinion on Crete that the Abrami had been members of the Great Council.[46] Nevertheless, they were not admitted until the early fifteenth century. In another case from the same year, the grandson of Nicolò Auduino claimed that his grandfather had belonged to the Forty in 1276 and 1301 but not subsequently. Again admission was not granted until the beginning of the fifteenth century.[47] During an investigation into the eligibility of Filippo, son of Donato di Mare, Tommaso Longo, Pietro Barozzi, and Marino Pisani, all swore that fifty years earlier Pietro di Mare had been a member of the Great Council.[48] Yet such petitions failed again and again, though the reasons for their failure are unclear. Bearers of distinguished names such as Paolo Grilioni (1331) and Natale Mauro (1336) were rejected by the Forty.[49] All in all, the nobility followed a clear policy. Until the War of Chioggia (1379–81) no new families were admitted per gratiam. Only in that time of great need were men who had rendered outstanding service admitted to the Great Council and thus also to the Venetian aristocracy. After that the per gratiam procedure was again used sparingly.

What is the explanation for this course of events? According to traditional Venetian historiography, two rival factions existed within the nobility at the end of the thirteenth century: the conservatives around the Dandolo and Gradenigo and their opponents, the Tiepolo and Querini, along with their supporters. The former wished to maintain the leadership of the old families, while the latter wanted to integrate at least the newly rich into the ruling elite.[50] In the end the oligarchs succeeded. But this explanation is no longer tenable since it is based on a misinterpretation of the rivalry between the Dandolo and Tiepolo families, of the rebellion of Baiamonte Tiepolo, and indeed of the Serrata itself.[51] In the twentieth century, Roberto Cessi, Giorgio Cracco, and Frederic Lane have posed alternative explanations, all of which move away from the traditional idea of a closing of the Great Council.

As we have already seen, Roberto Cessi offered a purely technical explanation for the reforms of 1297.[52] According to Cessi, during the course of the thirteenth century Venetian offices had developed and increased in number, and the custom of consulting officials as ex-officio members led to greater and greater disproportions between them and the regularly elected Great Council members. However, since the ex-officio members doubtless had the majority in the council, the one hundred regularly elected council members were in danger of losing their significance. According to Cessi, the reforms of 1297 were intended to do away with the fixed number of regular seats in the council.

In this way the number of council members was increased and the Great Council was confirmed in its role as the central organ of the Venetian constitution. The main strength of Cessi's argument is its faithfulness to the sources, but he overestimates the significance of purely institutional developments and underestimates the role of party interests, foreign affairs, and economic factors in shaping those events.

By contrast, Giorgio Cracco bases his explanation of the events of 1297 and the policies of Doge Pietro Gradenigo on an analysis of the various social groups that shaped Venetian politics.[53] Cracco shows that the lines dividing noble and commoner, rich and poor, and old and new families were not clear. He locates the social origins of the Serrata in the struggle of disenfranchised merchants against the *grandi,* or *magnati,* a conflict exacerbated by the collapse of a long-term economic boom and the commercial difficulties that came in its wake. While the old great families, whose leader was the doge, were able to overcome the new threats to commerce with the help of their secure wealth, other merchants were not. Therefore, they strove for more political power in order to enjoy the financial benefits of officeholding as well. According to Cracco, Pietro Gradenigo played the members of this group against one another. By smoothing the way for part of this bourgeoisie to enter the Great Council, he split the middle class and drew the wealthier and the more important members to his side and that of the grandi. Cracco recognizes that economic factors played a part in the events surrounding 1297, but he is hampered by the difficulty of clearly delineating these social groups in the sources.

For Frederic Lane, problems within the nobility itself were the immediate reason for the change in the electoral law.[54] In the years 1261–82 between four hundred and five hundred noblemen had to be nominated in by-elections each year to take the place of those who had become ex-officio members. The large number of nominees ensured that no family that enjoyed the right to participate in political power was excluded. However, in the years immediately before 1297 posts were increasingly filled by men who were not members of the Great Council, so that the number of men nominated in by-elections declined. This created the dangerous possibility that individual factions might try to exclude their enemies from power through control of the nominating process. The inclination of the electors to nominate members of their own families in the largest possible numbers only increased this danger. Furthermore, there are signs that the unity of the Venetian upper class that had characterized the thirteenth century was coming to an end. The situation in northern Italy, where the Guelfs and the Ghibellines were fighting each other, probably increased the fear of established parties still further. For Lane the enlargement of the council—and it was nothing but this—prevented individual noble factions from seizing power, while the admission of groups of common people reduced the threat of those looking for allies in the guilds.[55]

Each of these interpretations has merits, but none fully explains events from 1286 to 1321. My own interpretation combines these three views and takes into consideration all the major events from 1286 until 1321. First, as I have argued above, it is crucial to view the events of 1297 in the context of previous changes in electoral procedures. Elections took place by various means, with the Great Council determining the procedure. In fact, at least sixty-five different resolutions concerning electoral procedures are known before the so-called Serrata.[56]

Second, with regard to the specific changes in the electoral law of 1297, the difficulties of the war with Padua may have triggered the decision to change the rules in such a way that political experience would be secured for the new session. Many of the most experienced politicians doubtless were needed as military leaders in the war effort. This meant that the new council, the decisive body of the Venetian constitution, might be made up primarily of young and inexperienced members of the nobility. Therefore, it seemed sensible to vote on those who had gained experience as members in the previous four years before adding new members.[57] The electoral process underwent further alternations, and the resolution of 1297 should be seen in this context. In 1298 the number of councilors again declined, probably because of a shortage of suitable applicants in the city. The terrible Venetian defeat at the hands of the Genoese near Curzola in the same year may have further exacerbated this problem. The provisional and experimental character of these electoral changes is apparent, for the new procedure had to undergo a trial period of eighteen months.

Third, in the period 1298–1310 a group within the nobility who supported the election of new families into the Great Council clearly emerged. Lane was correct to characterize this change as an enlargement. The proponent of this policy was Doge Pietro Gradenigo; as long as he was the head of state those who favored this strategy were rather successful. Beyond this, however, the records are confusing, and it is prudent not to assign particular groups or families within the nobility to a particular party. The Dandolo, for example, are traditionally seen as allies of Doge Gradenigo, but we know that in 1286 Doge Giovanni Dandolo, a member of the family later chroniclers perceived as the leader of the oligarchic faction, thwarted the first attempts to change the electoral law. And in 1317 Tommaso Dandolo, leader of the Forty, requested that a register of the nobility be started. What we know for certain is that about 1300 a number of new families were admitted to the council. The families returning from Acre may have exacerbated the problem of political participation. The old ruling class could integrate individual new families easily, but larger groups posed a problem. In this regard a comparison of the size of the Great Council in selected years is revealing:[58]

Year	Members	Year	Members
1297	589	1308	458
1298	582	1311	1,107
1299	513	1314	1,150
1300	607	1349	960
1302	586	1350	897

These figures show a significant increase in the number of council members immediately after the Querini-Tiepolo conspiracy of 1310. Later chronicles state that Doge Gradenigo hated the populace. But if contemporary sources are to be believed, this was not the case. On the contrary, we have ample evidence of nonnobles holding public offices during his reign. In 1296, for example, Domenico Schiavo commanded a squadron, and in 1300 he was a *capitaneus* of a fleet. Normally only aristocrats could become admirals in Venice.[59]

Nevertheless, opposition to Gradenigo's policy did develop shortly afterwards, though it is difficult to identify who his opponents were. By frequently pressing for increases in the number of votes required for the admission of new members per gratiam, the opposition was successful in limiting entry only to those supported by the entire nobility. Even so, admission per gratiam was only used in the aftermath of the War of Chioggia and fell into desuetude in the fifteenth and sixteenth centuries. This policy of closure is in line with the general tendency during the fourteenth century toward more hierarchical arrangements in Venetian society.[60] Indeed, nothing better illustrates this new sense of hierarchy than the Ducal Council's defeat of a motion in 1403 to ensure that a commoner family would be admitted to the Great Council whenever a noble family died out.[61]

The clear presence of two factions clashing over the question of admission to the Great Council raises the difficult issue of political parties in Venice, a problem that continues to engage historians of other Italian city-states.[62] The older historiography accepted the myth of a unified noble caste that felt responsible for the welfare of Venice. This historiography relied on chroniclers of the late Middle Ages, who were deliberately silent about factional fighting.[63] Council meetings, in which conflict was likely to break the surface, were secret affairs, and the only evidence of factions we have are occasional allusions to riots, which the chroniclers felt compelled to mention.

But historians must exercise caution and not assume the existence of factions—as they have done, for example, in making a connection between the Dandolo-Tiepolo feud and the Querini-Tiepolo conspiracy. The feud between the Dandolo and Tiepolo families, after all, probably dates to 1229, when a stalemate between Marino Dandolo and Jacopo Tiepolo in the ducal election was solved by drawing lots.[64] Tiepolo won the office, but Pietro Ziani, who had resigned from the dogeship, refused to receive a doge who had been elected in this manner. In the middle of the century the feud between the families reached its bloody climax in violent actions in the piazza San Marco. Then, in 1268, when Lorenzo Tiepolo was elected doge, a reconciliation that was apparently one of the conditions for his election, was achieved.[65]

All of the alleged representatives of the commoners', or people's, party are so identified on the basis of their later participation in the Querini-Tiepolo conspiracy in 1310, which fifteenth-century chroniclers wrongly interpreted as a consequence of the Serrata. A similar interpretation was applied to the shadowy rebellion of Marino Bocco against Doge Pietro Gradenigo in 1300.[66] Yet the Tiepolo family had been accepted into the highest ranks of Venetian society at the beginning of the thirteenth century and for about a hundred years had been one of the city's most distinguished families. Nonetheless, the popolo supported the Tiepolo, even though their lifestyle had long been similar to that of the Ziani, Dandolo, Gradenigo, and Morosini.[67] After the death of Doge Giovanni Dandolo, commoners demanded the election of Jacopo Tiepolo. But pressure from the nobility forced him to leave the city until the election of a successor had taken place. The intent was clear: the Tiepolo should be prevented from providing a doge in the third generation (both Jacopo's father and grandfather had been doge), which would risk the possibility of rulership by a single family. It was typical for the candidate of the common people to bow to pressure from the nobility. When Baiamonte Tiepolo and his conspirators planned the murder of Doge Pietro Gradenigo, they did it for very personal reasons, namely, to revenge the slight to Baiamonte's father, Jacopo. Only much later did historians draw a connection between the conspiracy and the Serrata.

The question of factions leads to the greater question whether Guelf and Ghibelline parties existed in Venice as they did elsewhere in Italy.[68] It should be noted that Venice lay outside the Holy Roman Empire. Thus, it had less reason than other cities to take a clear stand in the conflict between Emperor Frederick II and the papacy. Nominally Venice, fearing imperial hegemony in northern Italy, was a member of the coalition against the Hohenstaufen. After the deposition of Frederick II at the Council of Lyons in 1245 a peace was negotiated.[69] Party conflict, which was often only a pretext for local animosities, therefore did not lead to programmatic opposition in Venice. Only when Venetian families extended their political activities to the mainland did they have to take sides. This was the case with the Querini, who owned property in the Ferrarese and provided a bishop in Ferrara. They were generally assumed to be Guelfs.[70] When, however, Doge Pietro Gradenigo started a war with Pope Clement V over Ferrara, bringing Venice under interdict, the Guelf-Ghibelline division became an issue in Venice as well. One story, that ladies of the Tiepolo and Querini families wore bonnets "alla Ghibellina" while the Dandolo and Badoer women wore them "alla Guelfa," is almost certainly apocryphal.[71] And while it is certainly possible that the conflict with the church, which damaged Venetian trade through confiscations, may have temporarily introduced Italy's traditional party patterns to the city, we do not hear of this conflict after this time. This does not mean that factions did not exist within the Venetian nobility; indeed, we can clearly detect efforts to prevent their development, such as a 1274 prohibition on carrying arms into council meetings.[72] But more important than these efforts at preventing the problems that occurred in the other northern Italian city-states were the economic expansion of the thirteenth century and the opportunities Venice was able to exploit as a maritime power.[73]

At the end of the thirteenth century, after a long period of growth, western Europe entered a period of economic stagnation, and the era in which significant numbers of new men were able to become rich came to an end.[74] Statistics for this economic crisis are difficult to come by, but Italy's coastal cities must have felt it immediately. What we can trace in this period is a change in the trade policy of Venice, which from 1315 on assumed an increasingly hostile attitude toward foreigners. Although Venice had relied on foreign capital to finance its war effort as recently as the Second Genoese War, it now rejected foreign influences. The *provveditori di comun,* a newly established authority, now required every merchant to prove his Venetian citizenship. If he could not do so, he had to pay high customs like all foreigners.[75] In 1305 the Great Council declared that those who had lived in the city for twenty-five years should receive citizenship and those who had been there for ten years should be permitted to stay.[76] However, since only full citizens with the right *de intus et extra* were entitled to the city's trade privileges, the nobility had basically secured its commercial interests against competitors.

WHAT CONCLUSIONS can we draw about the so-called Serrata of the Great Council of Venice? Our analysis of the documentary evidence indicates that in the first years after 1297 a policy of opening and enlarging the council occurred. Doge Pietro Gradenigo advocated this policy. Soon, however, other forces came into play that limited admission even though the procedure of admission per gratiam was in place. The question whether officials in the year 1297 intended to close the Great Council when they passed their resolutions remains open, but the political situation immediately after the so-called Serrata suggests that this was not the case, and admissions increased dramatically in the aftermath of the Querini-Tiepolo conspiracy of 1310. It was Frederic Lane who first drew attention to the fact that the tendency of the upper class to cut itself off from the rest of the society, something unknown in Venice up until then, was a clear reaction to increasing economic difficulties after 1315. The economic crisis explains why the changes regarding admission to the council, which began as an enlargement, changed into a closing.

What fifteenth-century chroniclers described when they discussed events at the end of the thirteenth century was actually the state of affairs in their own time, when the Venetian aristocracy had indeed become an increasingly closed and well-defined group unwilling to share power with the newly rich. Searching for the origin of this situation, fifteenth-century chroniclers believed they had found it in the electoral law of 1297, for there they identified a fundamental change that put its mark on society for centuries. What is clear is that, in contrast to men of the thirteenth century and first two decades of the fourteenth century, the generations after the reign of Doge Pietro Gradenigo were no longer willing to allow successful new merchants to share in power as equals. The difference between commoners and nobles, defined by eligibility for membership in the council, became more and more pronounced. For those who came too late, qualification as *cittadini* provided a field of activity and prestige and distinguished them from the mass of inhabitants. Thus Marco Barbaro was correct when he wrote that as a consequence of the events of

1297, "ogni giorno più cresceva la distinzione di cittadino e cittadino nobile" (every day the distinction between citizen and noble grew greater).

NOTES

1. Gherardo Ortalli, "Venedig," in *Lexikon des Mittelalters,* 9 vols. (Munich, 1980–98), 8:1459–1466, esp. 1465.

2. Because it supposedly guaranteed stable structures in the midst of a changing world, the Venetian constitution has long fascinated students of European political history. For the traditional view of the Serrata in the history of the Venetian constitution, see G. B. Muazzo, *Del Governo antico, delle Alterazioni, e Regulationi de esso, e delle Cause e Tempi che sono Successo fino a nostri Giorni e precisamente del Maggior Consiglio della Republica Veneta* (Venice, 1671); and Cristoforo Tentori, *Saggio sulla storia civile, politica ed ecclesiastica della Republica de Venezia* (Venice, 1785). In this narrative, the Serrata, which supposedly set the seal on noble rule for more than five hundred years, is a salient feature of the myth of Venice that recent research has done so much to illuminate. On the myth, see especially James S. Grubb, "When Myths Lose Power: Four Decades of Venetian Historiography," *Journal of Modern History* 58 (1986): 43–94; and John Martin and Dennis Romano's introductory essay in this volume. But while many elements of this myth have been revealed as fictions, the myth of the Serrata lives on (see, e.g., Donald E. Queller, *The Venetian Patriciate: Reality versus Myth* [Urbana, 1986]; and Anthony Molho, Kurt Raaflaub, and Julia Emlen, eds., *City States in Classical Antiquity and Medieval Italy* [Ann Arbor, 1991], where Venice continues to be portrayed as a city free of political conflict).

3. Gerhard Rösch, *Der venezianische Adel bis zur Schließung des Großen Rats: Zur Genese einer Führungsschicht* (Sigmaringen, 1989), 121–34.

4. Margarete Merores, "Der große Rat von Venedig und die sogenannte Serrata vom Jahre 1297," *Vierteljahrschrift für Sozial- und Wirtschaftsgeschichte* 21 (1928): 52–54.

5. Rösch, *Der venezianische Adel,* 134–41.

6. Ibid., 157–60.

7. Andrea Dandolo, *Chronica per extensum descripta,* ed. Ester Pastorello, Rerum Italicarum Scriptores, 12, pt. 1 (Bologna, 1933), 314, 321.

8. Rösch, *Der venezianische Adel,* 158–59.

9. Gisella Graziato, ed., *Le promissioni del doge di Venezia: Dalle origini alla fine del Duecento* (Venice, 1986), 90.

10. Stanley Chojnacki, "In Search of the Venetian Patriciate: Families and Factions in the Fourteenth Century," in *Renaissance Venice,* ed. J. R. Hale (London, 1973), 47–90; Dennis Romano, *Patricians and Popolani: The Social Foundations of the Venetian Renaissance State* (Baltimore, 1987), 141–58.

11. Stanley Chojnacki, "Social Identity in Renaissance Venice: The Second Serrata," *Renaissance Studies* 8 (1994): 341–58. See also his "Identity and Ideology in Renaissance Venice: The Third *Serrata*" in this volume.

12. Margarete Merores, "Der venezianische Adel: Ein Beitrag zur Sozialgeschichte," *Vierteljahrschrift für Sozial- und Wirtschaftsgeschichte* 19 (1926): 193–237; idem, "Der große Rat von Venedig," 33–113; Heinrich Kretschmayr, *Geschichte von Venedig*, 3 vols. (Gotha, 1905–34), 2:74–76; Jean-Claude Hocquet, "Oligarchie et patriciat à Venise," *Studi Veneziani* 17–18 (1975–76): 401–10; Frederic C. Lane, "The Enlargement of the Great Council of Venice," in *Florilegium Historiale: Essays Presented to Wallace K. Ferguson,* ed. J. G. Rowe and W. H. Stockdale (Toronto, 1971), 236–74; Rösch, *Der venezianische Adel*, 168–84.

13. "Questa dignità de nobili cittadini del gran Consiglio dopo il 1296 fino al presente et stata et e una istessa; perche non abbiamo alcun del gran Consiglio, che non sia nobile cittadino nostro, ne abbiamo alcun cittadino nato nobile che non sia o vero esser possa del gran Consiglio. E se bene abbiamo cittadini di nobile e gentil sangue, tamen quando dicemo ovvero scrivemo semplicemente cittadino Veneto s'intende e si deve intendere di quel cittadino, che non e ne puo esser del gran Consiglio se suo padre fosse stato imperatore. E quando dicemo ovvero scrivemo nobile cittadino nostro s'intende e si deve intendere di quel cittadino, che che sia, vero esser possa dal gran consiglio, se bene il suo padre, prima che li fosse data la dignita, fosse stata di vilisima stirpe, ed alla cancelleria da poi serrata il consiglio maggiore averti erano mosta a scrivere su i libbri publici il titolo di nobilita a coloro che non erano ne poterano esser del gran consiglio" (quoted in Merores, "Der große Rat von Venedig," 85).

14. Some accounts attributed the Serrata to a 1214 plan to move the entire city to Constantinople (see Biblioteca Nazionale Marciana [BNM], Ms. It. cl. VII, 519 [8438], Nicolò Trevisan, "Cronaca di Venezia continuata da altro autore sine all'anno 1585" [hereafter cited as Trevisan, "Cronaca di Venezia"], fol. 86v; and Merores, "Der große Rat von Venedig," 35–36).

15. Rösch, *Der venezianische Adel,* 168–69.

16. Andrea Dandolo, *Chronica brevis,* ed. Ludovico A. Muratori, Rerum Italicarum Scriptores, 12 (Milan, 1728), 409. Lane makes this point in "Enlargement of the Great Council," 261 n. 1, in opposition to Merores, "Der große Rat von Venedig," 82. See also Rösch, *Der venezianische Adel,* 169 n. 4.

17. *Venetiarum Historia vulgo Petro Iustiniano Iustiniani filio adiudicata,* ed. Fanny Bennato and Roberto Cessi, Deputazione Veneta di Storia Patria, Monumenti Storici, n.s., 18 (Venice, 1964), 205; Lane, "Enlargement of the Great Council," 261 n. 2.

18. Trevisan, "Cronaca di Venezia," fol. 86v; Rösch, *Der venezianische Adel,* 169; Lane, "Enlargement of the Great Council," 262 n. 4.

19. Trevisan, "Cronaca di Venezia," fol. 89r; Lane, "Enlargement of the Great Council," 262–63 n. 4.

20. Trevisan, "Cronica di Venezia," fol. 89r; the translation is from Lane, "Enlargement of the Great Council," 239.

21. Here I follow the 1668 Italian edition: Marco Antonio Sabellico, *Dell'Historia Venitiana libri XXXIII* (Venice, 1668), 148, 154, 156–57; Lane, "Enlargement of the Great Council," 241.

22. In his *Lives of the Doges,* written at the end of the Quattrocento, Marino Sanudo gave a classic description of the Serrata of the Great Council, establishing the standard

account that would be used to the end of the Republic (Marin Sanuto, *Vitae ducum venetorum,* ed. Ludovico A. Muratori, *Rerum Italicarum Scriptores,* 22 [Milan, 1733], col. 580. Additional fifteenth-century chronicles of the later Middle Ages are cited in Merores, "Der große Rat von Venedig," 83 n. 61).

23. Merores, "Der große Rat von Venedig," 84 n. 62.

24. Ibid., 45ff.; Lane, "Enlargement of the Great Council," 251; Rösch, *Der venezianische Adel,* 171–72; Roberto Cessi, ed., *Deliberazioni del Maggior Consiglio di Venezia,* 3 vols. (Bologna, 1931–50), 2:88–101, 225–26, nos. 1–3.

25. Cessi, *Deliberazioni del Maggior Consiglio di Venezia,* 3:156–57, nos. 119–20; Rösch, *Der venezianische Adel,* 172–73.

26. Cessi, *Deliberazioni del Maggior Consiglio di Venezia,* 3:157, no. 123.

27. Ibid., 3:396, no. 6.

28. Ibid., 3:417–18, no. 104.

29. Lane, "Enlargement of the Great Council," 255; Rösch, *Der venezianische Adel,* 174.

30. Cessi, *Deliberazioni del Maggior Consiglio di Venezia,* 1:xiv–xx.

31. Ibid., 3:446, no. 43; Rösch, *Der venezianische Adel,* 176.

32. Archivio di Stato, Venice (ASV), Maggior Consiglio, Deliberazioni, "Magnus Capricornus," fol. 6r; Merores, "Der große Rat von Venedig," 77 n. 53.

33. Merores, "Der große Rat von Venedig," 77–78 n. 54.

34. ASV, Maggior Consiglio, Deliberazioni, "Magnus Capricornus," fol. 165r.

35. ASV, Maggior Consiglio, Deliberazioni, "Presbiter," fol. 52v.

36. Rösch, *Der venezianische Adel,* 177.

37. Merores, "Der große Rat von Venedig," 78; ASV, Maggior Consiglio, Deliberazioni, "Clericus-Civicus," fol. 58r.

38. Lane, "Enlargement of the Great Council," 258.

39. ASV, Maggior Consiglio, Deliberazioni, "Clericus-Civicus," fol. 121v.

40. ASV, Maggior Consiglio, Deliberazioni, "Neptunus" (copia), fol. 226r.

41. ASV, Maggior Consiglio, Deliberazioni, "Fronensis," fol. 80r.

42. Rösch, *Der venezianische Adel,* 179.

43. Ibid., 180.

44. Merores, "Der große Rat von Venedig," 55.

45. Cessi, *Deliberazioni del Maggior Consiglio di Venezia,* 2:87, no. 35; Merores, 53; ASV, Maggior Consiglio, Deliberazioni, "Fractus," fol. 66 (25 Oct. 1277): "Capta fuit pars quod aliquis bastardus de cetero non possit eligi de maiori consilio vel in officio quod sit de eum per maiorem consilium" (Approved, that henceforth no bastard may be elected to the Great Council or to any office reserved for those of the Great Council). In 1338 Gabriele Dolfin's petition for noble status was rejected in the Forty "because he is not of legitimate marriage" (Merores, "Der große Rat von Venedig," 92 n. 70).

46. Vienna, Nationalbibliothek, Ms. 6155, Marco Barbaro, "Famiglie nobile venete," vol. 3, fol. 9r; Merores, "Der große Rat von Venedig," 92 n. 69: "et alcuni testimonii Grechi giurano, che in Candia era publica fama et voce che questi Abrami sono stati del Maggior Consiglio."

47. Merores, "Der große Rat von Venedig," 92 n. 69.

48. R. Predelli, ed., *I libri commemoriali della Republica di Venezia: Regesti,* tome 1, Deputazione Veneta di Storia Patria, Monumenti Storici, 1st ser., *Documenti,* vol. 1 (Venice, 1876), 93, no. 401; Merores, "Der große Rat von Venedig," 92 n. 69.

49. Merores, "Der große Rat von Venedig," 92 n. 69.

50. Samuele Romanin, *Storia documentata di Venezia,* 3d ed., 10 vols. (Venice, 1973), 2:244–50; Giuseppe Maranini, *La costituzione di Venezia,* 2 vols. (Venice, 1927–31), 1:332–64.

51. Chojnacki, "In Search of the Venetian Patriciate"; Rösch, *Der venezianische Adel,* 151–56.

52. Cessi, *Deliberazioni del Maggior Consiglio di Venezia,* 1:xiv–xx.

53. Giorgio Cracco, *Società e stato nel medioevo veneziano (secoli XII–XIV)* (Florence, 1967), 337–50; idem, *Un "altro mondo": Venezia del medioevo dal secolo XI al secolo XIV* (Turin, 1986), 105–15.

54. Lane, "Enlargement of the Great Council," 250–53.

55. Ibid., 252–55.

56. Cessi, *Deliberazioni del Maggior Consiglio di Venezia,* 2:88–101.

57. Rösch, *Der venezianische Adel,* 174.

58. Merores, "Der große Rat von Venedig," 90; Rösch, *Der venezianische Adel,* 175.

59. Merores, "Der große Rat von Venedig," 100 n. 97.

60. Romano, *Patricians and Popolani,* 141–58.

61. Chojnacki, "In Search of the Venetian Patriciate," 53–54; Elisabeth Crouzet-Pavan, *"Sopra le acque salse": Espaces, pouvoir, et société à Venise à la fin du Moyen Age,* 2 vols. (Rome, 1992), 1:386.

62. Giorgio Cracco, "Social Structure and Conflict in the Medieval City," in Molho, Raaflaub, and Emlen, *City States,* 309–29.

63. Rösch, *Der venezianische Adel,* 151–56.

64. Dandolo, *Chronica per extensum descripta,* 251–52; Rösch, *Der venezianische Adel,* 152–53 n. 150.

65. Dandolo, *Chronica per estensum descripta,* 314, 316.

66. Rösch, *Der venezianische Adel,* 169.

67. Ibid., 153–54.

68. F. Cardini, "Ghibellinen" and "Guelfen," in *Lexikon des Mittelalters,* 4:1436–38 and 4:1763–65; P. Herde, "Guelfen und Ghibellinen," in *Friedrich II: Tagung des Deutschen Historischen Instituts in Rom* (Tübingen, 1996), 50–66.

69. Gerhard Rösch, *Venedig und das Reich: Handels- und verkehrspolitische Beziehungen in der Deutschen Kaiserzeit* (Tübingen, 1982), 24–26.

70. Rösch, *Der venezianische Adel,* 155.

71. Albertino Mussato, *De gestis Italicorum post mortem Henrici VII caesaris,* ed. Ludovico A. Muratori, Rerum Italicarum Scriptores, 10 (Milan, 1727), cols. 583–86; Merores, "Der große Rat von Venedig," 106–7 n. 83.

72. Cessi, *Deliberazioni del Maggior Consiglio di Venezia,* 2:84 no. 23.

73. Rösch, *Der venezianische Adel,* 155–56.

74. See Roberto S. Lopez, *The Commercial Revolution of the Middle Ages* (Berkeley,

1971); Philip Jones, "La storia economica dalla caduta dell'Impero Romano al secolo XIV," in *Storia d'Italia,* ed. Ruggiero Romano and Corrado Vivanti, vol. 2, *Dalla caduta dell'Impero Romano al secolo XVIII,* pt. 2 (Turin 1978), 1469–1931; idem, *The Italian City-State from Comune to Signoria* (Oxford, 1997), 152–332; and the essay by James S. Grubb in this volume.

75. Lane, "Enlargement of the Great Council," 258–60; Roberto Cessi, "L'Officium de Navigantibus e i sistemi della politica commerciale veneziana nel secolo XIV," in *Politica e economia di Venezia nel Trecento,* ed. Roberto Cessi (Rome, 1952), 23–61.

76. Rösch, *Der venezianische Adel,* 187–88.

3

Hard Times and Ducal Radiance
Andrea Dandolo and the Construction of the Ruler in Fourteenth-Century Venice

DEBRA PINCUS

The shift in interest among historians over the past generation from diplomacy and high politics to social class and patronage has tended to obscure the fact that a prince presided over Venice's republican government. According to most formulations, after the constitutional adjustments of the thirteenth century the duke, or doge, of Venice was little more than a figurehead. Yet the prominent historical roles of several doges—Francesco Foscari, for instance, or Andrea Gritti and Leonardo Donà—would seem to belie such an interpretation and raise important questions about the exact nature of ducal power. The apparatus and ritual of the republican government supported ducal authority. The doge personally presided at the meetings of all important councils, and he alone, with the exception of the procurators of San Marco and the grand chancellor, held office for life. As much recent work has made clear, the doge stood at the charismatic center of most Venetian state ceremonies. In this essay Debra Pincus examines developments in the fourteenth century, fundamental to the later image of the doge, that made the doge a sacral figure. Through an examination of four ducal tombs from the Trecento she demonstrates how a series of doges, in particular Andrea Dandolo, moved toward a reformulation of the office in the wake of the Serrata. As her analysis of these tombs and related monuments indicates, the doge was brought forward in the course of the fourteenth and early fifteenth centuries as a visionary of the divine plan and the embodiment of God's special relationship with the city.

FOURTEENTH-CENTURY VENICE is something of a stepchild in Venetian historiography. To one side stands the thirteenth century, whose trajectory was set by the Fourth Crusade—that abortive venture that began with the goal of reconquering the Holy Land and ended with the storming of Constantinople. The enterprise known as the Fourth Crusade earned for Venice enormous wealth and an unequivocal international profile. Substantial territories were acquired in the East; the doge of Venice gained an imperial title; and the image of a shrewd ruler brilliantly skilled at diplomatic maneuvering became a fixture of Venetian legend.[1] The period following the Fourth Crusade, when Venice was extending its maritime outreach and consolidating its role as the primary trading power in the eastern Mediterranean, has captured the imagination of generations of scholars. To the other side stands the fifteenth century, the century that saw Venice bind itself inextricably to mainland Italy and begin to play a major role in the social, political, and cultural developments that we call the Early Renaissance and whose remarkable outpouring of creative energy has long claimed the attention of scholars in many fields.

Sandwiched between these two periods of expansion and growth is the problematic fourteenth century. Venice's claim to dominance of the Adriatic and the Mediterranean had come under siege. The decisive defeat of Pisa at the hands of Genoa in 1284 and the resurgence of Byzantine power in the eastern Mediterranean once again made Genoa a formidable threat to Venetian commerce in the East. Venice's hegemony in the Adriatic was challenged by Bologna and Ancona. The key port of Zara, on the Dalmatian coast, essential to Venetian control of the Adriatic, was in rebellion, encouraged by the Hungarians, who had ancient claims to the territory. At home, food shortages and a constricting economy resulted in general unrest marked by sporadic uprisings, and there were serious problems with the currency.[2] The badly deteriorating political situation in the latter part of the thirteenth century resulted in the much-discussed piece of legislation that has come to be called the *Serrata* of the Maggior Consiglio.[3] In 1297, culminating reorganization attempts that had begun in the late 1280s, the Maggior Consiglio (Great Council) set up a regularized system of membership, accepting as members those who had previously served in the council and the legitimate male descendants of all past and present members. The immediate effect was to increase the size of the council, but ultimately it limited access to a discrete group of families.[4] Recent scholarship, in contrast to an earlier literature, has emphasized the Serrata not as the resolution of Venice's political problems but as initiating an intense period of adjustments, fine-tuning, and rethinking about the institutions of the city that affected all levels of Venetian society.[5]

Intersecting with the shifting economic and political scene was a series of developments that deeply affected the cultural profile of the city. Toward the early fourteenth century the ducal chancery was established. In the first instance it served as a bureaucratic arm of the Maggior Consiglio, bringing into the sphere of government the active participation of the citizen class. Equally important, the chancery institutionalized a challenging interchange between humanist scholars and Venice's patrician politicians.[6] The rising tide of humanism and the historical vision that accompanied it resulted in an upsurge in the writing of history, as well as the involvement of both patricians and nonpatricians in the activity of chronicle writing, which now featured a vernacular component.[7] The past of Venice was being looked at in newly analytical ways.

An important question remained at the heart of the changes taking place in fourteenth-century Venice: what sort of ruler was to head this newly configured state? Canonized in Venetian history is the concept of the doge as the inspired ideator of the regularized, stable government purportedly ushered in by the Serrata. By the time of the late sixteenth century the success of the restructured Venetian state was being attributed with positive fulsomeness to ducal agency. For Francesco Sansovino, writing in the sixteenth century, the doge of the Serrata, Pietro Gradenigo (1289–1311), was "circumspect [accorto], prudent, his soul invincible, and he cast for eternity . . . the foundation of this Republic with his excellent ordering of the elements [cose] of government."[8] By the late seventeenth century, as an intriguing commemorative medal bearing the date 1310 but entirely consonant with medallic conventions of the 1670s and 1680s shows, the concept of the doge's guiding the state onto a new level of solidity and security was an established part of the Venetian vision. We know the medal through the drawing by Jan Grevembroch in the collection prepared for the Doge Pietro Gradenigo's descendent and namesake, the eighteenth-century patrician Pietro Gradenigo (Fig. 1).[9] The medal presents on one side Doge Gradenigo in commanding three-quarter view. On the reverse is the "fortress" of the Venetian state, solid and secure on a rocky escarpment. The seas below are active but controlled. The legend, "PORTVS SECVRVS ET LVNA IN MEDIO MARIS, 1310," suggests the "safe port" arrived at after governmental reorganization and the overturning of the assassination plot of 1310, aimed at the doge.

The reality was much different. Not only was there no such ducal acclamation at the time of the Serrata but the chronicles show us quite a different picture. That same Pietro Gradenigo treated with reverence by Sansovino began his dogado with a conspicuous lack of popular acclaim, and he died in 1311 reviled and detested. His funeral, the "Cronaca Caroldo" tells us, took place without public ceremony not only because of the interdict but also "because the doge was so hated by the people during his lifetime that there was fear of violation of his corpse."[10] His successor, so the story goes, was a pious

FIG. 1. Drawing, commemorative medal of Doge Pietro Gradenigo (1289–1311), by Jan Grevembroch, "Varie venete: Curiosità sacre e profane," Ms. Gradenigo 219, vol. 1 (1755), fol. 32, no. 99, Biblioteca del Museo Civico Correr, Venice. Courtesy of Museo Civico Correr.

nobody, Marino Zorzi (1311–12), carrying bread to distribute to poor prisoners in the cells of the Palazzo Ducale when he was spotted through the window by one of the electors and catapulted into the chief office of state, which nobody wanted now.[11] In 1310, bringing into full relief the frustrations and tensions of the period, there occurred the well-planned assassination attempt on the doge alluded to in Pietro Gradenigo's commemorative medal. Organized by members of some of Venice's most prestigious families, it has come down in Venetian history as the Baiamonte Tiepolo conspiracy, under the name of the most prominent Venetian noble involved, *il gran cavaliere* of the prestigious Tiepolo family. But it drew in both nobles and citizens, signaling the unrest that affected a broad swath of the Venetian population. The breakdown in central authority that the assassination attempt brought to the fore resulted in the institution of a new administrative body, the Council of Ten, the secretive, broadly empowered, so-called law-and-order council.[12] There was a desperate need not only for cohesiveness but for a ruler who could serve as the binding agent within a dramatically changed political construct.

The volatile period of change and reorganization summoned forth a new type of politician, the statesman joined to the man of learning and scholarship. Over the course of two centuries the Venetian version of the blend of the *vita attiva* and the *vita contemplativa* would produce an extraordinary group of Venetian noblemen who have left a conspicuous mark on both the Venetian state and the world of the arts.[13] Coming forward during the first half of the fourteenth century was the most important early exemplar of the type, the scholardoge Andrea Dandolo. Catapulted into the inner circle of Venetian government at the unprecedentedly young age of twenty-one as *procuratore de supra di San Marco* (1328–43), Dandolo was elected doge in 1343 at thirty-six, unusually young for Venice. In his early years he spent a period of time at the University of Padua, probably pursuing legal studies. It has been suggested that he was a student of the celebrated jurist of Padua, Riccardo Malombra.[14] His grand chancellor, Benintendi Ravagnani, who moved in the same circles as Petrarch, was Dandolo's close associate, perhaps even collaborator, throughout his dogado. Petrarch addressed several letters to Ravagnani; in one memorable characterization, written shortly after the start of the Dandolo dogado, he described Dandolo as "a man no less famous for his studies of the arts than for his many badges of office."[15]

Scholars have focused on Andrea Dandolo as jurist and historian, organizer of Venetian statutes, and orchestrator of Venetian history in his *Chronica extensa*. Less often noted is the Dandolo of the transcendental, whose history of Venice opens with Mark sailing across the lagoon and hearing Christ's message "Pax tibi Marce," a phrase that has become famous—because of Dandolo. Alive to its superb literary compression, Dandolo extracted the *Pax tibi* phrase from another moment in the Mark legend and brought it to the *praedestinatio,* whence it became virtually the catch phrase of Venice triumphant.[16]

All the evidence suggests that Andrea Dandolo could maneuver with equal confidence in both the visual and the literary spheres. It may well have been under Dandolo that the secular portraits of the Pala d'Oro were reworked to include a Venetian doge in close proximity to the sacred—and with a halo.[17] This is the Andrea Dandolo who put on Venetian coinage an image of himself with the great Paschal candle, one of the key liturgical objects of the Easter ritual, the symbol of the Risen Christ. Andrea Dandolo's mezzanino shows, on the obverse, Mark and the doge together holding the Paschal candle (Fig. 2). On the reverse, Christ rises from the tomb (Fig. 3). To the fourteenth-century Venetian it was a resonant motif, summoning up the image of the doge in procession in the Piazzetta on Easter Sunday carrying the heavy lighted Paschal candle, of white wax, "very large and extraordinarily beautiful," as we know it from Martino da Canal.[18] Beginning in the early 1340s, Dandolo spearheaded a program for the embellishment of San Marco on a scale not seen since the

FIG. 2. Mezzanino of Doge Andrea
Dandolo (1343–54), obverse: Mark
and the doge holding the Paschal
candle. Courtesy of American
Numismatic Photographic Services,
American Numismatic Society, New
York.

thirteenth century, designed to put into sharper focus the singularly ducal
character of the church.

Intersecting in Dandolo's vision were the two dominant intellectual currents
of the mid-fourteenth century: on the one hand, the scientific, law- and
medicine-focused Aristotelian current, with its scholastic roots, and on the
other, the literary current, involved with language, poetry, and rhetoric, given
to large and compelling visions of history. Drawing on ideas already embedded
in the Venetian ethos, Dandolo came to his understanding of how law and the
structures of government could be illuminated by the aura of the *princeps*. Jurist
and protohumanist that he was, Andrea Dandolo grasped in a remarkably vivid
way the need for codification and systematization of the apparatus of government as well as the crucial importance of attaching divine sanction to that
apparatus. This mix—what Guido Ruggiero has termed the "blend of the
bureaucratic and transcendent"[19]—is one of Andrea Dandolo's most enduring
contributions to that enameled work of art known as the Venetian government.

For Dandolo it was the doge who would provide the sacral aura that could
irradiate the increasingly complex structures of government. In his major literary work, the *Chronica extensa,* Dandolo made the doge a figure of individuality
and continuity, a central and unifying element in the history of Venice.[20] In his
artistic projects Dandolo gave presence to a newly orchestrated ducal persona,
the church of San Marco being the preeminent structure for bringing that
ducal persona forward.[21] Considerable scholarly attention has focused on the
decoration campaigns of San Marco in the thirteenth century. Relatively little

attention has been paid to the meaning of the additions and recasting of the fourteenth century. It is a major gap in the Venetian historical picture. San Marco was the site that could most dramatically project a ducal aura onto the city, and it was used as such by Andrea Dandolo with all the flourish of an expanding artistic culture.

The work of defining the persona of the doge in ways that would shed glory on the political entity of Venice had deep roots in the thirteenth century. Dandolo, as he himself well understood, was operating with the full force of Venetian tradition behind him. With the Byzantine model in the background, Venice had moved in the course of the thirteenth century toward developing a stressed visual association between the doge and Christ. In the heady years following the 1204 *impresa* and the takeover of Constantinople by the Venetians and the French, the tomb of the doge of Venice began to be used to announce both to Venetians and to outsiders Venice's special status. Shortly after the death of Doge Jacopo Tiepolo (1229–49) his tomb was set up outside the Dominican church of Santi Giovanni e Paolo (Fig. 4).[22] It stands as the first truly public ducal tomb, the first of a class of monuments that served as carriers of Venetian political ideas.[23] An evocative tomb type was chosen, one with deep roots in northern Italy, a type specifically associated with Ravenna's impe-rial past.[24] The lid of the tomb chest was marked prominently with a great jeweled cross on steps (Fig. 5), an image recalling the cross potent on steps of Byzantine imperial coinage (Fig. 6) as well as the *crux gemmata* erected by the emperor Theodosius on Golgotha, crosses that were meant to publicize the participation of the *basileus* in the divine script.[25] The tomb chests of doges

FIG. 3. Mezzanino of Doge Andrea Dandolo (1343–54), reverse: Christ rising from the tomb. Courtesy of American Numismatic Photographic Services, American Numismatic Society, New York.

FIG. 4. Tomb of Doge Jacopo Tiepolo (1229–49), exterior facade, Santi Giovanni e Paolo, Venice. Photograph by author.

FIG. 5. Tomb of Doge Jacopo Tiepolo, Santi Giovanni e Paolo, Venice, detail of lid, jeweled cross on stepped base. Photograph by author.

FIG. 6. Solidus of Tiberius II (578–82) with cross potent on steps. Courtesy of the Byzantine Collection, Dumbarton Oaks, Washington, D.C.

Marino Morosini (1249–53) and Rainieri Zeno (1253–68), who succeeded Tiepolo, encase the body of the doge in images of Christ as a ruler, perpetuating the message of the doge's association with divine power.

Thirteenth-century ducal ceremonial further enhanced the ties between the doge and Christ. Martino da Canal tells us that in the mid-thirteenth century Doge Ranieri Zeno, as part of the Easter Sunday celebration, attended Mass in San Marco, where he was elevated above the crowd in the splendid hexagonal porphyry pulpit. On entering the church, pausing at the steps to the Cappella Maggiore, he was lauded with the formula of Christ as supreme ruler—"Criste vince, Criste regne, Criste inpere" in Da Canal's French—and greeted in a booming voice with all of his titles.[26] It was also under Zeno that the great Venetian feast of the *Sensa,* the feast of Christ's Ascension, was developed, in which the doge in great splendor cast a gold ring into the Adriatic, joining Venice to the sea in an echo of Christ's marriage to the church.[27]

Culminating thirteenth-century Venice's involvement in promoting a doge tied to the divine was the imagery developed at the end of the century for Venetian coinage. When an important new piece of money, the ducat, was minted in Venice in 1284, a new design was created: the doge receiving authority through Saint Mark.[28] On the verso is the triumphal figure of the ascending Christ (Fig. 7), enclosed within a starry mandorla, the Christ of San Marco's great center Ascension dome. The obverse tells us that it is the doge, by way of Mark, in whom Christ's power is invested (Fig. 8). Mark is specifically identified as "Mark of Venice": S. M. VENETI. He hands the banner of rule to the

FIG. 7. Ducat of Doge Giovanni Dandolo (1280–89), reverse: Ascension of Christ. Courtesy of American Numismatic Photographic Services, American Numismatic Society, New York.

kneeling doge, identified by costume, name, and the word DUX floating prominently in the upper field.[29] As seen on the ducat of 1284, the first of a long series, it is Doge Giovanni Dandolo (1280–89), his name placed along the rim to the right, complementing Mark's name to the left. Francesco Sansovino, writing in the late sixteenth century, did not hesitate to describe the doge on Venice's coinage as a figure of sacral resonance: "quasi come Principe che partecipasse . . . del sacro."[30]

What we see in the fourteenth century is the refocusing and reshaping of the concept of a doge with connection to divine power, the skillful orchestrating of a ducal persona that would meet the needs of a fragmented period. In charting the development of the doge in the post-Serrata years I am using as evidence the information provided by four ducal tombs. Two of the tombs are of doges who died while Andrea Dandolo was one of the powerful procurators of San Marco—and one of these doges was a kinsman of Dandolo. The third tomb was prepared for Dandolo's immediate predecessor in the ducal office; arrangements for the tomb would have been completed early in Dandolo's dogado. And the fourth is Andrea Dandolo's own tomb, whose installation he began to consider during his lifetime.[31] The four tombs are diverse in style, but in terms of tomb politics they form a distinct group with a common set of strategies. Each of the tombs is axially placed opposite a major entranceway, giving it a commanding presence in the space that it occupies. Each, in the decoration of the tomb chest, makes reference to the specific dedication of that space, bonding the doge to the religious and institutional setting of the tomb. From an administrative point of view, it was certainly the case that Andrea Dandolo, first as a procurator of San Marco and then as doge with the church as his special precinct, was involved in the planning of at least three of the tombs of this group. I am arguing that his mindset pervades all of them.

Andrea Dandolo was already a procurator of San Marco, a member of the influential administrative body that included among its wide-ranging responsibilities the overseeing of the fabric of the church,[32] some seven months before the radical decision was made to erect the tomb of Doge Giovanni Soranzo in the Baptistery of San Marco.[33] Baptisteries were structures of high importance in the political units of late medieval Italy. The great wave of baptistery building in twelfth-century Italy, part of the celebration of communal identity, had an important aftermath in the thirteenth and fourteenth centuries.[34] As the communes entered a fractious period in their political development, major decorative and restoration programs focused on the baptistery as an important symbol of civic unity. The baptistery in Italy had come to embody both civic and Christian identity; it was the site of entrance into the local Christian community, on the one hand, and identification with the universal message of Christ's triumph and promise of afterlife, on the other. As a place of burial it had been reserved for clerics, in the first instance for the bishop, the official administrator of baptism. The insertion of Doge Soranzo's tomb in the Baptistery of San Marco opens up a new chapter in the use of the baptistery space in the West, standing at the beginning of a series of elaborate ruler tomb ensembles in baptistery spaces rich with layers of political and religious meaning.

The Baptistery of San Marco is built into the south arm of the narthex of the church,[35] abutting the bay of the now walled-up south, or sea, entrance into San Marco, the Porta da mar. Like the church to which it is attached, the Baptistery combines aspects of East and West. In plan it is both a basilica-type

FIG. 8. Ducat of Doge Giovanni Dandolo (1280–89), obverse: Mark hands the vexillum to the doge. Courtesy of American Numismatic Photographic Services, American Numismatic Society, New York.

space, long and narrow with the altar at one end, and a structure additively made up of central-plan units. The structure is divided into three spaces: the western bay, serving as a vestibule; the domed center bay, sheltering the font; and the domed eastern bay, marking the space of the altar. The principal entrance, a door that today is almost never opened, is the entrance from the public space of the Piazzetta. Emmanuele Cicogna, writing in the early nineteenth century, described it as "the door by which one enters the Chapel from the street."[36] At some point this entrance received a considerably heightened emphasis. One of the *pilastri d'acri,* the famous trophies that Lorenzo Tiepolo supposedly brought back to Venice in the thirteenth century from a Genoese stronghold, was shifted from its original placement flanking the sea entrance to allow for the two markers to serve as approximate framing posts for the Piazzetta entrance into the Baptistery.[37] Sited opposite the Piazzetta entrance, on the north wall of the vestibule, confronting the viewer entering "dalla strada," is the tomb of Doge Giovanni Soranzo (Fig. 9).[38]

The placement of the Soranzo tomb on axis with the doorway is not accidental. The view from the door functioned in fourteenth-century chapel decoration to give the visitor a pointed, meaningful message at the moment of entry into the sacred space.[39] In a baptismal structure the "view from the door" carried a particularly vibrant meaning, for baptism, as an established tradition of theological exegesis had made clear, was the sacrament that opened the way to heaven, the "portal of Paradise." One passed through the doors of the baptistery as if entering through the gates of heaven, poised to receive the gift of salvation.[40] As the viewer/celebrant prepared to enter the Baptistery of San Marco from the public space of the Piazzetta, this message was inextricably bound up with the ducal presence that faced one on the wall immediately opposite. The connection was made explicit by the figure of John the Baptist at the center of the tomb chest holding in his hand the medallion of the *agnus dei,* an image encompassing both Christ's death and his triumph over death.[41]

The Soranzo tomb commands the entire wall.[42] Beginning with the tomb chest that houses the mortal remains of the doge, the presentation moves upward with the display of the Soranzo coat of arms and culminates just below the molding with the cosmological statement of the interlace plaque. The *cipollino verde* marble panels of the chest present green and white wavelike formations that interact dramatically with the formal "book-matched" proconnesian marble of the wall's revetment, the marbles of the wall and the marbles of the tomb echoing and at the same time contrasting with each other in a dynamic counterpoint. The expansion of the tomb statement onto the

FIG. 9. Tomb of Doge Giovanni Soranzo (1312–28), Baptistery of San Marco, Venice. Photograph by Dino Zanella, Venice.

wall, combined with the scintillating interplay between the cipollino verde of the tomb and the proconnesian of the wall, marks an important step in the integration of the ducal tomb with the architectural space into which it is set. In the course of the fourteenth century this integration would become more and more pronounced.

Ducal burial in the baptistery summons up the tradition coming from both East and West of baptism as a frame for highlighting the sacral nature of the ruler. Baptism was a ritual that allowed for the ruler's specially appointed role to be revealed, analogous with the revelation of Christ's role that took place at Christ's baptism.[43] A significant association between baptism and the ruler in the peripheral spaces of Eastern churches has been traced in churches in Serbia as a reflection of the role of the ruler to lead his people toward light and wisdom.[44] In a situation analogous both to Christ, who at baptism was infused with the divine spirit, and to the Baptist, the prophet who pointed the way to the new evangelical era, the ruler becomes a figure of divine vision who can lead his community to a new age. Within French royal propaganda going back to the ninth century but promoted with particular fervor in the thirteenth and fourteenth centuries, baptismal ceremony had been programmatically utilized as the frame for the presentation of a sacral ruler. Legend maintained that Clovis, the first Christian king of France, had been baptized immediately before his coronation and anointed with oil miraculously provided by a dove sent down from heaven. This supernatural unction gave the kings of France a near identity with Christ, endowing the ruler with Christ-like miraculous powers, including the famous "royal touch," which could cure disease. The heaven-sent baptismal oil was preserved at Reims, used for subsequent royal baptisms and coronations, and given a carefully defined role within the *ordines* of the French royal coronation ceremony. Illustrations in the French chronicles capture with marvelous clarity the concept of the ruler, already crowned, infused with divine powers as the dove descends from heaven at the moment of baptism (Fig. 10).[45]

With the insertion of the Soranzo tomb into the multilayered space of the Baptistery of San Marco, the ducat's message of a doge glossed with sacral power was writ large to address the Venice of the post-Serrata period. A few years after the production of the Soranzo tomb the message would be set forth in Venetian chronicles. In the charged climate of social engineering the doge is brought forward as the figure of overriding importance in implementing the promise of success that comes to Venice by way of divine agency. As the vernacular chronicle of Enrico Dandolo succinctly puts it: "And God through his mercy and divine grace illuminates the mind of each doge, chief and rector

FIG. 10. Baptism of Clovis, *Grandes Chroniques de France*, Bibliothèque Nationale, Paris, Ms. fr. 2813, fol. 12v. Courtesy of Bibliothèque Nationale.

[*cavo e rettor*] of that [Venice], so that his state may always grow and expand, and so that each may accordingly support and govern and preserve his state."[46]

In the thirteenth century, as the imagery and inscriptions of the ducat make clear, Christ, with Mark as an adjunct, were the dominant figures of Venetian divine patronage. The Virgin occupied a secondary role, and largely in terms of the orant Virgin favored by Byzantine tradition.[47] In the fourteenth century the Virgin comes forward, joining Mark and Christ to form a powerful patronage team. The tomb of the doge who followed Soranzo, Doge Francesco Dandolo (1329–39), presents the most extensive use of Virgin imagery in a tomb context in Italy up to that point. Against the background of the use of the Virgin by Italian city-states, and with the impetus of Franciscan Marian devotions, Mary was thrust forward to assume a central position in Venetian state imagery. No documents have turned up relating to the commissioning of the tomb;[48] it is not without interest, however, that Francesco Dandolo and Andrea Dandolo, distant cousins, were both members of "Ca' Dandolo."[49]

The tomb of Francesco Dandolo (Fig. 11) was placed in the chapter house of the major Franciscan church in Venice, Santa Maria Gloriosa dei Frari. It was sited in the space so as to be directly opposite the entrance into the chapter

FIG. 11. Tomb of Doge Francesco Dandolo (1329–39), chapter house, Santa Maria Gloriosa dei Frari, Venice. Photograph from Osvaldo Böhm, Venice.

FIG. 12. Reconstruction drawing of tomb of Doge Francesco Dandolo (1329–39). Drawing by Bronwen Wilson.

house from the cloister.[50] The tomb consists of three parts: a heavy, free-floating arch that serves as an honorific sheltering canopy,[51] a large lunette-shaped painted panel under the canopy,[52] and the tomb chest sheltered below. The consoles supporting the canopy display a thick leaf overlay that represents an early use of a lush leafage type, the *foglie grasse*,[53] a mainstay of the Venetian architectural vocabulary well into the fifteenth century. The front surfaces of the leafage consoles bear the arms of the Dandolo family, a halved shield, the top white and the bottom black. The tomb chest presents a narrative sculptural relief across its entire front face. A long epitaph on a large plaque directly below the tomb chest fills the space between the two consoles. The reconstruction drawing (Fig. 12) shows the winged angels that originally filled the spandrels, giving to the sheltering canopy overtones of the triumphal arch.[54] Parts of the chest were polychromed and gilded, some of which has been recalled as a result of the restoration completed in 1989.[55] Its parts once scattered in various parts of the city, the tomb has been largely reassembled since 1979 and is now on view in its original site after a series of wanderings that lasted more than a century. Unfortunately, the lunette remains detached and is on view in the adjoining sacristy, so that the viewer must imagine the tight upward-moving program—the Death of the Virgin carved in deep relief on the tomb chest, surmounted by the depiction of the enthroned Virgin in glowing jewel-tone colors in the panel above.

The lunette panel presents the Virgin, placed against a gold background, as Queen of Heaven, dressed in luxurious garments that bespeak her royal status.[56] Her heavy blue silk robe is strewn with gold-embroidered pomegranates and edged in gold, with a gold silk lining, and under it she wears a shimmering vermilion undergarment shot through with gold threads. Behind the Virgin, a silky yellow cloth of honor, strewn with still another type of pomegranate blossom, is held up by four angels. Into the Virgin's throne room have been admitted the doge and the dogaressa. At the left is the kneeling doge, presented by his patron saint, Francis; at the right is the dogaressa, Elisabetta Contarini, presented by her patron, Saint Elizabeth of Portugal.[57] The depiction of the two is sharply contrasted. The doge is shown in the robes of state, while the dogaressa is dressed in the nunlike habit of a Franciscan tertiary, giving her a visual identity with her patron. The Christ child in the Virgin's lap turns ostentatiously to the left to face the doge, bestowing a blessing directed exclusively toward him.

As the first major Venetian state monument to elevate the Virgin to a position of primary honor, the Francesco Dandolo tomb plays a central role in setting a new direction in Venetian state imagery. The Virgin as a civic figure begins to be promoted with an intensity that follows on and parallels the bringing forward of the Virgin as a protector figure in Italian communes on the mainland. In Venice the immediate impetus seems to have come from the Franciscans. As the choir of Assisi pointedly demonstrates, the Virgin had become installed at the center of Franciscan devotions by the end of the thirteenth century.[58] In the Francesco Dandolo tomb the doge takes possession of Marian devotion, focusing on the death and elevation of the Virgin, which was the particular focus of the Franciscans of the Frari.[59] The Virgin's elevation is made palpably explicit in a narrative that foils the materiality of her death, in the earthly medium of sculpture, against the transcendence of her elevation, in the glowing jewel tones and sumptuous fabrics of Paolo Veneziano's lunette. The Francesco Dandolo tomb puts this iconography into a thrilling pictorial language, initiating a series of triumphant Virgin images with direct relevance to Venice, among them Titian's compelling *Assunta* on the Frari's high altar. The ducal office and the Virgin have come together in a union that would decisively shape the future of religious and political imagery in Venice.

The tomb of Bartolomeo Gradenigo (1339–42), Francesco Dandolo's successor and Andrea Dandolo's immediate predecessor, would have been prepared during the first years of Andrea Dandolo's dogado. The ducal tomb is brought back to that central monument of the Venetian civitas, the focus of Andrea Dandolo's artistic projects, the church of San Marco. Gradenigo's tomb (Fig. 13) was superbly sited in the northernmost bay of the entrance narthex of San Marco, installed as the focal point of one of the church's most important processional routes, the one leading from the water, across the Piazzetta, and into the church of San Marco through the monumental barrel-vaulted Porta da mar. The placement of ducal tombs in the narthex of San Marco during the middle years of the previous century had marked it as a space for ducal burial.[60] The placement of Bartolomeo Gradenigo's tomb went considerably further, absorbing the entire space of the west narthex in a triumphal setting. The closing off of the sea portal in the sixteenth century and the elimination of the entrance from the sea have destroyed the distinction of the tomb's placement.[61] Set in what now seems a gloomy corner of the narthex, the bustle of postcard and souvenir vendors generally in place immediately below it taking away anything that it might retain of ceremonial grandeur, the tomb has slipped away as one of the less noticed productions of fourteenth-century Venetian sculpture.

The tomb itself, a rectangular chest with rather restrained decoration, is deceptively simple, a masterpiece of compressed state propaganda in which the Virgin, Christ, Mark, and the doge are seen together in a context that, through the use of the Annunciation, joins the history of the Venetian state to the whole of Christian history. The center relief (Fig. 14) continues the Virgin focus of the Francesco Dandolo tomb, but now, for the first time in Venetian ducal tomb imagery, bringing the image of the enthroned Virgin and Child together with the doge directly onto the tomb chest. Enthroned and crowned, the Virgin is shown seated in an interior space, as defined by the curtain that hangs behind her from a rod, and flanked by saints. At her side, kneeling in prayer, is the tiny figure of the doge, depicted at approximately one-third the scale of the sacred figures. The doge's patron saint, Bartholomew, has been

FIG. 13. Tomb of Doge Bartolomeo Gradenigo (1339–43), narthex, San Marco, Venice. Photograph from Osvaldo Böhm, Venice.

plausibly identified as the figure who stands on the Virgin's right, with Saint Mark on the Virgin's left.[62] It is Mark, the patron saint of Venice, who has the major role. Mark stands behind the doge, presenting Gradenigo to the Virgin while lightly touching, and thereby calling attention to, the ducal *corno*, the emblem of office. There is a suggestion of individual characterization in the portrait of the doge, his face bearing the creases of age. The Christ child, poised on the Virgin's left knee, turns away from the Virgin in a movement that highlights the bestowal of his blessing on the doge, repeating the action seen in the lunette of the Francesco Dandolo tomb.

But it is the end reliefs, presenting the Annunciation, that stand as the tomb's most innovative aspect, bringing Venice, through the doge, into the grand design of Christian history.[63] As a powerful theme of compression that, using only the figures of the Virgin and Gabriel, could carry a full Christological message, the Annunciation had come to the fore in the late thirteenth century in a variety of decorative programs.[64] Already in the thirteenth century the Annunciation had played an important role in the civic life of Venice. Da Canal describes in enthusiastic detail the annual parade in which two clerics dressed as

FIG. 14. Enthroned Virgin with Saints Bartholomew and Mark and Doge Bartolomeo Gradenigo, tomb of Doge Bartolomeo Gradenigo (1339–43). Photograph by Dino Zanella, Venice.

the Virgin and Gabriel were carried separately with great pomp through the city, pausing at the ducal palace, where each salutes the doge before going on to meet at Santa Maria Formosa to reenact the sacred drama.[65] It was also in the thirteenth century that the Annunciation was prominently placed on the front facade of San Marco, at the sides of the central doorway, to be seen as part of the program that included the archivolts of the Labors of the Months and the Trades of the Venetians.[66] Together they convey the sense of the devout, well-ordered city, in harmony with the cycle of the seasons and the work cycle of the Venetian year. The Gradenigo tomb has a claim as the first use of the Annunciation in official Venetian imagery with a very different meaning, one tied closely to the prehumanist sense of historical time. Padua, the intellectual center that provided Andrea Dandolo with his formative education, looms large in the background. The political ties established in 1339 brought Venice into a new alliance with this leading intellectual center of the Veneto. With its rich prehumanist culture, Padua led the way in exploiting the political possibilities of the Annunciation theme. In approximately the middle of the 1330s, there developed within the circle of the city's intellectuals an interest in carving out for Padua and for eminent Paduan families a historical role in the colonizing of the Veneto. The script worked out by the Paduans included the founding of Venice by Paduans, an event that was precisely located on the day of the Annunciation in the year 421, thus joining the foundation year already being used in Venetian chronicles with the evocative day of the Annunciation.[67] On the tomb prepared for the first Carrara lord of Padua, Marsilio da Carrara, who died in 1338—four years before Bartolomeo Gradenigo—the Annunciation prominently anchored the corners of the sarcophagus in reference to Padua's foundation on Annunciation day (Fig. 15).[68]

Venice could always recognize a good idea and was never loath to annex it. The tomb of Bartolomeo Gradenigo took over the Annunciation theme for Venice, and from there it spread into the city at large. The praedestinatio had already configured Venice as the city favored by Christ. The Annunciation on the ducal tomb, through its doge, emphasizes this connection. The Annunciation statement of the Bartolomeo Gradenigo tomb was at some point pulled out into the public space of the Piazzetta, as shown on the Jacopo de' Barbari map of 1500 (Fig. 16), when the narthex still functioned as part of the processional route. On the de' Barbari map we see the upper portion of the large triumphal-arch opening of the sea portal braced with a tie beam on which stands an Annunciation group. The image is somewhat summarily handled, but the interaction of the two figures—one in the act of presenting, the other in

FIG. 15. Tomb of Marsilio da Carrara, Church of S. Stefano, Carrara Santo Stefano. Photograph from Gabinetto Fotografico, Musei e Biblioteche di Padova.

a receiving pose—makes the motif clear. I see the Annunciation of the Gradenigo tomb and the Annunciation of the Porta da mar as chronologically related statements.[69]

Andrea Dandolo's twelve years as doge (1342–54) are characterized by an impressive list of artistic accomplishments. San Marco was without question the site of most importance to him. Within San Marco there are the remounting of the Pala d'Oro, the building and decoration of the Cappella di San Isidoro, and the mosaic program added to the Baptistery of San Marco—all of which give the church a new level of ducal emphasis. It was during Dandolo's dogado that the most explicit statement of a doge touched with divine revelation was made during the fourteenth century. The great Crucifixion mosaic above the altar in the Baptistery is the capstone of Dandolo's concept of the doge (Fig. 17). Nothing equaled it in scale and ambition. Enfolded into the religious moment we have a portrait of the Venetian state. Anchoring the scene on either side are figures that speak to the order of the Venetian system: the grand chancellor, "capo dei cittadini," and on the opposite side, a young noble, entering the *cursus honorum*. In the privileged position at the foot of the cross, displacing even the Virgin, directly below the sacramental flow of blood and

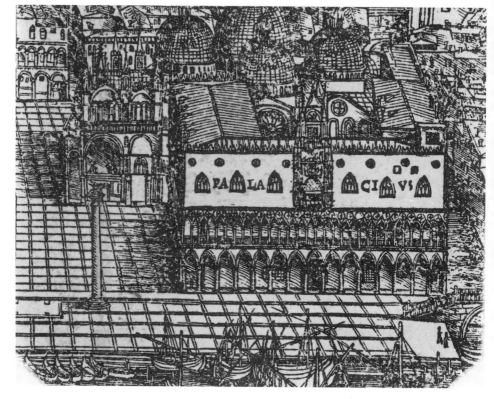

FIG. 16. Porta da mar, south flank of San Marco, Jacopo de' Barbari map (detail). Rosenwald Collection, National Gallery of Art, Washington, D.C.

water that gushes from Christ's side, is the head of state, Andrea Dandolo (Fig. 18). Dandolo looks up at the Crucifixion, his eye opened wide in a trans-fixed gaze, the single glossy black tessera conveying the look of a rapt vision. We are not left in doubt with regard to what Dandolo sees. The divine plan and the divine order are graphically set forth in the cupola overhead, where a resplendent Christ clothed in white and shooting forth rays of gold, sur-rounded by the nine orders of angels, reigns in the Eternal Kingdom (Fig. 19).

It should not be surprising that Andrea Dandolo was involved in arrange-ments for his own tomb. His burial plans, if realized, would have constituted another level of ducal privileging. Drawn up in the last year of his life, on 3 September 1354, Dandolo's will provides the unique extant record of a doge's choosing the church of San Marco as his burial site: "eligimus sepulturam nostrum in ecclesia Sancti Marci."[70] It was no modest site that Dandolo desig-nated. His first choice, as specified in his will, was the north transept chapel, the chapel dedicated to San Giovanni Evangelista. The tomb would have been located close below the dome in which the words of the *laudes* sung to the doge were inscribed in the twelfth-century mosaics.[71]

The choice of the chapel of San Giovanni Evangelista was freighted with implications, not least of which was the concept of bringing the ducal tomb into the main body of the church. The positioning of Andrea Dandolo's tomb in the space dedicated to John the Evangelist would have set up an association between the doge and the Evangelist, who more than any other signified a vision of the eternal plan. Dandolo's intended placement brings forth intriguing parallels with the message of the mosaic of the Crucifixion in the Baptistery. The depiction of the martyrdom of John the Evangelist on the front of the tomb chest, paired with the martyrdom of Andrew, Dandolo's name saint, leaves one with the impression that he was confident that his request would be honored, given the probability that the tomb was designed, and perhaps even in part carved, during his lifetime.

Dandolo clearly realized that he was aiming high. The final decision, as he acknowledged in his will, would be up to the Signoria and the procurators. Chosen was the Baptistery of San Marco, where Dandolo's tomb was shoe-

FIG. 17. Crucifixion mosaic, Baptistery, San Marco, Venice. Photograph from Osvaldo Böhm, Venice.

FIG. 18. Doge Andrea Dandolo (1343–54) at the foot of the
cross, Crucifixion mosaic, Baptistery, San Marco, Venice.
Photograph from Osvaldo Böhm, Venice.

horned into an awkward space on the south wall (Fig. 20). The tomb itself,
disregarding its tight, uncomfortable placement, is an important one, introducing another level of ducal presence. The curtains of the effigy enclosure are
open, and within we see Dandolo on display, laid out in full ducal dress,
serenely smiling (Fig. 21), the first monumental effigy of the Venetian ducal
tomb tradition. Dandolo's half-closed eyes underscore the sense of movement
between worlds, while the corners of his lips turn upward in a subtle but
distinct expression of well-being, that of the ruler who bequeaths the legacy of
inspired rule and leaves behind the well-ordered state.

Venice was not alone, of course, in its development of a ruler linked to
divine power. The sacral ruler had proved an important, even essential con-

struct as European states of the Middle Ages came into being. The French involvement in establishing a sacral ruler called into play a sophisticated arsenal of ceremony, legend, and visual imagery that has been dealt with at length in a long and distinguished literature.[72] What distinguished the Venetian situation was the particular flexibility of the concept of the sacral doge and how imaginatively it was shaped to the historical moment. Particularly to be noted in the Venetian situation is the near simultaneous attention to the government of laws and the government of divine favor. And apparently it was Andrea Dandolo who had the striking and sophisticated understanding of the construct of a near-divine doge as a useful—perhaps even indispensable—accompaniment to the increasingly complex structure of government.

The concept of the Venetian ruler as a transmission agent bringing divine revelation into the deliberations of state would take a variety of visual forms in the years following Dandolo. Ducal tomb structures worked increasingly elaborate variations on the theme of the mortal/immortal doge. Within the pre-

FIG. 19. Christ in glory, mosaic of cupola above altar, Baptistery, San Marco, Venice. Photograph from Osvaldo Böhm, Venice.

FIG. 20. Tomb of Doge Andrea Dandolo (1343–54), Baptistery, San Marco, Venice.
Photograph from Osvaldo Böhm, Venice.

cinct of the Palazzo Ducale a new image of ducal rule was produced that elucidated the concept by reworking the imagery of the ducat, using Mark in his heraldic form of Winged Lion. The Winged Lion of Saint Mark had entered the decoration program of the Palazzo Ducale in the early part of the fourteenth century, in a project with which Andrea Dandolo's name is associated.[73] Early in the fifteenth century the doge came to be paired with the Lion of Saint Mark in a relationship that transformed power delegation into power sharing. The statement began in 1400 with the embellishments of the grand window on the *piano nobile* of the south facade of the Palazzo Ducale, overlooking the sea. The contract of 2 October 1400 only specified a winged lion, to be executed in the local stone of *pietra d'Istria,* with the wings in the salmon-pink *pietra di Verona.*[74] Later, very likely during installation of the decorations of the window, as we know from the mid-eighteenth-century wash and water-color drawing by Jan Grevembroch (Fig. 22),[75] a figure of the doge was added

FIG. 21. Effigy of Dandolo, tomb of Doge Andrea Dandolo (1343–54). Photograph by Dino Zanella, Venice.

FIG. 22. Doge and lion group, Palazzo Ducale, south facade, wash and watercolor drawing by Jan Grevembroch, "Monumenta veneta ex antiquis ruderibus," Ms. Gradenigo-Dolfin 228, vol. 2, fol. 26, Biblioteca del Museo Civico Correr, Venice. Courtesy of Museo Civico Correr.

FIG. 23. Porta della Carta, Palazzo Ducale, Venice. Photograph from Anderson/Alinari.

alongside the lion. There is a disparity in the two figures: the lion is of monumental size, commanding the space of the platform, whereas the doge is on a much smaller scale, squeezed into the open space at the right end of the platform. The somewhat adventitious arrangement strongly suggests that the idea of bringing the doge closely into Mark's purview came forward only after the initial layout had been determined. We are in the first stages of the crafting of a new type.

Some fifty years later, in the execution of the Porta della Carta, the showy gateway leading from the Piazzetta into the Palazzo Ducale (Fig. 23), executed under Doge Francesco Foscari (1423–57) and one of the most prestigious

FIG. 24. Doge and Lion group, Porta della Carta, Venice. Photograph: Italo Ballarin, Courtesy of Palazzo Ducale.

FIG. 25. Porta della Carta, wash and watercolor drawing by Jan Grevembroch, "Monumenta veneta ex antiquis ruderibus," Ms. Gradenigo–Dolfin 228, vol. 2, fol. 88, Biblioteca del Museo Civico Correr, Venice. Courtesy of Museo Civico Correr.

FIG. 26. Giovanni Bellini, Doge Leonardo Loredan (1501–1521), courtesy of National Gallery, London.

stonework projects of the city during the first half of the fifteenth century,[76] the type effloresced into a monumental group. The group is seen on the Porta della Carta today in a nineteenth-century reconstruction (Fig. 24) based on the eighteenth-century drawing by Jan Grevembroch in his "Monumenta veneta" (Fig. 25).[77] Doge Foscari and the Lion of Saint Mark are at equal scale, in a position of maximum visibility directly over the doorway. Mark holds the open Gospel book inscribed with the famous greeting "Pax tibi Marce, Evangelista meus." The *Pax tibi* phrase had entered the praedestinatio script earlier, as we have seen, under Andrea Dandolo. The Porta della Carta marks the first extant use of the phrase in what would become its canonical form, functioning as virtually an emblem for the concept of Venice's divinely sanctioned success, with Mark and the Doge as partners in managing the divine destiny of Venice.

By the sixteenth century the statement of a connection to the divine would be a mandatory part of virtually every ducal representation. I end this essay with a work that puts us at the threshold of the sixteenth century: Giovanni Bellini's ca. 1501 depiction of Doge Leonardo Loredan, now in the National Gallery in London (Fig. 26).[78] The legacy of a doge touched by divinity that Andrea Dandolo did so much to further and relate to the state bears fruit in one of the great ruler images of the Renaissance. Despite its disarming simplicity, it is one of the most complex and subtle ducal portrait images produced in Venice. The stiffness and abstract quality of Loredan have sometimes encouraged its use in illustration of the idea that later commentators have attached to the doge: figurehead/slave of the state. This misses the point. Bellini's Loredan incorporates into his being the statement of direct communication with divine power. Solid and eternal like an icon, head turning slightly out of the frontal position so that he receives full on his face light from an unseen source, Loredan is the carrier of divine wisdom to a triumphant Venice. Loredan sees what Dandolo saw at the foot of the cross, that is, Venice's privileged place within the divine plan. Now it is physiognomy alone that transmits the concept of a conduit to the divine that this constitutional state has come to embody in its ruler.

NOTES

This chapter is dedicated to the memory of Wendy Stedman Sheard, dear friend and colleague, who followed this work on the doges of Venice closely and was ever ready with informed suggestions, support, and encouragement. The last letter I received from her, shortly before her death on 25 March 1998, was, generously as always, brimming over with valuable perceptions and responses, which have assisted me in the shaping of this essay. I have felt her presence very near in bringing this work to completion.

Much of the material brought forward here is dealt with at greater length in my book *The Tombs of the Doges of Venice* (Cambridge, 2000). For help of various kinds in the present essay, I would like to thank my colleagues JoAnne Gitlin Bernstein, Jack Freiberg, Michael Jacoff, Christine Smith, Alan Stahl, and Shelley Zuraw. I am indebted to Bronwen Wilson for tackling the reconstruction drawing of the Francesco Dandolo tomb. I would like to express my profound thanks to Architetto Ettore Vio, *proto di San Marco;* Monsignor Antonio Niero, *canonico* and *procuratore di San Marco;* Monsignor Antonio Meneguolo, *delegato patriarcale* and *procuratore di San Marco;* and the staff of the Procuratoria di San Marco, above all Dottoressa Maria Da Villa Urbani, Geometra Giuseppe Fioretti, and Ingener Davide Beltrame, all of whom have been gracious and infinitely helpful. Grants from the Gladys Krieble Delmas Foundation and from the Social Sciences and Humanities Research Council of Canada have facilitated the Andrea Dandolo component of the research. Presenting this material at the "Venice Reconsidered" conference in September 1997 was an incomparable professional experience, and I am grateful to Dennis Romano and John Martin for their outstanding job of organization and to the comments of fellow participants. The sharp eye and passion for accuracy of Joseph Pincus have vastly improved the final product.

1. See Donald M. Nicol, *Byzantium and Venice: A Study in Diplomatic and Cultural Relations* (Cambridge, 1988), 124–65; Donald E. Queller and Thomas F. Madden, with an essay on primary sources by Alfred J. Andrea, *The Fourth Crusade: The Conquest of Constantinople, 1201–1204,* 2d ed. (Philadelphia, 1997); Charles M. Brand, *Byzantium Confronts the West, 1180–1204* (Cambridge, Mass., 1968); and Joseph Gill, "Franks, Venetians, and Pope Innocent III, 1201–1203," *Studi Veneziani* 12 (1970): 85–106.

2. Samuele Romanin, *Storia documentata di Venezia,* 3d ed., 10 vols. (Venice, 1972–75), vol. 3; Heinrich Kretschmayr, *Geschichte von Venedig,* 3 vols. (1905–34; reprint, Darmstadt, 1964), esp. vol. 2; Gino Luzzatto, *Storia economica di Venezia dall'XI al XVI secolo* (Venice, 1961), esp. ch. 2; Frederic C. Lane, *Venice: A Maritime Republic* (Baltimore, 1973); Robert S. Lopez, "Venice and Genoa: Two Styles, One Success," *Diogenes* 71 (1970): 39–47.

3. For the use, first occurring in Venetian chronicles of the fourteenth century, of the term *serar* or *serata,* see Frederic C. Lane, "The Enlargement of the Great Council of Venice," in *Florilegium Historiale: Essays Presented to Wallace K. Ferguson,* ed. J. G. Rowe and W. H. Stockdale (Toronto, 1971), 236–74, esp. 255.

4. The bibliography on the Serrata is large and complex. See Giorgio Cracco, *Società e stato nel medioevo veneziano (secoli XII–XIV)* (Florence, 1967); and Roberto Cessi, *Storia della Repubblica di Venezia,* 2 vols. (Milan, 1944), 1:265ff. Reinhold C. Mueller, "Espressioni di *status* sociale a Venezia dopo la 'serrata' del Maggior Consiglio," in *Studi veneti offerti a Gaetano Cozzi* (Venice, 1992), 53–61, esp. 54f., documents the early-fourteenth-century use of membership in the Maggior Consiglio as an unequivocal way of indicating noble status. For the definition of Venetian nobility prior to the Serrata, see Gerhard Rösch, *Der venezianische Adel bis zur Schließung des Großen Rats: Zur Genese einer Führungsschicht* (Sigmaringen, 1989), and the useful review of Rösch by Reinhold C. Mueller in *Studi Veneziani,* n.s., 21 (1991): 413–19.

5. Stanley Chojnacki, "Social Identity in Renaissance Venice: The Second *Serrata,*" *Renaissance Studies* 8 (1994): 341–58. A recent discussion that fully accepts Chojnacki's thesis is Victor Crescenzi, *"Esse de maiori consilio": Legittimità civile e legittimazione politica nella Repubblica di Venezia (secc. XIII–XVI)* (Rome, 1996), esp. 318ff.

6. The importance of the ducal chancery as a governmental body closely associated with protohumanist currents in both Padua and Venice has been emphasized in a number of studies. See Lino Lazzarini, *Paolo de Bernardo e i primordi dell'umanesimo in Venezia* (Geneva, 1930); Nicholas Mann, "Petrarca e la cancelleria veneziana," in *Storia della cultura veneta,* ed. Girolamo Arnaldi and Manlio Pastore Stocchi, 6 vols. (Vicenza,

1976–86), 2:517–35; and Girolamo Arnaldi, "La cancelleria ducale fra culto della *legalitas* e nuova cultura umanistica," in *Storia di Venezia: Dalle origini alla caduta della Serenissima,* vol. 3, *La formazione dello stato patrizio,* ed. Girolamo Arnaldi, Giorgio Cracco, and Alberto Tenenti (Rome, 1997), 865–87.

7. A superb collection of essays on the history and development of Venetian chronicle writing is Agostino Pertusi, ed., *La storiografia veneziana fino al secolo XVI: Aspetti e problemi* (Florence, 1970), to be supplemented by Silvana Collodo, "Temi e caratteri della cronachistica veneziana in volgare del Tre-Quattrocento," *Studi Veneziani* 9 (1967): 127–51, and Gherardo Ortalli, "I cronisti e la determinazione di Venezia città," *Storia di Venezia,* vol. 2, *L'età del comune,* ed. Giorgio Cracco and Gherardo Ortalli (Rome, 1995), 761–82.

8. "Accorto huomo, prudente, d'animo invitto, & molto eloquente, & che gettò si può dire il fondamento della eternità di questa Republ. con la ottima regolatione ch'egli fece delle cose del governo" (Francesco Sansovino, *Venetia città nobilissima et singolare, con aggiunta da Giustiniano Martinioni,* 2 vols. [1663; reprint, Venice, 1968], 2:565).

9. Museo Civico Correr (MCC), Ms. Gradenigo 219, Jan Grevembroch, "Varie venete: Curiosità sacre e profane," vol. 1, fol. 32, no. 99. Andrea Da Mosto, *I dogi di Venezia nella vita pubblica e privata* (Milan, 1966), an expansion of his earlier *I dogi di Venezia, con particolare riguardo alle loro tombe* (Venice, 1939), apparently also knew the medal only through a drawing, reporting that "tale medaglia si vede disegnata nelle genealogie del Barbaro" (119; attempts to confirm Da Mosto's reference have not proved successful). The mid-eighteenth-century compilation by Fra Rocco Maria Curti, *Inscriptiones sepulchrales,* Biblioteca Nazionale Marciana (BNM), Ms. Lat. cl. XIV, 103–4 (4280–81), vol. 2, carta 691, also contains a reference to the Pietro Gradenigo medal, again with a somewhat ambiguous tone regarding the existence of the medal itself. From captions in Grevembroch's *Curiosità* we learn that there was a "Museo Gradenigo," evidently an object-oriented history of Venice with pieces that evoked key moments of the Venetian past. The commemorative medal reproduced by Grevembroch follows models developed in Florence toward the end of the seventeenth century and used extensively in the eighteenth (see Fiorenza Vannel and Giuseppe Toderi, *La medaglia barocca in Toscana* [Florence, 1987], e.g., nos. 62, 163). I am grateful to Douglas Lewis, Curator of Sculpture and Decorative Arts at the National Gallery of Art, Washington, D.C., for his assistance in dating the Gradenigo design.

10. See Da Mosto, *I dogi di Venezia* (1966), 115, for the bitterness attending Pietro Gradenigo's election; and Romanin, *Storia documentata di Venezia,* 3:61f., quoting the "Cronaca Barbaro" on the harsh nature of Gradenigo's personality, and 61 n. 1, for the passage from the "Cronaca Caroldo" on the highly private aspect of Gradenigo's funeral.

11. Marin Sanudo, *Vitae ducum venetorum,* ed. Ludovico A. Muratori, Rerum Italicarum Scriptores, 22 (Milan, 1733), col. 592; see also Francis C. Hodgson, *Venice in the Thirteenth and Fourteenth Centuries* (London, 1910), 336f., which captures admirably the colorful nature of the event.

12. Kretschmayr, *Geschichte von Venedig,* 2:76ff. See also Romanin, *Storia docu-*

mentata di Venezia, 3:21–39; and Dennis Romano, "The Aftermath of the Querini-Tiepolo Conspiracy in Venice," *Stanford Italian Review* 7 (1987): 147–59.

13. For a documentation of the type in its fully developed fifteenth-century form, see Nella Giannetto, *Bernardo Bembo: Umanista e politico veneziano* (Florence, 1985). A distinction between the Venetian and Florentine manifestations of the type is still absent from the literature, but the groundwork for such an analysis is to be found in Wendy Stedman Sheard, "Bernardo e Pietro Bembo, Pietro, Tullio e Antonio Lombardo: Metamorfosi delle tematiche cortigiane nelle tendenze classicistiche della scultura veneziana," in *Tiziano: Amor Sacro e Amor Profano,* ed. Maria Grazia Bernardi, exh. cat. (Milan, 1995), 118–32.

14. See Ester Pastorello, introduction to Andrea Dandolo, *Chronica per extensum descripta,* ed. Pastorello, Rerum Italicarum Scriptores, 12, pt. 1 (Bologna, 1938–58), iii–lxxvii; see also Henry Simonsfeld, "Andrea Dandolo e le sue opere storiche," *Archivio Veneto* 14, pt. 1 (1877): 49–149, translation by Benedetto Morossi of Simonsfeld's *Andreas Dandolos und seine Geschichtswerke* (Munich, 1876); and Giorgio Ravegnani, "Andrea Dandolo," *Dizionario biografico degli italiani,* vol. 32 (Rome, 1986), 432–40. Various aspects of the cultural life of Dandolo's dogado are dealt with in the essays in Giorgio Padoan, ed., *Petrarca, Venezia, e il Veneto* (Florence, 1976); particularly noteworthy in the context of this discussion are Lino Lazzarini, "*Dux ille Danduleus:* Andrea Dandolo e la cultura veneziana a metà del Trecento," 123–56; and Michelangelo Muraro, "Petrarca, Paolo Veneziano, e la cultura artistica alla corte del doge Andrea Dandolo," 157–68. The most complete discussion of Dandolo's work as a historian is Girolamo Arnaldi, "Andrea Dandolo Doge-Cronista," in Pertusi, *La storiografia veneziana,* 127–268. Lazzarini, in *Paolo de Bernardo,* 26, following Sanudo, accepts the tradition that in his early years Dandolo was in contact with Malombra, which is very likely given that Malombra was adviser to the Venetian Republic in the period ca. 1314–30. For Malombra, see Andrea Gloria, *Monumenti dell'Università di Padova (1222–1318)* (Padua, 1884), 243–47.

15. "Non minus bonarum artium studiis quam tanti magistratus insignibus vir clarus" (Petrarch to Luca Cristiani, 19 May 1349, from Padua, in *Epistolae de rebus familiaribus,* VIII, 5, quoted here from Petrarch's later definitive version, Francesco Petrarca, *Le Familiari,* ed. Vittorio Rossi, vol. 2 [Florence, 1934], 342). The relevant passage in both its original and revised versions is quoted and commented on by Mann in "Petrarca e la cancelleria veneziana," 518, 526. Petrarch lived in Venice off and on for various periods beginning in 1354, shortly before Dandolo's death; this characterization was written before the two had met.

16. The *praedestinatio,* the "pre-destiny" of Venice, first appeared, in both literary and visual form, in the late 1260s and early 1270s. It was almost certainly developed during the dogado of Ranieri Zeno (1253–68). As transmitted in the chronicle of Martino da Canal, datable to 1267–75, Christ, speaking through a messenger angel, tells Mark that Venice is the place where his body will ultimately be honored. Hagiographical texts include the phrase "Pax tibi, Marce, noster Evangelista" as the phrase of greeting when Christ appears to Mark in prison in Alexandria. The greeting "Pax tibi Evangelista Meus Marce" appears in the titulus of the prison scene on the Pala d'Oro.

For the textual traditions, see Thomas E. A. Dale, "*Inventing* a Sacred Past: Pictorial Narratives of St. Mark the Evangelist in Aquileia and Venice, c. 1000–1300," *Dumbarton Oaks Papers* 48 (1994): 53–104, esp. 65f.; and Silvio Tramontin, "Origini e sviluppi della leggenda marciana," in *Le origini della chiesa di Venezia,* ed. Franco Tonon, Contributi alla Storia della Chiesa di Venezia, 1 (Venice, 1987), 167–86, esp. 179f. Andrea Dandolo, then, in an inspired act of literary appropriation, interpolates the *Pax tibi* phrase into the praedestinatio episode in his *Chronica extensa* (Andrea Dandolo, *Chronica per extensum descripta,* ed. Pastorello, 10). Both Dale and Tramontin note the phrase's migration from the mystical meeting in the prison in Alexandria to the mystical meeting in the Venetian lagoon. For further discussion of the uses of the praedestinatio in the hands of Dandolo and later, see Debra Pincus, "Mark Gets the Message: Mantegna and the *praedestinatio* in Fifteenth-Century Venice," *Artibus et Historiae* 35/XVIII (1997), Essays in Memory of Carolyn Kolb, 135–46. As far as we know, the phrase did not appear in its canonical form—"Pax tibi Marce, Evangelista meus"—before the fifteenth century (see Giuseppe Pavanello, "San Marco nella leggenda e nella storia," *Rivista Mensile della Città di Venezia* 7 [1928]: 293–324, esp. n. 34). The diffusion of the Lion of Saint Mark throughout the lagoon and elsewhere is being systematically charted by Alberto Rizzi, who is preparing a corpus of both painted and sculpted examples.

17. See Hans R. Hahnloser, ed., *Il tesoro di San Marco,* vol. 1, *La Pala d'Oro* (Florence, 1965); and Hans R. Hahnloser and Renato Polacco, eds., *La Pala d'Oro* (Venice, 1994).

18. "Mult grant et beaus a mervoille" (Martin da Canal, *Les estoires de Venise,* ed. Alberto Limentani [Florence, 1972], 248–49). For a discussion of the doge's central role in the Easter rites, focused on his special custodianship of the sepulcher of Christ, see Thomas E. A. Dale, "Easter, Saint Mark, and the Doge: The Deposition Mosaic in the Choir of San Marco in Venice," *Thesaurismatica* 25 (1995): 21–33. For the Easter ritual and the importance of the Paschal candle in the ritual, see Fernand Cabrol and Henri Leclerq, *Dictionnaire d'archéologique chrétienne et de liturgie* (Paris, 1907–53), s.v. "Pacques" (vol. 13, pt. 2, cols. 1521–74, esp. 1559–71) and "Semaine sainte" (vol. 15, pt. 1, cols. 1151–85, esp. 1175–85).

19. Guido Ruggiero, "Modernization and the Mythic State in Early Renaissance Venice: The Serrata Revisited," *Viator* 10 (1979): 245–56, esp. 253.

20. A particularly useful analysis of Dandolo's *Chronica extensa* from the standpoint of its handling of the ducal persona appears in Cracco, *Società e stato,* 399ff.

21. There is a small but interesting literature on Dandolo's artistic projects. See, in addition to the articles in *Petrarca, Venezia, e il Veneto,* Hugo Buchthal, *Historia Troiana: Studies in the History of Mediaeval Secular Illustration,* Studies of the Warburg Institute, 32 (London, 1971); Ranee A. Katzenstein, "Three Liturgical Manuscripts from San Marco: Art and Patronage in Mid-Trecento Venice" (Ph.D. diss., Harvard University, 1987); Rona Goffen, "Paolo Veneziano e Andrea Dandolo: Una nuova lettura della Pala Feriale," in Hahnloser and Polacco, *La Pala d'Oro,* 173–84; and Debra Pincus, "Andrea Dandolo (1343–1354) and Visible History: The San Marco Projects," in *Art and Politics in Late Medieval and Early Renaissance Italy,* ed. Charles M. Rosenberg (Notre Dame, Ind., 1990), 191–206.

22. An extremely useful study of the early stages of mendicant insertion into the body politic in Venice is Fernanda Sorelli, "I nuovi religiosi: Note sull'insediamento degli ordini mendicanti," in *La Chiesa di Venezia nei secoli XI–XIII*, ed. Franco Tonon, Contributi alla Storia della Chiesa di Venezia, 2 (Venice, 1988), 135–52. See also Rona Goffen, *Piety and Patronage in Renaissance Venice: Bellini, Titian, and the Franciscans* (New Haven, 1986). The placement and history of the Tiepolo tomb underscores what has been brought forward in other contexts, namely, that the Dominican order early understood the value and benefits of tomb display. See Anita Fiderer Moskowitz, "On Sources and Meaning of Nicola Pisano's Arca di San Domenico," in *Verrocchio and Late Quattrocento Italian Sculpture*, ed. Steven Bule, Alan Phipps Darr, and Fiorella Superbi Gioffredi (papers of conferences held under the auspices of Brigham Young University and the Harvard University Center for Italian Renaissance Studies at Villa I Tatti) (Florence, 1992), 271–81; and idem, *Nicola Pisano's Arca di San Domenico and Its Legacy* (University Park, Pa., 1994). For further material regarding the active role of the Dominicans in promoting tomb display, see discussions focused on the tomb of Pope Clement IV (d. 1268), now located in the church of San Francesco in Viterbo but originally prepared for the Dominican church of Santa Maria in Gradi in Viterbo (Peter Cornelius Claussen, *Magistri doctissimi romani: Die römischen Marmorkünstler des Mittelalters*, Corpus Cosmatorum, 1 [Stuttgart, 1987], esp. 196f.; Ingo Herklotz, *"Sepulcra" e "monumenta" del medioevo: Studi sull'arte sepolcrale in Italia*, 2d ed. [Rome, 1990], 163ff.).

23. Placement beside the main portal was likely a special honor (see Ingo Herklotz, "Grabmalstiftungen und städtische Öffentlichkeit im spätmittelalterlichen Italien," in *Materielle Kultur und religiöse Stiftung im Spätmittelalter*, Österreichische Akademie der Wissenschaften, philosophisch-historische Klasse, Sitzungsberichte, 554 (Vienna, 1990), 233–71, with specific reference to the Tiepolo tomb, 247f. The Tiepolo tomb was raised off the ground and attached to the facade of Santi Giovanni e Paolo in 1431, presumably representing a last stage of the rebuilding program initiated in the fourteenth century (see Pincus, *Tombs of the Doges*, ch. 2; and Franca Zava Boccazzi, *La Basilica dei Santi Giovanni e Paolo in Venezia* [Venice, 1965], 47f.).

24. Fernando Rebecchi, "Sarcofagi cispadani di età imperiale romana: Ricerche sulla decorazione figurata, sulla produzione e sul loro commercio," *Mitteilungen des Deutschen Archäologischen Instituts, Römische Abteilung* 84 (1977): 107–58; and Johannes Kollwitz and Helga Herdejuergen, *Die ravennatischen Sarkophage*, in *Die antiken Sarkophagreliefs*, vol. 8, *Die Sarkophage westlichen Gebiete des Imperium Romanum*, pt. 2 (Berlin, 1979).

25. The importance of the jeweled cross on Golgotha as an object of intense devotion associated with a major pilgrimage site was emphasized by Anatole Frolow in "Numismatique byzantine et archéologie des lieux saints," in *Mélanges d'histoire et d'archéologie byzantines: Memorial Louis Petit* (Bucharest, 1948), 77–94, esp. 84ff.

26. Da Canal, *Les estoires de Venise*, 248–49. See also Ernst H. Kantorowicz, *Laudes Regiae: A Study in Liturgical Acclamations and Mediaeval Ruler Worship* (Berkeley, 1946), 147–56. Gina Fasoli, "Liturgia e cerimoniale ducale," in *Venezia e il Levante fino al secolo XV*, ed. Agostino Pertusi (Florence, 1953), 261–95, reprinted in Fasoli, *Scritti di storia*

medievale, ed. F. Bocchi, A. Carile, and A. I. Pini (Bologna, 1974), suggests that the lauding of the doge in Venice has a history prior to Zeno.

27. Da Canal, *Les estoires de Venise,* 250–51. Giustina Renier Michiel, *Le origine delle feste veneziane,* 2d ed. (Milan, 1829), 1:196f., puts the feast of the Ascension of Christ among the five most solemn civic and religious feasts of the Venetian year. In light of the Dominicans' importance for promoting miracles in Venice during the Zeno dogado, it is tempting to speculate on their role in bringing high drama to the Sensa. See Debra Pincus, "Christian Relics and the Body Politic: A Thirteenth-Century Relief Plaque in the Church of San Marco," in *Interpretazioni veneziane: Studi di storia dell'arte in onore di Michelangelo Muraro,* ed. David Rosand (Venice, 1984), 39–57, for Dominican involvement in the campaign to promote a group of key Venetian relics as the objects of a miracle, with the indication that these relics were being displayed once more on the day of Christ's Ascension, "according to custom" (see p. 57 for Zeno's letter of 30 May 1265).

28. The minting of the gold ducat was legislated by a decree of the Maggior Consiglio of 31 October 1284 (see Roberto Cessi, *Problemi monetari veneziani fino a tutto il secolo XIV* [Padua, 1937], xl f. and 40f. [doc. 36] for publication in full of the 1284 decree); the decree informs us that the imagery of the ducat was to be chosen by the "doge and his counselors and the heads of the Quarantia." See also Cracco, *Società e stato,* 312f.; José-Gentil Da Silva, "La politique monetaire à Venise: Motifs techniques et motifs économiques," *Studi Veneziani* 11 (1969): 57–74; and Nicolò Papadopoli Aldobrandini, *Le monete di Venezia,* 4 vols. (1893–1919; reprint, Bologna, 1997), 1:123.

29. The Byzantine image of the transfer of the banner, presenting two standing figures of parity—one divine, the other temporal—had been brought virtually intact to Venetian coinage under Enrico Dandolo on the silver grosso, initiated near the beginning of the thirteenth century. For discussions of the imagery of the grosso, see Alan M. Stahl, *Zecca: The Mint of Venice in the Middle Ages* (in press), ch. 6. The presentation of the Mark-doge relationship on the ducat makes a statement of power delegation, emphasizing the hierarchy of command and drawing on the use of the vexillum in Western imagery (see Debra Pincus, "Venice and the Two Romes: Byzantium and Rome as a Double Heritage in Venetian Cultural Politics," *Artibus et Historiae* 26 [1992]: 101–14, esp. 104). I am grateful to Alan M. Stahl for his assistance in dealing with the imagery and inscriptions of the ducat.

30. Sansovino, *Venetia città nobilissima et singolare,* 1:470. See also Fasoli, "Liturgia e cerimoniale ducale," 261–95, esp. 266f., for a characterization of the imagery of the ducat as embodying "il concetto di una diretta investitura dell'Apostolo al doge."

31. The *Pro capellanis ecclesie Sancti Marci venetiarum,* dated 6 June 1353, a revealing document that is ostensibly involved with reasserting the right of the doge to nominate the clerics of San Marco, speaks eloquently of Dandolo's sense of San Marco as a ducal structure (included by Pastorello in her introduction to Dandolo, *Chronica per extensum descripta;* see cii–civ). The document underscores the doge's *jus patronatus* over San Marco—"the church was and is ours"—and reviews the long history of ducal involvement in the construction of the church. In view of what can be posited as Dandolo's

involvement in tomb projects of doges preceding him, combined with his documented involvement with his own tomb arrangements, it is intriguing that the final clause of the document asserts the doge's decisive voice in determining burials in San Marco: "Patet etiam quod Duces quamplurimi sepulturas apud ipsam ecclesiam, motu proprio, elegerunt."

32. Reinhold C. Mueller, "The Procurators of San Marco in the Thirteenth and Fourteenth Centuries: A Study of the Office as a Financial and Trust Institution," *Studi Veneziani* 13 (1971): 105–220. The role of the procurators as commissioners of works of art, as well as their role in terms of artistic decisions regarding San Marco, is a subject very much in need of exploration; however, see Katzenstein, "Three Liturgical Manuscripts from San Marco," 227f. For a discussion of the important role of the procurators in the development of the piazza San Marco, see Juergen Schulz, "Urbanism in Medieval Venice," in *City States in Classical Antiquity and Medieval Italy*, ed. Anthony Molho, Kurt Raaflaub, and Julia Emlen (Ann Arbor, 1991), 419–45; and idem, "La piazza medievale di San Marco," *Annali di Architettura: Rivista del Centro Internazionale di Studi di Architettura Andrea Palladio* 4–5 (1992–93): 134–56.

33. The placement of the tomb in the Baptistery represents a return to the Church of San Marco as the locus for ducal burial after three-quarters of a century (see Pincus, *Tombs of the Doges*, ch. 6).

34. See Enrico Cattaneo, "Il battistero in Italia dopo il Mille," *Miscellanea Gilles Gerard Meersseman,* Italia Sacra, vol. 15 (Padua, 1970), 1:171–95; and idem, "La *Basilica baptisterii:* Segno di unità ecclesiale e civile," *Ravennatensia* 7 (1979): 9–32.

35. The mention of the display of Doge Pietro Gradenigo's body in the "Cappella di S. Z. Battista delli Putti" at his death in 1311 is the first specific reference to a baptistery in San Marco (BNM, Ms. It. cl. VII, 141 [7146], "Cronaca Caroldo," vol. 1, fol. 282). Physical evidence suggests that there was a structure of some sort on at least part of the Baptistery site as early as the twelfth century. In current literature the present architecture of the Baptistery is seen as fourteenth century in date (see the discussions in Otto Demus, *The Church of San Marco in Venice*, Dumbarton Oaks Studies, 6 [Washington, D.C., 1960], 78ff.; Gabriele Horn, *Das Baptisterium der Markuskirche in Venedig: Baugeschichte und Ausstattung* [diss., Bonn, 1990; Frankfurt am Main, 1991]; and Ettore Vio, "The Baptistery, the Chapel of Saint Isidore, and the Sacristy," in *San Marco: Patriarchal Basilica in Venice*, vol. 1, *The Mosaics, the History, the Lighting*, contrib. Otto Demus et al. [Milan, 1990], 183–89, esp. 183). Otto Demus, "Eine Wandegemälde in San Marco, Venedig," *Okeanos: Essays Presented to Ihor Ševčenko on His Sixtieth Birthday by His Colleagues and Students, Harvard Ukrainian Studies* 7 (1983): 125–44, esp. 127 n. 6, has suggested that an earlier font for baptism by immersion was reused in the fourteenth century as a foundation for the altar. For a discussion of the baptismal organization of Venice, which appears to go back to the late twelfth century and in which San Marco served as one of the five *matrici*, or baptismal churches, see Debra Pincus, "Geografica e politica nel battistero di San Marco: La cupola degli apostoli," in *San Marco: Aspetti storici e agiografici, Atti del Convegno internazionale di studi, Venezia, 26–29 aprile 1994*, ed. Antonio Niero (Venice, 1996), 459–73.

36. "La porta per cui s'entra nella Cappella dalla strada" (Emmanuele Cicogna,

Delle inscrizioni veneziane, vol. 3 [1830; reprint, 6 vols. in 7, Bologna, 1969], 405). Cicogna describes Soranzo's tomb in his *vita* of the doge, appended to the epitaph of his descendant Pietro Soranzo.

37. See Michael Jacoff, *The Horses of San Marco and the Quadriga of the Lord* (Princeton, 1993), 9f.; and idem, "L'unità delle facciate di San Marco del XIII secolo," in *Storia dell'arte marciana: L'architettura, Atti del Convegno internazionale di studi, Venezia, 11–14 ottobre 1994,* ed. Renato Polacco (Venice, 1997), 77–87.

38. See the discussion of the tomb in Wolfgang Wolters, *La scultura veneziana gotica 1300/1460,* 2 vols. (Venice, 1976), vol. 1, cat. no. 17, p. 156, vol. 2, figs. 48, 51; and Pincus, *Tombs of the Doges,* ch. 6. My own work on the tombs of Venice has been enormously facilitated by Wolters's massive compilation of information and his carefully conceived ordering of the material.

39. The importance of the "view from the door" is emphasized by Marilyn Aronberg Lavin in *The Place of Narrative: Mural Decoration in Italian Churches, 431–1600* (Chicago, 1990), 231f.

40. For a discussion of the baptistery and the doors of the baptistery as the gates of heaven, see Eloise M. Angiola, "'Gates of Paradise' and the Florentine Baptistery," *Art Bulletin* 60 (1978): 242–48. The Baptistery of Pisa was characterized as "speculum Civitatis . . . et . . . porta Paradisi" by Federigo Visconti, archbishop of Pisa, in a sermon of the 1250s or 1260s (idem, "Nicola Pisano, Federigo Visconti, and the Classical Style in Pisa," ibid. 59 [1977]: 1–27, esp. 7 n. 53). The fourteenth-century tomb of Fina Buzzacarini, wife of the Carrara lord of the city, is built into the interior wall of the entrance in the Baptistery in Padua, and the fifteenth-century tomb of John XXIII is positioned on the west wall of the Baptistery of Florence, opposite the main entrance. The longstanding association between baptism and burial has been laid out in the classic article by Richard Krautheimer, "Introduction to an 'Iconography of Medieval Architecture,'" *Journal of the Warburg and Courtauld Institutes* 5 (1942): 1–33, reprinted in Krautheimer, *Studies in Early Christian, Medieval, and Renaissance Art* (New York, 1969), 115–50.

41. For the Lamb of God as a symbol of Christ's sacrificial death, see Gertrude Schiller, *Iconography of Christian Art,* 2 vols. (Greenwich, Conn., 1971–72), 2:117–21. For the history of the motif and its early banning in the East, see Klaus Wessel, "Agnus Dei," in *Reallexikon zur byzantinischen Kunst,* 4 vols. (Stuttgart, 1966–90), vol. 1, cols. 90–94.

42. Standard photographs showing only the sarcophagus unit—e.g., Wolters, *La scultura veneziana gotica,* vol. 2, pl. 51—are not, in fact, true representations of the tomb. The chest is the only part of the presentation that has been dealt with in detail in the literature.

43. Two magisterial treatments of the link between the sacrament of baptism and the *rex et sacerdos* theme are Robert Deshman, "Otto III and the Warmund Sacramentary: A Study in Political Theology," *Zeitschrift für Kunstgeschichte* 34 (1971): 1–20; and Konrad Hoffmann, *Taufsymbolik im mittelalterlichen Herrscherbild* (Dusseldorf, 1968). For a valuable treatment of the connection between baptism and the ruler, see also Sarah Blake McHam, "Donatello's Tomb of Pope John XXIII," in *Life and Death in Fifteenth-*

Century Florence, ed. Marcel Tetel, Ronald G. Witt, and Rona Goffen (Durham, 1989), 146–242, esp. 165f.

44. The theme has been explored in a number of articles by Zaga Gavrilović; see esp. "Divine Wisdom as Part of Byzantine Imperial Ideology: Research into the Artistic Interpretations of the Theme in Medieval Serbia," *Zograf* 11 (1980): 44–52.

45. For the legend of Clovis, see Georges Tessier, *Le baptême de Clovis* (Paris, 1964). The first mention of the holy oil sent down from heaven is in the thirteenth-century ordines for the coronation of the French king (see R. A. Jackson, *Vivat rex in aeternum: Histoire des sacres et couronnements en France, 1364–1825* [Strasbourg, 1984]; see also Danielle Gaborit-Chopin, *Regalia: Les instruments du sacre des rois des Frances: Les "Honneurs de Charlemagne"* [Paris, 1987], 44–47). For full treatment of the illustrated French chronicles, see Anne D. Hedeman, *The Royal Image: Illustrations of the "Grandes Chroniques de France," 1274–1422* (Berkeley, 1991).

46. "Et Dio per la sua misericordia e divina gratia inlumina sì la mente de zaschun doxe, cavo, et rettor de quella, ch'el stado sempre accressa, et amplificha e che cadaun reza, e governa, et mantegna segondo el stado suo" (MCC, Codice Cicogna 2831, Enrico Dandolo, "Chronicha de Venexia," fol. 6r; see also Collodo, "Temi e caratteri della cronachistica veneziana," esp. 148f.).

47. See Otto Demus et al., *Le sculture esterne di San Marco* (Milan, 1995), no. 87, pp. 87f. (entry by Guido Tigler); and Demus, *Church of San Marco,* 131f. A useful compendium of orant Virgin icons in Venice is given by Christa Belting-Ihm in "*Sub matris tutela:* Untersuchungen zur Vorgeschichte der Schutzmantelmandonna," *Abhandlungen der Heidelberger Akademie der Wissenschaften,* philosophisch-historische Klasse, 3 (Heidelberg, 1976), 65 n. 18.

48. For documentation on the tomb, see Wolters, *La scultura veneziana gotica,* vol. 1, cat. no. 32, pp. 163f.; and Pincus, *Tombs of the Doges,* ch. 7.

49. See the condensed genealogy of the branches of the Dandolo family in Simonsfeld, "Andrea Dandolo e le sue opere storiche," 17 in *estratto.* The San Luca branch of the family, the branch to which Andrea Dandolo belonged, was the main branch of the family and is discussed in detail in Juergen Schulz, "The Houses of the Dandolo: A Family Compound in Medieval Venice," *Journal of the Society of Architectural Historians* 52 (1993): 391–415.

50. The fourteenth-century systematization of the Frari, its auxiliary spaces, and the attached cloisters was radically altered in the early nineteenth century. Following the nineteenth-century deconsecration of the church, the space in which the Dandolo tomb was placed appears to have lost its identity as the chapter house of the Frari (see, e.g., Giannantonio Moschini, *Guida per la città di Venezia all'amico delle belle arti,* 2 vols. [Venice, 1815], 2:200: "Sotto il primo chiostro v'è una cappella con pitture abbandonate"). Both Giannantonio Moschini, *La Chiesa e il Seminario di Santa Maria della Salute in Venezia* (Venice, 1842), 75, and Leo Planiscig, "Geschichte der venezianische Skulptur im XIV. Jahrhundert," *Jahrbuch der Kunsthistorischen Sammlungen des Allerhöchsten Kaiserhauses* 33 (1916): 31–212, esp. 51, place the original location of the tomb in the cloister of the Frari. The chapter house was never returned to its original function. Today the main sacristy is located, as it evidently was in the fourteenth century, to the

west of the former chapter house; in the fifteenth century it came under the special patronage of the Pesaro family (see Goffen, *Piety and Patronage in Renaissance Venice,* ch. 2).

51. In late-thirteenth- and early-fourteenth-century Italy Arnolfo di Cambio gave currency to the concept of the freestanding honorific canopy both as a covering for the altar, as in his ciboria for Santa Cecilia and Santa Maria Maggiore, and as a major component of both the ecclesiastical and the secular tomb. The variety of formats that the ruler's ceremonial baldacchino can take, including that of tomb canopy–ciborium, is laid out by Percy E. Schramm in "Der Baldachin," *Herrschaftszeichen und Staatssymbolik,* vol. 3 (Stuttgart, 1956), 722–27.

Ingo Herklotz, "Mittelalterliche Baldachingräber in S. Lorenzo fuori le mura, Rom," *Zeitschrift für Kunstgeschichte* 43 (1980): 11–20, focused attention on the late-twelfth-century tombs with honorific sheltering superstructures in San Lorenzo fuori le mura. However, it was apparently Tino di Camaino, in the landmark tomb of Emperor Henry VII, commissioned in 1315 and set up in the choir of Pisa cathedral, who brought the ciborium-type sheltering canopy into the sphere of the ruler tomb. For the reconstruction of the architectural frame of the Henry VII tomb as a deep canopy arch, see Gert Kreytenberg, "Das Grabmal von Kaiser Heinrich VII. in Pisa," *Mitteilungen des Kunsthistorischen Instituts in Florenz* 28 (1984): 33–64.

52. The panel is now a bit shorter on either side than the sheltering arch; it was apparently cut down when the tomb and the panel were separated in order to give it more the look of an easel painting. Probably the wooden frame, which is still attached to the panel, was added at the same time.

53. For use of the term *foglie grasse* and a valuable discussion of the leafage capital in Venice in the fourteenth and early fifteenth centuries, see Edoardo Arslan, *Venezia gotica: L'architettura civile* (Venice, 1986), 113ff. According to Arslan, the foglie grasse came into use in Venice ca. 1340, which would make the consoles of the Francesco Dandolo tomb an early example of this decorative vocabulary.

54. The reconstruction drawing is based on Jan Grevembroch's drawing of the tomb, MCC, Ms. Gradenigo-Dolfin 228, "Monumenta veneta ex antiquis ruderibus," vol. 2, fol. 52.

55. Giuseppe Marino Urbani de Gheltof, "La policromia delle sculture in Venezia," *Bullettino di Arti, Industrie e Curiosità Veneziane* 1 (1877–78): 53–56; Giambattista Soràvia, *Le chiese di Venezia,* 3 vols. (Venice, 1822–24), 1:148, noted heavy gilding on the sarcophagus.

56. Philippe Verdier, *Le couronnement de la Vierge: Les origines et les premiers développements d'un thème iconographique* (Montreal, 1980), esp. ch. 7, "Le couronnement de la Vierge en Italie"; for the implications of the theme of the coronation of the Virgin in a civic space, see Staale Sinding-Larsen, *Christ in the Council Hall: Studies in the Religious Iconography of the Venetian Republic,* in *Acta ad archaeologiam et artium historiam pertinentia,* 5 (1974), esp. 45–56.

57. For the introduction of Saint Elizabeth of Portugal into Franciscan spirituality in the fourteenth century, see Alberto Ghinato, *Spiritualità francescana* (Rome, 1974), 164.

58. Hans Belting, *Die Oberkirche von San Francesco in Assisi* (Berlin, 1977). See also Dieter Blume, *Wandmalerei als Ordenspropaganda: Bildprogramme im Chorbereich franziskaner Konvente Italiens bis zur Mitte des 14. Jahrhunderts* (Worms, 1983). The Franciscan focus on the Virgin was fueled by both civic and papal imagery. For the revival of the royal Virgin, Maria-Regina, within the sphere of papal iconography of early-twelfth-century Rome, see Ursula Nilgen, "Maria-Regina—Ein politischer Kultbildtypus?" *Römisches Jahrbuch für Kunstgeschichte* 19 (1981): 1–33. For the lunette of the Dandolo tomb within the context of a far-ranging discussion of Trecento intercessory panels, see Rona Goffen, "*Nostra Conversatio in Caelis Est:* Observations on the *Sacra Conversazione* in the Trecento," *Art Bulletin* 61 (1979): 198–222, esp. 215.

59. The Frari was specifically dedicated to the Virgin of the Assumption (see Goffen, *Piety and Patronage in Renaissance Venice,* 6 and n. 25, 168–69).

60. See Pincus, *Tombs of the Doges,* ch. 3.

61. Bertrand Jestaz, *La chapelle Zen à Saint-Marc de Venise d'Antonio à Tullio Lombardo* (Stuttgart, 1986), 79–82; see also the document appendix, 204–15.

62. The identity of the saints remains somewhat ambiguous. However, the saint on the Virgin's left has the cap of short hair in tight ringlets that is consistent with the iconography of Mark, and the saint on the Virgin's right has a book as attribute, linking him to the Apostles and thus consistent with his identification as Bartholomew (see Hans van der Gabelentz, *Mittelalterliche Plastik in Venedig* [Leipzig, 1903], 244; and Wolters, *La scultura veneziana gotica,* 1:165). The major role given to Mark as the figure who presents the doge and the secondary role given to the doge's patron saint, Bartholomew—placing Gradenigo's official persona before his private person—speaks to the intentions of the tomb as a civic monument.

63. I take the phrase "grand design" from C. A. Patrides, *The Grand Design of God: The Literary Form of the Christian View of History* (London, 1972).

64. The influential tomb of Bishop Castellano, prepared for the Cathedral of Treviso in the early years of the fourteenth century, had brought the Annunciation into the tomb imagery of the Veneto (see Wolters, *La scultura veneziana gotica,* vol. 1, cat. no. 15, p. 155; and Pincus, *Tombs of the Doges,* chs. 7, 8).

65. Da Canal, *Les estoires de Venise,* 254–57.

66. Demus et al., *Le sculture esterne di San Marco,* cat. nos. 87, 90 (orant Virgin and Gabriel), 136–48 (Labors of the Months), 164–78 (Trades of the Venetians) (entries by Guido Tigler).

67. For summaries of the development of the legend of the Annunciation foundation in Paduan historiography, see Edward Muir, *Civic Ritual in Renaissance Venice* (Princeton, 1981), 70f.; and Patricia Fortini Brown, "*Renovatio* or *Conciliatio?* How Renaissances Happened in Venice," in *Languages and Images of Renaissance Italy,* ed. Alison Brown (Oxford, 1995), 127–54, esp. 142f. There appears to have been an important tradition in Padua as well as in Venice for the Annunciation *sacra rappresentazione.* As early as 1278 Padua was regulating the performance of an annual Annunciation play, regulations that were renewed in 1331 (Bruno Brunelli, "La Festa dell'Annunciazione all'Arena e un affresco di Giotto," *Bollettino del Museo Civico di*

Padova, n.s., 1 [1925]: 100–109). References to a twelfth-century legend for the founding of Venice on the day of the Annunciation that sometimes occur in the literature do not appear to rest on firm evidence. Da Canal places the founding of Venice in "the year of our Lord 421"—"cele bele cité que l'en apele Venise fu faite en l'an de l'incarnacion de nostre seignor Jesu Crist .ccccxxj"—but makes no reference to the day of the Annunciation (Da Canal, *Les estoires de Venise,* 6).

68. Wolters, *La scultura veneziana gotica,* vol. 1, cat. no. 30, pp. 162–63; Pincus, *Tombs of the Doges,* ch. 8.

69. It should be noted that Andrea Dandolo also appears to have been responsible for the addition of an Annunciate group placed on columns behind the Pala d'Oro (see Wolters, *La scultura veneziana gotica,* vol. 1, cat. no. 27, p. 160).

70. Vittorio Lazzarini, "Il testamento del Doge Andrea Dandolo," *Nuovo Archivio Veneto,* n.s., 7 (1904), 139–48, esp. 143.

71. Otto Demus, *The Mosaics of San Marco,* vol. 1 (Chicago, 1984), text, 84.

72. See Joseph R. Strayer, "France: The Holy Land, the Chosen People, and the Most Christian King," in *Medieval Statecraft and the Perspectives of History* (Princeton, 1971), 300–314; and Ernst H. Kantorowicz, *The King's Two Bodies: A Study in Medieval Political Theology* (Princeton, 1957), 238. For the refocusing of history in other Italian city-states during the thirteenth century to include the component of a divinely favored foundation, see Nicolai Rubinstein, "The Beginnings of Political Thought in Florence: A Study in Medieval Historiography," *Journal of the Warburg and Courtauld Institutes* 5 (1942): 198–227.

73. A notice of 1 June 1335 records a payment from the procurators of San Marco, one of whom was Andrea Dandolo, and two stonemasons for the piece of *pietra d'Istria* out of which was made the lion placed "above the door of the Palace" (see Giuseppe Cadorin, *Pareri di XV architetti e notizie storiche intorno al Palazzo Ducale di Venezia* [Venice, 1838], 189). A notice in Francesco Sansovino's 1581 guidebook to Venice, in the context of the description of the Porta della Carta, notes that "nel luogo istesso l'anno 1335 fu portato un gran masso del quale si fece un leone che fu posta sopra la Porta del Ducato" (Francesco Sansovino, *Venetia città nobilissima e singolare* [Venice, 1581], carta 118v). Sansovino's notice, perhaps based on old reports, raises the possibility that the lion ordered by Andrea Dandolo and Marco Loredan may have decorated the entrance into the Palazzo Ducale that preceded the Porta della Carta. Cadorin, *Pareri di XV architetti,* 131, and Pietro Paoletti, *L'architettura e la scultura del Rinascimento a Venezia* (Venice, 1893), 37 n. 4, interpret the Sansovino notice—mistakenly, in my opinion—as a garbled reference to work on the Porta della Carta.

74. Paoletti, *L'architettura,* 3–4.

75. MCC, Ms. Gradenigo-Dolfin 228, Grevembroch, "Monumenta veneta ex antiquis ruderibus," vol. 2, fol. 26. The group was destroyed at the end of the eighteenth century as part of the systematic wholesale destruction of lion emblems during the French occupation of Venice (see Antonio Santalena, *Leoni di S. Marco* [Venice, 1906]).

76. An important recent discussion of the Porta della Carta, placing it in the context of important building projects in mid-fifteenth-century Venice, is Richard J. Goy,

The House of Gold: Building a Palace in Medieval Venice (Cambridge, 1992), ch. 43; see also Debra Pincus, *The Arco Foscari: The Building of a Triumphal Gateway in Renaissance Venice* (New York, 1976), ch. 2.

77. MCC, Ms. Gradenigo-Dolfin 228, Grevembroch, "Monumenta veneta ex antiquis ruderibus," vol. 2, fol. 88. The single piece from the group to have been recovered is the head of Foscari, on display in the Museo dell'Opera, Palazzo Ducale.

78. See Rona Goffen, *Giovanni Bellini* (New Haven, 1989), 207–10, signaling the newness of the type. For the Bellini portrait within the lineage of Andrea Mantegna's remarkable portrait of Saint Mark in the Städelsches Kunstinstitut, Frankfurt am Main, see Pincus, "Mark Gets the Message," esp. 144. A compelling discussion of the Loredan portrait is given by Daniele Ferrara in "Il ritratto del doge Leonardo Loredan: Strategie dell'abito tra politica e religione," *Venezia Cinquecento* 1 (1991): 89–108, with considerable discussion of the import of Loredan's white damask brocade ducal robes.

Was There Republicanism in the Renaissance Republics?

Venice after Agnadello

EDWARD MUIR

San Marco a le sue spese, e forse invano,
tardi conosce come li bisogna
tener la spada e non il libro in mano.
> Niccolò Machiavelli,
> *Dell'ambizione*, lines 166–68

Although republicanism has long been a dominant theme in the study of the Italian Renaissance, the recent history of Renaissance politics has underscored the profound limits of the traditional historiography. For one thing, when cities such as Venice and Florence expanded their territory, they failed to extend the privileges of citizenship and instead imposed their rule on the subjects brought under their control. Accordingly, it is reasonable to ask, as Muir does in this chapter, if it mattered "whether one lived under a prince or a republic during the Renaissance." In his classic and influential study Nobiltà e popolo nella società veneta del Quattrocento e Cinquecento, *first published in 1964, the Italian historian Angelo Ventura suggested that Venetian republicanism mattered very little on the* terraferma *since the evidence he had gleaned from the subject cities suggested a general aristocratization of Italian culture and an eclipse of communal and republican liberties. Muir offers a more nuanced view that demonstrates how at least one group of peasants and notaries in the Friuli preserved their liberties through appeals to Roman law and the intelligent use of the Venetian court system. According to Muir, republican traditions did matter. He finds a curious survival of republicanism after Agnadello: a peasant republic that was based in concrete practice and resistance rather than learned theory, a republic, in short, that drew its strength from the mediation of conflicts rather than from humanist ideals of concord and social harmony.*

ON 14 MAY 1509, the French expeditionary force in Italy, allied to the
German Empire, Spain, Mantua, Ferrara, and Rome, defeated the mercenary
army of Venice a few miles east of Milan near the village of Agnadello.[1] The
Venetian army was broken up, the French took prisoner the badly wounded
second-in-command, the famously daring *condottiere* Bartolomeo d'Alviano,
and within a matter of days nearly the entire *terraferma* dominion of the Venetian Republic was lost as town after town rebelled against the Venetian governors. Machiavelli's judgment was emblematic: "In one battle they lost what in
eight hundred years they had won with so much effort."[2] The French attack
was merely the first salvo in the War of the League of Cambrai (1508–17), a
campaign of all the major European powers except England to dismantle the
Venetian mainland empire. Venice gradually reacquired most of what it lost in
1509 only to face ruin again in the summer of 1513, when the whole terraferma was once more given over to the enemy and even Mestre, on the banks
of the Venetian lagoon, was burned. "At an hour before sunset," the Venetian
senator Marino Sanudo reported from his safe perch on the bell tower of St.
Mark's basilica, "the sun was so red from the smoke of so many fires that it
seemed to be blood," a sanguinary portent that Venice itself was about to fall.[3]
But the city of Venice never fell, never saw a single inhabitant killed, never
witnessed a single errant soldier loot or rape. By the time the fighting finally
abated in 1516, Venice had again regained nearly all of its mainland territories
and survived with its own "liberty" intact, but its mainland subjects had been
devastated and impoverished by a vicious war of siege and occupation.

This polarizing war provoked a generation of political ferment in the terraferma towns and villages, revealing the otherwise hidden conceptions and
contradictions of the Venetian Republic, especially the bitter antipathy of
provincial elites toward the Venetian oligarchs, to whom artisans and peasants
seem to have had a curious loyalty. During the war years two alternative social
and political systems came into stark relief, alternatives over which political
theorists debated and for which many who knew nothing of Aristotle and
Polybius were willing to fight and die. On the mainland, aristocrats and notables embraced the foreign monarchs who offered to guarantee the elites' privileges, while peasants stood by the Venetian Republic, which at least offered
the expectation, if not the assurance, that it might respect the communal statutes and legal practices of the rural communities. The reverberations of Agnadello allow us to investigate fundamental questions: Did it matter whether one

lived under a prince or a republic during the Renaissance? If so, how did it matter? Did it matter differently for different classes and groups of people? And when looking beyond the ruling elite, was there indeed republicanism in the Renaissance republics?

Although these conflicts have been characterized as a struggle between princely and republican conceptions of the state, such theoretical dichotomies occlude the complexities of political practice, especially the ways of doing things ingrained in juridical procedures. The Venetian Republic certainly neither granted its provincial subjects complete equality under the law nor consistently safeguarded communal liberty from aristocratic tyranny, but it did perpetuate a system of nearly continuous litigation, which gave provincials access to appellate courts that bound local tyrants in the formalities of judicial practice. Continuous litigation gave rural communities an arena for dodging and maneuvering against feudal privilege, which was probably all that could be achieved in the absence of the utopian republic that some contemporaries imagined.[4]

As a political system the Venetian Republic was many, sometimes not completely compatible things. For the Venetian oligarchs "republicanism" became, especially during the War of the League of Cambrai, a means of dominating provincial elites, who considered the republic a form of tyranny. For leaders of the rural communities most subject to exploitation by those provincial elites republicanism created a slightly more open political space than would have been available in the feasible alternatives.

An otherwise obscure event in the now obscure Italian wars of 1494–1530, the Venetian defeat at Agnadello is significant to the history of republicanism for two reasons. First, the trauma of the loss set up a debate within the tradition of republican thought about what should be required of the virtuous citizen to safeguard the liberty of a republic, a type of government notoriously indecisive in the face of crisis, susceptible to internal divisions, and therefore vulnerable to determined tyrants. By their very nature republics do not last long, and in 1509 it seemed to many that Venice's time had come. By the early sixteenth century Venice was the only remaining medieval city-republic worthy of the name, and would be the only living republic until the foundation of the American one, with the exception of the brief English, tentative Dutch, and ruinous Polish flirtations with republicanism in the seventeenth century. Those who wanted to think about republics had to think about Venice.[5] Venetian patricians who lived through Agnadello pondered what had gone wrong, which led to criticisms of the moral lassitude of their fellow citizens and pleas for more money to hire more mercenaries.[6] However, the republic of St. Mark's eventual escape from the Valois and Habsburg grip reassured Venetians that they need not think very hard. They could relax in the complacent assurance that they enjoyed the perfect embodiment of the Polybian ideal of mixed government, a view most fully expressed after Agnadello by their fellow patrician Gasparo Contarini, whose little book *De magistratibus et republica Venetorum* became the standard guide to the Venetian constitution for the next two centuries.[7]

The Florentines thought harder about Venice. Florence also had a powerful republican tradition, but after sixty years of Medici domination, from 1434 to 1494, the Florentines had had difficulty making their revived republic work very well, and for nearly a century no one but local chauvinists had seriously held up Florence as a model republic. The mechanics of the Florentine republic always seemed to need adjusting, and for some critically minded Florentines Venice was the place to look to for constitutional engineering.[8] The great Florentine theorists of republicanism, Niccolò Machiavelli, Francesco Guicciardini, and Donato Giannotti, all reexamined the Venetian model after the Medici return to Florence in 1512 suspended the republic. Machiavelli vigorously argued against imitating Venice because he thought the Venetian defeat proved his point about the dangers of relying on mercenaries, and in *The Prince* and *The Discourses* he recurrently brought up Agnadello, inferring that the effete, feminized Venetians, lovers of luxury and leisure, simply had not been men enough to defend themselves. In short, they had lacked the masculine qualities of *virtù* necessary to make good republican citizens. Venetian failures helped him make the case for the alternative model of the ancient Roman republic, which, in contrast to pacific Venice, secured liberty through the institutionalization of class conflict between the plebeians and the senators. Less critical of Venice than Machiavelli and more attracted to its patrician self-possession, Guicciardini and Giannotti wrote when Venice's survival was assured and hopes of reviving the Florentine republic had become an evanescent dream. The aristocrat Guicciardini admired Venice for its cautious prudence, while Giannotti imagined that the Venetian electoral routines had, in the words of John Pocock, "mechanized *virtù*," blending chance and choice in such a way as to free every voter from coercion and avarice, allowing him to make rational decisions.[9]

The history of republican political thought has been punctuated by moments of reflection in response to crises, usually civil disturbances or threats of military conquests. Besides Venice after Agnadello, there was Athens in the wake of the Peloponnesian War, Rome during the civil wars of the first century B.C.E, Florence after the death of Giangaleazzo Visconti in 1402, Venice again during the papal interdict of 1606–7, England during the Civil War and Commonwealth, and America and France during the American and French Revolutions.[10] This genealogical conception of republican political thought lays out a patrilineage of texts that has been periodically reinvigorated by infusions of new blood from thinkers who married their experiences in the real world of governmental and diplomatic affairs to the canonical textual tradition. As Pocock recognized, to think and write about republics demands reflection about these moments of punctuation because unlike empires and monarchies, which found comfort in a timeless hierarchic order that linked heaven and nature, "the republic was not timeless. . . . The one thing most clearly known about republics was that they came to an end in time, whereas a theocentric universe perpetually affirmed monarchy. . . . To affirm the republic, then, was to break up the timeless continuity of the hierarchic universe into particular moments: those periods of history at which republics had existed and which were worthy of attention, and those at which they had not and which consequently afforded nothing of value or authority to the present."[11] It would be a dubious enterprise to employ this republican genealogy as the master plot for the history of Renaissance Italy or, even worse, of Western Civilization, but here I merely want to note how republican theory attends to certain moments in history, such as the Venetian defeat at Agnadello.[12]

The second reason why the Venetian defeat at Agnadello might be significant for the history of republicanism, and the one I wish to pursue here, has more to do with space than with time. In contrast to monarchic political thought, which posited an intrinsic, organic connection between the king and his subjects, republican theory imagined that republican institutions could be exported anywhere. During the early modern period exportable republicanism consisted in following either ancient Rome or contemporary Venice, the latter choice supplying a living example of the Aristotelian ideal of mixed government and useful practices such as the secret ballot. The Agnadello defeat and ensuing turmoil on the terraferma make it possible to test the exportability of Venetian republicanism to the feudal countryside and subject towns, several of which had been communes or mini-republics at some time before their absorption into the Venetian regional state during the late fourteenth and early fifteenth centuries. Agnadello supplied the provincial aristocrats, citizen elites, urban artisans, and village peasants with the singular opportunity of choosing between living in a republic and living under a prince. Because of the recurring presence of armies these choices were hardly free choices, and constraint either from armies or from local tyrants always played a role, but the numerous changes of allegiance and the many rebellions against either the Venetians or the foreigners, especially during the seven years of warfare after Agnadello, offer numerous glimpses into the practices of politics on the terraferma.

The diverse terraferma dominion of Venice included large, once independent and still self-assertive cities such as Treviso, Padua, Vicenza, Verona, Brescia, and Bergamo; vast rural areas still dominated by feudal landlords, as in the Veronese and Friuli; and thousands of scattered rural towns and villages that retained communal statutes and privileges. The picture is not a simple one, but it is clear that the rhetoric and practices of Venetian republicanism slipped a kind of juridical wild card into the playing deck of local politics and meant different things to the different classes and communities: in the large cities Venetian practice served as an instrument of domination, for the aristocracy it checked the most flagrant abuses of jurisdictional privileges, and for the peasants it enforced the agrarian contracts that supplanted serfdom and provided access to the large Venetian market.

If attaching the suffix *ism* to the noun *republic* implies a distinctive ideology or set of practices, then the first task is to establish what those might be. The term *res publica* had a long medieval history that did not necessarily distinguish elective from hereditary forms of government and did not share, at least not until the time of the humanists, Cicero's understanding that only elective regimes, such as Rome under its traditional constitution, could be considered *res publicae*.[13] Outside of juridical or humanist parlance *res publica* had a certain vague currency for distinguishing matters pertaining to the public. In Rodez, France, in 1370 a builder named Huc del Cayro was asked in court to define the *res publica*. "I'm not absolutely sure," he replied, "but I think the Res Publica is something that's of use to all the people who live in one place." Johan Gasc, also a builder but a master in the trade, answered the same question with more assurance: "I know that churches, squares, fairgrounds, drinking fountains and streets are *res publicae,* and are called that because whoever wants to can go and pray in churches, whether they're strangers or not—as long as the churches are open, that is—and they can draw and drink water from fountains, and stand and walk about in squares and streets and fairgrounds, and it's a perfectly free activity for whoever wants to do it."[14] This practical, materialist, localized conception that there are places open to all and objects of utility available for common use might be considered the bedrock meaning of *res publica,* and republicanism in this sense would simply imply the recognition of public over private interests. In the Venetian terraferma a similar conception of republicanism was widespread, but it derived not from the dominion of the Venetian Republic but from the various communal governments that, in contrast to Venice, had adapted precepts from Roman law in statutes that in most cases had been promulgated before the Venetian conquest.

Although any form of government could embody the *res publica,* the communes seemed closest to Cicero's ideal. The word *commune* indicated a particular kind of regime *(reggimento)* in which citizens, in the words of Brunetto Latini writing in 1266, "are able to elect, as *podestà* or *signore,* those who will act most profitably for the common good of the city and all their subjects."[15] In this sense *republicanism* might refer to the body of laws *(statuti)* and the tradition of customs and practices *(consuetudine)* that guaranteed "the common good of the city" through the election of officials.[16] When Venice conquered new cities in the late fourteenth and early fifteenth centuries it habitually guaranteed that it would respect the local *statuti e consuetudine,* a pattern that in theory affirmed local autonomy by allowing the selection of local officials by traditional means but also created a problem concerning how Venice was to exercise the privileges of *dominio* over its territories because, of course, none of these cities had elected the Venetians to uphold the common good. The communes had been conquered or absorbed by the more powerful Venetian reggimento. The Venetian system in effect pitted its own republican institutions against provincial ones, which were sometimes communal in origin but typically were controlled by local aristocratic or citizen elites.

The Venetian regional state at the time of Agnadello hardly resembled the Weberian conception of a modern state administered by trained officials who carried out their duties in a routine, legal, and impartial manner.[17] Lacking a professional bureaucracy, administrative centralization, and uniform procedures, the Venetian state can best be understood as a network of diarchies in which the patrician families and institutions from Venice established bilateral relationships with the dominant families and institutions in the subject cities. The semiautonomous groups that composed these asymmetrical diarchies were called *corpi e ceti,* literally "bodies and classes," comprising territorial organizations such as the parliament of Friuli; cities, towns, and villages incorporated as communes; and aristocratic jurisdictions. Governing the terraferma required continuous negotiations, which often took the form of litigation between Venice, on the one hand, and these various corporate groups and privileged families, on the other, so that administrative and legal procedures tended overwhelmingly to privilege the power relationships of the moment over procedural norms and legal precedents.[18]

The diarchic structure of the Venetian regime was not especially unusual among the regional states of northern Italy, where all regimes tended to link local oligarchies through some form of indirect government, but Venice and Genoa may represent extreme forms. The decentralized government of Venice was especially unsystematic because the jurisdictions and responsibilities of its various councils overlapped or conflicted and because Venetian law was more "oracular" than guided by statute or precedent.[19] Venetian law had never been brought into conformity with principles of Roman law, whereas most of the terraferma cities had revised their own statutes on the basis of Roman law and hired bureaucrats trained in jurisprudence at Padua. The judges in Venetian courts were politicians who lacked legal training and who were elected to serve for limited terms, which prevented them from relying on past experience and knowledge of precedents, a system that guaranteed the domination of the patrician class by making the courts a mechanism of patronage and a site for the systematic distribution of bribes and favors in exchange for political support.[20] In this sense the Venetian regional state functioned through informal and highly adaptable forms of political organization such as family networks and alliances, ties of protection, and factions, but since these informal organizational structures worked sufficiently well to sustain a successful regional state, they ought not be dismissed as archaic or dysfunctional, which a Weberian model of the modern state would imply.[21]

The Venetian case isolates the conundrum of the exportability of republicanism. How can republican institutions be imitated or be imposed and local laws and practices be respected simultaneously? How can the first principles of republicanism, the liberty of the city and the equality of citizens, be exported through a system devoted to guaranteeing privilege? How can republicanism in such a regime be anything more than a rhetorical ploy for masking domination?

When the Venetians conquered or absorbed the terraferma dominion during the late fourteenth and early fifteenth centuries, they largely evaded answering these crucial questions in order to establish control at the least cost to themselves and with the least disruption to the social stability that sustained trade. Venetian rule betrayed the merchant's contempt for lawyers and intellectuals, who valued precise definitions. Given the mercantile interests of the Venetian patricians, it should not be surprising that they ignored political theory and legal precept for a regime that opened the mainland to Venetian economic penetration and asserted the primacy of the Rialto market. As a result Venetian political domination weighed most heavily where the most profit was to be gained, especially in the fertile bottom lands and lucrative trading centers of Padua, Vicenza, and Verona. Where little money was to be made, such as in Friuli, the Bellunese, and Bergamo, the Venetian presence was lighter, and local aristocrats continued to rule much as before. If there was an operative principle of government, it was the respect of privilege, most of all the privileges of Venetian patricians. Unlike the ancient Roman republic or the Renaissance principalities, where many notables from provincial towns were given citizenship or at least access to the prince's court, Venice very rarely granted non-Venetians membership in the governing patriciate, just as it failed to extend political privileges to Venetian commoners, Venetian patrician women, and resident foreigners.[22] This failure to incorporate provincial elites into the ruling class sustained the diarchic character of the regime and maintained asymmetries in favor of the Venetians.

Conquered towns signed formal pacts agreeing to Venetian sovereignty in exchange for local statutes' and practices' being respected. In some places the Venetians went so far as to create a board of jurists who were charged with making a particular administration subject to Venetian influence, but in most places legal contradictions remained unresolved.[23] As a result a peculiar fissure opened between the principles and practice of government, so that political rhetoric overreached the usual hyperbole and exaggeration to slip into a surreal landscape of indeterminate meaning. "The Venetian style," as James Grubb has put it, "was less to confront than to shift the terms of debate, sometimes investing similar language with different implications, often deploying generic terminology to devalue the precise claims of local, technical descriptive terms."[24]

No term suffered more distortions than *res publica*. For example, after the Venetian conquest Vicenza continued to describe itself as a *res publica*, implying that it had the autonomy of a medieval commune but still somehow allowing for Venetian sovereignty. The eight deputies of the city, who served for the "utility of the Vicentine *res publica*," even amplified their provincial authority after the Venetian conquest by taking advantage of the elasticity of the term to extend jurisdiction over other towns and the rural communities, many of which had in the past been themselves autonomous communes or *res publicae*. Although the Venetian authorities do not seem to have encouraged this process, they did not stop it either, and as a result provincial capitals such as Vicenza and Verona strengthened control of the countryside as they became administrative intermediaries between Venice and the hinterland.[25] In this situation which of the corpi e ceti that claimed to protect the public interest composed the real *res publica?* In the turmoil after Agnadello the failure of Venice to resolve this question made it possible for competing entities to assert themselves as *res publicae*. In 1510 the village of Schio, for example, sent a representative to the Collegio of Venice requesting separation from Vicenza, relying on the superior power of Venice to overrule the republican aspirations of Vicenza and to guarantee the republican status of Schio.[26] Recognizing the problems with the term, some jurists attempted to restrict the use of *res publica* to the Venetian regime but found themselves ignored in the subject territories. Venetian magistrates, for their part, employed the words *civitas, communis,* and eventually the bland *communitas* to refer to the subject towns, but in local contexts even these terms could imply the same autonomies and liberties as *res publica*. The problem was not so much with the terms employed as with the contradictions of the system, especially with the ways in which its diarchic structure left the distribution of authority over specific *corpi e ceti* in the hands of provincial elites, so that whatever Venice avowed about the nature of its regime, the practice of government was often bent to serve the interests of those elites whose only restriction before Agnadello had been not to directly challenge Venice's hegemony.

Despite the prevailing tendency toward indirect government, Venice did create the fragments of a provincial administration that symbolized sovereign authority more than it executed it and that at best served, as Alfredo Viggiano has put it, to mediate between the governors and the governed. Venetian patricians were elected to sixteen-month terms to serve as provincial governors *(podestà* and *capitani),* who heard judicial appeals, collected taxes, and managed police and military affairs. In effect, the juridico-political sinews of the Venetian Republic on the terraferma consisted in its willingness to hear appeals of civic and criminal cases, which were heard in the first instance and sometimes for the first appeal by those who held the privilege of *merum et mixtum imperium cum potestate gladii* (civil and criminal authority with the power of capital punishment) for the local jurisdiction, which could range from a fraction of a village to a large city or fief, and could be exercised through hereditary privilege by a lord or through elections by the members of a town council. Untutored in Roman law and often serving reluctantly, the Venetian governors who heard appeals habitually committed gross procedural errors and often considered financial gain a perk of the job.[27] In order to create some measure of equity, Venice constrained both local judges and Venetian governors through a three-tiered structure of higher appellate courts made up of itinerant judges (Auditori Novi), state attorneys (Avogadori di Comun) in Venice, and ultimately the increasingly powerful and efficient Council of Ten, which after Agnadello usurped in the name of state security many of the functions of other magistracies, including the special committee of the Collegio devoted to terraferma affairs.[28]

The hodgepodge of terraferma administration was especially evident in the arbitrariness of Venetian judicial procedures, the very stuff of day-to-day government, and yet the quality of provincial administration became one of the linchpins of the Republic's self-presentation. The cultural gap between provincials and Venetian patricians was especially acute with respect to theories of government. During the fifteenth century the most characteristic feature of the Venetian republican ideal became *unanimitas,* defined by Margaret King as "the convergence of a multitude of wants and aspirations into a single will." The ideal of unanimitas permeated the writings of Venetian humanists, influencing how Venetians understood their own politics and depriving all dissenters of legitimacy through the principle of the consensus of all parties *(consensus partium),* derived from Aristotle's *Politics.*[29]

The Aristotelian principle of unity found its most complete statement in Gasparo Contarini's influential *De magistratibus et republica Venetorum,* composed in the wake of Agnadello, published in 1543 and often republished, and translated into several vernacular languages. Book 5 treats the government of subject cities that, Contarini argues, Venice acquired reluctantly, "yielding to the instant petition of the oppressed bordering people," in the language of the Elizabethan translation, "who could not endure the rapines and cruelties of several tyrants, that had brought them into subjection." "With an infinite applause and willingnes of the people," Venice brought the mainland cities under its protection, "as though they had never beene disunited thereby setting them free from out the servitude of insolent strangers, which being the remainder & offspring of those Barbarians, that had wrought that general devastation in *Italy,* had then nestled themselves and helde the people in a most cruell and miserable bondage." Venice sought to "comfort and cherish" its terraferma subjects by maintaining "wholesome and profitable lawes" that respected municipal privileges and traditional institutions. According to Contarini, the towns of the dominion were self-governed but guided by doctors of law and natural principles of moderation.[30]

The trauma of Agnadello had led Contarini and several of his compatriots to find solace in an Aristotelian myth of the republic, but the sudden collapse of the terraferma dominion made it all too evident that many influential provincials felt neither comforted nor cherished by Venetian rule. Whereas the humanists of Venice tried to represent the conquest of the terraferma a century earlier as liberating cities from "the rapines and cruelties of several tyrants," the officials of Padua depicted the relationship very differently. In submitting to the emperor some five weeks after Agnadello the Paduan delegates asserted that their city had been obliged to support

> Three thousand Venetian tyrants, all of whom because of their proximity contin-uously subject us to ruin and damage, gnawing at our poor viscera, which they have ravished and completely consumed, so that to rational men of whatever degree we have become shadows and phantoms of what we were. In that city of Padua, which should be the city of the Paduans, no part remains for them, neither the town walls, nor houses, nor churches, nor civic offices, nor church benefices, nor any position of preeminence, and also outside of town, neither cultivated fields, nor mountains, nor plains, nor woods, nor valleys, nor lakes. Nothing is ours anymore, but everything has been extorted and torn from our hands by these Venetians, in part through usury and in part through other indirect means.

The Paduans offered themselves, their children, and their children not yet born to the emperor as "vassals, servants, and most faithful subjects" so that they might be "liberated from such a dark tyranny."[31] The usury charge against the Venetians found echoes throughout the terraferma, even among families who were otherwise friendly to Venice.[32] After a century of Venetian domination, the Paduan elites who chose the delegates clearly found the ancient tyranny of a distant emperor more desirable than a return to the recent tyranny of a nearby merchant republic.

In contrast to Contarini, who elided anti-Venetian incidents, Machiavelli took seriously the Paduans' justification for their submission to the Empire. While on a legation to Mantua and Verona late in the autumn of 1509 he reported that throughout the dominion aristocrats and citizen elites rebelled against Venice when given the chance.[33] In *The Discourses* he distilled his mis-cellaneous observations into a general proposition: "Of all hard slaveries, the hardest is that subjecting you to a republic: first, because it is more lasting and there is less hope of escape from it; second, because the purpose of a republic is to enfeeble and weaken, in order to increase its own body, all other bodies."[34] For the Paduans the most galling aspect of Venetian tyranny was not the deprivation of civic liberty, which they were perfectly willing to surrender to the emperor, but the dispossession of property and privilege. In Machiavelli's famous formulation, rulers become most despised when they seize what their subjects most value, especially property or women.[35]

Although the Paduan revolt especially troubled Venice given Padua's proximity and the huge Venetian investment in the Padovano, the traditional citizen elites *(cives onorifices)* in Verona and Vicenza demonstrated similar attitudes toward Venetian tyranny by seizing the opportunity of the flight of the Venetian governors to declare themselves subjects of the emperor. Sanudo recorded that "in their fury the Vicentine citizens knocked down a marble [lion] of St. Mark that was in the piazza, which broke into pieces, but the common people gathered all the pieces up and tried to save them because they were greatly afflicted by this change of government; and all this was caused by our bad government. And it should be known that the city [of Venice] has been distressed by the Collegio and the poor preparations it made, and [the members of the Collegio] are desperate, seeing how they have lost the beautiful state."[36] In Friuli the great castellans resented Venice because the magnetic draw of the huge Venetian market for agricultural produce had deprived them of a free hand in exploiting local resources, and accepting the suzerainty of the emperor offered the additional bait of resubjecting their tenants to serfdom.[37]

In rebelling against Venice provincial oligarchs did not overtly seek to re-establish their own independent republics but to construct an imperial bulwark against the economic hegemony of Venice. The issue, however, was not so much ideological—a choice between republicanism and monarchism—as strategic, and it was conceivable that the provincial towns of the Veneto might have achieved greater autonomy as *Reichsstädte* under the emperor than as *res publicae* in the Venetian dominion. In addition, these rebellions were a natural consequence of diarchy because once the long-established equilibrium became unbalanced, the local elites, who had never been accepted as full partners in the Venetian system, wanted to negotiate for better terms. Whether as vassals of the emperor or as subjects of Venice, however, these families anticipated that they would continue to dominate their communities. The crucial questions involved the terms of domination and which local families would predominate under imperial or Venetian patronage. Lurking behind the form of government in these towns was the persistent fact of oligarchy. In the Veneto as elsewhere in Italy, there was no real alternative to government by oligarchs no matter what they called themselves.[38] Nevertheless, the institutional alternatives presented by the Agnadello crisis were hardly inconsequential. The struggle over these alternatives discloses competing groups who were searching for autonomy and a form of government that would best serve their particular interests and reveals that one man's free republic could be tyranny to another.

The established oligarchic families constituted one of the competing interest groups on the terraferma. The scene of the Vicentine plebeians gathering up the shards of the statue of the Lion of St. Mark, which had been shattered by their rebellious masters, might serve as metaphor for the deepest social conflicts. If at one level Agnadello opened a political rivalry among the layers of the privileged, it also bestirred a social struggle between, on the one hand, the provincial oligarchs, who had been so ready to join the enemies of Venice, and, on the other, the artisans and peasants of the terraferma, who in massive numbers and in the face of great danger stood by St. Mark. In June 1509 Sanudo reported that after the imperial governors arrived in Padua, the local peasants continued to chant "Marco! Marco!" and were so menacing that the gates of Padua remained closed, driving up the price of grain and wine.[39] A week later boatmen demonstrated in front of a gate, again chanting "Marco, Marco!" and waving the Venetian flag.[40] Five months after that, while on a diplomatic mission to meet the emperor, Machiavelli described a similar situation in Verona:

> Yesterday a thousand Gascons came from Peschiera, and today two hundred men-at-arms, Frenchmen as well, arrived; and it is said that at Peschiera there are many men on foot and horse, who must arrive here with the Grand Master within two days, when the Emperor is expected to be here. After they arrive, it is said, they will proceed on to purge the sins of Vicenza, and the soldiers have been looking forward to this expedition because of the hope for loot and because of the weakness of the town, where they hope to make a very big haul with little effort and less danger. It is understood that the Venetians have neither fortified it nor made any extraordinary preparations, but they stay with their men in certain strongholds around the city. The peasants, who wait to steal into the town and sack it, have seen and experienced misery without precedent to such a degree that a willingness to die and a desire to avenge themselves has entered their souls. They have become more obstinate and enraged against the enemies of the Venetians than the Jews were against the Romans, and every day one of them who has been captured gets killed for refusing to deny the Venetian name. Yesterday evening one of them, who was taken before this bishop [George of Neydeck, bishop of Trent and the emperor's representative], said that he was a Marchesco [partisan of St. Mark] and that [if he could not be a] Marchesco he wanted to die and did not want to live anymore, so that the bishop had him strung up, but neither a promise to save him nor other kindnesses would shake him of this opinion. Thus, considering everything, it will be impossible for these kings to hold onto these lands as long as these peasants are alive.[41]

Everywhere across the terraferma witnesses from both sides reported a similar pattern in which aristocrats and citizen elites embraced the French king or the German emperor while the urban plebeians and rural peasants remained ardent "Marcheschi."[42] In Friuli the two years after Agnadello produced a dangerous state of tension that finally snapped in 1511, when the largest peasant revolt in Renaissance Italy broke out, leaving scores of philo-imperial aristocrats murdered, Udine in ruins, and numerous rural castles sacked and burned.[43] The popular disturbances on the Venetian mainland even had echoes in the Venetian colonies in Dalmatia and Albania, where there was no prospect of assistance from the allies of the League of Cambrai.[44]

At first glance, the willingness of peasants and artisans of the terraferma to support Venice so zealously and at so much cost seems curious. After all, where Venetians did own land, as in the Padovano, Polesine, Trevigiano, and lower Friuli, they exploited the peasants to their own advantage, collecting rents, enjoying as much of the surplus peasant production as they could, and buying up the lands of peasant proprietors who had fallen into debt.[45] In other areas more distant from Venice the Venetian presence concentrated along navigable waterways or was largely a legal figment, as in upper Friuli, Carnia, Cadore, Brescia, and Bergamo. For the peasants, however, it was not Venetian landlords they liked so much as access to the Venetian market. Producing few artisanal products itself and completely dependent on external sources for its food supply, Venice was a huge consumer that drove up prices of all kinds of products but especially agricultural staples such as grains and wine. The Venetian merchant Martino Merlini wrote to his brother from the mainland in June 1509 that when the popolo and peasants realize that they "will not be able to sell their cloth, wool, silk, merchandise, wine, fruit, poultry, eggs, cheeses, and other things that they sell to this city [Venice]. . . , [which] will never be able to hold firm against the citizens and gentlemen who are the rebels of the towns, [the people and peasants] will be forced to cut [the rebels] to pieces and will return to St. Mark."[46]

The centripetal pull of the Venetian market had a powerfully disturbing effect on the economy of the terraferma not just because it potentially enriched peasant proprietors of freeholds but also because it encouraged peasant tenants, many of whose grandfathers may have been serfs before the arrival of the Venetians, to find ways to take advantage of market conditions. The pull of the Venetian market worked against the practices of the traditional manorial economy, such as requiring all peasants to haul their grain to the lord's mill, relying on traditional *corvée* obligations to supply labor, preserving common lands from the plow, and most especially tying peasants to the land through *livello* contracts that fixed tenancy and rents for a generation, usually calculated as twenty-nine years. Most provincial landlords resisted any erosion of what they viewed as aristocratic privilege and resented the ability of the new Venetian landlords to buy up land. The enterprising landlords who adapted to market forces, whether provincials or Venetians, embraced the short-term *affittanza* contracts, which created greater flexibility in managing labor and negotiating rents but also broke the traditional ties between tenant families and particular plots of land, creating a vast pool of peasants whose sustenance depended on their ability to sell their labor and produce in a market dominated by Venice. One of the most powerful indications of the energy of the Venetian market was the relative absence of sharecropping *(mezzadria)* in the terraferma, a system that during the fifteenth century spread to other parts of central and northern Italy and tied peasants to the land through debt-peonage. The market for agricultural produce, however, created tremendous vulnerabilities as well as opportunities for peasants, who when faced with the crisis of war (represented by higher taxes, billets of soldiers, and pillaging armies) could be driven from the land in one bad season. Those peasants who stood by St. Mark during the crisis found Venice to be a bulwark against a return to serfdom and manorial restrictions, which provincial aristocrats imagined they would be able to accomplish under the Empire, and against local oligarchs who wished to restrict access to the market for their own benefit.[47]

The economic integration of the terraferma with Venice had quickened dramatically in the decades before Agnadello. In particular, many small peasant proprietors, especially near the cities, were tempted to sell their holdings to large landholders and were then either forced to emigrate or transformed from independent farmers into tenants with short-term leases. As a result of market forces, commercial crops, especially cereals, were favored; community ties weakened with the turnover of land tenure; social inequalities in the villages grew as some few profited and bought land from others who were ruined; common and communal lands, traditionally reserved for collective use, were grabbed for private profit; and community budgets were stretched to the breaking point as traditional sources of income disappeared through the loss of the communal lands.[48] Agnadello pushed an already grave malaise into a crisis.

The most complete statement of the peasants' collective views about their situation during the post-Agnadello crisis can be found in the Eleven Articles, presented to the Venetian *luogotenente* in Friuli in November 1509.[49] Seven of the articles dealt with economic issues, including complaints about taxes, the behavior of creditors, and impediments to full access to local markets; three dealt with difficulties created by the war; and one grumbled about the cost of justice. Among the peasants of Friuli the dominion of the Venetian Republic meant, besides the temporary condition of war, two things: an expanded market economy and the administration of justice.

Whatever the economic preoccupations of the Friulan peasants, the very framing of their grievances in the legal terms of formal articles reveals an understanding of that most basic meaning of *res publica,* "commonweal," the capacity of governments to protect the public good. This important document anticipated the demands of the more famous peasant articles, those promulgated under the inspiration of Martin Luther, which transformed widespread peasant discontent into the great German Revolution of 1525.[50] The most radical of the articles, the Articles of Merano, or *Landesordnung,* composed by Michael Gaismair in the south Tyrol, laid out the constitution for an elective republic of peasants and miners that would have abolished all distinctions of rank and class, reformed religion, introduced systematic social welfare, and overturned the economic system to integrate production and commerce into a collectively owned enterprise. After the revolution in Germany failed, Gaismair and some two thousand followers found refuge in the Veneto, where the republic of St. Mark gave him a free hand and eventually a pension that enabled him and his family to retire to Padua, where bounty hunters assassinated him in 1532.[51] The Articles of Merano envisioned a revolutionary republic that had little in common with Venice's timid, oligarchic republic, but the willingness of the Venetians to tolerate Gaismair offers a clue to why during the War of the League of Cambrai the peasants of the terraferma, who had asked for far less than Gaismair promised, looked to Venice as a protector and court of appeal from their philo-imperialist landlords.

In the constitutional territory between the conservative oligarchy of the Venetian patriciate and the utopian project of Gaismair can be found the practice of communal government, which may not exactly have constituted a form of republicanism in the sense that it betrayed a coherent ideology, much less a body of theory, but it provided the peasants with the legal instruments for opposing feudal privilege and bolstering community identity. Fostered by the same practical, materialist, and localized conception of the *res publica* as that voiced by the builders of Rodez, the communal governments of the Veneto (and much of north-central Italy for that matter) were sustained by the durable craft of notaries, who helped to construct familial, corporate, and communal memories through a disciplined, rule-laden written legal procedure. Written culture was more essential in northern Italy than elsewhere in Europe for the conduct of daily life even though only a minority possessed the skills of literacy.[52] The professionals who made writing so important were notaries, trained specialists who registered virtually every human transaction: the contents of trousseaus, marriage contracts, wills, real-estate deals, the terms of tenancy or apprenticeship, and business partnerships. The literate culture of notaries probably permeated Italian life more than the literate culture of priests, especially in rural areas, where educated priests were rare. There were about eight notaries per a thousand inhabitants in Florence in 1427 and Verona in 1605, and even isolated villages that might not be able to afford a priest still needed the services of a notary.[53] Areas that did not have a resident notary were served by itinerate notaries who traveled from village to village and for a small fee laid out parchment and pen on the wall of a well or pigsty and carefully counted, described, and recorded in the proper form the linens, sheets, and utensils in a peasant bride's dowry chest or described in fastidious detail a plot of land that was being sold.[54] The very ubiquity of notaries meant that even illiterates had an appreciation for the value of written records.[55]

In the villages of the terraferma notaries safeguarded and interpreted the laws, customs, and practices of the community. Most rural localities had some kind of assembly *(vicinia)* for heads of families that followed traditional norms originally passed down orally from father to son. In many cases the common law of tradition was transformed under the influence of notaries trained in Roman law into the civil law of statute.[56] These written statutes, most of which were drawn up between the eleventh and fifteenth centuries, constituted the legal basis for communal government.

In serving the public good of a commune the principal task of the village notary and other notables would have been to manage very carefully the community's relations with external authorities, usually the relations between either a local feudal lord or a provincial town with superior jurisdiction and distant Venice. Examining in microhistorical detail the circumstances during and after the War of the League of Cambrai in one rural community reveals one of the crucial strategies of notarial practice, the pursuit of continuous litigation. The commune of Buia consisted of a grouping of small hilltop settlements of perhaps two thousand inhabitants in the Tagliamento River valley of Friuli.[57] Because of its exemplary communal statutes, Buia provides an ideal test case perhaps more of what was possible than of what was normal. As a local historian has put it, "Buia represents the extreme case: the collectivity least dependent on its 'feudatory,' the one most capable of autonomous initiative."[58] If republicanism existed anywhere in the Venetian terraferma, it was here.

Buia was insulated from external interference by three levels of legal privileges. In 1371 the patriarch of Aquileia, who was then the reigning prince of Friuli, granted Buia its own communal statutes, which established a Council of Twenty-four that each year elected a mayor *(massaro)* from among its own membership, regulated the local economy through its own chosen officials, and most importantly, named two judges *(giudici giurati)*, who presided over legal trials in conjunction with a captain sent in from the outside. Four years later Buia was incorporated into the feudatory of the Savorgnan family, who were obligated by the terms of the feudal concession to respect the statutes of Buia. In 1420, when Venice conquered Friuli with the help of the Savorgnan, the Venetians granted this powerful aristocratic family a unique degree of control within their own feudal jurisdictions, making the Savorgnan territories the freest entity in the Venetian terraferma. In addition, the legal hold of Venice over the Patria del Friuli was so flimsy that Friulan governmental institutions remained virtually intact, a situation represented by the Venetian governor's tentative title of luogotenente.[59] Thus, between the citizens of Buia and the authority of Venice stood the commune's own statutes, the jurisdictional autonomy of its Savorgnan lords, and the quasi independence of the provincial government of Friuli. Two kinds of republics were enmeshed in this twisted legal web, a grubby little *res publica* of fiercely independent peasants living in the commune of Buia and an ostentatious oligarchic republic of merchant princes in Venice.

The precise definition of communal powers in Buia's statutes did not prevent infringements of its autonomy or abuses of power by the Savorgnan lords, but it did provide Buia with a juridical basis for resistance. The result was virtually continuous litigation from the fifteenth to the eighteenth century by the notaries of Buia on behalf of the commune. Buia's suits were typically attempts to outflank the Savorgnan lords by appealing to Venice on the basis of Buia's statutory privileges. Specific disputes concentrated on feudal obligations and access to local resources, particularly the Buiesi's desire to irrigate their fields with water from the Ledra River, a desire that conflicted with the Savorgnan's wish to maintain a high water level to move timber rafts. The most contentious cases arose from the presence of the nearby Savorgnan fortress of Osoppo, which subjected peasants in the vicinity to extraordinary obligations, especially during times of war, such as special levies, work details, and guard duty.[60] At the heart of Buia's self-conception as a communal *res publica* was its ability to assert its statutory exemption from these feudal dues and duties, and the notaries of Buia seem never to have hesitated to appeal to the Venetian courts to enforce the distinction between a *res publica* and a fief. Buia's persistent appeals accentuated the dilemma of the Venetian system because Venice could not afford to alienate the Savorgnan since their loyalty was crucial for the military defense of Friuli, especially while threats from the Germans and Turks made Osoppo a strategic necessity, but at the same time Venice feared giving the Savorgnan too much slack since their arrogant self-assertion tended to infuriate provincial aristocrats who were tempted by the lure of a countervailing connection to the Empire. Into this dangerous arena of delicate political calculations, to which Venetian justice was so notoriously vulnerable, stepped the notaries of little Buia.

Notaries, like millers and less often priests, were able to mediate between literate and nonliterate cultures because they understood both how to work within the complex legal and shifting patronage structures of urban society and how to communicate with the rural masses.[61] In Buia the Rizzardi family created a notarial dynasty and served for several generations as the spokesmen and leaders of the community, becoming minor oligarchs whose power derived from professional skill rather than from an inherited position or privileged status. Substantial property owners in Buia, the Rizzardi were trained in the notary school of Udine, which hired a doctor of laws to interpret Justinian's Code and the Digest and to teach the notarial craft. Although many of the notaries produced at Udine were the sons of local notables who were given token preparation for sinecures, the notary school could offer a serious legal education and included among its masters the distinguished humanist Marcantonio Sabellico. Simone Rizzardi and his son Costantino, who became the official notary of Buia in 1514, were masterful at employing the law to protect the privileges of the commune of Buia and earned a reputation as ardent opponents of feudal authority. The protests of the Rizzardi became something of a family tradition that matured in the subsequent generation into evangelical Protestantism.[62]

The war years provoked a confrontation between Buia, led by Costantino Rizzardi, and Girolamo Savorgnan, the lord of Buia and Osoppo, that brought to the surface the manifest contradictions between communal law, feudal privilege, and Venetian republicanism. The legal basis for the dispute was an accord drawn up in 1506 between Buia and the Savorgnan that was designed to govern the relations between the two. Article 15 of the accord states that the Buiesi were exempt from any requirements to work on the castle at Osoppo that were not in conformity with "the liberty of the commune through its humanity and not by obligation."[63] The war, however, threatened Buia's exemption from work on Osoppo. In the summer of 1513 Croat mercenaries sacked Buia, and the following winter the provincial capital of Udine surrendered for the second time during the war to the imperial forces, leaving the castle at Osoppo under the command of Girolamo Savorgnan as the last outpost of Venetian authority in Friuli. During the early spring the imperialists placed Osoppo under siege, pillaged the neighborhood yet again, and systematically destroyed Buia's crops. The winter of 1515 was notable for its severity, and then in June news arrived that peasants across the border in Carinthia had rebelled against their lords. In March of 1516 Maximilian again invaded the Veneto via the Brenner Pass, and Girolamo Savorgnan again began to prepare Osoppo for a siege, this time by Bosnian Turks, who had been tempted to take advantage of Venetian weakness by mounting their own invasion of Friuli through Slovenia.[64]

Girolamo Savorgnan desperately needed all the help he could get, but Venice was too preoccupied with the imperial invasion in the west to provide anything more than honeyed words. When he asked for help from Buia to repair the fortifications and to provide men for guard duty, the commune refused on the basis of the exemption in the 1506 accord.[65] Savorgnan retaliated by sending men to arrest the commune's leading citizen and most able defender, the notary Costantino Rizzardi, who was surprised in the Buia tavern on Easter Monday, a day famous for drunken revelry. Held at knife point, Costantino called out to his neighbors eating in the tavern, "Oh my commune, now is the time to help me." They did: the tocsin was rung calling the citizens to arms, and Savorgnan's henchmen were surrounded, beaten, threatened with death, and then driven from town. Costantino called a meeting of the communal assembly, which agreed to resist with force any further attempt to arrest him or anyone else. Girolamo Savorgnan complained to Venice that the Buiesi were so arrogant that they thought themselves "one of the cantons of Switzerland." Costantino appealed the trumped-up charges against him, a process that took a leisurely tour through the Venetian courts lasting more than ten years.[66]

The case exemplifies not just the complexities of Venetian justice but how a clever provincial notary could use the law to preserve the "liberty" of his commune. In the litigation the Savorgnan claimed that Costantino had forged the 1506 accord, even though a copy of it can still be found in the Savorgnan family archive. The luogotenente in Udine, who tended to value military concerns over his responsibility to adjudicate legal appeals, found in favor of the Savorgnan, but Costantino appealed to the Quarantia Civile in Venice, which reversed the decision in favor of Buia. Buia's exemption was allowed to stand until 1525, when the Council of Ten confirmed it, but then the Ten reversed themselves on the basis of a technical error by the notary who had written up the accord and required the Buiesi to work on the castle. Costantino then appealed to the Avogadori di Comun, who found again in Buia's favor and sent the case back to the Quarantia. At this point the record peters out, perhaps because Girolamo Savorgnan was ill by the late 1526 but also because with the end of fighting the castle at Osoppo was abandoned, eventually to be replaced in the Venetian defensive system by the fortress city of Palmanova.

As part of an answer to a question about the presence of republicanism in the Venetian Republic, this complex litigation demonstrates how the conflicting jurisdictions and competing powers of the various Venetian judicial bodies created a space for legal resistance by a rural community against local oligarchs and feudal lords. The ground for resistance was not some imagined utopia of God's elect but the statutes of a commune. The leaders of resistance were neither millenarian prophets nor reform-minded priests but notaries willing and able to employ legal procedures on behalf of the liberty of the commune. The consequence of resistance was hardly ever a firm resolution of differences but a semipermanent state of litigation that allowed clashing privileges to be subject to continuous negotiation through the court system and minimized the possibilities for violence. Strong communal customs offered many benefits. During the violent peasant rebellions in Friuli in 1511 Buia's exceptional statutes served it well since Buia, unlike its neighbors, remained peaceful and even became a haven for refugees.

The liberty of the commune of Buia and other rural communities did not rely on a concept of rights or even Venetian guarantees, which were regularly ignored or abrogated by powerful oligarchs, but was preserved through community resistance, especially the consuetudine, which had to be constantly asserted and vigilantly defended through litigation. What appear from the Weberian point of view to be the contradictions, inefficiencies, and ineptitude of Venetian justice were the very features that made communal *res publicae* possible. The Venetian legal system did not render justice for rural communities so much as it created a space for maneuver and negotiation. In effect, the Venetian legal system, rather than its political system, mediated class conflict, and the institutionalization of class conflict was, of course, the very principle that Machiavelli argued was essential for a free republic: "In every republic there are two opposed factions, that of the people and that of the rich, and . . . all the laws made in favor of liberty result from their discord."[67] The irony is that this is precisely what Machiavelli, who was writing in the wake of Agnadello, when the fate of Venice's terraferma empire was in doubt, thought the Venetian Republic had failed to do.

After its victory in the war, Venice faced a crucial constitutional dilemma. On the one hand, the councils and magistracies of the provincial capitals had to be reformed to make them more subject to Venetian control and to limit the privileges of the local oligarchs who had led the rebellions against St. Mark. On the other hand, in reclaiming the terraferma Venice could not brusquely push aside the artisans and peasants who in their animosity to aristocratic privilege had been faithful to St. Mark. Angelo Ventura has argued that Venice's solution was to offer the lower classes some modest access to power and to reform the provincial city councils in the image of Venice. In other words, Venice exported its own oligarchic institutions to the provinces, "demonstrating yet again that the Venetian patriciate could not imagine any alternative to the aristocratic structure, and that the classes of nobles and 'citizens,' no matter how unfaithful and rebellious, still remained the only legitimate and natural repository of the right to administer the city."[68]

My argument would be somewhat different. By looking just at the constitutional structures of the Venetian regime, one can see only exportable oligarchic institutions, but by searching for the often hidden forms of legal practice that constituted a form of resistance, one sees that there was considerable openness in the Venetian government that undercut the power of provincial oligarchs and made Venice's own courts subject to influence from below. These practices were not so much exported from Venice as licensed by Venice. In the end, to use his own standard for judging politics, Machiavelli was wrong: St. Mark was well advised to hold the book of laws rather than the sword in his hand. The republicanism found in the hinterlands of the Venetian Republic did not emanate from Venice.[69] Republicanism arose out of the resistance by communal governments to princely pretensions, and the liberty of these many little *res publicae* was preserved through the institutionalization rather than the suppression of conflict, an institutionalization that took the form of continuous litigation.

NOTES

I wish to dedicate this essay to two historians whose work has always kept sight of the larger moral and intellectual purposes of our endeavor. My mentor, Donald Weinstein's *Savonarola and Florence: Prophecy and Patriotism in the Renaissance* (Princeton, 1970) continues to inspire me and my own students. The late Felix Gilbert is best known among Renaissance scholars for his masterpiece, *Machiavelli and Guicciardini: Politics and History in Sixteenth-Century Florence* (Princeton, 1965), but late in his career he turned to Venice, especially the period of the War of the League of Cambrai. See esp. his "Venice in the Crisis of the League of Cambrai," in *Renaissance Venice,* ed. J. R. Hale (London, 1973), 274–92; and idem, *The Pope, His Banker, and Venice* (Cambridge, Mass., 1980).

Epigraph: "St. Mark, to his cost, and perhaps in vain, understands late that he needs to hold the sword and not the book in his hand." The reference is to Venice's traditional iconographic image of the lion of St. Mark, shown holding under his paw a book open to a page that reads, "Pax tibi Marce, Evangelista meus." The image was generally interpreted to represent Venice's peaceful dominion (see Edward Muir, *Civic Ritual in Renaissance Venice* [Princeton, 1981], 78–92).

1. The battle is also known as the battle of Ghiaradadda or Vailà. For a good synopsis of the War of the League of Cambrai, see M. E. Mallett and J. R. Hale, *The Military Organization of a Renaissance State: Venice c. 1400 to 1617* (Cambridge, 1984), 222–24. On the background of the war, see Nicolai Rubinstein, "Italian Reactions to Terraferma Expansion in the Fifteenth Century," in Hale, *Renaissance Venice,* 197–217.

2. *The Prince,* ch. 12, in *Machiavelli: The Chief Works and Others,* trans. Allan Gilbert, 3 vols. (Durham, N.C., 1965), 1:50. The statement is an accurate enough summation of contemporary opinion, but the dating is exaggerated: a hundred years would be closer to the truth.

3. Marino Sanuto, *I diarii di Marino Sanuto,* ed. Rinaldo Fulin et al., 58 vols. (Venice, 1879–1903), 17:102.

4. Continuous litigation might be imagined as a form of resistance. In the terms of James C. Scott, the transcript of the litigation was not as "hidden" as it might have been in other forms of resistance practiced by persons who found themselves in situations of extreme domination, but the public transcript of court cases certainly hid to some degree the actual political issues behind the litigation. In the example from Buia discussed below, the crucial legal case concerned allegations about a forged document, but when the community of Buia defended its notary it was resisting a feudal lord (see Scott, *Weapons of the Weak: Everyday Forms of Peasant Resistance* [New Haven, 1985]; and idem, *Domination and the Arts of Resistance: Hidden Transcripts* [New Haven, 1990]).

5. William J. Bouwsma, "Venice and the Political Education of Europe," in Hale, *Renaissance Venice,* 445–66.

6. Gilbert examines the reactions in "Venice in the Crisis of the League of Cambrai."

7. Bouwsma, "Venice and the Political Education of Europe." A measure of the remarkable conservatism of Venetian political thought is evident in the work of Marco Foscarini, the most important eighteenth-century Venetian political theorist; he ignored virtually all political thinkers after Machiavelli and Contarini (see Foscarini, *Necessità della storia e della facoltà di ben dire per gli uomini di Repubblica* and *Della perfezione della Repubblica veneziana,* ed. Luisa Ricaldone [Milan, 1983]).

8. Nicolai Rubinstein, "Oligarchy and Democracy in Fifteenth-Century Florence," in *Florence and Venice: Comparisons and Relations,* ed. Sergio Bertelli, Nicolai Rubinstein, and Craig Hugh Smyth, vol. 1, *Quattrocento* (Florence, 1979), 99–112.

9. The literature on this subject is quite vast, but the most important works are Innocenzo Cervelli, *Machiavelli e la crisi dello stato veneziano* (Naples, 1974); J. G. A. Pocock, *The Machiavellian Moment: Florentine Political Thought and the Atlantic Republican Tradition* (Princeton, 1975), 183–330 (284–85 on mechanized *virtù*); and Quentin Skinner, *The Foundations of Modern Political Thought*, vol. 1, *The Renaissance* (Cambridge, 1978), 139–44. Cervelli and Pocock see the Venetian model as more influential than does Skinner, who emphasizes the roots of republican concepts in the communal period. Cf. Quentin Skinner, "The Vocabulary of Renaissance Republicanism: A Cultural *Longue-Durée?*" in *Language and Images of Renaissance Italy*, ed. Alison Brown (Oxford, 1995), 87–110; and G. Bock, Q. Skinner, and M. Viroli, eds., *Machiavelli and Republicanism* (Cambridge, 1990).

10. Hans Baron argued that the Florentine reaction to military crisis that culminated in 1402 with the death of Giangaleazzo Visconti, the duke of Milan, stimulated the articulation of a new appreciation for republican liberty, especially in the works of Leonardo Bruni (see Baron, *The Crisis of the Early Italian Renaissance: Civic Humanism and Republican Liberty in an Age of Classicism and Tyranny*, new ed. [Princeton, 1966]; and idem, *In Search of Florentine Civic Humanism: Essays on the Transition from Medieval to Modern Thought*, 2 vols. [Princeton, 1988]). Baron's civic-humanism thesis still engenders critical debate. See esp. Riccardo Fubini, "Renaissance Historian: The Career of Hans Baron," *Journal of Modern History* 64 (1992): 541–74; the review essay on Hans Baron by John M. Najemy in *Renaissance Quarterly* 45 (1992): 340–50; James Hankins, "The 'Baron Thesis' after Forty Years and Some Recent Studies of Leonardo Bruni," *Journal of the History of Ideas* 56 (1995): 309–38; and the "*AHR* Forum" on Baron with papers by Ronald Witt, John M. Najemy, Craig Kallendorf, and Werner Gundersheimer in *American Historical Review* 101 (1996): 107–44. I wish to thank William J. Connell for allowing me to see in advance of publication his perceptive essay "The Republican Idea," forthcoming in *Rethinking Civic Humanism*, ed. James Hankins.

The papal interdict against Venice in 1606–7 provoked a sweeping defense of republican liberty against claims of papal universal authority (see William J. Bouwsma, *Venice and the Defense of Republican Liberty: Renaissance Values in the Age of the Counter Reformation* [Berkeley, 1968]; for a critical assessment, see Renzo Pecchioli, *Dal "mito" di Venezia all' "ideologia americana": Itinerari e modelli della storiografia sul repubblicanesimo nell'età moderna* [Venice, 1983]).

Although a commonplace in the history of ideas, systematic comparisons of ancient and Renaissance city-republics have been few. See esp. Anthony Molho, Kurt Raaflaub, and Julia Emlen, eds., *City States in Classical Antiquity and Medieval Italy* (Ann Arbor, 1991).

11. Pocock, *Machiavellian Moment*, 53–54.

12. On the use of republicanism for the plotting of history, especially by American historians of Europe, see Edward Muir, "The Italian Renaissance in America," *American Historical Review* 100 (1995): 1095–1118.

13. Skinner, "Vocabulary of Renaissance Republicanism," 101.

14. Huc del Cayro and Johan Gasc quoted in Ann Wroe, *A Fool and His Money: Life in a Partitioned Town in Fourteenth-Century France* (New York, 1995), 48 and 51, respectively.

15. Latini's statement is cited and discussed in Skinner, "Vocabulary of Renaissance Republicanism," 101. The passage is from Brunetto Latini, *Li Livres dou Trésor* (Berkeley, 1948), 392. Cf. the important article by Ronald Witt, "Medieval 'Ars dictaminis' and the Beginnings of Humanism: A New Construction of the Problem," *Renaissance Quarterly* 35 (1982): 1–35.

16. I use the word *practice* in this chapter both in its narrow juridical sense to describe legal customs and in the broader analytical sense of "ways of doing." On the later sense, see Pierre Bourdieu, *Outline of a Theory of Practice,* trans. Richard Nice (Cambridge, 1977); and Michel de Certeau, *The Practice of Everyday Life,* trans. Steven F. Rendall (Berkeley, 1984).

17. Cf. Julius Kirshner, ed., *The Origins of the State in Italy, 1300–1600* (Chicago, 1996), 1–10.

18. On the Venetian territorial state, see Marino Berengo, *La società veneta alla fine del Settecento: Ricerche storiche* (Florence, 1956); for the concept of diarchy, see Angelo Ventura, *Nobiltà e popolo nella società veneta del '400 e '500,* 2d ed. (Milan, 1993); and on cultural differences throughout the terraferma, see Gaetano Cozzi, "Ambiente veneziano, ambiente veneto," in *L'uomo e il suo ambiente,* ed. Stefano Rosso-Mazzinghi (Florence, 1973), 93–146; idem, "Considerazioni sull'amministrazione della giustizia nella Repubblica di Venezia (sec. XV–XVI)," in Bertelli, Rubinstein, and Smyth, *Florence and Venice,* 1:101–33; idem, ed., *Stato, società e giustizia nella Repubblica Veneta (sec. XV–XVIII),* 2 vols. (Rome, 1980–85); idem, "Politica, società, istituzioni," in Gaetano Cozzi and Michael Knapton, *La Repubblica di Venezia nell'età moderna,* vol. 12, pt. 1 (Turin, 1986), 3–252; Edward Muir, *Mad Blood Stirring: Vendetta and Factions in Friuli during the Renaissance* (Baltimore, 1993), 49–67; Furio Bianco, *1511: La "crudel zobia grassa": Rivolte contadine e faide nobiliari in Friuli tra '400 e '500* (Pordenone, 1995); Marco Bellabarba, *La giustizia ai confini: Il principato vescovile di Trento agli inizi dell'età moderna* (Bologna, 1996); and the excellent synthesis of work on the Veneto, Alfredo Viggiano, *Governanti e governati: Legittimità del potere ed esercizio dell'autorità sovrana nello stato veneto della prima età moderna* (Treviso, 1993).

19. On the regional state, see Giorgio Chittolini, *La formazione dello stato regionale e le istituzioni del contado: Secoli XIV e XV* (Turin, 1979); idem, ed., *La crisi degli ordinamenti comunali e le origini dello stato del Rinascimento* (Bologna, 1979); idem, "Stati padani, 'Stati del Rinascimento': Problemi di ricerca," in *Persistenze feudali e autonomie communitative in stati padani fra Cinque e Seicento,* ed. G. Tocci (Bologna, 1988), 9–29; and idem, "The 'Private,' the 'Public,' the State," in *The Origins of the State in Italy,* 34–61. On "indirect government" in the Genoese state, see Osvaldo Raggio, *Faide e parentele: Lo stato genovese visto dalla Fontanabuona* (Turin, 1990), xiv. Cf. Maurice Aymard, "La transizione dal feudalismo al capitalismo," in *Storia d'Italia: Annali,* ed. Ruggiero Romano and Corrado Vivanti, vol. 1, *Dal feudalismo al capitalismo* (Turin, 1978), 1131–92. One comparative historian of Mediterranean empires has described the Genoese empire in terms of the "'absence' of the state" (Felipe Fernández-Armesto, *Before Columbus: Exploration and Colonization from the Mediterranean to the Atlantic, 1229–1492* [Philadelphia, 1987], 96–120). The best synthetic study of the Genoese state is Steven A. Epstein, *Genoa and the Genoese, 958–1528* (Chapel Hill, N.C., 1996).

20. On corruption among Venetian governors and judges, see Donald E. Queller, *The Venetian Patriciate: Reality versus Myth* (Urbana, 1986). This view of Venetian legal administration derives from the work of Gaetano Cozzi and his students found in *Stato, società, e giustizia nella Repubblica Veneta* and summarized in Viggiano, *Governanti e governati*.

21. See Muir, *Mad Blood Stirring*, for an analysis of the most prominent case of politics pursued through informal factions. For an argument that clientalism and feuding should not be viewed as antimodern but as ways of consolidating states during the early modern period, see Chittolini, "The 'Private,' the 'Public,' the State."

22. The legal status of *cittadino* was available to provincials and commoners of substantial property who were resident in Venice, but the status only granted trading privileges, access to technical and clerical jobs in Venetian government, and the opportunity to join certain charitable institutions, such as the *scuole grandi;* it did not carry any political privileges (see Brian Pullan, *Rich and Poor in Renaissance Venice: The Social Institutions of a Catholic State to 1620* [Cambridge, Mass., 1971]). Very little is known about the cittadini as a class, but James Grubb's contribution in this volume constitutes the best work on them. Before the seventeenth century only a very small number of provincials received membership in the patriciate, usually because of military services, but Venetians were shocked when one of them had the temerity to exercise his privilege by showing up at meetings of the Senate. Girolamo Savorgnan caused scandal when he actually exercised the office of senator (Muir, *Mad Blood Stirring,* 239). On the suicidal reluctance of the Venetian patriciate to recruit new members, see James C. Davis, *The Decline of the Venetian Nobility as a Ruling Class* (Baltimore, 1962); and Volker Hunecke, *Der venezianische Adel am ende der Republik, 1646–1797* (Tübingen, 1995).

On the structural history of the Italian states, see Federico Chabod, *Scritti sul Rinascimento* (Turin, 1981); and idem, *Lo stato e la vita religiosa a Milano nell'epoca di Carlo V* (Turin, 1977). On the Tuscan grand ducal state, see Elena Fasano Guarini, ed., *Potere e società negli stati regionali italiani del '500 e '600* (Bologna, 1978); and idem, "Center and Periphery," in *The Origins of the State in Italy,* 74–96.

23. Giovanni Scarabello, "Nelle relazioni dei rettori veneti in terraferma: Aspetti di una loro attività di mediazione tra governanti delle città suddite e governo della dominante," in *Atti del Convegno: Venezia e la terraferma attraverso le relazioni dei rettori, Trieste, 23–24 ottobre 1980,* ed. Amelio Tagliaferri (Milan, 1981), 491.

24. James S. Grubb, *Firstborn of Venice: Vicenza in the Early Renaissance State* (Baltimore, 1988), 23.

25. Ibid., 23–25.

26. Sanuto, *I diarii,* 10:154.

27. Queller, *Venetian Patriciate.*

28. Venetian judicial history has been the subject of an extraordinary research effort inspired by Gaetano Cozzi. On the expansion of the powers of the Council of Ten after Agnadello, see Cozzi, "Authority and the Law in Renaissance Venice," in Hale, *Renaissance Venice,* 293–345. For a synthesis, see Viggiano, *Governanti e governati.*

29. On Venetian humanism, see Margaret L. King, *Venetian Humanism in an Age of Patrician Dominance* (Princeton, 1986), 92, 150–57, 333–35, quotation on 92.

30. Gasparo Contarini, *The Commonwealth and Government of Venice,* trans. Lewes Lewkenor (London, 1599), 125–49, quotations on 129–30. The original Latin edition is *De magistratibus et republica Venetorum libri quinque* (Venice, 1545). On the dating of the treatise, see Felix Gilbert, "The Date of the Composition of Contarini's and Giannotti's Books on Venice," *Studies in the Renaissance* 14 (1967): 172–84. On Contarini's career, see Elisabeth G. Gleason, *Gasparo Contarini: Venice, Rome, and Reform* (Berkeley, 1993). On the place of Contarini's book in the history of republican thought, see Pocock, *Machiavellian Moment,* 320–30. On the inadequacy of Contarini's views for explaining Venice's terraferma dominion, see James Grubb, "When Myths Lose Power: Four Decades of Venetian Historiography," *Journal of Modern History* 58 (1986): 43–94. On the theoretical problems presented by the terraferma dominion, see Cervelli, *Machiavelli e la crisi dello stato veneziano,* 165–217.

31. The speech is quoted at length in Cervelli, *Machiavelli e la crisi dello stato veneziano,* 47–48. Sanudo recorded that the Paduan delegation met Maximilian on 22 June 1509 (*I diarii,* 8:431).

32. Venice's most important supporter in Friuli, Antonio Savorgnan, complained bitterly about Venetian usury (see Muir, *Mad Blood Stirring,* 116).

33. Niccolò Machiavelli, *Legazioni e commissarie,* ed. Sergio Bertelli, 3 vols. (Milan, 1964), 3:1188–89.

34. Niccolò Machiavelli, *Discourses on the First Decades of Titus Livius* 2.2, translation from Allan Gilbert, *Machiavelli,* 1:333.

35. See Machiavelli, *The Prince,* chs. 17, 19.

36. Sanuto, *I diarii,* 8:374.

37. This is the major theme in the most violent conflict between terraferma aristocrats and peasants in the wake of Agnadello, the famous "Cruel Fat Thursday" in Friuli in 1511 (see Muir, *Mad Blood Stirring,* 135–51; and Bianco, *1511: La "crudel zobia grassa"*).

38. P. J. Jones points out that oligarchic hegemony characterized all Italian city-states, whether principalities or republics (see Jones, "Communes and Despots: The City State in Late-Medieval Italy," *Transactions of the Royal Historical Society,* 5th ser., 15 [1965]: 71–96; and idem, "Economia e società nell'Italia medievale: La leggenda della borghesia," in *Storia d'Italia: Annali,* 1:187–372). Angelo Ventura has made a similar argument for the Venetian terraferma in *Nobiltà e popolo.*

39. That, at least, is my interpretation of one of Sanudo's characteristically obscure passages: "Et lì a Padoa sono quelli do todeschi governadore, stanno im palazo. . . . Et le intrade di nostri pur si devano, et ne veniva qualche parte di padoana, *tamen* per li vilani, cridando: Marco! Marco! Si batevano. Et il formento valeva a Padoa soldi . . . el staro, il vin soldi 36 il mastello. Et le porte di Padoa erano tenute serade *etc.*" (*I diarii,* 8:431, dated 22 June 1509, second set of ellipses in Sanudo's text).

40. J. Bruti, *Annalia quaedam,* cited in Ventura, *Nobiltà e popolo,* 122.

41. Machiavelli, *Legazioni e commissarie,* 3:1193–94, letter from Verona dated 26 November 1509.

42. The evidence is neatly summarized in Ventura, *Nobiltà e popolo,* 121–87.

43. Muir, *Mad Blood Stirring*, 111–88.

44. Ventura, *Nobilità e popolo*, 150–68.

45. Gaetano Cozzi, Michael Knapton, and Giovanni Scarabello, *La Repubblica di Venezia nell'età moderna: Dal 1517 alla fine della Repubblica* (Turin, 1992), esp. 433–35.

46. G. Dalla Santa, *La lega di Cambrai e gli avvenimenti dell'anno 1509 descritti da un mercante veneziano contemporaneo* (Padua, 1903), 13, cited and discussed in Ventura, *Nobilità e popolo*, 128n.

47. My interpretation of the situation among the peasantry has been strongly influenced by the extreme case, the agrarian revolt in Friuli (see Muir, *Mad Blood Stirring*, 135–51, which is largely confirmed by Bianco, *1511: La "crudel zobia grassa,"* 14–32). There are many gaps in the rural history of the rest of the terraferma, but the pattern does seem to be general at least across the heavily populated plain and the eastern regions most fully enmeshed in the Venetian market. The literature is summarized in Knapton, "Tra dominante e dominio," 419–47.

48. Knapton, "Tra dominante e dominio," 424.

49. Archivio di Stato, Venice (ASV), Luogotenente della Patria di Friuli, filza 132, fol. 239. I have analyzed the articles in *Mad Blood Stirring*, 149–51.

50. For the German revolts in general, Peter Blickle, *The Revolution of 1525: The German Peasants' War from a New Perspective*, trans. Thomas A. Brady and H. C. Erik Midelfort (Baltimore, 1981).

51. For the Articles of Merano, see Manuela Acler, ed., "La completa versione in volgare italiano degli articoli di Merano," *Studi Trentini di Scienze Storiche* 56 (1977): 225–53. The best study is Giorgio Politi, *Gli statuti impossibili: La rivoluzione tirolese del 1525 e il "programma" di Michael Gaismair* (Turin, 1995).

52. Peter Burke, *The Historical Anthropology of Early Modern Italy: Essays on Perception and Communication* (Cambridge, 1987), 130.

53. On notary statistics, see ibid., 128.

54. For an account of the career of one such notary who specialized in peasant clients in the Padovano, see Marino Berengo, "Africo Clementi, agronomo padovano del Cinquecento," in *Miscellanea Augusto Campana*, vol. 1, Medioevo e Umanesimo, 44 (Padua, 1981), 27–69.

55. An illiterate Sienese peasant in the sixteenth century found writing so alluring that he hired various people to keep a diary for him (see Duccio Balestracci, *La zappa e la retorica: Memorie familiari di un contadino toscano del Quattrocento* [Florence, 1984], an English translation, *The Renaissance in the Fields: Family Memoirs of a Fifteenth-Century Tuscan Peasant*, by Paolo Squatriti and Betsy Merideth [University Park, Pa., 1999]).

56. Since the medieval statutes have long played a crucial role in forming communal identities, they have received a great deal of attention by local historians, and many have been published. For a list of the published statutes for Friuli alone, see Gaetano Perusini, "Gli statuti di una vicinia rurale Friulana del Cinquecento," *Memorie Storico Forogiuliesi* 43 (1958–59): 213n. A useful recent example is the superb critical study and edition of the statutes of Rovereto in the Trentino, *Statuti di Rovereto del 1425*, ed. Federica Parcianello (Venice, 1991). On notarial practice in general, see Claudio

Povolo, "Aspetti e problemi dell'amministrazione della giustizia penale nella repubblica di Venezia, secoli XVI–XVII," in Cozzi, *Stato, società e giustizia nella Repubblica Veneta,* 1:153–258.

57. This population figure is a guess guided by the known population figure of 2,706 for the period 1766–70.

58. Gian Paolo Gri, "Giurisdizione e vicinia nell'età moderna: Il caso di Buia," in *I Savorgnan e la Patria del Friuli dal XIII al XVIII secolo* (Udine, 1984), 178. On local institutions in Friuli, see esp. Michele Zacchigna, "Note per un inquadrimento storico della produzione statutaria friulana," in *La libertà di decidere: Realtà e parvenze di autonomia nella normativa locale del medioevo,* ed. Rolando Donardini (Cento, 1995). On the role of statutes in communal life, see Giorgio Chittolini and Dietmar Willoweit, *Statuti, città, territori in Italia e Germania tra medioevo ed età moderna* (Bologna, 1991); see also idem, *L'organizzazione del territorio in Italia e Germania: Secoli XIII–XIV* (Bologna, 1994). I wish to thank Julius Kirshner for his advice on the literature about *statuti.*

59. For the crucial legal documents for Buia, Archivio di Stato, Udine (ASU), Archivio Savorgnan, busta 33, pacco 3, "Summario generale de' titoli e carte della casa Eccellentissima Savorgnan per la giurisdizione di Buja e contro la general vicinia di Buja." These documents, however, have been selected to justify Savorgnan infringements on Buia's autonomy and can be only used with caution. For the governmental functions of Buia, see Gri, "Giurisdizione e vicinia," 183 nn. 9–11. On the Savorgnan and Friuli, see Muir, *Mad Blood Stirring,* 32–48, 78–82.

60. On these disputes, see Biblioteca Communale, Udine (BCU), Ms. Joppi 689c, vol. 3, docs. 2 (on work details, *pioveghi*), 3 (on special levies, *gravezze*), and 8 (on the Ledra water disputes). On the typical work obligations owed to feudatories in Friuli, see Ferruccio Carlo Carreri, "Del buon governo spilimberghese," *Archivio Veneto* 36 (1888): 331–32.

61. On millers and the mediation between literate and nonliterate culture in Friuli, see Carlo Ginzburg, *The Cheese and the Worms: The Cosmos of a Sixteenth-Century Miller,* trans. John Tedeschi and Anne C. Tedeschi (Baltimore, 1980).

62. On the Rizzardi, see ASU, Notarile, busta 373, "De Rizzardis Costantino Pichissivi Eusebio notaio in Buia, 1512–1556," fasc. 1512–15; for Costantino Rizzardi's commission as notary of Buia, dated 5 January 1513 (1512 *mv* [*mv* = *more veneto;* the Venetian year began on 1 March]), see ASV, Luogotenente della Patria di Friuli, Processi ed investiture, filza 134, "Investiturarum liber unicus," fol. 33v. On the condemnation of Dionisio Rizzardi in 1558 for Lutheranism, see Gri, "Giurisdizione e vicinia," 186 n. 28.

63. The crucial passage reads, "Volendo Noi [the Savorgnan] mai in alcun tempo fabbricar lo Castello suso lo Monte non possiamo astringere il Comun nè con piovigo, nè con persona, nè con carro, ma sia in libertà del Comun per sua umanitade, e non per l'obligazion" (ASU, Archivio Savorgnan, busta 33, pacco 2, fol. 24v). The explicit assertion of Buia's privileges caused controversy when the commune formally swore loyalty to Girolamo Savorgnan on 29 April 1514 (BCU, Ms. Joppi 689d, vol. 3, fols. 141v–142v).

64. For an account of local disasters during these years, see Sebastiano Mulioni di

Gemona, *Chronicon glemonense dal 1300 al 1517* (Udine, 1887), 13–26. On damage caused by the siege and enemy action, see ASV, Luogotenente della Patria di Friuli, filza 135, fol. 131r; ASV, Inquisitori di stato, busta 1037, processo 115, document dated April 1514; and Girolamo Savorgnan, "Lettere sulla guerra combattuta nel Friuli dal 1510 al 1528 scritte alla signoria di Venezia," *Archivio Storico Italiano*, n.s., 4 (1856): 31–32, 34. On the news of peasant rebellions in Carinthia, see Sanuto, *I diarii*, 20:317–18, 324–25, 384; and for reports of Turkish incursions, see ibid., 22:167.

65. On the first signs of trouble in Buia, see BCU, Ms. Joppi 689d, vol. 4, doc. 89, dated 28 August 1515.

66. The records of the case are in BCU, Ms. Joppi 689c, vol. 3, "processo." For the quote about Switzerland, see doc. 6, Inc.: "Le parolle de la oblation. . . ." Girolamo Savorgnan's full statement reads, "Ma se fussero ben stati uno de li Cantoni de Sviceri in sonar campane in segno de letitia in far procession et pastizarlo l'un l'altro, et dicendo parolle superbe de non poterle suportare le qual tute cose se offerimo prevar in Casa, che le sian negate." For the depositions regarding the aborted arrest of Costantino Rizzardi, see BCU, Ms. 1042, busta 1, filza 3, "Deposizioni di testimoni sopra una baruffa successa in Buja 1516." On the Swiss cantons as models of communal freedom, see Benjamin R. Barber, *The Death of Communal Liberty: A History of Freedom in a Swiss Mountain Canton* (Princeton, 1974); and Thomas A. Brady Jr., *Turning Swiss: Cities and Empire, 1450–1550* (Cambridge, 1985).

67. Machiavelli, *Discourses*, 1.4, translation from Allan Gilbert, *Machiavelli*, 2:203.

68. Ventura, *Nobiltà e popolo*, 169.

69. For a parallel case that emphasizes the criminalization of aristocratic violence through the cooperation of locals with Venetian courts, see Claudio Povolo, *L'intrigo dell'onore: Poteri e istituzioni nella Repubblica di Venezia tra Cinque e Seicento* (Verona, 1997). See also the studies in *Crime, Society, and the Law in Renaissance Italy*, ed. Trevor Dean and K. J. P. Lowe (Cambridge, 1994).

5

Confronting New Realities
Venice and the Peace of Bologna, 1530

ELISABETH G. GLEASON

As Edward Muir's essay makes clear, the 1509 defeat of Venice at Agnadello by the League of Cambrai has long been seen as a major turning point in Venetian history. In this chapter Elisabeth Gleason challenges this orthodoxy, suggesting not that scholars abandon the significance of Agnadello but rather that they view this event in a broader context of the wars of Italy, which concluded only with the Treaty of Bologna in 1530. But Gleason does more than develop a larger context in which to chart Venice's transition from a self-confident, expanding, even militant power to one both humbled and hemmed in by the hegemonic power of the Habsburg presence in Italy. She also offers a new framework for understanding how emerging international realities shaped what was undoubtedly one of the most influential books in the making of the myth of Venice: Gasparo Contarini's De magistratibus et republica Venetorum. In this work Contarini, a Venetian ambassador deeply involved in the shifting diplomatic and international world of the early sixteenth century, presented Venice as a city of peace, concord, and constitutional excellence. Its significance, he realized, could rest no longer on its military power but derived from the apparent perfection of its political institutions. Thus, the myth of Venice found its most notable expression in the wake of Venetian defeat and humiliation.

IN HISTORIES OF VENICE from the sixteenth century to our own the events of the summer of 1509 have occupied a special place. A European league against Venice, the spectacular defeat of the Republic's forces at Agnadello, and the loss of almost the entire mainland state provided high drama for accounts of the period. According to Machiavelli, Agnadello laid bare the essence of the Venetian character: arrogant in victory but dejected, despondent, and dispirited in defeat.[1] Guicciardini's analysis of the meaning of Agnadello focuses on the battle's repercussions for all Italian states, which realized that "the fall of Venice meant the cutting off of their most glorious member, that Italian state which more than any other maintained the fame and reputation of them all."[2] Yet Guicciardini's ambivalence toward Venice, like that of many Florentines, is obvious: he thought that Venetian politicians, despite their republican values and "their displays of lucidity and gravity," turned "down the wrong road, blinded by their own sense of intrinsic virtue and superiority. . . . driven by self-interest and delusion, the patricians of Venice, like the princes they scorn[ed], [became] playthings of Fortune."[3] For Venetian conservatives like Girolamo Priuli, the terrible fall from greatness was divine retribution for the vices of their state and an unmistakable sign that it had taken a wrong turn in abandoning glory at sea for expansion on land.[4] Doge Leonardo Loredan saw in the defeat divine punishment for the immoderate luxury in which the Venetians indulged.[5]

Modern historians, while using different categories, continue to stress the magnitude of the disaster of Agnadello and its effects on the political and economic position of Venice.[6] The name of the battle has come to symbolize the end of the age of Venice's triumphalism, expansion, and status as a major European power. The war the Republic had to wage was immensely expensive and weakened her financially.[7] Recent scholarship has emphasized the critical changes for Venice in the wake of Agnadello, such as the alteration of the constitution with the establishment of a narrow governing oligarchy and the concomitant diminution of the Great Council's power, the split of the nobility according to wealth that resulted from the venality of offices,[8] and the changed power relationship between the *dominante* and the *terraferma*. The Treaty of Bologna in 1530, when emperor and pope decided the fate of Italy, is often seen as little more than a coda to events of the two previous decades.

Without denying the importance of the Venetian defeat in 1509 or its results, above all its impact on the self-image of the Venetian ruling class, I would like to argue that it should be regarded not as *the* major watershed but as one of several major watersheds in the political history of early-sixteenth-century Venice. To be sure, it was a traumatic event, but it did not deprive the Republic of the ability to maneuver, recoup its forces, regain its mainland possessions, and at least temporarily cherish the illusion that it could reestablish itself as a key player in Italian and European politics. Most importantly, the immediate crisis caused by the War of the League of Cambrai had come to an end by 1517. The political and military history of the period following, although often slighted, clearly shows that the Venetian ruling class conducted business as usual and proceeded in accordance with lines of policy that had been well established before Agnadello. This is best demonstrated by the adherence of the Venetians to the League of Cognac in 1526 and the readiness with which they went to war in Apulia the following year.

The fortunes of Venice took an irrevocable turn only as a consequence of the extent, weight, and threatened permanence of Habsburg power. The Venetian ruling elite was forced to face the reality that a new period had begun with the powerlessness of Italian states, including its own, before the might of Charles V. This time the crisis showed no likelihood of ending. The issue was not the outcome of a war. Unlike the ephemeral League of Cambrai, the Habsburg empire had come to stay. In 1517, Venice, though scarred, strove to return to her normal place among European states; in 1530 the very idea of regaining that place was a chimera of the past.[9] The perception of the decline of Venice as a European power, whether expressed as generalization, analogy, or judgment,[10] came to permeate Venetian political discourse in the late 1520s. What an individual senator had said some years before in another context now could have been said by almost all members of the Senate and the Collegio: "El mondo è mutado" (the world has changed).[11] If one must periodize Venetian history, then the trauma of the defeat at Agnadello in 1509 appears as a prelude to events leading to the Treaty of Bologna in 1530, which truly marked the end of an era.

The years leading up to this peace are well documented.[12] The cardinal event on the international scene of the 1520s was the evolution of Charles V from a colorless nineteen-year-old at the time of his coronation to an emperor with a well-defined vision of his dominant role in Europe.[13] The hundreds of letters written by the Venetian ambassador at the imperial court from 1521 to 1525, Gasparo Contarini, and avidly read at home, where they helped to shape Venetian attitudes toward the emperor, chronicle the growth both of Charles's political maturity and of the ambassador's understanding of its implication for Venice.[14]

Like most of his peers, Contarini was pro-French.[15] While he was fair rather than hostile to Charles V, he remained unenthusiastic about his vast empire and skeptical toward the ideology of its protagonists. If anything, his years in Spain confirmed his admiration for a republican form of government. When Venice was constrained to join an alliance with the Habsburg brothers in 1523, Contarini shared with many of his fellow nobles the sense of unease at the narrowing of Venetian political options. In his reports during 1524–25, the last year of his embassy, we find a move from apprehension to anxiety concerning the emperor's might. Both were echoed with increasing frequency in the Collegio and the Senate and help explain the volte-face of the Republic, which in

December 1524 signed a secret treaty of alliance with Pope Clement VII and Francis I. Only two months later the French king was defeated and captured in the decisive battle of Pavia.[16] In May 1526 Venice readily joined France and the papacy in the anti-imperial League of Cognac. In a very real sense the preservation of *libertà* for both Venice and Italy was not only a slogan;[17] the French king, despite his territorial ambitions in Italy, was no longer perceived as a major threat, unlike the feared emperor and the accompanying specter of Spanish domination of Italy.[18]

While not directly affected by the sack of Rome in May 1527, Venice was nevertheless pushed to the wall and considered the freedom of Italy to be vital to her own survival.[19] Acquiescing in Charles V's claims to southern Italy and the Milanese state would mean acknowledging the emperor as the arbiter of Italy and thereby accepting that the Republic was only a minor player in a game it neither had initiated nor could control. Going to war against him, given the parlous situation of the pope and the French king, at various times both prisoners of the Spanish, would put the Venetians in an extremely exposed position but would reaffirm the self-image of Venice, a state of powerful warriors and conquerors with a long history of victories on sea and land protected by divine providence and glorying in the excellence of their unique institutions. The Venetian decision to wage war in Lombardy as well as in Apulia upheld that self-image.

The war years 1528–29 form the immediate background to the Peace of Bologna. Decisions by the government at home and events on the battlefields abroad are interwoven to form a gripping drama. A romantic poet might see in them the Venetian ideals of liberty pitted against the ruthless politics of new monarchs. The historian finds in them evidence of monumental change in the relations between Venice and western Europe and the tightening of the inescapable vise that was to constrict the Republic.

A key player in this complex drama was the unequivocally pro-French Doge Andrea Gritti, who possessed the sort of clear-sightedness in military matters that only personal experience in war could give.[20] Gritti was not afraid to go beyond the established limits of ducal authority in times of war. His impatience with the slowness of deliberations in the Senate and the Collegio and his willingness to expedite matters by resorting to appointment in preference to election provoked a public rebuke by the outspoken Lunardo Emo: "We are under a republic, not under a *signore,* and everything must be done by ballot," the doge was reminded.[21] But the doge was at times prepared to cut the Gordian knot of tradition and together with the majority of the Senate and the

Collegio did not hesitate to enlarge Venetian territory at the expense of the much-weakened Clement VII. When the pope was a prisoner, Venice had occupied Ravenna and Cervia, two papal cities important for both economic and logistic reasons. Their retention became one of the chief objectives of the Republic after 1527 despite her alliance with Clement VII and the perception of her governing class that "the destruction of the papacy as an independent power was a threat to Italy as a whole."[22] The irony of this was not lost on the pope. Venice was trying to accomplish two incompatible aims: supporting Clement VII against the emperor while stubbornly holding on to his two cities.

The Venetian commitment of troops and ships to Apulia had two purposes: to aid the French commander Lautrec in reconquering Naples and to carve out a foothold for Venice in an area that was an important source of grain and saltpeter. In northern Italy the Venetian objective was to prevent the emperor from incorporating Milan into his domains and to support both the French and Duke Francesco Sforza, whose claims to Milan were rejected by Charles V.

A paradoxical situation arose on Venice's far eastern flank after the Ottoman Turks obliterated the Hungarian kingdom in 1526. While Venetians were fighting a war on two fronts in Italy, they encouraged the Turks to attack Austria from the southeast so that the Habsburg brothers would be occupied with the defense of the Empire and consequently Charles V might reduce his pressure on both Venice and Italy. Sultan Suleiman the Magnificent in fact organized an immense military enterprise in the Balkans, and in 1529 the news reached Venice that more than 300,000 Turkish troops were moving toward Vienna. The pope did not view the Turkish threat to Austria as "mala nova," as the Venetian ambassador reported: Clement was pleased by anything that might diminish Habsburg power.[23] But Venice saw the news differently: while secretly in favor of the Turkish campaign, the Venetian rulers also realized that Turkish troops would be within a few days' march of Friuli, a border area they might (and eventually did) raid.[24] The Venetian governor of Udine, Marcantonio Contarini, wrote that the Turks were moving near Buda and that "all this land is in great fear."[25] Defending Friuli would mean fighting on three fronts. Besides, the presence of Alvise Gritti, the doge's son, in the sultan's camp was a public-relations disaster for Venice at the Habsburg courts.[26] The imperial ambassador in Rome even reported that Alvise was at the head of the Turkish army.[27] According to Girolamo Pesaro, one of the most influential Venetian senators, "there was nobody who did not believe" that the Signoria was guilty of conniving with the Turks in order to divert Charles V from Italy.[28]

The day-to-day deliberations of the Collegio during 1528 and even more during 1529 reveal an array of remarkable personalities both at home and abroad. Among the latter was the Venetian commander in southern Italy, Giovanni Vitturi, *proveditore generale* in Apulia, whose numerous letters have not received the careful study they deserve.[29] His clear, well-informed reports chronicle the decline of Venetian power in the Regno. The letters of Girolamo Pesaro, *capitano general di mar,* of the doge's namesake, Andrea Gritti (of the San Salvatore branch of the family), the governor of Monopoli, and of Vettor Soranzo, the governor of Trani, confirm Vitturi's analysis by their accurate judgment of military affairs. Together the reports of these men by degrees brought home to the Signoria the futility of the attempt to maintain Venetian control over the Apulian coast. The primary reason was not a lack of Venetian determination but the lack of money with which to counteract the emperor's vast power.

The day-by-day account in Sanudo's volumes for 1528 and 1529, showing the disproportion between the demands on Venetian resources and the Republic's ability to satisfy them, cannot fail to impress. Vitturi's letters concisely list how much money, ammunition, and other supplies were necessary if the southern Italian ports were to be defended against imperial troops. At critical points the unpaid Venetian and French troops mutinied, sacked and pillaged. Similar messages reached the Signoria from its *condottieri* in Lombardy. At the same time, the emissary from the anti-Medicean Florentine republic was pleading for money, especially after the beginning of the siege of the city by papal and imperial troops in the fall of 1529.

Faced with the urgency of raising money, the Venetian government resorted to the usual forced loans, taxation of ecclesiastical corporations, especially monasteries, borrowing against future income from monopolies, and imposing new taxes on Jews and on producers of luxury cloth and other high-priced articles. A lottery was instituted. Public lands were sold, as were offices. No avenue for increasing income was left unexplored. The desperate need of more revenue was the most urgent internal problem for the government during this period. Gaetano Cozzi has argued that in 1529–30 the need for money became truly obsessive and that under Gritti's influence money became a substitute for waning military power and a symbol of the Venetian brand of statecraft.[30]

To war with all its terrors were added two more horsemen of the apocalypse, famine and plague.[31] The opening sentence of Sanudo's entry for almost every day during 1527–29 chronicles the number of the dead. Mortality was persistent in Venice and the terraferma, but it reached catastrophic proportions

among the ill-provisioned and mutinous troops in southern Italy.[32] The French
commander Lautrec succumbed to it in August 1528, and his unpaid army
promptly shrank from 25,000 to 4,000 men.[33] The same summer brought the
bad news that Andrea Doria had changed sides, to the great chagrin of the
Signoria, which promptly ordered Venetian ships to avoid encounters with
Doria's fleet at all cost. That plainly meant abandoning the Tyrrhenian Sea and
regrouping the navy to defend the Adriatic.

When Charles V announced that he would come to Italy in the spring
of 1529, the Venetian government was greatly worried. "Everyone perfectly
understands the importance of this news, and what imminent danger it is
bringing not only to our state, but to all of Italy," we read in the deliberations of
the Senate.[34] Now the French were Venice's last hope. On 3 June a motion was
made to offer 20,000 ducats a month to Francis I for an expedition to Italy. In
the debate that followed this desperate move, Francesco Morosini made a hard-
hitting parallel between Venice and Carthage; by proposing to shoulder the
entire cost of the war, he argued, Venice had embarked on a course of self-
destruction.[35] Gritti and the pro-French majority of the Signoria disagreed; in
the doge's view, Venetians were caught between "the two greatest emperors in
the world," Charles V and Suleiman. Only Francis could save Venice. But
many in the Collegio thought otherwise and believed that there was no point
in continuing to pay Venetian troops to oppose Charles V.[36] A proposal to offer
the emperor a large sum of money in return for peace provoked Lunardo Emo
almost to frenzy. Not only did he caution against giving the Turks grounds for
suspicion but "he raised many fears about making an enemy of the Turk, and
wept at the speaker's platform."[37] Even the letter to the Signoria of Master Calo,
a Jewish physician and astrologer who encouraged the government to persevere and remain constant, had little effect, although he predicted that the
emperor and the French king would acquiesce in Venice's wishes.[38]

Much more trenchant was the almost palpable fear in the report of Giovanni
Francesco Corner from Lombardy that the Spanish soldiers were burning and
sacking and "are devils, not men; they fear nobody."[39] The sense of imminent
danger after Charles V landed in Genoa on 12 August 1529 explains the sad fate
of the loud-mouthed Venetian Hieronimo Tron, who remarked in a gathering
in a tailor's shop that the emperor's troops would soon be sacking Venetian
territory and that he too would like to sack a house. Two days later he was
executed between the two columns of the Piazzetta "for having talked scan-
dalously in favor of the emperor."[40] Venice clearly put no trust in the proclama-
tions of the Spanish ambassador, as Contarini reported from Rome: "When

the emperor comes to Italy, he will show all Italian princes and all the world that he does not desire to be a monarch or lord it over Italy, but wishes to be a friend of all and in peace with all."[41]

Two events proved to be turning points in the politics of the Republic. At the end of June 1529 Clement VII and Charles V concluded the Treaty of Barcelona. Charles was invested by the pope with the Kingdom of Naples, and he, in turn, promised to help Clement regain Ravenna, Cervia, and other possessions in northern Italy. The pope did not bother to consult or even inform his Venetian allies, despite their previous pleas that he not conclude a separate peace but hold out for a general settlement with the emperor.[42] Most humiliating for Venice were the provisions regarding Ravenna and Cervia. Despite Contarini's frequent and eloquent defense of their incorporation into the Venetian state in many discussions with Clement VII, their fate was a bargaining chip of pope and emperor without any regard for the Republic's views.[43] In retaliation for this treatment, the Senate voted overwhelmingly not only to pay Francis I 20,000 ducats a month if he came to Italy but also to give him 13,000 soldiers.[44] More money and men were to be sent to Vitturi in southern Italy, and the Florentine Republic was to receive 1,000 additional troops.[45]

These decisions were the last stand of the Venetian government made in the old spirit of political independence. On 15 August letters from the Venetian ambassador to France brought news of the peace treaty concluded between Francis I and Charles V; "et fono cative lettere," added Sanudo. The French king had entirely ignored his erstwhile allies, the Venetians. "The whole state, upon hearing such bad news, remained astounded, seeing so great a betrayal by the king of France of his allies, in contravention of the provisions of the League and against all reason," wrote Sanudo.[46]

A week later the complete articles of the Peace of Cambrai arrived in Venice. They made it crystal clear that neither monarch considered the Venetian Republic a serious player in international politics. Francis I agreed to return to Charles V within forty days everything the French and the Venetians had conquered in southern Italy, without even informing his Venetian allies. A crumb was thrown to Florence and Venice: they would be included in the peace if they settled their differences with the emperor and his brother within four months.[47] Guicciardini considered this last provision tantamount to a tacit exclusion of both Italian states.[48]

The next four months are a singularly revealing period of Venetian history. Despite continued and often sharp disagreements in the Collegio and the

Senate, the majority proved extraordinarily realistic. Within days of learning about the Peace of Cambrai the government put out peace feelers to Charles V and instructed its ambassador in Rome to inform the pope of its new attitude.[49] Meanwhile, the naval and military commanders in southern Italy received orders to extricate Venice from involvements there. This included lifting the siege of Brindisi and shifting the ships to Corfu.[50] In effect, Venice acknowledged her defeat.

Against this background Contarini was instructed to treat for peace on behalf of Venice with the emperor and the pope in Bologna.[51] Bowing to the inevitable, Venice agreed to restore the southern Italian cities to Charles V and to offer him very substantial monetary payments. But some senators thought that the restitution of Ravenna and Cervia would represent a great loss of honor. In the course of a telling debate of 9 November these senators spoke the old-fashioned language of Venetian patriotism, clashing with the realists, who proclaimed that their priority was peace.[52] The details of this and succeeding debates have been preserved by the Venetian statesman, ambassador, and finally doge (1578–85) Niccolò Da Ponte, who was a witness to the history of his *patria* during his remarkable lifespan of almost a century.

Girolamo Pesaro spoke for the hawks, castigating his compatriots who were willing to cede Ravenna and Cervia to the pope and attacking his opponents by name. Alvise Mocenigo was more politic, proposing that Venice first approach the emperor as a mediator and return the cities to the pope "through the good graces of the emperor." As for Clement, Mocenigo declared, he was entirely untrustworthy and selfish; he should more properly be called heresiarch instead of pope and head of all Christians.[53] Marco Dandolo expressed a third opinion, counseling against alienating the pope by drawing Charles V too closely into Venetian affairs. At least the pope did not object to Venice's existence, and unlike the emperor, he did not rejoice in her misfortunes.[54] The Senate voted 141 to 42 to inform Clement that Venice would return the cities at the conclusion of the peace.[55] The politic ambassador thereupon told the pope that Venice would return the cities and then informed the emperor that this would be done "in order to please His Majesty."[56]

The clearest evidence of the Signoria's awareness of the decline in Venetian influence on international affairs was the shift in discourse. Instead of the language of warriors defending their state on land and sea and fighting for their honor and right, we find in the deliberations of the Senate and the Collegio the language of peace, even altruism: "In order to arrive at a good conclusion that can be beneficial to all Italy, as well as satisfactory to our state, and having a constant mind and [unchanging] intentions so that the whole world will know that we are most desirous of peace, Ravenna and Cervia will not be reasons to disturb the peace of Italy."[57] A striking change of tone in regard to the emperor occurs in Gritti's letters to Contarini, who was told that Venice was "most inclined" toward His Majesty, whose ability to give peace to Italy will bring him more glory than all his other victories.[58] At the same time, Venice continued to pay tribute to the Turks, showering their ambassador, Janus Bey, with presents until he was "well satisfied."[59] The Signoria anxiously explained to him why it had to make peace with the emperor, almost as if it owed the Turks an apology. Gritti minced no words: Venice had no choice because "the Signoria remained alone, abandoned by all princes of Italy and by the king of France; and the duke of Milan, our only ally, has also come to an agreement with the emperor."[60]

Charles V and Clement VII met in Bologna in early November. The ceremonies accompanying this momentous meeting have been carefully and repeatedly chronicled, and scholars have begun to study their symbolism in detail.[61] But the hard reality behind all the splendor of triumphal arches, processions, receptions, masses, dinners, and music was encapsulated in the treaty signed on 23 December.[62] Venice was the loser. Ravenna and Cervia were returned to Clement VII, and the southern Italian cities to Charles V. In addition to having to make punishing money payments to the emperor, Venice was constrained to join a league made up of the pope, the emperor, King Ferdinand, Ferrara, and Milan.[63] The only short-lived achievement of Venetian diplomacy was the restitution of Milan to Francesco Sforza. His death in 1535 brought about what Venice had feared most: Spanish rule over Milan and therefore the Habsburgs on the Republic's western, eastern, and northern frontiers. According to the figures given in the Venetian Senate, the cost of the war from January 1526 to September 1529 was 4 million ducats, an enormous sum.[64] When the expenses of the following months and the payments to the Turks are added, it becomes obvious that Venice had reached the limit of her financial capabilities.

Under these circumstances, Andrea Gritti and those who thought like him were able to face realistically the decline of their state as an important European political and economic power. As early as the fall of 1529 Contarini was instructed by the doge to continually stress and if necessary repeat that Venice loved peace: "You will clearly state that we desire peace and wish that Italian affairs should be resolved in a tranquil and peaceful fashion. We shall always embrace all honorable and reasonable conditions for peace with his Imperial

Majesty, to whom we are naturally most inclined."[65] All of a sudden Venice was "most inclined" to the ruler she feared above all others! The Signoria of course had no way of knowing that Charles V had written to his brother Ferdinand at great length about his own eagerness for peace in Italy since he had no means of making himself ruler of the whole peninsula. In passing he mentioned that he should have invaded Venetian territory at the beginning of the war in order to make Venice more amenable to coming to terms with him.[66] Thus, Venetians clearly had good reason to fear the emperor.

The Peace of Bologna signaled a remarkable paradigm shift on the part of the Venetian ruling elite. In their diplomatic and political discourse the old ideal of a powerful, militant, victorious republic was superseded by that of Venice as the city of peace, governing only a small Italian state. The speed with which this shift occurred is astounding and testifies to the adaptability, or better, creativity, of the Venetians.

On 9 November Contarini met in Bologna with the emperor's chancellor, Gattinara, and the concillors De Prat and Granvelle. In a masterful opening speech the ambassador laid out the image of the new Venice. Contarini declared that Venice had no cause for war against Charles V personally.[67]

> Every time one takes up arms against another, it is because of hatred one bears him, or in order to obtain something, or for self-defense, or because of fear. That the Signoria did not take up arms against the emperor is certain; at all times the Signoria had the utmost respect and reverence for him and felt the appropriate joy at his prosperity and success. That Venice did not go to war to obtain anything is evident; if two desire the same thing, they should be equals. It is obvious that there is no equality between the emperor and the Signoria, and no relation between our Republic and the greatness and power of the emperor. . . . If we have taken up arms against the emperor, it was because of fear and the desire to defend ourselves against his [armies] that were in Italy, threatening to do great things, as then happened.[68]

In this new view Venice emerges as having been forced into war. Her empire-building in Apulia is forgotten. The rhetoric of peace prevails. Eventually Venice was to represent herself as the center of a peace-loving state that could not only offer Italy and Europe a fresh vision of political, intellectual, and artistic life but also play a key role in European culture.[69]

Not surprisingly, the best expression of this vision came from a member of the Gritti circle, Gasparo Contarini. He was one of the chief architects of the new image of Venice not only during his diplomatic mission of 1528–29 but above all through his treatise on the Venetian state, *De magistratibus et republica*

Venetorum, which in recent scholarship has been called "the authoritative text for political literature on Venice" in the early modern period that "fixed the myth" of the Venetian mixed constitution.[70] It was, to be sure, "the most famous work ever composed on Venetian government."[71] But beyond this, and most importantly, Contarini's work is the political testament of the Gritti period, completed under the impact of the Peace of Bologna.[72] *De magistratibus* was written by a man without illusions about the political realities after 1530. While it presents the myth of Venice in its fullest and most mature form, Contarini's work is pervaded by the consciousness of the inevitability of change and of Venice's decline as a major European and Italian power.

Contarini's praise of the Venetian constitution and of the institutions of the Republic, down to minor offices, is the major key of the treatise, which preserves in amber, as it were, the picture of the perfect state, with its balance between monarchy, aristocracy, and democracy, that deeply influenced political thinkers in subsequent centuries. However, a minor key is discernible to the careful reader.[73] Contarini was sensitive to the fact that the beautiful edifice he was describing had developed cracks that could not be made whole again.

For all its perfection, established by the superhuman wisdom of its founders and perpetuated in official rhetoric, the Republic had changed. As an insider, Contarini was fully aware that the Peace of Bologna was a turning point in the political fortunes of a Venice now sharply reduced in importance. This consciousness of outward decline spurred him to seek another and deeper meaning of the Venetian state for Italy as well as Europe. As he was putting the finishing touches on his treatise in the early 1530s, Contarini's personal beliefs coincided with the program of Gritti and members of his closest circle. The doge championed reform of the entire Venetian legal system in order to create an efficient machinery of government in which officials would be technicians rather than amateurs.[74] Both Contarini and Gritti as a matter of principle favored the concentration of power in the hands of a small oligarchy composed of the doge, his six councilors, the Council of Ten, and its *zonta,* or committee of advisers. Although vesting ultimate decision-making power in thirty-one men would alter traditional relations between the doge, the Council of Ten, and the Senate, and beyond that the Great Council, the smaller group could lead a movement for reform of the state and the revitalization of Venice. For Gritti such a revitalization was primarily a matter for scientists and technicians, whereas for Contarini it involved spiritual and moral reform as well.

The new vision of Venice came out of de facto defeat and is an important monument to the intellectual vitality of the Gritti period. Checkmated politically by Habsburg power, Venice fashioned herself into a city of peace and concord, art, architecture, and music, and thus a major player once more on the European scene. Contarini believed that Europe needed what the Venetian state could offer to her cultural and political education.[75] Knowledge of the philosophical and moral bases of the Venetian constitution could enlighten other European states, especially those that emerged as the victors in the Peace of Bologna.

But Contarini's treatise spoke not only to outsiders. He challenged the Venetian ruling class to rise to great heights of political wisdom, and the rest of Europe to emulate what was best in Venice. Then people would live under just rulers and be able to lead morally good lives. Venice would have fulfilled her destiny by moving beyond the sphere of change and corruption, instructing and enlightening other states. As conquered Greece had taught victorious Rome, so defeated Venice could teach the countries whose political star was on the ascendant, unlike her own.

NOTES

1. Niccolò Machiavelli, *The Discourses of Niccolò Machiavelli,* trans. Leslie J. Walker, S.J., with a new introduction and appendixes by Cecil H. Clough (London, 1975), 551.

2. Francesco Guicciardini, *The History of Italy,* ed. and trans. Sidney Alexander (New York, 1972), 203.

3. Robert Finlay, "The Myth of Venice in Guicciardini's *History of Italy:* Senate Orations on Princes and the Republic," in *Medieval and Renaissance Venice: Studies in Honor of Donald E. Queller,* ed. Ellen E. Kittell and Thomas F. Madden (Urbana, 1999), 297. I would like to thank Professor Finlay for sharing an early version of his contribution with me.

4. Felix Gilbert, "Venice in the Crisis of the League of Cambrai," in *Renaissance Venice,* ed. J. R. Hale (London, 1973), 275.

5. Ibid., 277.

6. See, e.g., Pietro Pieri, *Il Rinascimento e la crisi militare italiana* (Turin, 1952): 455–69; and Gilbert, "Venice in the Crisis of the League of Cambrai."

7. Although the entire cost of the war has not been determined precisely, the wage bill alone from 1509 to 1516 was 3.5 million ducats (Michael E. Mallett and John R. Hale, *The Military Organization of a Renaissance State: Venice, c. 1400 to 1617* [Cambridge, 1984], 475).

8. See Gaetano Cozzi, Michael Knapton, and Giovanni Scarabello, *La Repubblica di Venezia nell'età moderna: Dal 1517 alla fine della Repubblica* (Turin, 1992), ch. 1 and pertinent bibliography, 184–85. See also Cozzi's two essays "Venezia Regina," in *Crisi e*

rinnovamenti nell'autunno del rinascimento a Venezia, ed. Vittore Branca and Carlo Ossola (Florence, 1991), 1–5, and "Venezia dal Rinascimento all'età barocca," in *Storia di Venezia dalle origini alla caduta della Serenissima,* vol. 6, *Dal Rinascimento al Barocco,* ed. Gaetano Cozzi and Paolo Prodi (Rome, 1994), esp. 3–23; and Gilbert, "Venice in the Crisis of the League of Cambrai."

9. Robert Finlay, *Politics in Renaissance Venice* (New Brunswick, N.J., 1980), 225.

10. Randolph Starn discusses these categories in "Meaning-Levels in the Theme of Historical Decline," *History and Theory* 14 (1975): 7.

11. Cozzi, "Venezia nei secoli XVI e XVII," 5, quoting from Marino Sanuto, *I diarii di Marino Sanuto,* ed. Rinaldo Fulin et al., 58 vols. (Venice, 1879–1903), 27:456–57.

12. In addition to the rich information in Sanuto, *I diarii,* vols. 45–52, see Niccolò Da Ponte's detailed report about the discussions in the Senate and the Collegio, "Maneggio della pace di Bologna tra Clemente VII, Carlo V, la Repubblica di Venezia e Francesco Sforza, 1529," in *Relazioni degli ambasciatori veneti al Senato,* ed. Eugenio Albèri, ser. 2, vol. 3 (Florence, 1846), 142–253. Other important sources are the instructions from Doge Andrea Gritti to Gasparo Contarini in Museo Civico Correr (MCC), Codice Cicogna 3477; Contarini's dispatches from his embassy to Pope Clement VII in Biblioteca Nazionale Marciana (BNM), Ms. It. cl. VII, 1043 (7616); and the deliberations of the Senate in Archivio di Stato, Venice (ASV).

13. See Frances Yates, "Charles Quint et l'idée d'empire," in *Fêtes et cérémonies au temps de Charles Quint,* vol. 2 of *Les fêtes de la Renaissance,* ed. Jean Jacquot (Paris, 1956–72), 57–99; Vicomte Terlinden, "La politique italienne de Charles Quint et le 'triomphe' de Bologne," ibid., 29–43; and Peter Rassow, *Die Kaiser-Idee Karls V. dargestellt an der Politik der Jahre 1528–1540* (Berlin, 1932), ch. 1.

14. Contarini's dispatches from the imperial court are in BNM, Ms. It. cl. VII, 1009 (7447).

15. However, there were also open admirers of Charles V among Venetian patricians (see Federica Ambrosini, "Immagini dell'Impero nell'ideologia del patriziato veneziano del '500," in *I ceti dirigenti in Italia in età moderna e contemporanea,* ed. Amelio Tagliaferri [Udine, 1984], 67–68).

16. Cozzi, "Venezia nei secoli XVI e XVII," 8–14; Angus Konstam, *Pavia, 1525: Charles V Crushes the French* (Osprey, 1996). Contarini's reaction to the emperor's victory is telling: one way of deflecting Charles V from Italy, he said, was to suggest that the real seat of his empire was Constantinople and to wish that he could assume his crown there (dispatch of 12 March 1525, BNM, Ms. It. cl. VII, 1009 [7447], fol. 420v).

17. Judith Hook, "The Destruction of the New 'Italia': Venice and the Papacy in Collision," *Italian Studies* 28 (1973): 12.

18. Guicciardini, *History of Italy,* 347.

19. Hook, "Destruction of the New 'Italia,'" 16.

20. Gritti counseled the Venetians to adopt a strategy of fortifying cities rather than relying on the fortunes of battles fought by unreliable troops (Gaetano Cozzi, "Authority and the Law in Renaissance Venice," in Hale, *Renaissance Venice,* 327).

21. Sanuto, *I diarii,* 50:149.

22. Hook, "Destruction of the New 'Italia,' " 15.

23. ASV, Capi del Consiglio dei Dieci, Lettere di Ambasciatori, Roma, 1515–38, busta 22, Contarini's letter of 17 February 1530 (1529 *mv*).

24. Sanudo reports repeatedly about news from Friuli concerning the northward march of the Turks (see, e.g., *I diarii*, 50:509, 18 June 1529). Even today one can still see fortified hilltops in Friuli, called *tabor* by Slovenes in the border area, to which the population could flee together with their livestock when fire signals warned of approaching Turks.

25. Ibid., 51:428.

26. For Alvise Gritti's colorful career, see Robert Finlay, "Al servizio del Sultano: Venezia, i Turchi e il mondo cristiano, 1523–1538," in *"Renovatio urbis": Venezia nell'età di Andrea Gritti (1523–1538)*, ed. Manfredo Tafuri (Rome, 1984), 78–118.

27. Ibid., 87.

28. Sanuto, *I diarii*, 51:45.

29. Vitturi's letters are included in ibid., esp. 50–53.

30. Cozzi, "Authority and the Law in Renaissance Venice," 331.

31. For the effects of the famine of 1527–29 on Venice and responses to it, see Brian Pullan, *Rich and Poor in Renaissance Venice: The Social Institutions of a Catholic State, to 1620* (Cambridge, Mass., 1971), ch. 3, esp. 239–55.

32. Sanuto, *I diarii*, 50:574, 576, 577.

33. Vito Vitale, "L'impresa di Puglia negli anni 1528–1529," *Archivio Veneto*, 3d ser., 13 (1907): 29.

34. "Laqual [the news of the emperor's coming] di quanta importantia sia, et che imminente pericolo apporti secco non solamente al stato nostro, ma a tutta Italia, cadauno benissimo comprehende" (ASV, Senato, Deliberazioni Secrete, reg. 53 [1528–29], fol. 166r).

35. Sanuto, *I diarii*, 50:424.

36. Ibid., 51:9.

37. Ibid., 45.

38. Ibid., 34.

39. Ibid., 607.

40. Ibid., 341.

41. Contarini to the Senate, 28 July 1529, BNM, Ms. It. cl. VII, 1043 (7616), fol. 277r; Gasparo Contarini, *Regesten und Briefe des Cardinals Gasparo Contarini*, ed. Franz Dittrich (Braunsberg, 1881), 59 (no. 189).

42. ASV, Senato, Deliberazioni Secrete, reg. 53 (1528–29), fols. 189v–190r. Contarini was instructed to influence the pope against signing a separate peace.

43. For the provisions of the treaty, see Sanuto, *I diarii*, 51:79–80; see also 137, 252, 377.

44. Ibid., 207.

45. Ibid., 118, 209.

46. Ibid., 322.

47. Ibid., 377.

48. Guicciardini, *History of Italy*, 413.

49. The Senate to Contarini, 31 August 1529, ASV, Senato, Deliberazioni Secrete, reg. 53 (1528–29), fol. 225r.

50. Sanuto, *I diarii,* 51:355.

51. "Instructio mittenda V.N. Gaspari Contareno oratori apud S. Pont. pro pace tractanda Bononiae cum Caesarea maiestate," ASV, Senato, Deliberazioni Secrete, reg. 53 (1528–29), fols. 247r–v. Of the ceremonial copy of this commission only the miniature remains. It shows the persistence of an anachronistic iconography: the pope sits on his throne, flanked by the emperor and the doge, both of whom stand on the same level.

52. Da Ponte, "Maneggio della pace di Bologna," 166–67.

53. Ibid., 168.

54. Ibid.

55. Ibid., 173; 10 November; and ASV, Senato, Deliberazioni Secrete, reg. 53 (1528–29), fols. 254r–v.

56. Contarini's letters of 10 and 12 November, ASV, Senato, Deliberazioni Secrete, reg. 53 (1528–29), fols. 254r–v.

57. Letter of 10 November 1529, ASV, Senato, Deliberazioni Secrete, reg. 53 (1528–29), fol. 254r. Heinrich Kretschmayr, *Geschichte von Venedig,* 3 vols. (Gotha, 1905–34), 3:14, was struck by expressions of Venetian concern with the idea of Italy after the League of Cognac. Judith Hook argues that the foundation stone of the "New Italy" was Venice's close cooperation with the pope, which the Venetians had selfishly destroyed by their insistence on keeping Ravenna and Cervia ("Destruction of the 'New Italy,' " 25, 28).

58. Gritti to Contarini, 26 September and 28 December 1529, MCC, Venice, Codice Cicogna 3477, nos. 21 and 5.

59. Sanuto, *I diarii,* 52:408, 496.

60. Da Ponte, "Maneggio della pace di Bologna," 225.

61. See the bibliography in Tiziana Bernardi, "Analisi di una cerimonia pubblica: L'incoronazione di Carlo V a Bologna," *Quaderni Storici,* n.s., 61 (1986): 171–99.

62. Two older works are still useful for the details of ceremonies and entertainments during the meeting at Bologna: G. Romano, *Cronaca del soggiorno di Carlo V in Italia (dal 26 Luglio 1529 al 25 Aprile 1530): Documento di storia italiana estratto da un codice della Regia Biblioteca Universitaria di Pavia* (Milan, 1892); and Gaetano Giordani, *Della venuta e dimora in Bologna del Sommo Pontefice Clemente VII. per la coronazione de Carlo V Imperatore celebrata l'anno MDXXX* (Bologna, 1842).

63. For the provisions see Da Ponte, "Maneggio della pace di Bologna," 217–18; ASV, Senato, Deliberazioni Secrete, reg. 53 (1528–29), fols. 265r–267r; and Giordani, *Della venuta e dimora,* 50–57. There is a summary of the treaty in Sanuto, *I diarii,* 52:383–86.

64. Mallett and Hale, *Military Organization of a Renaissance State,* 476.

65. Gritti to Contarini, 26 September 1529, in MCC, Venice, Codice Cicogna 2223.

66. The original French text of this letter is in *Correspondenz des Kaisers Karl V.,* ed. Karl Lanz, vol. 1, *1513–1532* (Leipzig, 1844), 360–72. An English translation is in

Calendar of Letters, Dispatches, and State Papers Relating to the Negotiations between England and Spain . . . 1529–30, vol. 4, pt. 1, ed. Pascual de Gayangos (London, 1879), 396–409, paraphrased passage on 401.

67. Sanuto, *I diarii* 52:218.

68. Da Ponte, "Maneggio della pace di Bologna," 173.

69. I agree with the general thrust of Manfredo Tafuri's " 'Renovatio urbis Venetiarum': Il problema storiografico," in *"Renovatio urbis,"* which argues for a "program" of renewal. But in my view, he stated his case brilliantly though somewhat too absolutely; it needs more nuances.

70. Contarini's treatise was published posthumously in Paris in 1543, translated into French and Italian in 1544, and translated into English in 1599. Numerous printings of the Latin, Italian, and French versions continued into the seventeenth century. The quotations are from Franco Gaeta, "L'idea di Venezia," in *Storia della cultura veneta,* ed. Girolamo Arnaldi and Manlio Pastore Stocchi, 6 vols. (Vicenza, 1976–86), 3, pt. 3: 632; and James S. Grubb, "When Myths Lose Power: Four Decades of Venetian Historiography," *Journal of Modern History* 58 (1886): 46, respectively.

71. Lester J. Libby Jr., "Venetian History and Political Thought after 1509," *Studies in the Renaissance* 20 (1973): 18.

72. Felix Gilbert, "The Date of Composition of Contarini's and Giannotti's Books on Venice," ibid. 14 (1967): 176–77.

73. Elisabeth G. Gleason, "Reading between the Lines of Gasparo Contarini's Treatise on the Venetian State," *Historical Reflections / Réflexions Historiques* 15 (1988): 251–70.

74. On this topic, see Cozzi, "Authority and the Law in Renaissance Venice"; Manfredo Tafuri, *Venezia e il Rinascimento: Religione, scienza, architettura* (Turin, 1985), esp. 162–71; and Antonio Foscari and Manfredo Tafuri, *L'armonia e i conflitti* (Turin, 1983).

75. William J. Bouwsma, "Venice and the Political Education of Europe," in Hale, *Renaissance Venice,* 451.

6

"A Plot Discover'd?"
Myth, Legend, and the "Spanish" Conspiracy against Venice in 1618

RICHARD MACKENNEY

The Spanish conspiracy of 1618 remains one of the most enigmatic events in the history of Venice. Embedded in myth and rumor, this conspiracy, in which the viceroy of Naples and the Spanish ambassador to Venice allegedly attempted to coordinate an armed takeover of the Venetian Republic, may or may not have existed. In this chapter, however, Richard Mackenney takes a novel approach to this subject, using the case of the "Spanish" conspiracy to cast light on the changing nature of the state in early-seventeenth-century Europe. In particular, by tracing the role of the Venetian Paolo Sarpi in stirring up anti-Spanish feelings in Europe at this time—which corresponded with the outbreak of the Thirty Years' War—he demonstrates how Venetian foreign policy became increasingly concerned with appearances and the strategic manipulation of information. Not only was the Venetian government deliberate in its use of secrecy and deception in the pursuit of its own ends but it became notorious for such practices. Mackenney charts a significant shift in Venice's reputation between the interdict crisis of 1606–7, when Venice appeared to be a defender of republican liberty, and 1618, when Venice emerged as a polity defined primarily by principles of "reason of state." This shift played a significant role in the development of the antimyth of Venice, the myth of Venice as an oppressive and secretive tyranny.

IN THE SPRING of 1606 Pope Paul V excommunicated the doge and the Senate of Venice and placed all the territories of the Republic under an interdict. The immediate cause was a dispute over whether priests should be tried as criminals in secular or ecclesiastical courts. On one level, this was merely the latest in a long series of quarrels between Rome and the Republic over matters of jurisdiction. Yet few would deny that the interdict of 1606–7 was accompanied by dramatic changes in the character of the Venetian state and that these changes would have an equally dramatic effect on how the Republic and its place in history would be perceived. After all, in its struggle with Rome the Venetian state appears to have undergone both an ideological revitalization and a reinvention for posterity. The group of politicians in the circle of Doge Leonardo Donà, known as the *giovani* (young), uncompromisingly asserted the Republic's independence from Rome and reasserted Venice's religious autonomy.[1] They did so by turning the cause of Venice into an international one, of significance to all European states concerned over matters of sovereignty. A bitter dispute about ecclesiastical property rights and the jurisdiction of civil law over the clergy was thus transformed into a historic confrontation between the last, flowering articulation of Renaissance republicanism and the repressive authoritarian dogmatism of the Counter Reformation papacy.[2] Historians have continued to portray the conflict in these terms down to the present day. As William James Bouwsma has written, "Thus during the years when Venice, under the leadership of the *giovani,* was increasingly conscious of her heritage as a free republic, the papacy was deepening its universalism and growing rapidly more articulate and aggressive in promoting its own authoritarian perspectives and values."[3]

Recent studies have also suggested that the same period was critical in the history of states in Europe as a whole. For the first time the nature of the state was a matter for general discussion. The history plays of Shakespeare explored before a wide audience the nature of the body politic and the gulf between the rhetoric fed to the mob and the realities of power and ambition. This was a world trapped between a fear of tyranny and a fear of anarchy, for resistance to the one seemed only to bring the prospect of the other.[4] It was a world in which Machiavelli had apparently triumphed, yet the anxiety increased with the question how a master of appearances would be recognizable as a Machiavellian. In 1641 Cardinal Richelieu became the first statesman openly to extol Machiavelli's ideas, and "he could not sufficiently wonder at the fact that all who wrote politics attended to this rare spirit without one of them ever having had the courage or the heart to defend the indispensable and reasonable maxims of this solid and truthful writer."[5] Secretaries were advised that dissimulation was praiseworthy because prudent; it was simulation that was wrong: "One simulates something that is not, the other dissimulates something that is," according to Torquato Accetto.[6] There was general discussion among the populace at large: "not only the counselors in the courts and the doctors in the schools, but even the barbers and the most humble artisans in their shops and gathering places talk and dispute about reason of state, and persuade themselves that they know what things are done for reason of state and what not."[7]

In a penetrating book, Maurizio Viroli suggested that the period around 1600 witnessed the triumph of reason of state, that is, the preservation of dominion, over the art of good government. The rhetoric of civic humanism began to appear naively utopian in a world of squalid realities bred out of—and breeding—a new cynicism. In that world Venice's commitment to republican liberty shone like a beacon and seemed all the more unique.[8] Maria Luisa Doglio sees the Venetian Republic's renewal as a reward for the exercise of reason of state in Giovanni Botero's terms, as the product of a unique combination of political virtue and constitutional perfection: "The durability of Venice analysed by Botero, the most eminent theorist of the reason of state, is the result of the test of the relationship between perfection and virtue—unrepeatable elsewhere and in Venice manifest to the eyes of all through that struggle against the Interdict, the strenuous collective resistance, the common will for autonomy," and it was subsequently proven by "the backing off of the Uskoks, the reinforcement of the lordship over the Adriatic with the withdrawal of Ossuna, the treaty of mutual aid with Carlo Emmanuele I, the most effective repression of the 'Spanish conspiracy' ordered by the Marquis of Bedmar."[9]

Yet, from the perspective of the so-called Spanish conspiracy of 1618, such changes, it might be argued, take on a rather different aspect, presenting a state retreating in on itself, rejoicing in its own secretiveness and delighting in its capacity to deceive. Ironically, the latter characterization is entirely in keeping with Viroli's picture of the triumph of reason of state. In this process the period following the interdict is critical.[10] The fashioning of the Republic's image in the quarrel with the papacy had been entrusted to Paolo Sarpi, Servite friar and official historiographer. The interdict had been resolved through compromise. As Doge Donà himself put it to the Senate:

> Let us not deem it the duty of a prudent man always to have the same opinion, but that which the accidents and rather variable conjunctures of human affairs counsel. And certainly, since the principles and accidents of things vary, it is essential for the deliberations based on them also to vary. Thus he who otherwise might pretend to the title of consistency and constancy in his opinions should rather deserve a reputation for imprudent pertinacity and unconsidered obstinacy, since everyone, even of superficial intelligence in things of state, knows that civil matters are variable and subject like the sea to the diversity of the winds, to

the violence and diversity of accidents. For this reason man should regulate his opinions exactly as on a sea voyage, according to the quality of the winds. Nor is he obliged always to have the same opinion, but rather the same end: the good and safety of the Republic.[11]

Such compromise may have been distasteful to Sarpi, whose views apparently became marginalized after the settlement.[12] Nevertheless, he was also to play a central and in many ways definitive part in providing an official version of the "conspiracy" of 1618. His particular role is of special relevance to our general theme. In 1606 he fashioned the image of Venice as a free state. In 1618 he was the unwavering agent of reason of state. In an important sense, then, the writings of Sarpi spread through Europe both the myth of Venice—that it was a free republic—and the antimyth—that it was an oppressive and secretive tyranny.[13] Put another way, Sarpi's role in the transmission of the very different things that came to be admired or deplored in the Venetian Republic may tell us something about the ambiguities at the center of our conception of "the state."

The myth of Venice also owed much to the intensification of the "black legend" of Spanish tyranny. Usually the notion that "where the Spaniard sets his foot no grass grows" was expressed by the English and the Dutch as a warning that the tyranny the Spaniards had imposed on the New World would become the lot of all of Europe. For the Venetians, increasingly isolated as an independent power in an Italy dominated by the Spaniards, Spain and the papacy became closely associated, with Spanish power serving as the means to enforce papal pretensions. Paolo Paruta, another of the giovani, "particularly insisted on the traditional opposition of Venice to the Italian designs of Spain."[14]

Historiographically, the Venetians have always enjoyed a myth tempered with an antimyth. There has been no antidote to the "black legend" of the Spaniards.[15] Yet the Spaniards had grounds for mistrusting the Venetians, particularly in matters of the faith. In 1571 the two states had a shared vision of Christendom, and victory over the Turks in the great naval battle of Lepanto seemed a triumph for that vision—the Spanish ambassador was present in St. Mark's for the celebratory Mass. Yet within two years the Venetians had put a strict price on their Christianity, ceding Cyprus to the Turks and withdrawing from the Holy League. The news was passed to Philip II by the Venetian ambassador, one Leonardo Donà, whose tenure of that office marked a steep decline in relations between the two states. He emphasized to Philip that "it was in His Majesty's interest as well as ours."

The king listened to us very attentively. The more he realized that we were explaining our position in a suitably friendly and respectful manner, the more His Majesty gave us his attention and directed his gaze right at us. His face gave no hint of what he was thinking, except that at the moment when he heard that the conditions of the peace treaty had been accepted his mouth moved ever so slightly in the very fleetest of ironic smiles, almost as if His Majesty wanted to say, without interrupting us, "In short, you've done it, just as everyone told me you would!"[16]

Perhaps it is no coincidence that some of the most penetrating comments on the operations of the Venetian state were made by the Spanish ambassador in Venice in the early seventeenth century, the marquis of Bedmar, whom, along with the viceroy of Naples, the duke of Ossuna, the Venetians often name as the author of the "conspiracy" of 1618.

They hold anything legitimate which promotes the security of ruling, and they applaud losses of Your Majesty. Out of self-interest they consider your profit to be the destruction and ruin of their things; and for reason of state they embrace and destroy at one blow all piety and fear of God, maintaining intelligence with enemies of God and of the Roman Church, having dealings with various perverse princes. And under the pretext of conserving the Republic, they cause the ruin of plans for the increase of the holy faith, consulting, discussing and deciding everything according to their habitual way of political government.[17]

Bedmar may also have been the author of another damaging work, one published anonymously as the *Squitinio della libertà veneta* (Scrutiny of Venetian liberty).[18] The suppression of Bedmar's "conspiracy" was a convenient way of demonstrating the continuing validity of the "myth" because internal stability was maintained and the external threat was repulsed. Thus, the thoroughly pro-Venetian writer Horatio Brown commented in his vivid account, which is very close to what the Venetian government had prepared: "It is necessary to bear in mind that there were two distinct lines of action on the part of the viceroy, his declared and open intention to challenge Venetian supremacy in the Adriatic, and the secret plot by which he hoped to strike a blow at Venice from the inside."[19]

It is important to stress that there is nothing new about Venetians' putting a strongly pro-Venetian gloss on international events, however tawdry the reality. This tendency could be said to go back to the Peace of Venice, in 1177, which was used to demonstrate the Republic's neutrality between the papacy and the Empire and therefore its independence from both. Similarly, the events of the Crusade of 1204 were reinvented to show that the Republic was independent of Byzantium. However, the changing social and political contexts in which the "Spanish" conspiracy was constructed make the incident eminently worthy of careful attention in its own right. This chapter should be set against a background of other research on the city of Venice, suggesting a more general process of redefinition of the public and private spheres in the years around 1600, with a developing polarity between the state and the family. The evidence suggests that traditionally in Venice there had been no clear distinction between public and private. First, the city itself was an intensely crowded urban space in which real privacy was difficult to attain. Second, public and private were unified by the sacred within that space, with the orientation and identity of the Venetians largely defined by one of the seventy or so churches. Moreover, the Virgin Mary played a special role as the object of both private devotion and of great public occasions, which often made her something very close to the personification of the city itself. Finally, a large number of institutions—neighborhoods, parishes, confraternities (especially the *scuole grandi*), guilds, and workshops—operated in a broad area that we might call "semipublic" and mitigated against the polarity of state and family by filling the gap between them.[20]

The corollary in political life—on which the present study concentrates—was the assertion of a sovereign authority that governed by dominion and could not readily accommodate the semipublic sphere because that sphere compromised the absoluteness of sovereignty by allowing people to identify with the state rather than merely be subject to it. One symptom of the change about 1600 was the immersion of the individual in the life of the state, a sort of sacrifice of the private to the public again mediated by a certain sacrality of office, to which the individual was subordinate. The life of the state as a machine of dominion, however, became increasingly arcane, and self-consciously so. Thus, according to Bouwsma, Doge Leonardo Donà "felt an almost sacerdotal devotion to public office in which he aimed totally to submerge his private identity." According to one contemporary, his discussions with the giovani focused on "the government of the republic, the preservation of liberty, political life, and reason of state, of which he was a great professional."[21] According to Fulgenzio Micanzio, Sarpi's biographer, Sarpi "entered public life with a sense of religious mission." Micanzio recorded that when Sarpi took up his appointment as "consultore teologico-canonico" (consultant in matters theological and canonical), it can be said that his quiet studies ended along with his private life; and from this time to the end of his years, he entered another world, or rather the world, and it pleased God to call him to works to which he would never have thought of applying himself. But man is not born for himself alone, but principally for his country and for the common good. I leave it to others to discuss [in general terms] whether the wise man should apply himself to government. Our Padre [Sarpi] will give us a [practical] example of one who rejects neither labours nor dangers for the service of God and of country. [He shows] that the wise and good man is far from [accepting] the false doctrine invented by a rabble of seditious deceivers that nothing but evil should be said of secular politics, although it is instituted by God. [He also shows] that in politics the good man can serve the divine majesty with a vocation so pious and excellent that nothing equals it, or at least nothing surpasses it.[22]

These characterizations of two key figures in the specifically Venetian context of statehood raise the question whether the Republic's apparently exceptional nature in the seventeenth century can also seem to typify general European developments. In Donà's case, was it possible to reconcile the "preservation of liberty" with the exercise of "reason of state"? Viroli's argument suggests that it would not have been. Moreover, as King James I of England announced to Parliament after his escape from death in the Gunpowder Plot—in November 1605, just months before the interdict—this was an age "when every kind of iniquity is covered by the mantle of religion." How does the picture change if we take a Hobbesian view of Sarpi's vocation to public life, in which the state itself is godlike? What if the religious dimension of his calling was zeal for reason of state? David Wootton has, after all, made a strong, though controversial, case for the idea that Sarpi was both an atheist and an absolutist.[23]

WITH REGARD to the assessment of changes in the character of the state— in Venice and elsewhere—in the seventeenth century, Thomas Otway's play *Venice Preserv'd or, A Plot Discover'd* is an unusual but surprisingly useful starting point. It sets one thinking about the "myth" of Venice and perhaps even the myth of the state.[24] First performed in 1682 before the future James II, whose push toward Catholic absolutism was to result in his dethronement in the revolution of 1688, Otway's play was also a mistaken choice for posterity. His view was a Tory one, royalist and antiparliamentarian, but it was a Whiggish reinvention of Venice ("il venezianismo whig") that was to have the more lasting influence, especially in the New World through figures such as William Penn.[25]

The play unfolds roughly as follows. The patrician Priuli is resentful of his daughter Belvidera's marriage to the hapless Jaffeir. Jaffeir is a close friend of the mercenary captain Jacques Pierre, who also happens to be the ringleader of a plot to overthrow the Venetian state, a corrupt entity represented by the appalling Antonio, who seeks sadomasochistic sexual satisfaction from Pierre's mistress. Jaffeir is drawn into the plot but is persuaded by Belvidera to denounce it in the public interest. His private feelings are then torn between his love for Belvidera and his loyalty to Pierre. Jaffeir is overcome with remorse, especially since the state does not honor its guarantee of pardon to the conspirators. He renews his friendship with Pierre by killing him on the wheel in order to save him further torture, and he then stabs himself. At this, Belvidera dies of grief. Priuli asks to be left alone and grimly enjoins the bystanders, "Sparing no tears when you this tale relate, / But bid all cruel fathers dread my fate." All in all, it is a relentlessly bleak view of youth and love crushed by age and decay.

There is, however, one significant omission. The episode on which the play is based is usually referred to—and always by the Venetians—as the "Spanish" conspiracy, "the conspiracy of Bedmar," or "the conspiracy of Ossuna." Apart from one desultory and fleeting appearance by the ambassador, "Bedamar," Otway makes no mention of Spanish involvement. In the aftermath of the Exclusion Crisis, the Popish Plot, and fears of French absolutism, this may have been for reasons of topicality.[26] But by his omission Otway goes directly against his principal source, *The Conspiracy of the Spanish against the Republic of Venice*, a dreary historical novel by the abbé de Saint-Réal (misleadingly included on the history shelves in Edinburgh University Library). For Saint-Réal, an author much admired by Voltaire, Spanish involvement was all-important. In his version, Bedmar was "one of the most exalted geniuses and most dangerous spirits that Spain has ever produced," and he involved Don Pedro de Toledo, governor of Milan, and the duke of Ossuna, viceroy of Naples, in a plot to overthrow the Venetian state. The tenacity of the tradition of Spanish machination is evidenced by Wootton's insistence, perhaps deriving from his positive reading of Saint-Réal, that "for Otway the Venetians and the *Spanish* conspirators were both images of evil."[27]

But what in fact do we know about events in Venice in 1618? It was a momentous year, characterized by rumor and counter-rumor on the eve of a general European war that would last three decades.[28] For once, Venice may be firmly placed in the broad European predicament. In 1615 a simmering dispute with the Austrian Habsburgs had become a dirty war in the Gulf of Venice with the piratical Uskoks of Senj.[29] The city of Venice was filled with armed men as mercenary units assembled.[30] Those used to being on horseback looked conspicuously odd. "The captains of them wore boots with spurs on their feet, and there were so many of them, that throughout the Merceria, you could see nothing else, which was a source of amazement to all."[31] To the west, Spanish troop movements threatened the Valtelline in an effort to secure an alternative to the "Spanish Road," which led northward.[32] Exchanges with London communicated a mounting anxiety. On 29 December 1617 the ambassador Piero Contarini wrote to the doge and the Senate: "Here everyone is astounded at the policy now adopted by the Spaniards. They appear not to comprehend it, coming to the conclusion, either that the governors have rendered themselves absolute and rule according to their own caprice, without reference to the royal commands, or what is more probable that it is all a fraud, in order to put other powers off their guard that they may be the better able to attack those territories of which they seem so desirous." By 6 January 1618 the Senate was informing its ambassadors that "we have less reason than ever to hope for peace, and more cause to suspect the insidious practices of the Spaniards . . . such tricks and artifices have never before been seen." A few days later, on 11 January, the Senate determined to summon the Spanish ambassador to be reprimanded since the Spaniards' "actions differ so entirely from their words." On 25 January James I reportedly replied to the ambassador's request for support that, "in short, alone and merely [sic] for the Venetian territories it was impossible to raise a force sufficient to withstand the immense preparations which Spain was hastening in every direction."[33]

On 27 January 1618 the Senate tells the ambassador to inform the king that more than Venice is at stake and asks for support against "the certainty that the Spaniards mean to subdue Italy." The "immense preparations" seem to have been launched by Don Pedro de Toledo, governor of Milan, and the duke of Ossuna, viceroy of Naples. On 13 January the Senate sends ambassadors the news that "at Naples the Duke of Ossuna continues his naval preparations." The government learns on 23 January that Ossuna is "collecting metal to make a number of culverins." The eventual flashpoint of the conflagration, Germany, appears almost as an aside with the news from Contarini, in London, in a letter of 22 February, that Frederick of the Palatinate intends to prevent Ferdinand from becoming king of the Romans. In the event, the "Spanish" conspiracy in Venice took place in May, the same month as the Defenestration of Prague, which set in train the Thirty Years' War.[34] The report of the Venetian ambassador in Madrid in 1620 catches the mood of the time in retrospect:

In this time, albeit a period which did not exceed forty months, there took place fierce encounters and troublesome incidents between that crown [of Spain] and Your Serenity, aid reciprocally given by the King to the enemies of Your Serenity, and by Your Serenity to the enemies of the King; seizures of our ships, our galleys taken, encounters of fleets and the beginnings of a general conflict, incursions of borders and the preludes to a general breach. The King's ships were held up by ours, the galleons of Naples were damaged and fled, whence the outward appearance of friendship and peace, but the realities, and from terms used on both sides, were hostility and war.[35]

The allegation—quite open in Saint-Réal's account[36]—was that there was collusion between Bedmar, who was in touch with mercenary groups in Venice, and Ossuna, who had already turned the screw by seizing Venetian ships and disputing Venice's legal authority in the Adriatic. Letters from Gasparo Spinelli, a Venetian envoy in Naples, implicated Ossuna in the following plan. The suborned mercenaries led by the sea captain Jacques Pierre were to attack the Great Council while it was in session, slaughter the patricians, seize the Arsenal, and secure the Piazza San Marco. Pierre had many French accomplices: Nicholas Regnault, who acted as translator, an explosives expert called Langrand, the brothers Charles and Jean Bouleaux, and two other mercenaries, Juven (Otway's Jaffeir) and Moncassin. Meanwhile, Ossuna was to send hundreds more soldiers in troopships disguised as merchantmen under the command of an Englishman, Robert Elyot. However, the plot was revealed by Juven and Moncassin; the papers carried by another, Brouillard, were alleged to be directed to Ossuna complaining of delay. Pierre and one accomplice were jailed aboard ship and then executed; and three conspirators were strangled in prison, their corpses, suspended by one leg to indicate the crime of treason, displayed at San Marco on 18 May. A parallel plot to subvert Crema was conveniently discovered at the same time. Several hundred mercenaries who had been packing the taverns melted away, some supposedly drowned as conspirators. Bedmar left Venice in June, perhaps in some fear for his own safety, and Ossuna was subsequently disgraced and imprisoned until his death.[37]

Historians used to be fascinated by these complex goings-on. Writing on England and the Mediterranean in a work published in 1904, Julian Corbett pronounced that "of all the mysteries of Italian history, there is none more dramatic or more difficult to probe in all its dark recesses than what is known in Venice as the Spanish conspiracy."[38] Horatio Brown was still more assertive of the fact that "there can be no doubt about Ossuna's participation in the conspiracy from the beginning to the end," and he quoted Venetian evidence that clinched Ossuna's responsibility since "not even his immediate dependents deny that the plot had its origin in Naples." But he acknowledged from the outset the complexity of the enigma: "Indeed, it would be difficult to find a more tangled skein for the historian to unravel; yet the process reveals so curious a condition of society in Europe, and in Venice especially, at the opening of the seventeenth century, and throws so strong a light upon the causes which first corrupted and then destroyed the Republic, that the effort to follow each clue through the labyrinth is repaid with interest."[39] The Venetian historian Samuele Romanin trumpeted that Venice offered the only resistance to Spain in Southern Europe.[40] Heinrich Kretschmayr's general history of Venice (1934) included a meticulous identification of the conspirators and their tasks: Jacques Pierre the leader, Regnault the interpreter, Langrand the explosives expert, and Moncassin and Juven coordinators of the companies of troops. He was also careful to point out that any connection between the plot and Bedmar was insecure.[41]

However, in many ways the most powerful and penetrating account remains that of Leopold von Ranke. His *Verschwörung gegen Venedig* (Conspiracy against Venice) communicates the scale of the crisis. Here we find agents of the conspirators viewing routes of entry for the ships from a campanile, arranging to check the depths of canals to ensure that the invading ships could pass, French mercenaries about to seize the impregnable capital of a state with which France and Spain were at peace. He also destroys the credibility of Saint-Réal in a way that really should have gotten the abbé removed from history shelves, and he emphasizes that there is no decisive evidence of Jacques Pierre's having contacted Ossuna. In some ways it may be a rather uncharacteristic piece: full of the machinations within the corridors of power, granted, but also acknowledging in a powerful aside the dangers of working with the official version of events. Whatever the Venetians may have said to their ambassador in London, Ranke is categorical in pointing out that "the Venetians knew that Spain did not want a war in Italy." It remains a brilliant account of loose talk among soldiers in taverns that conveys a quite magnificent sense of drama, though Ranke's remark "if this were a piece of theater" (wäre es ein Theaterstück) suggests that he was unaware of Otway's play. Certainly, the need for wariness in the face of the official documentation and the sense of an unfolding drama show how difficult it is for the historian to reconstruct such an episode "wie es eigentlich gewesen."[42]

For the most part, the details of the "conspiracy" have to be tracked down in specialist literature. This is a corpus of scholarly work that merits careful examination. One early-twentieth-century scholar, Lamberto Chiarelli, discussed correspondence between a writer called Alessandro Granzini and the Inquisitori di Stato that reveals Bedmar's "ignoble deceits" and records an angry confrontation with the Senate in which the ambassador was not allowed to speak but was shown a letter and asked, "Is this a letter in your own hand? Can you deny it? Read it! And believe in your unworthiness!" The confrontation left Bedmar "dead and beside himself with shame." However, as Chiarelli acknowledges, this does not prove his guilt.[43] Italo Raulich suggested that pinning the blame on Bedmar may have been a convenient way of having him removed, especially since his understanding of the workings of Venetian government may have been uncomfortably close to reality, and that Jacques Pierre may have been acting on his own initiative.[44] Amelia Zambler saw Ossuna as the villain of the piece, "one of the principal instigators of these vile manipulations," all part of "the deceits, hidden and open, directed by the Spaniards against the Venetian government."[45] On the other hand, the question, Who started it? bears asking, as Giuseppe Coniglio's work points out. Ossuna's promotion of piracy may have been a response to Venice's payments of subsidies to Spain's enemy, Savoy. And Bedmar had been concerned about the scale of Venetian preparations for war, which may suggest "the hypothesis that the Republic had profited from the Pierre episode, in order to involve therein, by false accusations of complicity, its two haughty adversaries: Bedmar and Ossuna." Coniglio found that the duke of Infantado, had remarked in the Council of State, like Bedmar, that "in Venice it is natural to value reason of state above conscience."[46]

Scholarly attention has also focused on documentation from less obvious archives than those of Venice, Madrid, and Naples. Working with the Florentine materials, Achille de Rubertis found a letter from the French ambassador to Venice, Bruslart, that was defensive regarding accusations about French involvement, accusations that were natural enough given the national origins of the identifiable conspirators. Bruslart wrote that "whatever [the Venetians] say, one discerns no apparent sign, either outside the city or inside it, that this enterprise has any foundation, and the death of the leaders of it, who were impeached, has no other basis than the letter of recommendation from the Spanish ambassador." Perhaps to deflect further investigation of the French, Bruslart recorded his suspicion that Bedmar had fomented a mutiny among Dutch mercenaries, but he acknowledged that the only hard evidence of a conspiracy was the executions of the alleged conspirators: "The public acts of the case were suppressed by the Senate with much secrecy. Nor, if you set aside

the many executions, is there the slightest indication of such a conspiracy
before, or any vestiges after, the proceedings against some of those conspirators." He also remarked that the Venetians "with every light novelty, have a
habit of making exaggerated claims in the courts of princes against the Spanish
name, and [this] to further the idea that the ministers of that king were out to
take possession of what belonged to others by violence or subterfuge."[47] Documentation studied by Alessandro Luzio in Mantua, much of it Spanish, suggests
that the Venetian populace had been stirred up against Spain at a time of
political instability in Venice, where there were divisions in the Senate, two
ducal elections, and a continuing confrontation between the giovani and their
vecchi opponents. Ossuna could claim to be acting under orders in his naval
actions; Pierre had sought to ingratiate himself with the viceroy after being
rejected for service with the Republic. Bedmar had sworn to the doge in the
presence of the Senate that "as the nobleman that I am, and by the chrism on
my forehead," he had heard nothing of the matters with which he was now
being confronted.[48]

Perhaps this is a subject on which there is really little more to say. Apart from
a characteristically stylish treatment by Hugh Trevor-Roper, the episode has
rather faded from general view. Even Trevor-Roper, that most notable of
historical detectives, could not demonstrate that a conspiracy took place, concluding that: "The reality of 'the Spanish conspiracy' has often been doubted.
Possibly there was no precise plan. The complicity of Ossuna and Bedmar
cannot be demonstrated. But there can be no doubt that both were con-
templating a *coup* against Venice even if the particular episode illustrated the
suspicion they incurred rather than the plans they had laid."[49] Recent accounts
such as that in the great scholarly work of Gaetano Cozzi, Michael Knapton,
and Giovanni Scarabello continue to describe the event as the "conspiracy of
Bedmar" while acknowledging that the Venetian government used it to stir up
anti-Spanish feeling.[50] Even the remarkable study by Paolo Preto sheds no new
light on this specific incident.[51]

For all these reasons, as well as the intrinsic attractiveness of an unsolved
mystery, the conspiracy merits another look. But there are disclaimers to be
made. First, what follows is no attempt to provide definitive solutions; rather, I
hope to suggest ways in which Venetian sources have deliberately intensified
the confusion. Second, I do not claim that the Spanish protagonists were not
seeking to further Spanish interests at the expense of Venice: I merely argue
that there is no proof that they were responsible for the alleged conspiracy of
1618. Ossuna was clearly a saber rattler who was challenging Venetian su-

premacy in the Adriatic—in defense of which supremacy Sarpi had published. Contemporary opinion was that Ossuna was a man "of lively and turbulent spirit. . . . a forward friend of enterprises and innovations . . . his prodigality was rash" (de ingenio vivo y turbolento. . . . levantado amigo de impresas y novedades . . . su prodigalidad era inconsiderada).[52] However, Ossuna's fall from grace cannot be directly linked to events in Venice alone. Admittedly, he was at pains to protest his innocence to his king. The Venetians, he wrote to Philip III, "proceed with the same artifice in all their actions, and to frighten France and its king they have sought to attribute it [the conspiracy] to the dealings of Don Alonso de la Cueva [Bedmar] and me."[53] His naval actions against Venice in the Gulf were not unprecedented, and booty from other people's ships was collected like dues by the viceroys of Naples.[54] It seems likely that Ossuna was removed from office as a result of a projected coup in Naples; at least that was the allegation of a group of disaffected nobles. Then again, his downfall may have been caused by court intrigue, which made him vulnerable after the fall of Lerma.[55] However, the evidence consulted *in extenso* by Michelangelo Schipa exonerated Ossuna from any planned coup in Naples and suggested that hostility to him at court had been fomented by the Venetians. The viceroy admitted hiring large numbers of French mercenaries, but in defending this action he maintained that he had done so in order to keep them out of Venetian service.[56] Bedmar, it should be remembered, was not recalled from Venice but chased out; however, he proved a survivor, becoming a cardinal in 1622. He went on to serve in the Netherlands, where his severity led to his disgrace and a return to Rome. He became bishop of Malaga in 1644 and died at eighty-three in 1655.[57] There seems every likelihood that the Spaniards were involved in a plot of some sort. But even if they were, they were not alone, and any "Spanish" conspiracy against Venice must be set in the context of the early seventeenth century, a time of secrecy and subterfuge, along with dramatic shifts in loyalty dictated by reason of state.

Such changes, and some of the plots, can be traced in the years 1605–6, to which we should now return our attention. In 1605 Venetian ambassadors' reports from England were full of fears for Catholicism in that country. Robert Cecil, the king's most influential counselor was reported as saying that "there is no doubt that the object of these laws is to extinguish the Catholic religion in this kingdom." As late as October the ambassador reported in cypher that Catholics "live in perpetual dread of their property today, their liberty tomorrow, their life the day after, as has happened to many." On Christmas Eve the

Venetian Inquisition sent James I's justification of royal absolutism, the *Basilikon Doron,* to the Congregation of the Index to be placed on its list of prohibited books because of its "many impious and detestable sentiments." In the meantime, of course, the Gunpowder Plot of November 1605 had intensified anti-Catholic sentiment. However, such sentiment owed much to allegations of papal involvement. As the ambassador Nicolò Molin reported on 17 November 1605, "There is also a grave suspicion that the Pope may be the source of the plot, for, as it is a question of religion, it seems impossible that he should not have assented, even if he took no active part in it." An awareness of this suspicion is vital to an understanding of how, and how quickly, the situation changed. English policy could be anti-Catholic because it was antipapal. Venetian policy could be pro-Catholic and antipapal. Despite the apparent distance between the two powers, all that was needed to unite them was a policy that was antipapal rather than pro- or anti-Catholic. Resistance to Rome would become the cause of all princes—and republics. By 6 January Molin was reporting an audience with the king in which James had said: "I do not know upon what they found this perfidious and cursed doctrine of Rome that they are permitted to plot against the lives of princes . . . a doctrine invented certainly not for the benefit of souls, as they pretend, but to augment the temporal power and authority of the Popes, and to furnish them with opportunity to satisfy that cupidity and ambition of theirs to be held the lords of the whole world, and authorised to enrich and aggrandise their own relations."[58]

The election of Doge Leonardo Donà apparently made the giovani supreme. Tension with the papacy increased in the aftermath of a papal brief "menacing the excommunicatory sentence," as the English ambassador Sir Henry Wotton recorded in a letter of 20 January to Sir Thomas Edmondes. "We have here lost the old Prince, and the Cavalier Leonardo Donato is chosen in his room, a wise and beaten [experienced] man in the world, eloquent, resolute, provident; and of all this the State seemeth to have very much need, being fallen into terms of great contumacy with the Pope."[59]

The recognition of a common English and Venetian interest in an anti-papal stance grew as relations deteriorated between Rome and the Republic. On 10 February the new Venetian ambassador in London, Zorzi Giustinian, wrote in cypher to the doge and the Senate: "Here they freely discuss the quarrel between the Pope and the Republic. They are pleased at this disaccord, for they consider that one of the principal supports of the Holy See is the reverence and devotion of the Republic. . . . As to yielding to Papal pretensions, as we did not know what these were, it was impossible for us to say anything, except that the Republic would always continue in her ancient devotion to the Holy See, with the same constance, that she would maintain her rights as an independent sovereign." Two weeks after that, Giustinian was still expressing concern about anti-Catholic measures, but he referred to the implementation in England of a general oath "that they do not believe the Pope has authority to depose or excommunicate a Sovereign."[60]

That was an oath that many Venetians could have taken. Venice's increasing hostility toward the papacy resulted in the interdict declared by Paul V on 17 April.[61] In mid-June James I interrupted ambassador Giustinian's explanation of Venice's legal position and said, "They are pious, most just, most necessary laws . . . . The world would indeed be fortunate if every Prince would open his eyes and behave as the Republic does." There were some apparent foreshadowings of the events of 1618 as Spanish intervention began to seem likely, taking the form of a challenge to Venetian sovereignty in the Gulf and the threat of action against Crema. By late September Giustinian could report from London that "the printed discourse of master Father Paolo (Sarpi), the Servite in defence of the Republic in its contest with the Pontiff, has arrived here. Everyone appreciates and praises it." It was complemented in December by an account of the Gunpowder Plot by the Catholic earl of Northampton, "a treatise hostile to the pretended superiority of Popes over Princes in matters temporal."[62]

Yet we race ahead, overlooking developments in Venice itself. After the interdict of 17 April, as early as the end of May Sir Henry Wotton was hopeful that Venice could be converted to Protestantism, and he was pushing in a direction that would have startled his king.[63] In a letter in which he described the magnificence of the Corpus Christi procession that the government had ordered in defiance of the interdict, Wotton added: "The State useth me with much kindness, and I protest unto your Lordship I think hereafter they will come nearer unto his majesty, not only in civil friendship but even in religion. I have, upon the inclination of things that way, begun to take order for an Italian preacher from Geneva whatsoever it cost me, out of shame that in this kind, the disseminators of untruth do bear from us the praise of diligence."[64] The preacher concerned was Giovanni Diodati, who arrived in Venice two years later with every intention of converting the Venetians. Accompanying him was one Monsieur de Liques, who had strict instructions on his course of action from no less a figure than Philippe du Plessis Mornay, who, like Sarpi, was no stranger to disguised authorship and whose biography de Liques helped to write.[65]

With M. Diodati he will decide how to plan his journey, either with him or separately, according to what seems best, and according to that will agree on a rendez-vous for their meeting . . . . He will take the route via Geneva, Zurich, and Coire [Chur], then on to the Valtelline. . . . If he arrives in Venice before M. Diodati, if he is to be followed soon by him, I am of the opinion that he does not present himself with any letters to My Lord the Ambassador of England, or Padre Paolo, or the pastor in the house of My Lord the Ambassador, that he does not get there until he has assessed the lie of the land and has prepared them first, and in order not to sin against discretion, which above all must be observed.[66]

The planned velvet revolution in religion would then be followed by a political realignment:

It will be possible to gain the ears of the most notable people through the words of M. Diodati, in order to bring about this holy mutation, if it pleases God to lead us there, that there would be need, taking the opportunity of the quarrels with the pope, or the doubts of the king of Spain, that the Signoria may ally itself closely with the Swiss cantons, the Elector Palatine, and other princes of Germany, who, on these stirrings between the emperor and the Archduke Matthias, have lately become closely united and in consequence have reviewed their forces; the same is true of the Low Countries, matchless today in their forces on the Ocean sea and capable of launching a very powerful diversion in favour of their friends, and this before they are finished with the Spaniard; and when one wishes to reach an understanding there, one will be able to make overtures and give more precise points of contact.[67]

One has the sense that Mornay was trying to activate a final push for a coalition at once anti-Spanish and anti-Roman. In the aftermath of the Venetian interdict he began his work on the papacy under the title *Le mystère d'iniquité*. Politically, he was operating through contacts at the highest levels, ensuring, for instance, that the Venetian Republic would give full ceremonial and formal recognition of ambassadorial status to the representative of the United Provinces. This was cemented by the Venetians' reciprocal embassy, and there was talk of "a closer alliance between the Republics for some great matter in the future."[68] There were real possibilities of an alliance with France and, despite the confessional obstacles, with Protestant powers for "the kind of league that was aligned against the Habsburgs in the Thirty Years' War." Sarpi appears to have encouraged hopes of this.[69]

Mornay's agent, Diodati, certainly expected much of the Republic's official historiographer. In his own account Diodati describes Sarpi as "the foremost instrumental wheel of this holy affair." However, those involved did not have full confidence in Sarpi: "One might say that seeing Father Paolo connive and dissimulate so profoundly in the matter of his faith, alarm made them go cold again and held them back."[70] Sarpi's defense was that an open declaration would deny him access to the secrets of the state. He was intimate with matters of great importance and would be informed promptly of matters political and religious, means that would be denied him if he made an open declaration.[71] By his own admission, openness was not characteristic of him: "My character is such that, like a chameleon, I imitate the behaviour of those amongst whom I find myself. Thus if I am amongst people who are reserved and gloomy I become, despite myself, unfriendly. I respond openly and freely to people who are cheerful and uninhibited. I am compelled to wear a mask. Perhaps there is nobody who can survive in Italy without one."[72] Perhaps it may have appeared to Diodati that just this once the mask of which Sarpi was so proud had slipped a little.

While much has been written on Sarpi's role in the interdict, less attention has been given to his role in the presentation of the events of 1618. This may be because some scholars feel that after the interdict his influence was on the wane.[73] However, his contribution was decisive in producing a Venetian version of events. The surviving documentation reveals with startling clarity the problems the Republic faced over the conspiracy. To publicize the event had its disadvantages since the successful suppression of a plot did not necessarily enhance the reputation of a state famed for its immunity to external threat and internal subversion. Sarpi's memorandum to the state, a document confidently attributed to him by many authorities and still accepted as his work by Paolo Preto, sets out the pros and cons with scientific coldness.[74] The draft account that he offers has been influential, matching almost exactly that of Horatio Brown, for example. Even its title is categorical, relating to the "Conspiracy ordered by Pietro Giron di Ossuna, Viceroy of Naples." (When the plot was first referred to as "the conspiracy of Bedmar" has yet to be discovered.) It is coldly divided under different headings, which nevertheless reveal a real tension between fashioning an image of the Venetian state as all-seeing and biding its time, on the one hand, and a number of more or less obvious inconsistencies and loose ends that may tarnish that image. "Since the present account must be in the hands of anyone and might be read by some with malicious intent, it is necessary for it to conform to what is true and what looks true at one and the same time and, however, to order it according to how things are presumed to have happened, describing them as one thing depending on another."[75]

The grounds for not publishing details of the event include keeping the Society of Jesus guessing (since "their souls and pens are wickedly tempered"), avoiding inconsistency with any details already revealed (especially what was contained in the notice placed at Rialto on 17 October 1618), and not having to justify the executions of Pierre and Langrand,

> since in this matter, for the best of reasons, many details are not expressed but were related in the account of 17 October, people will ask why, and they will take it as a sign of ill faith. In writing, either it will be necessary to record the death of Jacques Pierre and Langlad [Langrand], and in recording it to defend it, or not. It cannot be suppressed, because it is notorious. To defend it, even though it is not to be doubted that there were good reasons that made it possible, will be to sound a trumpet for a great controversy, and invariably whoever defends the more malicious side is given greater credence. (61)

Then there are *taciute* (things to leave unsaid), for instance,

> on the 10 or 15 nobles and merchants who were in the know with the conspirators, because of the difficulty of not detracting from the confessions of the guilty or indeed to make believe that this was true and then disguised because of the government's weakness. (62)

These in turn are followed by the *inverosimili* (things that it would be difficult to make seem true), for example:

> That Moncassin, who knew so much, did not know even one of the 200 or 300 [men] whom Jacques Pierre said he had in Venice.
> That Juven was allowed to walk free after his revelation to the Doge.
> That such an enterprise could be undertaken without the knowledge of the city, and that if it was known, it was not discovered earlier.
> That it was not likely that one or two men could betray Crema. (62–63)

Another series of features is *imminente* (hanging over our heads):

> [Then] again it does not appear that the danger was so threatening because Jacques Pierre said to Moncassin in January that they could wait [until] September or October, so March does not have confirmation.
> And why Jacques Pierre, who had the main responsibility, would not have left and gone to the fleet at that precise time.
> And why we do not know who stayed behind to do Langlad's work with the explosives and pyrotechnics, which is the main thing, absolutely the main thing.
> That the conspiracy was to be carried out at a time when the Great Council was in session, and that all were to be killed, and that once the city was taken, the Council was to be summoned and the poor nobles suborned. (63)

Rimanenti (matters outstanding) include that "it will remain a marvel that in so many discussions between Jacques Pierre, Robert, and the Ambassador [Bedmar] and Moncassin none of them has said how they wished to make use of him" and that the executions were carried out without trial or "other use of justice" (64) All of this Eugenia Levi cited as evidence of Sarpi's prudence and patriotism.

Perhaps appropriately, the eventual publication remains obscure.[76] There is no specific official account, but there is evidence of a heightening stridency in expressions of anti-Spanish sentiment. Yet, with that chilling capacity for disguise noted by Diodati, Sarpi published his own version as an anonymous, supplementary updating and completion of a history of Venice's relations with the Habsburgs and the Uskoks written by Minuccio Minucci, archbishop of Zara.[77] In this piece Sarpi disguises polemic as history: avoiding rhetoric, he still puts across the view that his "Relatione" had expressed as *propaganda,* in the literal sense of "things that are to be spread." According to Sarpi, Ossuna himself had made known his intention to damage the Republic and had raised soldiers for that specific purpose, and it was known "for certain" that they were to "assault and sack Venice."[78] "So well conducted was the machination" that Venice was only saved by divine intervention (295). The number of conspirators has risen to 400. Twenty galleys were due to invade, with four galleons posing as merchant ships. They concealed 2,000 musketeers who were to disembark onto twenty barges. They were to land at San Marco and meet up with "a large number of bandits and no-goods who had gathered together on shore leave." No fewer than 500 would seize the piazza, and 300 others were to enter the palace, take over the armory, and hold the Great Council, "cutting to pieces those who sought to escape" (296). Sarpi repeats that "so well devised was this machination" that "written instructions had been drawn up for it, setting out the manner and order to use, with all the details of the plan, which by the effective joint action of the leaders had been studied and discussed." "It was amazing that the discovery of the conspiracy in Venice threw into confusion other plotters in the city of Crema." And it was still more to be wondered at that "the confessions of so many in such different places were all exactly the same." Is it significant that he adds about the confessions that it was "as if they had issued forth from one mouth" (297)? This device covers the objection in the "Relatione" that Moncassin could not provide a single name for his 300 accomplices, and it is rendered all the more convincing by the embellishment that the confessions were the same whether volunteered or extracted by torture (298). There is a wonderfully slippery characterization of rumor: "Throughout the city it was divulged that a mighty conspiracy had been discovered, and according to the custom of the people—among them the less one of them knows, the more they talk—various matters without foundation were discussed" (299).

The Spanish ambassador sought protection and "could not deny having kept, protected and looked after in his own house a person much burdened with the guilt [of the plot], nor could he even absolutely plead an exception for himself" (299). The language here is particularly interesting, "to plead an exception for himself" (eccettuare se stesso) a phrase using the technical language of the jurist, as though this were a matter of court record. The government, in its wisdom, "judged it proper to imitate other great princes, who in similar circumstances, the guilty having been punished, kept their maturity and a reserve suitable to the end of maintaining calm and not exciting rumor" (299). On the other hand, rumors that "the conspiracy was between Frenchmen and Dutchmen acting as private individuals" were "easily recognized as false." Having woven in the "conspiracy" so deftly, he returns to the main subject, the peace treaty with the Austrian Habsburgs (300).

That account leaves much unsaid but nothing hanging over us and no matters outstanding. Cozzi's comments on the text are particularly insightful. He notes that it is a controlled polemic, that it reflects an interaction between history and politics, that the events must be understood in the context of Europe as a whole, and that Sarpi frequently resorts to the phrase "more likely than true"—all of which bring the supreme Sarpi expert closer, perhaps rather surprisingly, to Wootton's views.[79]

Sarpi, then, played a key role in fashioning for posterity a particularly misleading account of a "Spanish" conspiracy that was not necessarily Spanish and may not have been a conspiracy. One is tempted to conclude with a reminder of the general condition of a Europe anxiously seeking to tell the difference between what was real and what was not. The first folio of Shakespeare's works was published in 1623, the year of Sarpi's death. The Servite friar's account of the "Spanish" conspiracy as recorded in a work of "history" is double-talk worthy of the prologue to Shakespeare's *Henry IV, Part II,* spoken by Rumour, clad in a robe "painted full of tongues" and bringing "smooth comforts false, worse than true wrongs." However, while that is one minor way of showing that Shakespeare's plays were very much "of their time," it neglects Sarpi's legacy to posterity and the ambiguities and contradictions at the center of that legacy.

A terse but overt expression of Sarpi's anti-Spanish views is concentrated in his *Breve relatione di Valtellina* (1621). This work reflects the Senate's opinion that Venice had a pivotal strategic importance, "being the only dividing border between the House of Austria in Germany and that of Spain in Italy" (essendo solo termine divisorio fra la casa d'Austria in Germania con quella di Spagna in

Italia).[80] Sarpi, Spain, and the Valtelline were subsequently to have a curious relationship. In 1624, a year after Sarpi's death, a violent attack on Spain addressed to Philip III (who also had died in 1623) appeared under the title *Discorso sopra le ragioni della resolutione fatta in Val Telina*. It appeared in English in 1628, as *A Discourse upon the Reasons of the Resolution Taken in the Valtelline,* at which point someone, probably the translator, Sir Thomas Roe, attributed it to "the Author of the Historie of the Councell of Trent." It seems impossible that the Italian original, published anonymously, was Sarpi's work. (Indeed, Dedouvres attributed the French edition to Father Joseph.) It was published again in 1650, when it was described as "shewing the only way in Policie to counterplot the designes of promoting unjust interests of state."[81] The Valtelline had been "possessed under the colour of religion," Venice had been "conspired," Piedmont "assaulted," France "twice corrupted into combustion with holy leagues and open armes," England "practiced and invaded," and then "a scelerous peace sought with the Turke, to whom, in truth, Spaine is only a true friend." The pseudo-Sarpi also assaults that most sensitive feature of the Spanish monarchy, its reputation, "If your Maiestie be not more then heedful, you shall be certainly induced to such actions, that being added to the other three Narrations of your Ancestors, will serve for an example to Posteritie, of an impious and wicked Enterprise, under a religious and godly vaile," and points to the dangers of a Spanish world conspiracy:

> If then a Vice-King of Naples hath once surprised some castles of the pope, which after with difficulties were restored: if another did rob the Merchant Gallies of Venice, which yet they have not restored; if a Governour of Millan did once attempt to take Casall of Monteferrat, a Citie of the Duke of Mantua by treason, and the Castle of Bresse from the State of Venice; If another did leape out to ransack the land of Cremasco; Another did procure to betray the Citie of Crema subiect to the senate: If one of your Ambassadours, with intelligence of the Vice-Roy of Naples, and the Governour of Millan, did machinate a most detestable conspiracie against the Citie of Venice it selfe: If now the present Governour of Millan hath caused the Valtellines to rebell from the Grisons: And if all these things have been done, with the Armes, the men, and the money of your Maiestie, and in times that you have professed to bee a good friend both to the Grisons, Venetians, Duke of Mantua, and the Pope, the world cannot imagine other, but that Your Maiestie hath given these orders. From whence it is publikely spoken, that the King of Spaine doth attend to nothing else, but to raise Rebellions, to contrive Conspiracies, to sollicit treasons, to ransacke, rob, and assassinate his friends. Thus by the meanes of his Ministers, his Royall name, without any his owne fault, is stayned with Infamy.[82]

There is a just irony here: when he was alive, Sarpi disguised himself; when he was dead, others disguised the work of others as Sarpi's.

By 1650, when the *Discourse* was published again, we have begun to move closer to Thomas Otway's world. While the play itself has contemporary resonance for 1682, when it was first performed, Shaftesbury variously identified with Regnault and Antonio, this world too had its Venetian links, once again giving weight to Viroli's views. Another work attributed to Sarpi, translated by William Aglionby as *Advice Given to the Republic of Venice,* setting out the rules for acquiring "perpetual Dominion," was published in 1693, having first appeared under a slightly different title in 1689. Both derived from an Italian original under Sarpi's name that in some variants was called *Opinion falsely ascribed to Father Paul.*[83] One can imagine how Sarpi would have enjoyed the uncertainty generated by the proclamation in the title that he was *not* the author.

In the 1693 edition the translator's "epistle dedicatory" sets the tone. It is addressed to Viscount Sidney, who, with the generals Charles Trelawny and Percy Kirke, had deserted James II. There is a deep satisfaction in the secrets of the state, "as it was made for the perusal of those only who were the participants of all the Arcanums of the Empire, it is writ with less regard to the Publick Censure, to which he suppos'd it would never be subject." The work is "directed to those whose interest it was to conceal it." Types of constitution are irrelevant to the exercise of power, for "all is just that contributes to the preservation of the government." It is a natural deduction from this that one might "advise in some cases not to stand upon common proceedings."[84] Oppression and the exercise of reason of state are now to be admired in the Republic: in an important sense, the myth of Venice has become the antimyth. Or perhaps it is more accurate to say that the myth of Venice has become the myth of Sarpi.

In any case, those sorts of sentiments circulating in late-seventeenth-century England go some way to confirming the terrible bleakness of Otway's vision. What his play provides is a messy human reality a world away from the official version. He juxtaposes age and corruption in public life with youth and purity in private sentiment. Why single out the Spaniards, when all public life will corrupt whatever is young and beautiful and brave? Efforts to reform the public weal are misconceived because it is preserved precisely through its own corruption. According to Bouwsma, what Donà, Sarpi, and the giovani had recognized was that "change and corruption were inescapable."[85] What is the Venice that is eventually preserved in Otway's play?

> . . . to see our senators
> Cheat the deluded people with a show
> Of liberty, which yet they ne'er must taste of;
> They say, by them our hands are free from fetters,
> Yet whom they please they lay in basest bonds;
> Bring whom they please to Infamy and Sorrow;
> Drive us like wracks down the rough tide of power,
> Whilst no hold's left to save us from destruction;
> All that bear this are villains; and I one,
> Not to rouse up at the great call of nature,
> And check the growth of these domestic spoilers
> That makes us slaves and tells us 'tis our charter!   (1.1)

And what is lost when Belvidera persuades Jaffeir to reveal what he knows?

> . . . thou'rt my soul itself; wealth, friendship, honour,
> All present joys, and earnest of all future,
> Are summ'd in thee: methinks when in thy arms
> Thus leaning on thy breast, one minute's more
> Than a long thousand years of vulgar hours.
> Why was such happiness not given me pure?
> Why dash'd with cruel wrongs and bitter wantings?
> Come, lead me forward now like a tame lamb
> To sacrifice, thus in his fatal garlands
> Deck'd fine and pleas'd, the wanton skips and plays
> > Trots by the enticing flattering priestess' side,
> > And much transported with his little pride,
> > Forgets his dear companions of the plain
> > Till, by her bound, he's on the altar lain,
> > Yet then too hardly bleats, such pleasure's in the pain.   (3.2)

Otway, whose play was the starting point for this essay, was at one time regarded as "next to Shakespeare" as a tragedian, and he might be compared with Schiller, who wrote on the conspiracy of Count Fieschi in Genoa and, indeed, like Otway used Saint-Réal as his source for a play about Don Carlos. Otway was also mentioned favorably by Byron. So perhaps one way of making this misfit fit is to place him between Shakespeare and the romantics.[86]

Those are speculations by way of acknowledgment, and one cannot be confident in one's judgments of literary merit. That said, it is a humbling experience for a historian to learn that sometimes it takes poetic insight to show what a dangerous subject history is, especially when it is entrusted to the servants of the state. This long investigation suggests that actually there is no single decisive piece of evidence to link Bedmar, or Ossuna, or any other

Spaniard to what is known as the "Spanish" conspiracy, but there is evidence of a conspiracy against Venice, and of a conspiracy to ensure that the Spaniards were made to look responsible for—a conspiracy. Perhaps the conspiracies of 1618 in Venice might best be understood in relation to another theatrical comment on history. In act 3 of Shaw's play *The Devil's Disciple,* when General Burgoyne receives news that the loss of the colonies is now certain, he is asked, "What will History say?" The general replies, "History, Sir, will tell lies, as usual."

But asserting that the historian can never reliably get to the bottom of anything would be a negative way to conclude. Moreover, such a conclusion would lurch toward an antimyth giving credit to Sarpi as puppet master of confusion. What the episode prompts in a positive way is a reconsideration of the microcosm of Venice and the macrocosm of the European political experience. The context of the incident known as the Spanish conspiracy was a changing relationship between the public and private spheres in which each increasingly kept itself to itself. At the same time that the private citizen was estranged from public affairs, so affairs of state became increasingly shut in on themselves. Rather than being polar opposites, the myth of Venice and the antimyth became one and the same. This development in turn can be linked to the general European tendency that Viroli has identified, in which reason of state and mastery of appearances triumphed over civic humanism. Thus, in Venice reason of state can appear as republican freedom. Viewed from the perspective of the "Spanish" conspiracy of 1618, the ambiguous reputation of the Venetian Republic in the seventeenth century may reveal something about the ambiguities in the concept of the European state itself.

NOTES

The research for this chapter was made possible by the Master and Fellows of Saint Catharine's College, Cambridge, through their generous award of a Visiting Fellowship in the summer of 1992. I owe a special debt to Paul and Wendy Hartle. Paul's expertise in Restoration literature contributed more than he knew, as did the kind advice of Jonathan Scott on Restoration politics. The wonderful open shelves and the efficient photocopying service, as well as the Rare Books Room of the Cambridge University Library, were indispensable, as were the expertise and friendship of Stephen Lees. Previous versions were delivered at the College, Winchester, at the Modern History Seminar and the Early Modern Intellectual History Seminar in Edinburgh, at the Early Modern Europe Seminar in Oxford, and at the Venetian Seminar in York. I am very grateful to Rob Wyke, John Gooding, Nick Phillipson, John Robertson, and Nick Davidson for inviting me to speak, to all those whose comments and questions were so useful in Britain and at the "Venice Reconsidered" conference in Syracuse, and to Simon Adams for his illuminating advice on early-seventeenth-century international relations. Jean Archibald saved me from a monstrous error just before the Syracuse conference.

1. See esp. Gaetano Cozzi's imperious *Il doge Nicolò Contarini: Ricerche sul patriziato veneziano agli inizi del Seicento* (Venice, 1958), reprinted in his *Venezia barocca: Conflitti di uomini e idee nella crisi del Seicento veneziano* (Venice, 1995); idem, *Paolo Sarpi tra Venezia e l'Europa* (Turin, 1979); Gaetano Cozzi, Michael Knapton, and Giovanni Scarabello, *La Repubblica di Venezia nell'età moderna: Dal 1517 alla fine della Repubblica* (Turin, 1992), 69–102; and Gino Benzoni, *Venezia nell'età della controriforma* (Milan, 1973).

2. William J. Bouwsma, *Venice and the Defense of Republican Liberty: Renaissance Values in the Age of the Counter Reformation* (Berkeley, 1968).

3. Ibid., 321.

4. See, e.g., Alexander Leggatt, *Shakespeare's Political Drama* (London, 1988); Andrew Gurr, *Playgoing in Shakespeare's London* (London, 1987); and idem, "The Shakespearean Stage," in *The Norton Shakespeare,* ed. Stephen Greenblatt et al. (New York, 1997), 3281–3301.

5. Louis Machot, quoted in Peter Donaldson, *Machiavelli and Mystery of State* (Cambridge, 1988), 187.

6. Torquato Accetto, quoted in Salvatore S. Nigro, "The Secretary," in *Baroque Personae,* ed. Rosario Villari, trans. Lydia G. Cochrane (Chicago, 1995), 94. For case histories of political behavior, see David Wootton, *Paolo Sarpi: Between Renaissance and Enlightenment* (Cambridge, 1983); and John Bossy, *Giordano Bruno and the Embassy Affair* (New Haven, 1991).

7. Ludovico Zuccolo, quoted in Bouwsma, *Venice and the Defense of Republican Liberty,* 300–301. See also Roland Mousnier, "The Exponents and Critics of Absolutism," in *New Cambridge Modern History,* vol. 4, *The Decline of Spain and the Thirty Years' War,* ed. J. P. Cooper (Cambridge, 1970), 101–31.

8. Maurizio Viroli, *From Politics to Reason of State: The Acquisition and Transformation of the Language of Politics, 1250–1600* (Cambridge, 1992), 1–2, 231–37, 265.

9. Maria Luisa Doglio, "La letteratura ufficiale e l'oratoria celebrativa," in *Storia della cultura veneta,* ed. Girolamo Arnaldi and Manlio Pastore Stocchi, 6 vols. (Vicenza, 1976–86), 4, pt. 1: 174, 175.

10. On the Venetian situation, see Paolo Preto, "Le grandi paure di Venezia nel secondo '500: La paura del tradimento e delle congiure," in *Crisi e rinnovamenti nell'autunno del rinascimento a Venezia,* ed. Vittore Branca and Carlo Ossola (Florence, 1991), esp. 204.

11. Doge Leonardo Donà, quoted in Bouwsma, *Venice and the Defense of Republican Liberty,* 410–11.

12. Ibid., 512–16.

13. William J. Bouwsma, "Venice and the Political Education of Europe," in *Renaissance Venice*, ed. J. R. Hale (London, 1973), 445–66.

14. Bouwsma, *Venice and the Defense of Republican Liberty*, 190, 243; see also Hugh Trevor-Roper, "Spain and Europe, 1598–1621," in *New Cambridge Modern History*, 4:260–82.

15. See William S. Maltby, *The Black Legend in England: The Development of Anti-Spanish Sentiment, 1558–1660* (Durham, N.C., 1971); and for Spain in Europe, Richard Mackenney, *Sixteenth Century Europe: Expansion and Conflict* (London, 1993), esp. 10, 47, 299–309.

16. See Alberto Tenenti, "La Repubblica di Venezia e la Spagna di Filippo II e Filippo III," *Studi Veneziani*, n.s., 30 (1995): 112, 115. For Donà's interview with Philip II, see James C. Davis, ed., *Pursuit of Power: Venetian Ambassadors' Reports on Spain, Turkey, and France in the Age of Philip II, 1560–1600* (New York, 1970), 104.

17. Italo Raulich, "Una relazione del Marchese di Bedmar sui veneziani," *Nuovo Archivio Veneto* 16 (1898): 21. I have used the translation from Bouwsma, *Venice and the Defense of Republican Liberty*, 503.

18. Franco Gaeta, "Venezia da 'stato misto' ad aristocrazia 'esemplare,' " in Arnaldi and Stocchi, *Storia della cultura veneta*, 4, pt. 2: 469–70 and n. 116.

19. Horatio F. Brown, "The Spanish Conspiracy: An Episode in the Decline of Venice," in his *Studies in Venetian History*, vol. 2 (London, 1907), 267.

20. See Richard Mackenney, "Public and Private in Renaissance Venice," *Renaissance Studies* 12 (1998): 109–30; idem, "The Guilds of Venice: State and Society in the Longue Durée," *Studi Veneziani*, n.s., 34 (1997): 15–43; idem, "The *scuole piccole* of Venice: Formations and Transformations," in *The Politics of Ritual Kinship: Confraternities and Social Order in Early Modern Italy*, ed. Nicholas Terpstra (Cambridge, 1999), 172–89.

21. Giuseppe Malatesta, quoted in Bouwsma, *Venice and the Defense of Republican Liberty*, 234.

22. Fulgenzio Micanzio, quoted in Bouwsma, *Venice and the Defense of Republican Liberty*, 362–63.

23. James's speech is quoted by the Venetian ambassador to England, Nicolò Molin, in a report of 23 November 1605, in *Calendar of State Papers and Manuscripts relating to English Affairs, existing in the Archives and Collections of Venice, and in other Libraries of Northern Italy*, 38 vols., ed. Rawdon Brown (vols. 1–6), Rawdon Brown and the Right Honorable George Cavendish Bentinck, M.P. (vol. 7), Horatio F. Brown (vols. 8–12), and Allen B. Hinds (vols. 13–38) (London, 1864–1947; hereafter *CSPV*), 10:303. On Sarpi as atheist and absolutist and on similarities to Hobbes, see Wootton, *Paolo Sarpi*, esp. 1–7. For a contrasting view, see Gaetano Cozzi and Luisa Cozzi, "Paolo Sarpi," in Arnaldi and Stocchi, *Storia della cultura veneta*, 4, pt. 2: 1–36.

24. The play is available as Thomas Otway, *Venice Preserv'd or, A Plot Discover'd. A Tragedy. As it is Acted at the Duke's Theatre* (London, 1682), in *The Works of Thomas Otway: Plays, Poems, and Love-Letters*, ed. J. C. Ghosh, 2 vols. (Oxford, 1932); and also in the Everyman volume *Restoration Plays*, intro. Sir Edmund Gosse (London, 1932). On the context see David Wootton, "Ulysses Bound? Venice and the Idea of Liberty from

Howell to Hume," in *Republicanism, Liberty, and Commercial Society, 1679–1776,* ed. Wootton (New York, 1994), 341–67; and the classic by Ernst Cassirer, *The Myth of the State* (New Haven, 1946), esp. 116–75.

25. It is important to acknowledge one's debt to Otway (1652–85), not least because such a writer is now largely unheard of. There can have been few people who managed to get so much wrong in life. In seeking a patron he attached himself to the earl of Rochester, who blew hot and cold, but more cold than hot. When successful as a duelist, Otway crossed swords with John Churchill, the future duke of Marlborough. When he sought a military career, he enrolled in the regiment of the luckless duke of Monmouth. When he was funny, it was—rashly—at the expense of John Dryden. To his credit, Otway himself related the anecdote that, living on the opposite side of the same street as Dryden, he returned home one evening the worse for drink and wrote on Dryden's door, "Here Dryden lives, a poet and a wit." The next night he found that his neighbour had added the subscription, "Here Otway lives, exactly opposite." For biographical details, see Otway, *Works,* 1:1–37; Aline Mackenzie Taylor, *"Next to Shakespeare": Otway's Venice Preserv'd and The Orphan and Their History on the London Stage* (Durham, N.C., 1950); Gaeta, "Venezia da 'stato misto' ad aristocrazia 'esemplare,' " 488.

26. Taylor, *"Next to Shakespeare,"* 39–58; John Robert Moore, "Contemporary Satire in Otway's *Venice Preserved," Publications of the Modern Languages Association of America* 43 (1928): 166–81. See also John P. Kenyon, *The Popish Plot* (London, 1972).

27. César Vischard, abbé de Saint-Réal, *The Conspiracy of the Spaniards against the Republic of Venice,* translated from the French (London, 1770), quotation on 8–9; Gustave Dulong, *L'Abbé de Saint-Réal: Etude sur les rapports de l'histoire et du roman au 17e siècle* (Paris, 1921); Wootton, "Ulysses Bound?" 352, emphasis added.

28. See the vivid evocation by Hugh Trevor-Roper, "The Outbreak of the Thirty Years' War," in his *Renaissance Essays* (London, 1985), 275–94.

29. Gunther E. Rothenberg, "Venice and the Uskoks of Senj, 1537–1618," *Journal of Modern History* 33 (1961): 148–56; Wendy Catherine Bracewell, *The Uskoks of Senj: Piracy, Banditry, and Holy War in the Sixteenth-Century Adriatic* (New York, 1992).

30. Frederic C. Lane, *Venice: A Maritime Republic* (Baltimore, 1973), 399; Brown, "Spanish Conspiracy," 246–47.

31. The chronicler Girolamo Priuli, quoted in Leopold von Ranke, "Die Verschwörung gegen Venedig im Jahre 1618: Mit Urkunden aus dem venezianischen Archiv," in *Sämmtliche Werke,* vol. 42, *Zur venezianischen Geschichte* (Leipzig, 1878), 203.

32. Geoffrey Parker, *The Army of Flanders and the Spanish Road: The Logistics of Spanish Victory and Defeat in the Low Countries Wars* (Cambridge, 1972), 70–74.

33. *CSPV,* 15:86, no. 145; 96, no. 162; 103, no. 171; 114, no. 189.

34. Ibid., 118, no. 191; 104, no. 173; 120, no. 198; 150, no. 242.

35. Pietro Gritti, *Relazione,* in *Relazioni di Ambasciatori Veneti al Senato,* vol. 9, *Spagna,* ed. Nicolò Barozzi and Guglielmo Berchet (1856; reprint, ed. L. Firpo, Turin 1978), 497.

36. Saint-Réal, *Conspiracy,* 35–36.

37. See, e.g., the account in Lane, *Venice,* 398–400; and Brown, "Spanish Conspir-

acy," 246–48. Other details cited are drawn from S. Romanin, *Storia documentata di Venezia*, 10 vols. (Venice, 1853–61), 7:113–60, with documents on 581–84.

38. Julian S. Corbett, *England in the Mediterranean: A Study of the Rise and Influence of British Power within the Straits, 1603–1713*, 2 vols. (London, 1904), 1:44.

39. Brown, "Spanish Conspiracy," 267, 294, 246.

40. Romanin, *Storia documentata di Venezia*, 7:113.

41. Heinrich Kretschmayr, *Geschichte von Venedig*, 3 vols. (Gotha, 1905–34), 3:284, 287.

42. Ranke, "Die Verschwörung," 140 (on the official history), 141–42 (on the conspirators), 144–71 (on Saint-Réal), 203–6 (on Ossuna's involvement or the lack of it); quotation on 167.

43. Lamberto Chiarelli, "Il Marchese di Bedmar e i suoi confidenti come risultano dalla corrispondenza segreta del 'novellista' Alessandro Granzini con gli Inquisitori di Stato a Venezia," *Archivio Veneto-Tridentino* 8 (1925) 144–73, quotations on 150 and 162 n. 1.

44. Italo Raulich, "La congiura spagnola contro Venezia (contributo di documenti inediti)," *Nuovo Archivio Veneto* 6 (1893): 5–86, esp. 25; see also idem, "Una relazione del Marchese di Bedmar sui veneziani."

45. Amelia Zambler, "Contributo alla storia della congiura spagnuola contro Venezia," *Nuovo Archivio Veneto* 11 (1896): 15–121, esp. 17–27, quotations on 17 and 27.

46. Giuseppe Coniglio, "Il Duca d'Ossuna e Venezia dal 1616 al 1620," *Archivio Veneto*, 5th ser., 54–55 (1955): 42–70, esp. 43, 52, 54. See also, more generally, idem, *Il Viceregno di Napoli nel sec. 17* (Rome, 1955).

47. Achille de Rubertis, "La congiura spagnola contro Venezia nel 1618 secondo i documenti dell'Archivio di Stato in Firenze," *Archivio Storico Italiano*, n.s., 105 (1947): 11–49, 153–67, quotations on 18, 35, and 20, respectively.

48. Alessandro Luzio, *La congiura spagnola contro Venezia nel 1618, secondo i documenti dell'Archivio Gonzaga*, Miscellanea di Storia veneta ed. R. Deputazione di Storia Patria, 3d ser., vol. 13 (Venice, 1918), 12, 23, 47, 49.

49. Trevor-Roper, "Spain and Europe," 275.

50. Cozzi, Knapton, and Scarabello, *La Repubblica di Venezia nell'età moderna*, 101–2. See also Giorgio Fedalto, "Stranieri a Venezia e a Padova, 1550–1700," and Giovanni Scarabello, "Paure, superstizioni, infamie," in Arnaldi and Stocchi, *Storia della cultura veneta*, 4, pt. 2, 167 and 352–54, respectively.

51. Paolo Preto, *I servizi segreti di Venezia* (Milan, 1994), 147–54.

52. Paolo Sarpi, "Scrittura seconda che tratta del titolo del legitimo dominio sopra il Mar Adriatico. 1612, 12 Aprile," in Paolo Sarpi, *Opere*, ed. Gaetano Cozzi and Luisa Cozzi, La Letteratura Italiana, Storia e Testi, 35, Storici, Politici e Moralisti del Seicento, 1 (Milan, 1969), 615–31; see also idem, *De iurisditione ser. reipublicae Venetae in mare Adriaticum* (Eleutheropoli, 1619). See esp. Coniglio, "Il Duca d'Ossuna," 43–52; the quotation is from Coniglio, *Il Viceregno*, 231 n. 34.

53. Raulich, "La congiura spagnuola," 59 n. 1.

54. Tenenti, "La Repubblica di Venezia," 120.

55. On the alleged coup, see Rosario Villari, *La rivolta antispagnola a Napoli: Le*

origini, 1585–1647, 2d ed. (Bari, 1980), 204; on his vulnerability at court, see Ranke, "Die Verschwörung," 223. A recent study by Domenico Ligresti suggests that he had done something to stabilize Sicilian finances ("L'organizzazione militare del Regno di Sicilia [1575–1635]," *Rivista Storica Italiana* 105 [1993]: 647–78). I am most grateful to Anthony Wright for pointing out to me the importance of noble opposition within the viceroyalty.

56. Michelangelo Schipa, "La pretesa fellonia del Duca d'Ossuna (1619–20)," *Archivio Storico per le Provincie Napoletane* 35 (1910): 459–84, 637–60; 36 (1911): 56–85, 286–88; 37 (1912): 211–41, 341–411 [*sic*]; for references to the specific points made here, see 35:462–63, 460, and 36:64.

57. Raulich, "Una relazione del Marchese di Bedmar," 6. I am most grateful to John H. Elliott for information on Bedmar's career after the "conspiracy."

58. *CSPV,* 10:230, no. 353; 279, no. 432; 306, no. 459; 292, no. 443 (in cypher); 308, no. 463.

59. *The Life and Letters of Sir Henry Wotton,* ed. Logan Pearsall Smith, 2 vols. (Oxford, 1907), 1:340.

60. *CSPV,* 10:319, no. 482; 322, no. 486.

61. Bouwsma, *Venice and the Defense of Republican Liberty,* 372.

62. *CSPV,* 10:359–60, no. 532, 14 June 1606; 400, 461; 403–4, no. 583; 439, no. 635.

63. For an English perspective on the position see Simon Adams, "James I, Salisbury, and the Failure of Realpolitik, 1603–1610," ch. 5 of "The Protestant Cause: Religious Alliance with the West European Calvinist Communities as a Political Issue in England, 1585–1630" (D.Phil. thesis, University of Oxford, 1972), 154–82.

64. Wotton to the earl of Salisbury, n.d., sent with a letter of 26 May 1606, in Wotton, *Life and Letters,* 1:350–51.

65. See the superlative edition of Stephanus Junius Brutus, the Celt, *Vindiciae, contra Tyrannos: or, concerning the legitimate power of a prince over the people, and of the people over a prince,* ed. and trans. George Garnett (Cambridge, 1994); for a discussion of Mornay's version, see lv–lviii.

66. Philippe du Plessis Mornay, *Mémoires et correspondance de Duplessis-Mornay,* with notes by A. D. de la Fontenelle de Vaudoré and P. R. Auguis, 10 vols. (Paris, 1824–25), vol. 10, *Ecrits politiques et correspondance, 1604–1610,* 237–38. The pastor referred to was William Bedell, on whom see E. S. Shuckburgh, ed., *Two Biographies of William Bedell, Bishop of Kilmore with a Selection of his Letters and an Unpublished Treatise* (Cambridge, 1902).

67. Mornay, *Mémoires,* 10:240.

68. David de Liques, René Chalopin, and Jules Meslay, *Histoire de la vie de . . . P. de Mornay . . . contenant outre la relation de plusieurs evenements . . . en l'estat . . . divers advis politiqs . . . & militaires sur beaucoup de mouvemens . . . de l'Europe; soubs Henry III. Henry IV. & Louys XIII* (Leiden, 1647), 335–36.

69. Bouwsma, *Venice and the Defense of Republican Liberty,* 506–7.

70. Giovanni Diodati, quoted in E. de Budé, *Vie de Jean Diodati théologien génévois* (Lausanne, 1869), 52–53, 54.

71. Ibid., 58.

72. Sarpi to Jacques Gillot, 12 May 1609, quoted and trans. in Wootton, *Paolo Sarpi,* 119. The whole chapter is tellingly entitled "The Man and his Masks."

73. See, e.g., Bouwsma, *Venice and the Defense of Republican Liberty,* 512–13.

74. Eugenia Levi, "Per la congiura contro Venezia nel 1618: Una 'Relatione' di Fra Paolo Sarpi," *Nuovo Archivio Veneto* 17 (1899) 5–65; Preto, *I servizi segreti di Venezia,* 147 and n. 2.

75. Levi, "La congiura," 60.

76. De Rubertis, "La congiura spagnola," 16, 27; Preto, *I servizi segreti di Venezia,* 147.

77. *Trattato di pace et accommodamento delli moti di guerra eccitati per causa d'Uscochi tra il re Ferdinando di Austria e la Republica di Venezia per fine dell'istoria principiata da Minuccio Minucci arcivescovo di Zara,* in Paolo Sarpi, *La Repubblica di Venezia, la casa d'Austria e gli Uscocchi. Aggionta e supplemento all'istoria degli Uscochi. Trattato di pace et accommodamento,* ed. Gaetano Cozzi and Luisa Cozzi, Scrittori d'Italia, 231 (Bari, 1965), 139–415. The "conspiracy" is described on 291–300. On the history of the text, see the editor's "Nota storica," on 419–24. For examples, not directly related to the "conspiracy," of how Sarpi altered his sources in order to emphasize the need for Venice to take an anti-Spanish stance, see 445–50. See also Paolo Negri, "La politica veneta contro gli Uscocchi in relazione alla congiura del 1618," *Nuovo Archivio Veneto* 17 (1909): 338–84.

78. Sarpi, *La Repubblica di Venezia,* 291.

79. Ibid., 433, 439, 440.

80. Sarpi, *Opere,* 1185–97; the Senate is quoted in the editors' introductory notes, 1183.

81. "The authorship of the *Discorso* which was published anonymously, appears to be exceedingly doubtful," notes Margaret A. Scott in *Elizabethan Translations from the Italian* (Boston, 1916), 285–86. She also provides the following entry: Paolo Sarpi, *A Discourse upon the reasons of the resolution taken in the Valteline against the tyranny of the Grisons and Heretiques,* trans. Sir Thomas Roe (London, 1628). This title is embellished in 1650, when the identical text is published as *The Cruell Subtilty of Ambtoin, discovered in a Discourse concerning the King of Spaines Surprising the Valteline* (London, 1650). *The British Museum General Catalogue of Printed Books* notes under "Valtelline" that "The Discourse which was published anonymously, is certainly not by Sarpi." *The National Union Catalog* notes Dedouvres's attribution of the work to Père Joseph. I am very grateful indeed for the expert guidance to all these references that was generously provided by Jean Archibald, of Edinburgh University Library Special Collections.

82. Sarpi, *A Discourse upon the reasons of the resolution taken in the Valteline* (1628), 5, 55, 73–74.

83. *Advice Given to the Republick of Venice. How they ought to Govern themselves at home and abroad, to have perpetual Dominion. First written in Italian by that Great Politician and Lover of his Countrey, Father PAUL the Venetian, Author of the Council of Trent,* trans. Dr. Aglionby (London, 1693), deriving from the Italian *Opinione falsamente ascritta al Padre Paolo Servita, come debba governarsi internamente, e esternamente la Republica venetiana, per havere il perpetuo dominio. Con la quale si ponderano anco gli interessi di tutti i Prencipi* (Venice, 1685).

84. Ibid., A4v–A5r. I am grateful to Professor Harry Dickinson for the precise identification of Trelawny and Kirke. Remarkably, the assessment foreshadows that of Federico Chabod, *La politica di Paolo Sarpi* (Venice, 1962), 85: "Il *bene comune* è il bene dello Stato . . . e cioè come governo."

85. Bouwsma, *Venice and the Defense of Republican Liberty,* 231.

86. Taylor, *"Next to Shakespeare,"* 263, 266.

Opera, Festivity, and Spectacle in "Revolutionary" Venice

Phantasms of Time and History

MARTHA FELDMAN

As this chapter and the one by Claudio Povolo later in this volume make clear, the sudden capitulation in May 1797 of the Republic of Venice to Napoleon raised important questions for the Venetians about how the old republican aristocratic regime would be understood and remembered. The process of reinterpreting Venice's republican past in light of new circumstances began almost immediately and occurred on many levels. In this chapter Martha Feldman examines how a social space—the La Fenice opera house—and a cultural form—opera seria—both long associated with aristocracy and oligarchy, were reinvented and transformed in the months following the fall of the Republic. The house and operas staged therein proved amazingly elastic as libretti and music that once glorified a patriarchal and absolutist order were reworked to produce a new kind of "happy ending" based on democratic principles. This involved not merely a reworking of the social and political orders but also, as Feldman argues, a reimagining of time and space. In typical fashion Venetians felt that to turn the clock forward, they had to turn it backward, in this case to the period prior to the Serrata of 1297. The creation was a restoration. Feldman underscores the role that mythologizing played not only during the republic but afterward as well and illustrates that in order for Venetians to plot their future, they had to make sense of their past.

IN THE EIGHTEENTH CENTURY Venetian opera was still wedded to the festive machinery that proliferated throughout early modern Italy. The hubbub of sociability that prevailed in commercial theaters, which put opera at center stage during festive seasons of the church calendar, make this evident. Nor is it hard to see the dramaturgy of opera through a festive lens, particularly the dramaturgy of *opera seria,* which glorified the ruling class through its lavish stagings and stories of princely magnanimity.

These phenomena help explain why Venetian nobles sought to resuscitate opera seria just as their aged oligarchy was breathing its last. Nevertheless, to have done so in the 1790s, when numerous voices across Europe had been sounding the case against the festive rites and forms that still dominated eighteenth-century social life, was ironic, since most opera seria plots seized on the dilemmas not of republics but of ancient rulers, whose direct analogue in modern times was the prince. Moreover, "serious" opera was linked with the often raucous atmosphere of Italian theaters, theaters caught in contradictions that became ever more obvious as the century wore on: the time of Carnival, when theater had its principal season, implied hierarchy inverted, yet opera seria served up tales of absolutist hierarchies with the prince indisputably at their top; Carnival implied that time would change, even as seria's narratives claimed that history was fixed unto eternity; and while the practices of Carnival remained fraught with pagan symbols, seria libretti proposed ruling monarchs as agents of a Christian god.[1] These disjunctions were just a few of the reasons why later-eighteenth-century reformers denigrated the institution of opera seria in favor of more compatibility between the content of opera and its function—between propositions made onstage and offstage conditions—and why ultimately they found fissures in the very premises of opera seria.

All the same, festivity and spectacle remained deeply rooted in the practices of commercial Italian institutions wherever opera seria was produced, tied, if elusively, to the mystifications of absolutist power that opera seria elaborated and the illusions of an august eternal present that such power presupposed. Conditions in late-eighteenth-century Venice elaborated below reveal something of how these ties were maintained in a crumbling old political order and how the same festive practices that had long been integral to it could later be exploited (much as in revolutionary France) in a purportedly antiabsolutist project. This is the story of a festive theater created within an "absolutist oligarchy" and its subsequent remaking under the auspices of a provisional "democracy."

STRUCTURE AND EVENT

In 1792 a society of Venetian nobles founded a new theater devoted to the (by then) old institution of opera seria, the *nobilissimo* Teatro La Fenice. At a time when both opera seria and the Venetian oligarchy that called upon it were fast fading, La Fenice conjured up a lavish emblem of old aristocratic pride. The

Society of La Fenice sponsored an architectural competition to construct the theater and embarked on an elaborate building program. The finished edifice was the third largest theater in Venice, edged out only by the theaters of San Luca and San Giovanni Grisostomo, and indisputably the most elegant.[2] Nobles who bought boxes paid dearly to cover singers' fees, opulent productions, and amortization costs of construction and furnishing. In return they spent festive seasons amid sumptuous appointments and stagings that attested their supremacy as uniquely independent, a republic still ruled by indigenous nobles on a peninsula swollen with foreign despots.[3]

But the moment was fragile. The republic, once robust and imperial, had long since melted into spectral monumentality, a shadowy relic made of myth and spectacle. When it fell to Napoleonic forces on 12 May 1797, it was as a result not of invasion at home but of succumbing to ultimatums it was too weak to refuse.[4]

Such a turn of events was not unexpected, since Napoleon had been pressing his armies into Lombardy and the Veneto *terraferma* for many months. By mid-April he had occupied Milan, Brescia, Mantua, and Bergamo, among other towns. Though Venice was still far from Napoleon's grasp, two events took place thereafter that quickly spelled Venice's tactical doom. Around Easter French troops in Verona were attacked in repeated popular uprisings, uprisings that the French claimed were provoked by Venetian hostilities and that caused serious losses of French soldiers. Days afterwards a French lugger was sunk in the port of Venice. Already provoked—or feigning provocation—Napoleon reacted to the last with demands that the Venetians abdicate their oligarchy or face war, a war Venice was totally unprepared to sustain. The nobles whose ancestors had collectively run the republic for a millennium saved the city and themselves from destruction by handing it over to the French, an act of cowardice by feudal standards but one of prudence by established Venetian mores of practical wisdom and reverence for the city.[5]

Since Venice had been the supreme icon of oligarchic independence for longer than any other major state on the Continent, the fall of the republic carried a distinct symbolic currency in the redistribution of power taking place across Europe even though its practical implications were negligible. It was a powerful sign of the times, of a new era when time itself would be remapped and reimagined; and it was precisely in this reimagining that La Fenice took center stage. No other new institution so visibly condensed and reiterated the symbols of elite and everlasting oligarchic power. Yet a terrible paradox lay waiting to be exploited, for in the wake of the fall the same monument that had served to enshrine patrician status through the pliable media of opera seria could easily be co-opted once the old order and premises were no longer in place. This was the tactic of the new regime, which quickly appropriated La Fenice to its own ends, transforming opera seria by borrowing its meanings while inverting many of them. By asserting that the allegedly indestructible old republic was vulnerable and suspect, the new regime also proposed time anew; a previously timeless past became the burden of a problematic history.

The significance of such views—and the susceptibility of opera seria to transmute at the hands of its co-opters—yield themselves only on close analysis of various events that took place in Venice between May and October 1797. I use the word *events* pointedly, for these were such in the bona fide sense distinguished by narrative historians: they were disruptions to the normal flow of activity, bringing frailties in existing forms and ideologies of social life to a visible surface. And yet, as William H. Sewell Jr. has recently written, "the uncertainty of structural relations that characterizes events can stimulate bursts of collective cultural creativity" and thus ultimately lead to important cultural transformations.[6] So it was in Venice, where the fall of the republic brought about decisive revisions to numerous institutions, political and cultural, of which theater was but a single, if highly condensed, example. In this spirit I examine events here as part of a historical category, capable of revealing fault lines in the premises and sociabilities of eighteenth-century festivity as evinced at La Fenice even as they affirmed the resilience of the theater's festive practices.

Ultimately the phenomenon of opera seria in 1797 raises two central questions: first, how a monument of the old order could be transformed in the face of new premises and a new regime; and second, how a project devoted to consolidating patrician identity could fall prey, at the moment of its ruin, to new fantasies of identity, new narratives of history, and new instruments of power.

FROM ITS INCEPTION La Fenice was intended as a shrine to the elite classes, the most deluxe of Venice's theaters and the only one exclusively given over to opera seria. Erection of the theater took all the membership's considerable clout, financial and political.[7] Among other obstacles, a sumptuary decree of 1756 had prohibited building new theaters beyond the seven that already existed, principally because competition among them had reached detrimental levels. Furthermore, houses needed to be demolished in the area of San Fantin, where the theater was to be erected, and some owners asked exorbitant prices for them. Then, too, this came at precisely the moment in the republic's history

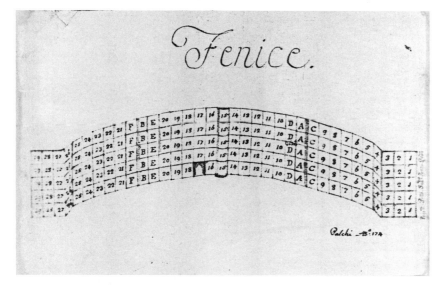

FIG. 1. Eighteenth-century plan of the Teatro La Fenice, Museo Civico Correr, Venice. Reproduced by permission.

when the numbers of nobility had declined sharply, governmental funds were most depleted, noble offices remained unfilled for lack of noble bodies, and trade had severely diminished.[8] Yet in 1787 the Society easily succeeded in having the decree in question waived and its petition for an eighth theater approved by the Council of Ten.[9]

Surviving lists of boxholders reveal that members of the Society (as constituted through ownership of boxes) came overwhelmingly from the local nobility and secondarily from the haute bourgeoisie.[10] Of the five tiers of boxes that were ultimately built, the bottom three bore the greatest concentration of nobles, in keeping with customs elsewhere (see Fig. 1).[11] The second tier, the so-called *primo ordine,* housed exclusively nobles, save in one box. Twenty-six nobles held boxes in the *pepian* (the bottommost tier of the theater), eighteen in the *secondo ordine* (third tier), six in the *terzo ordine* (fourth tier), and two in the *quarto ordine* (fifth tier). In each of the first three tiers exactly five of the noble families came not from the ranks of old nobility, those whose noble status was conferred with the *Serrata* of 1297, but from families newly added to the *Libro d'Oro,* mostly in the mid-seventeenth century.[12] A number of bourgeoisie also bought their way into the lower tiers, although most of them were steered into the slightly less desirable pepian (where eight boxes were owned by bour-

geoisie) and secondo ordine (where there were fourteen).[13] Such a mix made
up the Society's central power base from its inception, as reflected in the four or
five noble and bourgeois "presidents" who ran it at any given time throughout
the 1790s.[14]

Once the theater got under way it was intermittently plagued with serious
financial difficulties, the most notorious of which led in 1793–94 to the dis-
missal of the impresario Michele Dall'Agata (who subsequently poisoned himself at the end of the Carnival season).[15] Setbacks, material or otherwise, did not
discourage the Society's policies of extravagance, however. Dall'Agata's successor, Onorato Viganò, began his term with a contract that mandated an
elaborate annual cycle of operas and ballets.[16] Four opere serie were to be given
each year—one in Autumn, two at Carnival, and one during Ascension. Two
ballets were always to be inserted between the three acts, and all operas were to
be new except possibly that for Autumn, which was an abbreviated season
owing to the nobles' late return from summer villeggiature. Of the two ballets,
one was always to be of a "carattere serio." The other could be of "mezzo
carattere, ma non mai basso, nè indecente," and hence potentially less extravagant, and both were always to be premiered at the same time as the operas with
which they were paired. All ballets were to be magnificent, "corrispondente
alla Nobiltà, e grandezza del Teatro," with lighting, scenery, and costumes to
match and without ever stooping to the "mockable" stage effects of artificial
animals and the like. The orchestra too was to be choice so as to match the
"grandezza del Teatro" and the composer "di conosciuta riputazione," like the
composer of music for the ballets.

The theater's showy image, heralding its aristocratic, old-world conservatism, did not go unremarked by local observers. Reviewers for the Gazzetta
Urbana Veneta repeatedly noted the "pompa delle decorazioni" and the "sempre
gran gente" who populated the theater.[17] In the years leading up to 1797 pomp
and luxury extended to the repertory, which was heavily Metastasian: Alessandro nell'Indie was performed in Autumn 1792, Antigono for Ascension 1794
and Achille in Sciro the following Autumn, both Artaserse and Demofoonte in
Autumn 1795, and Issipile in Autumn 1796.[18]

Conservatism at La Fenice was of a markedly Venetian kind, however.
Unlike many theaters in eighteenth-century Italy, La Fenice had no royal or
ducal box. Even though class stratifications were palpable across its hierarchized
tiers of boxes, the theater's semiotics bespoke dispersal, not centralization. Nor
were the most coveted boxes massed together in given tiers: evidently, levies
imposed on boxes were based as much on the desirability of the sight lines they

provided as on the visibility of their positions within the hall.[19] Such were the economies of oligarchic republicanism.

B Y D A Y 5 after the fall, however, in "Year One of Italian Liberty," oligarchic republicanism was to be deemed no republicanism at all. On that day the new provisional municipal government announced its division into various committees, staffed by natives but designed to mimic those of the French revolutionary government and overseen by watchful leaders of the French garrison. Among these, the Committee of Public Instruction, whose Venetian officers included some of the liveliest, and most rabid, sympathizers with the French, was to manage the moral and educational program of the new order. Central to its goals was the organization of a zealous educational program designed to inculcate new "democratic" precepts while insisting on a total break with the past. To that end the committee installed orators in every campo to teach the tenets of democracy, extended the hours of the public library, eliminated various forms of aristocratic "vanity" (by simplifying public uniforms and the like), supervised the publication in Italian and dialect of tracts by Rousseau, Thomas Paine, and other enlightened "democrats," as well as the publication of various democratic constitutions from abroad, published the minutes of its open sessions, organized public festivals, and posted endless decrees on matters moral, from prostitution to domestic life, schooling, and church. They also quickly adopted the revolutionary clocks and calendar of the French, which had been authorized in France by the National Convention of the French Revolution three and a half years earlier as a way of rupturing any symbolic, and especially Christian, connections to the old Gregorian calendar. In this way timekeeping under the new system was intended not just to replace the church's real and implicit social controls with the secular controls of government—the new arbiter of nationhood—but to do so through the highly rationalized French decimal system, which counted all weeks, hours, and minutes in tens and emphasized seasonal connections to agriculture in ways intended to make the new calendar seem natural and inevitable.[20]

Yet these strategies of change did not relinquish festive models of old; rather, much like the French—indeed prodded by them—the new municipal government appropriated festivity to instruct the masses in the new ideals. A central instrument of their democratic propaganda was the theater. Not only did the Committee of Public Instruction field all petitions from theaters regarding rules of management and assume the role of political censor, previously the role of the Inquisitori di Stato; it also became involved directly and centrally in the

establishment of a theater for the "common people," a class more or less com-
mensurate with the *popolani,* which did not categorically dissolve with the fall
of the oligarchy but hardened into a totem to be worshipped in the more
flattering arena of revolutionary drama.[21] Indeed, a statement by the committee
addressed to authors of theatrical works, directors of troupes, and impresarios
made explicit its role vis-à-vis a theater of the people: "One of the principal
objects of Public Instruction must be theater. The performances done in it are
sometimes more efficacious than laws. To change the spirit of a people abased
by long slavery, to inspire a salutary honor by great delights, to light the sacred
fire of liberty—these must be the principal aims of tragic works; just as enlightening the people, refining the Nation, and correcting it of its habits must be
those of the painter of true comedy."[22]

OPENING THE ASCENSION SEASON IN ''DEMOCRATIC'' VENICE

Since the Committee of Public Instruction constituted the prime organ of
theatrical propaganda, it also adjudicated the reopening of La Fenice for the
impending Ascension season. Just days after the republic collapsed, the then
impresario Alberto Cavos began negotiating with the committee in a series of
petitions. The first opera planned was a revival of *Gli Orazi e i Curiazi,* with
libretto by the Paduan lawyer Antonio Simeone Sografi and music by Domenico Cimarosa, a shocker in the genre of the *tragedia per musica* that had premiered during the previous Carnival. As a revival, *Gli Orazi* was easy enough
to mount in a time of such chaos, but the question which ballets were to be
inserted between its acts still had to be decided. Even though time constraints
induced the committee to give permission for a ballet called *Il Cesare nelle
Gallie,* it worried lest people assume that the ballet had passed governmental
inspection. Therefore, it ordered that the title *Riconciliazione degli Edui* be
used in place of the proposed one so as to avoid any "inappropriate allusion"
(though neither title appears in the published libretto).[23] Similar quandaries
beset permissions for the opera, since there was no time to order changes in
it either if the theater was to open on schedule. To circumvent the whole
problem the committee directed on 19 May that a note be inserted in the
libretto indicating that neither opera nor ballet had been revised owing to lack
of time.[24]

The messages projected by the works onstage were not the only matters
plaguing the reopening of the theater. The running of the Ascension season,

for which preparations at La Fenice were already under way, had to be accommodated to new procedures of which the management was totally uncertain; for despite the continuities that sustained La Fenice as the theater of the elite, the collapse of the oligarchy had fractured a potentially vast range of cultural mechanisms, if not all of its systems of belief, and virtually all modes of finance, management, and power hung in a state of structural uncertainty. Many questions related directly to theater management since, as elsewhere, the practices of running the theater were bound up with local ideologies.

On Day 6, "Year One of Italian Liberty," Cavos began forwarding a string of queries and petitions to the Committee of Public Instruction. He petitioned on Day 7 to open the following evening but needed advice on rules—on masking by theatergoers, when to start the show, whether ministers of foreign courts were to pay at the door, how to treat infractions, how to make financial deposits, and many others he could not yet think to name.[25]

That same day an anonymous official of the committee jotted down a checklist of demands made and met, numbering five in all.[26] The theater, he noted, had been given permission to open, and the libretto and ballet programs had been cleared. Deposits were to be made to the Committee of Finance. Dedications, now the blight of an older patronage system, were forbidden in libretti. And a plan was to be instituted for producing patriotic arias. All demands had been met save the last, "ancora non eseguita."

Since La Fenice was prized as cultural capital, the Committee of Public Instruction succumbed to reviving as the season opener *Gli Orazi ed i Curiazi,* which had triumphed in the previous Carnival season and could be staged virtually unchanged and hence with little delay. Permission was granted for an opening on 20 May, though it was finally delayed until the twenty-first.[27]

Paradoxically *Gli Orazi* offered a fanatical defense of the old patriarchal political order even as it radically demystified through a particularly bloody ending its allegorical assurances of a happy outcome. In Sografi's libretto the Roman Orazio kills off his Alban foe Curiazio, member of an old enemy nation, in a duel designed to settle a war between the nations. But Curiazio is beloved of, and newly husband to, Orazio's sister Orazia. When Orazia in her mad grief denounces Orazio's would-be "valor" before a great crowd of citizens and curses Rome, her brother stabs her and hurls her down a flight of stairs.

Death onstage was still a relatively new phenomenon in Italian theaters, and the murder audiences witnessed here surpassed all precursors not only in intensity but in defying the principle of familial loyalty common to Settecento stageworks, whose endings had generally reconciled the exigencies of familial ties with principles of loyalty to the state.[28] Furthermore, Orazio's double transgression—forcing fratricide before the delicate eyes of eighteenth-century spectators (onstage and off) and wresting judicial power from the state to mete out punishment—meets with mixed responses within the opera's own narrative. The father of the Orazi and Orazio's wife Sabina (also sister to Curiazio) react with horror to Orazio's monstrous act, his contempt for family bonds, and his defiance of public process. But their voices are nearly drowned by a sea of public praise: by those of the Roman senators and populace cheering Orazio for loyalty to the state, as if the solo voices of Orazio and Sabina were no match for the grand choruses of the vox populi. *Gli Orazi* thus opened a subversive chink in the heroic Metastasian armor of nobility even as it claimed to perpetuate the trope of Roman valor that had traditionally been purveyed by the aristocracy. It is unclear how many performances of *Gli Orazi* took place, but in the eyes of French sympathizers its importance surely paled beside that of the second opera for Ascension, *La morte di Mitridate*,[29] based on a libretto written the previous year for Vicenza and Trieste.[30] Again the librettist, and this time also the reviser, was Sografi, by now the leading author of Jacobin stage rhetoric.[31]

Sografi had already honed a protorevolutionary style in spoken drama and in the bloody new operatic genre of tragedia per musica, of which he had been the prime practitioner throughout the 1790s.[32] After Venice fell, he pursued a frenzy of projects toward the installation of a popular "democratic" theater. Among his first tasks was to write what he called an *azione teatrale,* for the benefit of the "popolo," based on the Serrata of 1297 and the abortive plot of 1310 to topple the oligarchy, which was to serve as the main fare for a new civic theater. In Sografi's construction the Serrata, which had stood for centuries as the definitive event in the formation of the oligarchy, had been consolidated shortly after its occurrence by the failed attempt to overthrow it in 1310, to be reversed only after five hundred years in 1797. Replying to the Committee of Public Instruction on 23 May, Sografi borrowed the new antiaristocratic rhetoric of clipped propositions to affirm to his fellow "Cittadini" the vitality of a project that sought to discredit the aristocracy on the theatrical stage. One salient justification for his project was that theater had been the abiding "pulpit of the great French." "Can you," he urged,

> intent on the good of the people, with your constant concern, forget that at such a moment? [Within the theater] it is time for the voices of Liberty and Equality to sound again; there it is necessary for the People to obtain knowledge of their rights—usurped, reviled, abused; there . . . but this is not the moment to discuss: it is time to resolve. The undertaking is a difficult one with the time constraints,

but liberty has its miracles. Witness: shrink back; make up your minds. The uniting of the two epochs would be of no little instruction to the people. I speak of the closing of the Maggior Consiglio in 1296 and of the Conspiracy of Bajamonte in 1310. These two deeds united would form an Azione Teatrale, Democratic.[33]

In a follow-up letter on his progress, Sografi claimed to be treating his subject "popolarmente, *ad utilitatem* e non *ad pumpam,*" in such a way that his play would show the people that they were regaining what five hundred years ago they had lost and why they had great reason to be happy.[34] As a venue for Sografi's "Teatrale Patriotico" (so called by the new government) the committee had selected the Teatro San Giovanni Grisostomo, owned by Virginia Chigi Grimani, a theater larger but less richly appointed than La Fenice. Grimani was asked to relinquish it throughout the whole summer season so that it could be made into a popular patriotic theater, the site of the so-called Teatro Civico.

It may be useful to review the process by which such a theater was founded, since it was a matter of strenuous concern to the Committee of Public Instruction, which devoted much time in its initial planning sessions to urgent discussions over its location and mien. Already on 21 and 22 May, in reviewing plans for an imminent public *festa* ordered by the president of the Municipalità Provvisoria, Nicolò Corner, the matter of a popular theater had become paramount. In requesting a report from the committee Corner had stressed that the reason a special festa was needed was to "animate the people," adding that it was "necessary to do so with public spectacles" and furthermore that "a patriotic meal . . . decreed by law" had in any case already been linked to the occasion.

It seems that in settling on a "Festa in Teatro gratis al popolo" as part of the proposed plans committee members had first recommended La Fenice as the obvious site, only to deem it inappropriate once their discussions turned from the question of a one-time event to a broader proposal for an ongoing popular theater. All agreed that it was useful to promote public spirit through festivity, but one member argued successfully that on a daily basis a comic theater would please the general populace better than would La Fenice, whose repertory had always consisted entirely of opera seria.[35] Ironically, in the delirious first weeks after the fall it was these discussions that led to the simultaneous founding of the Teatro Civico within the old Teatro San Giovanni Grisostomo[36] and the targeting of La Fenice to be symbolically purged of oligarchic evils in the public festa of 28 May.

Rejecting La Fenice as the regular theater of the masses and commandeer-

FIG. 2. Engraving of the "Festa in Teatro gratis al popolo," held at La Fenice, 28 May 1797, Museo Civico Correr, Venice. Reproduced by permission.

ing it instead to fuel fantasies of revolution whose valences could match the theater's social register, the Committee of Public Instruction succumbed to its mystique as a "nobilissimo teatro." While San Giovanni Grisostomo would be turned into the people's theater, La Fenice was to be the arena of exultant bourgeoisie, humbled ex-patriciates, new government officials, French officers, and prestigious visitors, its noble character called upon to embellish the magnificence of the new regime. To this end the management had to hand over for regular use by French officials and members of the provisional government six boxes in the lower tiers that had traditionally been reserved for ministers of foreign courts.[37] In summertime, moreover, it became the site of thirty special performances ordered by the French to celebrate the arrival of Bonaparte. For these the genres remained the *dramma serio* and the *tragedia per musica*, thus assigning the French a luminous position in the present by allowing them to appropriate the symbolic space of its timeless past.

Meanwhile, La Fenice's impresario was busy arranging the free "Festa in Teatro" for the popolo. When the evening of 28 May arrived, an onstage orchestra played revolutionary songs and hymns to accompany workmen, gondoliers, and other popolani who danced on the stage dressed in three-cornered hats.[38] Behind them streamed liberty banners and French flags in red, white, and green, and in the midst of it all stood a liberty pole crowned with the Phrygian cap, ancient symbol of freedom from slavery. The event was commemorated with an engraving, now in the Museo Correr, that shows a stage bedecked with winged cupids and statues of Liberty carrying tribunes aloft (Fig. 2): "Il Popolo viviano riconoscente verso il suo liberatore," "La virtù e il carattere d'un popolo veramente libero," "Virtù e indivisibilità della repubblica italica," "Viva il Bravo General Commandante Baragras d'Illiers," "La Uguaglianza [e] la Libertà formano la Felicità de' Popoli," "Viva la Brava Armata Francese in Italia," "La Democrazia è l'Impero della Ragione." A campaign was in full swing to exalt the French as redeemers of justice and liberty and to propose festivity in a new light, not as a privilege bestowed by benevolent autocrats but as a fruit of revolution and individual sovereignty.[39]

In all of this, members of the committee imagined themselves as agents, acting upon the realm of cultural production toward social change. Forgetful of their puppeteers on high, they believed in their power to shape values, symbols, and rules of culture as the French had done, and they appealed to their most skilled rhetoricians to furnish the same textual force and "unity" that marked revolution in France.[40]

16 PRATILE (4 JUNE)

Originally the festivities of 28 May were to commemorate the change of government as part of a large complex of spectacles designed to encompass the whole city, solemnly joined together to celebrate its newfound liberty. But the vision of the Committee of Public Instruction, working with and, albeit semi-invisibly, under the French, had grown. In addition, rains had come, and in view of the elaborate preparations planned for the piazza it was necessary to put the event off for a week.[41] As it turned out, 28 May was a minor preamble to the ambitious festival that finally took place on Pentecost, the following Sunday, 4 June.

When the day arrived, piazza San Marco was strung with banners proclaiming peace and liberty through the strong arm of the law. Three tribunes bore the slogans "Liberty is preserved by obeying the laws," "Dawning liberty is protected by force of arms," and "Established liberty brings about universal peace," and the motto "Regenerated peace" was ubiquitous.[42] Again, a liberty pole topped with a Phrygian cap stood high in the center of it all. The piazza reverberated with the din of four huge bands and received a vast train of "liberated" "citizens" who processed twice around the piazza to the sound of the bands' thunder. At the head of the procession were members of the Municipality and the commander of the French garrison, Baraguey d'Hilliers. Following them were two children holding lighted candles and a banner with the words "Grow up, hope of the fatherland," succeeded by an engaged couple whose banner read "Democratic fecundity." Next came an elderly couple, who carried farming tools and "words alluding to their advanced age, at which time liberty was instituted,"[43] and lastly the national guard, foreign consuls, guilds, and civil servants.

The processions culminated in a variety of rituals performed by the new president of the "sovereign People of Venice," Angelo Talier, at the center of the square, where the tree of liberty was erected. The central image of the festival was that of regeneration, an image metaphorized through rebirth, fruitfulness, fertility, and productivity and symbolized by the tree of liberty, with its links to the earth, life, growth, and nature. Extending the metaphor of regeneration, the speech recited by the president at the crux of the ceremony elided nature's progenitors and progeny: wind, sun, and rain; temperance, health, and learning.

> In the replanting that is solemnly and festively carried out, this prosperous plant, oh Venetian Men (as the Athenian democrats in another age called themselves), brought to my mind the charming images of the poet Catullus: the zephyrs caress it, the sun strengthens it, the rain makes it grow and nourishes it.
>
> Tempered social passions are the caressing breezes, exertion adapted to robust people hardens it, just as (conversely) softness and luxury stunt it; finally the rain of manly and healthy education makes it thrive.[44]

Even as Talier called on the tropes of solidarity, fellowship, and harmony, perceptible in the symbols and referents they conjured up were two nearly contradictory rhetorics. Beginning with the more familiar of them, the president retooled longstanding Venetian mythologies of civic virtue by linking the tree to traditional Venetian virtues of goodness, moderation, wisdom, and justice. The tree, he declared, was a native son of Venice, as topographic entity if not as symbolic genus, for Venice had been settled long before by uncompromising lovers of liberty and equality, who prized those gifts over the more material ones of Ceres: "Remember that such a precious plant is not something exotic but indigenous and suited to this fortunate soil. Our Venice was born over there in the Rialto; she dispersed herself in these estuaries, shelter and refuge of a few poor people, but lovers of liberty, equality, and goodness, who, animated by the fire of virtue, preferred true equality and liberty to every other comfort and pleasure, succumbing even to the lack of salubrious waters and vegetated earth from which to procure the gifts of Ceres." Venetians' insistence on liberty, even at the expense of physical rewards, had made for resistance to invasion: that, so Talier claimed, was Venice's native "plant," its true nature, the fruits of which he called "incessant activity, military courage, industry in trades, growth of commerce, and a navy formidable for those times."[45]

In the latter half of his speech the president praised the French while turning to a new rhetoric of sacrifice tinged with violence—one that had developed in the climate of revolutionary France and found its way into Venetian rhetoric as a mere borrowing.[46] "History," Talier went on, "that portrayer of human actions, bears witness [to the consequences of a passion for liberty], so that when joining your forces with those of the magnanimous French troops whom we honor here, not to mention memorable feats of yours, and [who] with their hand and with counsel sustain us, you would topple the already degenerated eastern empire." In the spirit of sacrifice the Empire, glory and honor of Venice in times past, had to be forfeited. Such was the message that had already been disseminated in numerous broadsides and pamphlets, including an attempt of 23 May to herald the forthcoming festivities, which located them in the linguistic domain of the sacred: "Our regeneration must be celebrated with the *solemn happiness* of a people returned to their rights. The day destined for the erection of the *sacred Tree of liberty* will be a day of joy for all true citizens, who may begin to live the worthy life of man, and it will be a monument of gratitude to our descendants, who will *bless the generosity of France*. The Municipality is setting up a Spectacle *consecrated to Liberty*."[47]

We must not forget that amid this heady rhetoric of liberty and equality Venice was undergoing the trauma of occupation, a trauma that had ruptured for the first time in its history the mythology evoked at the beginning of the president's speech. Because of this, its myth of origins now had to be summoned up as a victory over homegrown Venetian tyranny, as a guarantee against internal affliction and a testimonial of innate redemptive power.[48] A hymn sung in dialect reviled the despotic bonds that had lacerated the people and praised those who had made them reborn.[49] All of this naturalized an event that was extraordinary—the demise of Venetian sovereignty—suggesting that the French were merely there to guide them from their degenerated oligarchic state back to their true natural origins.

Indeed, the president's reference to the French was prelude to a set of culminating rites of particular symbolic weight, what in a proclamation of 31 May were explicitly named "sacrifices," designed to ritualize the final destruction

232 ～ MARTHA FELDMAN

of the oligarchy.[50] The language of violent overthrow was of course merely
mimetic since Venice had barely any military forces at all and had not joined
them concretely with those of the French.[51] Yet through such rhetoric mythologies of Venetian freedom and impenetrability to invasion that had sustained Venice for a millennium could be recast as a triumph over Venice's
native oppression. The speech culminated in a sacrifice of particular symbolic
weight, the burning of the *Libro d'Oro*—lone symbol of the aristocratic body
and a highly fetishized object—and of the ducal insignia. The significance of
the former to the nobility was matched by the significance to the populace of
expunging the highly visible doge's crown, an object it would have witnessed at
every prior procession in the square. Designed to ritualize the final destruction
of the oligarchy,[52] the two were turned to ash as the president made the following appeal: "May the vain and imposing titles scatter themselves to the winds—
veils with which ineptitude largely wished to cover itself and other depraved
vices of the mind and good morals. May perfidy and political suspicion stay far
from us forever, which, after having imposed on us the hateful and detestable
aristocratic yoke, removed our calm of spirit with the fear of hired spies, with
the example of insulting ostentation, of depraved softness, and of their private
discords, and made us torpid and nearly paralyzed with the sweet sentiments of
brotherly philanthropy."[53]

With the burning of the *Libro d'Oro,* which listed members of the noble
rank and file along with the ducal insignia, the old Venice of 1297–1797 was
surrendered, its most exalted members symbolically destroyed to appease and
empower the moral and political forces of the new. From such an offering a
new Venice was to rise, transformed, from the ashes of the old. The (feminine)
"softness" of aristocratic vanity and luxury would be turned into the manly
hardness of democratic industry.[54] Signs of despotism condensed in aristocratic
symbols were dispersed, scattered by the beneficent winds of nature that had
stood by Venice since its inception and were to be its savior. In this way they
would "come back to their land of origin,"[55] the untamed Venice of times past.
The president returned to the naturalistic theme of the sacred tree of liberty,
enjoining the populace to sing hymns to the nation of Italy and the heroes of
France. Now, however, the tree was articulated with the specter of death:

> Having sung hymns of praise and paid adoring tribute to the highest Creator
> and Governor of all beings—who by unexpected paths wanted to make bloom
> among us the precious plant of mislaid Liberty and fraternal Equality—pervaded
> with true jubilation, drunk with internal joy, we all cry out in a full voice: "Long

live the first Nation of the universe, Long live the heroes of France, lightnings of war, who without shedding a drop of blood here among us, knew how to break our harsh bonds, who have regenerated us, and with the mirror of their virtue plant on this day the most happy vegetation that can take root, to the profit and relief of miserable humanity." People of Venice, sovereign People, vested with a new nature, engrave in your mind and, most piously, in your heart this golden motto: "Democracy, or death." I have spoken.[56]

Having staged these outdoor festivities, French and municipal authorities proceeded to an exclusive gala performance at La Fenice of Sografi's *La morte di Mitridate,* as set by Nicola Zingarelli, the second opera of the Ascension season and, unlike *Gli Orazi,* well honed, at least in crucial parts, to the new ideologies.[57] Thus ended the day, marked by an ironic cleavage in vertical class relations that could only have reminded observant commoners of what the previous Sunday of populist festivity had urged them to forget. Yet the two events—popular ceremonies and elitist opera—shared a common set of themes and symbols that illuminate the situation into which La Fenice, as a temple of opera seria, had been enigmatically thrust.

LA MORTE DI MITRIDATE

"Democracy, or death": this was a duality thematized in numerous, often bizarre variations throughout La Fenice seasons in which the municipal government reigned. Like the festivities of 4 June, the three operas put on for the rest of the spring and summer seasons all tacitly claimed sacrifice as the basis of sovereignty, and not by accident. We might identify two forgers of such a proposition, suggestive and ambiguous though it sometimes was. First was the chief librettist of the time, Sografi, whose revolutionary sympathies had already capsized the absolutist trope of the *lieto fine* in earlier libretti composed for La Fenice and elsewhere. Under the guidance of the French and the short-lived democratic government, Sografi's new texts shattered oligarchic axioms by turning those sympathies to tales of violent release from tyranny. Sografi was on hand to revise *Mitridate* and almost undoubtedly both of the libretti for the summer season that followed (only one of which was his own). But he would not have done so without direction from the provisional government and the French who oversaw it, who collectively formed the prime instrument behind La Fenice's sudden new representations of freedom and violent rebellion against tyranny.[58]

La morte di Mitridate was first set by Sebastiano Nasolini for the summer of

1796 in Vicenza, where the French had arrived the previous April, and was then restaged the following autumn at Trieste.[59] The principal difference between the story told at both Vicenza and Trieste and that told at Venice entailed the extent of the choruses and, most importantly, the nature of the ending. In two acts, the opera is set in the city of Nymphaeum, on the Black Sea, in the second century B.C. Both versions turn on a central problem involving an attempt by Farnace, son of the tyrannical king of Pontus, Mitridate, to usurp the throne from his brother Zifare at a moment when King Mitridate is believed to have died in battle against the Romans and to make the young Vonima his queen. Vonima is betrothed to Mitridate but has given her heart to Zifare, prince of Cochlis and hence rightful heir to Pontus, in the wake of Mitridate's presumed death. When Mitridate unexpectedly returns from triumphant battle, Vonima and Zifare are forced into an impossible impasse that is resolved only by Mitridate's suicide in act 2.

According to Sografi's directions, the opera opened to reveal upstage, at increasing perspectival depths, a portico opening onto Mitridate's palace, the buildings of Nymphaeum, and behind them the Caucasus Mountains.[60] Closer to the proscenium the stage was marked by a prophetic partition: on the right, a temple of Venus, readied for wedding festivities; and on the left, a mausoleum for the funeral of Mitridate. As a chorus of subjects urged the populace to celebrate the marriage, Zifare appeared mourning at the mausoleum, outraged at the insult to Mitridate's honor (though as yet unaware that the would-be bride was his beloved Vonima). Inflecting this scene was a repertory of forms and symbols drawn from imaginary pagan ritual; hence the procession of a wedding party from Mitridate's palace included "pompously" dressed guards, the sacrificer of Juno, four priests, and a group of four *donzelle* (girls) dedicated to Venus, followed by Vonima draped in an ancient virgin's veil.

The spatialized stage served as a kind of primeval dais for the scenic tableaux with which the opera began and by which its development was plotted throughout. The effect must have been part elegiac, part celebratory, and thoroughly monumental. In keeping with this, the final redaction of the musical score rendered scenes as seamlessly as possible, with a minimum of simple recitative, an abundance of dramatic obbligato, and maximum continuity between set numbers, orchestral interludes, recitatives, and choruses, even introducing unconventional interpolations by individual characters or choral groups.

Such a dynamic dramaturgy could serve to release the libretto's mounting emotional charge, particularly once the plot thickened with the appearance of a disheveled Mitridate in act 1, scene 3. Mitridate's return makes the "Freudian" dimensions of the family drama loom large since the first thing he learns is that his sons have been vying for Vonima in his absence.[61] One son has forced her hand in his bid to usurp the throne and, with it, the father's power, while the other has conquered her heart. But both, in stalking their father's prey, incur his fury, and in the remainder of act 1 Mitridate is racked by wrath and suspicion.

Nevertheless, by act 1, scene 3, the evil Farnace is all but forgotten, and Mitridate can subsequently appear as the emoting sovereign, saddened by his sons' desertions and insisting on true love from Vonima in place of her dutiful assents to wedlock (1.8). This was a reversion to the old prototype of the feeling tyrant and to an amorous superplot, here dominated by the triangle of Mitridate, Vonima, and Zifare. As such it did little harm to the new political agenda the opera was destined to project and meant that much of Sografi's original 1796 story could therefore be left standing.

Indeed, not only the libretto but also the music would have had to be revised. Zingarelli's autograph, now in the Archivio Storico Ricordi, Milan, leaves little doubt that the composer had already been at work on the score for a good month or more, setting a version of the libretto close to the Vicenza/ Trieste version, when the republic collapsed.[62] His score adds a fascinating component to the cultural transformations precipitated by the changed political situation since it had to reflect what was fit for the new patriotic stage, or at least what could, and could not, be tolerated.

Evidently neither the management nor the authorities were prepared to have all of Zingarelli's work redone when the republic collapsed. The love intrigues of the somewhat banal first act remained mostly unchanged, easing the task of staging the opera in time for the 4 June celebrations.[63] With the second act things proceeded differently, since Sografi and the committee cared above all how the mechanics of resolution would work upon the sense of an ending. Before the opera opened, numerous alterations changed or eliminated portions of act 2 that most contradicted the new social order (see table 1). In Sografi's Vicenza/Trieste version Mitridate represented the same benign and malleable tyrant encountered in act 1, a figure who could realize his true inner core over narrative time through the indulgence of obsequious subjects. He was a variant of the benevolent despot (familiar from the 1767 libretto of Cigna-Santi set most famously by Mozart for Milan in 1770), whose ultimately redemptive nature served to pacify potential evil in the imaginings of the absolutist body politic. (The initial and ultimate stages of Zingarelli's work on act 2 can be compared in the schematic digest given in table 1.)

TABLE I

Reconstruction of Compositional Stages of La morte di Mitridate, Act 2 (Venice, 1797)

| Preliminary Stages[a] (1796 or 1797 libretto) | | | Final Stage[b] (1797) | | |
Scene	Section	Folios	Scene	Section	Folios
			1	Introduzione: "Amor che l'alme accendi"	89r–91v
			1–2	Recit.: Mitridate, Farnace "Basta, gran parte"	92r–v
2 (end)–3 (1797)	Recit: Mitridate, Vonima ("–tite e sol Vonima resti" crossed out, followed by "Vonima, s'io t'amai")	92v	2 (end)	Recit.: Mitridate: "Vonima s'io t'amai"	93r–v
				Obblig. recit.: Vonima "I tuoi sospetti"	93v–94v
3	Vonima's fainting music from aria (duet?)	97v–98r		Aria (duet?): Mitridate, (Vonima) "Morrai lo merti" (excluding fols. 97v–98r)	95r–103r
	(crossed out)	99v			
	Coda of Mitridate's aria shortened				
			4	Recit.: Fedima, Farnace "Tutta scorsi"	107r–v
				Aria: Fedima "Già so che m'intendi"	108r–110r
				Recit.: Farnace "Sempre più la vendetta"	110r
			5	Recit.: Zifare, Vonima "Vonima, idol mio"	104r
			6	Obblig. recit.: Arbate "Cedi il . . . signor"	104v–105v
				Aria (with chorus): Zifare "Per queste amare lagrime"	123r–128v
				Recit.: Farnace "Respira il cor al fin"	106r
				Aria: Farnace "Vedrò que' perfidi"	138r–140r
			7	Recit.: Mitridate, Vonima "Vonima a me"	111r–v

8 (1797)	111v	Recit.: Mitridate "Che vuoi da me?"	8	129r–v	Obblig. recit. (excerpt): Mitridate, Vonima "… volta io ti possa parar … versa il mio"
9 (1796)	118r–122v	Aria: Vonima "Al pianto mio concedi"		130r–137r	Aria: Vonima "Per pietà del mio tormento"
				112r	Recit.: Mitridate "E l'ascoltai" "Scena e Duetto":
9–12 (beg.) (1797)	112r–v	Recit.: Farnace, Mitridate, Fedima "Salvati, genitor" (through "Siam traditi")	9–11	113r–114v	Obblig. recit.: Farnace, etc. "Salvati, genitor"
				115r	Marcia
14 (1796)	116v–117v	Obblig. recit.: Mitridate "Ma dove andrò"	12	115v–116r	Obblig. recit.: Arbate, Mitridate "Siam traditi"
				150r–161r	Duet: Mitridate and Zifare "Cadrà l'altera Roma" ("Notturno": Mitridate, Vonima "Dove i Romani" here?)
13 (= 15 in 1796)	162r	Recit.: Zifare, Vonima (with expansion, fol. 162r, 3rd system ff.)	13	142r–162r	Recit.: Zifare, Vonima "Ah! non l'abbandonar" (without expansion)
14 (1797)	141r–v	Obblig. recit.: Vonima "Fedima, Arbate, tutti, salvate il nostro Re"	14	141v–142r	Orchestral interlude
14 (1797)	144r–145r	Obblig. recit. (cont.) (= continuation of 141r–142v in earlier redaction, an expansion of dialogue later cut for the final version, of which 141r–143r = music)			

TABLE I
Continued

Preliminary Stages[a] (1796 or 1797 libretto)			Final Stage[b] (1797)		
Scene	Section	Folios	Scene	Section	Folios
17 (1796)	Aria: Mitridate "Nume del ciel"	145v–146v	15	Obblig. recit.: Mitridate, Vonima "Ombra" scene: "Dove i Romani" (or after 12; duet?)	142r–143r
	"Finale"			"Finale"	
18 (1796, much altered)	Trumpet fanfare	147r	15 (middle–end)	Chorus with Mitridate, Zifare "Viva il Roman valor . . . Viva la libertà"	163r–168r
	Obblig. recit.: "Che ascolto" (new) → "Pompeo fu vinto, il vincitor son io . . . a nuova gloria	147r–149v		(Mitridate and Zifare die)	
			16	Chorus (cont.) with Vonima and Farnace "Proteggeranno i Dei la nostra libertà" (everything in libretto cut from "La tromba ormai c'invita" except last line, "Viva la libertà")	

SOURCES: For the score, Zingarelli, *La morte di Mitridate* (Venice, 1797), Archivio Storico Ricordi, Milan; for the libretti, Sografi, *La morte di Mitridate* (Trieste, Autumn 1796, and Venice Ascension 1797).

NOTE: Scene numbers indicate Venice libretto unless "1796," for Trieste, is indicated. Folio numbers refer to the Zingarelli autograph. "Recit." indicates simple recitative; "obblig. recit." indicates obbligato recitative.

[a]Portions eventually excluded.
[b]Version probably performed.

Knotting Mitridate to this type, Zingarelli had evidently already set the Vicenza / Trieste act 2, scene 3, or a part of it at least, wherein Vonima maintains her innocence and dedication to Mitridate in the face of his death threats and thereby manages to win his good grace. Unlike its counterpart in the Vicenza / Trieste version, Zingarelli's Venice setting of the scene (Fig. 3) culminates in an enraged aria by a menacing Mitridate with duetlike interjections by Vonima, who sing together the following (from the 1797 libretto):

> M. Morrai lo merti. Il voglio
> Ma dell'amante in seno
> Vedrò quel core almeno
> La morte a paventar.
> Dove si vidde mai?
> Affanno più tiranno?
> Più barbaro dolor.
> V. T'Amai . . .
> M.   Mentisci . . .

> V. Il giuro . . .
> M. Ah! nel mirar quel ciglio
>   Sento il primiero affetto
>   Si parta! il mio periglio
>   Numi mi fa terror.
> V. Mi và mancando il cor.
>   *(cade svenuta . . .*
> M. Sommi Dei! qual son guerriero
>   Roma cada. Il figlio mora
>   Non resisto al mio furor.
>   Tornerò, ben mio, lo speri
>   La del campo vincitor.
>   *(partono.*

At a key moment Vonima breaks Mitridate's tirade with a swooning spell with the words "Mi và mancando il cor," marked by drooping, minor-sixth portamenti to a sighing violin accompaniment, to which he responds with energetic if suspicious concern, repeating his avowals of "fear not, I love you" (Fig. 4). Indeed, in the eyes of the new censors Mitridate evidently seemed all too concerned. Once final revisions were made to the score, the passage was deleted to cut straight to the chase: Mitridate rages until distracted by the sound of "bellicose" trumpets, then promptly abandons Vonima to go off warring with Rome.

Subsequent parts of act 2 were similarly altered to make Mitridate more barbaric. Zingarelli had already set Vonima's supplication aria midway through act 2, in scene 10, using text from the 1796 versions, wherein she was depicted in tearful self-reproach while beseeching Mitridate to take pity on Zifare.

> *1796, act 2, scene 10*
>   Al pianto mio concedi
> elemente i giorni suoi;
> un sangue reo, se vuoi
> tu lo ritrovi in me.
>   Ah! se sperar mi lice
> da te così bel dono,
> più lieto, più felice
> di questo cor non v'è.
>   Lo vedi,
> lo comprendi,
> lo credi,
> e già m'intendi . . . .
>   La mia speranza è in te.
>   Trieste version

FIG. 4. Nicola Zingarelli, *La morte di Mitridate,* excerpt from "Morrai lo merti,"
showing deleted exchange with Vomina, fol. 97v. Property of Archivio Storico
Ricordi, Milan. All rights reserved. Reproduced by permission.

In revising the text for a new setting, Sografi intensified Vonima's diction with
laments of misery and entreaties that Mitridate curb the barbarian in him to
play the nobler part of the father figure:

> *1797, act 2, scene 8*
> Per pietà del mio tormento
> Al tuo sen ricevi il figlio
> Che sei padre a te ramento
> Frena il barbaro rigor.
>> Nella calma, e nel contento
> Deh ritorni il genitor.
> Tu consola tu 'l difendi
> Tanto affanno: e questo cor.
>> Venice version

Similarly, Zingarelli had set Vonima's plea in act 2, scene 14, to save the king
(despite her predicament) using an impassioned obbligato recitative. The text
of the scene, in which she begs the elder confidantes Arbate and Fedima to

"guard his days," survived even until the Venice libretto was printed for La Fenice, which must have been done just days before the premiere.

> Fedima, Arbate, tutti
> Salvate il vostro rè, de giorni suoi
> Cura prendiam. Ver questa parte il vidi
> Portar il piè; vacillante . . . io tremo . . .
> (*Mitridate comparisce improvisamente sopra il Tempio semivivo.*
> Ma s'apre il Tempio! . . .
> (*con sorpresa,*
> Egli s'appressa . . . oh Dio! . . .
> Come squallido in volto! . . .
> (*attonita,*
> Vieni mio prence a noi? . . .

But this too was ultimately struck from Zingarelli's autograph.

Moments like this, in which the sovereign's inferiors vouchsafe his power, were of course crucial to the earlier narrative paradigm of opera seria, wherein the king, supreme among all males, holds an axiomatic claim on women—a claim he forgoes only as an act of benign will—and wherein the women, in order to maintain the social order, acknowledge his prerogative even when they hope to put off his advances for private reasons. In excising this passage from the version performed, the new regime rejected the exemplar of the obsequious subject in tacit favor of the new self-determining citizen. By rejecting the right of the paternal king to seize female quarry, it implicitly rejected as well the analogous right of the paterfamilias to dispose of women as he pleased. Both were of course based on the absolutist political model of the patriarchal family, in which the king sat atop the social hierarchy directly below god and Christ as a universal father figure, from which position he derived his power to settle matters of affinal relations and alliance. Concomitantly, rejection of such a hierarchy meant rejection of the imperative of collective protection for the monarch, or some monarchical surrogate (here the oligarchic body), in favor of the autonomous, even recalcitrant individual. Saving the monarch was no longer the subject's job.

The version produced for the final performance made Mitridate meaner and more barbaric—in short, less worthy of being saved—than he had been on the terraferma in 1796, and it meant that the new version could fail to save him, even spiritually. Consequently, while both versions culminate in the invasion of Mitridate's realm in Asia Minor by Roman armies and in Mitridate's defiant claim to "show how heroes leave . . . life" by answering their invasion with a

FIG. 5. Nicola Zingarelli, *La morte di Mitridate,* excerpt from Mitridate's death aria, "Nume del ciel," fol. 145v; text from Vicenza / Trieste version, 1796. Property of Archivio Storico Ricordi, Milan. All rights reserved. Reproduced by permission.

slow suicide, only the final La Fenice version visited a truly gruesome death upon him in exchange for his treatment of Vonima and his antagonism toward mythical Rome. Once again, Zingarelli had originally set the death scene from the Vicenza / Trieste version (act 2, scene 17) using Mitridate's tender solo aria "Nume del ciel," which the tyrant had sung in his death throes following a passage of broken recitative (Fig. 5).

> [Recitative]
> Contra i Romani! Andiam: coraggio, amici,
> quà si soccorra; là si voli, è certa
> la mia, la vostra gloria:
> alla pugna, al trionfo, alla vittoria.
>   (Mancando.)
> Ah che vacilla . . . ahi lasso!
> Tardo . . . tremante il passo . . . in tal momento . . .
> Figlio, mi lasci! . . . Oddìo! morir mi sento.

[Aria]
Nume del ciel, ridona
  a queste braccia il figlio:
  con moribondo ciglio
  tel chiede un genitor.
E tu all'ardor perdona *(a Von.*
  del misero mio cor.   *morendo.*

"Nume del ciel" is a classic *aria d'affetto.* As such, it allowed Mitridate to regain his lyric composure long enough to plead with Heaven that he might embrace Zifare one last time before dying and be forgiven his ardor for Vonima. It allowed Zingarelli to project him as the dying despot with a special dignity and pathos, a stately, triple-meter cantabile aria in B-flat.

For the sake of "revolutionary" Venice, however, Sografi ultimately replaced "Nume del ciel" with a new passage of blank verse, "Dove i Romani."

Dove i Romani son . . . Dove Pompeo? . . .
Venga già del velen! . . .
  (mancando.
V. Veleno? oh Dei.
  (da sè.
M. Ancora ho il ferro in questa man io tremo . . .
  (cade in braccio alle guardie.
Già di nera caligine si adombra
La moribonda luce! . . . Eterna notte . . .
Mi circonda d'intorno! . . . un freddo orrore . . .
Sento che in sen mi piomba . . . a poco a poco . . .
Cedasi al fato estremo! . . .
Roma trionfa! . . . io vo mancando . . . e fremo . . .
  (s'ode gran strepito di trombe, e Coro di Romani vittoriosi.
  Mitridate resta sorpreso con gran stupore.
Coro.
Viva il roman valore   *(di dentro.*
Viva la Libertà.
Viva Pompeo . . .   Act 2, scene 15

With this in hand, Zingarelli could now send Mitridate to Hell in a dramatic scene of orchestral recitative, a scene he probably sketched shortly before opening night (see Fig. 6). Just before the opera ends he staggers onto the temple half-alive with his dagger in hand. After gasping out a parlante speech to the accompaniment of shuddering violins and diminished chords ("tremo" and "Eterna notte"), he suffers one final torment as cries of Roman victory begin to sound in the distance.

FIG. 6. Nicola Zingarelli, *La morte di Mitridate,* excerpt from Mitridate's obbligato death *scena,* "Dove i Romani," fols. 142r–v; text from Venice libretto of 1797. Property of Archivio Storico Ricordi, Milan. All rights reserved. Reproduced by permission.

All of these revisions pushed the opera away from the segmented drama-turgy of old opera seria toward a harsher, more grisly stage action underwrit-ten by an increase in dramatic orchestral recitative, the construction of scenic tableaux that avoided the closure of the set number, and a sharpening of the *parola scenica,* fraught with emotional, broken speech.[64] The new, overwrought genre could be harnessed to help demonize Mitridate through concerted acts of iconoclasm, acts that turned the tyrant into a figure of aristocratic villainy to be symbolically crushed in the very temple in which the aristocracy exalted itself.

The crowning blow was dealt in the final scene, which introduced a sudden chiasmus in the original trajectory toward a quasi-happy ending. It is important to note here that even though the Vicenza/Trieste version ended with Mitri-date's suicide, he nevertheless died happily, surrounded by grief-struck subjects and visited finally by a triumphant Zifare decked with insignia of the con-quered Romans, whom his troops had just pushed into the sea. In Venice, by contrast, Mitridate was made to die miserably, afflicted by shades of Hell, to the glee of the populace: the Romans win, Zifare is killed, and the populace rejoices, while Vonima is simply forgotten. Moreover, the final scenes of the Venice version throw Zifare under an evil light at the eleventh hour and make Farnace—the Roman sympathizer—into the noble offspring who suddenly appears in triumph after conquering the evil Eastern empire of "Asia."

Vast amounts of time and space were thus phantasmatically compressed into a few minutes of dramatic time. If this belied geographical and historical truth, not to mention every concern for verisimilitude, it offered a transformative narrative for spectators at La Fenice that June. Through the medium of a merciless death, aristocratic claims could be denied and choral lament con-verted into collective euphoria, as the Venice version resolved in victory cho-ruses.[65] Sografi's revolutionary enthusiasms probably got the better of him before the final redaction was made, for sixteen lines that appear in the printed libretto—but not in the score—have the populace rushing to take up arms with Roman warriors.[66] The ideology behind Venetian myth made popular vio-lence anathema, nor would it have been sanctioned by French occupying forces, whom Venetian "democrats" repeatedly praised for ridding Venice of tyranny through peaceful intervention.[67] Whatever cathartic power popular violence may have held in France was here displaced onto symbolic and narra-tive forms to become at most a figurative undercurrent, and not too real a one at that. No trumpets call the crowd to battle ("All'armi, all'armi") as in Sografi's text, and the chorus simply resounds with "Viva la libertà!"[68] Thus ended *Mitridate* on 4 June, and with it an intelligible ritual sequence that had begun earlier that day in piazza San Marco.

THE SUMMER SEASON

Eight days later, on 12 June, the Society of La Fenice was facing orders from on high to stage an unprecedented summer season, with thirty performances of *opere serie* to honor the arrival of Bonaparte.[69] Within the next four days boxholders were required to announce their intention either to retain or to give up for the summer the boxes that they alone owned and were accustomed to outfitting, curtaining, and lighting throughout the festive calendar, which stretched from roughly November through June with breaks principally for Christmas and Lent.[70] The fantasies of revolution that led architects of the revised *Mitridate* to falsify history by making ancient Rome the originary source of a revolutionary Venice now worked to suppress time in the realm of the everyday, brushing away centuries of cyclic time embedded in the theatrical calendar with a sweep of the hand.[71] For the economic elite, moreover, the concept of a summer season contradicted the very foundations of theatergoing, since wealth was largely predicated on real estate and the wealthy traditionally spent summers up to five months long at rural residences in the Veneto. Despite the antipathy they must therefore have felt toward such a demand, the patricians in the audience were accustomed to their summer *villeggiature*, and few were in a mood to change their plans for such a reason. By 16 June two-thirds of the boxes in the first two ranks, which were mostly owned by nobles, had been relinquished for the summer, in contrast to fewer than a quarter in the fourth and fifth ranks, dominated by the bourgeoisie.[72]

It was to be a summer of democratic theater for Venice. While the Teatro Civico staged a succession of patriotic dramas with a regular company of amateur *cittadini,* the Fenice put on two additional operas, Gaetano Sertor and Francesco Bianchi's *La morte di Cesare* and Antonio Sografi and Giovanni Andreozzi's *Giovanna d'Arco.* One valorized Brutus's murder of Caesar, thus rehabilitating once again the greater glory of republican Rome, while the other exalted the rebellious courage of Joan of Arc. Both were retooled from pioneering libretti of 1789,[73] and both claimed liberty over life as their central proposition. Like *Mitridate,* they aimed for realism through the *parola scenica* and an unbroken series of scenic tableaux.

Of the two, the opening *dramma serio, Cesare,* echoed the Venetian condition most closely, since it glorified Brutus's murder of a tyrannical Caesar in order to reclaim Roman liberty. Like *Mitridate* before it, *Cesare* aimed for high drama and narrative sweep, so much so that it was performed without ballet intermezzi, the ballets being delayed until after the opera proper, when a four-act *ballo tragico* was given. Many passages that had been done as simple recitative in Bianchi's 1788–89 setting for the Teatro San Samuele in Venice were cut, raising the dramatic pitch, while added passages of broken obbligato recitative intensified the possibilities of psychological verisimilitude.[74] By dwelling on Brutus's vain attempts to dissuade Caesar from his tyrannical course, the 1797 version could enhance the effect of "realism" and prepare audiences for the opera's shocking end, when Caesar would be murdered onstage (unlike the 1789 version or the revivals of 1790 and 1791 mounted in Livorno, Reggio, and Milan).[75] The love talk originally given by Sertor to Calphurnia shortly before Caesar's death was cut for Venice, in keeping with the more graphic ending, while interruptions to the narrative flow, such as Caesar's three-stanza love aria to Calphurnia in the penultimate scene, were eliminated.[76] Indeed, the ending did more than merely prepare the audience; it facilitated the intended identification of the spectators with the political situation depicted by calling on a popular chorus as co-conspirators: just before Brutus deals Caesar a mortal blow the chorus intervenes to urge his death with shouts of liberty and then cries out "O morte, o libertà," culminating in the requisite "Viva la libertà!"[77]

Given the enormity of the occasion that prompted the summer season, it is not surprising that both operas were staged on a scale even grander than that of the previous Ascension. The chorus swelled from sixteen members during Ascension to thirty-six strong for the summer, and the numbers of choral bodies who figured in the drama increased as well.[78] For example, to *Cesare's* original choruses of the 1789 version, comprising the Popolo Romano (i.e., the magistrates), priests, conspirators, soldiers, and lictors, the 1797 version added choruses of senators, the "Popolo," sacrificers, Roman matrons, and Briton slaves. The cast was also expanded, with two additional Roman senators, who added weight to the anti-Caesar (hence antityrannical) camp.[79]

MORALIZING THE SPECTATOR

Despite these resonances with events and ideologies in France, however, the "revolution" in which opera participated was vicarious, mimetic, and in the end chimeric. By January 1798 Venice was occupied by a despotic Habsburg Austria. Moreover, Venetians cared little for the wholesale creation of a mythic present that had taken place in revolutionary France, preferring to harken back to their own mythic past.[80] Thus, though time was suddenly calculated *alla francese,* subtracting the entire past from 1797 did not really result in Year One: for Venetians, 1797 was always reduced by five hundred to highlight the year 1297, the moment from which Venetian history had rolled forward and from which some now hoped to roll the clocks symbolically back. Even Venice's steeliest Jacobins, like Sografi and the poet Ugo Foscolo, focused less on the "Anno primo della libertà italiana" than on recovering for Venice its mythic prehistory before the Serrata, when the Venetian empire sat poised to triumph. Venice, they claimed, was born a true republic when Roman sovereigns claimed its muddy waters in their natural, prelapsarian state. Thus for "revolutionaries" in Venice, democracy was figured not so much through a calculus of rupture and genesis as through one of restoration and regeneration of an ancient past.

Central to the regeneration they sought was a renewed morality that would breed communities of patriots by edifying their moral outlooks and animate the spirits of crowds. Ironically, the cultivation of similar loyalties was already presupposed by conditions immanent to opera seria, whose festive nature aimed to reproduce the rites and rules of spectating communities.

Already in the 1780s Stefano Arteaga, Italy's most prominent opera historian, had chastised the festive effects of opera in Italy by insisting that the Italians' love of pleasure so compromised the possibility of political virtue that their numerous theaters could be blamed for their loss of political freedom.[81] Consider, though, that opera seria in its classic guise traded on a varied, disjunct succession of closed forms over and above the formal continuities of narrative, its arias jolting to recitatives and its ballets inserted unrelatedly between acts. In like manner, its scenery was meant not to create illusions of reality but to provide mere referential backdrops, placing singers in reciprocal relation to audiences. All of this promoted a carnivalesque flux of social and spectating activities in the opera house. In contrast, "revolutionary" Venice now put scenographic, poetic, and musical continuities to use in order to help secure the attentions and loyalties of collectivities and individuals alike. Vast scenes, oblique perspectives,[82] and continuous tableaux in open, syntagmatic forms, combined with a new raw realism, so that opera could more easily draw spectators into absorbed states that allowed the messages of tragedy to be interiorized for personal as well as collective betterment.[83]

Perhaps it is not so surprising, then, that ultimately the new genre of tragedia per musica undermined its ostensibly tragic claims through a bloody ending designed, like French rescue opera of the 1790s, to signal gaiety, not gloom, and through revolutionary choruses that affirmed a new-styled lieto fine. In this sense, "revolutionary" opera at La Fenice shattered the axioms of the aristocratic body only to reclaim collective celebration in the form of a dubious "democratic" populism.

Even as an idea, of course, revolutionary festivity at Venice was imposed largely from without and embraced only by a slice of the indigenous population. The spontaneous effervescence that theoretically should have united the collective imagination existed in an impossible tension with the organizational mechanisms that loomed behind it, and with the internal resistance to them of many Venetians. But married to a bureaucratic machine, festivity was nevertheless deployed to colonize Venetians by rupturing assumptions of time and history rather than helping to sustain them, as it had in the past. This arrogation of purpose was a danger Venetians had long avoided, but it was one immanent in the festive practices of which they were Europe's reigning experts. Even at the oligarchic La Fenice festivity was a gift of the nobility to itself and of the nobility to the nonnoble, a display of beneficence that claimed that the splendors and pleasures of the present were destined for time immemorial.

NOTES

This essay is for Tom.

Research for this chapter was generously supported by a residence fellowship at the Chicago Humanities Institute (1993–94), a Junior Faculty Fellowship from the University of Chicago (1994), and a fellowship from the Gladys Krieble Delmas Foundation for Research in Venice (1994–95). I am grateful to Thomas Bauman, Alberto Rizzuti, Dennis Romano, and Valerio Valeri for insightful comments on earlier drafts and to Sergio Perini for his generous help in transcribing passages from some of the more difficult documents used herein.

1. The history of this claim, particularly in England and France, is elaborated in Ernst H. Kantorowicz's classic work *The King's Two Bodies: A Study in Medieval Political Theology* (Princeton, 1957), esp. chs. 4 and 5, pt. 2.

2. Eighteenth-century plans of the theaters are preserved in Museo Civico Correr (MCC), Ms. Correr, busta 970, fasc. 25.

3. On La Fenice's early history see Manlio Brusatin and Giuseppe Pavanello (with essays by Cesare De Michelis and documents by Susanna Biadene), *Il Teatro La Fenice: I progetti, l'archittetura, le decorazioni* (Venice, 1987); Nicola Mangini, *I teatri di Venezia* (Milan, 1974), 165–76; and Thomas Bauman, "The Society of La Fenice and Its First Impresarios," *Journal of the American Musicological Society* 39 (1986): 332–54. The research carried out by Bauman on the pre-1797 years formed the starting point for my research in this chapter.

4. For accounts of these events see George B. McClellan, *Venice and Bonaparte* (Princeton, 1931); and Giovanni Scarabello, "Gli ultimi giorni della repubblica," in *Storia della cultura veneta,* ed. Girolamo Arnaldi and Manlio Pastore Stocchi, 6 vols. (Vicenza, 1976–86), 5, pt. 2: 487–508. For a lively fictionalized account from the nineteenth century see Ippolito Nievo, *Le confessioni di un italiano,* vol. 1 (Milan, 1980), ch. 11, ostensibly based on the eyewitness accounts of his grandmother, a Venetian noblewoman.

5. Indeed, as Nievo put it, the Council that voted itself out of existence maintained agency over its own fate instead of facing bloody defeat in war.

6. See William H. Sewell Jr., "Historical Events as Transformations of Structures: Inventing Revolution at the Bastille," *Theory and Society* 25 (1996): 841–81 (quotation on 845), which attempts to theorize more precisely than has been done in the past the nature of the "event" and its relationship to historical structure, using the storming of the Bastille as a case study.

7. See Mario Nani Mocenigo, *Il Teatro La Fenice: Note storiche e artistiche* (Venice, 1926), 16.

8. See James Cushman Davis, *The Decline of the Venetian Nobility as a Ruling Class* (Baltimore, 1962); and Franco Venturi, *Settecento riformatore: La chiesa e la repubblica dentro i loro limiti* (Turin, 1976).

9. One factor that allowed the Society to obtain permission for a fancy new theater may have been the dilapidated state into which poor finances and neglect had driven Venice's other theaters by the later eighteenth century (see Lodovico Zorzi, "Venezia: La Repubblica a teatro," in *Il teatro e la città* [Turin, 1977], 278).

10. What follows is based on my analysis of records in Fondazione Ugo e Olga Levi, Archivio Storico del Teatro La Fenice, Partitario Canoni 2, 1792–1800.

11. See above, n. 2.

12. Desperate attempts to expand the pool of noble families, and with them the eligible membership for governmental offices and the amount of governmental funds available, were far less successful in the eighteenth century than in the seventeenth (see Davis, *Decline of the Venetian Nobility,* 119–25).

13. Box ownership began in 1789, when families first had to pay levies on boxes they wished to reserve for the theater's opening. The vast majority of owners retained their boxes through the 1790s, even during and beyond the period of the fall of the Republic.

14. Lists of presidents were compiled by Sandro Dalla Libera in "La Presidenza del Teatro La Fenice dalle origini al 1968" (Venice, 1968), typescript conserved at Fondazione Ugo e Olga Levi, Archivio Storico del Teatro La Fenice. See also Michele Girardi and Franco Rossi, *Il Teatro La Fenice: Cronologia degli spettacoli, 1792–1936* (Venice, 1989).

15. See Mangini, *I teatri di Venezia,* 173.

16. For a transcription of the contract see Bauman, "Society of La Fenice and Its First Impresarios," 351–54.

17. *Gazzetta Urbana Veneta,* nos. 86 (28 Oct. 1795) and 12 (11 Feb. 1795), respectively.

18. It is probably no accident that these old classics were done mostly during the Autumn season since it was the least promoted of the three theatrical seasons.

19. For example, in 1797 levies for boxes in the pepian were affixed as follows: the proscenium boxes (1–3 and 27–29) and the single box at dead center (15) cost the most, at 285.18 lire, followed by the boxes surrounding the centermost one (10–14, 16, 18–20, D, and E) at 238 lire; least expensive in the first tier were boxes that fell in the curve of the arc (4–9, C, A, B, F, and 21–26), which cost 190.12 lire (Fondazione Ugo e Olga Levi, Archivio Storico del Teatro La Fenice, Partitario Canoni 2, 1792–1800). By designating prime-viewing boxes in locations scattered throughout the theater rather than in contiguous locations, the Society of La Fenice imitated the demographics of fancy real estate throughout Venice, which traditionally had ensured through various legal mechanisms that noble palaces be built off the Grand Canal (as well as along it) and throughout all six of the city's *sestieri*. This feature of aristocratic demography in Venice distinguished it from most other Italian cities.

20. See Eviatar Zerubavel, *Hidden Rhythms: Schedules and Calendars in Social Life* (Chicago, 1981), ch. 3, "The Calendar," for a basic explanation of the French revolutionary decimal system.

21. On the Teatro Civico see Cesare De Michelis, ed., *Il teatro patriottico* (Padua, 1966), with an introduction on 9–43 and a chronology on 44–49, followed by various texts produced at the theater (including Sografi's *Il matrimonio democratico*). See also Franca R. Barricelli, "Civic Representations: Theatre, Politics, and Public Life in Venice, 1770–1806" (Ph.D diss., University of Wisconsin at Madison, 1994), 153–59.

22. The text is addressed to "Autori di Teatrali Rappresentazioni, . . . Capi Comici, ed Impresarj di Opere": "Uno tra i principali oggetti della Pubblica Istruzione esser deve il Teatro. Le Rappresentazioni, che in esso si fanno sono talvolta più efficaci delle stesse leggi. Cangiare lo spirito di un Popolo per lunga schiavitù avvilito, ispirare un onor salutare pei gran delitti, accendere il sacro fuoco di libertà esser devono le principali mire di una tragica rappresentazione; siccome illuminare il Popolo, ingentilire la Nazione, correggerne i costumi, quelle esser debbono della pittrice del vero la Commedia" (Archivio di Stato, Venice [ASV], Democrazia, 167, n.d., unpaginated).

A historical discussion of the state archives during the Municipality, with a guide to the contents, is given by Francesca Cavazzana Romanelli, "Archivistica giacobina: La Municipalità Veneziana e gli archivi," in *Vita religiosa e cultura in Lombardia e nel Veneto nell'età napoleonica,* ed. Gabriele De Rosa e Filiberto Agostini, Biblioteca di cultura moderna, 995 (Bari, 1990), 325–47.

23. ASV, Democrazia, 88.6, 18 May 1797.

24. Ibid., 88.6.4, 19 May 1797, and 88.6.18, 20 May 1797.

25. "Cittadini Municipalisti Provisorj. Il Cittadino Alberto Cavos Impressario del Teatro la Fenice, chiede il permesso di poter Sabbato ventuno sarà li 20. Maggio corrente aprire con opera seria il Teatro stesso, come pure chiede il metodo, ed il luoco apposito onde poter eseguire il Deposito a cautela certa de' virtuosi, che si presteranno al servizio del Teatro medesimo. Chiede altresì quali metodi si debbano tenere, et osservare per le maschere alla porta, e scena del detto Teatro, chiede pure l'ora precisa da incominciarsi l'opera, non che se debba far pagare alla porta li Ministri delle Corti

estere, e il metodo per poter togliere l'abbuso di aprire senza il dovuto biglietto li scagni nel teatro stesso. E' finalmente chiede di essere avvertito di tutte quelle discipline, regole, e metodi, che saranno credute opportune da questa provisoria municipalità" (ibid., 88.6.14, 20 May 1797).

In a meeting of the Society of La Fenice on 19 May members expressed similar confusion about whether and how to make deposits for the impresario (Fondazione Ugo e Olga Levi, Archivio Storico del Teatro La Fenice, Processi verbali delle convocazioni sottrati all'incendio 1817 del Palazzo Cornei, box 1, fasc. 12).

26. ASV, Democrazia, 88.6.9.

27. An ironic commentary was published in anticipation of the occasion in *Il nuovo postiglione, ossia Compendio de' più accreditati Fogli d'Europa. MDCCXCVII. 26 Maggio. Anno I. della Democrazia Veneta:* "Domenica notte probabilmente si darà un Pubblico Veglione nel Teatro *la Fenice,* dove si rappresenta da alcuni sere l'Opere dello scorso Carnevale; *Gli Orazj, e Curiazj.* Oh qual soave spettacolo si fù il vedere molte delle amabili nostri Ex Patrizii, dimesso quel grave carattere che il pregiudizio della nascita le accordava, abbandonarsi colla loro presenza e ilarità a quella dolce filantropia che diresse i loro Sposi, i Genitori, i Parenti. Oh quanto più care esse divennero ai lor Concittadini! Possa l'esempio virtuoso di queste, il lor trionfo, la Patriotica loro fermezza, esser seguiti da tutte l'altre, che intempestive combinazioni ritennero fino ad ora. Esse nate per dominar su' cuori, e non su' dritti de' Cittadini, formeran sempre più l'oggetti della commune estimazione" (360).

28. On the Italian reintroduction of onstage death see Marita P. McClymonds, "'La morte di Semiramide ossia La vendetta di Nino' and the Restoration of Death and Tragedy to the Italian Operatic Stage in the 1780s and 90s," in *Report of the Fourteenth Congress of the International Musicological Society, Bologna 1987,* pt. 3 (Bologna, 1990), 285–92.

29. Staging two operas for Ascension was unprecedented; the rule had always been one. Most probably *Gli Orazi* was only revived once the Republic fell because *Mitridate,* planned as the sole opera of the season, had to be put off while revisions were made (see below).

30. I am indebted to Alberto Rizzuti for bringing the Vicenza performance to my attention and sharing with me the typescript of his "Giovanna d'Arco all'opera: Diario Rivoluzionario di una debuttante (1789–1797)," forthcoming in the proceedings of the conference "L'aere è fosco, il ciel s'imbruna," held at the Fondazione Levi, Venice, 10–12 April 1997.

31. By 1797 opera seria and its outgrowth, the tragedia per musica, were both embedded in a history of tensions between young librettists of revolutionary bent and the old nobility (see Alessandro Pepoli's *Due lettere,* cited in Bauman, "Society of La Fenice and Its First Impresarios," n. 10; and idem, "Alessandro Pepoli's Renewal of the Tragedia per Musica," in *I vicini di Mozart,* ed. Maria Teresa Muraro, Studi di musica veneta, 15, Fondazione Giorgio Cini, vol. 1, *Il teatro musicale tra Sette e Ottocento* (Florence, 1989), 211–20.

32. See Marita P. McClymonds, "The Venetian Role in the Transformation of Italian Opera Seria in the 1790s," in Muraro, *I vicini di Mozart,* 1:221–40.

33. On the outside is written, "23 Maggio 1797 / Petizione del Cittadino Sograffi per Rappresentazione teatrale," and on the inside, "Cittadini / [inserted: '23 Maggio 1797'] / Petizione del Cittadino Sografi. / Cittadini, Il Pulpito de' bravi Francesi è stato sempre il Teatro. Voi, intenti al bene del Popolo colle vostre assidue cure, potrete dimenticarlo in siffatto momento? Di là è tempo che tuonino ancora le voci di Libertà di Eguaglianza, di là è necessario che tragga il Popolo la cognizione de' suoi diritti, usurpati, avviliti, abusati: di là . . . ma non è il momento di discorrere; è quello di risolvere. L'impresa è malagevole per la ristrettezza del tempo, ma la libertà ha i suoi miracoli. Assiste: temi, decidetevi. L'unire due epoche sarebbe di non poca istruzione al popolo; parlo del chiudersi il [?] fu Maggior Consiglio nel 1296 e della Congiura di Bajamonte nel 1310. Uniti questi due fatti, formerebbesi un Azione Teatrale, Democratica" (ASV, Democrazia, 88.6.68, ellipses in the original). Sografi uses the old Venetian calendar in dating the Serrata to 1296.

34. "Salutate il Gritti, e ditegli che tratterò questo soggetto come siamo rimasti d'accordo, cioè, popolarmente, ad utilitatem e non ad pumpam. Faremo vedere al popolo com'egli oggi acquista ciò che cinquecent'anni sono ha perduto e che ha gran motivo di star allegro" (ibid., 88.6.157 [163], 28 May 1797, from Padua).

35. Ibid., 90.67, 22 May 1797.

36. Ibid., 167.73. Grimani answered on 30 May with a list of requests for maintaining the theater in good order throughout the summer (88.6.126). A further petition to Grimani for the opening, now on behalf of a Società Patriotica del Civico Teatro, was submitted on 6 July (88.6); interestingly, on 13 July Sografi submitted another petition protesting that his work had been "defraudato" and rescinding rights of publication from the Committee of Public Instruction in accordance with ever-growing ideologies that viewed authorial labor as an author's property (88.3).

The San Giovanni Grisostomo, albeit an aristocratic theater, had staged a good deal of comic opera. It had the reputation of being architecturally awkward and having a public "formed for the most part of footmen and gondoliers," who could enter the theater for free on the first day of the season. The Spanish comic playwright Moratin observed that in the middle of the parterre there was a stand for selling chestnuts and cooked pears, that during intermissions glasses of wine were passed around, and that there was much noise, simple happiness, clapping, and shouting (see Mangini, *I teatri di Venezia,* 150).

37. The information comes from the account books of La Fenice in Fondazione Ugo e Olga Levi, Archivio Storico del Teatro La Fenice, Partitario Canoni 2, 1792–1800 (year 1797).

38. ASV, Democrazia, 167.107. Vittorio Malamani, "Giustina Renier Michiel: I suoi amici, il suo tempo," *Archivio Veneto,* n.s., 38 (1889): 5–95, 279–367, mistakenly gives the date of the occasion as 28 March, which is wholly misleading (24).

39. See the report in *Il nuovo postiglione* (26 May 1797), 360.

40. I borrow the notion "textual unity" here from Lynn Hunt, *Politics, Culture, and Class in the French Revolution* (Berkeley and Los Angeles, 1984). For a treatment of these attempts in Venice see McClellan, *Venice and Bonaparte.*

41. The initial announcement of 23 May appears in ASV, Biblioteca Legislativa, vol. 1, no. 40, and the announcement of the postponement on 31 May, in vol. 1, no. 97. The former is reproduced in *Il codice della libertà italiana rigenerata nell anno MDCCXCVII. Conterrà una serie completa delle carte pubbliche, leggi, proclami ecc. di tutte le municipalità d'Italia,* 2 vols. (Venice, 1797), 1:240 (housed in Biblioteca Nazionale Marciana [BNM] under the call number 68.c.50).

42. For a general description see McClellan, *Venice and Bonaparte,* 246–47

43. *Monitore Veneto,* 5 June, Year One (= 1797), quoted in McClellan, *Venice and Bonaparte,* 247.

44. The text, which provides a major record of the day's rites, survives as a published broadside in ASV, Biblioteca Legislativa, vol. 1, no. 122.

45. From these origins, of course, had grown up a millennium and more of mythology linking Venice to the Virgin as pure, just, inviolate, and unconquered, a lagoon in a maiden sea (see Edward Muir, *Civic Ritual in Renaissance Venice* [Princeton, 1981]).

46. For an analysis of the link between popular sovereignty and popular violence with respect to the taking of the Bastille see Sewell, "Historical Events as Transformations of Structures."

47. *Il codice della libertà italiana rigenerata nell anno MDCCXCVII,* 1:119, emphasis added.

48. In Barricelli's interpretation it was precisely this capacity to reinterpret French revolutionary events and symbols in terms of Venetian history and myth that made the trauma of occupation bearable ("Civic Representations," 141).

49. The text was printed as *Ino patriotico per el zorno dell'inalzamento dell'albero della libertà* (MCC, Op. Cicogna XXII [op. 291.11]).

50. The former survives in ASV, Biblioteca Legislativa, vol. 2, no. 100, and in a copy in *Il codice della libertà italiana rigenerata nell anno MDCCXCVII,* 1:23.

51. Nor do I mean to invoke the classic associations of sacrifice with violence now widely derived from René Girard's psychological theory of sacrificial violence as collective catharsis (see *Violence and the Sacred,* trans. Patrick Gregory [Baltimore, 1977]). Girard's theory, wherein violence inheres in sacrifice because sacrifice is an outlet for the violence that is immanent in all human relationships, is too universalizing to be fitted to analyses grounded in historical and cultural particulars, as Valerio Valeri has argued in *Kingship and Sacrifice: Ritual and Society in Ancient Hawaii,* trans. Paula Wissing (Chicago, 1985), 67–70. Still I would suggest that the theory finds a good exemplar, perhaps the motivating one, in French revolutionary rhetoric, especially in its claim that violence tends to be concentrated in a particular victim or scapegoat toward the collective good of the many.

52. A proclamation of 31 May announcing the event explicitly calls it a sacrifice (ASV, Biblioteca Legislativa, vol. 2, no. 100; there is a copy in *Il codice della libertà italiana rigenerata nell'anno MDCCXCVII,* 1:230).

53. On the pairing of sacrificial rites with prayers see Valerio Valeri, "Credenze e culti," in *Enciclopedia delle scienze sociali,* vol. 2 (Milan, 1992), 574, col. 1; and on the case of ancient Hawaii, idem, *Kingship and Sacrifice,* 52–55.

54. Recall earlier in the speech the words "gli esercizj adattati alle robuste genti ne la rassodano, come per lo contrario mollezza e lusso la intristiscono" (ASV, Biblioteca Legislativa, vol. 1, no. 122).

55. I adapt the notion from Marcel Mauss, *The Gift: The Form and Reason for Exchange in Archaic Societies*, trans. W. D. Halls (1950; reprint, New York, 1990), 15.

56. See Marcel David, *Fraternité et la révolution française, 1789–1799* (Paris, 1987); David claims, however, that the related phrase *fraternité ou mort* did not sound as threatening then as it now does.

57. For the dates of performance see Girardi and Rossi, *Il Teatro La Fenice*, 24.

58. The *Indice de' teatrali spettacoli* was explicit about the government's role, listing the ballets for *Mitridate* as having been performed "per ordine di quella Municipalità" (*Indice de' teatrali spettacoli*, spring 1797–Carnival 1798, pt. 13 [Milan, n.d.], 134). Furthermore, copies of the libretto preserved at BNM and Casa Goldoni include on the recto preceding the title page the notice "I balli descritti nella presente opera anderà in scena fra' pochi giorni," confirming that the whole production had undergone difficulties and delays.

59. Their respective libretti are titled *La morte di Mitridate tragedia per musica del signor Sografi poeta del nob: Teatro La Fenice e del Teatro Comico S. Angelo da rappresentarsi nel Nuovo Teatro di Vicenza l'estate MDCCXCVI. Vicenza per Gio: Battista Vendramini Mosca;* and *La morte di Mitridate tragedia per musica del Signor Sografi poeta del nobile Teatro la Fenice e del Teatro Comico S. Angelo da rappresentarsi nel Ces. Reg. Teatro di Trieste l'autunno MDCCXCVI. Dalla ces. reg. privilegiata Stamperia governiale.* Both were produced under the impresario Antonio Zardon, who handled the productions at theaters in both seasons. Like many smaller cities, they seem to have taken advantage of the availability of superior personnel in "off" seasons. In what follows I refer to the two jointly as the Vicenza/Trieste version, since the libretti, the casts, the personnel, the management, and evidently the stagings were all quite similar. While I have seen both libretti, I have not been able to compare them directly; therefore, I cite text from the Trieste libretto (as the later of the two 1796 texts) and also compare with it passages of text appearing in Zingarelli's score.

60. None of Antonio Mauro's scenographic designs for the opera survives.

61. In Racine's drama, which is much closer to the ancient histories, Mitridate amasses mistresses obsessively, only to have most of them killed off out of jealousy, hence making the function of women as prey more plain and raw.

62. I base this estimate on the fact that a full-length opera typically required at least two months to complete; such an estimate is probably too low for most composers writing in the 1790s.

63. In view of the fact that a hastily composed ending was suddenly to valorize Farnace instead of Zifare at the end of the opera, some tinkering did have to be done to act 1. The autograph shows, for instance, that Zingarelli had already set the earlier version of act 1, scene 4, "Esitar non poss'io, Farnace è il traditor," as simple recitative (fol. 54), but it was struck from the score.

64. On these aspects of revolutionary opera see Giorgio Pestelli, "Reflessi della

rivoluzione francese nel teatro musicale italiano," in *Eredità dell'Ottantanove e l'Italia,* ed. Renzo Zorzi, Civiltà veneziana, Saggi, 39 (Florence, 1992), 261–78.

65. See ibid., 270–71, on the reason for tableaulike ensembles in revolutionary opera, as opposed to the action-packed concertato finales otherwise common between 1790 and 1810.

66. The final lines in the libretto printed for La Fenice read:

Coro: Corriamo all'armi Al campo?
Farnace: Venite? . . .
Tutti: All'armi, all'armi . . .
Farnace: Vi seguo . . .
Tutti: Al campo al campo Si vinca oppur si mora De nostri ferri al fulmine No non si può resistere Paventino i nemici Di nostra Libertà! . . .
Farnace: Io vi precedo andiamo. Da noi si vincerà. In libertà si viva, Si mora in libertà . . .
Tutti: Ah fortunato istante Viva la Libertà.

For the finale Zingarelli's score set only the last line of Sografi's text.

67. Indeed, revolution itself was a concept toward which Venice harbored a long-standing enmity, an enmity that continued into the period of municipal government (see Barricelli, "Civic Representations," 152).

68. Zingarelli's score also suggests that Sografi's final stage direction, calling for the whole cast to arrange itself in military formation to the sound of a march—"e ponendosi in ordine militare segue gran marcia, e così termine il Dramma"—also was not carried out, since no march follows the last chorus.

69. The document revealing these orders was first reported in Bauman, "Society of La Fenice and Its First Impresarios," 350; it is conserved in Fondazione Ugo e Olga Levi, Archivio Storico del Teatro La Fenice, Processi verbali delle convocazioni sottratti all'incendio 1817 del Palazzo Corner, box 1, fasc. 4. Most of the receipts for the summer season are preserved in ibid., Fabbrica del Teatro La Fenice, Spese 1789–1794–1798, filza 6, and a few others scattered throughout ibid., Cassa, 1792–97.

70. Boxholders who failed to claim their boxes would lose them for the whole summer. Boxes given up went back to a special commission.

71. The standard theater calendar in Venice began with an autumn season around mid-November (for which not all nobles returned in time), followed by the prime season of Carnival beginning on 26 December. It ended with the Ascension season, which ran during May and June, generally for a month or more. By July 1797 the old system of theatrical seasons at La Fenice not only had been toppled but had received a frontal assault of a more general kind in the *Teatro Moderno Applaudito* 13 (July 1797), which pronounced it "una delle più ridicole ed insieme più tiranniche leggi del passato governo di Venezia" (quoted in Barricelli, "Civic Representations," 157 n. 30).

72. Boxes given up and boxes retained are listed in Fondazione Ugo e Olga Levi, Archivio Storico del Teatro La Fenice, Partitario Canoni 2, 1792–1800, fol. 191. All

told, only seventeen out of seventy in the fourth and fifth ranks gave up their boxes; indeed, merely four boxes were given up in the fifth (and top) rank.

73. The original libretto for *La morte di Cesare* was conceived for the Teatro San Samuele in Venice and published as *La morte di Cesare. Dramma per musica del signor D. Gaetano Sertor da rappresentarsi nel nobilisssimo Teatro di S. Samuele il carnovale dell'anno 1789. Dedicato a . . . Gio. Battista Pignatelli principe di Mariconuovo . . . . Giovanna d'Arco* was premiered the following summer (also 1789) at Vicenza, with the libretto published as *Giovanna d'Arco dramma in quattr'atti per musica del Signor A. S. Sografi da rappresentarsi in Vicenza nel nuovo teatro la state dell'anno 1789. Umiliato agli eccellentissimi rettori. In Vicenza per Antonio Giusto con permissioni. Si vende da detto stampatore a S. Michele.*

74. As in the inserted act 1, scene 9, in which Calphurnia begs Caesar not to leave Rome.

75. Act 2, scene 17, begins with the following description: "Apresi la scena, che dimostra il Senato di Roma con magnifici Sedili d'intorno. Nel mezzo la statua di Pompeo elevata sopra varj gradini, così pure la sedia curule. Veggonsi dei Senatori seduti ma varj posti vuoti. Entra Cesare preceduto da molti Littori. Tutti si levano in piedi, e gli vanno incontro, sopra tutto Bruto, Antonio, e varj congiurati, ma Antonio è trattenuto con arte in iscorso vicino ad una delle due porte che introducono da Decimo, e Trebonio. Tutti mostrano una simulata indifferenza, e tutti osservano Cesare."

76. In the 1789 version the aria "Rasserena i mesti rai" occurs in act 3, scene 7, the scene equivalent to act 2, scene 15, in the 1797 version.

77. Ironically, Sertor's original version of *La morte di Cesare,* which played at the Teatro San Samuele in Venice during Carnival 1788–89, had ended with a *licenza* in praise of Venetian republicanism, contrasting Venice with the corrupted image of ancient Rome:

> Non turbarti, Venezia, oggi al tuo sguardo
> La Romana Repubblica fa solo
> Spettacolo de'suoi casi, ma non osa
> Paragonarsi a te. Conosce anch'essa,
> Quanto minor del vero
> L'immagine sarebbe, e troppo è chiara
> Tra voi la differenza. E' tutto in lei
> Violenza, Discordia,
> Tumulto, eccesso, orrore; in te non regna
> Che virtù, che ragion, che amor del giusto,
> Che concorde voler. V'ha tra i suoi figli
> Chi vuol la Libertà le patrie Leggi
> Vederne oppresse; un sol non v'hà tra i tuoi,
> Che a sostenerle il sangue
> Non sia pronto a versar. Mille perigli,
> Mille vicende ella provò; tu illesa,
> E intatta ti conservi, qual nascesti;

Passaggera ella fù, tu eterna resti.
Serbati, o vivo Tempio
D'onor, di fè, di gloria
E un luminoso esempio
Abbiano i Regni in te.
Del tuo felice Impero
Quanto soave è il freno,
Ah! non l'intende appieno
Se non chi lo perdè.

(quoted from the copy at Conservatorio Santa Cecilia, Rome, p. 80). In 1797 even Caesar acknowledges the liberty-or-death motif, but in the guise of the intrepid ruler. Knowing that his life is in danger, he boasts, "Morte piuttosto eleggo," to which Brutus replies, "E morte avrai" (act 2, scene 16). Brutus kills Caesar as the latter tries in vain to defend himself, while Cassius proclaims, "Roma trionfa," and the chorus sings "O morte, o libertà."

78. The *Indice de' teatrali spettacoli,* spring 1797–Carnival 1798, pt. 13, lists "num. 16. Coristi" and "num. 16. Coppie Figuranti" for the Ascension season. For the summer season (Estate) it lists "num. 36. Coristi" and "num. 32. Ballerini per Corpo di Ballo." Evidently, then, the number of dancers did not change, but the chorus more than doubled.

79. Antonio Mauro's sets must have been imposing too, judging from Sografi's descriptions, particularly for the final scene of Caesar's murder.

80. The point is made by Barricelli, "Civic Representations."

81. Stefano Arteaga, *Le rivoluzioni del teatro musicale italiano dalla sua origine fino al presente,* 3 vols. (1783–88; facs. reprint, Bibliotheca Musica Bononiensis, ser. 3, no. 6, Bologna, 1969).

82. Extensive stage directions in the libretto describing the opening scene as semi-circular with a "vastness of objects [represented]" suggest something of the character of Mauro's (now lost) stage designs. The Meotide Marsh created an obstruction within "the empty space around the center," and "the periphery . . . [was] composed of the magnificent buildings of the city of Nymphaeum." At the extreme ends of the semicircle were placed, to the right, the Temple of Venus, "from which all breathes pleasure," and, to the left, a newly built mausoleum for the believed death of Mitridate, from which "all breathes sadness." Upstage left is described as animated by "a portico leading to the palace of Mitridate," and upstage right, by a sacred grove. Still further back the Caucasus Mountains could be seen in the distance. This dramatically packed and expansive stage set was typical of late-eighteenth-century scenographic style, which aimed to draw the spectator into the viewing space.

83. Such individualist modes were in line with the intense concerns of Venetians to ensure that citizens take charge of their education, their moral decisions, and their judgments, concerns that were taken up by the Committee of Public Instruction in endless sessions and edicts on schools, speeches, sumptuary laws, and so on, and that can

also be seen in its anxieties over women's role in theater. Relevant to the last are also the lengthy and pointed criticisms of women's presence on the stage of the Teatro Civico voiced by an anonymous pamphleteer in *Opinione di un libero cittadino sulla nuova istituzione d'un teatro civico* (Venice, 1797), included in "Scritti sortitti nella Revoluzione di Venezia seguita li 12 maggio 1797. Tomo Primo," 65–80 (BNM, call number 183.c.88).

III

Society and Culture

8

Identity and Ideology in *Renaissance Venice*
The Third *Serrata*

STANLEY CHOJNACKI

Over the last generation historians have largely abandoned the traditional view, once widely held, that the Serrata, or Closing, of the Great Council in 1297 resulted in a clearly de-fined constitution and social structure. As Gerhard Rösch's contribution to this volume makes plain, the Venetian ruling group was in fact defined by a gradual process of adjust-ment and negotiation that lasted well over a generation. In this chapter Stanley Chojnacki examines a similar process of patrician self-definition that took place at the end of the fifteenth and the beginning of the sixteenth century. In particular he demonstrates how a series of crises in this period led to legislation that required the registration of noble births and marriages. Of special interest is the emphasis Venetians placed on the mother's status as well as the father's in the determination of noble identity. But Chojnacki's title is also of interest. Here, as in an earlier essay on an early-fifteenth-century season of legislative activity in which Venetian nobles sought to stabilize their political power and to prevent the admission of new men into the Great Council, he has deliberately and provocatively used the term serrata to describe the efforts at self-definition. As a consequence, he completes the critique that Rösch began. We can no longer think of the Venetian constitution and nobility as the creation of late medieval legislation. Rather, we must think of both the constitution and the nobility as recurrently renewed and redefined by new strategies of collective self-fashioning. Indeed, this new perspective may go a long way in explaining the apparent stability of the Venetian patriciate from the Middle Ages to the fall of the Republic.

IN DECEMBER 1506 the Council of Ten, the most powerful body in the Venetian government, passed a law regulating attendance at dinner parties.[1] The law applied to banquets of the *compagnie della calza,* exclusive clubs of wealthy younger members of Venice's hereditary ruling patriciate.[2] The Ten's purpose in enacting it was to prevent ambitious nobles, as members of the class called themselves, from campaigning for government office by hosting sumptuous banquets for their voting fellow nobles.[3] Part of a vigorous new assault by the Ten against electioneering, the measure amplified an earlier one of 1497 that had condemned such lobbying as "foreign to the sacred customs of our forefathers and to the peaceful institutions of our republic."[4] The perennial (and perennially futile) effort to curtail vote-seeking among nobles has been thoroughly studied, but the 1506 law is of special interest because of its concern with patrician women.[5] It expressly prohibited attendance at *calza* company dinners by women other than wives of members. If other women should violate this stricture and be present at such an occasion, not only the host but the women's husbands would suffer the severe penalties decreed in 1497: a doubling of their *decima* (tax) liability, deprivation of the right to hold governmental office, and the forfeiture of all the other benefits of patrician status.

The 1506 banquet law encapsulates the features of a revolutionary body of legislation enacted between the 1490s and the 1530s that sought to regulate political behavior by asserting the government's authority in the social life of the patriciate. It invoked as justification Venice's venerated past and the benign effectiveness of its governmental institutions, distinguished between different groups of nobles, and made the identities of patrician wives the crux of the issue. The dinner guests whose votes were being lured were men, most likely rank-and-file nobles accustomed to negotiating their franchise with their richer and more powerful fellow patricians; because poorer men depended on the stipends of governmental posts, they were especially vulnerable to the Ten's threatened deprivation of office.[6] Yet it was not their presence at calza dinners that the Ten tried to prevent but their wives'. The Ten reasoned that men whose wives were excluded from campaign banquets were unlikely to be swayed to pledge their votes because the presence of the wives of calza members would make these unaccompanied invitees appear to be second-class participants. The Ten thus combated electioneering by exploiting the patriciate's taste for sociability between men and women, a phenomenon well documented by the contemporary diarist Marino Sanudo.[7] By sanctioning the presence of members' wives at calza dinners, it gave governmental validation to the presence of noblewomen in the social activity of the ruling class.

The focus on wifehood in the Ten's December 1506 antielectioneering law was anything but exceptional. Other laws of the 1490s–1530s put even greater emphasis on patrician marriage, with implications for more than electoral propriety. The outcome was a recasting of patrician identity, a reconfiguration of the regime's sociopolitical structure that constituted the final phase of the long process of defining the ruling class that had begun at the end of the thirteenth century. That it occurred at the beginning of the Cinquecento is not surprising. Since the 1970s the early sixteenth century has come to be regarded as the great turning point in Venice's history. This marks a major change in historiographical fashion. To earlier generations of historians the so-called *Serrata,* or closing, of the Great Council between 1297 and 1323 was the formative moment, the period when Venice's aristocratic regime was permanently constituted and its ruling class made fixed and hereditary. But over the last three decades changes in scholarly interest and methods have pushed the chief focus of research two centuries forward. A major reason is that the great institutional result traditionally credited to the Serrata, the entrenchment of a hereditary ruling class, is largely taken for granted. When they have been studied, the events of the late thirteenth and early fourteenth centuries have been downgraded to one stage in a process of ruling-class formation that had begun earlier, would be continued later, or both, as Gerhard Rösch's chapter in this volume illustrates.[8] With Venice's underlying social and political structure securely and timelessly established, historians interested in Venice's politics have turned their attention elsewhere: to constitutional and legal adjustments, as in the work of Gaetano Cozzi; to patterns of political relationships and conflicts, as in Robert Finlay's synthesis; and to political culture, notably in the work of Innocenzo Cervelli, Edward Muir, and Manfredo Tafuri.[9]

All of this scholarship coalesces around the early Cinquecento for two principal reasons. One is the shattering of the Republic's power and self-confidence as a result of the War of Cambrai (1509–17), most dramatically by the defeat of the Venetian forces at Agnadello in May 1509. What Cervelli calls "the crisis of the Venetian state" has provoked an outpouring of scholarship exploring its immediate origins, the recriminations and adjustments on the home front that followed it, and reform efforts in the 1520s and 1530s to undo its effects and restore the strength and prestige of Venetian government and public life.[10] The other reason is the availability of unprecedentedly rich sources. The period abounds in contemporary diaries and chronicles, foremost those of Domenico Malipiero, Girolamo Priuli, and above all Marino Sanudo, and an equally rich body of contemporary political analysis, the most prominent examples of which are treatises by the Venetians Gasparo Contarini and Domenico Morosini and the Florentine Donato Giannotti. The powerful impact of these sources on scholarship is due to their availability in print, enabling historians to engage issues on the basis of a shared vocabulary of sources.[11] Supplementing those printed sources are the manuscript materials generated by the Venetian government, which for the sixteenth century are more voluminous and systematic owing to greatly expanded governmental oversight and recordkeeping. Some of these new types of documentation are important to the argument of this chapter.

To be sure, a notable vein of scholarship has helped to bridge the chronological and thematic gap between the older Serrata-centered historiography and the newer concentration on the early sixteenth century. Elisabeth Crouzet-Pavan, Richard Mackenney, Dennis Romano, Guido Ruggiero, and I have discerned evolutionary changes in politics and society during the fourteenth and fifteenth centuries.[12] Nevertheless, much scholarship still accepts that the decades around 1300 witnessed the definitive establishment of the hereditary aristocracy that would rule Venice for the next five hundred years.[13] Yet the devastating events of the late Quattrocento and early Cinquecento and the innovations put into operation to weather them raise the question whether indeed the crisis could have been ridden out by a regime shaped two centuries earlier. Taking an even longer view, it is hard to see how the changes in Venice's economic, political, and geographical contours during the fourteenth and fifteenth centuries could have failed to stimulate adjustments in Venice's basic political, social, and cultural structures. In an earlier study I proposed that legislation enacted in the first third of the Quattrocento sufficiently altered how the ruling class constituted itself to warrant being called the second Serrata.[14] The present chapter is an effort to show that not only the turbulent events around 1500 but processes at work during the Quattrocento also lay behind the legislative campaign of the 1490s–1530s, which built on the innovations of the early fifteenth century. The larger argument is that the policies and procedures adopted during the early Cinquecento achieved the full and final elaboration of Venetian patrician status: the substantive meaning of nobility, who was noble, and how, and with whom, nobles were to act. They thus completed the long process that had begun in the thirteenth century, constituting the third and final Serrata.[15]

At many points the findings presented here accord with those of an important recent book by Victor Crescenzi, which has been of great value to the discussion that follows.[16] However, whereas Crescenzi emphasizes the juridical significance of the new configuration of noble status, I draw three different lessons here. First, I argue that the early-sixteenth-century redefinition of patrician status was a consequence of social and economic difficulties weighing on nobles throughout much of the Quattrocento and exacerbated by the political upheaval of the first third of the new century. Measures to specify what nobility was and to identify who qualified for it were provoked by strains within and between noble families. Second, the redefinition of patrician status was conditioned by the new ideological thrust publicized in the profusion of analysis and celebration of Venice's government by noble "scrittori politici," to use Angelo Ventura's term.[17] This ideological program cloaked unprecedented state initiatives in a vision of Venice's venerated past. Third, the nature of the social and political challenge to which the legislation of the third Serrata responded instigated governmental intrusions into the most intimate areas of private life, making marriage, birth, and wifehood the pivotal elements in the new patrician order. The result was a redefinition of noble identity—of the class as a whole, of its various components young and old, female and male, and of the relationships between them—according to the tenets of the political ideology of the early Cinquecento.

AT THE HEART of the legislation was the perennial issue of the qualifications for membership in the Great Council. A law of the first Serrata, enacted in 1323, had established patrilineal heredity as the sovereign principle and instituted procedures for applying it.[18] But the procedures were applied only spottily in the Trecento, principally because the dominant houses, secure in their historically grounded status, had no need to demonstrate it to governmental officials.[19] Since those houses dominated the Quarantia, which had the final say on Great Council membership, and the Avogaria di Comun, which had broad discretion in accepting credentials, they were in a position to induct their own clients and to reject the clients of their opponents.[20] Throughout the Trecento the Avogadori di Comun kept no records of their discretionary approvals of candidates; the only cases that made it into the documents were those uncertain ones that they chose to take to the Signoria (the doge, his six councilors, and the three heads of the Quarantia) for adjudication, and the first of these is dated 1342, nearly two decades after the legislation that made patrilineal heredity the qualification for membership in the ruling class.[21] That, plus the inconsistent use of titles denoting status and the easy sociability between nobles and the *popolo grande* identified by Dennis Romano, made the boundaries around the patriciate uncertain and permeable.[22]

In the last third of the Trecento, however, social and economic difficulties, brought to a head during the War of Chioggia (1379–81), triggered a tightening up as the ancient houses lost their political domination to comparative newcomers and impoverished families struggled to hold onto their noble status and to exclude competitors of uncertain status from the new noble-welfare programs created by the government in the wake of the crisis.[23] The legislation enacted between 1414 and 1430 directed the Avogadori di Comun to implement new procedures for checking the credentials of men claiming eligibility for the Great Council and to keep records of those credentials proofs, which became the first systematic documentation of the patriciate's membership.[24] The tightening up was justified in a new language of patrician purity that identified nobles as different in character from the flawed *popolani,* now marked more sharply than ever as a separate, inferior class. Along with that came laws setting status requirements on, and recording the identities of, the mothers of would-be nobles, which had the effect of encouraging patrician endogamy, as did measures restricting dowry levels and assigning different dowry privileges to different categories of wives.[25] The second Serrata thus reinforced the first by making governmental attention to marriage and the women whom male nobles married the keys to the integrity and exclusiveness of the ruling class.

Thus, when in the early Cinquecento the government systematically undertook to regulate the patriciate's private life, it was building on a century-long precedent of scrutinizing nobles' marriages in order to ascertain patrician identity.[26] By 1500, however, its motive was no longer concern about infiltration by nonnoble families. The legislation of the early fifteenth century had effectively closed the class by finally giving the Avogadori di Comun a firm grasp of its membership. The Avogadori's records actually reveal a decline in the number of patrician houses during the Quattrocento, from 165 to 142, which should have enhanced the access of individual families to the benefits of noble-welfare programs.[27] The problem was that those fewer families were producing more sons and hurrying them into the Great Council. Attendance at Council sessions more than doubled, from 500–600 in the 1420s to 1200–1400 in the 1490s.[28] This noble population explosion was a product of both sheer demographic increase and greater assiduity by noble fathers in qualifying their sons for the benefits of patrician status. Their eagerness was all the greater owing to reduced commercial opportunities, which impoverished many families and inevitably increased the competition for the remunerative offices. The government responded to the pressure by creating new posts. But as Donald Queller showed with massive documentation, there still were not enough "welfare jobs for the nobles," leading them to devise all manner of machinations in order to get the available ones.[29]

The results were "confused and scandalous" violations of the procedures for proving eligibility for the Great Council, where elections to the eagerly sought offices were held. The words are from a law enacted by the Council of Ten on 19 December 1497, one day before it passed the antielectioneering law mentioned above.[30] The Ten found the violations "concocted by men's wickedness" so widespread and found deceiving the Avogadori di Comun, which was responsible for ascertaining eligibility, so easy that it now required all men admitted to the Great Council during the previous thirty-three months to prove their status anew or be expelled forever from that body and all other governmental posts. The Ten imposed this "strict rigor" on the review of nobles' credentials, "in the interests of justice and equality among those in whose hands rest the peaceful government and preservation of our republic."[31] Like the reverence for wise ancestors and the praise for Venice's constitution that would be evoked the next day in the antielectioneering law, the references here to justice, equality among nobles, and the governing mission of the patriciate were to be recurrent themes in the legislation of the early Cinquecento, encasing in an elaborately articulated political ideology newly devised solutions to pressing new problems. Infiltration of the Great Council by unqualified interlopers menaced the political integrity of the ruling class and exacerbated the tensions arising from competition for remunerative offices. But the economic and demographic squeeze on many noble families created a problem that alarmed the Council of Ten, and the Senate as well, even more than did underage Great Council members or even electoral corruption, for it threatened the social distinctiveness and cultural dignity that, as the language of the second Serrata had repeatedly declared, set nobles apart from the popolo.

The problem stemmed from nobles' difficulty in arranging marriages for their proliferating sons and daughters. At a time when many families were hard-pressed, dowry levels were being relentlessly pushed up by a variety of forces: the flaunting of wealth by the richest patricians, the value to all nobles of prestigious and politically influential or at least supportive in-laws, and the desire by mothers to recycle their own dowry wealth into dowries for their daughters.[32] Faced with the soaring cost of marrying daughters, which more than doubled between the later fourteenth and the early sixteenth century, the patrician rank and file could participate in the marriage market only by betting their resources on dowries for one or two girls, consigning the others to convents.[33] But that meant marriage for only one or two sons because the marriage legislation of the early Quattrocento, creating an official record of the identities of mothers of registered nobles, put pressure on nobles to find wives within the patriciate.[34] Also limiting the marriage prospects of male patricians were the desire not to fragment patrimonies among several married brothers and the requirement that bridegrooms secure their brides' dowries on their own or their family's property.[35] But whereas unmarried daughters could be placed in convents, often with the unedifying results recounted by Guido Ruggiero and Giovanni Scarabello, unmarriageable sons were left to find sexual satisfaction where they might, usually out of wedlock and most often with women of the popolo.[36] The ignoble taint borne by the sons of such unions, however, did not stop them from trying to follow their fathers into the Great Council. As the Ten tirelessly reiterated, it was the presence in government councils of these men, tainted by illegitimate birth and related to patrician society through only one parent, that now undermined the cultural image and the social structure of the patriciate. Hovering over the legislation of the early Cinquecento was the threat bastardy posed to the nexus between marriage and government in the patrician regime.[37]

Since marriage was the problem, the solution had to be found in marriage. Accordingly, wives and mothers became the overriding preoccupation of the third Serrata. In dealing with it the Council of Ten and the Senate pursued complementary tacks, the Ten addressing the bastard problem, the Senate that of the high cost of marrying, which contributed to the former.[38] The opening salvo of the third Serrata was a Senate law of November 1505 raising the ceiling on dowries that had been set in 1420. Such action was needed, the preamble stated, because over and above its severe impact on the wealth of "our nobles and *cittadini*," the "pernicious practice" of giving "excessive dowries" was the source of many other "inconveniences, of which every prudent person is aware."[39] This hint of tensions between the rich and poor nobles, exacerbated by the former's capacity to assemble huge dowries, also alludes to the problem of illegitimacy stemming from the inability of many nobles to marry.[40]

The Senate's response was actually to raise the legal limit, from 1,600 to 3,000 ducats, but it wrote in two enforcement measures that give the act its chief importance. First, it brought marriage under state supervision by requiring that all future contracts be personally registered with the Avogadori di Comun by the groom, the father or some other close relative of the bride, and the *golo* (marriage broker). This put into government records not just the amount of the marriage settlement but the names of all the parties to the contract: the marrying couple, their parents, and all contributors to the dowry and guarantors of the husband's capacity to restore it to his widow; the signatures of all these persons were appended to the document, together with those of the Avogadori. The web of relationships in a marriage transaction, which could be extensive, thus became part of the official record. The second feature of the act was its focus on the property of women. On one hand, the senators allowed wives to receive legacies larger than 3,000 ducats as long as the surplus was treated as inheritance *(dimissoria)* rather than dowry and "remained freely in the hands of the woman, as is honest." But they also made the property of those women the target of the act's enforcement mechanism; any widow whose dowry was not recorded in the Avogadori's register would lose her traditional right to its restitution. What had until then been a private trans- action, usually, in contrast to Florentine practice, without even a notary pres- ent, was now a public one subject to governmental oversight.[41]

The identity of wives and the social context of patrician marriage were given still greater importance nine months later in a counterpoint measure en- acted by the Council of Ten. This was the famous *Libro d'Oro* law of 31 August 1506. Its declared purpose, to reinforce previous legislation denying noble status to men either not descended from Great Council members or born out of wedlock or to slaves or other low-status women, reaffirmed the early Quattrocento linkage between paternal, maternal, and matrimonial qualifica- tions for noble status.[42] But as in the dowry law the previous year, the method of achieving it was state registration and documentation of a hitherto private event. Henceforth, fathers, or in their absence mothers, must notify the Avoga- dori di Comun within eight days of the birth of a son, and parish priests were likewise to inform the Avogadori of all patrician baptisms they performed. The Avogadori were to record these notifications in apposite registers, the *Libri d'Oro,* or Golden Books, which would later document the sons' eligibility for the Great Council (as in fact they did).[43]

This law altered the meaning of nobility in Venice. Whereas the legislation of the first and second Serratas had made entry into political life the checkpoint for determining noble status, now it was birth itself. Patrician identity was to be associated not only and not even necessarily with government—the *Libro d'Oro* registers record the births of many sons who never entered the Great Council— but with a distinctive social location at the beginning of life. The law assigned that location precise coordinates, starting with the newborn's father. Only men who were actually members of the Great Council could inscribe their sons in the *Libro d'Oro.*[44] Claimants to noble status on the basis of paternal grandfathers or uncles in the Great Council must wait until adulthood, when, after more stringent examination of their credentials, they must gain the votes of two- thirds of the Signoria.[45] The favored status thus given the sons of actively and visibly noble fathers marked a further step, following the precedent set in the second Serrata, in the replacement of the traditional criterion of patrician status, membership in a noble clan, the more ancient the better, by the newer procedural one emphasizing the officially recorded continuity of father to son.[46]

In addition, a newborn's noble identity was henceforth officially framed within a wider circle of kin and friends. The law required that witnesses swear to the legitimacy of the marriage and stand surety for fines levied on fathers who provided false information.[47] These *fideiussores* occupied a wholly new sociopolitical role. One year earlier, in yet another attempt to curtail electioneering and patronage peddling, the Council of Ten had prohibited nobles from standing as baptismal godfathers to the sons of other nobles.[48] Now it completed that action by transferring the initial rite of social bonding among patricians from religious to governmental precincts. As if to underscore the state's takeover of the rite of patrician identification, entries in the Avogadori's register of baptisms do not include the names of godparents.[49] The witnesses at *Libro d'Oro* registrations thus became a newborn noble's officially recognized coparents, participants in a state ritual marking the entrance of an infant into the ruling class and patrician society.

However, the most important element of an infant's identity after the status of his father was that of his mother. The law decreed that "in order to determine whether [the child] was born of a woman acceptable [*concessa*] according to our laws," her first and last names and her *nation* (place of origin), if outside Venice, were also to be entered in the birth register. This was the key to achieving the law's purpose of preventing the Great Council from being, in the language of the preamble, "contaminated, blemished, or otherwise denigrated" by the admission of bastards or sons of servile women. It put an additional premium on intermarriage among patricians. The eminence or humbleness of a noble's maternal lineage would now be a matter of official record from his infancy; marriages between patrician families would also be more likely to attract noble fideiussores willing to attest to their legitimacy; and because anxiety about sexual honor led nobles to keep their unmarried daughters closeted away from temptation, a patrician mother offered the strongest assurance of the legitimacy of her offspring.

Married nobles responded by welcoming the opportunity to have their offsprings' credentials certified. Even more, the new procedure gave them an official forum in which to advertise and reinforce social relationships. The relationships they brandished were not the obvious ones of lineage but those formed by earlier marriages. In eighty-three registrations of infants from six patrician houses only one-quarter of the witnesses belonged to the mother's or father's patrilineage.[50] The others were marital kin, invited by the new parents or themselves volunteering to commit their credibility toward guaranteeing the patrician status and the reputable marriage of their affines. When Andrea di Alvise Arimondo inscribed his two-month-old son in 1510, one of the witnesses was Giannantonio Venier, whose relationship to the new father, Andrea, was through his mother, a sister of Andrea's father, who had married Venier's father four decades earlier, in 1471.[51] Giannantonio Venier's involvement with his Arimondo cousins did not end there. Sixteen years later, in 1526, he was commissioned by Arimondo's recently bereaved widow, Caterina Vendramin, to register the birth of their month-old last son. In this case Venier was documenting the noble identity of a child born to a family his mother had married out of nearly a half-century earlier.[52] The marriage connections in this 1526 registration spread further still, to embrace more distant affines of both parents. One of the *fideiussores* was a brother of the husband of the late Andrea Arimondo's sister, the other was the husband of a sister of the widowed Caterina Vendramin.[53]

Thus, one marriage and its offspring were vouched for by participants in three other marriages, showing the spreading bilateral links of the newborn Andrea Arimondo (who was given his late father's name) with three lineages other than his own. They offered official testimony of his noble identity at the time and would provide him with a valuable social network when he grew up. Giannantonio Venier's long-term involvement with the Arimondos shows how *Libro d'Oro* registrations demonstrated the lasting strength of marriage ties across generations.[54] Nor were his ties to his affines exceptional. In one six-month period in 1508–9 Girolamo Boldù acted as fideiussor at the registrations of sons of his two brothers-in-law, Alvise and Nicolò Balbi, whose sister he had married eighteen years earlier.[55] Fifteen years later Girolamo's own son, Nicolò Boldù, followed suit, going even deeper into his mother's patrilineage. He was a fideiussor at the registration of the son of Sebastiano Balbi, whose paternal grandfather and Nicolò Boldù's mother's paternal grandfather were brothers.[56] Most of the traced marital links were closer, however, solidifying relations between siblings and their respective spouses, as when in 1507 Marco quondam Benedetto Balbi registered his and Ludovica Vitturi's son with the husbands of both his sister and Ludovica's sister as fideiussores.[57]

These examples illustrate how the *Libro d'Oro* law, designed to weed out extramarital offspring, reinforced noble endogamy by assigning a new official function to the relationships created in marriage. Satisfying the requirement to inscribe infants in the government's register of the nobility gave parents and fideiussores alike the opportunity to obtain official acknowledgment of their own credentials, to display their noble associations, and to tighten the bonds and expand the reciprocal obligations between families joined by marriage. Together with the Senate's dowry-registration action nine months earlier and the Ten's measure regulating banquets of the compagnie della calza four months later, the Libro d'Oro law represented a major escalation of state direction of domestic life and social interaction. The Senate and the Council of Ten imposed new gauges of identity on the wives and sons of the ruling class, in the process shifting the boundary between government and private life by making the state the arbiter of birth and marriage.

The essential criterion of nobility in Venice was thereby altered. After 1506 that criterion was no longer merely inherited capacity for governmental office, displayed at the entry into political life, but birth into a particular nuclear family with its own distinctive social constellation, certified by governmental officials upon official notice by parents or their surrogates.[58] Henceforth patrician identity would be tied to a complex of paternity, maternity, and infancy devised and orchestrated by the state. The crux was supervision over marriage. Despite the new mechanisms, however, the aim of regularizing noble marriage continued to run up against the problem of extramarital noble generativity. Fathers of illegitimate sons found ways of circumventing the new requirement, aided, it appears, by lax enforcement by the Avogadori di Comun.[59] So a generation later the Ten and the Senate made another attempt to shore up the supremacy of marriage, in the second phase of the third Serrata.

In April 1526 rumors flew through the city as the Council of Ten held three secret sessions over six days. Their concern, Marino Sanudo reported, was that "many bastards had been approved as noble" and "the doge and his council are highly incensed [molto caldi] over it."[60] To put an end to these "pernicious and pestiferous" violations of existing laws, in the words of the preamble to the resulting legislation, the Ten took bold new steps "to keep immaculate and pure [neto] the rank and order of the nobility," on which rested "the honor, peace, and conservation of our state [stato nostro]."[61] First, all men admitted to the Great Council during the twenty years since passage of the 1506 law whose births had not been inscribed in the Libro d'Oro had to be recredentialed by a special examining board comprising the doge, his six councilors, and—breaking precedent—not the three capi of the Quarantia but the three capi, that is, the executive committee, of the Ten itself.[62] Any man unable to gain seven of those ten ballots would then be reconsidered by the entire Council of Ten, which at a stroke thus set itself up as the ultimate arbiter of noble status. If a man fell short of seven votes there, he would be forever excluded from the patriciate.[63] This recredentialing requirement for men who had reached adulthood from 1506 onward in effect imposed the rigor of the *Libro d'Oro* law retroactively on men born in the two decades before its passage.

Even those whose births had been duly recorded felt the effects of the Ten's reforming zeal.[64] Since the Avogadori had been slipshod, inscribing sons of nobles long after the eight-day postpartum deadline had elapsed, all men whose names had been recorded in the *Libro d'Oro* more than three months after their birth had to prove their credentials anew before the Signoria. To ensure that its order would be carried out, the three capi of the Ten were to pore over the *Libro d'Oro* register, noting *iterum probetur* (to be reexamined) beside each inscription recorded after the three-month grace period; in fact they did so.[65] At the same time the Ten bowed to reality by extending the eight-day registration window to one month, but with a new requirement: henceforth the Avogadori were to "interrogate the witnesses regarding the child's legitimacy and their knowledge of his mother" (de la legitima [et] de cognitione et scientia matrum). The oath regarding legitimacy had been part of the procedure from the start, but information on the mother had been scanty. Until 1526 only her given name and surname were recorded, with her father's name included only rarely. Now, however, the Ten realized that his mother's paternity was the surest indicator of a child's legitimacy, since the daughter of an identified noble father would almost certainly not bear a child out of wedlock. And indeed from April 1526 *Libro d'Oro* registrations do name the mother's father.[66]

Wives and mothers were thus the principal focus of the reforms of April 1526.[67] However important it was to revise *Libro d'Oro* procedures, the most far-reaching innovation was to make marriage, not birth, the critical juncture in the determination of noble identity for both men and women. This was done by instituting a civil marriage ritual. Henceforth every noble marriage had to be registered with the Avogadori di Comun within one month of its celebration; a son born of a marriage not so registered could not be inscribed in the *Libro d'Oro* or later be admitted to the Great Council except by a two-thirds vote of the Signoria.[68] Although the bride's presence was not required at the registration, her identity was the crux of the procedure. The groom was to present himself to the Avogadori together with two of his own close relatives ("propinqui parenti") and two of the bride's, all four of whom were to swear that she was his legitimate wife and to "declare the quality of her father and the woman's condition" (dichiarir la qualita del padre et condition de essa dona).

This information, signed by all three Avogadori, was then to be recorded "in a separate register." The official record of a noble's identity now began before his birth. For marriages celebrated elsewhere in Venice's possessions the Venetian governor of the place had to write to the Avogadori di Comun informing them of "le condition et qualita et genealogia de le done."

This act was the final step in the process begun in 1430 that made marriage and maternal identity, documented in governmental records, the keys to patrician status.[69] The elaborateness of the registration formula in the following example, dated 7 May 1529, shows the solemnity with which the government infused this civil act. It also displays the range and kind of kin invoked as *propinqui parenti* to bear official witness to the transaction that bound patrician families to one another's future.

> The noble ser Gianfrancesco Bragadin di ser Piero quondam ser Andrea appeared before the magnificent lords Piero Boldù, Melchiorre Michiel, and Marino Giustinian, Avogadori di Comun, and, in implementation of the April 1526 law of the most excellent Council of Ten, declared that he has taken as his legitimate wife the noble lady Elisabetta Trevisan, legitimate daughter of the quondam noble ser Vincenzo, whom he married [*desponsavit*] on the nineteenth of April just passed in the church of San Giacomo on the Giudecca. And in justification [and verification] of all the foregoing he produced on his own behalf the nobles ser Piero Bragadin quondam ser Andrea and ser Ettore Loredan quondam ser Nicolò; on the woman's behalf were produced the nobles ser Michele Morosini quondam ser Piero and ser Francesco Trevisan quondam ser Vincenzo. All four of whom, brought before the aforesaid magnificent lords Avogadori di Comun, affirmed under oath, on pain of all applicable sanctions if the truth is discovered to be otherwise, that they were present at [*interfuisse*] the aforementioned wedding, and are very well acquainted with this lady Elisabetta, now wife of the aforesaid noble ser Gianfrancesco Bragadin.[70]

Taken together, these clauses showed Elisabetta Trevisan to be the ideal mother of the noble sons she would bear Gianfrancesco Bragadin: her father's name, her title *nobilis domina*, her legitimacy, the verifiable date and location of her wedding, the oaths of not only her witnesses but also her husband's that they knew her personally. What gave their testimony special credibility was that they made the perfect combination of marriage witnesses. One was Gianfrancesco's father, another was Elisabetta's brother, and the other two had intertwined affinal ties to the two spouses. Michele Morosini was the bride's uncle by marriage, the husband of her mother's sister.[71] Ettore Loredan had a more remote connection with the groom, Gianfrancesco Bragadin, sharing a Loredan great-great-grandfather with Bragadin's mother.[72] But his involvement in the marriage was closer by reason of his also being the bride's cousin-in-law, married to a daughter of her father's brother.[73] Having the names of these witnesses in the documentation of the marriage meant that it would be permanently lodged in the official memory of the regime as a coalescence of four lineages and multiple marriages, all interconnected by ties, some quite distant, of blood or affinity. Other patricians fashioned the same coalescence. In a sample of fifty-five registered marriages involving grooms from twelve patrician houses only 40 percent of the 215 witnesses identified came from either the bride's or the groom's patrilineage.[74] As they had been doing since 1506 in registering their sons' birth, nobles seized on the new requirement to advertise their broad-based integration in noble society by displaying the obliging loyalty of their marital kin connections, now doubly ritualized in religious and civil ceremonies.

But that worked only when both spouses were nobles, their titles paraded as in the Bragadin-Trevisan marriage. When a male patrician married outside his class, which occurred in 16 of 150 registrations studied, the effect was the opposite.[75] The requirement that she provide witnesses from among her kinsmen, whose names would be duly noted in the official record, magnified the social disadvantage of her husband's marriage, marking him as lacking the extended circle of noble relations that Gianfrancesco Bragadin and most other bride-grooms fashioned for themselves when they married; he was documented as less socially and culturally noble than they were. When "vir nobilis" Bartolomeo Venier married Franceschina di Leonardo Graziabona in 1532 the witnesses on his behalf were his two brothers, identified as "viri nobiles." His bride's witnesses, however, were her father and brother, "ser" Leonardo and "ser" Marco Graziabono.[76] As a result, Bartolomeo, his brothers, and any children born of the marriage would lack the enlarged circle of patrician kin and collaborators that noble husbands, brothers-in-law, and sons acquired when they married noble wives. Even when brides from the popolo produced at least one noble relation as a witness, as did Cecilia Lanza and Laura Montorio when they married nobles in 1529, their sons would still be tagged by their less than lustrous maternal kin when their fathers' marriage registrations were checked, as now required, whenever they sought to take their seats in the Great Council or qualify for a governmental post.[77] The official record was very precise about status, as the Council of Ten had mandated in requiring information on the *condition* of brides. In 1531 "vir nobilis" Bernardo Cicogna married Stella Garzoni, and to ensure that she and her brothers, who acted as her witnesses, would not be mistaken for members of the noble Garzoni clan, the Avogadori

had their scribe specify that she was "dominam Stellam de Garzonibus popu-
larem."[78] Less derogatory but still explicitly nonnoble was the specification in
1537 of Chiara, bride of Marcantonio Querini, as the daughter of Paolo de
Franceschi, "civis veneti."[79]

It was doubtless the publicity incurred by mésalliances under the new documentary requirements that accounted for the rarity of such marriages. Of the
16 nonnoble brides only 5, fewer than 4 percent of the 150 brides in the sample,
belonged to popolano or cittadino families; the other 11 were daughters of
foreigners.[80] The Council of Ten's increased determination to restrict patrician
status led it to publicize status distinctions even among witnesses. In 1532
Maffeo Bollani married "nobilem dominam" Bianca Zeno, the daughter of
"viri nobilis" Jacopo Zeno. Her credentials as a patrician were clearly impecca-
ble, but the Avogadori's scribes were careful to note that although one of her
witnesses was "vir nobilis" Marco Zeno, the other was "ser" Girolamo Zeno,
son of "ser Joannis civis."[81] Despite belonging to a cittadino offshoot of the
noble Zeno clan, Girolamo retained strong enough ties to his patrician kinsmen to be called upon by them in matters of family business. But to Venetian
officialdom his inferior status, itself probably originating in an ancestor's illegitimacy, must now be acknowledged and permanently inscribed in governmental records.

In contrast with the enduring disadvantage that patrician men incurred by
marrying nonnoble women, however, illegitimate daughters of nobles were
easily accepted as wives of nobles. Their presence in the patriciate's matrimonial activity reveals the complex interplay of the status and gender dimensions of the official patrician culture taking shape in the third Serrata. At a time
when the government was taking unprecedented steps to ensure the exclusion
of illegitimate sons of nobles from the regime, their bastard daughters were
welcomed into its social substructure.[82] Ettore Loredan, the witness at the
Bragadin-Trevisan marriage registration in 1529 reproduced above, was connected with the Trevisan family through his wife, who was the illegitimate
daughter of the noble Marino Trevisan.[83] His marriage was far from unique
because with a large enough dowry a father could make his bastard daughter an
attractive spouse for a fellow noble, and one with few social liabilities. Along
with the dowry, her husband gained the association with another noble family
that was critical to patricians' political and social well-being.

The marriages of two Barozzi men show how attractive such arrangements
could be. In 1529 Vincenzo Barozzi registered his marriage to Elena, "filiam
naturalem" of Girolamo Querini, with a dowry of 3,000 ducats, plus another

3,000 in dimissoria. In their marriage contract Elena's father authorized him to administer the 6,000-ducat package. In addition, Vincenzo was also to assume supervision of the income and expenses of the Querini household he was marrying into because in the contract his father-in-law "obligated himself to take the *magnifico miser* Vincenzo into his house, treat him as his own son, and pay living and clothing expenses for him and his children."[84] Four years later Antonio Barozzi married the doubly illegimate Marina, "filiam naturalem" of ser Alvise Trevisan, who was the "filii naturalis" of the noble Nicolò Trevisan.[85] Like his kinsman Vincenzo, Antonio received a handsome marriage settlement from his bastard wife: a dowry of 3,000 ducats and her dimissoria of 2,000 ducats, both of which Antonio was to administer. On top of these 5,000 ducats, his father-in-law promised to bequeath half of his estate to Marina and her heirs, who as Antonio's heirs would thus be the channels of a large infusion of wealth into his Barozzi line.[86]

These were alluring economic inducements, but they were by no means the only attractions offered by illegitimate wives.[87] Unlike nonnoble brides, they brought their husbands arrays of noble kin as well. Elena Querini's witnesses were "viri nobiles" Carlo Querini, her paternal uncle, and Giambattista quondam Jacopo Morosini. By marrying her, Vincenzo Barozzi thus established ties with as many as three noble houses: her father's, Giambattista Morosini's, and perhaps Morosini's Dolfin in-laws as well.[88] Marina Trevisan conveyed similar ties to Antonio Barozzi; for all her and her father's bastardy, she connected him not just with her own tainted family but also with two branches of the Morosini clan, represented by the *viri nobiles* who were her registration witnesses.[89] In nine other registrations involving illegitimate wives the brides' witnesses were also all patricians. All but one of the eleven women had witnesses representing at least two different clans.[90] Bridegrooms thus sacrificed little or nothing by marrying the bastard daughters of nobles.

It is not surprising that at a time when economic difficulties and rising dowry standards were forcing many women out of the marriage market illegitimate daughters with substantial dowries and patrician relations found husbands among the mass of noble bachelors. Validated as wives by private demand, they were also legitimated, as it were, in the Avogadori's marriage register. Their *condition* as *filie naturales* was acknowledged, then ignored, in a kind of official purging of the stain of their birth, for they served a purpose for the government as well as for wife-seeking men. By enlarging the pool of marriageable patrician women they eased resentment among nobles who would otherwise have been excluded from marriage and thereby reduced, however slightly, the danger that illegitimate men would infiltrate the government. These benefits were conferred also by the nonnoble women whom patricians married. But illegitimate daughters of nobles, vouched for by their noble kinsmen, had the additional virtue of tightening the reticulating marriage ties that contributed to stability within the patriciate.

THE COUNCIL OF TEN'S determined campaign against infiltration of the patriciate by bastard sons created new structures of noble womanhood and, indirectly, of noble manhood as well. Although for many prospective husbands a woman with two noble parents doubtless had greater appeal, what really counted was the capacity to bear legitimate sons who would have patrician support on the maternal as well as the paternal side. This illegitimate daughters could offer. Ironically, their importance in both domestic and governmental spheres also validated a generative role in patrician social relations for unmarried male nobles. A man who fathered a son out of wedlock was the target of increasingly rigorous measures of exclusion and denigration, but a man with a bastard daughter could now participate with an official stamp of approval in the marriage politics that served as the deep structure of his class's political functioning.[91] At least five of the eleven fathers of illegitimate brides in the sample fall into this category because they apparently never married, and a sixth, Girolamo Querini, whose daughter Elena married Vincenzo Barozzi, reportedly married one of his servants and in any case did not contract a patrician marriage.[92] Administrative and documentary innovations by the government thus revised the range of approved noble identities, excluding bastard sons more rigorously than ever but officially enfranchising bastard daughters, who could even be referred to as *nobel dona* in marriage contracts countersigned by the Avogadori di Comun.[93] In the process, they also gave official recognition to the generativity of unmarried noble fathers of such women as participants in the increasingly regulated social functioning of the ruling class, with its checkpoints and its constituent relationships built on marriage.

In the language of the preamble to the 1526 legislation, the purpose of these new constructions of patrician identity was to ensure "the honor, peace, and preservation of our state." This was the lofty "ethical intention" of the third Serrata, to use Paul Ricoeur's term for one of the essential dimensions of selfhood, the realization of one's self in purposive action. Ethical intention is defined by Ricoeur as "aiming at the 'good life,' with and for others, in just institutions."[94] When the Council of Ten premised Venice's civic well-being on the matrimonially secured distinctiveness of its ruling class, it was implementing its notion of the patrician polity's "good life." It was in pursuit of that objective, presented as a consensual value of the patriciate, that it created institutions to acknowledge the various noble selfhoods and to regulate nobles' relations with one another. The honor, peace, and preservation of the regime was Venice's supreme "hypergood," Charles Taylor's term for the good "which not only [is] incomparably more important than others but provide[s] the standpoint from which these must be weighed, judged, decided about."[95] In seeking that dominant good, the Ten, acting as the state, was bound to intervene institutionally in the private transactions of patricians with and for one another in order to ensure that the benefits and responsibilities of membership in the patriciate were reserved to suitably identified nobles and apportioned equitably among them.[96]

But defining the rules and roles of patrician interaction did not necessarily mean that they would be observed. We have already noted that some illegitimate daughters—and not only illegitimate ones—were getting dowries double the limit set in 1505. Technically, these were not violations of the letter of the dowry law because the excess was designated as the bride's dimissoria, or bequest, in theory not part of the package conveyed to the husband but in practice given to him to administer and even in some cases to profit from without having to give an accounting.[97] The zeal for well-connected sons-in-law led to wholesale flouting of the 3,000-ducat ceiling by means of the dimissoria loophole. Out of twenty-four marriage contracts registered with the Avogadori di Comun between 1526 and 1534 eleven included dimissorie that brought the total settlement well over 3,000 ducats; in one particularly egregious case Maria Priuli tacked a dimissoria of 7,000 ducats onto the 3,000-ducat dowry she gave to Gianalvise Badoer.[98] So in April 1535 the Senate responded with another effort to stem the tide. The allowable dowry amount was increased to 4,000 ducats, but that was to include the dimissoria.[99] However, the interest of the law lies not so much in its tinkering with dowry totals as in its invocation of traditional ideals and its elevation of enforcement mechanisms to the highest level of the state.

High dowries are bad, reads the preamble, because they cause disdain for law by fathers of daughters, dereliction of responsibility by officials—the Avogadori di Comun are meant—and the abandonment by young men of the ancient model of patrician manhood: "Our young men no longer engage in business in the city or overseas commerce or any other praiseworthy enterprise; instead they put all their hopes on their wives' extravagant dowries." To all the other reasons for stemming the inflation in marriage settlements was added that of returning the ruling class to its revered ancient ways. The way to bring about the honor, peace, and preservation of the state was to reenergize the worthy old mercantile traditions by getting young nobles to adopt the practices and values of their ancestors, to shape their male identities to the model of the past, not dependent on their wives' wealth but boarding galleys to make their own. The yearning for that nostalgic dream linked two of the most interesting Venetians of the 1530s, both of whom sought a renewal of their city's morale after the disasters of the War of Cambrai and its sequel, but with different emphases that capture the ideological complexity of the third Serrata.

One of the two authors of the 1535 dowry law was Gasparo Contarini, his great treatise *De magistratibus et republica Venetorum* completed only two or three years earlier, his elevation to the cardinalate coming only three weeks later.[100] Throughout the *De magistratibus* Contarini's emphasis is on the wise traditions of "nostri antichi," whose balancing of ancient lineage with honorably acquired wealth was the key to Venice's constitutional success.[101] Restricting dowries would help maintain the balance by preventing the wealthy from consolidating an endogamous plutocracy. The lament in the law over the *gioventù*'s abandonment of overseas commerce also echoed Contarini's regret in the *De magistratibus* over the decline of maritime skills among the nobles.[102] As Elisabeth Gleason points out, Contarini's solution for the current decline was to provide in the *De magistratibus* an idealized picture of the Venetian past to be used as a model for rehabilitating the polity, and particularly the nobility, in the reform effort headed by the reigning doge, Andrea Gritti.[103]

Historians differ about the relationship between Contarini's orientation toward Venice's past and Gritti's program of "radical renewal," in Manfredo Tafuri's phrase, but there is no disputing that they both were animated by a desire to reestablish Venice's political prosperity after a generation of doubt and defeat.[104] The whole aim of Gritti's reform was, again in Tafuri's words, the "recovery of identity and internal prestige" lost after the disasters of the War of Cambrai.[105] Venice's political identity was the central issue for both Contarini and Gritti, and their approaches to its recovery were complementary, Contarini emphasizing the authority of the past, Gritti promoting wholesale reform of laws and procedures.[106] Those approaches were the two streams that converged in the third Serrata, and the dowry law of 1535 symbolizes their confluence. In order to deploy the most politically and culturally powerful authority in the effort to restrain the seductive dowries that deterred young patricians from the vigorous traditions of their ancestors, the Senate instructed that every marriage contract registered with the Avogadori di Comun be read aloud at a special weekly session of none other than the doge and the Signoria because "the most serene prince in his goodness will want that morning devoted to this purpose." It would be Andrea Gritti, the radical innovator, collaborating with Gasparo Contarini in promoting the ancient values by presiding over yet another new ritual marking the state's spreading mastery over the making of marriage.[107]

That blend of tradition and innovation runs through the legislation we have been reviewing, as the Senate and the Council of Ten invested their wresting control over birth, marriage, and the identities and relationships that flowed from them with the authority of Venice's past. The registration of marriage contracts decreed in 1505 was associated with "our forefathers [*li mazor nostri*], ever vigilant to eliminate all practices offensive to our exalted creator and harmful to our nobles and citizens." The same was true of the *Libro d'Oro* law the following year: requiring the registration of noble births followed the precedents laid down by "our most wise forefathers [*progenitores nostri*] . . . in their zeal to guard and ensure that our Great Council never be contaminated." The marriage-registration law of 1526 also invoked "the heartfelt concern of our wise and benign forefathers [*mazori nostri*]" to keep the patriciate immaculate and pure.

It is a basic characteristic of ideology that "claims [to domination] are embedded in stories which recount the past and treat the present as part of a timeless tradition."[108] In Venice, legislation had long been associated with the patriciate's forefathers, but in the years around 1500 those invocations were given a new rationale. According to the Senate in 1505, it was the duty of "a well instituted republic" to restrain dowry excesses "out of reverence for God and for the benefit of our city." Similarly, requiring registration of births in the *Libro d'Oro* was a way of "preserving the peaceful unity and, God be thanked, the glorious reputation of our state," just as instituting marriage registration in 1526 was in the interest of "the honor, peace, and preservation of our state." What was at stake was the common good, and new departures in state regulation of private life were justified as carrying out a well-instituted republic's responsibility to maintain the dignity and unity of its ruling class, "in whose hands," declared the Council of Ten in 1497, "rest the peaceful government and preservation of our republic."[109] This is the preeminent theme in Gasparo Contarini's *De magistratibus* as well as in Domenico Morosini's *De bene instituta re publica*—the title quotes the Senate in 1505 verbatim—written sometime before 1509. Like his counterparts in the Senate and the Council of Ten, Morosini advocated sweeping institutional changes in the way noble identity was recognized and apportioned in order to return to the ancient virtues.[110] For Morosini, Contarini, Gritti, and the legislators of the third Serrata, the legitimacy of the regime demanded a ruling class purified of illegitimate men but purifying illegitimate women. Toward both these ends the authority of the past was joined to new state initiatives to control private life in the present in order to regulate and encourage intermarriage among nobles. Such intermarriage was the commanding purpose of gendered patrician identity and the matrix of the patriciate, which in the early Cinquecento completed the two-hundred-year-long process of defining its collective identity, the individual identities of its members male and female, and the ideology of the patrician regime.[111]

NOTES

1. Archivio di Stato, Venice, Consiglio dei Dieci, Miste (Dieci, Miste), reg. 31, fol. 95r (18 Dec. 1506). Unless otherwise noted, all source references are to documents in the Archivio di Stato in Venice. I would like to thank Barbara J. Harris, Benjamin G. Kohl, and Dennis Romano for valuable suggestions on the preparation and revision of this essay.

2. On the calza companies, see Maria Teresa Muraro, "La festa a Venezia e le sue manifestazioni rappresentative: Le compagnie della calza e le *momarie*," in *Storia della cultura veneta,* ed. Girolamo Arnaldi and Manlio Pastore Stocchi, 6 vols. (Vicenza, 1976–86), 3, pt. 3: 315–41; and Edward Muir, *Civic Ritual in Renaissance Venice* (Princeton, 1981), 167–72.

3. On banquets and electioneering, see Robert Finlay, *Politics in Renaissance Venice* (New Brunswick, N.J., 1980), 203–4.

4. Dieci, Miste, reg. 27, fol. 173r (20 Dec. 1497).

5. On antielectioneering efforts, see, in addition to Finlay, *Politics in Renaissance Venice,* 196–221, Donald E. Queller, *The Venetian Patriciate: Reality versus Myth* (Urbana, 1986), 51–112; and Gaetano Cozzi, "Authority and the Law in Renaissance Venice," in *Renaissance Venice,* ed. J. R. Hale (London, 1973), 293–345, esp. 325–27.

6. On poorer nobles' dependence on governmental office, see Queller, *Venetian Patriciate,* 21–50; Finlay, *Politics in Renaissance Venice,* 70–81; Cozzi, "Authority and the Law in Renaissance Venice," 298–301.

7. Marin Sanudo, *I diarii di Marino Sanuto,* ed. Rinaldo Fulin et al., 58 vols. (Venice, 1879–1903). For examples of patrician men and women socializing, see vol. 6, col. 437; vol. 7, col. 45; vol. 18, cols. 299–300; vol. 29, cols. 536, 547, 567; vol. 36, col. 459; vol. 37, cols. 447, 470–71; and vol. 57, cols. 525–26.

8. On the Serrata as continuing a process begun decades earlier, see Gerhard Rösch, *Der venezianische Adel bis zur Schließung des Großen Rats: Zur Genese einer Führungsschicht* (Sigmaringen, 1989); and Giorgio Cracco, *Società e stato nel medioevo veneziano (secoli XII–XIV)* (Florence, 1967). For its continuation into the Trecento, see Frederic C.

Lane, "The Enlargement of the Great Council of Venice," in *Florilegium Historiale: Essays Presented to Wallace K. Ferguson,* ed. J. G. Rowe and W. H. Stockdale (Toronto, 1971), 236–74; and Stanley Chojnacki, "La formazione della nobiltà dopo la Serrata," in *La Storia di Venezia: Dalle origini alla caduta della Serenissima,* vol. 3, *La formazione dello stato patrizio,* ed. Girolamo Arnaldi, Giorgio Cracco, and Alberto Tenenti (Rome, 1997), 641–725. For an interpretation of the Serrata as completed during the 1290s–1320s, see Guido Ruggiero, "Modernization and the Mythic State in Early Renaissance Venice: The Serrata Revisited," *Viator* 10 (1979): 245–56.

9. Cozzi, "Authority and the Law in Renaissance Venice"; idem, "La politica del diritto nella Repubblica di Venezia," in *Stato, società e giustizia nella Repubblica veneta (sec. XV–XVIII),* ed. Cozzi, vol. 1 (Rome, 1980), 15–152; Finlay, *Politics in Renaissance Venice;* Innocenzo Cervelli, *Machiavelli e la crisi dello stato veneziano* (Naples, 1974); Muir, *Civic Ritual in Renaissance Venice;* idem, "Images of Power: Art and Pageantry in Renaissance Venice," *American Historical Review* 84 (1979): 16–52; Manfredo Tafuri, "'Renovatio urbis Venetiarum': Il problema storiografico," in *"Renovatio urbis": Venezia nell'età di Andrea Gritti (1523–1538),* ed. Manfredo Tafuri (Rome, 1984), 9–55; idem, *Venezia e il Rinascimento: Religione, scienza, architettura* (Turin, 1985).

10. In addition to the works cited in the previous note, see Frederic C. Lane, "Naval Actions and Fleet Organization, 1499–1502," and Felix Gilbert, "Venice in the Crisis of the League of Cambrai," in Hale, *Renaissance Venice,* 146–73 and 274–92, respectively.

11. Domenico Malipiero, *Annali veneti dall'anno 1457 al 1500,* ed. Francesco Longo and Agostino Sagredo, 2 vols., *Archivio Storico Italiano* 7 (1843–44); Girolamo Priuli, *I diarii di Girolamo Priuli [AA. 1499–1512],* ed. Arturo Segre and Roberto Cessi, Rerum Italicarum Scriptores, 24, pt. 3, vols. 1, 2, 4 (Bologna, 1912–38); Sanuto, *I diarii;* Gasparo Contarini, *La Republica e i magistrati di Vinegia* (Venice, 1544); Domenico Morosini, *De bene instituta re publica,* ed. Claudio Finzi (Milan, 1969); Donato Giannotti, *Libro della republica de' Viniziani,* in *Opere politiche,* ed. Furio Diaz (Milan, 1974).

12. Elizabeth Crouzet-Pavan, *"Sopra le acque salse": Espaces, pouvoir, et société à Venise à la fin du Moyen Age,* 2 vols. (Rome, 1992); Richard Mackenney, *Tradesmen and Traders: The World of the Guilds in Venice and Europe, c. 1250–c. 1650* (Totowa, N.J., 1987); Dennis Romano, *Patricians and Popolani: The Social Foundations of the Venetian Renaissance State* (Baltimore, 1987); idem, *Housecraft and Statecraft: Domestic Service in Renaissance Venice, 1400–1600* (Baltimore, 1996); Guido Ruggiero, *The Boundaries of Eros: Sex Crime and Sexuality in Renaissance Venice* (New York, 1985); Stanley Chojnacki, "In Search of the Venetian Patriciate: Families and Factions in the Fourteenth Century," in Hale, *Renaissance Venice,* 47–90; idem, "Social Identity in Renaissance Venice: The Second Serrata," *Renaissance Studies* 8 (1994): 341–58.

13. See, for a recent example, Reinhold C. Mueller, "Espressioni di *status* sociale a Venezia dopo la 'serrata' del Maggior Consiglio," in *Studi veneti offerti a Gaetano Cozzi* (Venice, 1992), 53–61.

14. Chojnacki, "Social Identity in Renaissance Venice."

15. I wish to acknowledge the importance of Dennis Romano's insights in helping me to clarify this point.

16. Victor Crescenzi, *"Esse de maiori consilio"*: *Legittimità civile e legittimità politica nella Repubblica di Venezia (sec. XIII–XVI)* (Rome, 1996).

17. Angelo Ventura, "Scrittori politici e scritture di governo," in Arnaldi and Stocchi, *Storia della cultura veneta,* 3, pt. 3: 513–63. For a review of the literature on these writers as well as a valuable contribution to it, see Giovanni Silvano, *La "Republica de' Viniziani": Ricerche sul repubblicanesimo veneziano in età moderna* (Florence, 1993), esp. 9–37.

18. Lane, "Enlargement of the Great Council," 258; Crescenzi, *"Esse de maiori consilio,"* 335–37.

19. Chojnacki, "La formazione della nobiltà."

20. Ibid.; Crescenzi, *"Esse de maiori consilio,"* 335.

21. Chojnacki, "La formazione della nobiltà," 689, 704.

22. Romano, *Patricians and Popolani,* 36–37, 50–56, 144–47.

23. On adjustments after the War of Chioggia, see ibid., 152–58; Stanley Chojnacki, "Political Adulthood in Fifteenth-Century Venice," *American Historical Review* 91 (1986): 797–98; and idem, "La formazione della nobiltà," 706–12.

24. James S. Grubb, "Memory and Identity: Why Venetians Didn't Keep *Ricordanze,"* *Renaissance Studies* 8 (1994): 378–79; Chojnacki, "Social Identity in Renaissance Venice," 344–46.

25. Stanley Chojnacki, "Nobility, Women, and the State: Marriage Regulation in Venice, 1420–1535," in *Marriage in Italy, 1300–1650,* ed. Trevor Dean and K. J. P. Lowe (Cambridge, 1998), 132–39.

26. The escalation of exclusivist policy through the fourteenth and fifteenth centuries to its culmination in the early sixteenth is a central theme in Crescenzi, *"Esse de maiori consilio."*

27. In the early Quattrocento the Avogadori di Comun identified 236 houses as noble houses, though only 164 were in fact extant. One additional house was not on the Avogadori's list. In the early Cinquecento, by contrast, the Avogadori identified only 146, of which 142 are elsewhere documented as extant (Chojnacki, "Social Identity in Renaissance Venice," 345–46).

28. Maria-Teresa Todesco, "Andamento demografico della nobiltà veneziana allo specchio delle votazioni nel Maggior Consiglio (1297–1797)," *Ateneo Veneto,* n.s., 27 (1989): 152–53. Registrations for the Barbarella (or *Balla d'Oro*), the yearly lottery for young nobles, which enabled winners to enter the Great Council at twenty rather than waiting until the statutory age of twenty-five, also increased by 55 percent between the first and second halves of the Quattrocento (see Chojnacki, "Political Adulthood," 802; on the Barbarella, see 800–804).

29. See the chapter "Corrupt Elections" in Queller, *Venetian Patriciate,* 85–112.

30. Dieci, Miste, reg. 27, fol. 171v (19 Dec. 1497). The measure also raised the registration age for entrants in the Barbarella from eighteen to twenty. In his diary Marino Sanudo discusses this law as one of several important measures passed by the Ten at sessions of 19–21 December; he notes that rumors coursed through the city about the false credentials proofs ("alcune prove fate indebitamente contro le forme di le leze"), which the Ten now invalidated (*I diarii,* vol. 1, col. 835).

31. "Pro iustitia et equabilitate servanda inter omnes quibus mediantibus respublica

nostra per dei gratia et clementiam adaucta pacifice gubernetur et conservetur." Crescenzi reads "equalitate" rather than "equabilitate" (*"Esse de maiori consilio,"* 374).

32. On alliance strategies, see Bianca Betto, "Linee di politica matrimoniale nella nobiltà veneziana fino al XV secolo: Alcune note genealogiche e l'esempio della famiglia Mocenigo," *Archivio Storico Italiano* 139 (1981): 3–64, esp. 54–59. On the pursuit of desirable sons-in-law, see Stanley Chojnacki, "From Trousseau to Groomgift in Late Medieval Venice," in *Medieval and Renaissance Venice: Studies in Honor of Donald E. Queller,* ed. Ellen E. Kittell and Thomas F. Madden (Urbana, 1999), 141–65. On women's wealth as an engine of dowry inflation, see Donald E. Queller and Thomas F. Madden, "Father of the Bride: Fathers, Daughters, and Dowries in Late Medieval and Early Renaissance Venice," *Renaissance Quarterly* 46 (1993): 685–711, esp. 694–99.

33. Sampling indicates that average noble dowries grew from 873 ducats in 1361–90 (139 cases) to 1,732 ducats in 1505–7 (72 cases) (Cancelleria Inferiore, Notai, busta 114, Marino, S. Tomà, protocollo 1366–91; Avogaria di Comun, Contratti di Nozze, Misti, reg. 140/1, fols. 1r–66r). The practice of consigning unmarriageable girls to convents is documented anecdotally in wills and in a 1420 law limiting dowries; there is, however, no systematic study of its extent in practice. On the legislative reference, see Stanley Chojnacki, "Marriage Legislation and Patrician Society in Fifteenth-Century Venice," in *Law, Custom, and the Social Fabric in Medieval Europe: Essays in Honor of Bryce Lyon,* ed. Bernard S. Bachrach and David Nicholas (Kalamazoo, Mich., 1990), 164. Diverging from the general tendency in the scholarship, Queller and Madden argue that marriages were contracted without expectation of political or social advantage ("Father of the Bride," 700–704).

34. On recording mothers' names, see Chojnacki, "Marriage Legislation," 167–68. In a sample of 890 men from 16 patrician houses who married in the Quattrocento, only 81, 9.1 percent, married women from the cittadino, or popular classes (see the table in ibid., 174). In his chapter in this volume James Grubb finds a higher rate of male patrician exogamy.

35. See Stanley Chojnacki, "Subaltern Patriarchs: Patrician Bachelors in Renaissance Venice," in *Medieval Masculinities: Regarding Men in the Middle Ages,* ed. Claire A. Lees (Minneapolis, 1994), 78–79.

36. On sexual scandals in convents, see Giovanni Scarabello, "Devianza sessuale ed interventi di giustizia a Venezia nella prima metà del XVI secolo," in *Tiziano e Venezia: Convegno internazionale di studi, Venezia 1976* (Vicenza, 1980), 78–79; and Ruggiero, *Boundaries of Eros,* 72–84. The exploitation of women of the populace by male nobles is a major theme of Ruggiero's study (see, e.g., 97–108).

37. The evolving distinction between legitimacy according to the *ius civile* and the Venetian definition of political legitimacy is the principal theme in Crescenzi, *"Esse de maiori consilio";* see esp. the concluding chapter, "Legittimazione politica e legittimità civile nel sistema di *ius commune,"* 353–430.

38. For fuller discussion of the marriage legislation of these years, see Chojnacki, "Nobility, Women, and the State," 140–51.

39. On the cittadini, or the citizen status group mediating between patriciate and popolo, see James Grubb's chapter in this volume.

40. Senato, Terra, reg. 15, fols. 93v–94v. In the 1490s, reported Sanudo, nearly all dowries surpassed 3,000 ducats and some were as high as 10,000 (*I diarii*, vol. 1, col. 885). Sanudo reports that the author of the 1505 act was Marcantonio Morosini (vol. 6, col. 253). According to Finlay, Morosini was "beloved by patricians" (*Politics in Renaissance Venice*, 152). However, Antonio Tron, described by Finlay as an opponent of the rich, a supporter of poorer nobles, and a champion of intraclass equality, sought to delay it (241–42). Uncertainty thus hovers over the politics of dowry restraint.

41. On the participation of notaries in Florentine marriage contracts, see Christiane Klapisch-Zuber, *Women, Family, and Ritual in Renaissance Italy*, trans. Lydia G. Cochrane (Chicago, 1985), 184–85.

42. Dieci, Miste, reg 31, fols. 109v–110r. The fullest discussion of the import of this and other legislation of the early Cinquecento in the context of the intensifying concern with the identity of nobles' mothers is in Crescenzi, "*Esse de maiori consilio,*" 197–204, 217–22, and passim; on the terminology applied to objectionable mothers, see, 372–74. See also on legislation of 1422 spelling out conditions under which women of the populace could give birth to qualified nobles, Chojnacki, "Marriage Legislation," 167–71.

43. The first of the registers of baptisms is Avogaria di Comun, Registri di Battesimi, reg. 37/1, which includes several fascicles recording baptisms through the 1530s. The first entry, noting the baptism of Donato Stefano Nani, whose father's name is left blank, at San Giovanni Novo on 3 January 1506 *mv*, was recorded four days later, on 7 January. A rapid survey of the fascicles indicates that the names of mothers were entered only in cases of baptisms performed outside Venice.

The birth registrations in the *Libri d'Oro* begin in Avogaria di Comun, Nascite—Libro d'Oro, reg. 51/1 (NLO 51/1). Entries are listed alphabetically by surname, with a list of the lineages included on fol. 1r–v, followed by the text of the law of 31 August and a preface indicating the purpose of the register and the names of the current Avogadori. The first entry, dated 18 October 1506, records the birth of Piero Giovanni Alberto, son of Marino Alberto q. Piero and Elisabetta Donato (fol. 4r). The Avogadori's scribes noted in the margins of entries their subsequent use to establish the registrants' credentials for admission to the Great Council. For example, the entry on 8 March 1510 recording the birth of Paolo Girolamo Arimondo, son of Andrea di Alvise Arimondo and Caterina Vendramin (fol. 6r), includes in the margin a note dated 25 November 1530 that Piero Alberto, now twenty years old, had been issued a *bulletinum* attesting his qualifications to register for the Barbarella competition.

44. The precedent for this restriction was a law of 1414 refining Barbarella procedures (Crescenzi, "*Esse de maiori consilio,*" 349–52; Chojnacki, "Political Adulthood," 802–3).

45. The 31 August act explicitly limited the *Libro d'Oro* to sons of Great Council members. The requirement of a two-thirds majority in the doge's Collegio had been imposed in another act of the Ten twelve days earlier, on 19 August (Dieci, Miste, reg. 31, fol. 101r–v).

46. On the father-son tie as critical in the legislation of the early Quattrocento, see Chojnacki, "Social Identity in Renaissance Venice," 344, 347. The essential role of the

father in announcing his son's birth to the Avogadori di Comun is central to Crescenzi's configuration of a new political legitimacy as the most significant innovation of the early Cinquecento *("Esse de maiori consilio")*.

47. The fines were 500 lire for false claims of legitimacy and 200 lire for a false birth date.

48. A law of 12 August 1505 forbade nobles to act as "copatres" of other nobles either at baptism or confirmation (Dieci, Miste, reg. 30, fol. 191r. On this law see Finlay, *Politics in Renaissance Venice,* 203; and on the roles of witnesses at noble birth registrations see Crescenzi, *"Esse de maiori consilio,"* 77–84).

49. Avogaria di Comun, Registri di Battesimo, esp. reg. 37/1.

50. NLO 50/1. The entries record the names of 166 of the witnesses, of whom 30 were members of the father's lineage, only 12 of the mother's. The six houses were the Alberto, Arimondo, Balbi, Da Canal, Priuli, and Venier.

51. Ibid., fol. 6r. The marriage of Giannantonio's father, Jacopoalvise Venier, to the sister of Alvise di Piero Arimondo is recorded in Marco Barbaro, "Libro di nozze patrizie," Biblioteca Nazionale Marciana, Venice, Ms. It. cl. VII, 156 (8492), fol. 9r.

52. NLO 50/1, fol. 6v. Giannantonio registered the infant Andrea under the authority of a *procura* made to him by Caterina Vendramin.

53. They were, respectively, Francesco q. Piero da Molin and Andrea q. Marino da Molin. The marriages are recorded in Avogaria di Comun, Contratti di Nozze Misti (CN), reg. 140/1, fols. 3r, 64v.

54. At the 1510 *Libro d'Oro* inscription of Andrea and Caterina's first son, noted above, Giannantonio Venier's fideiussor colleague was Francesco Longo, who represented the third generation of Longos to vouch for the nobility of their Arimondo connections, which had been forged in the 1432 marriage of the confusingly named Arimonda Longo and Andrea di Alvise Arimondo's grandfather, Piero (Barbaro, "Libro di nozze patrizie," fol. 8v). The other Longo-Arimondo collaborations are recorded in Avogaria di Comun, Balla d'Oro, reg. 164/3, fols. 2r (8 Apr. 1465), 2v (1 May 1496). The relationship among these Longos is not clear owing to ambiguity in the sources about the given name of Arimonda Longo's father.

55. NLO 50/1, fol. 47r. The Boldù-Balbi marriage of 1490 is recorded in Barbaro, "Libro di nozze patrizie," fol. 40r.

56. NLO 50/1, fol. 48r. The Balbi relationships are given in Marco Barbaro, "Arbori de' patrizi veneti," vol. 1, fols. 115, 135 (copy in Archivio di Stato, Venice).

57. The fideiussores were, respectively, Francesco da Lezze and Piero da Pesaro (NLO 50/1, fol. 47r). The Balbi–Da Lezze and Vitturi–Da Pesaro marriages are recorded in Barbaro, "Libro di nozze patrizie," fols. 40r and 433r, respectively. Another brother-in-law fideiussor was Francesco Foscari, who vouched for the son of his wife's brother, Domenico Priuli, in 1509 (NLO 50/1, fol. 106v).

58. On the significance of the requirement that fathers *dare in nota* to the Avogadori the births of their sons, see Crescenzi, *"Esse de maiori consilio,"* esp. 46–57, 281.

59. On the power struggle between the Council of Ten and the more traditionalist Avogadori di Comun, see Crescenzi, ibid., esp. 173–79; Cozzi, "Authority and the Law in Renaissance Venice," esp. 322ff.; and Finlay, *Politics in Renaissance Venice,* 208–10.

60. Sanuto, *I diarii,* vol. 41, cols. 201, 203.

61. Consiglio dei Dieci, Comuni (Dieci, Comuni), reg. 2, fols. 14v–17v.

62. Ibid., fols. 14v–15r (21 Apr. 1526). The credentials-proof reform of 1497, discussed earlier, had also assigned the recredentialing of men approved during the previous thirty-three months to the capi of the Ten, who would join the Avogadori di Comun. But 1526 was the first time the Ten participated in what since 1323 had been the body with ultimate authority over proofs of nobility. On the Ten's growing authority in this period, see the extended discussion in Cozzi, "Authority and the Law in Renaissance Venice."

63. Two of the Ten, Luca Tron and Francesco Pesaro, proposed that the required majority be six of ten, not seven; they received no support. Since Luca Tron had the reputation of supporting the poorer nobles and the traditional authority of the Avogadori di Comun, his intervention likely indicates that it was the rank-and-file nobles, those least able to marry, who benefited from the Avogadori's evidently lax enforcement of the 1506 law, which the Ten now sought to correct (Dieci, Comuni, reg. 2, fol. 15r. On Luca Tron, see Cozzi, "Authority and the Law in Renaissance Venice," 322ff.; and Finlay, *Politics in Renaissance Venice,* 234–41).

64. Dieci, Comuni, reg. 2, fol. 17r–v (27 Apr. 1526).

65. They made the notation—in full, *iterum probetur iuxta legem*—even in cases where the interval was only two or three weeks beyond the three-month limit (see, e.g., NLO 50/1, fols. 48r [28 Dec. 1519] and 95v [27 Jan. 1518 *mv*]. See also the discussion, with examples, in Crescenzi, *"Esse de maiori consilio,"* 164–71).

66. For example, an entry for a Da Canal newborn dated 20 February 1525 *mv* followed normal practice in identifying his mother simply as "domina Maria Trivisano." But the subsequent two entries on the folio (also for Da Canal infants), dated 5 September and 18 December 1526, refer to the mothers as "domina Helisabeth Cornaro quondam ser Petri" and "domina Helisabeth Moro ser Augustini," respectively. Evidently, the new requirement took some adjusting to; in the Cornaro reference the notary squeezed the "quondam ser Petri" above the line, after inserting a carat after "Cornaro" (NLO 50/1, fol. 97r).

67. Crescenzi argues that the legislation of 1526 institutionalized a new "ideologia" that made birth to a low-born woman tantamount to illegitimacy (*"Esse de maiori consilio,"* 205–22). He examines the act and its application with detailed thoroughness on 107–56; the text of the legislation is on 107–9.

68. Dieci, Comuni, reg. 2, fols. 15v–17r (*sic:* there is no fol. 16; 26 April 1526).

69. A law of 1422 had required all claimants to noble status to identify their mothers, but it was not until 1430, in the wake of another law, that names of mothers were recorded in the registers of the Avogadori di Comun. On these measures, see Chojnacki, "Social Identity in Renaissance Venice," 350–51.

70. Avogaria di Comun, Matrimoni—Libro d'Oro, reg. 87/1 (MLO 87/1), fol. 38r. In most other registrations the formula *ad verificationem et justificationem* is used. For a thorough discussion of the evolving formula in these declarations, see Crescenzi, *"Esse de maiori consilio,"* 113–31.

71. Morosini and Vincenzo Trevisan were both married to daughters of Benedetto Giustinian q. Pangrazio (Barbaro, "Libro di nozze patrizie," fols. 328v, 420v).

72. The connection is established in the marriages of the descendents of Alvise q. Paolo Loredan (ibid., fols. 244v–247v). It is likely that Ettore was closer in practice to his distant cousins in the Loredan branch into which Piero Bragadin had married than the seven degrees of kinship that separated them would suggest. In any event, three years after his son's wedding to Elisabetta Trevisan, Piero Bragadin acted as a groom's witness in the marriage of Marco q. Alvise Loredan, his wife's brother (MLO 87/1, fol. 228r [16 June 1532]).

73. He had married the daughter of Marino di Marchio Trevisan in 1508; Vincenzo Trevisan, the father of the bride, was Vincenzo q. Marchio Trevisan (ibid., fols. 247v, 420r).

74. In only three of the marriages were all four witnesses members of the spouses' patrilineages (MLO 87/1). The names of five witnesses are either missing or illegible. The houses examined were the Arimondo, Badoer, Balbi, Barozzi, Bellegno, Bembo, Da Canal, Priuli, Venier, Vitturi, Zane, Zulian.

75. This number includes marriages with foreign women as well as nonnoble Venetian women. It should be noted that entries frequently fail to identify as *viri nobiles* brides' fathers with noble names. Although this may be scribal oversight, it may also signal men who had not established their noble credentials.

76. MLO 87/1, fol. 316v.

77. Cecilia Lanza married Zaccaria Barbaro with "vir nobilis" Girolamo q. Luca Minio and "ser Augustinus Lanza" as witnesses; the witnesses of Laura Montorio's marriage to Marco Balbi were "vir nobilis" Giovanni di Domenico Minio and "ser Stephanus ab auro" (ibid., fols. 31v, 74r). Even Giovanni Minio's relationship with Laura Montorio is suspect since his brother was one of the witnesses for her bridegroom.

78. Ibid., fol. 137rv.

79. Ibid., fol. 69r. However, Chiara de Franceschi's witnesses were two brothers from the noble Manolesso clan.

80. Three of the eleven belonged to Greek families living in Venice; the others were from Greek islands or Venice's possessions on the Italian mainland. In his chapter in this volume James Grubb finds a higher incidence of cross-class marriages by male patricians.

81. MLO 87/1, fol. 41v.

82. Crescenzi, *"Esse de maiori consilio,"* 7–8.

83. She is identified as a "bastarda" in Barbaro, "Libro di nozze patrizie," fol. 247v (1508).

84. The marriage registration is in MLO 87/1, fol. 18r. The terms of the settlement are in CN, reg. 142/3, fols. 169v–170r.

85. MLO 87/1, fol. 18rv (10 June 1533).

86. The terms of the settlement are in CN, reg. 142/3, fol. 265rv.

87. I have found marriage contracts for 5 others of the 11 illegitimate brides encountered in the sample of 150 marriage registrations. One, though imprecise, may

have reached 6,600 ducats; the others were in the vicinity of 3,000 (CN, reg. 142/3, fols. 33r, 63v, 71r, 90v, 92r). Although 11 women were acknowledged as illegitimate, the actual number may be larger, since some of the registered wives may be daughters of nonnobles with noble surnames or of unenfranchised or illegitimate sons of nobles, such as Marietta Gritti, daughter of Doge Andrea Gritti's illegitimate son Andrea, who married Alvise Bragadin in 1533 (MLO 87/1, 39r).

88. Morosini's marriage in 1518 to the daughter of Alvise Dolfin is recorded in Barbaro, "Libro di nozze patrizie," fol. 329v.

89. They were Alvise q. Carlo Morosini and the same Giambattista q. Jacopo Morosini who had witnessed Alvise Barozzi's marriage to Elena Querini four years earlier.

90. The witnesses in the one exceptional case were the bride's paternal uncle and brother (MLO 87/1, fol. 24r). The suspicion that other wives in the 150-marriage sample not identified as bastards were nevertheless illegitimate arises from the absence in many cases of a statement of the bride's condition, whereas the great majority were explicitly identified as their fathers' *filiam legitimam*. Crescenzi's observation, by contrast, is that the legitimacy or illegitimacy of the bride was nearly always indicated from 1527 on (*"Esse de maiori consilio,"* 119–22).

91. Finlay, *Politics in Renaissance Venice,* 87–89.

92. The five unmarried fathers (Jacopo q. Daniele Bragadin, Alvise q. Girolamo Dolfin, Bartolomeo q. Luca Michiel, Alvise di Nicolò Trevisan, and Andrea q. Paolo Vendramin) are absent from the lists of their clans' marriages from the 1470s to the 1530s in Barbaro, "Libro di nozze patrizie." Girolamo Querini is recorded as having married "sua garzona" in 1513 (ibid., fol. 379v). It is not known whether that woman was the mother of Elena, who married Vincenzo Barozzi and who is in any case identified in the Avogadori di Comun's register as illegitimate. The marriages to patrician women of the other five fathers of illegitimate daughters are recorded in Barbaro's compilation.

93. In a marriage contract registered with the Avogadori di Comun in 1534 the marriage broker referred to "la *nobel dona* madona Helena di Prioli fiola naturale del magnifico miser Zacharia di Prioli" (CN, reg. 142/3, fol. 290v, emphasis added).

94. Paul Ricoeur, *Oneself as Another,* trans. Kathleen Blamey (Chicago, 1993), 169–202, quotation on 172.

95. Charles Taylor, *Sources of the Self: The Making of the Modern Identity* (Cambridge, Mass., 1989), 62–63. Like Ricoeur, Taylor sees selfhood as achieved in moral interaction with others: "The full definition of someone's identity thus usually involves not only his stand on moral and spiritual matters but also some reference to a defining community" (36).

96. For Ricoeur, just institutions are necessary "to govern the apportionment of roles, tasks, and advantages or disadvantages between the members of society," a process that involves "the intersection of the private and the public aspect of distributive justice" (*Oneself as Another,* 200, 199).

97. CN, reg. 142/3, fols. 232r, 382r. On the relationship between dimissoria and

dowry, see Marco Ferro, *Dizionario del diritto comune e veneto,* 10 vols. in 5 (Venice, 1778–81), 4:279–83.

98. CN, reg. 142/3, fol. 232r. Other large totals were 4,500 ducats (30v), 6,000 (169r, 255v), 6,720 (265v), and 5,000 (265r bis).

99. Senato, Terra, reg. 28, fol. 151r (29 Apr. 1535). An amendment passed on 12 May would have restored women's rights to inherit, and testators' right to bequeath, amounts greater than 4,000 ducats (154r v). However, it appears to have been re-scinded by a later act on that same day (155v–156r). For a fuller discussion of this law, see Chojnacki, "Nobility, Women, and the State," 148–49.

100. Contarini was joined in proposing the law by Alvise Mocenigo *eques;* both were ducal councilors. On the dates of the composition of *De magistratibus* and of Contarini's receiving the cardinalate, see Elisabeth G. Gleason, *Gasparo Contarini: Venice, Rome, and Reform* (Berkeley, 1993), 110, 129. Gleason notes Mocenigo's history of policy disagreements with Contarini, especially regarding the papacy (43, 44, 70), but also his generous statement of admiration for Contarini's statesmanship at the news of the latter's nomination as cardinal less than a month after they had collaborated on the dowry law (74).

101. "I nostri antichi huomini savissimi . . . giudicarono, che fosse meglio che questa diffinitione della ragione publica si facesse dalla nobiltà di sangue, che dalla grandezza della robba: con questo temperamento nondimeno, accioché gli huomini di grandissima nobiltà soli non hanno questa riputazione; che questa sarebbe stato della potentia de pochi, e non della Republica; ma anchora tutti gli altri Cittadini non ignobili. Tutti quelli adunque, che furono o no nobili di sangue, o chiari per virtù, o benemeriti della Republica, ricevettero da principio questa authorità di governare la città" (Gasparo Contarini, *La Republica e i Magistrati di Vinegia* [Venice, 1544], x).

102. Gleason, *Gasparo Contarini,* 118, 122.

103. Ibid., 126–28.

104. For the overall context, see Cozzi, "Authority and the Law in Renaissance Venice." For a view that emphasizes major differences between Gritti's program of "novità" and Contarini's celebration of "tradizione," see Silvano, *La "Republica de' Viniziani,"* 26–29. On Gritti's reforms, see, briefly, Tafuri, *Venezia e il Rinascimento,* 162–63.

105. Tafuri, *Venezia e il Rinascimento.* (The English translation of this work, *Venice and the Renaissance,* trans. Jessica Levine [Cambridge, Mass., 1989], is unreliable owing to many inaccuracies.) See also Tafuri, *"Renovatio urbis,"* 9–55.

106. For assessments of Gritti's program of institutional reform, see Cozzi, "La politica del diritto," 122–45; and Tafuri, *"Renovatio urbis,"* esp. 16; Victor Crescenzi, "Il modello veneto: Il Libro d'Oro delle leggi del Maggior Consiglio (secc. XVI–XVII)," in *L'educazione giuridica,* ed. Alessandro Giuliani and Nicola Picardi, vol. 5, *Modelli di legislatore e scienza della legislazione* (Rome, 1987), 166–67.

107. Senato, Terra, reg. 28, fol. 154v (12 May 1535). The doge's review was apparently proposed by Gasparo Malipiero, but the enforcement clause was the work of Gasparo Contarini, once again partnered with Alvise Mocenigo: the Avogadori di

Comun were not to register any marriage the contract for which had not been read before the doge, nor could any woman married to a noble, or any woman married to a cittadino with a dowry of 1,000 ducats or higher, reclaim her dowry unless the contract had been read before the doge (155v). On Gritti's program of solemnizing ritual occasions, see Muir, "Images of Power," 33–36.

108. John B. Thompson, *Ideology and Modern Culture: Critical Theory in the Era of Mass Communication* (Stanford, 1990), 61–62.

109. Dieci, Miste, reg. 27, fol. 171v; on this act, see above.

110. Morosini urged institutional reform with an oligarchical emphasis to address problems arising from the presence in the government of too many poor nobles who depended on the stipends they earned from government jobs and too many young nobles who disrupted government councils (Gaetano Cozzi, "Domenico Morosini e il 'De bene instituta republica,' " *Studi Veneziani* 12 [1970]: 405–58, esp. 421–27. See also Ventura, "Scrittori politici e scritture di governo," 546–48).

111. On the connection between identity and ideology, see Eric Erikson, *Identity: Youth and Crisis* (New York, 1968): "For the social institution which is the guardian of identity *is* what we have called *ideology.* One may see in ideology also the imagery of an aristocracy in its widest possible sense, which connotes that within a defined world image and a given course of history the best people will come to rule and rule will develop the best in people. . . . For it is through their ideology that social systems enter into the fiber of the next generation and attempt to absorb into their lifeblood the rejuvenative power of youth" (133–34).

Behind the Walls

The Material Culture of Venetian Elites

PATRICIA FORTINI BROWN

Perhaps more than any other city, Venice was built on worldly goods. The shops along the Merceria, the street running from Rialto to San Marco, and the palaces along the Grand Canal overflowed with items transported from abroad or hammered and chiseled by local artisans at home. But what did this profusion of goods mean? In this chapter Patricia Fortini Brown shows how both patricians and cittadini *used these objects to define their individual and familial identities and to map out a place for themselves in Venetian society. Yet the impulse of these elites to distinguish themselves through a display of material wealth threatened the mercantile virtues of prudence and frugality as well as the solidarity of a ruling class based first and foremost on hereditary right. The result was a long and generally unsuccessful campaign of sumptuary legislation. Brown argues that in Venice these laws served a unique purpose. They were not used, as they were elsewhere, to validate the social system and to distinguish one class from another. Instead, the Venetian government promulgated them both to maintain solidarity within the ranks of the patriciate and to narrow the gap between nobles and wealthy commoners. In Venice every effort was made to ensure that private wealth would not be used to destroy public life.*

RECENT STUDIES suggest that the consumption of luxury goods was a defining feature of a distinct Renaissance culture, as important as the rediscovery of the art and literature of classical antiquity in making a break from the world of medieval feudalism.[1] While the relative importance of the library vis-à-vis the marketplace is a matter of debate, one cannot deny that the golden age of Venice and other major European cities in the sixteenth and seventeenth centuries was golden indeed in terms of objects as well as ideas.[2] Indeed, Venice, perhaps more than any other city, played a central role in the nascent consumer culture described so well by Richard Goldthwaite and Lisa Jardine. As Padre Pietro Casola observed on a visit in 1494:

> Something may be said about the quantity of merchandise in the said city, although not nearly the whole truth, because it is inestimable. Indeed it seems as if the whole world flocks there, and that human beings have concentrated there all their force for trading. I was taken to see various warehouses, beginning with that of the Germans—which it appears to me would suffice alone to supply all Italy with the goods that come and go—and so many others that it can be said they are innumerable. . . . And who could count the many shops so well furnished that they also seem warehouses, with so many cloths of every make—tapestry, brocades and hangings of every design, carpets of every sort, camlets of every colour and texture, silks of every kind; and so many warehouses full of spices, groceries and drugs, and so much beautiful white wax! These things stupefy the beholder, and cannot be fully described to those who have not seen them.[3]

Given that Venice was unique in so many aspects—its site, its government, its social structure—it may be asked whether its use of, and experience with, this expanded world of beautiful objects was also distinctive. Any such query may well begin in the private spaces of Venetian palaces, and a short tour behind the walls with the Venetian writer Francesco Sansovino in 1581 will serve to define the issues. Son of the renowned sculptor and architect Jacopo Sansovino, he had a good eye and a voluble pen. Observing that Venetians referred to their homes as houses *(case)* instead of *palazzi* "out of modesty," he continued:

> In the past, although our ancestors were frugal, they were lavish in the decoration of their houses. There are countless buildings with ceilings of bedrooms [*camere*] and other rooms decorated in gold and other colors and with histories painted by celebrated artists. Almost everyone has his house adorned with noble tapestries, silk drapes and gilded leather, wall hangings [*spalliere*] and other things according to the time and season, and most of the bedrooms are furnished with bedsteads and chests, gilded and painted, so the cornices are loaded with gold. The dressers displaying silverware, porcelain, pewter and brass or damascene bronze are innumerable. In the reception rooms [*sale*] of great families there are racks of arms with the shields and standards of their ancestors who fought for Venice on land and at sea. I have seen sold at auction the home furnishings of a noble condemned by unfortunate incident that would have been more than a Grand Duke of Italy would wish. The same can be said of the middle and lower classes in proportion. Because there is no person so miserable, with a well-equipped house [*casa aperta*],[4] that he would not have chests and bedsteads of walnut, green draperies, carpets, pewter, copper, chains of gold, forks and rings

of silver. Such is the *politia* of this city. Therefore, practicing admirably the exercise of the arts and converging there all the foreign nations, the people participate in this profit so fertile, some more, some less, according to the quality and ingenuity of the persons, [but] made thereby too soft and licentious.[5]

Sansovino's choice of the word *politia* was probably no accident. The term had two distinct, if related, meanings in the sixteenth century. One usage derived from the Greek *politeia* and connoted good government, the political life, and civil comportment.[6] The other came from the Latin *politus,* meaning refinement in fashion, politeness of behavior, or the display of luxury.[7] Here Sansovino was referring to the manners and material goods that added up to an urbane lifestyle of civility and refinement. He attributes the opulence of the Venetian home to the city's long history without invasion or pillage and to mercantile activities that brought in goods from throughout the world. But for all his celebration of its material splendor, he introduces an ambiguous, if not discordant, tone on two points. First, his Venetian forefathers were both frugal and profligate. And second, while his contemporaries profited from a thriving culture of consumption and display, at least some had become overly addicted to a life of self-indulgence. They were, in short, a frugal people caught up in a sumptuous lifestyle about which he seemingly had mixed feelings.

Thomas Coryat, an Englishman who visited the city in 1608, also sensed ambiguities in Venetian society, but from the perspective of an outsider. He allowed that "the name of a Gentleman of Venice is esteemed a title of . . . eminent dignity and honour," and yet his view of the household arrangements of the Venetians was ambivalent. He asks: "Howbeit these Gentlemen do not maintaine and support the title of their gentility with a quarter of that noble state and magnificence as our English Noblemen and Gentlemen of the better sort doe. For they keepe no honourable hospitality, nor gallant retinue of servants about them, but a very frugall table, though they inhabit the most beautiful Palaces, and are inriched with as ample meanses to keepe a brave port as some of our greatest English Earles."[8] Indeed, as a recent study has shown, the typical patrician family in Venice employed few servants in comparison with their counterparts of the same social rank elsewhere.[9] Such restraint was due, Coryat learned, to "a certain kinde of edect made by the Senate, that they should not keepe a retinue beyond their limitation."[10]

Indeed, that anomalous image of frugality amidst material splendor sums up the dilemma of a society in transition. By the middle of the Cinquecento, *concordia* and *unanimitas,* the ethical linchpins of the longstanding Venetian myth of equality and consensus within the patriciate, were under increasing strain.[11] For an ever more transparent myth was called upon to mask ever greater disparities and concentrations of wealth within that same patriciate, as well as disjunctions between economic class and social caste within the society as a whole.[12] At issue was the public control of private *politia* in a society that privileged civic responsibility over individual or family glory. As a first step toward a better understanding of Venetian attitudes toward worldly goods in terms of personal and public identities, this chapter focuses on three questions. First, how did the Venetian experience relate to ideas about nobility that were being debated throughout Italy during this period? Second, how did the domestic environment in Venice express patrician ideals, or, to put it another way, how did the individual define and defend family identity through the accumulation of objects and works of art? And third, how did Venetian society deal with the tension between private aspirations and the need for communal solidarity that was engendered by those modestly named but sumptuously adorned *case* that not only lined the Grand Canal but were scattered through every *sestiere* of the city?

The debate on nobility was not new. Fourteenth- and fifteenth-century jurists and humanists in Tuscany, from Bartolo di Sassoferrato to Poggio Bracciolini, had struggled to define the relative importance of blood, *virtù* (i.e., fame, glory, virtue), and wealth in defining nobility in communes where a new mercantile oligarchy had gained power at the expense of an ancient military-feudal aristocracy. During the same period in Venice, where nobility had essentially been determined by bloodlines since the *Serrata* of 1297, writers were more concerned with the relationship between noble privilege and the sovereignty of the state (i.e., the Venetian senate). But during the first three decades of the sixteenth century, when class lines were becoming more strictly drawn and power was more narrowly held in states throughout the peninsula, an old debate took on new resonance. The presence of foreign armies in Italy, moreover, prompted comparisons with institutions and customs of other nations.[13] A growing body of literature, much of it published in Venice, began to grapple with changing definitions of nobility.

Niccolò Machiavelli, in his *Discorsi sopra la prima deca di Tito Livio*, probably written in 1513–17, sought to distinguish between *gentilhuomini* and *cittadini*. No admirer of nobility, he held that the caste was made up of gentiluomini, "who without working live in luxury on the returns from their landed possessions, without paying any attention either to agriculture or to any other occupation necessary for making a living." Such men, he charged, were "altogether hostile to all free government."[14] It was in fact the cittadini who created civility and the civil life. But how did Machiavelli account for Venice, which "ranked high among modern republics" elsewhere in his treatise[15] but was ruled by noble gentlemen? Indeed, in his view they were not gentlemen at all: "The gentlemen in that republic are so rather in name than in fact; they do not have great incomes from landed possessions, but their great riches are based on trade and movable property; moreover none of them holds castles or has any jurisdiction over men. Thus that name of gentleman among them is a name of dignity and reputation, without being founded on any of those things in other cities signified by the word *gentleman*. . . . so Venice is divided into gentlemen [among whom there were no distinctions] and people; and the rule is that the first shall hold or be eligible to hold all the offices; the others are wholly excluded from them."[16]

Since Machiavelli was concerned only with political power, he did not take account of *cittadini originari*, but his view was accurate enough for the early sixteenth century, when most of the patriciate were still actively engaged in trade. And yet by the late 1520s, when Gasparo Contarini composed his *De magistratibus et republica Venetorum,* the treatise was beginning to seem out of date.[17] The 1599 English translation of the treatise by Lewes Lewkenor captures the unabashed certainty of a privileged elite and will be used here. Observing that all political authority was vested in the Great Council, made up of a company of citizens [by which he meant the patriciate], Contarini explained: "Now first I am to yeeld you a reckoning how and with what wisedome it was ordayned by our auncestors, that the common people should not bee admitted into this company of citizens, in whose authority consisteth the whole power of the common wealth, then that this definition of citizens was not with lesse wisedome measured, rather by the nobility of lineage, then the greatnes of wealth, as in auncient commonwealthes it was wont, & as many old philosophers do prescribe."[18]

Contarini allowed that some of the founding fathers had argued that this "company of citizens" should be defined by ability and abundance of riches but argued that this was totally wrongheaded: "For it happeneth often that those of the basest sort, yea of the very skum of the people, do scrape together great wealth, as those that apply themselves to filthy artes, and illiberall occupations, never sparing the toilesome and carefull wearing out of their lives, but with an intollerable saving, defrauding themselves of the comforts of life, thereby to increase their substance." Conversely, the well brought up honest citizens (i.e., patricians) often fell into poverty either through adverse fortune or through spending their time on liberal studies rather than on increasing their wealth. In consequence, if "filthy and ill mannerd men favouring of nothing but gaine, utterly ignorant of good artes" came to govern, disaster would ensue. "Therefore our wise and prudent ancestors, lest their commonwealth should happen into these calamities, ordered that this definition of publike rule, should go rather by the nobility of lineage, than by the estimation of wealth."[19] Contarini would have been writing shortly after the passage of the landmark law of 1526 requiring registration of all noble marriages. Preceded by similar legislation in 1506 that called for the registration of all male noble births, it was the culmination of a series of laws passed over the past century designed to ensure the purity of noble blood.[20]

The hard edge on Contarini's words suggests that resentment of wealthy commoners among the poorer members of the patriciate must be held in check by stressing the membership of the latter in a community of noble equals who shared political privilege. His scheme thus far sounds much like Machiavelli's. But then he goes on to describe a political hierarchy within the citizen class of nobles. Aside from the doge, who "beareth the shew of a kingly power, representing in all thinges the glory, gravitie and dignity of a king," there was also a special group of officeholders who were elevated above their peers: "But the Senate, the tenne, the colledge of elders or chiefe counsellors, which amongst us of the common people are commonly called the sages: those I say which do consult of matters, & after from the commonwealth do make report unto the Senat, carry with them a certaine shew of an Aristocracy or government of the nobilitie."[21] Contarini's stratified patriciate, with some nobles more equal than others, reflected a political reality. But he chose to overlook another reality, namely, that wealth and power often went hand in hand, an inconvenient fact that would become increasingly divisive as the century went on.

The mercantile nobility of Venice was an anomaly often remarked upon by writers of the period. Giovambattista Nenna of Bari, who published a treatise on nobility in 1543, was struck by the diverse ways in which nobility was defined in different communities: "We see in the magnanimous and signorial city of Naples that the practice of trade—*mercadantia*—is alien to the noble caste." There, as in ancient Thebes, he observed, merchants were not allowed to hold public office. In Venice, however, "it is completely contrary: since not only plebes, but [also] nobles, including their senators, are engaged in trade. The purity of the blood of their ancestors is what distinguishes noble from non-noble, not their profession."[22]

Tommaso Garzoni expanded upon the same theme four decades later in his *La piazza universale*. Again looking at the Neapolitan barons, he wrote that "they constitute nobility in riding a beautiful *gianetto* [a Spanish horse], in jousting, in living a gallant life, in being escorted by a flock of pages, and in the exterior pomp of a beautiful and graceful company." He further observed that the Milanese lords were little different, if less affected. But "the noble Venetians are completely contrary in mood to these; because they go alone, with simple clothing, however finely dressed, they keep a single gondola in the cavana that is their stall, and they exercise *mercantia* [trade], however grand, which was not esteemed by the ancient Roman senators in any pact."[23] The contrast is clear in two woodcuts from Cesare Vecellio's costume book of 1590, where an elegantly accoutered Neapolitan nobleman may be compared with his soberly, if imposingly, dressed Venetian counterpart (Figs. 1 and 2).

Along with noble occupations, the relationship between nobility and wealth was also a major concern. Aristotle's theory of magnificence, which sanctioned, indeed required, great expenditures and appropriate display by the wealthy, had been part of the aristocratic rationale in Italy since the fifteenth century.[24] But in Venice the greater dilemma concerned not the noble rich but the noble poor. Accordingly, Girolamo Muzio in his treatise of 1565 sought to define who could truly be called a gentleman. He allowed that people were accustomed to honoring rich men who wore the most splendid dress, kept the most servants, and owned the most beautiful houses and the finest horses. But he held that not every rich man was noble and that in fact the most noble of men disdained riches, pleasure, and glory and might well not be rich. Such was often the case, he wrote, in Venice, where there was no one from a noble family so poor that he could not participate in the councils and hold political office. But Muzio admitted that Venice constituted a "miracolo."[25]

And yet, the famed solidarity of the Venetian patriciate was becoming less a miracle and more a mirage. With great wealth concentrated in ever fewer hands within the patriciate and even among wealthy commoners, a growing number of nobles lived in relative poverty.[26] Contarini's acclaim for rule "rather by the nobility of lineage, than by the estimation of wealth" was fine in theory but little comfort in real life. The Venetian patrician Paolo Paruta addressed the problem of how much wealth a nobleman needed in his treatise *Della perfettione della vita politica,* published in 1579. Rejecting proposals by several of the protagonists in his dialogue to pass laws limiting wealth, he suggested that honors and offices of the city be distributed harmoniously among the patriciate, equaling "according to a certain geometric proportion the diverse condition of persons."[27] But the overriding concern of the ever larger poor majority of the nobility was not simply officeholding or even hunger. At issue was personal

FIG. 1. Neapolitan gentleman, from Cesare Vecellio, *Degli habiti antichi et moderni di diverse parti del mondo libri due* (Venice, 1610). Reprinted by permission of the Folger Shakespeare Library.

FIG. 2. Venetian patrician with sleeves *a comedo,* from Cesare Vecellio, *Degli habiti antichi et moderni di diverse parti del mondo libri due* (Venice, 1610). Reprinted by permission of the Folger Shakespeare Library.

identity, for riches were necessary if one was to live in a noble manner. As Antonio Colluraffi later wrote in his *Il nobile veneto*, "It is not enough then for our noble to say: I am born *Nobile*; but he should also say: I want to live *Nobile*; I want to die *Nobile*."[28]

And the manner of living *nobile* was supported by its own literature in the sixteenth century.[29] The point of departure was Alessandro Piccolomini's translation of Xenophon's *Oeconomicus*, a fourth-century treatise on the art of governing the home, published in Venice in 1540.[30] Two years later, Piccolomini brought out his own treatise entitled *Della institutione de la felice vita dell'huomo nato nobile e in città libera* [The principles of the happy life of the man born noble and in a free city].[31] Similar works followed by other writers, who depended on Aristotle as well as Xenophon. The central premise was that the house, as the most tangible symbol of family identity and continuity, should balance *commodità* (comfort and utility) with *decoro* (honor) within its *fabrica* (structure). Its dimensions, its floor plan, its decorations, and its furnishings were eloquent signs of the family's status and quality of life. Although each writer had his own emphasis—some were oriented more toward rural than toward city life—they all presented principles and norms that were shared by the new aristocratic elite that had taken hold in most of the old citizen-republics of Italy.[32]

Several of the treatise writers insisted that every family should own its own home. Those who lived in the houses of others, wrote Nicolò Vito di Gozze, a gentleman of Ragusa, were "imperfectly *economico*" because just as it was necessary to have one's own sons and one's own wife, it was also necessary to have one's own house.[33] Giacomo Lanteri, a Brescian nobleman, stressed that "he who is born noble and rich should not in any way (if great necessity does not force him to) make himself a slave to the price of one hundred scudi a year."[34] And yet here again Venetians went their own way, for a number of patrician families—about 50 percent by 1582—rented palaces from others.[35] Their livelihoods long connected to trade rather than to the land, some did this in order to keep their capital liquid for investment rather than because they could not afford to purchase or build a house. Others were forced to rent by virtue of inheritance laws.[36] But if the palace was a major factor in family identity, was it less so if the family simply lived there and did not own it? The problem is worth further investigation, but one suspects that in such cases the family image was projected in the *mobili* (material goods), for which the palace provided a dignified and essential frame.

A second area of discussion in the treatises was the proper site and orientation of the house. The possibilities were limited in crowded Venice. The

Venetian writer Giovanni Maria Memmo urged that, if possible, it "should not be dominated by other palaces in order that they not impede air and the sunlight, and that it should not be subject to the view of neighbors so that the domestic activities could be seen and observed by them. I judge that this is one of the major drawbacks that a palace could have, being in such a way the servant of others."[37] But as Palladio observed, "Most commonly in cities, either the neighbours' walls, the streets, or publick places, prescribed certain limits, which the architect cannot surpass."[38]

Aside from the difficulty of finding an ideal location in Venice, there was also a greater dispersal of noble homes throughout the city than Lanteri might have sanctioned. For he had counseled that it was not good for noblemen to live on public streets and squares where there are *botteghe* (shops) of artisans because of the noise and lack of space. On the other hand, he had advised the merchant to locate his residence in the part of the city most convenient to his business and even to rent ground-floor rooms to others as botteghe or *fondachi* (warehouses or stores).[39] For Venice's mercantile nobility the demands of honor and utility might well be balanced between a magnificent facade facing the Grand Canal and a less imposing ground entrance amidst shops and small artisan establishments.

Within the house, principles of separation and specialization pertained, the size of each room being appropriate to its function. Lanteri held that rooms for everyday family use should be kept separate from those used by guests, and servants' rooms should be "in the most abject part of the house so that they will be hidden from the view of those who enter." While the father's chamber and study should be closest to the entrance, the women's rooms should be the furthest from it, connected to the garden and the places of washing and storage so that the women could go freely from one place to the other "without passing through the rest of the house, where they can be seen." Allowing that nobles and *grandi* of the highest rank are "more than all the others obligated to display grandeur and pomp," Lanteri advised that the same principles held true for all homes.[40] The plan thus controlled access and ordered traffic, with degrees of separation between public and private areas.[41]

In Venice and elsewhere in Renaissance Italy, *camere* (bedchambers) were quasi-public rooms, used not only for childbirth celebrations but also for marriage banquets.[42] A lithograph made after an 1830 drawing by the English artist Lake Price of just such a chamber in the Palazzo Corner-Spinelli, which still had much of its sixteenth-century decoration, gives us a sense of these multi-purpose spaces (Fig. 3). The bed, built into an alcove, was characteristically

FIG. 3. Chamber in Palazzo Corner-Spinelli, lithograph by Joseph Nash from the original drawings, from Lake Price, *Interiors and Exteriors in Venice* (London, 1843). Photograph from Osvaldo Böhm, Venice.

Venetian. Padre Casola must have seen something like it in 1494, when he attended a lying-in celebration for a lady of the Dolfin family and described a well-accoutered bedstead "fixed in the room in the Venetian fashion."[43] However, a dialogue in Anton Francesco Doni's *Ragionamenti,* published in Venice in 1552, suggests either a change or a disagreement over the custom of the commodious bedchamber. Representing the traditional view, a certain Nanni Unghero complains of a modern floor plan: "Those *camerine* so small that there is room only for a bed, a table, and two chests cannot be praised; and then to make a sala that seems to be a piazza!" But Betto Arrighi responds: "The *camere* are made for sleeping and not for passing through, nor for banqueting in, nor for dancing; however, they are sufficient. The *sala* is rightly so [large] because all the family comes together there all at once. . . . The ladies stand beneath the windows because of the light, to embroider and make fine things with the needle, . . . [the family] eats on the table at the head [of the room] and plays [games] on the one at the side. Some stroll around, others stand at the fire, and so there is a place for everyone."[44] Doni illustrated this point with a woodcut of a Venetian matron absorbed in her needlework next to a large window (Fig. 4).

Addressing the matter from a Venetian perspective, Memmo emphasized two features that are not so prominent in the other treatises. First, he called for a spacious loggia and a reception room—the *sala* or *portego*—that was cheerful and full of air because these were "the life and spirit of the palace, where the Citizen lives the greater part of his life."[45] Indeed, the portego, the most public room in the Venetian house, was also a defining space for the family who lived in it. The loggia gave visual access to the public world beyond the walls, and, conversely, denoted on the exterior facade of the house the heart of domestic space. In the luminous interior a family, surrounded by portraits and

FIG. 4. Venetian lady doing needlework, from Anton Francesco Doni, *I marmi* (Florence, 1863). Reprinted by permission of the Folger Shakespeare Library.

paintings of secular and religious subjects, presented itself as a cohesive unit to those who were invited inside the palace walls. The bedchambers may have contained more of the material wealth of the house and undoubtedly were the site of more of the day-to-day activity, but it was in the portego that families or individuals represented themselves in a formal way.[46] While the range of furnishings listed in porteghi in sixteenth-century inventories is great, they typically held works of art, a few large pieces of furniture, and a generous number of chairs or benches, ensembles well suited for the entertainment of many guests.

Well before Sansovino celebrated the politia of the Venetian house, many families already lived in luxurious surroundings that the writer would have considered suitable for a *casa aperta*. In the fourteenth century Lionardo di Niccolò Frescobaldi, a Florentine pilgrim on the way to the Holy Land who spent several days in Venice, described a dinner at the home of Remigio Soranzo, which "appeared to be a house of gold."[47] Likewise, at the end of the fifteenth century Padre Casola saw a fireplace of Carrara marble in the Dolfin bedchamber and "so much gold everywhere" that he was certain that its decoration would have cost 2,000 ducats or more. It should also be noted that he left the reception hungry and commented on the same penurious hospitality that Coryat would criticize a century later.[48]

But such reports, like those of Marino Sanudo and Sansovino, are hearsay. To get beyond them into all the rooms of a variety of Venetian homes, one must inevitably look to inventories. Drawn up by notaries, inventories listed all the objects (no matter how modest) in a house, in most cases room by room; they offer invaluable and reliable evidence of a material culture that is truly sumptuous at the high end and depressing indeed at the low. Such documentation provides a check on the ideal prescriptions of the treatises on the household and the reports of dazzled eyewitnesses such as Casola. But it is important to be aware of the limitations of inventories. They do not describe the immovable decoration of rooms, such as marble fireplaces, elaborately carved doors, and gold and ultramarine coffered ceilings. Nor was every household inventoried. Most often inventories were made upon the death of an individual with children of minor age or for a widow who was reclaiming her dowry.[49] And yet precisely because of the random nature of inventories that survive, embracing both lengthy catalogues of affluent houses and poignantly meager lists of the poor, they appear to offer a reasonably representative cross section of the levels of wealth in Venetian society.

Several inventories were published by Pompeo Molmenti in his ground-breaking study *La storia di Venezia nella vita privata,* first published in 1880 and expanded to three volumes in six subsequent editions.[50] But Isabella Palumbo-Fossati, writing in the 1980s, was, to my knowledge, the first scholar to look at them analytically.[51] Focusing primarily on the homes of artisans and artists, she documented a level of comfort that amply confirms Sansovino's claims for the availability of a lifestyle of *politia* even for "the middle and lower classes in proportion."

To get a sense of the domestic environments of the most privileged in terms of wealth and noble status, we will turn to the inventory of the patrician Domenico di Nicolò Capello, who died in 1532, leaving a widow and at least one minor child. During his life Capello moved among the *grandi.* Elected *capo* of the Council of Ten "per danari," as Sanudo put it, he was active in political life.[52] At the time of his death Capello had about 2,500 ducats in cash in his palace on the Rio di San Lorenzo in the parish of Santa Maria Formosa. Later praised by Sansovino as one of the hundred residences in the city worthy of the name *palazzo,* it was a traditional gothic-style structure with a frescoed facade that featured no less than three rooms denoted in the inventory as "golden."[53] Among the furnishings of the *camera d'oro grande* were four paintings: a Madonna with Saints Peter and John in a frame with gilded colonettes and painted images of Prudence, Temperance, and Justice, those secular patron saints of the Venetian household, each in its own gilt frame.[54] The room also held ten painted and gilded chests, a large gilded writing desk of walnut, and a mirror with a gilt frame. Likewise, the *camera d'oro piccolo* featured a black walnut writing desk, seven painted and gilded chests, a large mirror of tin with a walnut frame, a gilded *restello* (dressing mirror), and two paintings, a Madonna with Saints Nicholas and Anthony and the Madonna alone. Even the walls of the *mezado d'oro* were decorated with a mirror and paintings of the Madonna and a head of Christ.[55]

The portego was intended for aristocratic gatherings such as the dinner Domenico gave for nine gentlemen in 1530. According to Sanudo, it was "molto brava" and the talk of the city. For the variety of game that was served, "one could call it an ark of Noah."[56] Sanudo does not record the locale of the dinner, but if the guests had eaten in the portego, they would have been surrounded by eight paintings, six of which depicted religious subjects: "a large painting on canvas of Mary, Joseph, and the shepherds [probably a Nativity or possibly a Flight into Egypt], a Last Supper, an Assumption of the Virgin, a Prodigal Son, a Crucifixion," and "uno dela adultera," probably Christ and the Adulteress. The two secular paintings were an Ages of Man and a portrait of

Domenico's son Nicolò, then deceased. The room also contained a large wood chest, a small square bench of walnut, six dining tables on trestles, including one of cypress wood, and fifteen painted benches "around the portego."[57]

Although the inventories document a proliferation of wall paintings in Venetian porteghi over the course of the sixteenth century, some patrician walls remained relatively bare. The inventory made after the death of Donado di Michael da Lezze in 1582 is a case in point. While the wealth of objects attests to his affluence, his portego featured only three paintings, two of them portraits of Donado himself and his grandfather. And yet the room was clearly set up for large gatherings: twenty-four walnut benches, some decorated and some plain, twenty-two chairs, two tables (one fir and the other a small round one of walnut "to work on"), a campaign chest covered with horse skin, a credenza of walnut, five chests of various types, a copper bucket, and three stools.[58] The nobleman Cipriano di Nicolò Boldù, by contrast, exemplified penury more than restrained opulence. At the time of his death in 1572 his portego held only nine walnut chairs (six new and three old), a walnut credenza, a painted chest to hold dirty clothing, a *homo di legno*,[59] a trestle table, and an old chest containing some writings.[60]

By the early seventeenth century the portego walls of wealthy families had begun to spill over with paintings.[61] For example, an inventory of 1604 listing the possessions of Francesco Vrins, a Flemish merchant who lived in the parish of Santa Maria Formosa, cited no fewer than twenty-two. Among them were nine portraits; four of these were of named family members, including two of the deceased. There were also six landscapes, two kitchen scenes, a Judgment of Paris, a painting with five large figures, and three small pictures above the doors. The only piece of religious art in the room was "a Christ with the martyrdom of the column," presumably a sculpted figure of the Flagellation. A large framed *mappamondo* also hung on the wall.[62] Maps of the world or of continents, artifacts of an age of exploration and discovery of varying degrees of scientific accuracy, were already a popular form of decoration in the north. Although rare in Venice at the beginning of the sixteenth century—Marino Sanudo had one that was much admired—they appeared increasingly in Venetian inventories and by the seventeenth century were ubiquitous emblems of wealth and good taste. While Vrins may well have consulted his map in the course of his mercantile pursuits, in many—perhaps most—Venetian patrician homes in this period large wall maps would have been status symbols whose purpose was more ornamental than functional. Less actively engaged by this time in mercantile activities that required an accurate knowledge of the world,

FIG. 5. Chamber in Palazzo Barbarigo, from Lake Price, *Interiors and Exteriors in Venice* (London, 1843). Photograph from Osvaldo Böhm, Venice.

the patriciate had become "gentlemen in fact" as well as in name.[63] Vrins's portego also held a credenza, a harpsichord, a mirror with an ebony frame, a large gilded lantern, two tables (one surfaced with red leather, the other having drawers), nineteen chairs, and twenty stools or benches.[64] In his drawing of the portego in Palazzo Barbarigo, Lake Price attempted to reconstruct the original appearance of such a room in the sixteenth century, complete, in this case, with the lordly figure of Titian at the easel (Fig. 5).

Gardens, the second feature recommended by Memmo of particular relevance to Venetian householders, were also a particular sign of wealth in a city where there was little room for kitchen gardens. He counseled:

Try to have a large and spacious courtyard and a beautiful garden adorned with various and delicate fruits, herbs, and flowers of many kinds, qualities, and fragrances because for the citizen who spends a good part of his life in the palace such things will be of no small enjoyment and recreation, and he will be especially delighted in agriculture so located, appreciated, and used by the ancient sages: the garden, the loggia, and the courtyard will take away a great part of the worries and boredom that are part of human affairs. And delighting in the study of good literature, [the citizen] will find infinite recreation each time that, tired from study, he enters the garden and with a little knife in his hand will choose some fragrant and delicate flower; he will capture a salad leaf in his own hand, he will pick a mature fruit; and enjoying such a pastime and recreation, he will create the highest and divine concepts, with which he will then fill learned and honored pages upon returning to his study.[65]

Although Venetian courtyards are now often barren of vegetation, many must have looked like that of Palazzo Salviati at San Polo in a Lake Price drawing (Fig. 6). Beyond that, the taste for bringing the garden inside the house is evident in the large number of *spalliere a verdure* listed in the invento-ries, such as those decorating the throne room and St. Ursula's bedchamber in Carpaccio's *Reception of the Ambassadors,* a painting in his cycle of the Life of Saint Ursula (Fig. 7). These are tapestries woven with a vegetal or millefleur design that were hung like a wainscoting around the lower part of the walls. The wealthy cittadino merchant Nicolò Duodo, for example, had sixteen nutwood chests in the *camera grande* facing the garden in his palace at San Marziale. These were filled with spalliere, mostly *a verdure,* in pieces that were about 4 feet high and in lengths that ranged from 6 to 24 feet. Altogether, they

FIG. 6. Courtyard of Palazzo Salviati, near the Casa Bianca Cappello, at San Polo, from Lake Price, *Interiors and Exteriors in Venice* (London, 1843). Photograph from Osvaldo Böhm, Venice.

FIG. 7. Vittore Carpaccio, *Reception of the Ambassadors* (detail), Accademia, Venice.
Photograph from Osvaldo Böhm, Venice.

added up to 222 running feet, enough to adorn the walls of a fair-sized room several times over.[66] Domenico Capello's inventory listed both *antiporte* (door curtains) and *spalliere a verdure*, as well as *spalliere a verdure con paesi*, probably tapestries with pastoral or rustic scenes.[67]

Memmo also advises, betraying an attitude that seems particularly Venetian, that "beyond the obvious and open entrances, [the house] should have some secret doors where one can enter and exit without being seen by anyone."[68] Indeed, the palace took on a metaphorical function, with its arrangement expressing the attitudes and hierarchy of values of the inhabitants and activities that it housed.[69] Palladio compared the house to the human body, which has noble and beautiful parts but also ugly and ignoble but necessary parts, which are best kept hidden. In the house too the most beautiful parts should be placed in areas of greatest visibility, where they can be seen immediately, whereas the less beautiful places should be hidden away.[70]

Another theme that emerges from the treatises, and one that is closely related to the ideals of separation and specialization, is that of the primacy of order. Each thing in the house, whether it was a basket of fruit or a sack of grain, a kitchen implement, a tablecloth, or a bed, had its proper location. Piccolomini, who was particularly eloquent on this matter, wrote: "And the clothing of each has to have a different place—one place for the children's, another for the husband's, and finally another for that of his consort. As to [the wife's] ornaments, one place is appropriate for her dresses, another for a ring, or jewel, or necklace, or bracelet, or similar expensive things, which should be kept in the most secret place in the lady's bedchamber." He tells an anecdote to make his point. Asking what locale would be least disposed to be arranged in an orderly way, he points to the barges that transport passengers between Venice and Padua each day and night: "Not so much because they are small but because there is no separate room or compartment where things can be stowed away until they are needed." And yet he had seen such a barge come to Venice from Ancona loaded with every type of merchandise, and it was in such perfect order that each item could be located immediately.[71] The lesson was clear: the beauty of a thing, including the casa, lies in the order and the proportion of its parts.

Here, Piccolomini was speaking to the wife. It was her charge to keep the household in good order. The model of the good marriage that comes through in these treatises, while it may well be patriarchal, is one of a partnership. For both husband and wife are held to be necessary to the *economica* of the household. The husband's role was to acquire and provide; the wife's was to conserve. Although we cannot know what order was actually maintained in the Venetian palaces, household inventories document a frame of mind according to which the necessities and the adornments of everyday life were arranged in markedly similar ways in a wide variety of homes, from artisans' to patricians'. The number and diversity of containers inside the Venetian home is one of the most striking features of the inventories. The most common storage chest was the *cassa,* typically made of walnut and less often of fir or cypress, sometimes painted or gilded or both, or carved, or inlaid with intarsia *alla certosina,* or even painted *a marmaro,* that is, *faux marbre.*[72] In addition, there were the *cassoni,* the *cassele,* the *cassete,* the *forzieri,* the *cofani,* the *scrigni,* the *scatole,* the *ceste,* and the *cestellete,* a plethora of possibilities whose specificity of function is sometimes difficult to distinguish, designed to ensure the good order of the household.[73] The desire to organize is also reflected in the proliferation of furnishings designed for specific purposes. The restello is a case in point. A piece of furniture that was invented in the fifteenth century but had almost disappeared from the inventories by the end of the sixteenth, it typically consisted of a wall mirror set into a wood frame, often richly decorated with painting, gilding, and intaglio, with hooks from which articles for the toilette were hung: hairbrushes, combs, *code* (horse tail switches to clean combs), *scriminali* (styluses or needles of bone, glass, or silver for parting the hair), a *zebellino* (a small fur to hold in the hand), *profumego lavorado da pomo colla sua cadenella* (a perfume ball on a chain), *paternostri* (rosaries), *spugnette* (sponges), *bottigliette di profumi* (perfume bottles), *vasetti di pomette* (glass jars of pomade), and the like.[74] With such objects, organization became a work of art.

Assessing the abundance and wealth of material things that made up the Venetian interior, Palumbo-Fossati noted three constants.[75] First, the Renaissance Venetian was surrounded by a broad spectrum of colors—and to that we might add textures and stuffs—that are assiduously recorded in the inventories, now translatable only with guesswork and considerable imprecision. For example, among the abundant furnishings found in the camera grande of the recently deceased procurator Lorenzo Correr in 1584 were three door curtains of crimson wool and another of crimson *panno rosso* with a cut pattern of green velvet; a *turchino* (probably turquoise blue) damask bed ensemble with cords of gold; four velvet cushions, two black and two crimson; a coverlet of crimson *ormesino* (a silk often used for togas) lined with green *samito* (a heavy luxurious silk); three white quilted coverlets, a coverlet of columbine *raso* (silk satin) lined with yellow cloth; a coverlet of turchino and white *rasetti* (an extremely fine satin) lined with red cloth; two white bedspreads; and a seat cover of turchino *raso* with fringes of gold.[76] The fluid prose of the notary attests to an eye well practiced in distinguishing not only colors but silk fabrics of various sorts. Second, light was a tangible presence not only from the large windows, loggias, and interior courtyards but also through the types of materials that were common in the Venetian home, emanating from lamps and reflecting off mirrors, bronzes, shining terrazzo floors, and glass objects of every kind. And third, objects of diverse provenance, whether in fact or in inspiration—painted landscapes *alla fiandra,* bedcovers *alla suriana,* mosque carpets *alla turchesca* and *alla cimiscasa*—coexisted. In sum, the Venetian aesthetic taste of the mid-sixteenth century revealed a sensitivity to the decorative possibilities of light, privileging diversity and ingenuity in terms of types of objects, colors, textiles, and provenance.

Amidst all this splendor, how was *specific* family identity expressed? Muzio wrote of Venice: "For antiquity of blood there is no city in Italy that has more noble families; both from their order of magistrates and for the memory that they keep of their lineages, one can distinguish nobles from others better here than in any other part."[77] The most direct and visually powerful assertion of the antiquity and social rank of the family, whether cittadino or noble, was the coat of arms, as evidenced most eloquently and comprehensively by the compilations of noble *stemme,* a new literary genre that flourished in the period.[78] As Goldthwaite points out, heraldry was part of the language of medieval chivalry that expanded into the mercantile classes in the early Renaissance. However, the complex rules in use in northern Europe, with dividing and quartering of bloodlines on the coat of arms, were simply ignored in Italy in favor of personally invented insignia and impresa. Display of a stemma was thus no proof of nobility—simply the sign of a certain level of politia as Sansovino would have understood it.[79]

Outside the palace, the stemma was carved on wellheads and embedded in walls to proclaim and delimit the space of the casa. Inside the walls, it might be embroidered onto a spalliera like those being aired out on the *altana* (rooftop terrace) in Carpaccio's *Healing of the Possessed Man,* or woven into a backrest of padded silk fabric, or carved on a fireplace hood as in Mansueti's *Healing of the Daughter of Ser Nicolò Benvegnudo of San Polo.*[80] The inventory of Domenico Capello was typical: "an hourglass with its colonettes and the Capello arms . . . a damascene basin with the Capello and Bernardo arms . . . nine tapestries, that is spalliere, with beautiful figures and five others with the Capello and Bernardo arms."[81] Or the stemma might be tooled on book covers or incised on

FIG. 8. Bronze bells, Museo Civico Correr, Venice. Each incorporating a coat of arms in its decoration, the bells were probably of Paduan manufacture. Courtesy of Museo Civico Correr.

the handles of cutlery, bronze bells (Fig. 8), the covers of chests, or the frames of mirrors or paintings. Or it might be painted onto a ceramic or glass dish.

The display of weapons called the *lanziera di arme,* installed in the portego or sala, was the quintessential emblem of noble identity. In the aftermath of the disastrous events of the War of Cambrai, Doge Leonardo Loredan castigated himself and his peers for removing the weapons from the room to accommodate guests at large banquets and saw the growth in luxurious living as an offense to God.[82] But some houses maintained, or restored, the traditional arrangement, for not only did Sansovino describe them as typical items in the Venetian sala in 1581 but a number of inventories of the period include them as well.[83] A Lake Price drawing shows such an arrangement in the Palazzo Capello, on the Grand Canal, next to the Palazzo Barbarigo della Terraza, which can be seen through the window in the background (Fig. 9).[84] On a list of respectable but far from opulent household goods of the recently deceased Magnifico Michele Memmo were a silver cup and twelve gilded knives engraved with the Memmo and Ciera arms and a sparsely furnished portego. The sole furnishings in that room were twenty-four well-worn benches, twelve walnut chairs with straw seats, a gilded shield with a helmet bearing the Memmo arms, a standard, a *restelliera* (display rack with spears), and a regimental banner.[85]

This brings us to the overriding principle that informs the treatises on economica. Strongly rooted in the noble consciousness of the period throughout Italy was the insistence that the house conform to the social class and

FIG. 9. Portego of the Palazzo Capello, on the Canal Grande, looking out at Palazzo Barbarigo della Terraza, from Lake Price, *Interiors and Exteriors in Venice* (London, 1843). Photograph from Osvaldo Böhm, Venice.

economic level of the owner. The concept that had already been articulated by Alberti and Filarete in the fifteenth century was particularly important to the Brescian Lanteri. He insisted that each class or estate should have a house that was suitable to its own honor and dignity: "Because it would not be appropriate for a merchant to live in a sumptuous palace, built with great magnificence, or that a rich feudal lord living off his investments should live in a small habitation."[86] The same principle held true for dress, comportment, interior decoration, expenditures, and servants: each social rank had its own obligations and its own limits. It was just as wrong to push beyond as to fall short. Honor resided in respecting the requirements of rank and role and in renouncing excessive ostentation.[87] Silvio Antoniano wrote in 1584: "That the small artisan would wish to be equal to the citizen, the citizen to the gentleman, the gentleman to the titled lord, and the latter to the prince; these are things intolerable and beyond reason, akin, I say, to thefts and robberies, and there are no riches that could make up for such depths. From them are born debts and interest payments and bills and multiple usuries."[88] Again, Memmo considered the issue from a Venetian perspective: "I say that our city being divided into three qualities of men . . . I judge a different habitation to be appropriate for an honored citizen [patrician], another for a merchant [the cittadino and other well-to-do commoners], and another for an artisan." He warned, furthermore, that many a patrician had come to ruin for building a princely palace beyond his means and subjecting his family to shame and distress. He concluded that the palace should "be decorated and furnished according to the condition of the patron and the custom of the city."[89] At stake was the order of society.

Indeed, the all too human vices of pride, ambition, and envy were among the greatest threats to Venetian consensus and solidarity. Ostentatious public display by the rich could only exacerbate the inequities of rank and wealth that were becoming ever more obvious in the sixteenth century. Not surprisingly, admonitions of the church and the disapproval of conservative patricians adhering to the old values of frugality and discretion were insufficient to check tendencies toward acquisition and disruptive magnificence. So how did Venetians deal with the tensions produced by a sizable group of nobles who were not wealthy and a sizable group of rich commoners who were not noble?

Sumptuary legislation was the primary legal mechanism for controlling the display of wealth, and it was no more successful in Venice than elsewhere in Italy.[90] A summary look at Venetian initiatives reveals a succession of high hopes and repeated disappointments.[91] The earliest such law was passed by the Great Council in 1299 in an attempt to limit expenditures for marriage celebrations, events that marked the intersection between public and private life, and to a lesser degree for women's luxury clothing.[92] Although Venice had created a hereditary patriciate just two years earlier, the statute applied to all men and women across the board, of whatever rank, with the exception of the doge and his family—a privilege that was to remain until the end of the Republic. The egalitarian tone was typical of sumptuary legislation throughout Italy during this period, when other emerging communes sought to blur class distinctions, thus allowing new merchant elites to share power with, if not to replace, traditional hereditary elites.[93] In Venice, the aim may well have been to curb discontent on the part of those families who were excluded from the new noble caste.

Although the 1299 law was revoked in 1307, another attempt to curb spending came in 1334. With marriage celebrations and clothing again the primary targets, the Great Council framed the problem in economic terms, declaring that "inordinate and especially superfluous expenses by both men and women are continually being made in this city, beyond the possibility of any person, from which abundant expenditures much goes to waste, and men are reduced to nothing."[94] The Senate took a moralizing stance, arguing that legislation was necessary "because cupidity is the root of all evil and sin and hidden vice that easily creep up on men and women."[95] This dual charge, with the emphasis shifting according to the political and social circumstances, provided the rationale for all subsequent sumptuary legislation.

In the first half of the fifteenth century weddings were forgotten, and legislative attempts to control conspicuous display were centered almost exclusively on dress. In 1400 it was the *socha* or *pellanda,* a mantle worn by both men and women, whose sleeves had grown to considerable dimensions.[96] But if the wealthy could not have voluminous sochae, then they would line the cutdown versions with costly furs, such as ermine or marten. In 1403 these too were forbidden.[97] In 1425 it was the cost of brides' trousseaus that was "the consumption of their men and also the cause of much ill," and new restrictions were ordered. In 1442 it was gowns of cloth of gold or silver. With some outfits now costing as much as 600 ducats, husbands or fathers of ladies who wore gowns made of such luxurious fabrics would be obliged to make a forced loan to the government of 1,000 lire. The logic was irrefutable: anyone who could afford such clothing could also afford to support the state in a time of financial need.[98] The law was extended to male dress in 1456, when the Senate complained that the youth of the city had begun to wear clothing of similarly precious materials. As with the fur-lined sochae, ingenious tailors soon discovered ways to circumvent the rules and began to line sleeves with the forbidden stuffs. In 1473 a weary Senate affirmed that whatever was forbidden for clothing was also prohibited for linings.[99]

Excessive expenses for wedding celebrations and banquets of the *compagnie della calza* came under attack in 1460 and again in 1466, when a maximum cost of half a ducat per guest was set, with the substantial penalty for offenders of 200 ducats plus exclusion for two years from office for patricians and from piazza San Marco and Rialto for commoners. Informants were promised half the fine, and if they were slaves or indentured servants, they were also given their freedom.[100] In 1472 banquets were again the primary target. Realizing the futility of only setting a maximum cost per guest, the state now went inside the kitchen. Specifically forbidden were pheasants, francolins, peacocks, partridge, and doves. The number of dishes was limited to three, not counting confections, and food was not to be gilded. Nor would dinners in public (presumably in squares and courtyards and on *fondamente* [sidewalks next to canals]) be tolerated any longer: "rather only private ones in the chambers as the ancients were accustomed to do, and only with small sweets [served]."[101]

Indeed, even more private space was no longer beyond the reach of state inspectors. While lavish banquets and costly women's clothing and jewelry remained favored targets for regulation, the Great Council began to show concern for the decoration and furnishing of private palaces. In 1476 it went inside the bedroom with a decree that condemned "the immoderate and excessive expenses that are made in this city in the ornament of ladies and the decoration of beds and chambers to the great offense of our lord god and the universal damage of our gentlemen and citizens, that as a thing alien to every laudable and honorable custom and example, can no longer be tolerated in any way."[102] The cost of decorating the bedchamber itself with wood, gilding, and paint was not to exceed 150 ducats.[103]

In 1483 the Republic was embroiled in a war with Ferrara, and the response was predictable. As Pietro Bembo would later write in his *Della historia vinitiana,* "Since already before this war the city was inundated with every sort of license, at the beginning of the following year the laws regarding domestic expenses were renewed, and they forbade peacocks and pheasants at the banquets, and the most delicate viands; and in the chamber it was not permitted to use decorations of gold and silver and porphyry. [It held] that ornaments for women could not exceed 10 libre of gold; and promised great prizes to the accusers, and to servants their freedom."[104]

In 1489 the "many wise, useful, and profitable statutes" on clothing, banquets, and other immoderate expenses were reaffirmed, with a new commission made up of "three of our honorable gentlemen, ready and enthusiastic," elected to reform and enforce them. Under the title *Savij sora le pompe de le donne* they were given offices at Rialto and considerable discretion over all kinds of sumptuary violations, not just those involving women.[105] They immediately noted that two new items, "completely vain and superfluous, which exceed the private," had recently entered the bedchambers: "the restelli and gilded chests, very sumptuous and valuable." These were now to be prohibited, with fines levied on the owner and the masters who made them, and anyone who found them "could in fact possess them, and they would be freely his."[106]

The irrationality of a penalty that allows the accuser to possess a forbidden object does not seem to have occurred to the drafters of the law. Indeed, it reveals one of the basic flaws of sumptuary legislation, for it was grounded in ambiguity from start to finish. On the one hand, the consumption of "vain and superfluous" goods did, indeed, squander capital; but on the other, spending was necessary for a healthy economy. Luxurious display was not an evil in itself, since it was allowed to the church and to rulers like the doge; but the principle of *mediocritas* in Venice made it particularly difficult for the noble elite to distinguish itself from a wealthy citizen class without simply outspending it.[107]

Another troublesome form of home decoration would come under scrutiny in the Senate just a month later. The recently introduced custom of laying carpets atop tablecloths on dinner tables was found to be a "useless and unnecessary superfluity" and was now to be summarily banned for banquets for the compagnie, weddings, or any other occasion. Among the unseemly items of women's clothing that had recently appeared on the scene were wraps of luxury furs like sables, ermine, and lynx covered with iridescent silk. These too were held to be "detestable to god and the world" and were not to be tolerated.[108]

And yet, for all the high-minded rhetoric, and despite stiff monetary fines and other penalties, compliance was elusive. In 1497 the Senate concerned itself with "the immoderate use of pearls in our city," complaining that women were wearing pearls worth 600 to 800 ducats and more despite the statutory limitation of one single strand of pearls worth up to 50 ducats decreed in 1476.[109] A new across-the-board ban was passed forbidding all persons of whatever quality, condition, or sex, in the city or in its dominions, to use pearls on their person (head, neck, neckline, breast, fingers, or arms), their dress, or their home furnishings. Husbands or fathers of miscreant wives and daughters would be assessed an extra tax of 25 ducats at each *decima* (tax declaration) for the next ten years. Any person or official who observed a violator could appropriate the pearls for himself. Thus, one could possess pearls but not wear them. In this case, the contradiction had a rationale, for such laws were often temporarily revoked for receptions of distinguished visitors to the city. On such occasions the splendor of the pearl-bedecked matron became the splendor of the state.[110]

The tendency toward intrusion into the private spaces of Venetian palaces became even more pronounced in the sixteenth century. At a session in January 1509, only months before the humiliating defeat at Agnadello, the Senate spoke out once again on marriage banquets. It was a time for reassessment. The two banquets that were restricted to forty guests each in the statute of December 1489 were now being attended by three hundred guests and more. "And because it is impossible that such a small number would be observed at the wedding feast following the *sposar*, and this is a certain thing that each of this council by its prudence understands very well, if the orders and laws were not so very strict then almost everyone would willingly observe them."[111] The solution was ingenious: to entertain the guests in an expanded number of dinners. Now between the engagement and the marriage there could be six small dinners for twenty-five guests each and two large dinners for fifty or fewer, and after the marriage itself there could be a dinner for up to eighty guests "because it is impossible to do it with [only] forty persons, as everyone knows."[112] The same foods were forbidden as in the law of 1489, but collations were now to be served only in the chambers and not in the sala.

Ever-expanding reception parties were also an ongoing problem. Whereas previously only the closest female relatives had been invited to receive the other guests, as many as fifty, eighty, a hundred, and more ladies were now taking part, "so that there are more who receive than those who are received."[113] This "more than any other thing is the cause of great expense to our citizens, because in order to go to such offices and spectacles, everyone is forced to exceed the others with pomp and new fashions."[114] So it was now prohibited to have more than twenty ladies in the reception party, "whether in the portego or camera or elsewhere," for marriages, childbirth celebrations, election of officers and procuratorships, or the return from regiments.[115]

In addition to a share of the fines and manumission offered to slaves who reported on their masters and full payment of unfilled contracts to hired servants, all *scalchi* (dining-room stewards) and cooks who served at such banquets were obligated, under penalty of a 25 ducat fine and 6 months in prison, to go in advance to the office of the *savi* to report where they had been called to serve so that the inspectors could be sent there; similarly, on the day after the banquet they had to report on the number of persons as well as the quality and type of food served.[116]

These were difficult times. The registers of the Senate were filled with legislation on debtors, numerous patricians were asking their creditors for extensions, and there were special tax levies.[117] The fiscal situation remaining precarious, the Senate again rearranged the dinner tables of the wealthy. In May 1510 it decreed that "all worked silver, except for six cups and two salt cellars for each family, knives, forks, and spoons, and likewise all worked gold, except for glasses and rings and gold jewelry, cannot be used during the present war in any way, under penalty of forfeiting them permanently." Within eight days all were required to bring the remainder of their silver and gold to the Zecca, where it would be appraised. Credits were given for appropriated items, which were to be broken and melted down immediately "so that they cannot be presented more than one time."[118]

The travails were not over. In February 1511 the Senate criticized wealthy families who continued to spend lavishly in contravention of the laws, "throwing away a great sum of money," while they did not pay their special tax levies in these difficult times, which were "known to everyone." Stricter measures of enforcement were necessary, and it was decided to place two of the procurators, the highest officials in the city next to the doge, in charge for a one-year term "to moderate, correct, and castigate those who had committed and commit the stated transgressions, worthy of the greatest attention, and all other exorbitant and dishonorable expenses."[119]

The two procurators, for all their prestige, were no more successful than their predecessors. The Senate declared at the end of March 1512 that "many women as well as men" were spending even more than they had before, despite the great costs to the state of the continuing wars, "thinking up diverse costumes and new fashions [and] putting a great sum of money in many other frivolous things, from which one does not draw any utility."[120] In May the Senate was presented with a new redaction of the well-worn laws. This was intended to pull together all the previous regulations, passed at different times, into a single statute, thus eliminating contradictions, and to make some modifications "in order to quiet unbridled appetites." Women's fashions were targeted as usual, but with the greatest specificity to date. The *parte* (law) was, as Bistort put it, a true and proper "treatise of tailoring and dressmaking of its time."[121] From what it prohibits we can tell what was worn. Wedding gifts to the bride were now limited to six forks or six spoons. Indeed, all inhabitants of the city were forbidden to introduce "any fashion that could be imagined or excogitated." Masters who made any of the prohibited items would face a 25-ducat fine for each offense and six months in prison. As far as home furnishings were concerned, the old prohibitions held, with lavishly decorated bed linens, gilded chests, cradles, restelli, mirrors, and other implements decorated with silver, gold embroidery, or jewels strictly forbidden. To these were now added andirons worked from damascene gold or silver.

Momarie, theatrical performances, and masquerades, typically produced for wedding celebrations by the compagnie della calza, were now incorporated into general sumptuary legislation for the first time, reaffirming a similar decree of the Council of Ten of 1508 (and documenting its ineffectiveness). All such representations, whether public or private, whether tragedy or comedy or eclogue, were to be banned as threats to public morals and the corruption of youth.

The new law was no more successful than those it had augmented. Only three months later the Senate would declare: "The fickleness of unbridled appetites of men as well as women continues to grow so much, that few care about spending, and they throw their riches and goods to the winds; and few fear and hold in reverence our lord God." It reaffirmed by a less than over-whelming vote of 98 to 63 its firm intention to impose the penalties provided in the statute.[122] Prosecutions were made, but many judgments were appealed. According to a June 1513 decree of the Great Council, many came to the Collegio every day in order to appeal condemnations for infractions of the sumptuary laws, requesting their cases to be handled "cum instantia expedi-tione." The doge and his councilors were too busy to deal with these matters, and appeals were handed over to the XX Savij in Rialto for consideration.[123] Clearly, the piecemeal approach to sumptuary legislation was not working. Attempting once again to "extinguish the immoderate expenditures that not only offend the lord God but are also the cause of ruin of the faculties of our nobles and citizens," the Senate finally set up a permanent magistracy on 8 February 1514 *mv* called the Magistrato alle Pompe. Consisting of three nobles who carried the title *provveditori* and served terms of two years, it remained in place, presumably with little more success than its predecessors, for nearly five decades.[124]

A phrase appearing in an otherwise pro forma reiteration of the laws on banquets in 1526 suggests that compliance was not enthusiastic: "And truly, those who would act so dishonestly as to throw bread or oranges at our em-ployees, or push them or kick them out, will fall subject to a penalty of fifty ducats."[125] The entire set of laws was recapitulated several times in the decades that followed. Finally, in a tumultous meeting of the Senate in January 1560, another attempt was made to reform the statutes, with separate ballots taken on each of fifteen articles. The most controversial provisions concerned home decoration. It was proposed that all tapestries and spalliere more than four *quarte* high, as well as any hangings containing gold or silver thread, be banned. However, a provision that prohibited items could be registered with the office of the provveditori and used until they wore out barely passed by a vote of 100 to 77, with 11 abstentions. The matter was a divisive one. After a vote to enact the statutes into law that again resulted in a split vote, with 95 in favor, 45 against, and 39 abstentions, it was agreed to suspend the entire proceedings. Within a month a committee of five, including the provedditori, appeared before the Senate. Their statement is the first to articulate with unambiguous clarity the fundamental concern of the time: "We must in every respect give much consideration and use much study in conserving the equality between our nobles and citizens and in prohibiting those things that could give rise to any bad effect." Although the traditional moral and economic concerns under-lying sumptuary legislation were still present, now the social order itself was given the highest priority. The committee argued strenuously that the controversial provision allowing proscribed clothing and home decoration to be used until it was worn out should be annulled. Otherwise, it would "bring to destruction all that which has been decided so maturely in such matters. Not only would it be against the dignity of this council but it could give rise to diverse bad effects among our citizens." The provision was repealed; however, the vote testifies to a divided heart: 92 in favor, 27 against, and 21 abstentions.[126]

In 1562 the Senate brought to fruition the reform begun two years earlier, passing the most comprehensive sumptuary legislation to date. While women's clothing and jewelry and, as always, the adornment of courtesans received the usual critical concern, the list of proscribed room decorations had lengthened once again. Tapestries and spalliere more than five feet high were not to be tolerated, nor were spalliere *a figure* or leather wall hangings, whether gold-tooled or not. Also prohibited were gilded andirons and fireplace furnishings or those worked *alla damaschina,* as well as chairs upholstered with figured velvet or decorated with gilding other than studs. Rules on banquet fare had also become more specific and wide-ranging. With festoons over doorways and windows, "as in any other place," now forbidden, the types and amounts of meat, fowl, and fish to be served each guest were specified, with desserts to consist of only "small confections, pieces of ordinary pastry, and simple fruits of all types according to the season." Severe penalties were levied on cooks, stewards, and tailors whose services allowed rich families to flout the law. Moreover, new standards of austerity were also applied to servants' livery and decorations for gondolas and other boats. Beyond that, the doors of the family palace were to be thrown open to officials of the Magistrato alle Pompe during banquets and childbirth celebrations to ensure that the sumptuary laws were respected.[127]

Similar proscriptions had been announced before, with little lasting effect. What was significant in the new bill was the strengthening of the Magistrato alle Pompe as a body with full investigative, judicial, and legislative powers. With the addition of two *sopraprovveditori* elected yearly by the Senate, the number of magistrates was increased from three to five. Required to meet three times a week, the magistrates were able to change laws quickly in response to new fashions without a protracted Senate debate, and they were given considerable latitude in interpreting them. But their most significant, and controversial, prerogatives lay in the judicial area, where the accused had only limited rights and the magistrates held all the cards. A case would be assigned to one magistrate, who examined witnesses or accusers in secret and presented the case to the other magistrates for the final judgment. Although the accused was allowed to present written responses in his or her own defense, such evidence could not be entered into the court record if it concerned accusations that had already been clearly proven to the presiding magistrate's satisfaction. Four magistrates were required to be present to render judgment. Only two votes were necessary to condemn the accused, and the decision could not be appealed. Subsequent attempts by the Avogaria di Comun to force the Magistrato alle Pompe to release case records for review were rejected by the Senate. As the magistrates themselves put it, it was not possible to deal with "certain subterfuges, at times too pernicious, in ordinary ways."[128]

For all its rigor and comprehensiveness, the new law was only one more document in a tattered ledger of failed attempts at public control of private consumption. Legislation continued to be passed and ignored. The areas of Venetian life that conformed most closely to the sumptuary laws were in the realm of hospitality—the meanness of refreshments that Coryat and Casola had observed. But even in this area any such compliance was probably more a matter of tradition than of law. And Sanudo's diaries are full of sumptuous entertainments that flagrantly violated the most rigorous attempts to control them.

Perhaps the most significant thing about Venetian sumptuary laws is that, with few exceptions, they were binding upon all citizens, whether noble or commoner, "of whatever status, degree, or condition." By the later sixteenth century they allowed the poorer patricians to save face with an official justification to contain family expenses within affordable limits. Beyond that, there was a flourishing rental market in clothing, spalliere, and other types of household adornments for those who could not buy their own. And *strazzaruoli,* merchants in second-hand clothing, were among the most prosperous retailers in the city.[129] Still, the question of dress is more complicated than it seems at first glance. On the most basic level, the uniformity of male dress in public space would appear to level the playing field for those above the artisan level. But while the black toga was the standard uniform for patricians and cittadini, hierarchy was reinforced through the wearing of colors, the quality of the fabric, and the cut of the sleeve. The long lists of officials in Sanudo's *Diarii* who were dressed in *scarlatto* or *pavonazzo* or with sleeves *alla ducale* or *a comedo* on ceremonial occasions is an index of the value accorded dress as a sign (Fig. 10). But allowing that high office was usually secured by families with economic power and a high social status, the costumes displayed, at least in theory, a hierarchy of office and not a hierarchy of wealth.[130]

Women's dress was another matter, however. That the wives of rich com-

FIG. 10. Venetian senator or knight with sleeves *alla ducale,* from
Cesare Vecellio, *Degli habiti antichi et moderni di diverse parti del
mondo libri due* (Venice, 1610). Reprinted by permission of the
Folger Shakespeare Library.

moners were allowed to display more luxury than those of the poorer nobility was a paradox regarded with disdain by visitors like Coryat. Why were Venetian patricians reluctant to further reify their legally established social and political dominance over wealthy cittadini by adopting a privileged form of dress, in the manner of other aristocratic elites? It has been convincingly argued that such legislation in other states was essentially based upon the fear of deception: that an individual dressing outside his group norms could threaten the established stratified order.[131]

In Venice, by contrast, the greater fear was surely that the well-established order would be threatened by disparities within and between the groups. It was more prudent to insist on egalitarian rights while maintaining hereditary privilege. However, as in most societies, some members were more equal than others, and the exceptions are worth noting. First, there was the doge and his family: it was incumbent upon them, as symbols of the Republic, to express the state's full magnificence. Then there were the *cavalieri*, or knights; they too remained exempt from restrictions on dress throughout the period.[132] Beyond that, the reform law of 1562 extended this privilege to orators who represented the Republic at foreign courts and their families. Finally, the prohibition of colorful liveries for gondoliers and servants repressed not only the grandeur of a wealthy family but also ensured that servants would not be taken for their social betters. In any event, the accounts of contemporary observers like Sansovino suggest that all such measures were exercises in futility and failed to close the widening gap between those who *were* noble and those who simply *lived* in a noble manner.[133]

Was Venice's unwillingness to use sumptuary laws to reinforce the social hierarchy an example of "the consummate political wisdom of the republic," as the Venetian secretary Antonio Milledonne and the French jurist Jean Bodin saw it?[134] Perhaps it was simply a pragmatic acceptance of a *de facto* nobility that was born from ineluctable economic and social forces whose roots pushed deep into Venice's (ignoble) mercantile past.

NOTES

1. See, e.g., Richard A. Goldthwaite, *Wealth and the Demand for Art in Italy, 1300–1600* (Baltimore, 1993); Lisa Jardine, *Worldly Goods: A New History of the Renaissance* (New York, 1996); and Simon Schama, *The Embarrassment of Riches: An Interpretation of Dutch Culture in the Golden Age* (New York, 1987).

2. For a critical view, see Ingrid Rowland, "The Renaissance Revealed," in *New York Review of Books,* 6 November 1997.

3. M. Margaret Newett, *Canon Pietro Casola's Pilgrimage to Jerusalem in the Year 1494* (Manchester, 1907), 128–29.

4. Salvatore Battaglia, *Grande dizionario della lingua italiana,* 18 vols. (Turin, 1961– 96), 2:824: "Casa aperta: Avere, tenere casa aperta: ricevere spesso e con molta cordialità molti ospiti. Anche: possedere una casa provvista di tutto ciò che occorre per potervi abitare." Sansovino's use of the word appears closest to the second meaning. Cf. Vincenzo Giustiniani, "Discorso sopra la pittura (1610)," in his *Discorsi sulle arti e sui mestieri,* ed. A. Banti (Florence, 1981), 45: "in vero è cosa degna di maraviglia il considerare il gran numero de' pittori ordinari, e di molte persone che tengono casa aperta con molta famiglia."

5. Francesco Sansovino, *Venetia città nobilissima et singolare, con aggiunta da D. Giustiniano Martinioni,* 2 vols. (1663; reprint, Venice, 1968), 1:384–85. The translation is based in part upon David Chambers and Brian Pullan, eds., *Venice: A Documentary History, 1450–1630* (Oxford, 1992), 25.

6. See Istituto della Enciclopedia Italiana, *Vocabolario della lingua italiana,* 4 vols. in 5 (Rome, 1986–94), 3, pt. 2: 976 ("politia, s. f. . . . sopratutto per rendere un partic. uso del termine greco, proprio di Aristotele nel trattato della *Politica,* dove indica la forma di costituzione nella quale il governo è in mano al popolo, che lo esercita in vista del bene comune") and 979 ("polizia . . . Forma di governo; costituzione, ordinamento della città e dello stato; amministrazione, anche di istituzioni e di attività pubbliche; vita politica partecipazione alla vita pubblica; comportamento civile"); Manlio Cortelazzo and Paolo Zolli, *Dizionario etimologico della lingua italiana,* 5 vols. (Bologna, 1979–88), 4:950 ("polizia, s. f. sistema col quale si governa bene una città [av. 1449, D. Burchiello]"); and Carlo Battisti and Giovanni Alessio, *Dizionario etimologico italiano,* 5 vols. (Florence, 1975), 4:3002 ("polizia f. [XVI–XVII sec] . . . forma di governo").

7. Istituto della Enciclopedia Italiana, *Vocabolario della lingua italiana,* 3, pt. 2: 976 ("polizia . . "Forma ant. per *pulizia,* nel sign. proprio, e più spesso in quelli connessi con l'agg. *polito,* cioè finezza di modi e di comportamento, gentilezza e cortesia, raffinatezza, eleganza e anche probità"); Battaglia, *Grande dizionario della lingua italiana,* 13:772 ("Polizia . . . Raffinatezza di modi, finezza di tratto, compitezza di contegno [talvolta puramente formale o osservata per opportunità o con affettazione]; buona educazione, urbanità, cortesia, gentilezza; correttezza, scrupolosità.—Anche: ostentazione di lusso"); Battisti and Alessio, *Dizionario etimologico italiano,* 4:3001 ("polito agg., XIV sec., -*ezza* (XVII sec., Redi); liscio, terso; 'pulito'; v. dotta, lat. *politus* adorno, elegante, fine").

8. Thomas Coryat, *Coryat's Crudities,* 2 vols. (Glasgow, 1905), 1:415.

9. Dennis Romano, *Housecraft and Statecraft: Domestic Service in Renaissance Venice, 1400–1600* (Baltimore, 1996), 231–32.

10. Coryat, *Coryat's Crudities,* 415.

11. See Margaret King, *Venetian Humanism in an Age of Patrician Dominance* (Princeton, 1986).

12. Still fundamental is James Cushman Davis, *The Decline of the Venetian Nobility as a Ruling Class* (Baltimore, 1962). But see now Giuseppe Trebbi, "La società veneziana,"

in *Storia di Venezia,* vol. 6, *Dal Rinascimento al Barocco,* ed. Gaetano Cozzi and Paolo Prodi (Rome, 1994), 129–213.

13. Claudio Donati, *L'idea di nobiltà in Italia, secoli XIV–XVIII* (Bari, 1995), 3–17.

14. Nicolò Machiavelli, *Discorsi sopra la prima deca di Tito Livio* 1.55. English translation from *Machiavelli: The Chief Works and Others,* trans. Allan Gilbert, 3 vols. (Durham, N.C., 1965), 1:308–9. See also Donati, *L'idea di nobiltà,* 29–30.

15. Machiavelli, *Discorsi,* 1.34.

16. Ibid., 1.55; *Machiavelli,* 310.

17. Contarini composed the treatise in Latin between 1523 and 1531; it was first published in Paris in 1543. An Italian translation came out a year later in Venice: *La Republica e i magistrati di Vinegia* (Venice, 1544). See also Donati, *L'idea di nobiltà,* 56–58.

18. The English translation is taken from Gasper Contareno, *The Commonwealth and Government of Venice,* trans. Lewes Lewkenor (1599; reprint, Amsterdam, 1969), 16.

19. Ibid., 17–18.

20. Stanley Chojnacki, "Nobility, Women, and the State: Marriage Regulation in Venice, 1420–1535," in *Marriage in Italy, 1300–1650,* ed. Trevor Dean and K. J. P. Lowe (Cambridge, 1998), 128–51.

21. Contareno, *Commonwealth and Government of Venice,* 18.

22. Giovambattista Nenna da Bari, *Il Nennio: Il quale ragiona di nobiltà* (Venice, 1543), bk. 3 (no pagination).

23. Tommaso Garzoni, *La piazza universale di tutte le professioni del mondo* (Venice, 1595), 175. The book was first published in 1585 in Venice, with many subsequent reprintings. It is also available in a modern critical edition in two volumes edited by Giovanni Battista Bronzini (Florence, 1996). For Garzoni, see John Martin, "The Imaginary Piazza: Tommaso Garzoni and the Late Italian Renaissance," in *Portraits of Medieval and Renaissance Living: Essays in Memory of David Herlihy,* ed. Samuel K. Cohn Jr. and Steven A. Epstein (Ann Arbor, 1996), 439–54.

24. See A. D. Fraser Jenkins, "Cosimo de' Medici's Patronage of Architecture and the Theory of Magnificence," *Journal of the Warburg and Courtauld Institutes* 33 (1970): 162–70; and David Thomson, *Renaissance Architecture: Critics, Patrons, Luxury* (Manchester, 1993), 1–28.

25. Girolamo Muzio, *Il gentilhuomo del Mutio Iustinopolitano* (Venice, 1565), 1–55. See also Donati, *L'idea di nobiltà,* 126–28.

26. See Peter Burke, *Venice and Amsterdam: A Study of Seventeenth-Century Elites,* 2d ed. (London, 1994), 11–15, which speaks of three hierarchies within the patriciate: status (antiquity of the family), political power, and wealth; Trebbi, "La società veneziana," 129–52; Donati, *L'idea di nobiltà,* 198–205; and Davis, *The Decline of the Venetian Nobility.*

27. Paolo Paruta, *Della perfettione della vita politica di M. Paolo Paruta nobile vinetiano, cavaliere & procuratore di San Marco* (Venice, 1579), bk. 3, quoted in Donati, *L'idea di nobiltà,* 203: "secondo certa geometrica proporzione la condizione diversa delle persone."

28. Antonio Colluraffi da Librizzi, *Il nobile veneto* (Venice, 1623). Cf. Muzio, *Il gentilhuomo,* 1–11, who makes essentially the same point.

29. For a fine study of the tradition of living *nobile*, see Daniela Frigo, *Il padre di famiglia: Governo della casa e governo civile nella tradizione dell' "economica" tra Cinque e Seicento* (Rome, 1985). See also Romano, *Housecraft and Statecraft*, 3–42.

30. The original is available in English translation as *The Estate Manager (Oeconomicus)*, trans. Robin Waterfield, in Xenophon, *Conversations of Socrates*, trans. Hugh Tredennick and Robin Waterfield (London, 1990), 269–359.

31. Alessandro Piccolomini, *Della institutione de la felice vita dell'huomo nato nobile e in città libera* (Venice, 1545). Cf. Donati, *L'idea di nobiltà*, 60–61; and Mary Rogers, "An Ideal Wife at the Villa Maser: Veronese, the Barbaros, and Renaissance Theorists of Marriage," *Renaissance Studies* 7 (1993): 385.

32. Frigo, *Il padre di famiglia*, ch. 4.

33. Nicolò Vito di Gozze, *Accademico occulto: Nel quale brevemente, trattando la vera economia, s'insegna, non meno con facilità che dottamente, il governo, non pure della casa tanto di città quanto di contado, ma ancora il vero modo di accrescere e conservare le ricchezze* (Venice, 1589), 6. See also Frigo, *Il padre di famiglia*, 134–35.

34. Giacomo Lanteri, *Della economica: Trattato di m. Giacomo Lanteri gentilhuomo bresciano, nel quale si dimostrano le qualità, che all'uomo et alla donna separatamente convengono pel governo della casa* (Venice, 1560), 29. See also Frigo, *Il padre della famiglia*, 58 n. 72.

35. Laura Megna, "Comportamenti abitativi del patriziato veneziano (1582–1740)," *Studi Veneziani*, n.s., 22 (1991): 253–323, esp. 309. For a discussion of Lorenzo Priuli (1446–1518), who followed just such a strategy, see Romano, *Housecraft and Statecraft*, 86–89.

36. Megna, "Comportamenti abitativi," 272, 278.

37. Giovanni Maria Memmo, *Dialogo del Magn. Cavaliere M. Gio. Maria Memmo* (Venice, 1563), 80.

38. Andrea Palladio, *The Four Books of Architecture* (1738; reprint, New York, 1965), 38 (bk. 2, ch. 2); the Italian edition appeared in 1570.

39. Lanteri, *Della economica*, 125–27.

40. Ibid., 102–3.

41. See Peter Thornton, *The Italian Renaissance Interior, 1400–1600* (London, 1991), 284. For Florentine palaces and their use, see Brenda Preyer, "Planning for Visitors at Florentine Palaces," *Renaissance Studies* 12 (1998): 357–74.

42. Thornton, *Italian Renaissance Interior*, 288–90.

43. Newett, *Canon Pietro Casola's Pilgrimage*, 339–40.

44. Anton Francesco Doni, *I marmi* (Florence, 1863), 168:
Nanni. Quelle camerine sì piccolo, che a pena vi può stare un letto, una tavola e due forzieri, non saranno già lodate: a poi fare una sala che pare una piazza!
Betto. Le camere son fatte per dormire, e non per passeggiare o banchettarvi dentro, nè per ballarvi; però le son d'avanzo. La sala sta ben così, perchè vi si riduce tutta la casa a un tratto dentro: le donne si stanno a piedi delle finestre, sì per veder lume a lavorare con l'ago le cose sottili e i ricami; sì per potere esser comode a farsi alla finestra; alla tavola in testa si mangia, a quella da lato si gioca: alcuni passeggiano, altri si stanno al fuoco; e così v'è luogo per tutti.

Cf. Alison A. Smith, "Gender, Ownership, and Domestic Space: Inventories and Family Archives in Renaissance Verona," *Renaissance Studies* 12 (1998): 375–91.

45. Memmo, *Dialogo*, 81.

46. Manfredo Tafuri, "Il pubblico e il privato: Architettura e committenza a Venezia," in *Storia di Venezia*, 6:367–70.

47. Lionardo di Niccolò Frescobaldi, *Visits to the Holy Places of Egypt, Sinai, Palestine, and Syria in 1384 by Frescobaldi, Gucci & Sigoli*, trans. Theophilus Bellorini and Eugene Hoade, Publications of the Studium Biblicum Franciscanorum, 6 (Jerusalem, 1948), 33–34. I am grateful to Rosamond Mack for this reference.

48. Newett, *Canon Pietro Casola's Pilgrimage*, 339–40.

49. For the full range of possibilities, see Isabella Palumbo-Fossati, "L'interno della casa dell'artigiano e dell'artista nella Venezia del Cinquecento," *Studi Veneziani*, n.s., 8 (1984): 112.

50. The first three editions were published in one volume. A second revised and expanded edition was published in 1880, and a third edition was published in 1885. The book was expanded to three volumes in the fourth edition, of 1905–8, presumably the basis for Horatio F. Brown's English translation, *Venice: Its Individual Growth from the Earliest Beginnings to the Fall of the Republic* (Chicago, 1907). The work was again expanded and revised in three more editions. The final and seventh edition was published in Bergamo in 1927–29 and reprinted in Trieste in 1973. Another important early study is Cesare Augusto Levi, *Le collezioni veneziane d'arte e d'antichità dal secolo XIV ai nostri giorni*, 2 vols. (Venice, 1906).

51. Unlike Molmenti, Palumbo-Fossati limited herself to the sixteenth century. The fundamental essay is Palumbo-Fossati, "L'interno della casa dell'artigiano." Also valuable are idem, "Il collezionista Sebastiano Erizzo e l'inventario dei suoi beni," *Ateneo Veneto* 171 (1984): 201–18; idem, "Livres et lecteurs dans la Venise du XVIe siècle," *Revue Française d'Histoire du Livre*, n.s., 54 (1985): 481–513; idem, "La casa veneziana di Gioseffo Zarlino nel testamento e nell'inventario dei beni del grande teorico musicale," *Nuova Rivista Musicale Italiana* 20 (1986): 633–49; and Dora Thornton, *The Scholar in His Study* (New Haven, 1997). For the seventeenth century, see Simona Savini Branca, *Il collezionismo veneziano nel '600* (Florence, 1965); Wilfrid Brulez, *Marchands Flamands à Venise I (1568–1605)* (Brussels, 1965); and Greta Devos and Wilfrid Brulez, *Marchands Flamands à Venise II (1606–1621)* (Brussels, 1986).

52. Marino Sanuto, *I diarii di Marino Sanuto*, ed. Rinaldo Fulin et al., 58 vols. (Venice, 1879–1903), 22:346 (6 July 1516); see also ibid., 28:135 and 37:415.

53. See Sansovino, *Venetia città nobilissima et singolare*, 1:386. The side of the palace, with frescoes, is visible in the left background of Gentile Bellini's *Miracle of the True Cross at the Bridge of San Lorenzo*, at the Accademia in Venice.

54. See Patricia Fortini Brown, *Venice and Antiquity: The Venetian Sense of the Past* (New Haven, 1996), 62, 63, 69, for plates showing the frontispiece to a manuscript by Livy with the arms of the Cattaneo family and the figures of Justice/Temperance and Fortitude/Charity and fresco fragments of Temperance, Charity, Constancy, and Hope from a house near San Zulian.

55. Archivio di Stato, Venice (ASV), Cancelleria Inferiore, Miscellanea Notai Diversi, busta 35, no. 27 (22 June–11 July 1532), fols. 11v–12. For the *restello*, see Palumbo-Fossati, "L'interno della casa dell'artigiano e dell'artista," 141–43.

56. Sanuto, *I diarii,* 53:553 (19 Sept. 1530).

57. ASV, Cancelleria Inferiore, Miscellanea Notai Diversi, busta 35, no. 27, fol. 12.

58. Ibid., busta 42, no. 66 (19 Oct. 1582), fols. 11–12.

59. The *homo di legno,* a wood mannequin on which to hang clothing or armor, was a very common item in Venetian inventories; it was usually placed in the portego.

60. ASV, Cancelleria Inferiore, Miscellanea Notai Diversi, busta 41, no. 57, fol. 4.

61. For this period, in addition to the references cited in n. 51, see Cristina De Benedictis, *Per la storia del collezionismo italiano: Fonti e documenti* (Florence, 1991).

62. Brulez, *Marchands Flamands à Venise I,* 33.

63. Federica Ambrosini, " 'Descrittioni del mondo' nelle case venete dei secoli XVI e XVII," *Archivio Veneto,* 5th ser., 112 (1981): 67–79.

64. Brulez, *Marchands Flamands à Venise I,* 633.

65. Memmo, *Dialogo,* 80–81.

66. ASV, Cancelleria Inferiore, Miscellanea Notai Diversi, busta 35, no. 4, fol. 1v (1530–33).

67. Ibid., fols. 4–4v.

68. Memmo, *Dialogo,* 81.

69. Frigo, *Il padre di famiglia,* 137–39.

70. Palladio, *Four Books of Architecture,* 38 (bk. 2, ch. 2).

71. Piccolomini, *Della institutione de la felice vita,* fols. 259v–260, in an artful adaptation from Xenophon, who also used a boat metaphor to make the same point.

72. Palumbo-Fossati, "L'interno della casa dell'artigiano e dell'artista," 121–22.

73. For the variety and uses of Renaissance chests, see Thornton, *Italian Renaissance Interior,* 192–204, which states that in Venice the cassa was probably a large chest equivalent to the Florentine cassone.

74. For the restello, or *rastello,* see Thornton, *Italian Renaissance Interior,* 239–41. Gustav Ludwig, "Restello, Spiegel und Toilettenutensilien in Venedig zur Zeit der Renaissance," *Italienische Forschungen* 1 (1906): 187–387, discusses the restello at length, suggesting a reconstruction of one listed in the testament of the painter Vincenzo Catena and explaining that it had two roles, as both a piece of furniture and an ornament.

75. Palumbo-Fossati, "L'interno della casa dell'artigiano e dell'artista," 141–43.

76. The furnishings are listed in Molmenti, *La storia di Venezia nella vita privata,* 7th ed., 3 vols. (1927–29; reprint, Trieste, 1973), 2:486: "Tre portiere de panno cremesin tagiade—Una portiera de panno rosso cremesin intagià de veludo verde—Un fornimento turchin de damasco, con cordelle d'oro da littiera da campo, con suoi forcieri et stramazzi—Doi cossini di veludo cremesin—Doi cossini di veludo negro—Una coltra d'ormesin cremesin fodrà de samito verde—Tre coltre bianche di tela imbotida—Una coltra de raso columbin fodrà de tela zala—Una coltra di rasetti turchina e bianca fodrà di tela rossa—Una coltra de raso giala fodrà cremesin—Doi filzade bianche—Un banchaleto de raso turchin con franze d'oro."

77. Muzio, *Il gentilhuomo,* 1–55, quoted in Donati, *L'idea di nobiltà,* 126–28.

78. Brown, *Venice and Antiquity,* 262.

79. Goldthwaite, *Wealth and the Demand for Art,* 168–69.

80. Both works were part of the Miracles of the True Cross cycle made for the Scuola Grande di San Giovanni Evangelista ca. 1494–1506 and now in the Accademia Galleries in Venice (see Patricia Fortini Brown, *Venetian Narrative Painting in the Age of Carpaccio* [New Haven, 1988]).

81. ASV, Cancelleria Inferiore, Miscellanea Notai Diversi, busta 35, no. 27, fol. 3.

82. Sanuto, *I diarii,* 17:246 (25 Oct. 1513). Cf. Felix Gilbert, "Venice in the Crisis of the League of Cambrai," in *Renaissance Venice,* ed. J. R. Hale (London, 1973), 277, who must be incorrect in placing this room on the ground floor of the palace.

83. Sansovino, *Venetia città nobilissima et singolare,* 1:385. See also Palumbo-Fossati, "L'interno della casa dell'artigiano e dell'artista," 139.

84. This was a different, albeit equally noble branch of the Capello family from the Domenico Capello of Santa Maria Formosa.

85. ASV, Cancelleria Inferiore, Miscellanea Notai Diversi, busta 41, no. 48 (8 Jan. 1572 *mv*), fol. 3v.

86. Lanteri, *Della economica,* 14.

87. Ibid., 22. See also Frigo, *Il padre di famiglia,* 143–44.

88. Silvio Antoniano, *Tre libri dell'educatione cristiana dei figliuoli* (Verona, 1584), 296: "Che l'artefice minuto voglia agguagliarsi al cittadino, il cittadino al gentiluomo, il gentiluomo al titulato, e questi al principe; queste sono cose fuori d'ogni ragione e intollerabili, cose dico ai latrocini e alle rapine, e non è ricchezza alcuna che possa supplire a tanta voragine. Quindi poi nascono i debiti e gli interessi e le grose e multiplicate usure."

89. Memmo, *Dialogo,* 79 and 81.

90. See Maria Giuseppina Muzzarelli, *Gli inganni delle apparenze: Disciplina di vesti e ornamenti alla fine del medioevo* (Turin, 1996); and Alan Hunt, *Governance of the Consuming Passions: A History of Sumptuary Law* (New York, 1996).

91. See esp. Mary Margaret Newett, "The Sumptuary Laws of Venice in the Fourteenth and Fifteenth Centuries," in *Historical Essays First Published in 1902 in Commemoration of the Jubilee of the Owens College Manchester,* ed. T. F. Tout and James Tait (Manchester, 1907); Giulio Bistort, *Il Magistrato alle Pompe nella Republica di Venezia* (Bologna, 1912); and Pierogiovanni Mometto, "'Vizi privati, pubbliche virtù': Aspetti e problemi della questione del lusso nella Repubblica di Venezia (secolo XVI)," in *Crimine, giustizia e società veneta in età moderna,* ed. Luigi Berlinguer and Floriana Colao (Milan, 1989).

92. Bistort, *Il Magistrato alle Pompe,* 90–91, 323–29.

93. Muzzarelli, *Gli inganni delle apparenze,* esp. 14.

94. ASV, Maggior Consiglio, Spiritus, fol. 162v (22 May 1534), quoted in Bistort, *Il Magistrato alle Pompe,* 329: "Cum multe et maxime expense fiant continue in hac civitate inordinate et multum superflue in hominibus et feminis, ultra possibilitatem personarum, ex quibus multis expensis multi pereunt et homines ad nihilum deducuntur."

95. ASV, Senato, Misti, reg. 16, fol. 67v, quoted in Bistort, *Il Magistrato alle Pompe,*

331: "quia cupiditas est radix omnium malorum et pecatum et vitium latens, quod homines et mulieres subripiunt de facili."

96. Newett, "Sumptuary Laws of Venice," 275.

97. Ibid.

98. Ibid.; Bistort, *Il Magistrato alle Pompe*, 123.

99. Bistort, *Il Magistrato alle Pompe*, 123–24.

100. Ibid., 94, 207; Newett, "Sumptuary Laws of Venice," 273.

101. ASV, Senato, Terra, reg. 6, fol. 190v: "aza solamente privata in le chamere chome antiquitus far se voleva et de confecti menudi solamente." See also Newett, "The Sumptuary Laws of Venice," 273, 277; and Bistort, *Il Magistrato alle Pompe*, 207.

102. ASV, Senato, Terra, reg. 7, fols. 134–134v (28 Sept. 1476): "El sono intanto multiplicade le immoderate et excessive spexe che si fano in questa terra in ornamenti de done et apparati, sì de lecti, come de camere, cum grande offension del nostro signor dio et universal danno de nostri zentilhomeni et citadini che, come cossa aliena da ogni laudevole et honesto costume et exempio, non se po' più tolerar per alcun modo." See Bistort, *Il Magistrato alle Pompe*, 352–63, for a complete transcription of the *parte* (law) passed by the Great Council on 17 November 1476.

103. ASV, Senato, Terra, reg. 7, fol. 134v. See also Bistort, *Il Magistrato alle Pompe*, 239, 356–59.

104. Quoted in Bistort, *Il Magistrato alle Pompe*, 367 n. 3: "perciochè la Città già davanti a questa guerra in ogni sorte di licentia s'era allargata, furono nel principio dell'anno seguente rinnovate le leggi, che le spese domestiche riguardano, et vietato ne conviti i pavoni, et i fagiani, et le vivande più dilicate: et nelle camere i guarnimenti d'oro et d'argento et di porpora non fu permesso di usare. Che l'ornamento delle donne non potesse diece libre d'oro passare; et grandi premii a gli accusatori, et a servi la libertà promessa."

105. Ibid.

106. ASV, Senato, Terra, reg. 10, fols. 184–85 (10 Dec. 1488): "Preterea, perchè da poco tempo in qua se è posto in consuetudine far nove spexe al tuto vane e superflue, le qual exciedeno el privato, nè mai se ne pol trazer alguna utilità, zoè i rastelli et chasse dorata, molto sumptuose et de valuta. Et nunc, sia azonto che tuti i dicti rastelli et chasse quovismodo dorate, siano di facto prohibite et bandite, sichè da qui in avanti nullo modo se possino più uxar nè tegnir, soto tute le pene et structure contegnude in la parte di ornamenti de le camere, sì a quelli che decetero havesseno ardir de tegnirle, come ai maistri che le lavorasseno. Et oltra tute le altre pene e structure predicte, se algun maistro sarà trovado da qui in avanti lavorar alguna de le stesse casse prohibite in questo capitolo specificate, quelli che le troverano, siano chi se voglia, le possino de facto tuor et siano liberamente soe." Cf. Bistort, *Il Magistrato alle Pompe*, 368–73, which dates the statute to 1489.

107. See C. Kovesi Killerby, "Practical Problems in the Enforcement of Italian Sumptuary Law, 1200–1500," in *Crime, Society, and the Law in Renaissance Italy*, ed. T. Dean and K. J. P. Lowe (Cambridge, 1994), 118–19. Cf. Mometto, "Vizi privati, pubbliche virtù," 254–55, which argues that Venetians attempted to safeguard domes-

tic production of luxury textiles against foreign imports but does not find a direct connection between the sumptuary laws and the production of silk cloth.

108. ASV, Senato, Terra, reg. 10, fol. 185.

109. ASV, Maggior Consiglio, Regina, fol. 160, in Bistort, *Il Magistrato alle Pompe,* 353–54.

110. ASV, Senato, Terra, reg. 13, fol. 1. See also Bistort, *Il Magistrato alle Pompe,* 185.

111. ASV, Senato, Terra, reg. 16, fol. 69v (16 Jan. 1508 *mv*): "Et perche Imposibel è, che al sposar tal poco numero sia observato: et certa cossa, è Cadauno de questo Conseglio, per la prudentia sua molto ben lintende, che quando li ordenj & le lege non serani tanto strettissime quasi da ognj uno serano volentarie observate." The *sposar* was the public ceremony at which the marriage vows were exchanged. For the several stages of a Venetian wedding, see the fine summary in Patricia H. Labalme and Laura Sanguineti White, "How to (and How Not to) Get Married in Sixteenth-Century Venice (Selections from the Diaries of Marin Sanudo)," *Renaissance Quarterly* 52 (1999): 43–72.

112. ASV, Senato, Terra, reg. 16, fol. 69v (16 Jan. 1508 *mv*): "Perche impossibel è farlo cum persone quaranta come ogniun intende."

113. Ibid.: "Ita che sono più che accetano cha tuti quelle sono acetade."

114. Ibid.: "Il che più che ognj altra cossa è causa de gran spexa à li Citadinj nostri: perche ogniuna per andar a tal officij & spectaculj se sforza cum pompe & fozze nuove avanzar le altre."

115. Ibid.

116. Ibid.

117. Ibid., fol. 129v (14 Sept. 1509).

118. Ibid., reg. 17, fol. 14 (21 May 1510): "Landera parte che tutj li arzentj lavoradj exceptuate Tace sei, saliere do, per cadauna fameglia, cortellj, pironj & cuslier et similiter li orj lavoratj excepte vere & anellj & orj zoieladj. Non se possino usar durante la presente guerra per alcun modo: sotto pena de perder quellj inremissibiliter." The parte was repeated a number of times; see, e.g., ibid., fols. 17v, 23, 27v, 85v–86.

119. Ibid., fol. 62 (14 Feb. 1510 *mv*); see also Bistort, *Il Magistrato alle Pompe,* 51–52.

120. ASV, Senato, Terra, reg. 18 (30 Mar. 1512), fol. 4: "excogitando diversi habitj & foze inusitate: Ponendo gran summa de denarj in molte altre cosse legiere: delequal non se po trazer alcuna utilita." See also Bistort, *Il Magistrato alle Pompe,* 52–53.

121. Bistort, *Il Magistrato alle Pompe,* 133.

122. ASV, Senato, Terra, reg. 18, fols. 32–32v (25 Aug. 1512).

123. Bistort, *Il Magistrato alle Pompe,* 49, citing ASV, Maggior Consiglio, Deda, fols. 87–87v (5 and 17 June 1513). The XX Savij in Rialto was the tribunal that dealt with debtors to the Commune.

124. ASV, Senato, Terra, reg. 18, fols. 184v–185 (14 Feb. 1514 *mv*).

125. Quoted in Sanuto, *I diarii,* 40:751–52 (31 Jan. 1526). See also Labalme and White, "How to (and How Not to) Get Married in Sixteenth-Century Venice."

126. ASV, Senato, Terra, reg. 43, fol. 109v (12 Feb. 1559 *mv*): "Si die per ogni rispetto haver molta consideratione et usar molto studio in conservar l'equalita' fra li

nobeli et cittadini nostri et in prohibir quelle cose che potessero parturir alcun mal effetto, onde essendo stati presi diversi capitoli in questo Conseglio sotto di xx del mese prossimamente passato in materia di pompe, tra li quali si come vi sono 14 che provedeno che sia servato l'honesto et moderato viver et vestir di questa nostra città, cosi si ritrova qual xv per il qual e concesso, che si possino portar li habiti prohibiti nelli precedenti capitoli, et in altre parte prese per il passato fino alla consumatione di esse i col che vien ad esser distrutto tutto quello che cosi maturamente in tal materia e stato deliberato."

127. Ibid., reg. 44, fols. 55–62v (28 Sept.–15 Oct. 1562). For a transcription see Bistort, *Il Magistrato alle Pompe*, 373–414.

128. ASV, Senato, Terra, reg. 44, fol. 62v. See also Mometto, "Vizi privati, pubbliche virtù," 270.

129. See Patricia Allerston, "L'abito come articolo di scambio nella società dell'età moderna: Alcune implicazioni," in *Le trame della moda*, ed. Anna Giulia Cavagna and Grazietta Butazzi (Rome, 1995), 109–24; and idem, "Wedding Finery in Sixteenth-Century Venice," in *Marriage in Italy, 1300–1650*, ed. Trevor Dean and K. J. P. Lowe (Cambridge, 1998), 25–40.

130. See Stella Mary Newton, *The Dress of the Venetians, 1494–1534* (Aldershot, England, 1988). Cf. P. Venturelli, "La moda come 'status symbol': Legislazione suntuaria e 'segnali' di identificazione sociale," in *Storia della moda*, ed. R. Varese and G. Butazzi (Bologna, 1995), 27–54.

131. Bistort, *Il Magistrato alle Pompe*, 9.

132. For cavalieri, see Matteo Casini, "Gli ordini cavallereschi a Venezia fra Quattro e Seicento: Problemi e ipotesi di ricerca," *Atti dell'Istituto Veneto di Scienze, Lettere ed Arti, Classe di scienze morali, lettere ed arti* 156 (1997–98): 179–99.

133. Trebbi, "La società veneziana," 146–48.

134. Ibid. See also Jean Bodin, *I sei libri della republica tradotti di lingua francese nell'italiana da Lorenzo Conti* (Genoa, 1588), 620; and Antonio Milledonne, *Ragionamento di doi gentilhuomini, l'uno Romano, l'altro Venetiano: Sopra il governo della Republica Venetiana, fatto alli 15 di gennaro 1580 al modo di Venetia* (Venice, 1581), 52v.

IO

Elite Citizens

JAMES S. GRUBB

One of the enduring concerns in Venetian history is the Republic's social and political stability, especially when compared with other Italian states. Early commentators attributed Venice's harmony at least in part to its well-ordered social hierarchy and especially to the intermediate class of cittadini. *In recent years the cittadini have been the object of intense study by social historians. Building on the pioneering work of Brian Pullan, many scholars, including Stephen Ell, Mary Neff, Giuseppe Trebbi, Andrea Zannini, and others, have brought to light the role the cittadini played in the bureaucracy, charitable institutions, and commerce, as well as their easy sociability and intermarriage with patricians. Viewed in some analyses as Venice's bourgeoisie, in others as a kind of nobility of the robe, the cittadini have been seen as mediators or buffers between the nobility and the* popolo, *with their privileges providing a safety valve alleviating resentment against the aristocrats' monopoly of political power. In this chapter James S. Grubb does not challenge these interpretations. Instead he returns to the primary sources themselves to show that for much of the Republic's history the cittadini remained remarkably inchoate as a group, and their membership remained ill-defined. It was only in the latter part of the sixteenth century that an effort was made to formalize citizen status. Like Chojnacki, then, Grubb charts a growing trend toward social definition yet finds that Venetian society was less rigidly hierarchical and fixed than sixteenth- and seventeenth-century mythologizers claimed.*

NEITHER RENAISSANCE VENETIANS nor foreign observers of the city could reach a consensus about the structure of Venetian society. According to Marcantonio Sabellico, Venice held but two orders, that of the patriciate or aristocracy and that of the *populares*.[1] His bipartite assessment was followed by Gasparo Contarini, whose *De magistratibus et republica Venetorum* allowed only for *nobiles* and *plebs*, though it did acknowledge that the latter category was subdivided into the *honestior genus*, accorded some offices and honors, and the truly base plebeians *(infima plebs)*.[2] From 1459 (Poggio Bracciolini) to the later sixteenth century (Paolo Paruta), from Florence (Niccolò Machiavelli) to France (Claude de Seyssel, Philippe de Commynes, and an anonymous *Traité* of ca. 1510), a variety of authors portrayed a two-tier social order.[3]

Marino Sanudo, however, held another view. In a brief aside of 1493 he noted that Venice counted three sorts of inhabitants: "nobles [*zentilhomeni*]," "citizens [*cittadini*]," and artisans or "lesser people [*populo menudo*]."[4] When speaking of Venetians generally, his contemporary, the diarist Girolamo Priuli, frequently used a similar tripartite scheme, for example, in a 1509 reference to the loss of mainland goods by "Venetian nobles and citizens and commoners" in the War of the League of Cambrai.[5] The Florentine Donato Giannotti, writing in explicit opposition to Sabellico, saw Venice's society as composed of *popolari* or *plebei* (who exercized "the most miserable trades"), cittadini (who exercized "more honored trades" and so "acquired some splendor"), and *gentil-homeni* (who ruled the state).[6] In a 1581 dialogue chancery secretary Antonio Milledonne expanded upon that middle category, to which he belonged, noting that the highest offices in the chancery and leadership of the greater confraternities *(scuole grandi)* were reserved for the cittadini. He alone of the earlier commentators applied the more technical term "original citizens [*cittadini originari*]," and he distinguished them from the other principal category of Venetian citizens, those granted economic rights and citizenship *per privilegio* on the basis of long-term residency in the city.[7]

Despite the immense popularity of Contarini's model—the *De magistratibus* was quickly translated into European vernaculars and was many times reprinted—the bipartite reading of Venetian society was not destined to prevail.[8] Eighteenth-century writers, foremost among them the jurist Marco Ferro and the historian Vettor Sandi, affirmed both the presence of a distinct *ordine cittadinesco* and its monopoly of chancery and scuola grande positions.[9] At the dawn of modern historiography Leopold von Ranke picked up the theme as a partial explanation for Venice's legendary equilibrium.[10] Echoing leads of Contarini,[11] Milledonne, Jean Bodin, Giovanni Botero, and Niccolò Crasso,[12] he and many subsequent scholars located in the body of the cittadini originari one source of Venice's social pacification, as well as its wise and stable governance: the cittadini were given sufficient honors and rewards to bind them closely to the regime, and they, in turn, provided technical skills and continuity to magistracies of amateur patricians who constantly rotated in and out of office. In the most recent generation, though in less celebratory tones, that lead has been strengthened by several articles and theses and one book.[13]

This chapter does not challenge that tradition but finds it a partial reading. Early treatises were concerned to establish the political topography of Venice, and subsequent historiography has been overwhelmingly political in its attentions. With the exception of a few recent studies of the scuole and intellectual life,[14] the cittadini have been studied in terms of their place in the chancery. There is good reason for that concentration. The laws formalizing the most cogently defined of their ranks, the juridical category of original citizens, were intended to reserve for them broad swaths of public office. It has been natural for scholars to associate privileged status with the officeholders for whom it was most commonly defined. Moreover, patricians defined the chancery as "the heart of our state" in 1456 and granted cittadini originari a monopoly of its higher offices in 1478;[15] historiography accurately reflects the high regard in which contemporary nobles held both the institution and its upper-level functionaries.

I argue here, however, that chancery staff did not constitute the sole or even the predominant body of elite commoners. A number of nonchancery offices were reserved to cittadini: managers *(gastaldi)* in the offices of the procurators of San Marco, the captain of the port, the retired sailors who ran a pepper brokerage at Rialto (the *poveri ai peveri*), and even the custodian of the bell tower of St. Mark's church were cittadini.[16] But even if all citizen employees of the Republic are considered together, they formed only one subset of the cittadini. There were several alternative pools of honored citizens that only occasionally founded a claim to eminence on public service: a loosely defined social elite, a block of families granted original citizenship by the state, and in all probability a further body of eminent commoners descended from fallen nobles. Each was in some measure set apart from the mass of the populace, yet their attributes were somewhat different, and their memberships only partially overlapped. Only occasionally did they find identity in the category of original citizenship. Moreover, as we shall see, these non-officeholding groups claimed a good deal more than the right to hold higher administrative positions.

Patrician rulers knew that they were dealing with a composite citizen elite. When, for example, they entrusted commoners with special state missions, they showed no preference for those serving in the chancery. Eight of the thirteen cittadini guards of the captured cardinal Ascanio Sforza in 1500 came from nonchancery families; five of the nine "principal worthy Venetian citizens" selected to guard the captive marquis of Mantua in 1509 were not of families in government employ.[17] Of the approximately 140 commoners chosen to make a census in June of the latter year, well over half were from families with no representatives in the chancery.[18] Seeking support for the war effort, the doge in September 1509 summoned "ancient and worthy Venetian citizens and commoners of good and ancient family" to the palace, reaching out beyond the ranks of administrative personnel to a larger pool of subjects.[19]

Recognizing a difference between the officeholding elite and other worthy commoners, the patriciate sought to keep them distinct at least in a theoretical sense. In 1410 the Council of Ten had reserved the primary offices in the scuole grandi for cittadini originari and for those made original citizens who had been members of a scuola for twenty years; in 1438 this reservation was extended to other scuole offices. In 1442, however, a law was passed forbidding chancery officials to hold office in a scuola. It was relaxed slightly three decades later, allowing chancery notaries to hold office but only with the permission of the doge and the heads of the Council of Ten. The law was not strictly enforced, as indicated by the fact of its reiteration several times, and Brian Pullan has concluded that "office in the Scuole Grandi was the preserve of the entire citizen class."[20] But the law set principle, if not practice: the two major spheres reserved to citizens were to be occupied by different parties and were not to be monopolized by any single element.

Chancery citizens, the most visible body of public employees, can be identified via prosopography from a massively researched thesis by Mary Neff.[21] Two chronicles compiled in 1536 and 1540 listing and describing "ancient families of Venetian citizens" provide a quite different list of nonnoble worthies.[22] The ranks of cittadini in the chancery and those in the chronicles only partially overlapped. Only 53 of 208 families in the chronicles had members serving as a chancery secretary or chancellor. In nearly every case these families placed only one or two men in the civil service: governmental employment was clearly an occupation secondary to commerce or professions such as law or medicine. On the other side of the coin, the public-office elite was only sporadically represented in the cittadino chronicles: only 20 of 208 chronicle entries mention individuals serving as secretary, chancellor, or gastaldo of the procurators. The families of some of the most noteworthy of the civil servants—Giovanni Dario, who negotiated an end to the first Turkish war in 1479;[23] Alvise Manenti and Zaccaria Freschi, who negotiated an end to the second Turkish war;[24] Antonio Vinciguerra, many times solo envoy to courts in Italy and Hungary, including the Roman Curia;[25] and three of nine grand chancellors in the previous half-century[26]—are absent from the cittadino chronicles.

More to the point, the criteria for inclusion in the two groups were entirely different. Original citizenship as a qualification for public office was defined in a series of laws enacted over a century and a half. It always hinged on the distinction between original citizenship, by native birth *(per natione),* and acquired citizenship, granted to immigrants on the basis of long-term residency *(per privilegio* or *per grazia).* But the precise meaning of original citizenship was not fully clarified until 1569, when the Great Council defined cittadini originari as those able to prove formally to the Avogadori di Comun that they, their fathers, and their grandfathers had been born in Venice of legitimate marriages.[27]

Before that time various standards applied according to the position for which certification was sought and the magistracy setting the definition. A 1323 petition to have original citizenship recognized also invoked three generations of descent, but apparently more to prove merit than to fulfil a strict criterion;[28] the subsequent 1410 and 1438 laws required the original citizenship only of candidates for scuola office, and in 1471 the Great Council reserved priorates of hospitals for original citizens, defined as men born and raised in the city ("cives originarii Venetiarum id est nati Venetiis et educati") but with no reference to the birth status of father or grandfather.[29] The fundamental law of 4 March 1478, reserving places in the chancery to cittadini originari, likewise did not require the original citizenship of immediate progenitors. In 1484 and 1487 the Council of Ten set a two-generation rule, demanding that candidates for the chancery prove that they were sons of "worthy Venetian citizens"; they did not have to prove that their grandfathers had been born in the city.[30]

By 1492 the Council of Ten was ordering that no merchant could claim the rights of being Venetian ("Venetus") unless he, his father, and his grandfather had been born in the city.[31] Even then, however, the three-generation rule was not operative across the board, as the Ten in 1498 repeated the 1487 law requiring proof only of the original citizenship of chancery candidates and their fathers.[32] In 1507 the Great Council adopted a requirement that candidates for the post of gastaldo of the procurators of San Marco prove that they, their fathers, and their grandfathers were cittadini originari, and that three-generation standard was extended to candidates for some miscellaneous positions in 1539 and to candidates for lesser office in 1543. Giannotti, writing in the mid-1520s, assumed a three-generation rule. Still, it was not in effect in a 1537 law requiring the original citizenship of advocates, and it was not in effect in one *prova* (examination) of 1554.[33]

The requirement of legitimate birth was straightforward, set, at least for those wishing to enter the chancery, by the laws of 1484, 1487, and 1498. But the crucial issue of which magistracy was to authenticate original citizenship amidst this mass of partially contradictory norms remained tangled. Before 1569 at least seven different magistracies provided certification of original citizenship for various categories of public employment. After 1484 all candidates for the chancery had to prove their legitimacy and their descent from "boni cittadini nostri venetianii" before the heads of the Council of Ten.[34] The Quarantia Criminale, which distributed minor offices, evidently checked candidates' credentials.[35] After 1514 the qualifications of aspiring notaries in private practice, who were henceforth to be *cives originarii* only, were to be examined by the grand chancellor and the *cancellieri inferiori*.[36] In 1517 the Collegio de' Savi were given the task of nominating (and presumably checking the qualifications of) the *boni cittadini* that the Quarantia would vote on for lower office.[37] The Avogadori di Comun were to determine the original citizenship of candidates for the chancery by at least 1538.[38] In 1559 a candidate declared that he had previously (in 1553) proved his *cittadinanza* before the Conservatori ed Esecutori alle Leggi, a magistracy set up in 1537 to certify advocates.[39] After 1313 the petitions of all wishing to be granted citizenship per privilegio were examined by the Provveditori di Comun; in 1554, at least, the Provveditori were hearing similar petitions for recognition as cittadini originari.[40] Only in 1569 did the Avogaria di Comun become the sole licensing body.

The contours of the second body of eminent citizens, the 208 families defined in the 1536 and 1540 chronicles, were founded not on legal norms but on qualitative standards. They did not claim to be cittadini originari. Rather, some of these families, according to the chronicles, were immigrants eminent, even noble, in their cities of origin. The Amadi, for example, could boast of several ancestors who were bishops, cardinals, and counts palatine in the family's original base in Lucca; settled in Venice, the Amadi were still papal counts palatine and imperial nobles in the fifteenth and sixteenth centuries. The Arborsani claimed both Lucchese nobility and an imperial count palatinate. Barnaba Dardani was said to have been made *cavaliere* by Francesco il Vecchio da Carrara.[41] All cittadini families claimed to be ancient residents of the city, reporting a mean of slightly over two centuries since their arrival.

A further set of qualifications for prominence centered on proximity to the Venetian patriciate itself. Several cittadino families, declared the chronicles, had sat on Venice's Great Council in the distant past but had been excluded in the *Serrata* after 1297. Some claimed to belong to families admitted to nobility in 1297, though their own branches had been excluded. (These were not, it would seem, empty boasts: at least twenty-seven families in the 1536 and 1540 chronicles bore the surnames of members of the Great Council in the later thirteenth century.)[42] Thirty-two, it was said, were descended from noble families that had become extinct; a few belonged to families that currently had members on the council. Several cittadino lines, it was claimed, belonged to families ennobled when the Great Council accepted thirty commoner houses in 1381, but their own branches had not been admitted.[43] In total, 79 families listed in the chronicles, or 38 percent of the total, were said to possess blood kinship with noble clans past or present. A further pool had made worthy contributions to the state during the War of Chioggia but then lost in the voting for election to the Great Council in 1381; since a great number of commoners sought nobility at this time but only 59 or 60 were voted upon, even being considered in the vote gave one honored status.[44]

But the 1536 and 1540 chronicles do not exhaust the ranks of elite citizens either. A second type of original citizenship existed, that granted by the Signoria to foreigners not born in the city. The 1410 law reserving scuola office, for example, was specifically intended not to exclude "those made original citizens by privilege" (illis factis civibus originariis per privilegium) who had been scuola members for twenty years. This category of "new original citizens" was not numerically large, by one count accounting for 72 cases out of a total of more than 3,600 privileges of citizenship awarded in the period 1305–1500.[45] They do not seem to be an especially select group: only a dozen of their families were included in the 1536 and 1540 cittadino chronicles, and only a dozen placed sons in the chancery. However, this tabulation does not include the 31 Lucchesi families who later claimed to have been made cittadini originari by privilege early in the Trecento, to have introduced silk production and trade to Venice, to have held vast assets (real estate worth 273,000 ducats and a million ducats in bank deposits and commerce), and to have contributed heavily to the fisc (250,000 ducats). The numbers cannot be verified, but it is certain that the Lucchesi were indeed notable in many sectors of Venetian society.[46] Fifteen of their number were eminent enough to be assimilated into the 1536 and 1540 lists of prominent citizens, and two more were admitted to the Great Council.

Another feature of the cittadini, characteristic of chancery and nonchancery citizens alike but not exclusive to them, may point to still another pool of elite commoners: many had blood ties to, or at least shared surnames with, current patricians. Among the citizen families listed in the 1536 and 1540 chronicles, for example, are found fifteen names also held by patricians. Twenty-eight families working in the chancery bore noble names. More broadly based rolls of commoners—matriculation records of the scuole grandi, lists of city notaries

and candidates for minor government office—indicate an even higher incidence of ordinary citizens bearing noble surnames.

The first *Libro d'Oro* of the Venetian patriciate, dating from 1506, listed 142
noble clans resident in Venice.[47] A full 119 of their surnames (84 percent of the
total pool) are now known to have been held by commoners between the fourteenth and sixteenth centuries.[48] Many Venetians with the illustrious names
Bembo, Corner, Grimani, Giustiniani, Loredan, Sanudo, Querini, and Venier
were not eligible to sit on the Great Council. Angelo Corner and Girolamo
Balbi served in the chancery, Antonio Morosini and Francesco Gritti were
notaries, Tommaso Bragadin headed the Scuola Grande di San Marco. One can
only wonder about the thoughts of Gabriele and Alvise Contarini, minor
scribes in San Marco offices who worked alongside nobles who shared their
name.[49] Indeed, only the most insignificant of noble houses—Ballastro, Cao-
torta, Gussoni, Masolo, Paradiso, Ruzini—did *not* have commoner homonyms.

Where did these nobly named commoners come from? Some nobly named
commoner lines, as claimed in the 1536 and 1540 chronicles, may have been
excluded at the time of the Serrata or subsequent admissions to the Great
Council even though their kinsmen were accepted. In some cases simple coincidence may explain interclass homonyms: those with toponymic surnames
(Baffo, Pisani, Trevisan), those whose surnames were simply generic (Bon, da
Canal, Tagliapietra), and those whose surnames derived from widely shared
personal names (Donà, Marin, Michiel, Zorzi). It is not possible, however,
to explain away those dozens of commoners who bore the more distinctive
patrician names—Barbarigo and Gradenigo and Mocenigo and Pasqualigo,
Bondulmer and Condulmer, Diedo and Duodo, Foscari and Foscarini and
Foscolo, Lipomano and Pizamano and Vizamano.

The only plausible explanation is that at least some of these commoners
were blood relatives of patricians. Some may have descended from the illegitimate offspring of nobles, denied seats on the Great Council by laws of 1276,
1297 and 1376. Also excluded from councils, and hence excluded from nobility
itself, were those born to a patrician father and a slave or a very low-ranking
woman *(femena vil)* (unless, in the latter case only, the father had immediately registered his marriage with the Avogadori di Comun), by a law of 1422,
and those born to an *abietta* woman, by a law of 1533.[50] It has been asserted
that custom automatically admitted nobles' bastards into the ranks of cittadini
originari, though contemporary articulation of any such custom is lacking; if
this was the case, these would constitute yet another distinct pool of original
citizens.[51]

But illegitimacy and descent from unworthy women was only one reason why those of noble blood might find themselves ranked with the better commoners. Miscreant nobles were sometimes stripped of their status and probably were forced into the next level down.[52] A significant body of legislation in the early Quattrocento sought to maintain the purity of patrician blood by tightening mechanisms for probation and registration, to the point of constituting a "second *serrata*," and according to Giuseppe Maranini, the tests for admission to the Great Council became more "cautious, complex, and solemn" at that time;[53] those who failed increasingly rigorous *prove* may well have joined the ranks of elite commoners. Further legislation of the early Cinquecento, instituting registration procedures and intensifying oversight, would have served only to increase the likelihood that men of noble surname but ignoble qualifications would be denied seats on the Council. In the spring of 1526, for example, the Council of Ten ordered the reexamination of thirty self-styled nobles, fourteen who habitually sat on the Great Council and sixteen who, though politically inactive, had passed the test for eligibility in the past. Other *riprove* were offered in those years, either because would-be nobles had been registered too late or not at all or because they were suspected of illegitimacy; the riprove were to be decided not by the mid-ranking Avogadori di Comun but by a "solemn college" comprising the doge, his councilors, and the three heads of the Quarantia.[54] Some surely were decided negatively. Where could the unsuccessful go except into the ranks of the cittadini?

Sheer force of circumstances may also account for some of the nobly named among the commoners. Some men genealogically qualified for nobility simply chose not to prove their nobility because they did not wish to claim a seat on the Great Council. Although their sons were offered means for political rehabilitation if they chose to reenter public life,[55] these too became more stringent: after 1459 they were given a window of only five years after their twenty-fifth birthday, and in these cases too the "solemn college" was to hear petitions. After age thirty no probation was allowed.[56] It seems likely that those who declined political participation over several generations would de facto lose nobility itself, though they retained the noble name. As Paolo Paruta later put it, "The noble man, insofar as he is excluded from the honors of the city, doesn't always remain a noble."[57]

In another vein, Gasparo Contarini thought that loss of wealth might over time lead to loss of nobility, and a contemporary chronicler offered the picture of the da Colonna, once "made nobles of Venice," who were now of "low condition," operating a dry-goods shop.[58] It is also entirely possible, though firm proof is lacking, that grinding poverty might lead patricians to take up the sorts of trades that would ultimately disqualify them from nobility, trading shabby gentility and meaningless places on the Great Council for more substantial lives as commoners.

But it is hardly the case that all those commoners bearing noble surnames ranked with the higher-standing cittadini. Some were plebeian indeed: Lazzaro Gritti was a fisherman, Antonio Morosini a servant, Michele Basegio a carpenter, Alvise Tiepolo a boatman, Zuan Antonio Malipiero a prison guard.[59] Though they lacked personal occupational descriptives, Francesco Foscolo was listed among the tailors, Francesco Diedo among the butchers, Marin Foscolo among the laborers, Marco Diedo and Nicoleto Valier among the tanners.[60] Some of these may have descended from nobles who had fallen far. Others may always have been artisans: it seems plausible that when the lower orders of society took surnames, some adopted the names of noble employers or patrons. Brian Pullan has found some late cases of converts from Judaism who took the surnames of noble godparents.[61] Whatever their origins, they are so frequently found that sheer possession of a noble surname cannot be an automatic marker of cittadino status.

A feature of the cittadini not noted in the secondary literature is that they claimed a kind of cadet nobility. The full title of the 1540 text, in fact, is "Chronicle of all the ancient and noble families of Venetian citizens who are not of the Great Council." The notion of noble commoners was not new. In Giorgio Cracco's reading, it arose well before the Serrata closed the Venetian patriciate, as a way of identifying those populares whose wealth and standing distinguished them from the *popolo minuto*. Especially in the thirteenth century "noble commoner" denoted those who had gained access to some share of power, though they could not be ranked with the truly great.[62]

More to the point, the category survived the closure of noble ranks in the Serrata of 1297–1323. Even when nobility was firmly established as hereditary eligibility for the Great Council the possibility of a type of nobility attached to commoners remained. In the late fourteenth century, for example, matriculation records of the Scuola Grande di San Giovanni Evangelista established a separate category for *nobeli de puovolo* (nobles of the populace). Other scuole issued in-house nobility, probably for cash and probably as a means of exempting members from the requirement of regular ritual flagellation, well into the sixteenth century.[63]

There were other sorts of commoner nobility as well. In 1518 a member of the nonpatrician Vico family, in a document excerpted by the Avogadori di

Comun, was styled "nobel homo"; the same label was applied to the equally nonpatrician Anteo Amadi in 1517 and to commoner Stefano Ramberti in 1534. Graziosa Martini was styled "nobel madonna" in 1551; Laura Vidal too was "nobel."[64] Memoirs of the mid-Cinquecento proclaimed the nobility of the Arborsani and Dardani families, who assuredly were not represented on the Great Council.[65] In the next century, characterization of cittadini as constituting a "second order of gentlemen" or "private gentlemen" or "nobility of the citizens" became widespread, almost canonical.[66]

Some Venetian cittadini, that is, insisted on noble standing in their documents. They, at least, did not strictly equate nobility with eligibility for the Great Council, though that equation may already have been established by the early Trecento,[67] and that is the definition that historiography has left us. What did they mean by nobility? Not political nobility, certainly. At most one document from the dark autumn of 1509 asserts that a few frightened nobles may have interpreted popular unrest as threatening their position and discussed admitting a few cittadini to their ranks. Even this account stresses aristocratic fears but does not mention actual popular ambitions to noble standing. But the story comes from a Vicentine who was cut off from Venice by the war and may not have had direct knowledge of events. Venetian chroniclers did not report any such incident.[68] There is no other indication that Venetian citizens had pretensions to membership in the Great Council. As the 1540 chronicle and seventeenth-century texts affirm, they were content to remain "noble families of Venetian citizens who are not of the Great Council," those who "are born and live nobly but don't have a vote on the Council."

Nobles, in turn, were willing to concede such titles to higher-ranking commoners, even the titles *nobel homo* and *nobel madonna*. That the Avogadori di Comun, guardians of aristocratic purity, copied their documents and titles verbatim indicates that the highest levels of Venetian patricians accepted citizens' claims. Marino Sanudo, to take another example, thought that *missier* was one of two labels properly applied to a noble, yet he also gave that title to the commoner deputies called to make a census in 1509, along with their patrician colleagues.[69] He and Girolamo Priuli similarly styled as *sier* the commoner bankers of the Garzoni and Agostini families.[70] In the index to the Avogadori di Comun's second register of marriage contracts nobles and nonnobles alike were qualified as *ser* and *misser*. And those who successfully bid in auctions to collect tolls *(dazi),* whether noble (Bernardo da Lezze) or not (Jacomo Arian), were styled *ser.*[71] Sanudo's second preferred title for nobles was *magnificentia,* but the Avogadori also gave the honorific *magnifico* to nonnoble grand chancellors and other nonpatrician worthies, and the *generoso* that the Avogadori applied to the Turloni and Sagundino came close to a standard aristocratic descriptive. In Secretary Antonio Vinciguerra's tomb inscription (1517) he was described with the decidedly aristocratic *clarissimus*.[72]

Does any of this matter? For all practical purposes, citizen nobility counted for little. It counted for nothing in affairs of state. Still, for the cittadini it had immense social value, and they passed up no opportunity to inscribe it in their documents and memoirs. From their point of view, it could not be dismissed as affectation. In displaying titles with some regularity honored citizens looked upward, not toward any assimilation with the true aristocracy but toward establishing symbolic bonds with their superiors, and downward, to the mass of the populace from which they hoped to distance themselves. Already possessed of wealth and office, they saw honorific descriptives as one more element that set them off from the truly plebeian.

Intermarriage also bound the cittadini and the patriciate. As noted above, a string of laws were designed to establish and protect the blood purity of the aristocracy, disqualifying from the Great Council those born of slaves and requiring registration of marriages with servants or other base women. But no legislation discouraged unions of patrician men with respectable cittadine women or disqualified the offspring of those unions from seats on the Great Council.[73] Patrician legislators even expected such unions: the law of 1526 requiring registration of matrimonies, for example, was to apply to marriages of noble men "with any woman, whatever grade and condition she might be, whether noble or otherwise."

Whatever the bonds of patronage and intimacy—study of this phenomenon is still in its infancy—there were practical incentives for patricians to contract such unions, as the hefty dowries brought in by cittadino brides provided a relatively painless way to bolster the fortunes of straitened aristocratic houses. It may be doubted that the daughter of Zuan Speladi actually brought the enormous sum of 40,000 ducats to war hero Carlo Zen, as the later impoverished Bartolomeo Speladi tried to claim. But the list of thirteen Arborsani dowries transferred to patrician husbands in the period 1394–1496, totaling 36,600 ducats, does not seem out of line. Nor does the 25,000 ducats in dowries that eight Quartari brides were said to have brought to their noble spouses. Given that the ceiling on marriage portions was set at 1,600 ducats in 1420 and raised to 3,000 ducats in 1505 (though these limits were regularly ignored), cittadino dowries appear generous indeed. Also through marriage entire Arborsani patrimonies passed to patrician heirs, one of 6,000 ducats and some houses and another of 8,000 ducats.[74]

How frequent, in fact, was marriage between patricians and nonnobles? Stanley Chojnacki, working from a sample of 890 fifteenth-century marriages in sixteen noble families, concluded that class exogamy was relatively infrequent, occurring in about 9 percent of all cases. Furthermore, its incidence decreased over time, as male patrician marriages with commoners dropped from 9.7 percent in the first half of the century to 8.5 percent in the second half.[75] Calculation of a different source offers different results. An early-sixteenth-century register of the Avogaria di Comun was originally intended to list marriages of noble men in the period 1400–1502; later hands extended the accounting for another half-century. Tabulation of one-third of the volume records 2,473 male patrician marriages in the period 1400–1559. In total, a full 14.3 percent of patrician men married nonpatrician women in the fifteenth century.[76] This figure, 50 percent higher than Chojnacki's sampling, actually understates exogamous unions. All those with a surname held by a noble were considered noble. But as we have seen, most patrician surnames were shared with commoners. Since the register applied the title ser to all brides' fathers, noble and cittadino alike, it is impossible to know whether a given surname refers to a noble or a commoner. Given the frequency of shared surnames, it is likely that some of these marriages were in fact contracted with nonnobles, though they were not counted as such.

In this tabulation, as in Chojnacki's, the long-range trend was toward aristocratic exclusivity: the figure dropped to 9.9 percent in the first half of the sixteenth century. The fact remains, however, that in the Quattrocento one in every seven patrician men married outside the patriciate, and in the Cinquecento one in ten. Venetian aristocratic palaces were fairly replete with wives born outside the Venetian aristocracy.

Not all these brides were Venetian commoners. Many were foreigners, particularly from the notable families of subject lands.[77] In many cases the identity or origin of the nonpatrician bride's father (her name is not given) cannot be ascertained, and in several cases not even his surname is given. But it is certain, from a late-nineteenth-century compilation, that families of cittadini were indeed active in contracting marriages with patrician men: the Agostini counted seven such unions, the Amadi ten, the Cavazza seven, and the Ciera eleven. Here too the count is on the low side, as the compiler left out a number of cross-class marriages: he cited eight Arborsani marriages with patrician men before 1569, but the Arborsani memoir lists sixteen, as well as six marriages with patrician women. Still other records tell us that Francesco Sandei alone found noble spouses for five sons and a daughter, for a total of nine unions, counting remarriages.[78]

Again, to be blunt, did it matter? Whichever source is preferred, does a figure of 9–14 percent of patrician male unions with citizen women constitute a significant level of intermarriage? Probably not to patricians. They certainly did not find it unsettling enough to attempt to curb the phenomenon, at least not before the last decade of the sixteenth century.[79] But intermarriage did matter deeply to the citizens, and they regularly mentioned it in their memoirs. Marital alliances with the ruling group, even more than titles or bygone kinship, brought enduring legitimation of status. On ritual occasions of baptism and marriage well-connected cittadini might frequent the palaces of their superiors; at all times they knew that their blood mingled with aristocratic blood. Those with noble in-laws, nieces, nephews, and grandchildren could well feel themselves firmly set apart from the truly plebeian.

The ranks of the elite citizens were fluid and unfixed for all of the fifteenth century and most of the sixteenth. There were distinct if overlapping groups: the chancery secretaries, the group defined in the 1536 and 1540 chronicles (and it must be acknowledged that the latter offer different if overlapping lists),[80] original citizens by privilege, and perhaps some descendants of nobles' illegitimate offspring and some who declined or failed the tests for nobility. The legal definition moved toward the 1569 standard of three generations of legitimate birth in the city, but only in piecemeal and unsystematic fashion. In any case this standard would not have applied to those who based their status on criteria other than public office and had no need for formal ratification. The lack of a definitive tribunal and procedure for proving original citizenship no doubt provided contemporaries with additional grounds for confusion.

Ambiguity was gradually erased beginning in the 1530s and ending in the covering law of 1569. It would be an exaggeration to speak of a serrata, or closing, of ranks parallel to though trailing the serrata of the ranks of the patriciate since access from below was never cut off. Furthermore, patricians later forced something of an expansion of the formal boundary of cittadino ranks, adding a new category based on standards of honorable occupation: census forms in the late Cinquecento instructed officials to enroll as cittadini all "lawyers, physicians, notaries and others who exercise a civil profession, and also priests who are not noble."[81]

But the 1569 law did create definitive mechanisms and criteria for determining who was and who was not capable of claiming citizen status. Moreover, it was instantly effective: the Avogadori di Comun's registers of prove, dating from barely a month after passage of the law, are so complete that as a whole they are said to constitute a *Libro d'Argento,* parallel to the *Libri d'Oro* that inscribed the nobility.[82] Indeed, the overall impetus to establishing that *cursus* (legislative procedure) and archive might well have been the patrician Serrata. Certainly the early sixteenth century introduced a number of key pieces of legislation requiring the registration of patrician births and marriages and setting a standard cursus for proving eligibility for the Great Council. It seems only logical that the growing preoccupation with maintaining group purity through definition, probation, and registration would eventually extend from the patriciate to the cittadini, who loomed so large in Venetian public life.

Patricians also sought tighter definition of citizen status because they wished—or needed—to build a solid service class that could handle those tasks that they themselves could not or did not wish to manage and, perhaps, to coopt into their administration those commoners who could pose the only conceivable threat to their regime. In part their motivation for doing so was positive: they wished to reward those subjects, and only those subjects, who were "willing to risk not only their substance but their very lives for the Republic."[83] That, in turn, dictated exclusionary policies. Increasingly nativist, patrician legislators felt the need to ban foreigners from public employ; even those made citizen per privilegio might be assumed to have residual loyalties to the places of their birth and constantly were accused of shirking their tax obligations. Priests too had (or should have) competing loyalties, to God and Rome; they were denied chancery posts in 1475 and were excluded from the private notariate after 1514.[84]

But nobles' motivation in creating a service class of cittadini may also have been a response to perceived dysfunction within the nobility itself. Patricians increasingly depended upon public office for their economic base, yet the number of offices did not expand anywhere near as quickly as did the number of patricians, and thus competition grew more intense.[85] Electoral corruption, it would seem, was endemic, or at least they perceived it as endemic. Nobles were so inclined to "favor their own," for example, that in 1467 the task of carrying ballots was taken away from them and given to commoner youths.[86] Factional fault lines were everywhere: between the older and the newer houses *(case vecchie* and *case nuove),*[87] between exponents of an oligarchic vision and exponents of broad collegiality, between the old and the young.[88] Handing over sensitive aspects of government to loyal cittadini not only offered the practical advantages of technical skills and continuity in personnel but might serve to mitigate the worst of factionalism and help ensure that tensions within the patriciate did not infect the everyday business of administration. It also dictated exclusion of nobles from certain categories of public office.

Creation of a distinctive subaltern class was accomplished in the long run by the progressive reservation of certain types of office to the cittadini originari, beginning with leadership posts in the scuole grandi in 1410 and 1438 and extending to the upper chancery in 1478 and to lesser offices in 1507, 1517, and 1539.[89] It was accomplished in the second instance by the progressive delineation of standards for original citizenship, especially by the gradual imposition of the three-generation rule starting with merchants in 1492 and extending to gastaldi of the procurators in 1507 and to candidates for lesser office in 1543. It was accomplished, as well, by allowing some intermarriage, by admitting cadet nobility, and by conferring ceremonial entitlements: secretaries and grand chancellors marched just before the doge in processions; the chancellors could wear scarlet (as did the procurators) and received state funerals, and secretaries could wear the black velvet toga (as did patricians).[90]

But much of the impetus to define the ranks of honored citizens came from the cittadini themselves. Their immediate catalyst for doing so may have been a Senate law of 1534 relating to the other main category of Venetian citizenship, that granted per privilegio to immigrants who had resided in the city for a specified period. Rehearsing several past laws and ordering strict examination of suspect claims, the Senate almost as an afterthought ordered that citizens per privilegio be subject to the same laws governing cittadini originari "as it is appropriate that in all matters there be maintained equality" between the two categories of citizen.[91] But equality cut both ways: henceforth original citizens would find their status subject to the same scrutiny as the rights of those with acquired citizenship. Or perhaps the catalyst for the closing of the cittadini came in a law of 1538, requiring that candidates for the chancery prove their original citizenship before the Avogadori di Comun, according to the well-established and strict "form and procedure observed in proofs of nobility."[92]

Taken together, these measures gave cittadini a strong incentive for self-justification. Increasingly privileged, by the 1530s they were increasingly subject to scrutiny by patrician magistracies. Those claiming cittadino status by virtue of chancery employment were protected by legislation that both defined their ranks and guaranteed their office, but those cittadini partially or wholly outside the chancery needed to provide their own legitimating documentation. Thus, in 1536 and again in 1540 unknown compilers drew up chronicle lists of cittadino houses, clearly imitating the venerable genre of collective chronicles of noble houses.[93] For the cittadini too texts offered precise lists of families and provided information on their coats of arms, origins and antiquity, past heroes, and present locations, precisely the credentials offered by the chronicles of the patriciate. On a more pragmatic note, thirteen families in the 1540 chronicle were said to have contributed 1,409,000 ducats in taxes to the common good. Benedetto Arborsani likewise established the credentials of the body of Lucchesi made original citizens by privilege, chronicling the miseries of their home city, the ranks of families immigrating to Venice, the properties they owned in Venice, and the taxes they paid.[94]

Individual families too felt a need to prove their worthiness. They did so by drawing up composite dossiers of memoirs and documents that would prove the various facets of their worthiness. Known examples date from the mid-1530s, which surely is no coincidence, and extend to the 1550s.[95] None of the compilers claimed that his family held the juridical status of cittadino originario, as the 1536 and 1540 chronicles do not. Rather, their qualifications were of a sort that would bolster their claims to *publica fama* or ratification by general reputation, a criterion of eminence less precise yet no less powerful than legal distinctions.

Antiquity mattered: the Arborsani had arrived in 1316, the Amadi cited a ducal letter of 1287, and the Freschi claimed membership in councils since 1058. Accounts of taxes paid—the Speladi claimed 360,000 ducats, the Quartari 147,930 ducats, the Arborsani 59,482 ducats—proved that they had been responsible members of the body public and contributors to its endeavors.[96] Accounts of the personal sacrifices made in Venice's wars—like that of David Freschi, crippled in a naval battle in 1379—showed that they had long been prepared to offer not only their substance but their very lives to the Republic. Copies of documents illustrating the offices they had held testified to their service and their superiors' recognition of patriotic deeds. Anagraphic records, setting out their marriages and births, established longtime legitimacy. Records of unions with patricians established their good blood and high connections. Nobility itself, by one definition current in Venice, hinged on a combination of antiquity, wealth, and *virtù* (especially civic-minded *virtù*);[97] these dossiers proved all three.

Claiming proximity to the patriciate through antiquity, title, kinship, and patriotic service, that is, these cittadini aspired not to any amalgamation with the patriciate but to confirmation of a status analogous to that of the patriciate, one that would provide a foundation for their pretensions to eminence and ratify their definitive separation from the rest of the populace. In turn the patriciate, by reserving office for them, accepting their hyperbolic titles, marrying their daughters, and finally in 1569 providing a definitive mechanism for their certification, accepted the cittadini's aspirations. Having effected their own final serrata and now confident in their own exclusivity, the patriciate could afford to, and perhaps felt they had to, concede distinct and privileged standing to loyal subalterns.

N O T E S

I thank Matteo Casini, Stanley Chojnacki, Brian Pullan, and Giuseppe Trebbi for sharing their extensive knowledge of the subject.

　　1. Marcantonio Sabellico, *De Venetis magistratibus liber,* in *Thesaurus antiquitatum et historiarum Italiae,* ed. Joannes Georgius Graevius, vol. 5, pt. 1 (Louvain, 1722), cols. 31–32.

　　2. Gasparo Contarini, *De magistratibus et republica venetorum,* in ibid., cols. 8, 59. For the dating of this work, see Felix Gilbert, "The Date of the Composition of Contarini's and Giannotti's Books on Venice," *Studies in the Renaissance* 14 (1967): 172–84.

　　3. Poggio Bracciolini, paraphrased in Donald E. Queller, *The Venetian Patriciate: Realty versus Myth* (Urbana, 1986), 8; Paolo Paruta, *Discorsi politici,* in *Opere politiche* (Florence, 1852), 239; Niccolò Machiavelli and Claude de Seyssel, cited in Innocenzo Cervelli, *Machiavelli e la crisi dello stato veneziano* (Naples, 1974), 78, 221, 229, 240, 260; Philippe de Commynes, *Mémoires,* ed. Joseph Calmette, 3 vols. (Paris, 1965–81), 3:114; *Traité du gouvernement de la cité et seigneurie de Venise,* in *Histoire des relations de la France avec Venise,* ed. Paul Michel Perret, vol. 2 (Paris, 1896), 249.

　　4. Marin Sanudo, *De origine, situ et magistratibus urbis Venetae,* ed. Angela Caracciolo Aricò (Milan, 1980), 22.

　　5. Girolamo Priuli, *I diarii di Girolamo Priuli [AA. 1499–1512],* ed. Arturo Segre and Roberto Cessi, Rerum Italicarum Scriptores, 24, pt. 3, vols. 1, 2, 4 (Bologna, 1912–38), 4:8; see also 1:137–38, 2:193, 4:30, 39, 50, 73, 273, 281.

　　6. Donato Giannotti, *Della repubblica de' Viniziani,* in *Opere politiche e letterarie,* ed. F. L. Polidori, vol. 2 (Florence, 1850), 28–29. See also Gilbert, "Date of the Composition of Contarini's and Giannotti's Books on Venice."

　　7. Biblioteca Nazionale Marciana (BNM), Ms. It. cl. VII, 709 (8403), esp. fols. 3r–4r, 44r–46r, 51r–52v; see also Francesco Sansovino, *Venetia città nobilissima et singolare, con aggiunta da Giustiniano Martinioni,* 2 vols. (1663; reprint, Farnborough, Hampshire, Eng., 1968), 281.

　　8. For later echoes of the bipartite model, see Franco Gaeta, "Venezia da 'stato misto' ad aristocrazia 'esemplare,'" in *Storia della cultura veneta,* ed. Girolamo Arnaldi and Manlio Pastore Stocchi, 6 vols. (Vicenza, 1976–86), 4, pt. 2: 452–54, 463–64, 469,

491; and Maria Luisa Doglio, "La letteratura ufficiale e l'oratoria celebrativa," in ibid., 4, pt. 1: 168, 174.

9. Marco Ferro, *Dizionario del diritto comune e veneto,* 10 vols. in 5 (Venice, 1788–81), 2:137, 3:7–8, 9–10, 74, 189–90, 5:300; Vettor Sandi, *Principi di storia civile della Repubblica di Venezia dalla sua fondazione sino all'anno di N. S. 1700* (Venice, 1755–56), pt. 1, vol. 2, 811–12; pt. 2, vol. 1, 345–53. On the later tradition of the tripartite model, see Andrea Zannini, *Burocrazia e burocrati a Venezia in età moderna: I cittadini originari (sec. XVI–XVIII)* (Venice, 1993), 47–60 and ch. 5.

10. Leopold von Ranke, *Venezia nel Cinquecento con un saggio introduttivo di Ugo Tucci,* trans. Ingeborg Zapperi Walter (Rome, 1974), 148–49.

11. Contarini, *De magistratibus,* cols. 60–61. See also Franco Gaeta, "L'idea di Venezia," in Arnaldi and Stocchi, *Storia della cultura veneta,* 3, pt. 2: 638–39; and Lester Libby, "Venetian History and Political Thought after 1509," *Studies in the Renaissance* 20 (1973): 21–22.

12. Gaeta, "Venezia da 'stato misto' ad aristocrazia esemplare," 452–53 (Bodin); Angelo Ventura, ed., *Relazioni degli ambasciatori veneti al Senato* (Bari, 1976), xxix (Botero); Brian Pullan, "Service to the Venetian State: Aspects of Myth and Reality in the Early Seventeenth Century," *Studi Secenteschi* 5 (1964): 103 (Botero); Niccolò Crasso, commentary on Giannotti's *Dialogus de republica Venetorum,* in Graevius, *Thesaurus,* vol. 5, pt. 1, cols. 21–23.

13. In additions to works by Bellavitis, Casini, Neff, de Peppo, Trebbi, and Zannini cited throughout this essay, see Matteo Casini, *Cancelleria e cancellier grande nella Venezia seicentesca* (tesi di laurea, University of Venezia, Facoltà di Lettere e Filosofia, relatore prof. Gaetano Cozzi, 1987–88); and A. Doglioni, *La cittadinanza originaria nella Repubblica di Venezia* (tesi di laurea, University of Padua, Facoltà di Giurisprudenza, relatore prof. G. Zordan, 1989–90), neither of which was available to the author.

14. Patricia Fortini Brown, *Venetian Narrative Painting in the Age of Carpaccio* (New Haven, 1989); Margaret L. King, *Venetian Humanism in an Age of Patrician Dominance* (Princeton, 1986); Brian Pullan, *Rich and Poor in Renaissance Venice: The Social Institutions of a Catholic State, to 1620* (Oxford, 1971), esp. ch. 4; Lia Sbriziolo, "Per la storia delle confraternite veneziane, dalle deliberazioni miste (1310–1476) del Consiglio dei Dieci: Le scuole dei Battuti," in *Miscellanea Gilles Gerard Meersseman,* vol. 2 (Padua, 1970), 715–63.

15. Archivio di Stato, Venice (ASV), Consiglio dei Dieci (Dieci), reg. 15, fol. 114v (1456); ASV, Dieci, Misti, reg. 19, fol. 99v (1478). When volumes in ASV have both original and modern foliations, the latter are cited here. By the latter law, cives originarii of lands subject to Venice could enter the chancery with the approval of three-quarters of the Council of Ten; in fact, this did not happen.

16. Sansovino, *Venetia città nobilissima et singolare,* 295; Marin Sanudo, *Le vite dei dogi (1474–1494),* ed. Angela Caracciolo Aricò (Padua, 1989), 115; Samuele Romanin, *Storia documentata di Venezia,* 10 vols. (Venice, 1853–61), 4:269; BNM, Ms. It. cl. VII, 709 (8403), fols. 51r–52v.

17. Piero Dolfin, *Annali veneti,* in *Diarii veneziani del secolo decimosesto,* ed. Roberto

Cessi and Paolo Sambin, vol. 1 (Venice, 1943), 29, 31–32; Marino Sanuto, *I diarii di Marino Sanuto,* ed. Rinaldo Fulin et al., 58 vols. (Venice, 1879–1903), vol. 9, col. 42; quotation from Priuli, *I diarii,* 4:212. The tradition of citizen guards of illustrious captives dates at least to the mid-fifteenth century (Paola de Peppo, " 'Memorie di veneti cittadini': Alvise Dardani, cancellier grande," *Studi Veneziani,* n.s., 8 (1984): 416–19, 423.

18. Sanuto, *I diarii,* vol. 8, cols. 356–65, 385–86; Priuli, *I diarii,* 4:170.

19. Priuli, *I diarii,* 4:281–82.

20. ASV, Dieci, Misti, reg. 9, fol. 44v (1410), reg. 12, fol. 21r (1438); ASV, Scuola Grande di S. Giovanni Evangelista, reg. 8, fol. 35v (1473); ASV, Scuola Grande di S. Maria Misericordia, reg. 4, fol. 32v (dated 1474 but identical to the preceding); Pullan, *Rich and Poor in Renaissance Venice,* 109–11.

21. Mary Frances Neff, "Chancellery Secretaries in Venetian Politics and Society, 1400–1533" (Ph.D. diss., University of California at Los Angeles, 1985), 348–599.

22. The 1536 chronicle is Museo Civico Correr (MCC), Ms. Gradenigo 192, pp. 3–33 (ignoring the later interlinear and subsequent entries in a different hand). The 1540 chronicle is MCC, Cicogna 2156, 170–89; see also BNM, Ms. It. cl. VII, 27 (7761), fols. 82r–96r. These and many other manuscripts contain similar seventeenth-century chronicles, and there exist many later genealogies; these are ignored in the present study since they reflect later and very different perceptions of membership in the *ordo* of original citizens. See the works cited in Neff, "Chancellery Secretaries," 313–15; and de Peppo, "Memorie di veneti cittadini," 413–53.

23. Sanudo, *Le vite dei dogi,* 136–51, 163, 219–20; Gaetano Cozzi, "Politica, società, istituzioni," in Gaetano Cozzi and Michael Knapton, *La repubblica di Venezia dell'eta moderna,* vol. 12, pt. 1 (Turin, 1986), 60; Giuseppe Trebbi, "Il segetario veneziano," *Archivio Storico Italiano* 144, no. 1 (1986): 36. Dario, Manenti, Freschi, and Vinciguerra appear frequently in the diaries of Marino Sanudo and Girolamo Priuli and in Domenico Malipiero, *Annali veneti dall'anno 1457 al 1500,* ed. Francesco Longo and Agostino Sagredo, 2 vols., *Archivio Storico Italiano* 7 (1843–44) (see indexes).

24. BNM, Ms. It. cl. VII, 165 (8867), fols. 40r–41v; Mary Neff, "A Citizen in the Service of the Patrician State: The Career of Zaccaria de' Freschi," *Studi Veneziani,* n.s., 5 (1981): 33–61; Cozzi, "Politica, società, istituzioni," 86.

25. King, *Venetian Humanism,* 443–44; Neff, "Chancellery Secretaries," 583–86.

26. The families of Alessandro dalle Fornaci (elected 1470), Febo Capella (elected 1480), and Nicolò Aurelio (1523) were not included in the 1536 and 1540 chronicles; included were the families of Zuan Dedo (1482), Alvise Dardani (1510), Francesco Fasuol (1511), Gian Piero Stella (1516), Girolamo Dedo (1524), and Andrea Franceschi (1529).

27. ASV, Maggior Consiglio (MC), reg. 29, fol. 45r. The procedures outlined in this law were operative earlier, as seen in prove of 1558 and 1559 (ASV, Avogaria di Comun [AC], reg. 361, no. 7; reg. 365, no. 75). The 1569 law actually applied only to those seeking lesser positions as notaries and scribes at the San Marco magistracies, not to those seeking higher positions in the chancery or elsewhere in the administration (secretaries or gastaldi of the procurators). In actuality the standards and the procedures

outlined in the law were immediately applied to candidates for all offices and indeed to anyone wishing to prove *cittadinanza originaria* (see ASV, AC, Cittadinanza originaria [regs. 361–]).

28. Zannini, *Burocrazia e burocrati*, 32.

29. ASV, MC, reg. 23, fol. 105r.

30. ASV, Dieci, Misti, reg. 21, fols. 194r–v, reg. 23, fols. 108v–109v.

31. Ibid., reg. 25, fol. 105r; see also Luca Molà and Reinhold C. Mueller, "Essere straniero a Venezia nel tardo medioevo: Accoglienze e rifiuto nei privilegi di cittadinanza e nelle sentenze criminali," in *Le migrazioni in Europa*, ed. Simonetta Cavaciocchi (Florence, 1994), 846.

32. ASV, Dieci, Misti, reg. 27, fol. 202r.

33. ASV, MC, reg. 25, fols. 49v–50r (1507), reg. 27, fols. 49r–v (1539), 106v–107r (1543); BNM, Ms. It. cl. VII, 90 (8029), 1–2 (a 1554 prova demonstrating only the legitimate birth of the candidate). The 1537 law on advocates required only that they be "nobili et cittadini originarii over nativi di questa nostra città"; it made no mention of the birth status of fathers or grandfathers (ASV, Conservatori ed Esecutori alle Leggi, reg. 1, fols. 2v–7v).

34. ASV, Dieci, Misti, reg. 21, fols. 194r–v.

35. ASV, Quarantia Criminal, reg. 255 bis, records *probae* of 1488–1508, and several candidates are noted as cives originarii.

36. See ASV, Senato, Terra, reg. 18, fols. 132v–134r, 147r–148r, 175v–176r; and the 1531 revision of prova mechanisms in ibid., reg. 26, fols. 147r–148r.

37. ASV, MC, reg. 25, fols. 151r–152r.

38. ASV, Dieci, Comuni, reg. 12, fol. 161v; examples of 1558 and 1559 are in ASV, AC, reg. 361, no. 7, and reg. 365, no. 75.

39. ASV, AC, reg. 365, no. 75. For the Conservatori ed Esecutori alle Leggi, see Andrea Da Mosto, *L'Archivio di Stato di Venezia*, vol. 1 (Rome, 1937), 79; and ASV, Conservatori ed Esecutori alle Leggi, reg. 1, fols. 2v–7v.

40. ASV, Provveditori di Comun, reg. 2, fols. 6v–7r, 8r (1313); BNM, Ms. It cl. VII, 90 (8029), 1–2; see also Zannini, *Burocrazia e burocrati*, 42.

41. MCC, Ms. Gradenigo 56, pp. 53–54, 61–67, 89, 93–95, 132; Emmanuele Antonio Cicogna, *Delle inscrizioni veneziane*, vol. 6 (Venice, 1853), 377–78, 384–86, 842 (Amadi); BNM, Ms. It. cl. VII, 543 (7887), fol. 6r (Arborsani); de Peppo, "Memorie di veneti cittadini," 415 (Dardani).

42. Roberto Cessi, ed., *Deliberazioni del Maggior Consiglio di Venezia*, 3 vols. (Bologna, 1931–50), 1:269–362; Giorgio Cracco, *Società e stato nel medioevo veneziano* (Florence, 1967), 177 (Marioni); Raffaino Caresini, *Chronica (1343–1388)*, ed. Ester Pastorello, Rerum Italicarum Scriptores, 12, pt. 2 (Bologna, 1923), 10, 16 (Marioni, Rossi). Marco Barbaro's list of families accepted into the Venetian nobility in the period 1301–1406 contains many names later held by cittadini originari (BNM, Ms. It. cl. VII, 346 [8869]).

43. Romanin, *Storia documentata di Venezia*, 3:301. Individuals surnamed Alberto, Bolani, Cicogna, Condulmer, Darduin, Garzoni, Girardo, Lipomano, Longo, da Mezzo, Nani, Negro, Paruta, Pasqualigo, Pencin, Renier, Tagliapietra, Vendramin,

Vizamano and Zusti were admitted to the Great Council; commoners with those surnames are found throughout the fifteenth and sixteenth centuries.

44. As Gian Giacomo Caroldo declared in a sixteenth-century chronicle (BNM, Ms. It. cl. VII, 127, fols. 618v–619v). Other lists of those voted upon but not elected, with significant variations, are found in ibid., 52 (7604), fols. 7r–8v, 602 (7950), fol. 45r, 346 (8869), pp. 184–99. For lists of those offering service during the war, see Vittorio Lazzarini, "Le offerte per la guerra di Chioggia e un falsario del Quattrocento," *Nuovo Archivio Veneto*, n.s., 4 (1902): 205–13; and Fabio Besta, ed., *Bilanci generali della repubblica di Venezia*, 1, tome 1 (Venice, 1950), 68–78.

45. Matteo Casini, "La cittadinanza originaria a Venezia tra i secoli XV e XVI: Una linea interpretativa," in *Studi veneti offerti a Gaetano Cozzi* (Venice, 1992), 135–36, 149–50; Reinhold C. Mueller, "Espressioni di *status* sociale a Venezia dopo la 'serrata' del Maggior Consiglio," in ibid., 54 n. 3; Molà and Mueller, "Essere straniero," 840.

46. BNM, Ms. It. cl. VII, 543 (7887), fols. 6r–v, 7v–9r (probably the source for Sansovino, *Venetia città nobilissima et singolare*, 161), 69 (7728), fols. 482v–483v. On the Lucchesi community see Luca Molà, *La comunità dei Lucchesi a Venezia: Immigrazione e industria della seta nel tardo medioevo* (Venice, 1994).

47. ASV, AC, Nascite—Libro d'Oro, reg. 51/1, opened sections for 146 noble houses; four families habitually resident outside the city (the Avogaro and Martinenghi from Brescia, the da Colalto from Treviso, and the Savorgnan from Friuli) can be eliminated. The list should be compared with ASV, AC, reg. 106, which recorded noble marriages from 1400 to 1502 and opened sections for 153 houses. Marino Sanudo offers four lists that differ from one another and from the lists just cited: *De origine*, 68–70 (158 houses in 1493), 176–77 (158 houses in 1512); *Le vite dei dogi*, ed. Giovanni Monticolo, Rerum Italicarum Scriptores, 22, pt. 4 (Città di Castello, 1900), 17–47 (141 houses in 1522); *I diarii*, vol. 45, cols. 569–72 (143 houses in 1527).

48. BNM, Ms. It. cl. VII, 1667 (8459); ASV, Quarantia Criminal, regs. 255 bis, 255 ter; ASV, Scuola Grande di S. Giovanni Evangelista, reg. 4; ASV, Scuola Grande di S. Marco, regs. 3–5; ASV, Scuola Grande di S. Maria della Carità, regs. 233, 233 bis, 234; ASV, Scuola Grande di S. Maria della Valverde (or della Misericordia), regs. 4–5; Da Mosto, *L'Archivio di Stato di Venezia*, 228–34, 254–68; Neff, "Chancellery Secretaries," appendix; scattered cases in ASV, Giudici del Proprio, Testimoni, reg. 4, fol. 9r (I owe this reference to Stanley Chojnacki); ASV, MC, reg. 23, fol. 106v; ASV, Provveditori di Comun, reg. 2, fols. 89r, 92r–93r; and several noble surnames in ASV, AC, Contratti di Nozze—Cittadini I, reg. 144.

49. ASV, AC, reg. 140, fols. 109r–v; ASV, Quarantia Criminal, reg. 255 bis, fol. 18v; MCC, Ms. Gradenigo 56, p. 86.

50. Victor Crescenzi, *"Esse de maiori consilio": Legittimità civile e legittimazione politica nella Repubblica di Venezia (secc. XIII–XVI)* (Rome, 1996), 5, 8–9, 11, 74, 341, 343–44, 361, 369–70; Bartolomeo Cecchetti, "I nobili e il popolo di Venezia," *Archivio Veneto* 3 (1886): 424–25, 430; Cervelli, *Machiavelli*, 470; Romanin, *Storia documentata di Venezia*, 2:349; Giuseppe Trebbi, "La società veneziana," in *Storia di Venezia*, vol. 6, *Dal Rinascimento al Barocco*, ed. Gaetano Cozzi and Paolo Prodi (Rome, 1994), 131–32; Stanley Chojnacki, "In Search of the Venetian Patriciate: Families and Factions in the Four-

teenth Century," in *Renaissance Venice,* ed. John R. Hale (London, 1973), 53; idem, "Kinship Ties and Young Patricians in Fifteenth-Century Venice," *Renaissance Quarterly* 38 (1985): 246; idem, "Marriage Legislation and Patrician Society in Fifteenth-Century Venice," in *Law, Custom, and the Social Fabric in Medieval Europe. Essays in Honor of Bryce Lyon,* ed. Bernard S. Bachrach and David Nicholas (Kalamazoo, Mich., 1990), 167; idem, "Social Identity in Renaissance Venice: The Second *Serrata,*" *Renaissance Studies* 8 (1994): 351; Giuseppe Maranini, *La costituzione di Venezia,* 2 vols. (Venice, 1927–31), 1:209, 2.45–46; Ferro, *Dizionario,* 2:222, 7:74–75, 293.

51. Trebbi, "Il segetario veneziano," 42; idem, "La società veneziana," 162; Ferro, *Dizionario,* 7:160–61. For illegitimate sons of nobles as cittadini in the period after 1569, see Zannini, *Burocrazia e burocrati,* 99, 108–18.

52. For a 1327 case in which a noble was stripped of his citizenship, and by implication of his very nobility, see Rinaldo Fulin, "Gl'Inquisitori dei Dieci," *Archivio Veneto* 1 (1871): 39; see also Neff, "Chancellery Secretaries," 347.

53. Maranini, *La costituzione di Venezia dopo la serrata,* 55 (quotation); Chojnacki, "Social Identity in Renaissance Venice."

54. Sanuto, *I diarii,* vol. 41, cols. 227, 241–42; further *riprove* are in cols. 398–99, 411. See also Crescenzi, *"Esse de maiori consilio,"* pt. 3, chs. 1–2. For growing Cinquecento stringency, see Chojnacki's chapter in this volume.

55. Stanley Chojnacki, "Political Adulthood in Fifteenth-Century Venice," *American Historical Review,* 91 (1986): 803; idem, "Social Identity in Renaissance Venice," 347–48.

56. Crescenzi, *"Esse de maiori consilio,"* 5, 15–16, 28–29, 161–63, 225.

57. Paolo Paruta, *Della perfezione della vita politica,* in *Opere politiche* (Florence, 1852), 329.

58. For Contarini, see Cervelli, *Machiavelli,* 313; the quotation on the da Colonna is from BNM, Ms. It. cl. VII, 543 (7887), fols. 7r–v.

59. ASV, Scuola Grande di S. Marco, regs. 4–5.

60. ASV, Scuola Grande di S. Maria della Carità, reg. 233 bis.

61. Brian Pullan, *The Jews of Europe and the Inquisition of Venice, 1550–1670* (Totowa, N.J., 1983), 266–67 (I owe this reference to Brian Pullan).

62. Cracco, *Società e stato nel medioevo veneziano,* 108–10, 115, 206, 211, 217.

63. ASV, Scuola Grande di S. Giovanni Evangelista, reg. 4, fols. 12r–13v; the Quattrocento reference appears in Sbriziolo, "Per la storia delle confraternite veneziane," 726. According to Richard Mackenney, a noble title could be bought from a scuola and was valid "only within the confines of the confraternity" (*Tradesmen and Traders: The World of the Guilds in Venice and Europe, c. 1250–c. 1650* [Totowa, N.J., 1987], 54; I owe this reference to Brian Pullan).

64. ASV, AC, reg. 111, no. 17 (Martini), reg. 141, fols. 148v–149r (Amadi), 172r–v (Vico), reg. 142, fols. 120r–v (Vidal), 363v–364r (Ramberti).

65. BNM, Ms. It. cl. VII, 543 (7887), fol. 1r (Arborsani), 366 (7660), esp. fols. 1r–v (Dardani).

66. Ibid., 4 (7925), fols. 1r–v (and "gentilhomeni cittadini," who "nascono et vivono nobilmente ma non hanno voto nel predetto consiglio" [i.e, the Great Coun-

cil]); ibid., 27 (7761), fols. 97r–124r (and "gentilhuomini popolari" in fols. 130r–131v); MCC, Ms. Gradenigo 2156, 34, 127–38, 198–201 ("gentilhuomini popolari"). See also Ventura, *Relazioni degli ambasciatori veneti al Senato,* xxviii–xxix.

67. Mueller, "Espressioni di *status* sociale," 53–55. Jean-Claude Hocquet, however, dates the equation only to the fifteenth century ("Oligarchie et patriciat à Venise," *Studi Veneziani* 17–18 [1975–76]: 402).

68. Luigi da Porto, *Lettere storiche,* ed. Bartolommeo Bressan (Florence, 1857), 127–33, esp. 128–29; Cervelli, *Machiavelli,* 543–47. Sanudo's *Diarii* do not mention popular unrest; Priuli only gives an account (parallel to that of da Porto) of the doge summoning "antiqui et boni citadini et populari venetti de bona et antiqua famiglia" for a speech urging support of the war effort (*I diarii,* 4:281–82).

69. Sanudo, *De origine,* 23; idem, *I diarii,* vol. 7, cols. 356–65.

70. Priuli, *I diarii,* 1:111, 2:338–39; Sanuto, *I diarii,* 2:377, 775, 3:96 (commoner status from Sanudo, *De origine,* 27–28). The commoner Arborsani family applied *missier* and *ser* both to themselves and to the nobles they married (BNM, Ms. It. cl. VII, 543 [7887], fols. 10r, 11r–18v).

71. ASV, AC, reg. 141; Besta, *Bilanci generali,* 181–83.

72. ASV, AC, regs. 111, no. 17 (*magnifico* Appolonio Massa); 140, fol. 44r (*magnifici* Piero Franceschi and Bernardo Martini); 141, fols. 36v and 138r–v (*magnifico* Alvise Dardani) and 243r–v (Turloni and Sagundino); 142, fols. 164v–165r (*magnifico* Alvise Felleto, grand chancellor of Crete) and 189r–v (*magnifico* Febo Capella). On Vinciguerra's tomb inscription, see Sansovino, *Venetia città nobilissima et singolare,* 217.

73. A law of 1420 capped dowries at 1,600 ducats but allowed a ceiling of 2,000 ducats in the case of patricians marrying *populares;* however, it excluded cittadini from this special benefit (Chojnacki, "Marriage Legislation and Patrician Society," 164–65 and n. 7; idem, "Social Identity in Renaissance Venice," 350–51). Since dowry ceilings were regularly ignored, cittadini may not have been disadvantaged in practice.

74. ASV, Quarantia Criminal, reg. 255, fols. 28v–30r (Speladi) and 23v–25v (Quartari); BNM, Ms. It. cl. VII, 543 (7887), fols. 11v–18v (Arborsani); Stanley Chojnacki, "Dowries and Kinsmen in Early Renaissance Venice," *Journal of Interdisciplinary History* 4 (1975): 42; Anna Bellavitis, "La famiglia 'cittadina' veneziana nel secolo XVI: Dote e successioni: Le leggi e le fonti," *Studi Veneziani,* n.s., 30 (1995): 59–60.

75. Chojnacki, "Marriage Legislation and Patrician Society," 170; idem, "Kinship Ties and Young Patricians," 265. Chojnacki notes that patrician men were far more likely to marry commoner women (9.1%) than patrician women were to marry commoner men (1.4%) ("Marriage Legislation and Patrician Society," 174). Evidence from the Arborsani family corroborates that lead, though not to such a pronounced degree: six Arborsani men married noble women, but sixteen Arborsani women married noble men (BNM, Ms. It. cl. VII, 543 [7887], fols. 10r, 11v–18v).

76. ASV, AC, reg. 106. Included were all the interpolated marriages of the sixteenth century.

77. According to archivist Giuseppe Giomo's compilation (see n. 78), for example, Venetian men nine times married daughters of the Crespi family, lords of Milos.

78. The late-nineteenth-century compilation, by archivist Giuseppe Giomo, is

ASV, indexes 86 ter 1 and 86 ter 2. See also Molà, *La comunità dei Lucchesi a Venezia*, 134–35 (Sandei, with references to other cittadino-noble marriages); and BNM, Ms. It. cl. VII, 543 (7887), fols. 10r, 11v–18v (Arborsani).

79. After 1589–90, excluding from the Great Council those born to women whose fathers and/or grandfathers had exercized a manual trade (Trebbi, "La società veneziana," 169; Maranini, *La costituzione di Venezia dopo la serrata*, 71; Ferro, *Dizionario*, 7:78–79).

80. The 1536 chronicle lists 190 families; the 1540 chronicle 115, with 97 families in common. The 1536 chronicle has 93 families not found in the 1540 chronicle, and the 1540 chronicle has 18 families not found in the 1536 chronicle.

81. Zannini, *Burocrazia e burocrati*, 93.

82. Sixteenth-century registers are ASV, AC, regs. 361–69, 372. In addition, regs. 433–35 and 437 contain "suppliche e scritture inespedite," perhaps petitions withdrawn or denied.

83. This well-established legal principle justified the granting of *grazie* and the reservation of offices to those deserving of the Republic's favor (ASV, MC, reg. 12, fols. 44r–45v, reg. 22, fol. 156v, reg. 24, fols. 20v–21r, reg. 26, fols. 15v–16r, reg. 29, fol. 45r; ASV, Provveditori di Comun, reg. 2, fol. 90v; ASV, Quarantia Criminal, reg. 255, fols. 3v, 23v–25v, 28v–30r; ASV, Senato, Terra, reg. 18, fols. 132v–34r).

84. ASV, MC, reg. 23, fol. 153r, reg. 25, fol. 197r; ASV, Senato, Terra, reg. 18, fols. 132v–134r, reg. 26, 147r–148r.

85. Cozzi, "Politica, società, istituzioni," 119–20; idem, "Authority and the Law in Renaissance Venice," in Hale, *Renaissance Venice*, 298–301; Chojnacki, "Kinship Ties and Young Patricians," 244–45; idem, "Marriage Legislation and Patrician Society," 169; idem, "Political Adulthood," 797–98.

86. Malipiero, *Annali veneti*, 655–56; Queller, *Venetian Patriciate*.

87. For an ugly incident of 1486 see Malipiero, *Annali veneti*, 681–83; and Romanin, *Storia documentata di Venezia*, 4:420.

88. Cozzi, "Authority and the Law in Renaissance Venice;" idem, "Domenico Morosini e il 'De bene instituta republica,'" *Studi Veneziani* 12 (1970): 405–58; idem, "Venezia, una repubblica di principi?" ibid., n.s., 11 (1986): 139–57.

89. Laws of the Great Council from 1444 on, reserving positions of scribe, notary, coadjutor *(massaro)*, cancellieri inferiori, and gastaldi of the procurators to "boni cittadini originarii Venetiani," are in: ASV, MC, reg. 22, fol. 156v, reg. 24, fols. 20v–21r, reg. 25, fols. 40v–41r, 151r–152r, 183r, reg. 26, fols. 15v–16r, 62v–63r, reg. 29, fol. 45r; see also ASV, Senato, Terra, reg. 18, fols. 132v–134r, reg. 26, fols. 147r–148r.

90. ASV, MC, reg. 24, fols. 64r–v; Matteo Casini, "Realtà e simboli del cancellier grande veneziano in età moderna (secc. XVI–XVII)," *Studi Veneziani*, n.s., 22 (1991): esp. 222–23, 241; de Peppo, "Memorie di veneti cittadini," 438–39; Sansovino, *Venetia città nobilissima et singolare*, 411, 493.

91. ASV, Senato, Terra, reg. 28, fols. 71v–72v. The law did not then pass, and an alternative was also voted down; after some light revision the original version triumphed (see fols. 72v–73v and 78v–79r).

92. ASV, Dieci, Comuni, reg. 12, fol. 161v.

93. The genre of the collective chronicle of Venetian nobility dates back at least to the twelfth century (Gerhard Rösch, *Der venezianische Adel bis sur Schließung des Großen Rats: Zur Genese einer Führungsschicht* [Sigmaringen, 1989], 17–34). Early examples are *Origo civitatum Italie seu Venetiarum (Chronicon Altinate et Chronicon Gradense),* ed. Roberto Cessi (Rome, 1933), xxxx–xxxi, 46–47, 142–60; and *Venetiarum Historia vulgo Petro Iustiniano Iustiniani filio adiudicata,* ed. Fanny Bennato and Roberto Cessi, Deputazione Veneta di Storia Patria, Monumenti Storici, n.s., 18 (Venice, 1964), 255–76. Fifteenth-century manuscripts are BNM, Ms. It. cl. VII, 48 (7143), 52 (7604), 186 (7654), 2034 (8834), 2214 (8228), 2559 (12451), 2569 (12461); and ASV, Storia Veneta, 36, 42/I, 55, 61. There are dozens of sixteenth-century manuscripts in Veneto libraries and archives; several are cited in Antonio Carile, *La cronachistica veneziana (secoli XIII–XVI) di fronte alla spartizione della Romania nel 1204* (Florence, 1969), 14–15, 22, 53, 96–97, 99.

94. BNM, Ms. It. cl. VII, 543 (7887), fols. 2r–9r.

95. Ibid., 165 (8867) (Freschi; the majority was compiled by Tomà Freschi, who died in 1534); MCC, Ms. Gradenigo 56 (Amadi; mostly compiled by Francesco Amadi in 1535); BNM, Ms. It. cl. VII, 543 (7887) (Arborsani; Benedetto III dated his work to 1542–46); ibid., 366 (7660) (Dardani, dated 1556). Seventeenth-century collections of documents relating to commoner families seem to incorporate earlier, now lost compilations: ibid., 325 (8839) (Ramusio), 93 (8141) and 1980 (9114) (Padavino). Cicogna refers to "memorie che di Casa Franceschi" with a fifteenth-century entry (*Delle inscrizioni veneziane,* 6:848), which is perhaps the Franceschi memoir cited as the source of a 1513 entry (BNM, Ms. It. cl. VII, 341 (8623), fol. 12r) but which has not been located.

96. MCC, Ms. Gradenigo 56, 70–77, 85 (Amadi); BNM, Ms. It. cl. VII, 165 (8867), fol. 29v (Freschi); ASV, Quarantia Criminal, reg. 255, fols. 23v–25v (Quartari), 28v–30r (Speladi).

97. *Lauro Quirini umanista,* ed. Vittore Branca (Florence, 1977), esp. 78, 82, 99–100; Paruta, *Della perfezione della vita politica,* 315–59, esp. 324–25; Giovanni Silvano, *La "Republica de' Viniziani": Ricerche sul repubblicanesimo veneziano in età moderna* (Florence, 1993), 151–52.

II

Veronese's High Altarpiece for San Sebastiano
A Patrician Commission for a Counter Reformation Church

PETER HUMFREY

The establishment of a hereditarily defined ruling elite at the beginning of the fourteenth century created a dynamic that dominated Venetian political and cultural life until the end of the Republic. On the one hand, nobles had to work together to protect their collective interests. Humanists accordingly emphasized the virtues of unanimity and concord. On the other hand, both individual patricians and particular families wished to increase their wealth, power, and prestige and in so doing to distinguish themselves from their peers. One arena in which the competition between collective and individual or familial interests played itself out was art patronage. Ecclesiastical properties in particular provided rich opportunities for individuals and families to promote themselves, though by the late sixteenth century the church, in the wake of the Tridentine reforms, was attempting to rein in the impulses of patrons. In this chapter Peter Humfrey analyzes one particular example of patronage, the Soranzo family commission for the high altar of San Sebastiano. He evaluates the church's success in implementing the Tridentine program of church decoration. He also enriches our understanding of patrician patronage and identity by arguing that Veronese's altarpiece for San Sebastiano, unlike Titian's more famous Pesaro altarpiece in the church of the Frari, memorializes not only legitimate males of the Soranzo family but also illegitimate males as well as women who married into the family.

PAOLO VERONESE's noble painting above the high altar of San Sebastiano in Venice, enclosed in a multicolored marble frame of his own design, represents a fitting climax both to the architecture of the former Girolamite church and to the painter's decade-long work on the decoration of the nave (Figs. 1 and 2).[1] The painting itself is not documented, but a contract first

FIG. 1. Paolo Veronese, *Virgin and Child in Glory with Saints,* San Sebastiano, Venice. Photograph from Osvaldo Böhm, Venice.

published by Emmanuele Cicogna in 1834 shows that the frame was commissioned, together with other stonework in the chancel, by the Venetian noblewoman Lise Querini, widow of the recently deceased Giovanni Soranzo of Sant'Anzolo, on 29 June 1559. The mason responsible, one Salvador of San Maurizio, undertook to complete this work within the space of two years.[2]

Four years earlier, in December 1555, Veronese had been commissioned by the prior of the monastery, Fra Bernardo Torlioni, to paint the three large Old Testament scenes for the nave ceiling; in September 1558 he was paid by the prior for his frescoes on the upper part of the nave walls, and in October of the same year work was begun on the decoration of the organ according to a design by Veronese, who was subsequently to provide the pair of painted shutters.[3] The altarpiece, representing the Virgin and Child in glory with angels in the upper part of the composition and a group of five saints in the lower, was presumably designed, together with its frame, in the summer of 1559, but it has been plausibly argued on stylistic grounds that it was not actually executed until

FIG. 2. San Sebastiano, Venice, view of nave. Photograph from Osvaldo Böhm, Venice.

a few years later, perhaps about 1564–65.[4] A pair of vaguely worded documents dated September 1565 and October 1570 probably refer to the commission and completion of the final elements of the chancel decoration, the two rectangular wall canvases showing scenes from the life of Saint Sebastian, once more by Veronese.[5]

For the discipline of art history as traditionally practiced, the document of June 1559 is of obvious importance in providing at least an approximate date for a masterpiece of Veronese's middle career. Since the painter is mentioned as the designer of Salvador's frame, we may also give Veronese the chief credit for the beautiful way in which the picture is visually integrated with its surroundings. But the revelation that the prime responsibility for the commission of the altarpiece—unlike that of the nave ceiling and walls, the organ shutters, and the paintings on the chancel walls—resided not with the prior but with a patrician laywoman also raises a number of questions of broader historical relevance. How usual, for example, was it for patrician families to enjoy patronage rights over the high altars of major Venetian churches? How free were such families to choose the subjects of the paintings they commissioned, and how carefully were these coordinated with those elsewhere in the church? How usual was it for important public works of art to be commissioned by Venetian women? And how far were traditional practices in these respects affected by the advance of the Counter Reformation? Much of the research into the art of Renaissance Venice during the past two or three decades has been concerned with similar considerations of the roles played by patrons and with the social, political, and religious contexts in which works of art originated.[6]

Whatever the precise date of Veronese's San Sebastiano altarpiece, its conception and execution would have coincided closely with the final sessions of the Council of Trent and the publication of its decrees early in 1564. In most respects the painting may indeed be seen as conforming to the spirit and letter of the decree on the veneration of the saints and their images promulgated on 3–4 December 1563. Condemning Protestant iconoclasm, the Tridentine fathers declared that "the images of the saints are to be placed . . . in the churches, and that due honor and veneration is to be given to them . . . because through the saints salutory examples are set before the eyes of the faithful, so that they . . . may fashion their own life and conduct in imitation of the saints and be moved to adore and love God and cultivate piety."[7] This renewed emphasis on the didactic and inspirational value of saints' images bore typical fruit in Venetian altarpieces of the final third of the sixteenth century in scenes of martyrdom, as in Veronese's own *Martyrdom of Saint George* for the high altar of San

Giorgio in Braida, Verona, of about the same time. By contrast, the timeless grouping of assorted saints in the San Sebastiano altarpiece represents a much more traditional subject; yet compared even with those shown in the painter's own earlier *Sacra Conversazione* for San Francesco della Vigna of about 1551 (in situ), the saints of the San Sebastiano altarpiece have become more affectively enthusiastic in adoration.[8] No longer simply the passive recipients of intercessory prayers, the holy figures now implicitly encourage their devotees to imitate their own active religious fervor.

We must not, of course, assume that the publication of the Tridentine decrees early in 1564 had a more instantaneous effect on the character of religious imagery than it did on other areas of religious life. Over the past two generations historians have taught us that the Counter Reformation (if it is still legitimate to use the term) was a very gradual process, beginning well before Trent and enduring long after it; and similarly, we have learned that the decrees were implemented in different dioceses with widely varying degrees of speed and efficiency, depending on the energy and commitment of the local bishop and on a range of other local circumstances.[9] In Venice the traditional tensions between the government and the papacy ensured that the authorities did not rush to impose Tridentine conformity on religious life; and two decades later it was only with the greatest reluctance that the government was persuaded to permit an apostolic visitation of the city's parishes and houses of male regulars.[10]

Yet we should also have learned that works of art are themselves informative historical documents; and the case of San Sebastiano shows that by the 1550s there were already serious moves afoot to apply Tridentine thinking to the pictorial decoration of Venetian churches. Scenes of martyrdom connected with the story of Saint Sebastian are indeed included in the pictorial decoration of the chancel, in Veronese's two large wall canvases, and originally there were also frescoes by him in the area above the main cornice, including an *Assumption of the Virgin* in the cupola, which unfortunately was destroyed in the early eighteenth century.[11] These subjects are obviously intimately linked with that of the altarpiece, in which Sebastian, as titular of the church, is prominently placed at the center of the group of saints, while the Virgin, as titular of a previous, fifteenth-century church on the same site, called Santa Maria delle Grazie,[12] is surrounded, as in the lost *Assumption,* by clouds of glory, cherub heads, and jubilant musician angels. But the narrative paintings on the walls and in the cupola are also closely connected with those in the main body of the church, on the ceiling and on the upper part of the walls, and also with the ceiling decoration of the sacristy. Thus, the three large fields on the ceiling portray scenes from the Old Testament story of Esther, often chosen as a type for the Virgin, in particular for the Immaculate Virgin; the central rectangle showing the *Coronation of Esther* serves as an obvious parallel for the *Coronation of the Virgin,* painted by Veronese a year earlier (1555) for the center of the sacristy ceiling; and the transition from the Esther scenes to the *Assumption* in the cupola is made by way of the frescoed *Annunciation* on the exterior of the chancel. A similar link between the Old and New Testaments is made by the row of prophets and sybils placed in illusionistic niches between the Solomonic columns in the frescoes on the upper parts of the wall, while in the four broader fields between the columns appear four more scenes from the martyrdom of Saint Sebastian, complementing those of the chancel.[13]

All this is already recognizably Tridentine in spirit, not merely in its assertive glorification of the Virgin and of the martyr-intercessor Sebastian but in its evident purpose of imposing a coherent iconographic program of grand theological import on the pictorial decoration of an entire church. A recent precedent for decorating a church ceiling with Old Testament scenes that would serve as prefigurations of the theme of the chancel had been provided by the Augustinian church of Santo Spirito in Isola, where Titian's three ceiling paintings—*Cain and Abel, Abraham and Isaac,* and *David and Goliath*—were clearly devised as iconographic complements to his *Pentecost* above the high altar.[14] But this scheme dated from less than a decade earlier,[15] at a time when the Council of Trent was already in session; and before that one would have to go back to the Byzantine decoration of San Marco to find a Venetian precedent for the complex, integrated program seen at San Sebastiano. In the intervening centuries the pictorial decoration of Venetian churches had typically concentrated rather on the various altars and the cults embodied in them, corresponding to the particular devotional interests of the individual, usually lay patrons. It is unfortunate, therefore, that so little is known of the background to the program at San Sebastiano, such as who devised it, how it was financed, and how the still relatively young Veronese came to be chosen. A usual and reasonable assumption made in relation to the first question is that the program was devised by Torlioni, who served as prior of the Girolamite monastery from at least 1544 until his death in 1572;[16] and indeed, he seems to have had excellent credentials both as a theologian and as a reformer, and he is known to have been admired by the likes of Sadoleto, Carafa, and Pole.[17] In regard to the question of Veronese, it is usually assumed that since Torlioni was a native of Verona, he must have been responsible for persuading his young compatriot to settle in Venice by offering him the commission to paint the sacristy ceiling. This assumption is supported by the fact that the walls of the sacristy had already been decorated by Veronese (or Verona-born) painters, including Bonifacio de' Pitati, Domenico Brusasorci, and one Raffaello da Verona, Torlioni's own nephew.[18] On the other hand, as we shall see, there is also compelling evidence that Veronese owed the successful launch of his Venetian career at least as much to his preexisting contacts with patrician families, prominent among whom were the Corner and the Soranzo.

Although impressively comprehensive, the iconographic program at San Sebastian still does not embrace the pictorial decoration of the entire church; and not surprisingly, the side chapels retain their traditional thematic autonomy.[19] The altar on the right in the atrium, for example, founded by the eminent jurist Niccolò Crasso, was clearly dedicated to his name saint, and Titian's altarpiece accordingly provides an image of the enthroned Saint Nicholas (Fig. 3).[20] Similarly, above the first altar on the left, founded by Vincenzo Pellegrini (fig. 4), Schiavone's altarpiece shows a pilgrim at the center, perhaps identifiable as Saint James Major rather than Christ on the way to Emmaus,[21] but in any case clearly chosen as a punning allusion to the founder's family name. Again, above the third altar on the left (Fig. 4), founded by Marcantonio Grimani, are displayed the sculpted figures of his name saints, Mark and Anthony Abbot, while the highly personal and entirely un-self-effacing character of the imagery is emphasized by the presence of a handsome portrait bust of the donor by Alessandro Vittoria.[22] Few concessions to the Tridentine spirit are made in any of these chapel decorations; and although, by contrast, Veronese's *Crucifixion* painted for the Garzoni chapel about 1580 is imbued with a religiosity that may be judged characteristic of the Counter Reformation, it is unrelated in subject to any of Veronese's other paintings in the church.[23] The devotional autonomy of each of the side chapels is further emphasized by the differing sizes and frame designs of their respective altarpieces. An eloquent witness to the determination by an individual donor to make his own chapel as rich and dignified as possible while remaining indifferent to the character of neighboring spaces is provided by a document of August 1554 in which Marcantonio Grimani complained to the local clergy that funds he had donated for the construction and decoration of his own chapel were also being used for work in the chapel to the left and the area of the "transept" to the right.[24] As far as he was concerned, there was a clear distinction to be made between his own chapel and the church's other private and public spaces.

With respect to the *cappella maggiore* and the high altarpiece, it is apparent that similar though inevitably less clear-cut private concerns also came into

FIG. 3. Titian, *Saint Nicholas Enthroned,* San Sebastiano, Venice. Photograph by Richard Cocke.

play. Although the chancel naturally represented the liturgical focus of the church as a whole and may therefore be considered as belonging to the "public" space of the nave, patronage rights to the high altar, as was in fact traditional in conventual churches, were held by a lay patron, in this case the patrician Soranzo family. Thus it was that according to the previously mentioned document of January 1559 the mason Salvador received his commission from Lise Querini, the recent widow and executrix of Giovanni Soranzo of Sant'Anzolo (see chart 1),[25] and there is every indication that Veronese's painting too was commissioned not by the prior Torlioni but by Lise Querini Soranzo. In taking charge of the decoration of the chancel, Lise was acting as heir not just of her late husband but also of his paternal grandmother, Cateruzza Corner, who had originally acquired patronage rights to this most sacred and desirable part of the church in 1532, while it was still under construction.[26] Cateruzza was the daughter of the fabulously wealthy Zorzi Corner of San Maurizio and the

FIG. 4. San Sebastiano, Venice, view of chapels on left of nave, with the Pellegrini chapel on the left and the Grimani chapel on the right. Photograph from Osvaldo Böhm, Venice.

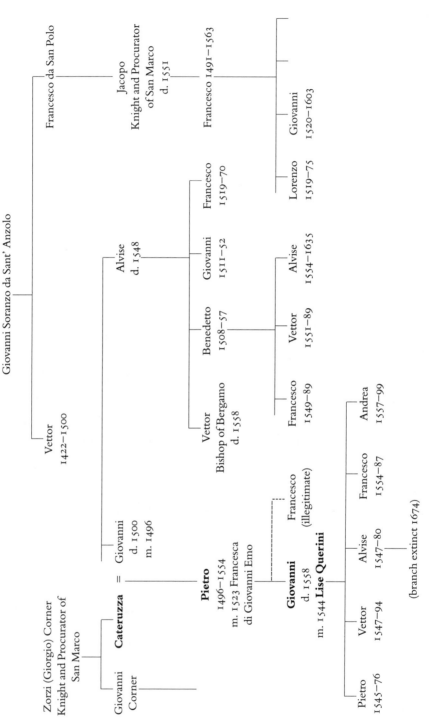

CHART 1. FAMILY TREE OF THE SORANZO DA SANT' ANZOLO

niece and namesake of the queen of Cyprus; in 1496, in a match that drew comment from the chronicler Malipiero on the magnificence of the dowry (4,000 ducats), she married the son of another member of a wealthy *casa vecchia,* Giovanni Soranzo.[27] Already widowed by 1500, Cateruzza had lost two more husbands by 1527; but her son Pietro Soranzo remained her only offspring, and when she made her will in 1546 her Soranzo heirs—Pietro and his son Giovanni—were made responsible for furnishing the chancel with the customary red and white paving stones, benches round the wall, a family sepulcher, and an altarpiece.[28] None of this was accomplished before Cateruzza's death in 1554; and the deaths in quick succession of both Pietro and Giovanni, in 1554 and 1558, respectively, left the latter's widow with the responsibility of finally implementing the wishes of his grandmother.

Scholars have often pointed out that the saints represented in Veronese's altarpiece constitute a repertory of the name saints of the members of the Soranzo family. This is obvious in the case of the three most closely clustered around the central figure of the titular, Sebastian: Catherine, in honor of Cateruzza Corner; the Baptist, in honor of Giovanni Soranzo; and Peter, in honor of Giovanni's father, Pietro.[29] The other female saint, just glimpsed between the two columns, is usually, and with apparent plausibility, identified as Elizabeth, the name saint of Lise herself. It should be pointed out, however, that she appears to hold a martyr's palm, in which case she could be neither the biblical Elizabeth nor Queen Elizabeth of Hungary; thus, her identity and the reason for her inclusion must both remain uncertain. Certainly incorrect is the identification by Carlo Ridolfi (1648), widely followed by scholars ever since, of the figure of Francis to the right as a portrait of Fra Bernardo Torlioni.[30] It is known that the Girolamite prior was born around 1491,[31] and so by 1565 he would have been in his mid-seventies, much older than the apparent age of the saint; in any case, it is hard to see why Torlioni, for all his importance as coordinator of the decorative program, should have been represented above the high altar of his church in the guise of the founder of another order. It is much more likely, in fact, that Francis, like his companions, is included as a name saint, either of Francesca Emo, wife of Pietro Soranzo and mother of Giovanni or more probably, perhaps, of Pietro's illegitimate son Francesco, who is mentioned as a beneficiary in the wills of both Cateruzza Corner and his legitimate brother, Giovanni.[32] Either would confirm the altarpiece as a celebration as much of the Soranzo family's private interests as of those of the local clergy; and despite the presence in fresco at the sides of the altarpiece of two hermit saints much venerated by the Hieronymite order, Paul the Hermit and

FIG. 5. Palma Giovane, *Virgin and Child in Glory with Saints Jerome and Charles Borromeo,* San Sebastiano, Venice. Photograph from Osvaldo Böhm, Venice.

Onuphrius, it may be noted that the altarpiece does not include the expected image of Jerome himself, who is celebrated instead in the neighboring chapel *in cornu epistolae* and in its altarpiece of about 1620 by Palma Giovane (Fig. 5).[33]

In its rich and grandiose double-columned frame Veronese's altarpiece serves, in fact, as an imposing monument to patrician dignity, and in this sense it continues to reflect the values much more of Venice's ruling class than of Gian Matteo Giberti's *Constitutiones* of 1542, which deplored displays of famil-ial pride in churches.[34] Although Giberti was referring more to excessively lavish tomb monuments than to altarpieces, he was also opposed to burial in church generally, whereas the Soranzo family sepulcher was placed, in a man-ner that by the more advanced Counter Reformation standards of the seven-teenth and eighteenth centuries would be condemned as indecent,[35] beneath the high altar itself, so that the altarpiece in part functioned as a monument to family members buried below. It is highly significant in this context that in his contract with Lise Querini in 1559 the mason Salvador was required to make his stonework of the same size and quality as that of Jacopo Sansovino's neigh-boring tomb monument of Livio Podocataro, archbishop of Cyprus (Fig. 6).[36]

While complementary, therefore, in theme and mood to Torlioni's didactic Mariological program of the nave, Veronese's altarpiece retains a high degree of iconographic autonomy; and as an ostentatious statement in a public setting of particular private interests, it resembles and indeed by far surpasses the other altarpieces in the church. It is surely no accident that its asymmetrical composi-tion and soaring columns clearly derive from one of the most complete expres-sions of patrician pride to be found in any altarpiece: Titian's Ca' Pesaro altarpiece in the Frari, painted some forty years earlier, in 1519–26 (in situ). As if to underline the relationship, Veronese's Saint Francis closely imitates the ecstatic pose and mediating role of his counterpart by Titian. At the same time, the comparison may serve to highlight two areas of ambivalence, or paradox, within Venetian patrician social attitudes. The first relates to the possibility, just mentioned, that the same Saint Francis refers to an illegitimate member of the family. In Venice a logical corollary of the emphasis laid on caste was that the bastard sons of the nobility should be debarred from the political process. This principle is clearly reflected in the Ca' Pesaro altarpiece, in which the group of male portraits does not include the donor's nephew Giovanni Maria, almost certainly because he was illegitimate.[37] Yet the difficult passage of a *parte* (law) in 1376 barring anyone of illegitimate birth from membership in the Great Council suggests a fairly widespread abuse of such restrictions;[38] and similarly, the fact that the Avogaria di Comun found it necessary to demand proof of

FIG. 6. Jacopo Sansovino, tomb monument of Livio Podocataro, archbishop of Cyprus, San Sebastiano, Venice.

legitimacy and to impose a fine of five hundred lire on the sponsors and guarantors of young nobles for the *Balla d'Oro* whose candidates proved not to be of legal patrician descent suggests a need for continuing vigilance.[39] It may be, therefore, that some families did not wish to exclude their bastard sons and brothers so categorically from patrician privilege, in which case Veronese's altarpiece may be read as a public statement that Francesco Soranzo was a valued member of his family and belonged with it even in death.

The second difference in social emphasis between the altarpieces of Titian and Veronese concerns the female members of the respective families. Again, the Ca' Pesaro altarpiece, with its rigid exclusion of any reference to mothers and daughters, provides the more accurate image of the concept of patriarchal dynastic lineage so fundamental to the Venetian political and social system. In keeping with this ethos, Venetian noblewomen did not, on the whole, share the important role in the patronage of art played by their counterparts in the courtly cultures of Florence and Milan, Mantua and Ferrara. Women were excluded from making any contribution to the commission of the great narrative cycles of the doge's palace and the scuole grandi, and no cultural leadership was required of the entirely self-effacing dogaressas.[40] But an important exception to the general rule, and one that deserves more systematic investigation, is represented precisely by the commissioning of chapels and altarpieces, which were not uncommonly the responsibility of female patrons. Sometimes these were patrician nuns, as in the well-known mid-fifteenth-century case of the three late Gothic polyptychs by Antonio Vivarini and Giovanni d'Alemagna and a set of choir stalls in the old church of San Zaccaria, commissioned by the abbess Elena Foscari (sister of Doge Francesco Foscari), her prioress, Marina Donà, and her housekeepers, Cecilia Donà and Agnesina Giustinian.[41] A more common scenario, however, was that of the childless widow who endowed a chapel in her own name and that of her deceased husband. A good documented example is that of Ursia Malipiero, wife of Simeone, who in 1525 commissioned Palma Vecchio's *Adoration of the Magi* for the high altar of the Montolivetan church of Sant'Elena (now Milan, Brera).[42] Or the female patron may have been acting on behalf of her own natal kin, as did Agnesina Badoer, sole heir of Girolamo di Giacomo Badoer, when she founded a chapel dedicated to Saint Jerome at San Francesco della Vigna,[43] or Elisabetta Dandolo, similarly acting in accordance with the testamentary wishes of her brother Bernardo when she founded a chapel in the same church.[44]

In such cases the deceased husband, father, or brother may have left quite detailed instructions regarding the character of the proposed monument, leaving the executrix little room to exercise her own personal taste. Certainly at San Sebastiano the essential task of Lise Querini was to realize the wishes of her deceased husband's family; yet interestingly in this case, as we have seen, those wishes had been formulated by another woman, Cateruzza Corner, who had also taken the original initiative for acquiring rights to the chapel. Ordinarily a Venetian woman's freedom for independent action was severely limited by the fact that on marriage her dowry became the property of her husband, and she lost any further claim to her father's estate,[45] but since Cateruzza was widowed only four years after her marriage, her very handsome dowry of 4,000 ducats quickly reverted to her, and she was able to make her own plans for endowing an exceptionally splendid chapel for the benefit of her Soranzo descendants. Even in misogynist Venice such a project, involving the dignified public expression of familial *pietas,* was evidently accepted as entirely worthy of the energies of a wealthy patrician female. Although in her will of 1546 Cateruzza merely listed work still to be done, it emerges from the mason Salvador's contract with Lise Querini that her predecessor had in fact gotten as far as commissioning and paying for the four marble columns of the frame, together with their bases and entablatures, and that in 1559 these were lying in storage in the monastery, awaiting installation.[46] There is some justice, therefore, in the fact that the arms of Cateruzza's own family, the Corner, should have been displayed, according to an eighteenth-century document, together with those of the Soranzo on the bases of the columns of the high altar.[47]

While it cannot be proved that Cateruzza played any part in the choice of Veronese for the commission, there is circumstantial evidence that the painter may have originally come to San Sebastiano, and perhaps even made the transfer from Verona to Venice, thanks to the good offices of her son Pietro Soranzo. One of Veronese's earliest commissions, executed in 1551, when he was still based in his native city, was for the fresco decoration of the family's country villa at Sant'Andrea di Castelfranco, near Treville, called La Soranza.[48] The architect of the villa, unfortunately demolished in the nineteenth century, was the eminent Veronese architect Michele Sanmicheli, and according to Vasari, it was Sanmicheli who was responsible for bringing in his young compatriot Paolo,[49] thereby introducing him to the wealthy and well-connected Soranzo family. It is true that it was probably not Pietro but his uncle Alvise who built La Soranza and Alvise's sons who had it decorated after their father's death in 1548.[50] But the ties between the two branches of the family would have been close, all the more since Alvise would have taken primary responsibility for the political and cultural education of his nephew after the premature death of the latter's father in 1500, and Pietro himself owned extensive property in the region of Sant'Andrea. (By contrast, these Soranzo were more distantly related, as second cousins, to Jacopo Soranzo of San Polo, whose preference for the art of Tintoretto over that of Veronese was inherited by at least three of his grandchildren.)[51] A further hint that Veronese was already in close contact with Pietro and his mother, Cateruzza, at the time of his first appearance at San Sebastiano in 1555 is provided by the fact that his earliest commission there, the decoration of the sacristy ceiling, is clearly indebted in its design to that painted by Vasari in 1542 in the palace of Giovanni di Giorgio Corner (now known as the Palazzo Corner-Spinelli), another uncle of Pietro and brother of Cateruzza.[52]

To round off this sketch of Veronese's initiation into the network of Venetian patrician families, which was to provide him with such constant and enthusiastic support throughout his subsequent career in the metropolis, it would be interesting to know if the Corner or Soranzo had any close connections with the Giustinian family of San Stae, which commissioned his very first Venetian altarpiece, around the time of the Soranza frescoes, for their chapel in San Francesco della Vigna.[53] It would also be interesting to know the relationship of the sitter in the splendid full-length seated portrait *Gentleman of the Soranzo Family* at Harewood House, usually dated on stylistic grounds to the 1580s, to our branch of the family;[54] and whether the Francesco Soranzo to whom Veronese addressed letters at the family estate at Sant'Andrea di Castelfranco in June 1584 and March 1586[55] was Francesco di Giovanni di Pietro, Francesco di Benedetto di Alvise, or the illegitimate Francesco di Pietro, honored by the inclusion of his name saint in the family's altarpiece. But in the meantime the case of Veronese's painting above the high altar of San Sebastiano may help shed light on issues of fundamental concern to historians of Venetian Cinquecento society and religion as well as of art. It illustrates, as we have seen, an early move to implement the Tridentine program of reform in the decoration of a Venetian monastic church; at the same time, it illustrates the continuing resistance to the full rigor of that reform in defense of traditional patrician privilege. Veronese's altarpiece may also have something to tell us about the ambivalent familial status of illegitimate patrician males and especially about the occasional ability of patrician women to transcend the usual restraints imposed on their freedom of action and commission works of art of enduring significance and beauty.

NOTES

1. The painting was executed on canvas and measures 420 by 230 cm (see Terisio Pignatti and Filippo Pedrocco, *Veronese*, 2 vols. [Milan, 1995], 1:259–60, and preceding bibliography. For Veronese's work at San Sebastiano in general, see ibid., 88–101; and Terisio Pignatti, *Le pitture di Paolo Veronese nella Chiesa di San Sebastiano di Venezia* [Milan, 1966]). I am grateful to Stephen Holt for allowing me to incorporate here material from ch. 2 of his doctoral dissertation, "Paolo Veronese and His Patrons" (Ph.D. thesis, University of St. Andrews, 1990).

2. Archivio di Stato, Venice (ASV), Provveditori al Sal, Miscellanea, busta 48, fasc. 4, A, published in full in Lionello Puppi, "Per Paolo Veronese architetto," *Palladio* 3 (1980): 53–75, app. 1, 75, and in part in Emmanuele Cicogna, *Delle inscrizioni veneziane,* vol. 4 (Venice, 1834), 182f., and in Pignatti and Pedrocco, *Veronese,* 2:554–55, doc. 16. For the identity of this Salvador, an associate of Jacopo Sansovino, see Bruce Boucher, "Sansovino e Veronese," in *Nuovi studi su Paolo Veronese,* ed. Massimo Gemin (Venice, 1990), 54–55.

3. For the documents, all of which were originally published by Cicogna in *Delle inscrizioni veneziane,* see Pignatti and Pedrocco, *Veronese,* 2:554–55, docs. 9, 10, 14, 15, 18.

4. This dating was first proposed on stylistic grounds by Pignatti, *Le pitture di Paolo Veronese,* 44–48; it has been accepted by, among others, Richard Cocke, *Veronese* (London, 1980), 62, and Rodolfo Pallucchini, *Veronese* (Milan, 1984), 176. Previous critics dated it to ca. 1559–61, contemporary with the documented stonework.

5. The suggestion was made by Pignatti, *Le pitture di Paolo Veronese,* 93; see also Pignatti and Pedrocco, *Veronese,* 2:557, docs. 28, 37.

6. Still useful in providing an overview of art patronage in Renaissance Venice is Oliver Logan, *Culture and Society in Venice, 1470–1790* (London, 1972), 148–219. More up-to-date surveys, in the context of Renaissance Italy as a whole, are Mary Hollingsworth, *Patronage in Renaissance Italy* (London, 1994), 95–154; and idem, *Patronage in Sixteenth-Century Italy* (London, 1996), 143–210, with references to recent bibliography. The fullest account of Venetian painters and their patrons in the late Renaissance period is Michel Hochmann, *Peintres et commanditaires à Venise, 1540–1628* (Rome, 1992), which has a valuable discussion on the Venetian response to the Counter Reformation. Detailed case studies on the impact of Counter Reformation religiosity on Venetian chapel decoration include Paul Hills, "Piety and Patronage in Cinquecento Venice: Tintoretto and the Scuole del Sacramento," *Art History* 6 (1983): 30–43; Stefania Mason Rinaldi, " 'Hora di nuovo vedasi . . .': Immagini della devozione eucaristica in Venezia alla fine del Cinquecento," in *Venezia e la Roma dei Papi* (Milan, 1987), 171–96; and idem, "Un percorso nella religiosità veneziana del Cinquecento attraverso le immagini eucaristiche," in *La chiesa di Venezia tra riforma protestante a riforma cattolica,* ed. Giuseppe Gullino (Venice, 1990), 183–94. For the impact of the Counter Reformation on Venetian altarpieces of the period, see Peter Humfrey, "La pala d'altare veneta

nell'età delle Riforme," in *La pittura a Venezia: Il Cinquecento,* ed. Mauro Lucco (Milan, 1999), with further bibliography; see also Peter Humfrey, "Altarpieces and Altar Dedications in Counter-Reformation Venice and the Veneto," *Renaissance Studies* 10 (1996): 371–87, and Richard Cocke, "Exemplary Lives: Veronese's Representations of Martyrdom and the Council of Trent," ibid., 388–404. Peter Humfrey, *The Altarpiece in Renaissance Venice* (New Haven, 1993), is concerned with the period before 1530 but attempts to set out broad parameters for the contextual study of altarpieces.

7. *The Canons and Decrees of the Council of Trent,* trans. H. J. Schroeder (Rockford, Ill., 1978), 215–16.

8. For the *Sacra Conversazione,* see most recently Peter Humfrey and Stephen Holt, "More on Veronese and His Patrons at San Francesco della Vigna," *Venezia Cinquecento* 5, no. 10 (1995): 187–214.

9. See esp. Paolo Prodi, "The Application of the Tridentine Decrees: The Organisation of the Diocese of Bologna during the Episcopate of Cardinal Gabriele Paleotti," in *The Late Italian Renaissance, 1525–1630,* ed. Eric Cochrane (London, 1970), 226–43; and more recently, with special reference to Venice, Paolo Prodi, "La chiesa di Venezia nell'età delle Riforme," in Gullino, *La chiesa di Venezia,* 63–75. For the Venetian *terraferma,* see Christopher Cairns, "Diocesan Studies of the Venetian *terraferma,*" *Studi Veneziani* 4 (1980): 79–97.

10. See Silvio Tramontin, "La visita apostolica del 1581 a Venezia," *Studi Veneziani* 9 (1967): 453–533. The effect of the visitation on art is discussed by Antonio Niero, "Riforma cattolica e Concilio di Trento a Venezia," in *Cultura e società nel Rinascimento tra riforme e manierismi,* ed. Vittore Branca and Carlo Ossola (Florence, 1984), 77–96.

11. The cupola was replaced by a new one decorated by Sebastiano Ricci, but this was in turn demolished in 1852. The images of St. Paul Hermit and St. Onuphrius, at either side of the altarpiece, are the only remaining fragments of Veronese's frescoes in the chancel (see Pignatti and Pedrocco, *Veronese,* 1:242).

12. The earlier dedication to the Virgin is recorded in Flaminio Corner, *Notizie storiche delle chiese e monasteri di Venezia e di Torcello* (Padua, 1758), 438–39. This earlier church was founded in 1398, but the dedication was changed when it was rebuilt beginning in 1455.

13. For the iconographic program of the nave, see Madlyn Kahr, "The Meaning of Veronese's Paintings in the Church of San Sebastiano in Venice," *Journal of the Warburg and Courtauld Institutes* 33 (1970): 235–47; Antonio Niero, "Il programma teologico di Paolo Veronese in San Sebastiano," in *Da Tiziano a El Greco: Per la storia del manierismo a Venezia,* exh. cat. (Milan, 1981), 327–29; and Sonia H. Evers, "The Art of Paolo Veronese: Artistic Identity in Harmony with Patrician Ideology" (Ph.D. diss., University of California, Berkeley, 1994), 71–96. Evers sought to play down the Catholic triumphalist message of the program stressed by Kahr and emphasized instead the patriotically Venetian resonance of Marian and especially coronation imagery. But an important distinction should be made between government buildings such as the doge's palace, where Guariento's great *Coronation* fresco in the Sala del Maggior Consiglio obviously did serve to convey a strongly patriotic message, and an ecclesiastical building belonging to an international religious order such as the Girolamites. At San

Sebastiano the Marian program may have been interpreted as carrying patriotic implications, but a more fundamental purpose would have been to restate the tenets of the Catholic religion.

14. For discussions of the theological program of Titian's ceiling paintings, all now located in Santa Maria della Salute, see Juergen Schulz, *Venetian Painted Ceilings of the Renaissance* (Berkeley, 1968), 77–80; and Richard Cocke, "Titian's Santo Spirito Ceiling: An Alternative Reconstruction," *Burlington Magazine* 113 (1971): 734.

15. Titian's Old Testament cycle is usually dated immediately before the painter's visit to Rome in 1545–46, but as argued by Paul Joannides, "On Some Borrowings and Non-borrowings from Central Italian and Antique Art in the Work of Titian, c. 1510–c. 1550," *Paragone,* no. 487 (1990): 21–45, 33–34, it probably dates from immediately afterwards.

16. "Fra Bernardo da Verona" is recorded as prior in 1544 in a document published by Pietro Paoletti, *L'architettura e la scultura del Rinascimento a Venezia* (Venice, 1893), 284. For Torlioni in general, see Luciano Rognini, "Bernardo Torlioni mecenate di Paolo Veronese e il suo nipote Raffaello, pittore e musico," *Studi Storici Veronesi L. Simeoni* 30–31 (1980–81): 143–65; for his role at San Sebastiano, see Evers, "Art of Paolo Veronese," 17–27. Evers draws attention to Torlioni's contacts with leading members of the Catholic Reform movement, such as Sadoleto, Carafa, and Pole.

17. See Cicogna *Delle inscrizioni veneziane,* 4:211; Rognini, "Bernardo Torlioni"; and Evers, "Art of Paolo Veronese," 17–21. The conformity of the program at San Sebastiano to the interests of Saint Jerome is stressed by Niero, "Il programma teologico di Paolo Veronese in San Sebastiano," 327.

18. Evers, "Art of Paolo Veronese." 22–25, rightly draws attention to the prevailingly Veronese character of the sacristy of San Sebastiano. Francesco Sansovino had already spoken of the works of "vari pittori veronesi" there (*Venetia città mobilissima* [1581], ed. Giustiniano Martinioni [Venice, 1663], 260–61); and Rognini, "Bernardo Torlioni," plausibly suggested on the basis of an eighteenth-century source that three of the canvases were by Torlioni's painter-nephew. This interesting pictorial ensemble remains to be properly studied.

19. The arguments by Niero, "Il programma teologico di Paolo Veronese in San Sebastiano," 329, that Veronese's various altarpieces in the side chapels are thematically linked to the decoration of the nave seem unduly forced.

20. For Niccolò Crasso, see Cicogna, *Delle inscrizioni veneziane,* 4:159; for Titian's altarpiece, see Harold Wethey, *Titian: the Religious Paintings* (London, 1969), 151–52.

21. For Vincenzo Pellegrini and his chapel, see Cicogna *Delle inscrizioni veneziane,* 4:131; for Schiavone's altarpiece, see Francis Richardson, *Andrea Schiavone* (Oxford, 1980), 151–52. The subject has been identified since the mid-seventeenth century as *Christ on the Way to Emmaus,* but it is worth noting that unlike in Florence, there was no particular cult of Gesù Pellegrino in Venice, and in 1568 Giorgio Vasari (*Le vite de' piu excellenti pittori, scultori ed architettori,* ed. Gaetano Milanesi, 9 vols. [1878–85], 6:596), called the central figure James. The issue would be resolved if the dedication of the chapel could be identified.

22. See most recently T. E. Martin, "The Portrait Busts of Alessandro Vittoria"

(Ph.D. diss., Columbia University, 1988), 163–67. The painting above the altar, Veronese's *Virgin and Child with St. Catherine and Fra Michele Spaventi* of ca. 1575, was placed there only in the twentieth century, and nothing is known of the original altarpiece.

23. For the Garzoni *Crucifixion,* see Pignatti and Pedrocco, *Veronese,* 2:393–94. It is not generally realized that the patrons of this chapel were the same family who commissioned Jacopo Sansovino to build the celebrated villa at Pontecasale. For the concession of the chapel to Girolamo di Nadal Garzoni in 1544, see Cicogna *Delle inscrizioni veneziane,* 4:141; in his will of 1588 (Museo Civico Correr [MCC], Ms., Provinenze Diverse, busta 2019, fasc. 13) Vincenzo di Alvise Garzoni maintains that the villa was built by his father, Alvise, and his uncle Girolamo. The latter died before 1566, when his brother was recorded as the sole proprietor of the villa, and Alvise died before 1582 (see A. Baldin, *Ville Venete in territorio padovano e nella Serenissima Repubblica* [Padua, 1986], 105–8). The *Crucifixion* is likely, therefore, to have been commissioned by Vincenzo as heir to the brothers.

24. ASV, San Sebastiano, busta 6, fol. 17.

25. The Soranzo family tree is based on the following sources: ASV, Marco Barbaro, "Arbori de' patritii veneti"; BNM, Ms. It. cl. VII, 156 (8492), Marco Barbaro, "Libro di nozze patrizie"; BNM, Ms. It. cl. VII, 16 (8305), Girolamo Cappellari Vivaro, "Campidoglio veneto." Cicogna *(Delle inscrizioni veneziane)* was apparently unaware of the relationship between the Corner and the Soranzo families, and Niero ("Il programma teologico di Paolo Veronese in San Sebastiano") was still confused on this point; the relationship was, however, clarified by Puppi, "Per Paolo Veronese architetto." See also Lionello Puppi, "La 'Città Ideale' di Paolo Veronese," in *Crisi e rinnovamenti nell'autunno del Rinascimento a Venezia,* ed. Vittore Branca and Carlo Ossola (Florence, 1991), 295–97.

26. Cicogna, *Delle inscrizioni veneziane,* 4:182; Puppi, "Per Paolo Veronese architetto," 54.

27. Domenico Malipiero, *Annali veneti dall'anno 1457 al 1500,* ed. Francesco Longo and Agostino Sagredo, *Archivio Storico Italiano* 7, pt. 2 (1844), 704.

28. ASV, Notarile, Testamenti, Angelo Canal, busta 209, no. 139, 14 July 1546, published in part by Cicogna, *Delle inscrizioni veneziane,* 4:182f. ("Io Catheruza fila del q. Clariss. D. Zorzi Corner el K. e P. de S. Marco et relitta il ult. matrimonia del Nob. H. Piero Mocenigo fo de Ms Franco . . . Item vogio sia compido la mia Cappella Grande nella chiesa de Ms S.Sebastian de V.tia e fatto la palla li banchi a torno et pavimento a quadri d. pera rossa di Verona biancha a mandole e tutte altre cose necessarie in caso che mi in vita non havesse fatto ogni cosa").

29. Niero, "Il programma teologico di Paolo Veronese in San Sebastiano," 329, is surely incorrect in relating Peter to Pietro Mocenigo, Cateruzza's second husband.

30. Carlo Ridolfi, *Le maraviglie dell'arte* (1648), ed. Detlev von Hadeln, 2 vols. (Berlin, 1914–24), 1:313.

31. See Rognini, "Bernardo Torlioni."

32. See the will of Giovanni Soranzo, ASV, Notarile, Testamenti, V. Maffei, busta 658, no. 485 ("Item lasso a ms Francesco Soranzo mi fratello ducati cento al anno in vita sua, e volendo star in casa . . . habbi le spese lui co' suo servitore").

33. For Palma's altarpiece, representing the Virgin and Child with Saints Jerome and Charles Borromeo, see Stefania Mason Rinaldi, *Jacopo Palma il Giovane* (Milan, 1984), 132.

34. See Kathryn Hiesinger, "The Fregoso Monument: A Study in Sixteenth-Century Tomb Monuments and the Catholic Reform," *Burlington Magazine* 118 (1976): 283–93.

35. See a document of 24 November 1746 in ASV, San Sebastiano, busta 3, carta 1): "Considerando il p. priore l'indecenza delle sepolture essistenti sotto le predelle de molti Altari especialm.te del Altar Maggiore della nostra chiesa, al riflesso della quale indecenza la leggi ecclesiastiche e canoniche esspressam.te probiscono tanto il sepelire cadavire sotto alle stesse predelle." As early as the last decade of the sixteenth century the patriarch Lorenzo Priuli decreed that any sepulchers in churches were to be placed underground and away from the altars (see Hiesinger "Fregoso Monument," 287).

36. Pignatti and Pedrocco, *Veronese*, 2:554–55, doc. 16 ("i pezzi delle pietre habbino ad esser di conveniente grandezza et della qualità che sono quelle della sepoltura dell'Arcivescovo di Cipro principiata nella medesima chiesa di s. Bastian").

37. This was deduced by Rona Goffen, *Piety and Patronage in Renaissance Venice* (New Haven, 1986), 124–25.

38. Stanley Chojnacki, "Crime, Punishment, and the Trecento Venetian State," in *Violence and Civil Disorder in Italian Cities 1200–1500,* ed. Lauro Martines (Berkeley, 1972), 184–228.

39. See Margaret King, "Caldiera and the Barbaros on Marriage and the Family: Humanist Reflections on Venetian Realities," *Journal of Medieval and Renaissance Studies* 6 (1976): 19–50. The ambivalent social and economic status of illegitimate sons in fifteenth-century Florence is discussed in Thomas Kuehn, *Law, Family, and Women: Towards a Legal Anthropology of Renaissance Italy* (Chicago, 1991), 157–93.

40. Probably for this reason Venetian studies have not yet greatly benefited from the recent growth of interest in women as patrons—or "matrons"—of art in the Renaissance period. See, however, Catherine King, "Medieval and Renaissance Matrons, Italian-style," *Zeitschrift für Kunstgeschichte* 55 (1992): 372–93, with a number of examples drawn from Venice and the Veneto. For a recent survey of the current state of research, see Jaynie Anderson, "Rewriting the History of Art Patronage," in *Renaissance Studies* 10 (1996): 129–38. This essay forms the introduction to an issue of the journal entitled *Woman Patrons of Renaissance Art, 1300–1600,* which includes a subsequent article by Catherine King, cited in n. 42 below.

41. The documents, first published in Paoletti, *L'architettura e la scultura,* 63, 84, are discussed in the wider context of Benedictine patronage in Venice by Victoria Primhak in "Women in Religious Communities: the Benedictine Convents in Venice, 1400–1550" (Ph.D. thesis, Warburg Institute, University of London, 1991), 103. Art patronage by nuns in Renaissance Venice remains an uninvestigated area; it would be interesting, for example, to know more of the circumstances of the commission of Veronese's *Mystic Marriage of St. Catherine* (Venice, Accademia), painted for the high altar of the Augustinian convent of Santa Caterina. It may, however, turn out that male religious and lay procurators still played the dominant role in architectural and decora-

tive projects involving Venetian nunneries, as they certainly did in the new church of San Zaccaria, in the Franciscan nuns' church of Santa Maria Maggiore, and in the church of the Zitelle.

42. See Philip Rylands, *Palma Vecchio* (Cambridge, 1990), 223–24. Other examples, including those of the Martini chapel in San Giobbe, the Benedetti chapel in Santi Giovanni e Paolo, and the Emiliani chapel at San Michele in Isola, are cited in Humfrey, *Altarpiece in Renaissance Venice*, 110. A major Veronese example, involving a female patron who showed an exceptional independence of outlook, is analyzed in Catherine King, "Margarita Pellegrini and the Pellegrini Chapel at San Bernardino, Verona, 1528–1557," *Renaissance Studies* 10 (1996): 171–89.

43. See Anne Markham Schulz, "The Giustiniani Chapel and the Art of the Lombardo," *Antichità Viva* 16, no. 2 (1977): 27–44; and Douglas Lewis, "Patterns of Preference: Patronage of Sixteenth-Century Architects by the Venetian Patriciate," in *Patronage in the Renaissance,* ed. Guy Fitch Lytle and Stephen Orgel (Princeton, 1981), 355–80. Lewis also provides a usefully detailed account of other aspects of Agnesina's activity as a patron; he is mistaken, however, in referring to the Soranzo family as belonging to the "lately arrived and aspiring nobility" (363).

44. See David McTavish, *Giuseppe Porta Called Giuseppe Salviati* (New York, 1981), 288.

45. See Stanley Chojnacki, "Dowries and Kinsmen in Early Renaissance Venice," *Journal of Interdisciplinary History* 5 (1975): 571–600; and James C. Davis, *A Venetian Family and Its Fortune, 1500–1900: The Donà and the Conservation of their Wealth* (Philadelphia, 1975).

46. ASV, San Sebastiano, busta 3, no. 4 ("Dechiarando appresso che oltre li sopra scritti ducatti trecento e ottanta, la detta madonna Lise da' alli detti maestri le quattro colonne con li suoi capitelli et base, che si ritrovano nel monsaterio di detta chiesa, gia per avanti comprate dalla chiarissima madonna Cataruzza Cornaro affine di meterle in detta opera"). See also Puppi, "Per Paolo Veronese architetto," 75.

47. ASV, San Sebastiano, busta 3, no. 4. It was perhaps usual for commissions by widows to display the arms of both their families: see the parallel instance in the Pellegrini chapel at San Bernardino, Verona, cited in King, "Margarita Pellegrini and the Pellegrini Chapel," 176 n. 22.

48. See Pignatti and Pedrocco, *Veronese,* 1:50–52.

49. Vasari, *Vite,* 6:369–70.

50. G. P. Bordignon Favero, *I Palazzo Soranzo Novello* (Castelfranco Veneto, 1981), 19–21, suggested that the villa was built by Pietro Soranzo, but Favero was apparently unaware that Bernhard Rupprecht, "Sanmichelis Villa Soranza," in *Festschrift Ulrich Middeldorf,* ed. Antje Kosegarten and Peter Tigler, 2 vols. (Berlin, 1968), 1:324–32, had already provided documentary evidence that its original patron was Alvise. According to Rupprecht, 331 n. 7, uncle and nephew were joint owners of a property "chiamato la Soranza" in 1537, but the building of the villa did not begin until after a *divisione* of the property in 1540.

51. For Tintoretto's frescoes on the facade of Jacopo Soranzo's palace behind San Marco, known as the Casa dell'Angelo, and the painter's *Assumption of the Virgin* com-

missioned by Jacopo's granddaughter for her altar in San Polo, see Rodolfo Pallucchini and Paola Rossi, *Tintoretto: Le opere sacre e profane* (Venice, 1982), 134, 206–7. For Tintoretto's portraits of Jacopo with his family and of his grandsons Lorenzo and Benedetto, see Paola Rossi, *Jacopo Tintoretto: Ritratti* (Milan, 1994), cat. nos. 8–11, 15, 18. For further observations on Tintoretto and this branch of the Soranzo see Tom Nichols, "Tintoretto: The Painter and His Public" (Ph.D. thesis, University of East Anglia, 1992), 86–92.

52. Veronese's indebtedness to Vasari is pointed out by Juergen Schulz in "Vasari at Venice," *Burlington Magazine* 103 (1961): 500–511. The argument presented in this chapter that Veronese owed his earliest commission at San Sebastiano more to his connections with the Soranzo family than to the prior Bernardo Torlioni would be weakened if the attribution to Veronese by Pignatti of the frescoes in the chapel of Marcantonio Grimani, completed by 1553, were to be accepted: see Pignatti, *Le pitture di Paolo Veronese,* 76; and Pignatti and Pedrocco, *Veronese,* 1:74–76. But although the attribution is accepted by Puppi, "La 'Città Ideale' di Paolo Veronese," 298, most other scholars more reasonably give them to Andrea Schiavone (see Richardson, *Andrea Schiavone,* 179–80).

53. See Humfrey and Holt, "More on Veronese and His Patrons at San Francesco della Vigna."

54. The *Gentleman of the Soranzo Family* was originally paired with a portrait of the sitter's wife, now lost (see Pignatti and Pedrocco, *Veronese,* 2:431). The late dating would preclude his identification as Alvise (1547–80), the only one of the five sons of Giovanni Soranzo and Lise Querini to marry; a possible candidate might therefore be Giovanni's second cousin, Francesco di Benedetto di Alvise.

55. Veronese's letters to Francesco Soranzo are reprinted in Pignatti and Pedrocco, *Veronese,* 2:562, docs. 63, 66. These letters, in which Veronese requests help in a dispute over a debt owed by one Giacomo Spinello, imply some sort of longstanding patron-client relationship between the painter and the addressee. It may also be noted that the parish church of Sant'Andrea contained frescoes attributed to Veronese by the eighteenth-century local writer Melchiori, but they are more likely to have been by his younger brother Benedetto. The frescoes were almost certainly commissioned by Giovanni Soranzo's second cousin Giorgio Corner, bishop of Treviso, since Benedetto did paint frescoes for the bishop's villa adjoining the church, the present-day Villa Piacentini Corner (see Nadal Melchiori, *Notizie di pittori e altri scritti,* ed. Giampaolo Bordignon Favero [Venice, 1964], 162).

12

Early Modern Venice as a Center of Information and Communication

PETER BURKE

Scholars have long recognized the importance of Venice as a center of publishing and printing in the Renaissance, and their studies have done much to highlight this history from a variety of vantage points, from the economic and business aspects of publishing, on the one hand, to the intellectual and cultural functions of the print shop, on the other. In this chapter Peter Burke shifts this discussion to the macrocultural scale and examines the history of printing from within what he calls "a regime of information and communication." Drawing on a far-flung network of merchants, diplomats, spies, and other agents that reached from Europe through the Ottoman Empire all the way to India, Ceylon, and Burma, Venice emerged as the major European center for political and economic news in the fifteenth and sixteenth centuries. Moreover, the cosmopolitan nature of the city made it a major source of cultural information as well, and indeed it was in this period an important center for books not only in Italian and Latin but also in Greek, Hebrew, Arabic, Old Church Slavonic, Croat, and even Spanish. Venetian presses instructed readers throughout Europe about foreign regions as diverse as Persia and America, though by the end of the seventeenth century the focus of the Venetian information industry—whether political, economic, or cultural— grew increasingly provincial or regional as new centers of communication developed along the Atlantic seaboard. This chapter exemplifies how narratives of transformation and adjustment have replaced those of rise and decline in the formulation of Venetian history.

EARLY MODERN VENICE as a center of information and communication stands at the crossroads of the history of Venice and the history of information. Here I shall attempt to be mindful of the uniqueness of Venice while dealing with the rise of what might be called a new regime of information and communication following the invention of printing with movable type. In the fifteenth and sixteenth centuries in particular Venice was the leading center of information and communication in Europe, its closest rivals being Genoa and Antwerp for economic information and Rome for political news. Even in the seventeenth century, when Amsterdam became a great information center, Venice still had a role to play. What made all these cities into centers was the regular arrival of information on many subjects—trade, war, politics, religion, and so on—from so many different places both inside and outside Europe. Given the relative cheapness of water transport, ports had an advantage over inland cities like Florence or Paris. Success bred success; some foreign traders and diplomats went to Venice to acquire information and in the process passed on some of their own. This chapter seeks to answer the following questions: How long did the centrality of Venice last? How and why and in what domains was it undermined? And by what city or cities was it replaced?

HISTORIOGRAPHY

The fundamental idea of Venice as a communication center is not new. It was fifty years ago that Pierre Sardella, in a study of news based on Marino Sanudo's diary, described Venice as "l'agence d'information le plus important du monde moderne naissant."[1] Fernand Braudel drew on Sardella's work in his famous study of the Mediterranean world, published only a year later, noting that Venice was almost exactly halfway between Madrid and Istanbul.[2] Since Sardella's day, especially since John Hale's volume on Renaissance Venice, intensive research on certain aspects of the topic has been carried out by economic historians, political historians, historians of religion, art historians, historians of literature, geographers, and bibliographers.[3] Indeed, it sometimes looks as if all roads lead to Venice.

The later 1970s, for example, saw studies of the Venetian press by Leonardas Gerulaitis, Paul Grendler, and Martin Lowry, as well as a substantial collection of essays on Venice as a center of mediation between East and West, a topic also discussed by William McNeill in an essay describing Venice as "a cultural metropolis," although "a marginal polity," between 1481 and 1669.[4] In the 1980s, contributions included Federica Ambrosini's book on the impact of the discovery of America on Venice, Claudia Bareggi's study of the activities of the *poligrafi*, Julian Raby on Venetian "orientalism," and a number of contributions to the multivolume *Storia della cultura veneta*.[5] In the 1990s, one thinks of Paolo Preto's monumental work on the Venetian secret service, John Martin on heresy, and a collection of essays on the impact of America on Venetian culture.[6]

After so many monographs, some of which have undermined traditional ideas and assumptions, there is obviously a need for synthesis, for arranging the material in other ways in order to reveal connections and to engage with the general themes of continuity and discontinuity in Venetian history. It is obviously important to discuss the relation between the shape of Venetian society and the kinds of information circulating, or failing to circulate, in the city. Hans Kissling was surely right to place an emphasis on Venice as a "mercantile state," but it is equally important to discuss the effects of the diffusion of information on the Venetian political system.[7]

In attempting the twin tasks of synthesis and reconsideration, this chapter focuses on two general problems and trends: the relation, or better the tension, between private and public information, secrecy and publicity, political pressures and economic ones; and the decline of Venice as a provider of information, or more exactly, its "intellectual involution," that is, its shift from a center of information about the world (especially the East) to a center of information about itself.

PRIVATE, ECONOMIC, POLITICAL, AND RELIGIOUS INFORMATION

Some scholarly debates were conducted more or less privately in the academies, on some occasions at least in order to restrict the flow of information.[8] Venice was also an important center for studies of "occult philosophy," on the edge between what we call "religion" and "science." The rise of interest in cabala is obviously linked to the growing importance of the Jewish community in the sixteenth century, but the adepts also included Christians, from the local friar Francesco Zorzi to the French scholar Guillaume Postel. Postel probably visited Venice in the first place because it was on the way to the Holy Land, but it was there he discovered the cabalist text *Zohar* and he went back several times to learn from people as diverse as the Jewish printer Daniel Bomberg and the living saint Madre Giovanna.[9] However, it was not esoteric knowledge so much as practical everyday information for which Venice was best known in this period.

The letters home written by merchants stationed abroad were an important source of information for the Venetians, a kind of "data bank," as a historian of Genoa has put it.[10] So it is not surprising to find that the Venetians were pioneers in the organization of a postal system. It was in the fourteenth century that the government founded the Compagnia dei corrieri. In the mid-sixteenth century, when the Tasso family of Bergamo set up their *corrieri or-dinari,* departing at fixed times, one of their main routes was between Milan and Venice. Even more important was the route between Rome and Venice.[11]

The latest "news on the Rialto" was of obvious economic importance, with serious consequences for the grain market and the spice market in particular.[12] No wonder four Venetian nobles once removed part of the roof of the Palazzo Ducale in order to listen to a confidential report from Istanbul.[13] When rumors about spices from India arriving in Lisbon reached Venice in 1501, the reaction of the government was to send an agent, Lunardo Masser, to Portugal to discover what was happening. His report still survives.[14] When Antonio Pigafetta of Vicenza returned from his voyage round the world with Magellan, he visited Venice, where the Collegio heard his account of India "con gran attention."[15]

Given the presence of a colony of Venetian merchants in Istanbul and their permanent representative, the *bailo,* Venice was a natural center for economic information about the East, especially about the Ottoman Empire. The role of the bailo in the collection and transmission of information about the Turks and some of his main sources, from the official translators or dragomans to the sultan's physicians, have been investigated.[16] Information arrived from Aleppo and Alexandria, where other Venetian merchants were established, and occasionally from more remote parts of the East. Nicolò Conti, for instance, spent nearly a quarter of a century, from 1419 to 1444, in India and Burma. Cesare Federici spent some twenty years in Bagdad, Hormuz, Ceylon, Sumatra, and Burma, returning to Venice in 1581. And Gasparo Balbi went first to Syria in 1576, then to India and Burma, returning in 1589.[17]

Given these economic interests, it is scarcely surprising that Venice was an important center of mapmaking in this period. In the fifteenth century, a Venetian mapmaker, Andrea Bianco, worked for the brother of the Portuguese prince Henry the Navigator. The Portuguese crown also bought a map from Fra Mauro of Murano. One of the earliest and most famous city maps of the Renaissance is the map of Venice by Jacopo de' Barbari.[18] In the sixteenth century, the Venetian Giovanni Andrea Vavassore was a major publisher of maps, of Spain, France, Greece, and Britain as well as of Italian provinces, and the Piedmontese Giacomo Gastaldi, an engineer in Venetian service, produced a series of detailed maps of Italy.[19] At the end of the seventeenth century this tradition was revived by Vincenzo Coronelli (discussed below).

By the late fourteenth century Italian diplomats were collecting information on behalf of their governments and sending it home in their dispatches. At first there seems to have been little interest in preserving these documents—the earliest collection of dispatches in the Venetian archives dates from 1477—but the practice changed in the sixteenth century, with the Venetians among the pioneers. It has often been noted that the Venetians were among the first European powers to adopt the system of resident ambassadors, as much to gather information about other countries as to negotiate with them. The government expected to receive from its representatives abroad not only regular dispatches but also formal reports at the end of the mission, the famous *relazioni,* describing the political, military, and economic strengths and weaknesses of the state to which the ambassador had been accredited.[20] These were read aloud in the Senate before being filed in the archives, as required by a decree of the Senate in 1524. However, these relazioni were better known abroad than the government would have wished. Indeed, they were used as models, not least for reports on Venice itself, which ranged from the objective to the satirical. A favorable example is Giovanni Botero's report, published in Venice itself in 1595 with a dedication to Doge Grimani and the Senate.[21]

The unfavorable, naturally anonymous, are perhaps most easily distinguished by their incipits. They include one addressed to Philip II ca. 1567 ("Se ad alcuno ambasciatore, cattolico re"), another ca. 1584 ("Tutto il governo della Repubblica di Venezia, si puo dire"), a third of 1620 ("Venetia sola tra tutte le città d'Italia"); and the report of about 1621 ascribed to the Spanish diplomat Alonso de la Cueva, marquis of Bedmar, beginning "Laboriosa impresa per certo è questo alla quale mi avingo," copies of which are still to be found in many European libraries.[22] This is not the place to discuss the genre further, although it surely deserves a monograph.

The Venetian government had other ways of acquiring information about foreign powers. The Council of Ten's cipher secretary Soro (active 1506–44), for example, was an expert in breaking the codes used by other states. The government also maintained a network of agents, or "spies." I put the word in quotation marks here not to suggest that the motives of the Venetians were idealistic but rather that the later division of labor between professional activities had not taken place: there was spying rather than spies.[23] Venetian interest in the Ottoman Empire was at least as much political as economic. The bailo was expelled in 1491, accused of spying.[24] In 1511 the consul at Damascus was accused of the same offense. In 1507 the *rettore* of Cyprus sent agents to Persia. More informally, Venetian merchants in Damascus and elsewhere in the Middle East sent political information to the government.[25] It seems appropriate that one of the ways to code information in this period was to describe political events in the language of merchants. At the time of Lepanto, for example, secret dispatches to Venice described the Turks as "drugs," the army as a "caravan," artillery as "mirrors," and so on.[26] Economic espionage was also practiced.[27]

The information was of course confidential, more or less. Considerable effort was expended in keeping it secret, but equal effort was expended in uncovering it. One duty of sixteenth-century Spanish ambassadors to Venice was to discover what the government knew about the Turks. Rome tried to do the same.[28] The government was extremely sensitive on the subject of secrecy, even for the early modern period, a time when, as recent research shows, material we might expect to be public was commonly regarded as confidential.[29] In the fifteenth century, a considerable number of individuals were put on trial on a charge of revealing secrets of state. In the sixteenth century, the topic was a major preoccupation of the Council of Ten and of a new institution, the Inquisitori di Stato (given this name in the 1590s but active earlier).[30] For example, in 1501 the Council of Ten forbade gossip about the ballots cast in the Great Council.[31] In 1515 the Ten gave permission to two patricians, Andrea Mocenigo and Marino Sanudo, to use the archives for their histories of recent events, but on condition that these histories be submitted for approval before publication.[32] The secret archives were guarded with such care—at least in theory—that even the doge was forbidden to enter the room in which they were kept unless he was accompanied, while the keeper was supposed to be unable to read and write.[33] As is well known, Venetian nobles were forbidden to have contacts with foreign ambassadors for fear that they would reveal what was being discussed in the Senate and other places. Some scholars have spoken of the government's "obsession" with secrecy. Their concern was not pathological but simply a reaction to a political system in which an unusually large number of people had access to *arcana imperii,* which in monarchies were the preserve of the few. As Paolo Giovio suggested, the leaking of confidential information may reflect conflicts between factions.[34] Despite official discouragement, secrets continued to be revealed. Among the more notorious cases were the accusation against Angelo Badoer in 1612 and the execution of Antonio Foscarini in 1622, part of the "witch hunt" following the recall in 1618 of the Spanish ambassador, Bedmar, who had a large network of agents in his service and was believed to have plotted to overthrow the Venetian government.[35]

Three examples of the sensitivity of the Venetian government, especially the Council of Ten, in this area are worth noting here. One might not have thought that Daniele Barbaro's famous commentary on Vitruvius (1556) was a politically dangerous work, but objections were made to its publication on the grounds that designs of fortifications might help Venice's enemies. The second case was the arrest of Lazzaro Soranzo by the Council of Ten in 1598, following his publication in Ferrara of an anti-Turkish treatise which the government considered to have divulged confidential information about the Ottoman regime.[36] The third case involved the request by the heirs of Doge Niccolò Contarini for permission to publish his history of Venice. The reply of the consultants in 1638 was that the history should not be published because it contained confidential political maxims that they thought should not be divulged ("massime molto intime del governo che per verità non sappiamo se stia bene divulgarle"). The manuscript was therefore to be kept "in a secret place" in the archives.[37]

Information about Venetian territory was also collected. For example, "the earliest state-sponsored maps" in Europe appear to be those commissioned by the Council of Ten in 1460.[38] Needless to say, they were highly confidential documents. The famous *Libro d'Oro,* begun in 1506, in which patricians' births were recorded, is another early example of the state's concern with recording information for practical purposes. Censuses of the population were carried out more frequently in Venice than elsewhere from at least the sixteenth century on, and the eighteenth-century census in particular is a model of precise and detailed information.

Like the Inquisition, the Venetian government encouraged ordinary people to denounce those who broke the law. Written denunciations were left in churches or on the stairs or at the doors of public buildings until the notorious *bocche di leone,* which fascinated foreign visitors such as Skippon, Saint-Didier, and Veryard, were constructed around the beginning of the seventeenth century, allowing delators to post their information to particular departments of government.[39]

Venice also has a special place in the history of archives. In 1586 an order was made to make a subject index of documents concerning the Senate, and in 1601 the first patrician was appointed to the new post of *sopraintendente.* The first holder of the office, Andrea Morosini, collaborated with Grand Chancellor Antelmi to make a catalogue, and a still more elaborate catalogue was compiled in 1669 under the supervision of Sopraintendente Battista Nani and Grand Chancellor Ballarin.[40] One of the first books ever published about archives, *De archivis,* by Balthasar Bonifacio, was published in Venice by Pinelli in 1632. It was indeed appropriate that Ranke, whom Lord Acton called "the real originator of the heroic study of records," paid so much attention to Venice, but he was fortunate enough to arrive after 1797.

Venice was a center of information about heresy, whether intended for the heretics themselves or for those who wished to persecute them. The city was the principal gateway through which the ideas of the German reformation reached Italy. A clandestine synod of Anabaptists was held in Venice in 1550. Clandestine publication also flourished. Italian translations of Luther (without Luther's name on the title page) could be found in the city. Sanudo notes that copies of a treatise by Luther were found in a Venice bookshop in 1520.[41] Heretical books were sometimes published in Venice, as in the famous case of the *Beneficio di Cristo,* published by Bindoni in 1543 (the only surviving copy, out of reach of censors and inquisitors, is still to be found in the library of St John's College, Cambridge). In the 1540s the smuggling of heretical books was well organized, with Pietro Perna in Basel as the chief supplier and a number of Venetian booksellers involved (Andrea Arrivabene, the Valgrisi, the Ziletti).[42]

In the first years after the Inquisition was established it was the clergy, parish priests and friars, who drew the Holy Office's attention to heretics. From the 1560s on, denunciations came from the laity.[43] Some printers, such as Valgrisi, were brought before the Inquisition on charges of owning or publishing heretical books.

THE COMMERCIALIZATION OF INFORMATION

Private information had its ways of becoming public. One famous institution for divulging confidential information, as well as criticizing individuals was the so-called Gobbo di Rialto. The Rialto was of course a place where official decrees were "published." Sanudo records an irreverent message attached to a column there in 1532. From the late sixteenth century on a statue that had been placed there in 1541 and nicknamed "the hunchback" was, like the "Pasquino" in Rome, a site for outspoken anonymous political comment.[44]

The crucial point of contact and tension between public and private was the news. Oral information about political events had its own geography. When the Florentine humanist Giannozzo Manetti was on a mission to Venice in 1448, he went to the Palazzo Ducale on Mondays and Saturdays to visit the Signoria, attend sessions of the Great Council, and learn the news from Lombardy, Tuscany, and elsewhere.[45] The Palazzo Ducale was also the main source for Sanudo's famous diary, which has been called a "news chronicle" because the entries so often begin with the formula "news came." However, as we have seen, private or even top-secret information had a way of becoming public property. In 1567 a German called Venice the metropolis of news.[46] By this time weekly manuscript *avvisi* (newsletters) were in circulation.[47] The Council of Ten outlawed the activities of the *novellisti,* as they were often called, in 1571, describing them as those "che fanno publica professione di scriver nove, per il che sono salariati di diversi."[48] All the same, the writing of manuscript newsletters by "reporters" *(reportiste)* continued to flourish in the eighteenth century.[49] Patricians needed information about one another, about offices, and about ballots in order to plan their careers, and by the early seventeenth century they were able to buy such information from clerks and *ballottini* in the form of manuscript pocketbooks such as the *zuccheta* and the *consegi* or *brogietti,* to the shock of the Council of Ten, who complained about this practice in 1618.[50] Manuscript copies were made of the official relazioni—by whom we do not know. Francesco Sansovino's biography of Charles V, for example, made use of relazioni by Bernardo Navagero and Marino Cavalli, ambassadors to the imperial court.[51]

By the seventeenth century at the latest, these relazioni were on sale in certain European cities, notably Rome (to the shock of Venetian ambassadors to Rome, such as Leonardo Donà in 1600 and Lorenzo Tiepolo in 1713), and some copies still survive in public and private libraries.[52] The ex-secretary to the French ambassador to Venice, Amelot de la Houssaie, was able to use letters, memoirs, and relazioni of ambassadors for a history of Venice that made public what he called "les mystères de la domination."[53]

It was only to be expected that sooner or later someone would be enterprising and bold enough to print some relazioni. One step was taken by a printer of Bergamo, Comin Ventura, who edited an anthology of texts under the title *Tesoro politico,* published, according to the title page, in Cologne in 1593. Later editions appeared in Milan and Vicenza but not, prudently enough, either in Bergamo or in Venice. Three more relazioni by Venetian ambassadors to Rome were published in 1672 under the title *Li tesori della corte romana.* The place of publication was given as Brussels, and there was no printer's name on the title page.

Given this flourishing trade in political information, one might have expected Venice to become an early center of newspapers. However, in comparison with other Italian cities, such as Genoa, Rome, Bologna, Milan, or Turin, Venice was slow to develop printed *gazzette* dealing with current events.[54] Presumably the authorities, concerned as usual with secrecy, discouraged these activities. What was printed was relatively anodyne. Albrizzi, for example, published a list of officeholders in 1673 under the title *Protogiornale Veneto,* and Coronelli published a similar *Giornale* for four consecutive years, 1713–16. Albrizzi also published flysheets about the wars with the Turks, for example, the *Giornale del Campo Cesareo sotto Buda* (1686).

All the same, when early modern Venice is described as a center of information and communication, it is above all on account of print. It was appropriate for Venice to become a printing center because it was already a center for other kinds of communication, as an international port, as the capital of what was still in part a maritime empire, and as an unusually large city for this period.

In the course of the fifteenth century more books were printed in Venice than in any other city in Europe (4,500 titles, in other words about 150 a year, and 2.5 million copies seems a reasonable estimate).[55] In the sixteenth century, when the city began to lose this relative lead over other centers, such as Paris, book production remained stable or even continued to increase. It has been estimated that about five hundred printers and publishers produced from 15,000 to 17,500 titles (150–75 a year) and possibly 18 million copies in the course of the century.[56] The work of Aldus was continued by such printers as Gabriele Giolito, who printed about 850 books at Venice before his death in 1578 and owned shops in Bologna, Ferrara, and Naples.[57]

Scholars have emphasized the oligarchic structure of the printing industry in the fifteenth century, the small group in control. Nicolas Jenson, for example, was supported by two merchants from Frankfurt. His press, with thirty employees, has been described as "possibly the largest private industrial establishment in Venice."[58] By the sixteenth century, on the other hand, the large number of rival printing houses was one of the attractions of Venice for Pietro Aretino and other professional writers of the time, like Ludovico Dolce, Ludovico Domenichi, Girolamo Ruscelli, and Francesco Sansovino. These were the famous *poligrafi,* men who made a living without depending on patrons by producing what publishers such as Marcolini, Giolito, or Valgrisi thought would sell—prose and verse, fact and fiction, translations, adaptations and plagiarisms from other authors.[59]

Domenichi, for example, translated Alberti, Polybius, and Xenophon. Dolce (who supposedly published no fewer than 358 works) wrote comedies, translated Euripides, edited Aretino, Boccaccio, Castiglione, and Petrarch, and plagiarized a treatise on the art of memory. Ruscelli edited a rival version of Boccaccio's *Decameron.* Sansovino in particular specialized in providing practical information, including a manual of letter writing and a guide to Venice for visitors (discussed below). In other words, there was by the mid-sixteenth century a "Venetian Grub Street," probably unparalleled until the seventeenth century in the Dutch Republic and the eighteenth century in London and Paris.[60]

Given the importance of rival information centers in early modern Europe, it is important to distinguish the domains in which Venice was strong from those in which it was relatively weak. One of the areas in which it was weak was mathematics and natural philosophy (with exceptions such as Euclid, Archimedes, and Tartaglia in mathematics, Vesalius and Colombo in anatomy, and Fracastoro and Falloppio in medicine).[61] The reason may have been that a university town such as Padua was an obvious place for publishing this kind of book. On the other hand, in the military field Venice played a dominant role. No fewer than 145 military books were printed there between 1492 and 1570.[62]

For books on the arts, Venice probably fell behind Florence, with the exception of illustrated treatises on architecture by Vitruvius, Alberti, Serlio, Palladio, Scamozzi, and so on, of which at least sixty editions appeared in two centuries, 1495–1694 (appendix table 1). Like Florence, Venice was a major center for the publication of classics of vernacular literature. The first edition of Castiglione's *Courtier,* for instance, was published by Aldus in 1528, followed by at least forty-three more editions by 1606.[63] Like the works of Petrarch and Ariosto, the *Courtier* was provided by the poligrafi with an editorial apparatus to help the reader—tables of contents, marginal glosses, summaries, indexes, and so on.[64] Venice was an early center of music publication, associated in particular with Ottaviano dei Petrucci, who had a monopoly in this field from 1498 to 1520, and later with the Gardano family, active in this field for more than sixty years (1538–1600).

In history and geography Venetian publishers were strong. Looking only at general books or reference books, we find at least eight editions of Ptolemy's geography (translated from the Greek by Ruscelli) published in the sixteenth century by Pedrezano and others. Botero's *Relazioni universali* went through nine editions in Venice between 1599 and 1671. Venetian-printed maps of the sixteenth century have an important place in the history of cartography. The Venetians published more than one edition of Guicciardini's classic history of Italy and at least three editions of Giovio's history of his own time (translated into Italian by Domenichi and edited by Ruscelli). They published chronologies such as Sansovino's world chronology (1580) and its rival, Bardi's universal chronology (1581), as well as Marco Guazzo's history of the world. The most important works of contemporary history published in Venice in the seventeenth century are listed in appendix table 4.

COSMOPOLITAN PUBLISHING

One reason for Venice's importance as a communication center was the temporary or permanent presence of many foreigners. Venice was a point of "confluence of divergent traditions," Greek, Jewish, German, "Slavonian," and so on.[65] It was via a diaspora of German printers that the process of printing with movable type spread through Europe, one of many examples of the importance of diasporas in European cultural history. In Venice the first printer was Johan von Speyer, who arrived in the city in 1469. By 1500 about twenty-five German printing firms had opened in the city.[66] Printers also included Frenchmen, including Nicolas Jenson, who arrived ca. 1471, and Vincent Vaugris, who arrived from Lyon in 1530s and became known as Valgrisi. Aldus Manutius, whose family came from Bassiano, near Rome, was also an immigrant.

The existence of subcultures within Venice made it possible for local printers to act as cultural middlemen more fully than elsewhere. Venice was not unique in this respect in the sixteenth and seventeenth centuries. Rome, Istanbul, Lyon, Antwerp, Seville, and Amsterdam were all cosmopolitan cities with ethnic subcultures. All the same, a distinctive feature of Venice as an information center was its polyglot nature, linked to the importance of its minorities.[67] For example, it was obviously easier to publish Greek books in Venice than in many other cities because Greek refugees from the Turks came to Venice, especially after the fall of the Byzantine Empire in 1453. The role of Greek scholars, such as Musurus, in editing classical Greek texts is well known, but the compositors presumably were Greeks as well.[68]

Publishing in ancient Greek in Venice has been studied in detail.[69] The first Greek text printed in Venice was in 1471, and Aldus entered this field in 1494.[70] The best-known of Greek printers were probably Zacharias Callergi (Kalliergis) and his partner the merchant Nicholas Vlastos, both originally from Crete. Janos Grigoropoulos corrected proofs for them and for Aldus.[71] Other Greek printers included Demetrios Zenos, active in the 1520s; Dominikos Hetepolonios, who was printing in 1602; and Nikolaos Saros, active in 1689–95.[72] These enterprises seem to have been small, but large firms like Sessa and Zanetti published in Greek occasionally, sometimes the classics, sometimes the liturgy. From 1509 on, Venetians also printed books in demotic Greek for export throughout the Greek-speaking world, beginning with the *Apokopos* of Bergadhis, which was reprinted more than once in Venice before the end of the century.[73]

From the beginning of the sixteenth century, when the Jews began to arrive from Spain, the Hebrew press in Venice was "the most important in Europe."[74] This aspect of Venetian publishing has also been studied in detail. Among the printers were Daniel Bomberg, originally from Antwerp, active in 1515–48, producing some two hundred titles, notably the Talmud (one assumes that the compositors too were Jewish). It is somewhat more surprising to find two Venetian patricians in the business, Marco Antonio Giustinian, active in 1545–51, who squeezed Bomberg out but was ruined when the Council of Ten forbade printing in Hebrew; and Alvise Bragadin, who accused Giustinian of trying to ruin him but was active in 1550–74 (the family continued the business). Jewish printers included the Parenzo family, Asher and Meir, who helped Bragadin, active in 1545–96; and Giovanni di Gara, active in 1563–1600.[75]

Venice was also a center of production of translations of Arabic books, thanks perhaps to the tradition of trade in the Middle East, but this aspect of Venetian publishing has attracted less attention. Arab works translated into Latin were already being published in the late fifteenth century. Avicenna, for instance, was published in Venice in 1486 and at least thirteen more times by 1595. Averroes did not do so well, though there were editions of works of his in 1542 and 1553, not to mention the commentaries. The astrologer Abd Al-Aziz was printed in 1482, 1491, 1512, 1521, and so on.[76] In 1538 the Venetian printer Paganino de Paganinis produced a Koran in Arabic, presumably for sale in the Ottoman Empire (despite the prohibition).[77] Another Venetian printer, Arrivabene, published a Koran in Italian in 1547.

The role of Venice (like its rival Tübingen) in the publication of books in Old Church Slavonic and Croat also deserves attention (see appendix table 2). A few "Slavonian" printers established there printed books in their own language: Jakov iz Kamene Reke, for instance, Jeronim Zagurović, Frano Ratkov, and above all the Vuković family, active in 1519–80. Other Venetian firms also catered to this market, including Andrea Torresano, Aldus's father-in-law: Marcolini; Bindoni; and Rampazetto. The majority of these books, sixty in all, were liturgical texts in Cyrillic or Glagolitic, in other words (as in the case of music publication) information for performance. However, there were also a few vernacular literary texts, now considered the early classics of Croat literature, by authors such as Marko Marulić, Marin Držić, Hanibal Lucić, Petar Hektorović, Petar Zoranić, Dinko Zlatarić, and Ivan Gundulić. These were printed in the Latin alphabet. There was one translation from Italian into Croat, Tasso's *Aminta,* as well as translations from Croat into Italian.[78]

Finally, the Spanish connection deserves to be emphasized. A considerable number of Spanish books were published in Venice. For example, the famous romance of chivalry *Amadís de Gaula* was published in Venice in Spanish by Pedrezano, a printer who seems to have specialized in Spanish books, in 1533. Giolito published the works of the Spanish poets Juan Boscán and Garcilaso de la Vega and even Spanish translations of Ariosto and Giovio, presumably for export either to Spain or to Milan. Medina's *Arte del navegar* was published in Spanish by Pedrezano, while Jorge de Montemayor's pastoral novel *Diana* was published by Comin de Trino (appendix table 3). Books translated from Spanish, some of which are discussed below, were much more numerous. An important figure in mediating between Venice and Spanish culture was Alfonso de Ulloa, a Spanish gentleman who became a leading *poligrafo* in Venice.

As in the cases of Greek, Hebrew, and Slavonic books, the presence in Venice of writers from the culture facilitated the task of the printers. The texts of the *Celestina, Amadís,* and *Primaleön* (another romance of chivalry) were all revised by the writer Francisco Delicado, who seems to have worked regularly for the publisher Pedrezano. The Spanish nobleman Alfonso de Ulloa spent more than twenty years in Venice (1548–70), beginning his career there as secretary to don Diego Hurtado de Mendoza, the Spanish ambassador to Venice, and later turning *poligrafo* and working for Giolito and other publishers not only as an original writer (the author of a biography of Charles V) but also as a translator and editor (Montemayor's *Diana* appeared "corregida y revista por Alfonso Ulloa").[79]

Venice was also a center for the publication of translations from Spanish into Italian, whether of moral works like those of Guevara (a sixteenth-century bestseller whose letters became a school textbook in Italy), works of piety such as those by Luis de Granada, or works of history, especially the history of the New World. Ulloa translated Columbus, Covarrubias, Mexía, Urrea, and Zárate into Italian. Works of Spanish fiction published in Italian in Venice included not only romances of chivalry such as *Amadís* and *Tirant lo Blanc* but also *Don Quixote* and the picaresque novels *Lazarillo, Guzmán,* and *Justina,* thanks in large part to the efforts of a single printer, Barezzo Barezzi, who translated most of them himself.[80]

THE WORLD BEYOND EUROPE

News of the discovery of America reached Venice later than it did Rome, Paris, and Florence.[81] All the same, thanks perhaps to the Spanish connection,

Venice was second only to Paris in terms of the amount of Americana published in the sixteenth century. It included accounts by Columbus, Vespucci, Cortés, and Oviedo (whose *Summario* was published in 1534), as well as a plagiarism of Pietro Martire d'Anghiera (the anonymous *Libretto de tutte le navigationi del Re di Spagna* of 1504), and the later histories of Mexico, Peru, and so on by López de Gómara, Cieza, Zarate, Benzoni, and others. For example, twelve editions of the Italian translation of López de Gómara were published in Venice between 1557 and 1599, and at least six editions of the translation of Cieza were published between 1555 and 1576.[82]

Some accounts of the discoveries were either written or compiled in Venice, like the three-volume *Navigationi e viaggi* (1550–59), edited by the Venetian civil servant Giovanni Battista Ramusio.[83] Ramusio, who had already edited Oviedo's *Summario,* was a member of a group of intellectuals interested in the New World, such as Bembo, Fracastoro, and Andrea Navagero, who used his time as a diplomat in Spain not only to study the peninsula but also to make friends with Pietro Martire and to forward information about the New World to Ramusio.

In any case, Venice was already a center of printed information about the "East" linked to travels of merchants and others.[84] At least four editions of Marco Polo were published there between 1496 and ca. 1555, including the first edition in Italian, and nine editions of the fictitious travels of "Sir John Mandeville" between 1491 and 1567.[85] Luigi Ronsaggio, a factor in Egypt and Syria who traveled in India, published his *Viaggio di Colocut* in 1539. Federici's *Viaggio nell'India Orientale* was published in 1587 (appearing in English translation in Hakluyt's famous collection only a year later), and Balbi's *Viaggio dell'Indie Orientali* appeared in 1590. The history of the East Indies by Lopes de Castanheda and the history of China by Gonzalez de Mendoza appeared in Venice in Italian translation in 1577 and 1586, respectively.

There was particular interest in Persia. Ambrogio Contarini's account of his mission to the shah of Persia in the 1470s (to arrange an alliance against the Turks) was published in 1487 and again in 1524 and 1543, and Caterino Zeno's account of a similar mission, also in the 1470s, was published in 1558.[86] G. T. Minadoi's history of the wars between the Turks and the Persians was published in 1588 and again in 1594. Pietro della Valle's account of the shah of Persia was published in 1628, and his description of that country appeared in 1661.

Needless to say, the Ottoman Empire attracted even more public interest in Venice, despite the qualms of the Council of Ten. Giovio's famous account of the Turks was published four times between 1538 and 1541. Benedetto Ramberti's *Le tre cose de' Turchi,* a firsthand account by a Venetian, was published in 1539. G. P. Contarini's account of the war between the sultan Selim and Venice was published in 1572. Probably the biggest publishing success, however, was Francesco Sansovino's *Historia universale de' Turchi,* first published in 1560 and reaching its eighth edition in 1600.[87] What was published was not always what the authorities would have liked. Three editions of Giovio on the Turks were anonymous, as if the printers were aware of the official concern with the subject.

I have tried to suggest that the Venetians produced, circulated, and received the information they deserved in the sense that in certain important respects the information structure was related to, if not a simple expression of, the economic, social, and political system. As Kissling has suggested, the fact that Venice was a "mercantile state' rather than a feudal-agrarian one was reflected in its information services, dependent, especially in the fifteenth century, on a network of merchants.[88] I have illustrated this point in the last few pages, as well as adding two of my own. First, I have emphasized the contribution of Venetian subcultures (Greek, Jewish, Slavonian, and so on) to the polyglot printing for which the city was famous. Second, I have discussed the relation between the circulation of political information in and around Venice and the distinctive structure of the state. A regime with a Maggior Consiglio of some two thousand members cannot keep its secrets. Hence both the leakage of politically sensitive information and the recurrent attempts to stop the leaks, from prohibiting patricians from meeting foreign ambassadors to discouraging printed journalism.

INTELLECTUAL INVOLUTION

Change in Venice during the early modern period has usually been presented in terms of decline, whether economic, political, or cultural, and assessments of the fortunes of the Venetian book trade are no exception. As early as 1603 the Senate expressed the fear that the printing industry was virtually disappearing, "annichilando grandemente."[89] Recent historians of Venetian publishing have told an almost equally sad story. Paolo Ulvioni emphasized the decline in the number of printers in the seventeenth century. Mario Infelise treated the period from 1600 to the 1680s as one of prolonged "crisis."[90] William McNeill is exceptional in his insistence that Venice remained a cultural "metropolis" as late as 1669.[91]

Decline in a relative sense over the long term there surely was, for at least two reasons. In the first place, Venetian tolerance for other cultures and other religions, the practical live-and-let-live attitude of merchants, was undermined by the spread of the Counter Reformation, at least from the arrival of Giovanni Della Casa as papal nuncio in 1544. The Inquisition was established in Venice in 1547, books were burned on piazza San Marco and near the Rialto in 1548, a Venetian *Index of Prohibited Books* was produced in 1549, and a ban on Hebrew printing was issued in 1554 (lasting until 1563). The fate of Guillaume Postel illustrates the change in climate. This unorthodox scholar returned to Venice around 1547. He was appointed chaplain of the Ospedaletto and censor of Hebrew books. He was also confessor to Madre Giovanna, a charismatic holy woman whom he believed to be the new Messiah. However, Postel was forced to leave Venice in 1549. He returned soon thereafter but was interrogated by the Inquisition in 1555, declared insane, and imprisoned in Ravenna.[92]

Booksellers began to be interrogated on charges of smuggling heretical or otherwise pernicious books from abroad. In 1570, for example, an Inquisition raid revealed copies of Machiavelli in the shops of Gilio Bonfadio, Vincenzo Valgrisi, Pietro da Fino, and Gabriele Giolito. Some printers migrated to cities such as Turin, Rome, and Naples, in sufficient numbers to alarm the Senate in 1601.[93] Others, such as Giolito, shifted their investments toward the publication of devotional books in Italian for a geographically more limited market. Giolito himself translated Luis de Granada.

In the second place, the discovery of the New World undermined the importance of Venice as an information and commercial center in the long run by shifting Europe's center of gravity westward toward the Atlantic. The Turkish occupation of Syria and Egypt reinforced the change. Lucien Febvre, writing to Henri Pirenne, once wished he could juxtapose two maps, one showing that in 1490 Venice was "le centre privilégié du monde économique connu," the other showing that in 1600 "elle n'était plus qu'une cité périphérique."[94] It was therefore time for another city to take over the role of Europe's center of information and communication. The immediate successor to Venice was Antwerp, about which a Venetian envoy admitted, "I saw Venice outdone."[95] In similar fashion the Venetian merchant Giovanni Zonca commented in the 1560s on the "grande libertade" of Antwerp.[96] After the Spanish recapture of Antwerp and the blockade of the Scheldt it would be Amsterdam's turn.

The decline of Venice relative to other centers should not be treated as absolute, or exaggerated, or dated too early, or linked too closely to the numbers of printers even if William McNeill may have been a little too generous in describing Venice as a "cultural metropolis" in the 1660s. Rather than a steady decline or a simple continuity, there was an ebb and flow of different kinds of information. For example, a revival of printing took place at the end of the seventeenth century, culminating (from the information point of view) in the ten-volume *Nuovo dizionario scientifico,* edited by Gianfrancesco Pivati and published by Miloco between 1746 and 1751.[97] From the 1750s on, however, the printing industry declined once more.[98]

Again, in the early seventeenth century Venice seems to have been more of a center of scientific information than ever before. Galileo was attracted to the city at the beginning of the seventeenth century, a time when a number of patricians were interested in "natural philosophy," and it was there that he learned of the new Dutch telescope, which he proceeded to imitate. At this time Paolo Sarpi was at the center of an international network of communication that included letters, visits to his convent by foreigners, and the bookshop Nave d'Oro, where he met his friends and held court.[99] The postal system continued to expand in this period. By the early seventeenth century couriers traveled weekly from Venice to Brussels (departing on Fridays) and Vienna (departing on Saturdays), fortnightly to Lyon, and monthly to Istanbul.[100] Giuseppe Miselli wrote in 1684 that letters could be sent via the ordinary Venetian couriers to the Netherlands, Germany, Sweden, Denmark, Poland, and Istanbul.[101] It is likely that political and geographical factors rather than economic ones underlay this expansion. It was not so much a matter of Venice's setting up a system as of the imperial court's, say, communicating with Istanbul through Venice.

In the sphere of clandestine publication there was continuity, despite attempts at repression. The satires of Ferrante Pallavicino, who lived in Venice from about 1636 and died because he let himself be tempted to leave, were probably published in the city under false imprints. A leading printer, Marco Ginammi, published Machiavelli in 1630 and 1648 and may have published the pornographic *Alcibiade fanciullo a scuola* ("Oranges," 1652).[102] In 1653 the Senate expressed alarm at the "clandestine printing of impious, obscene, and satirical works [*opere empie, obscene, malediche*]" and forbade printers to put false places of publication on the title page.[103] Two years later, however, Giovanni Maria Turrini, another leading printer (who had published what he called the "permitted works" of Ferrante Pallavicino in 1654), was accused of publishing heretical books.[104] It is likely that Meietti, who republished most of Sarpi's works between 1673 and 1685, occasionally claiming to do so not in Venice but in Mirandola, reprinted the forbidden *History of the Council of Trent.*

The Venetian poligrafi of the sixteenth century are well known. Less familiar are their equivalents in the mid-seventeenth century, a second wave. This second group specialized in publishing books on recent history and sometimes in supplying more up-to-date information on a private basis. They included Count Maiolino Bisaccioni, who lived and wrote in Venice for nearly thirty years, ca. 1635–63; Giambattista Birago Avogadro, who spent most of his life there; and Girolamo Brusoni, who was best known as a novelist but also active as a historian. Venetian publishers, notably Ginammi, Baba, Baglioni, and Combi, printed the work of a wide range of Italian historians, together with the occasional foreigner, such as Pierre Mathieu. In the age of the Thirty Years' War and the "revolutions" of the 1640s contemporary history seems to have sold well. Turrini published Ricci's account of the Thirty Years' War, *De bellis germanicis,* in 1649, only a year after the making of peace. The official printer Pinelli published regular accounts of Venetian naval engagements. As appendix table 4 shows, Venetian presses published a good deal about the history of central and eastern Europe, which was appropriate since the postal service from Italy to these regions went through Venice.

Books in Greek, especially liturgical books, continued to be printed by Antonio Pinelli (1603–31) and his family and also by Andrea Giuliano (1656–87). Given its links with the Ottoman Empire, it is not surprising to find that Venice was one of the first European cities to establish coffeehouses, about 1645. Florian's dates from 1720. Newspapers were available there in the eighteenth century, as they were in the Bottega di Cafè on Campo Santo Stefano. In 1778 a witness describes another café, La Regina d'Ungheria, as a center of novellisti.[105]

The wider world was not completely forgotten. For example, Venice was one of the few places in the world where Armenian books were printed, eight of them in the sixteenth century (all by Armenian printers), more than thirty in the seventeenth century, and still more in the eighteenth century, when the Bortali family specialized in this line of publishing.[106] Four works on the Americas by Bartolomé de Las Casas were printed by Marco Ginammi between 1626 and 1643 in both Spanish and Italian versions.[107] Three editions of the Italian translation of the *History of the Conquest of Mexico,* by Antonio de Solis, were published by Poletti in Venice in 1704, 1715, and 1733. The great tradition of Venetian geography was revived by Vincenzo Coronelli, who published his multivolume world atlas with Albrizzi between 1691 and 1697, at a time when the printing industry was beginning to revive.[108] It was in Venice that the contemporary historian Birago Avogadro published his history of Africa in 1650 and Giovanni Sagredo published his history of the Ottoman sultans in 1688.[109] Two editions of the travels of Pietro della Valle in the Orient were published by Baglioni in the 1660s. The Englishman Paul Rycaut's history of the Turks was published in translation by Combi in 1673. The Venetian physician Nicolao Manucci, who was inspired by Marco Polo's example to see the world and who lived in India from the 1650s on, sent the manuscript of his history of the Mogul Empire to the Venetian Senate, hoping that they would publish it.[110] A fellow physician who traveled the same route and met Manucci in India, Angelo Legrenzi, published *Il Pellegrino nell'Asia* in Venice in 1705.[111]

However, Manucci's hopes were disappointed. Indeed, a process of what might be called "intellectual involution" became evident quite early in the seventeenth century, if not before. *Involution* is not a euphemism for decline but a way of describing a shift. The city gradually became less metropolitan and more provincial. In the economic sphere, for example, Venice became a center of regional rather than international trade.[112] From the communication point of view, the city was most important in the later period as a center of information about itself. This was the positive aspect of involution, and a response to the increasing numbers of visitors to the city. Books published in Venice and about Venice included Gasparo Contarini's treatise on the government, with at least six Venetian editions in Latin or Italian between 1544 and 1591; the histories of Venice by Paolo Paruta (1605, 1645), Paolo Morosini (1637), and especially Battista Nani (1662, 1663, 1676, 1679, 1686); Stringa's description of the church of San Marco (1610); Luca Assarino's *Meraviglie dell'Arsenale* (1639); Marco Boschini's *Minere della pittura* (1664), oriented toward foreign tourism; and Cristoforo Ivanovich's history of Venetian opera, *Minerva al Tavolino* (1681). Gozzi's famous *Gazzetta Veneta* (1760), one of the most famous examples of Enlightenment moral journalism, also offered information about the city.

Especially important were Francesco Sansovino's guides to the city, the little dialogue *Cose notabili*, first published in 1556, and the massive treatise *Venezia città nobilissima*, of 1581. Between them, these guides had passed through at least 38 editions by 1692, from thirteen different publishers: Calepino, Cestari, Comin, Curti, Didini, Farri, Herz, Imberti, Miloco, Rampazetto, Salicato, Spineda, Tramontin, Valgrisi, Valvassori, Viani (appendix table 4). The dialogue appeared under various titles—*Cose maravigliose, Cose maravigliose e notabili, Cose notabili e maravigliose*—and even authors, Sansovino's name being replaced on occasion by that of Anselmo Guisconi or Girolamo Bardi. In the case of *Venezia città nobilissima*, the title pages proclaim the superiority of each successive edition, the information being "riformate, accommodate e grandemente ampliate," "con nuova aggiunta," and so on, thanks to the work of four different editors, Giovanni Niccolo Doglioni (disguised as "Leonico Gold-ioni"), Stringa, Martinioni, and Zittio. The number of copies of these works to be found in foreign libraries, notably in France, suggests their importance to foreign visitors for more than a century. They were eventually replaced by Coronelli's *Guida de'forestieri,* which had reached its fourth edition by 1700.

One might treat the fate of Sansovino's books as symbolic. His studies of the Turks were forgotten, whereas his guides to Venice continued to sell. At one time foreigners had gone to Venice to learn about the contemporary world. By the seventeenth century they were going to admire the city's past.

APPENDIX

TABLE I
Select Architectural Books Published in Venice, 1495–1694

1495	Vitruvius, Latin (Pensis)
1511	Vitruvius, Latin (Tacuino)
1524	Vitruvius, Italian (Sabio)
1535	Vitruvius, Italian (Zoppino)
1537	Serlio, 4 (Marcolini)
1540	Serlio, 3 (Marcolini)
1544	Serlio, 3 (Marcolini)
1544	Serlio, 4 (Marcolini)
1546	Alberti, Italian (Vaugris)
ca. 1551	Serlio, 1–2 (Sessa)
1551	Serlio, 3 (Sessa)
1551	Serlio (Marcolini)
1551	Serlio, 4 (Sessa)
1551	Serlio, 5 (Sessa)
1554	Cattaneo, 1–4 (Aldo)
1554	Palladio, *Antichità* (Pagan)
1556	Vitruvius, Italian (Franceschi)
1556	Vitruvius, Italian (Marcolini)
1557	Serlio (Sessa)
1558	Serlio (Sessa)
1559	Serlio, 5 (Sessa)
1560	Serlio 1–2 (Sessa)
1562	Serlio, 3 (Sessa)
ca. 1562	Serlio, 4 (Marcolini)
1562	Serlio (Rampazzetto)
1565	Alberti, Italian (Franceschi)
1565	Palladio, *Antichità* (Varisco)
1566	Serlio, 1–5 (Francesco Senese and Zuanne Krugher)
1567	Cattaneo, 1–8 (Aldo)
1567	Vitruvius, Italian (Franceschi)
1567	Serlio, *Libro estraordinario* (Sessa)
1568–69	Serlio, 1–5, Latin (Francesco Senese and Zuanne Krugher)
1569	Serlio, 5 (Sessa)
1569	Serlio (Franceschi)
1570	Palladio, *Due libri* (Franceschi)
1570	Palladio, *Quattro libri* (Franceschi)

TABLE I

Continued

1570	Vignola
1576	Labacco, *Architettura* (Porro)
1581	Palladio, *Quattro libri* (Carampello)
1582	Vignola (Ziletti)
1583	Scamozzi, *Antichità* (Ziletti)
1584	Serlio, 1–7 (Franceschi)
1584	Vitruvius, Italian (Francheschi)
1590	Rusconi (Giolito)
1596	Vignola (Porro)
1600	Serlio, 1–7 (Franceschi)
ca. 1600	Vignola (Doino)
1601	Palladio, *Quattro libri* (Carampello)
1603	Vignola (Franco)
1615	Scamozzi, *Idea* (Valentino)
1616	Palladio, *Quattro libri* (Carampello)
1618	Serlio (Franceschi)
1619	Serlio, 1–7 (Franceschi)
1629	Vitruvius, Italian (Vecchi)
1641	Vitruvius, Italian (Turrini)
1642	Palladio (Brogiollo)
ca. 1648	Vignola (Remondini)
1663	Serlio, 1–6 (Combi)
1663	Serlio (Hertz)
1694	Scamozzi (Albrizzi)

SOURCES: Alfred F. Johnson, Victor Scholderer, and D. A. Clark, eds., *Short Title Catalogue of Books Printed in Italy from 1465 to 1600 Now in the British Museum* (London, 1958); Suzanne P. Michel and Paul-Henri Michel, *Répertoire des ouvrages imprimés en langue italienne au XVIIème siècle conservés dans les bibliothèques de France,* 8 vols. (Paris, 1967–84); L. H. Fowler, *The Fowler Architectural Collection* (Baltimore, 1961). I should like to thank Juergen Schulz for helping me compile this list.

TABLE 2

Slavonic Texts Published in Venice, 1493–1599

1493	*Breviarium Croaticum* (Torresano)
1495	*Pishtule* (Damiano)
1512	*Molitvenik* (Ratkov)
1512	*Officia BVM* (Ratkov)
1512	*Officia S. Brigittae* (Ratkov)
1519	*Psaltir* (Vuković)
1519	*Molitvenik* (Vuković)
1519	*Sluzhabnik* (Vuković)
1521	Marulić, *Judit* (Fontanetto)
1522	Marulić, *Judit* (Benalio)
1522	Marulić, *Judit* (Negri)
1527	*Introductorium* (Torresano)
1527	*Molitvenik* (Vuković)
1527	*Sluzhabnik* (Vuković)
1528	*Bukvar*
1528	*Misali* (Bindoni)
1536	*Molitvenik* (Vuković)
ca. 1536	*Sobornik* (Vuković)
1537	*Oktoich* (Vuković)
1538	*Sobornik* (Vuković)

TABLE 2
Continued

ca. 1538	*Molitvenik* (Vuković)
1543	*Pishtule* (Sessa)
1546	*Psaltir* (Vuković)
1547	*Molitvenik* (Vuković)
1549	Dimitrović, *Sedam piesni* (Bascarini)
1549	Držić, *Tirena*
1551	Držić, *Pjesni*
1554	*Sluzhabnik* (Vuković)
1556	Lucić, *Skladanya* (Marcolini)
1560	*Molitvenik* (Vuković)
1561	*Breviarium* (Torresani)
1561	*Horarium* (Giunta)
1561	*Psaltir* (Vuković)
1561	*Triody* (Vuković)
1562	*Kato* (Temperica)
1562	*Missale*
ca. 1565	Divković, *Nauk karstianski*
1566	*Chasoslovec* (Jakov iz Kamene Reke)
1567	Gradić, *Libarze* (Guerra)
1568	Hektorović, *Ribanja* (Camotio)
1569	Hektorović, *Piesni*
1569	*Psaltir* (Zagurović)
1569	*Sluzhabnik* (Zagurović)
1569	Zoranić, *Planine* (Farri)
1570	*Trebnik* (Zagurović)
ca. 1570	*Sluzhabnik* (Zagurović)
1571	*Officia BVM* (Barom)
1571	*Officia S. Brigittae* (Barom)
1571	*Svjatki* (Barom)
1572	*Razlicnie potrebi* (Jakov)
1580	*Psaltir* (Vuković)
1580	Zlatarić, *Aminta* (Guerra)
1582	Jerković, *Bogoljubna* (Rampazetto)
1584	Krnarutić, *Vazetye Sigetta* (d'Albe)
1585	Lucić, *Robinja* (Mazoletto)
1585	*Nauk Katolicaski*
1586	Krnarutić, *Pirama i Tizbe* (Bindoni)
1586	Marulić, *Judit* (Bindoni)
1586	*Pishtole* (Rampazetto)
1595	Vrancić, *Dictionarium* (Moreto)
1596	*Pishtole*
1597	*Molitvenik* (Rampazetto)
1597	Zlatarić, *Elektra / Aminta* (Aldus)
1599	Cubranović, *Jeghiupka* (Salicato)

SOURCE: Josip Badalić, *Jugoslavia usque ad annum 1600* (Baden-Baden, 1959).

TABLE 3

Texts in Spanish Published in Venice, 1523–1644

1523	Celestina
1528	Delicado, Lozana
1531	Celestina
1533	Amadís (Pedrazano)
1534	Oviedo, Summario
1534	Primaleón (Pedrazano)
1548	Avila, Comentario (Çornoça)
1552	Avila, Comentario (Marcolini)
1552	Nuñez, Clareo y Floriseo (Giolito)
1553	Ariosto, Orlando, trans. Urrea (Giolito)
1553	Boscán, Obras, with Garcilaso de la Vega (Giolito)
1553	Celestina, ed. Ulloa (Giolito)
1553	Guevara, Libro aureo (Giolito)
1553	Homer, Ulyxea (Giolito)
1553	Mexia, Silva (Giolito)
1553	Questión de amor (Giolito)
1553	San Pedro, Carcel de Amor (Giolito)
1553	Ulloa (ed.), Processo de cartas de amores (Giolito)
1553	Ulloa (trans.), Sentencias y dichos (Giolito)
1555	Medina, Arte del navegar (Pederzano)
1558	Giovio, Impresas (Giolito)
1566	Urrea, De la verdadera honra (Grifo)
1567	Petrarch, Sonetos (Bevilacqua)
1568	Leone Ebreo, Diálogos, trans. Costa
1568	Montemayor, Diana (Comin)
1569	Ulloa, Commentarios (Farri)
1574	Montemayor, Diana (Comin)
1626	Las Casas, Relación (Ginammi)
1644	Las Casas, Conquista (Ginammi)

SOURCES: Antonio Palau y Dulcet, Manual del librero hispano-americano, 28 vols. (Barcelona, 1948–77); Antonio Rumeu de Armas, Alfonso de Ulloa: Introductor de la cultura española in Italia (Madrid, 1973).

TABLE 4

Select Seventeenth-Century Works on Recent History

1605	Paruta, Historia Veneta (Nicolini)
1623	Mathieu, Francia (Fontana), reprinted 1624, 1628, 1629
1623	Morosini, Historia de la Repubblica Veneta (Pinelli), 2d ed. 1637
1625	Mathieu, Guerre, trans. Canini (Barezzi: Fontana), reprinted 1628
1627	Pieri, Guerra di Fiandra (Ciotti)
1630	Davila, Guerre (Baglioni), new eds. 1634, 1638, 1642, 1650, 1664, 1692
1633	Noris, Guerre di Germania (Pinelli)
1634–38	Bisaccioni, Guerra in Alemagna (Baba)
1638	Pallavicino, Successi del mondo in 1636 (Tomasini)
1638	Pomo, Guerre di Ferdinando II (Sarzina)
1640	Bentivoglio, Fiandra (Baba), 2d ed. 1668
1640	Strada, Guerra di Fiandra (Baba)
1642	Bisaccioni, Gustavo Adolfo (Pavoni)
1642–46	Zilioli, Historie (Turrini)
1643	Tesauro, Campeggiamenti (Garzoni)
1644	Birago, Disunione
1645	Contarini, Guerra da Selim (Combi)

TABLE 4
Continued

1645	Paruta, *Historia Veneta* (Giunti)
1646–48	Gualdo Priorato, *Guerre di imperatori* (Bertani)
1647	Giraffi, *Rivolutioni* (Baba)
1648	Birago, *Mercurio veridico* (Leni)
1649	Ricci, *De bellis germanicis* (Turrini)
1652	Bate, *Moti d'Inghilterra*
1653	Birago, *Sollevationi* (Turrini)
1653	Bisaccioni, *Guerre civili* (Storti), reprinted 1655
1654	Birago, *Turbolenze di Europa* (Ginammi)
1655	Gualdo Priorato, *Rivolutioni di Francia* (Baglioni)
1655	Ricci, *Res italicae* (Turrini)
1656	Brusoni, *Historia d'Europa* (Turrini)
1657	Brusoni, *Historia Universale* (Storti)
1661	Brusoni, *Historia d'Italia* (Storti)
1662	Nani, *Historia de la Republica di Venezia* (Combi), reprinted 1663, 1676, 1686
1668	Bentivoglio, *Fiandra* (Miloco)
1671	Vimini [Bianchi], *Guerre Civili di Polonia* (Pinelli)
1671	Brusoni, *Historia d'Italia* (Storti), 2d ed. 1676
1673	Brusoni, *Historia dell'ultima guerra tra Venezia e Turchi* (Curti)
1679	Nani, *Historia de la Republica di Venezia,* pt. 2 (Combi), reprinted 1686
1679	Valier, *Guerra di Candia* (Baglioni)
1681	Gazzotti, *Guerre d'Europa* (Pezzano)
1684	Camuccio, *Assedio di Vienna* (Poletti)
1685	*Armi cesaree nell'Ungheria* (Cagnolini)
1687	Giustiniani, *Armi imperiali* (Curti)
1689	Brandano, *Guerre di Portogallo* (Baglioni)
1691	Locatelli, *Veneta guerra in Levante* (Albrizzi)

SOURCES: *Catalogue of Seventeenth-Century Italian Books in the British Library,* 3 vols. (London, 1986); Suzanne P. Michel and Paul-Henri Michel, *Répertoire des ouvrages imprimés en langue italienne au XVIIème siècle conservés dans les bibliothèques de France,* 8 vols. (Paris, 1967–84).

TABLE 5
Editions of Sansovino, 1556–1692

1556	Anselmo Guisconi [pseud.], *Tutte le cose notabili che sono in Venetia* (n.p.)
1560	*Tutte le cose notabili che sono in Venetia* (Rampazzetto)
1561	*Delle cose notabili che sono in Venetia* (Comin)
1562	*Delle cose notabili che sono in Venetia* (Farri)
1563	*Delle cose notabili che sono in Venetia* (Calepino)
1564	*Delle cose notabili che sono in Venetia* (Calepino)
1565	*Delle cose notabili che sono in Venetia* (Franceschi)
1565	*Delle cose notabili che sono in Venetia* (Rampazzetto)
1566	*Delle cose notabili che sono in Venetia* (Franceschi)
1566	*Delle cose notabili che sono in Venetia,* rev. Doglioni and Zittio (Cestari)
1567	*Delle cose notabili che sono in Venetia* (Franceschi)
1572	*Delle cose notabili che sono in Venetia* (Viani)
1581	*Venetia città nobilissima* (Farri)
1583	*Delle cose notabili che sono in Venetia* (Valvassori)
1587	*Delle cose notabili che sono in Venetia* (Zoppini)
1587	*Delle cose notabili che sono in Venetia* (Valgrisi, 24°)
1587	*Delle cose notabili che sono in Venetia* (Valgrisi, 8°)
1592	*Delle cose notabili che sono in Venetia* (Zoppini)
1601	*Delle cose notabili che sono in Venetia* (Salicato)

TABLE 5
Continued

1601	Bardi [pseud.], *Venetia città nobilissima* (Salicato)
1602	*Delle cose notabili che sono in Venetia* (Spineda)
1602	*Venetia città nobilissima* (Spineda)
1603	*Cose maravigliose*, rev. Goldioni [pseud.] (Imberti)
1604	*Venetia città nobilissima*, rev. Stringa (Salicato)
1606	*Delle cose notabili che sono in Venetia* (Salicato)
1612	*Cose maravigliose e notabili*, rev. Goldioni [pseud.] (Imberti)
1624	*Cose maravigliose e notabili*, rev. Goldioni [pseud.] (Imberti)
1629	*Cose notabili et maravigliose*, rev. Goldioni [pseud.] (Herz)
1641	*Cose maravigliose e notabili*, rev. Goldioni [pseud.] (Imberti)
1641	*Cose notabili et maravigliose*, rev. Goldioni [pseud.] (Herz)
1649	*Cose notabili et maravigliose*, rev. Goldioni [pseud.] (Herz)
1655	*Cose notabili et maravigliose*, rev. Goldioni [pseud.] (Herz)
1662	*Cose notabili et maravigliose*, rev. Goldioni [pseud.] (Herz)
1663	*Venetia città nobilissima*, rev. Martinioni (Curti)
1666	*Cose notabili et maravigliose*, rev. Goldioni [pseud.] (Cestari)
1671	*Cose notabili et maravigliose*, rev. Goldioni [pseud.] (Cestari)
1675	*Cose notabili et maravigliose*, rev. Goldioni [pseud.] (Cestari: Miloco)
1675	*Cose notabili et maravigliose*, rev. Goldioni [pseud.] (Miloco)
1692	*Cose notabili et maravigliose*, rev. Goldioni [pseud.] (Didini)
1692	*Cose notabili et maravigliose*, rev. Goldioni [pseud.] (Tramontin)

SOURCES: Alfred F. Johnson, Victor Scholderer, and D. A. Clark, eds., *Short Title Catalogue of Books Printed in Italy from 1465 to 1600 Now in the British Museum* (London, 1958): Suzanne P. Michel and Paul-Henri Michel, *Répertoire des ouvrages imprimés en langue italienne au XVIIème siècle conservés dans les bibliothèques de France*, 8 vols. (Paris, 1967–84); and information from Juergen Schulz.

NOTES

My thanks to the conference participants for their questions and comments and espe-cially to John Martin, Juergen Schulz, and Jonathan Walker. I should also like to thank Brendan Dooley for his constructive criticisms of an earlier draft of this paper.

1. Pierre Sardella, *Nouvelles et spéculations à Venise au début du XVIe siècle* (Paris, 1948), 10, 14.

2. Fernand Braudel, *La Méditerranée et le monde méditerranéen à l'époque de Philippe II* (Paris, 1949), 317; cf. Federico Melis, "La diffusione dell'informazione economica nel Mediterraneo," in *Mélanges Braudel*, ed. Emmanuel Le Roy Ladurie, 2 vols. (Toulouse, 1973), 1:389–424.

3. J. R. Hale, *Renaissance Venice* (London, 1973).

4. Leonardas V. Gerulaitis, *Printing and Publishing in Fifteenth-Century Venice* (Chi-cago, 1976); Paul Grendler, *The Roman Inquisition and the Venetian Press* (Princeton, 1977); Martin Lowry, *The World of Aldus Manutius* (Oxford, 1979); Hans-Georg Beck et al., eds., *Venezia centro di mediazione tra Oriente e Occidente (secoli XV–XVI): Aspetti e problemi*, 2 vols. (Florence, 1977); William McNeill, *Venice: The Hinge of Europe, 1081–1797* (Chicago, 1974).

5. Federica Ambrosini, *Paesi e mari ignoti: America e colonialismo europeo nella cultura veneziana (secoli XVI–XVII)* (Venice, 1982); Claudia di Filippo Bareggi, *Il mestiere di*

scrivere: Lavoro intellettuale e mercato librario a Venezia nel '500 (Rome, 1988); Julian Raby, *Venice, Dürer, and the Oriental Mode* (London, 1982); Girolamo Arnaldi and Manlio Pastore Stocchi, eds., *Storia della cultura veneta*, vols. 3 and 4 (Vicenza, 1980–83).

6. Paolo Preto, *I servizi secreti di Venezia* (Milan, 1994); John Martin, *Venice's Hidden Enemies: Italian Heretics in a Renaissance City* (Berkeley, 1993); Angela Caracciolo Aricò, ed., *L'impatto della scoperta dell'America nella cultura veneziana* (Rome, 1990).

7. Hans J. Kissling, "Venezia come centro di informazione sui Turchi," in Beck et al., *Venezia centro*, 1:97–109.

8. William Eamon, *Science and the Secrets of Nature: Books of Secrets in Medieval and Early Modern Culture* (Princeton, 1994).

9. Marion L. Kuntz, *Guillaume Postel* (The Hague, 1981), 73–83.

10. Giorgio Doria, "Conoscenza del mercato e sistema informativo: Il know-how dei mercanti-finanzieri genovesi nei secoli XVI e XVII," in *La repubblica internazionale del denaro tra XV e XVII secolo*, ed. Aldo de Maddalena and Hermann Kellenbenz (Bologna, 1986), 57–115.

11. Bruno Caizzi, *Dalla posta dei re alla posta di tutti* (Milan, 1993), 211–62.

12. Sardella, *Nouvelles et spéculations*, 119–37.

13. Donald E. Queller, *The Venetian Patriciate: Reality versus Myth* (Urbana, 1986).

14. Preto, *I servizi secreti di Venezia*, 218.

15. Marino Sanuto, *I diarii di Marino Sanuto*, ed. Rinaldo Fulin et al., 58 vols. (Venice, 1879–1903), 35:173.

16. See, e.g., Kissling, "Venezia come centro di informazione," 106; and Robert Mantran, "Venise, centre d'information sur les Turcs," in Beck et al., *Venezia centro*, 1:113–14.

17. Luca Campigotto, "Veneziani in India nel XVI secolo," *Studi Veneziani*, n.s., 22 (1991): 75–116; Alessandro Grossato, *Navigatori e viaggiatori veneti sulla rotta per l'India* (Florence, 1994).

18. Juergen Schulz, "Jacopo de' Barbari's View of Venice: Map Making, City Views, and Moralized Geography before the Year 1500," *Art Bulletin* 60 (1978): 425–74.

19. Numa Broc, *La géographie de la Renaissance*, 2d ed. (Paris, 1986), 51, 126; Luisa d'Arienzo, "La presenza veneziana in Portogallo," in Aricò, *L'impatto della scoperta dell'America*, 65.

20. Armand Baschet, *Les archives de Venise* (Paris, 1870), 331–61; Donald E. Queller, "How to Succeed as an Ambassador," *Studia Gratiana* 15 (1972): 665–71, esp. 670–71; idem, "The Development of Ambassadorial *Relazioni*," in Hale, *Renaissance Venice*, 174–96; Angelo Ventura, *Nobiltà e popolo nella società veneta del '400 e '500*, 2d ed. (Milan, 1993); J. Kenneth Hyde, "The Role of Diplomatic Correspondence and Reporting," in Hyde, *Literacy and Its Uses: Studies on Late Medieval Italy*, ed. Daniel P. Waley (Manchester, 1993), 217–59.

21. Giovanni Botero, *Relatione della repubblica venetiana* (Venice, 1595).

22. British Library, Department of Manuscripts, Sloan 697, fols. 1–32, 35–62; Add. 18, 660, fols. 137–46; Sloan 1834.

23. Cf. Ugo Tucci's intervention in the discussion in Beck et al., *Venezia centro*, 1:137.

24. Kissling, "Venezia come centro di informazione," 101.

25. Preto, *I servizi secreti di Venezia*, 248–49.

26. Ibid., 269; cf. Hyde, "Role of Diplomatic Correspondence and Reporting," 244.

27. Preto, *I servizi secreti di Venezia*, 381–96.

28. Giovanni K. Hassiotis, "Venezia e i domini veneziani tramite di informazioni sui Turchi per gli Spagnoli," in Beck et al., *Venezia centro*, 1:117–36; Peri in the discussion in ibid., 137.

29. Geoffrey Parker, "Maps and Ministers," in *Monarchs, Ministers, and Maps: The Emergence of Cartography as a Tool of Government in Early Modern Europe*, ed. David Buisseret (Chicago, 1992), 125.

30. Preto, *I servizi secreti di Venezia*, 55–57.

31. Queller, *Venetian Patriciate*, 75.

32. Gerulaitis, *Printing and Publishing in Fifteenth-Century Venice*, 55.

33. Baschet, *Les archives de Venise*, 175–76.

34. T. C. Price Zimmermann, *Paolo Giovio: The Historian and the Crisis of Renaissance Italy* (Princeton, 1995), 171.

35. Preto, *I servizi secreti di Venezia*, 66, 79, 123–28.

36. Ibid., 433.

37. Emmanuele Cicogna, *Delle inscrizioni veneziane*, 6 vols. (Venice, 1824–53), 3:287–90.

38. John Marino, "Administrative Mapping in the Italian States," in Buisseret, *Monarchs, Ministers, and Maps*, 6.

39. Preto, *I servizi secreti di Venezia*, 168–77.

40. Baschet, *Les archives de Venise*, 167–78, 194.

41. Martin, *Venice's Hidden Enemies*, 26.

42. Grendler, *Roman Inquisition and the Venetian Press*, 102–15; Martin, *Venice's Hidden Enemies*, 80–81.

43. Martin, *Venice's Hidden Enemies*, 67, 185–86.

44. Andrea Moschetti, "Il Gobbo di Rialto," *Nuovo Archivio Veneto* 5 (1893): 1–85.

45. Nadia Lerz, ed., "Il diario di Griso di Giovanni," *Archivio Storico Italiano* 422 (1959): 265; Hyde, "Role of Diplomatic Correspondence and Reporting," 242; Francesca Trivellato, "La missione diplomatica a Venezia del fiorentino Giannozzo Manetti," *Studi Veneziani*, n.s., 28 (1994): 213.

46. Biagio Brugi, *Gli scolari dello studio di Padova* (Padua, 1905), 27.

47. Valerio Castronovo, "I primi sviluppi della stampa periodica fra Cinque e Seicento," in *La stampa italiana dal '500 all '800*, ed. Valerio Castronovo and Nicolò Tranfaglia (Bari, 1976), 9–10.

48. Preto, *I servizi secreti di Venezia*, 89.

49. Mario Infelise, "Professione reportista: Copisti e gazzettieri nella Venezia del '600," in *Venezia: Itinerari per la storia della città*, ed. Stefano Gasparri, Giovanni Levi, and Pierandrea Moro (Bologna, 1997), 193–219; idem, "Le marché des informations à Venise au 17e siècle," in *Gazettes et information politique sous l'ancien régime*, ed. H. Duranton and Pierre Rétat (Saint-Etienne, 1999), 117–28.

50. Dorit Raines, "Office Seeking, Broglio, and the Pocket Political Guidebooks in '500 and '600 Venice," *Studi Veneziani*, n.s., 22 (1991): 137–94.

51. Alfred Morel-Fatio, *Historiographie de Charles-Quint* (Paris, 1913), 152.

52. Baschet, *Les archives de Venise*, 348–52; Ugo Tucci, "Ranke and the Venetian Document Market," in *Leopold von Ranke and the Shaping of the Historical Discipline*, ed. Georg G. Iggers and James M. Powell (Syracuse, 1990), 100; Preto, *I servizi secreti di Venezia*, 66.

53. A. N. Amelot de la Houssaie, *Histoire du gouvernement de Venise* (1676; reprint, Paris, 1685), preface.

54. Castronovo, "I primi sviluppi della stampa periodica fra Cinque e Seicento," 20.

55. Gerulaitis, *Printing and Publishing in Fifteenth-Century Venice*.

56. Grendler, *Roman Inquisition and the Venetian Press*, 5–6; Martin, *Venice's Hidden Enemies*, 77.

57. Salvatore Bongi, *Annali di Gabriel Giolito*, 2 vols. (Rome, 1890).

58. Lowry, *The World of Aldus Manutius*, 18.

59. Bareggi, *Il mestiere di scrivere*.

60. Martin, *Venice's Hidden Enemies*, 78n.

61. Ezio Riondato et al., *Trattati scientifici nel Veneto fra il XV e il XVI secolo* (Vicenza, 1985), is less useful than the title suggests.

62. J. R. Hale, "Printing and the Military Culture of Renaissance Venice," in idem, *Renaissance War Studies* (London, 1983), 429–70.

63. Peter Burke, *The Fortunes of the Courtier* (Cambridge, 1995), 158–62.

64. Brian Richardson, *Print Culture in Renaissance Italy* (Cambridge, 1994); Burke, *Fortunes of the Courtier*, 42–43.

65. McNeill, *Venice*, 157.

66. F. Geldner, *Die deutsche Inkunabeldrucker*, 2 vols. (Stuttgart, 1968–70), 2:61–97.

67. Lucien Romier, "Lyon et le cosmopolitanisme," *Bibliothèque d'Humanisme et Renaissance* 11 (1949): 28–42; Peter Burke, *Antwerp: A Metropolis in Comparative Perspective* (Antwerp, 1993); Guido Marnef, *Antwerp in the Age of Reformation*, trans. J. C. Grayson (Baltimore, 1996).

68. Burke, *Antwerp*.

69. Enrica Follieri, "Il libro greco per i greci nelle imprese editoriali romane e veneziane della prima metà del Cinquecento," in Beck et al., *Venezia centro*, 2:483–508; Léandre Vranoussis, "Les imprimeries vénitiennes et les premiers livres grecs," in ibid., 509–20.

70. Alessandro Pertusi, "Per la storia e le fonti delle prime grammatiche greche a stampa," *Italia Medievale e Umanistica* 5 (1962): 323–24. Pertusi corrected the traditional date of 1486.

71. E. Mioni, "Calliergi," in *Dizionario biografico degli Italiani*, 46 vols. to date (Rome, 1960–) 16:750–53.

72. *Catalogue of Seventeenth-Century Italian Books in the British Library*, 3 vols. (London, 1986).

73. Linos Politis, "Venezia come centro della stampa e della diffusione della prima letteratura neoellenica," in Beck et al., *Venezia centro*, 2:443–82; David Holton, ed., *Literature and Society in Renaissance Crete* (Cambridge, 1991), 4–6, 71–73.

74. Grendler, *Roman Inquisition and the Venetian Press*, 90.

75. Alfredo Cioni, "Bomberg," in *Dizionario biografico degli Italiani*, 11:382–87; Grendler, *Roman Inquisition and the Venetian Press*, 90–93, 255; Avraham Rosenthal, "Daniel Bomberg and His Talmud Editions," in *Gli Ebrei e Venezia*, ed. Gaetano Cozzi (Milan, 1987), 375–416; Fausto Parente, "La chiesa e il Talmud," in *Storia d'Italia: Annali*, ed. Ruggiero Romano and Corrado Vivanti, vol. 11 (Turin, 1996), 524–643, esp. 580–89.

76. Alfred F. Johnson, Victor Scholderer, and D. A. Clarke, *Short-Title Catalogue of Books Printed in Italy from 1465 to 1600 Now in the British Museum* (London, 1958).

77. A. Nuovo, *Alessandro Paganino* (Padua, 1990).

78. Josip Badalić, *Jugoslavia usque ad annum 1600* (Baden-Baden, 1959); cf. W. Schmitz, *Südslavische Buchdruck in Venedig* (Giessen, 1977).

79. Antonio Rumeu de Armas, *Alfonso de Ulloa: Introductor de la cultura española en Italia* (Madrid, 1973); Bareggi, *Il mestiere di scrivere*.

80. Alfredo Cioni and Claudio Mutini, "Barezzi," in *Dizionario biografico degli Italiani*, 6:336–40.

81. Angela Caracciolo Aricò, "Il nuovo mondo e l'umanesimo: Immagini e miti dell'editoria veneziana," in Aricò, *L'impatto della scoperta dell'America*, 25.

82. Ambrosini, *Paesi e mari ignoti*, esp. 81n; Donatella Ferro, "Traduzioni di opere spagnole sulla scoperta dell'America nell'editoria veneziana del Cinquecento," in Aricò, *L'impatto della scoperta dell'America*, 93–105.

83. Donald Lach, *Asia in the Making of Europe* (Chicago, 1965), 163–64, 180–81; Massimo Donattini, "Giambattista Ramusio e le sue *Navigationi*," in *Critica Storica* 17 (1980): 55–100.

84. Lach, *Asia in the Making of Europe*.

85. Johnson, Scholderer, and Clarke, *Short-Title Catalogue of Books Printed in Italy from 1465 to 1600*.

86. Ibid.

87. Stéphane Yérasimos, "De la collection des voyages à l'histoire universelle: La *Historia universale de' Turchi* de Francesco Sansovino," *Turcica* 20 (1988): 19–41.

88. Kissling, "Venezia come centro di informazione."

89. Quoted in Horatio F. Brown, *The Venetian Printing Press* (London, 1891), 218.

90. Paolo Ulvioni, "Stampatori e librai a Venezia nel '600," *Archivio Veneto* 54 (1977): 108; Mario Infelise, *L'editoria veneziana nel '700* (Milan, 1989), 9–11.

91. McNeill, *Venice*.

92. Kuntz, *Guillaume Postel*; Marion L. Kuntz, ed., *Postello, Venezia e il suo mondo* (Florence, 1988), esp. 119–36.

93. Brown, *Venetian Printing Press*, 175; Tiziana Pesenti, "Stampatori e letterati," in Arnaldi and Stocchi, *Storia della cultura veneta*, vol. 4, pt. 1: 103.

94. Lucien Febvre to Henri Pirenne, 31 May 1922 and 29 November 1927, in Bryce Lyon, *The Birth of Annales History* (Brussels, 1991), 95 and 38, respectively.

95. Quoted in John J. Murray, *Antwerp in the Age of Plantin and Breughel* (Norman, Okla., 1970), 43.

96. Marnef, *Antwerp in the Age of Reformation*, 3.

97. Silvano Garofalo, *L'enciclopedismo italiano: Gianfrancesco Pivati* (Ravenna, 1980).

98. Infelise, *L'editoria veneziana nel '700, 275–94.

99. Peter Burke, ed., *Paolo Sarpi* (New York, 1967); idem, *Venice and Amsterdam,* 2d ed. (Cambridge, 1994), 97.

100. Ottavio Cotogno, *Compendio delle poste* (Milan, 1623), 208–12, 454–55.

101. Giuseppe Miselli, *Il burattino veridico* (Rome, 1684), 172.

102. Grendler, *Roman Inquisition and the Venetian Press,* 165–67, 285.

103. Quoted in Brown, *Venetian Printing Press,* 227.

104. Preto, *I servizi secreti di Venezia,* 173.

105. Ibid., 92.

106. Baykar Sivazliyan, "Venezia per l'oriente: La nascita del libro armeno," in *Armeni, Ebrei, Greci stampatori a Venezia* (Venice, 1989), 23–38.

107. Ambrosini, *Paesi e mari ignoti,* 144–50; Angela Nuovo, "L'editoria veneziana del XVII secolo e il problema americano," in Aricò, *L'impatto della scoperta dell'America,* 175–86.

108. A. de Ferrari, "Coronelli," *Dizionario biografico degli Italiani,* 29:305–9; Teresa Colletta, "Vincenzo Coronelli," in *Libro e incisione a Venezia nei secoli XVII e XVIII,* ed. Colletta et al. (Vicenza, 1988), 1–32.

109. G. Birago Avogadro, *Historia Africana* (Venice, 1650); Giovanni Sagredo, *Monarchi Ottomani* (Venice, 1688).

110. Nicolao Manucci, *Storia do Mogor; or Mogul India,* trans. William Irvine (London, 1907–8); Grossato, *Navigatori e viaggiatori veneti,* 93–102.

111. Grossato, *Navigatori e viaggiatori veneti,* 103–6.

112. Jean Georgelin, *Venise au siècle des lumières* (Paris, 1978).

13

Toward a Social History of Women in Venice
From the Renaissance to the Enlightenment

In the last quarter-century one of the liveliest areas of research in Venetian history has been women's history, gender, and sexuality. For the most part this research has focused on the late Middle Ages and the Renaissance. In this essay Federica Ambrosini turns to a later period, offering a panorama of the social and cultural experience of women in Venice from the late Renaissance to the Enlightenment. Her analysis shows how familial expectations, economic pressures, and anxieties over the "dangers" of female sexuality tended to restrict the options for women to marriage or the convent. Indeed, girls were often forced into marriages and into the religious life against their will. While many women eked out precarious lives and remained subject to the whims of their fathers and brothers down to the fall of the Republic, the eighteenth century brought greater freedoms as Enlightenment ideas left their stamp on Venetian society. In this period women were less likely to be subjected against their will to life in the convent. New options, such as life as a pizzochera, a tertiary in a religious order, increased in number. At the same time, though the frequency of forced marriages remained high, affective ties came to have greater value for both men and women. And women in unhappy marriages were increasingly able to end their unions. These shifts, Ambrosini suggests, were not only the consequence of new social and institutional arrangements, as women found new ways to support one another in charity, patronage, and friendship. They were also the consequence of changes in Venetian culture. Literacy, in particular, played a decisive role in women's growing independence. Indeed, over the last few centuries of the Republic's history Venetian women found imaginative ways to draw on religious as well as libertine and Enlightenment texts to shape relatively independent lives in a predominantly patriarchal society.

UNTIL RELATIVELY RECENTLY historians largely ignored the varied roles women played in Venetian society. Even when they did turn their attention to the experience of women in the Republic, they generally drew on the conclusions of such scholars as Bartolomeo Cecchetti, who, in an essay published in 1886, tended to deny women a history of their own, holding that they could distinguish themselves only by their weakness, their beauty, or their missions as wives and mothers.[1] Pompeo Molmenti, in his *Storia di Venezia nella vita privata,* published at roughly the same time, more or less shared Cecchetti's perspective, though he did take a few renowned or notorious women into account. Indeed, Molmenti, who relied on a wide range of literary, archival, and iconographic sources, offered many useful details about the status of women in Venice from the origin to the fall of the Republic. Significantly, however, these details are scattered in his chapters devoted to family, worldly life and fashion, and the customs of the city and their corruption.[2] The position of women was not deemed worthy of much investigation. Nor, apparently, was it easy to deal with this subject without the strong moralistic bias typical of Cecchetti's and Molmenti's works. But a new era in the field was opened when the American scholar Stanley Chojnacki published an essay on Venetian women's history in 1974. Though he limited the scope of his research to the role of patrician women in family and interfamily relations during the Renaissance, Chojnacki's declared purpose was to confront "Cecchetti's view of Venetian women."[3] Further studies by Chojnacki and others followed. These works have proven decisive in reshaping our understanding of the social history of women in late medieval and early modern Venice. They have, however, tended to focus on the Renaissance and thus have tended to ignore the experience of women from the late sixteenth century down to the fall of the Republic. I wish to turn to this later period.

Not surprisingly, literacy played a significant role in the lives of women. We still know very little about the extent of schooling and literacy among the female population of early modern Venice.[4] Nonetheless, for the period we are considering (giving due attention to the fact that in the seventeenth century and even more in the eighteenth the habit of writing one's own will considerably decreased) the analysis of wills and other sources leads to a rather unexpected conclusion: some women of the lower classes and even servants were able to write, occasionally quite well. By contrast, many patrician ladies or women whose husbands were well educated had great difficulty in handling a pen or were even, by their own admission, simply unable to write. It would be extremely interesting to know what factors made patrician or *cittadino* fathers decide that teaching their daughters to write, or at least to make their signature on a document, was a profitable investment, chiefly, of course, in view of the marriage market. But this is very likely an unanswerable question.

Clearly, while many or most Venetian noblemen followed the custom of having their daughters educated in convents, even for patrician men of refined culture the literacy of their wives and daughters was not a matter of primary importance.[5] The careers of Cassandra Fedele and Elena Lucrezia Corner Piscopia, who in 1678 was the first woman to be granted a doctoral degree in Padua, give us reason to suspect that a father who encouraged his daughter's studies and gave her a good education was very likely motivated by ambition rather than by a sincere belief in the intellectual equality of men and women. Thus, those fathers, especially those of low social standing, who took the trouble to have their daughters taught how to write, were very open-minded indeed. By so doing, in fact, they invested women with a powerful weapon that could help them oppose men and fight for their rights. Abused wives, for instance, if they only could rely on some property of their own, at times used their holograph wills (i.e., wills they had written themselves) to punish their unworthy husbands. Doing without a notary was, after all, a guarantee of secrecy; besides, these pugnacious women liked to affirm that such wills, written out in their own hand, were no less valid than those drawn up "by a hundred notaries."[6] Some writing skill, in short, could be counted among those gifts that a father or another relative could add to a dowry. Perhaps it did not make a girl more desirable, but certainly it made her more self-reliant.

When a woman was taught to read, she was usually brought up on traditional devotional literature or on edifying books thought fit to improve her moral customs and her general behavior.[7] Fathers and husbands agreed on this point and joined in censuring such popular bestsellers as poems of chivalry and novels, which evidently were especially appealing to women.[8] Things began to change quickly in the eighteenth century, when women and not a few men came to consider some culture indispensable to ladies. In 1740 Giovanni Niccolò Bandiera, a Sienese priest, published anonymously in Venice his *Trattato degli studj delle donne,* in which he tried to prove that demanding studies were a woman's right and at the same time a duty to herself, to her father and husband, and to society in general. Upholding a thesis previously supported by several Venetian literati and by Erasmus, Bandiera considered learning a safeguard of women's morality as well.[9] Not just any sort of learning was healthy for women, though, according to Bandiera, who disapproved, for instance, of the prevailing fashion of studying French, so that the Italian language was marred with all sorts of Gallicisms, and of reading French books, which were in the best of cases useless and in the worst, harmful.[10] Not everyone agreed. At the beginning of the same year, 1740, a Venetian cittadino casually noted that his wife, Lucieta, was the owner of some "French books" and stipulated that she was to choose for herself a dozen more books, "excluding the Atlases," from his own library.[11] We do not know whether her father or her husband had helped Lucieta develop a taste for reading; nonetheless, it is easy to understand that this taste met with her husband's approval and that he was not in the least worried by those "French books" whose titles, regrettably, we do not know. If Lucieta was still living in the second half of the century, it is possible that she, like Caterina Dolfin Tron and other Venetian intellectual ladies, became an eager reader of forbidden works imbued with the spirit of the Enlightenment.[12]

In the sixteenth and seventeenth centuries a woman with a propensity for learning could find some opportunity for reading, studying, and even writing in a convent more easily than in her father's or her husband's house, though of course a nun's pen was expected to produce harmless and conventional devotional literature, not polemic, "feminist" treatises such as those that made Arcangela Tarabotti famous. Particularly in the seventeenth century, owing to dowry inflation and to the widespread practice of limiting the number of marriages, the convent became the fate of more and more girls, especially those from the upper classes. Life in the cloister did not necessarily imply unhappiness. Apart from real vocations, other factors could make life in the convent appealing. In addition to offering the possibility of improving one's learning, convent life was a shelter from the uncertainties of an arranged marriage with an unknown man. As a nun, a girl with a talent for business and administration could put it to good use, inside and outside the convent, no less satisfactorily than any married lady of good means.[13] An ambitious girl could hope to make a career and exercise a power that might be called political.[14] This means of self-fulfillment remained unknown to many women living outside the convent, where, it has been suggested, married ladies might try to reach this same goal in a much more "feminine" way, that is, through an exhibition of luxury in dress.[15]

But seventeenth-century wills generally confirm the view that entry into a convent was very often forced upon young women and was therefore a real tragedy not only for the young women who were so condemned but also for their parents. Parents made ruthless decisions for their children, often out of sheer economic necessity, though mothers did sometimes try to prevent their daughters from undergoing this life imprisonment.[16] Such was the case of Fiorenza Cappello, wife of Antonio Grimani di Zuanne, who in the early seventeenth century fought hard to save her nine-year-old daughter Chiara not only from a future life in a convent but also from being brainwashed—in the fashion so starkly described by Arcangela Tarabotti in her *Inferno monacale*—by the nuns in whose care Grimani had put her. "Let her be steady in her opinion, nor let herself be converted to their sanctimoniousness," Fiorenza urged, "let her keep her head and be resolute."[17] Mothers too, more than fathers, usually kept on trying, as they had since the fourteenth century, to offer their daughters the choice between three possible vocations: marriage, the cloister, and lay spinsterhood.

In the eighteenth century there was a decline in female claustration, though among the Venetian patriciate the percentage of young women taking the veil was probably still higher than in other European aristocracies. It is very likely that this meant a decline in forced claustration as well.[18] In any case the wills I examined no longer acquaint us with deeply troubled parents, often no less victims than the daughters they were about to sacrifice. Nor do we hear any longer echoes of the quarrels between husbands and wives about a daughter's state of life that had been so frequent in the previous century. No longer do we find so many mothers and grandmothers openly anxious to save their daughters and granddaughters from the convent.[19] And it had apparently become unusual for fathers to order their daughters to follow one life state rather than another.[20] The decline in the number of Venetian girls taking the veil could well have been related, though at present this cannot be ascertained, to an increase in the number of those who freely chose to remain virgins without retiring from the world.

Lay spinsterhood constituted another option for unmarried women. At this point we know little more about women who made this choice than what we can derive from their parents', or their own, dispositions by will. As Virginia Cox writes, "In a society that valued women primarily as breeding stock, the lives of these patrician spinsters have vanished almost without record."[21] Potentially liable to suspicion because they were not officially bound either to a man or to God, they were expected to spend their whole lives in the "invisibility" required of young girls. In his treatise *Modo di vivere proposto alle vergini che si chiaman dimesse* (1577), Agostino Valier, the bishop of Verona, clarified what was expected of lay spinsters: more than married women, more even than nuns, they were supposed to embody the "passive" virtues considered characteristic of their sex. Their role included tireless service to relatives without shrinking even from the humblest tasks, rejection of all sorts of vanity and luxury, steady self-control, and assiduous observance of their religious devotions.[22] Mothers and many fathers as well, especially in the seventeenth and eighteenth centuries, established a life annuity for their daughters destined to celibacy and entrusted them to the love and care of their brothers. Should cohabitation prove impossible, the spinsters were sometimes expected to retire to a convent or to some other "honorable place," spending the rest of their lives as boarders.[23]

Certainly very rare were the unmarried women who, like Corinna, a character in Moderata Fonte's dialogue *Il merito delle donne,* chose this way of life in order to express their personalities at their best in a patriarchal society. Especially in the sixteenth century the most immediate concern of these women far too often appears to have been their physical survival. Their wills tell sad tales of precarious lives in which they were exposed to all sorts of abuse by brothers or other unscrupulous relatives. Their role was often no higher than that of an unpaid servant or nurse.[24] Their fate was not different from that of nuns who had left the convents, provided they were lucky enough to avoid ending up as beggars or prostitutes.[25] Former nuns had lost their definite role in society, and unmarried women never had a definite role. Neither way of life was fully acceptable according to contemporary social standards. No wonder brothers or other relatives who were kind enough to shelter, feed, and clothe destitute single women expected their generosity to be somehow repaid.

Mothers were well aware of these drawbacks, from which married women were not necessarily spared. This is what was implied by Maria Donà di Zuanne, wife of Bortholamio Lippomano di Thomà, when she melancholically begged her daughter Lippamana, who was to spend her life with her brothers and sisters-in-law, "to suffer anything, as I myself have done," rather than leave her parents' house. Should she resolve herself to this, then she ought to go and stay "with any one of her sisters, either widows, or nuns, or married [i.e., endowed with a clearly defined status, exactly what would forever be denied to Lippamana] or with those who will show most loving kindness toward her, provided they be her brothers or sisters." The fact that Maria thought it prudent to see that Lippamana was able to remunerate the "loving kindness" of her siblings with a pecuniary reward tells us something about the precariousness of a lay spinster's situation.[26]

Lay spinsterhood was uncommon but by no means unknown before the sixteenth century; the same can be said for forced entry into a convent. The

1420 law that froze patrician dowries at 1,600 ducats made clear that the rise in dowries compelled patrician fathers not only to make their daughters enter convents but also to keep them at home "innuptas, cum rubore et periculo" (unmarried, in disgrace and danger).[27] Well into the sixteenth century several Venetians of the upper classes still held this opinion about the situation of the woman who could not or would not marry. In 1553 Tarsia, the widow of Piero Bembo *dottor,* who had not belonged to the nobility, was sure that her daughter Elena would "come to a bad end" if she neither married nor became a nun and therefore urgently entreated several patrician relatives to provide for the girl. In 1576 a patrician Bembo, Lorenzo di Andrea, dying of the plague, designated as his sole heir his sister Marietta. He urged her to marry quickly, "because, since she has no blood relatives who can help her and is unable to look after herself, there is no remedy other than this." We do not know whether Marietta's help-lessness was due to her youth or to other factors, though perhaps in Lorenzo's eyes this was the plight of all unmarried women, the single state being a sort of disease—a disease, we might add, against nature when it was not justified by a religious vocation—that could be healed only through the acquisition of a husband. At the end of the century, the nobleman Tommaso Morosini di Andrea, tackling the problem of what to do with his three daughters, declared himself able to marry Marina, whom a grandmother had benefited with an inheritance. He could "never believe" that any "need" would arise to marry Laura, but in this event he left his wife free to use her own dowry to this purpose if she wished (provided this would not mean damaging their seven sons) since he himself could grant Laura no more than the equivalent of a spiritual dowry. But Morosini clearly preferred that Laura become a nun, and as for his other daughter, Marietta, who was likely disabled, this was the only state of life he envisaged for her, though he did not discount the possibility that both Marietta and Laura might wish to "stay at home with their brothers." It is clear that this idea did not in the least appeal to him ("God forbid" and "I do not advise her to do so" were his comments on Marietta's and Laura's possible choice of lay celibacy), but he acknowledged that it was at least a tolerable option for a father with two or more daughters.[28]

Many Venetian fathers of all ranks shared Morosini's attitude. Thus, while mothers had supported this choice for centuries, many fathers too came to view lay spinsterhood as a reasonable option, though they usually considered it less desirable than the convent.[29] In 1525 Zuanne Barozzi di Giacomo wished his daughter Vienna to become a nun, but if she did not feel inclined to do so and wished to lead the life of a pizzochera at home instead, she would receive "victum et vestitum" (food and clothing). In 1573 Polo Correr di Zuanfran-cesco also intended his daughters, Franceschina and Contarina, to take the veil, but they might instead become pizzochere. Franceschina, more precisely, was required in this case to stay "as in a warehouse" in the very same monastery, San Girolamo, where she was already a boarder and where her father hoped she would spend her life as a nun.[30]

Pizzocharar, the word both Barozzi and Correr used to refer to lay spinster-hood, alludes to a parareligious state, that of a lay nun or tertiary. Although this was not always the case, since many women embraced this way of life without pronouncing any sort of vows, this term and the term *dimesse* no doubt proved reassuring for fathers and for society as a whole. By conferring on the single state a marked religious color, they implied that unmarried lay women were no longer to be feared for their potentially disruptive sexuality. Now such women were all assimilable to nuns, being, like nuns, chaste, humble, and selfless— exactly what pizzochere or dimesse were meant to be, and precisely the ideal that Bishop Valier held up for single women.[31] We can understand why fathers like Polo Correr felt even more reassured knowing that their unmarried daughters were not only practicing the virtues of nuns but living in a monastery as well, though without wearing a veil. But some fathers would go even further. In the early seventeenth century Alvise Loredan di Lorenzo declared that, having been prevented by his poverty from letting his seven daughters take the veil, notwithstanding their longing for a religious life, he had some-how put things right by renting a house where they could all live together. In short, he had established for them a sort of lay monastery, a surrogate of a real religious institution that would at the same time enable the girls to enjoy the benefits of family life without being obliged to live with their two brothers, which would perhaps have been an uncomfortable arrangement.[32]

In the seventeenth and eighteenth centuries fathers appear to have become more and more willing to support the option of secular spinsterhood for their daughters, often viewing it as a "vocation"; and in the eighteenth century this way of life seems to have become rather common.[33] This may have been the consequence of a greater willingness on the part of men, especially in the upper classes, to respect not only the choices but also the very persons of their daughters and, more generally speaking, of women in their families. Episodes of ill-treatment and exploitation of single women by their male relatives are less frequently reported, and it may be correct to argue that they had indeed become more exceptional. Of course there still is documentary evidence of tearful stories such as that of Angela Soranzo di Alvise, a poor, illiterate woman who, on the assumption that it would have been improper for her to live with strangers, had spent many years in the house of her uncle, Benetto Soranzo, resigning herself to acting as his servant and to handing over to him her only means of subsistence, the meager income to which she was entitled as the last of her lineage and the alms she received monthly from the Fraterna dei Poveri Vergognosi.[34] Undoubtedly the experience of one unmarried noblewoman, Vittoria Basadonna di Alvise, a wealthy and enterprising contemporary of Angela Soranzo who, owing to her business acumen, controlled her own and her family's property as well as that of Bernardo Gritti, the cousin in whose house she lived, was not representative, though in previous times as well owning some property could be an inducement for women to choose celibacy.[35] But it seems clear that in the final century of the Republic the life of single women was on the whole a little easier than before, owing somewhat to changes in the attitudes of men and to the larger number of charitable institutions available to women of good families. For poor and unmarried or widowed patrician and cittadino ladies, in particular, the Ca' di Dio, where the wretched Angela Soranzo also found at last a decorous and reliable shelter, had played a crucial role since the fourteenth century.[36]

In the eighteenth century it is not unusual to find unmarried patrician women clearly intolerant of the role to which age-old social and religious customs had consigned them. In the 1730s, for example, Contarina Trevisan was disinherited by her father for her disrespectful and threatening behavior to him and for her close friendship with an unworthy sister-in-law; and Caterina Pasqualigo, irreligious and adverse to marriage, was accused in 1773 of being a "public prostitute."[37] But noblewomen given to such patently disrespectful behaviors were by no means a novelty in the new cultural climate of the eighteenth century, with its weakening of religious feeling and of family ties and its emphasis on the rights of the individual. In the sixteenth century patrician status did not protect women from the possibility of drifting into prostitution.[38] In the early seventeenth century the patrician Zuanne Malipiero di Vettor ordered that his nephews or their heirs be disinherited if they married some "Venetian gentlewoman who was of no good fame, as it often is the case."[39] In wills women of high rank did sometimes mention their illegitimate children. It is difficult to say whether they had lost their virginity at an early age or at a relatively mature age, as young girls waiting to marry or enter the convent or as lay spinsters, though some of them eventually did get married, and not, or at least not always, to the fathers of their children.[40] What we know for certain is that young girls of good families did not always lead a cloistered life.[41] The noblewoman Bianca Cappello di Bartolomeo was only fifteen years old when she eloped with a young Florentine, a clerk in the Venetian branch of the Salviati bank, in 1563. Soon after the couple got married in Florence, Bianca became the mistress of the son of Cosimo I de' Medici, Francesco, whose legitimate wife she eventually became in 1578, thus ending her career as the grand duchess of Tuscany.[42] A much less famous but no less meaningful example of unconventionality and determination can be found in the story of strong-minded Cecilia Gabriel di Bertucci, who in 1559, after long vicissitudes, achieved the apparently unattainable goal of becoming the legitimate wife of a young converted Jew, already married and the father of two children.[43]

But for upper-class Venetian girls who dared to break the code of behavior society had devised for them—some were orphans and probably, as in the case of Cecilia Gabriel, not very strictly watched—such happy endings were not the rule. On the contrary, most of them appear to have been doomed to social alienation, claustration, or, in the best of cases, bleak marriages.[44] Single motherhood was also a source of anguish, at times leading women in this condition to long for their own death,[45] or it could destroy their self-esteem, as it probably did that of Sylvia Morosini, who in her will asked to be buried in the monastery of the repentant prostitutes, the Convertite, wearing their habit.[46] We should keep in mind that according to a law passed by the Senate in 1543, an unmarried woman—or a married woman separated from her husband—who had an affair with one or more men was condemned as a prostitute.[47]

It is not easy to determine whether children born out of wedlock were the issue of rape, of sexual intercourse under promise of marriage, of part-time prostitution, or of affairs into which patrician girls like Cecilia Gabriel could boldly launch of their own free will.[48] What we can rule out is any possibility that these single mothers, left to themselves, established steady relationships with their children's fathers and could therefore be said to belong to that intermediate state between the married and the unmarried woman, concubinage.[49] "A persistent phenomenon among the Venetian patriciate," concubinage did not meet with disapproval when, as was often the case, men of high standing chose as their concubines respectable women of good families and endowed with all those virtues that could be required of good wives.[50] Male partners might or might not cohabit with their companions, but between such couples mutual ties were still very close, and their offspring were usually lovingly cared and provided for. Nevertheless, between the sixteenth and the seventeenth century a change can be observed in the attitude of men involved in such relationships. In the earlier period they often sounded defiant in declaring that whatever the opinion of the church authorities, they considered their partners in every respect their wives.[51] Later on, as Tridentine precepts on marriage took root, the irregularity of these bonds was openly and meekly acknowledged. Sometimes the men, who very often belonged to the patriciate, eventually found suitable husbands for their companions. At other times— perhaps more frequently since the seventeenth century, when "patricians came under increasing pressure from the church to marry their concubines"—they ended in fact by marrying them themselves. Often they did so as a sort of reward and to ease their consciences after having for a long time benefited from the selfless assistance of their women, and usually the marriages were secret.[52]

A dramatic increase in the number of secret and, to a lesser degree, clandestine marriages, especially within the patriciate, is in fact a typical feature of seventeenth- and, even more, eighteenth-century Venetian society.[53] This suggests that, more than in the past, male partners, though unable or not wishing to have their marriages registered at the Avogaria di Comun, felt motivated to confer on their irregular relationships some sort of official character, granting the women they loved something like the status of married ladies. It seems, in fact, that many of those patricians who in the two last centuries of the Republic married nonpatrician women were driven by passion rather than by a desire for monetary gain.[54] Women too, by all appearances, had become much bolder and more demanding. In the sixteenth century it very likely came as a matter of fact to women like Gratiosa and Hortensia—the concubines of Alvise Bembo di Gaspare and of Francesco Falier di Marc'Antonio, and the mothers of their children—quietly to relinquish any hope of ever becoming the legitimate wives of their patrician partners, who in the past had indeed, sincerely perhaps, promised to marry them.[55] When Lorenzo Cappello di Silvan, inspired, as he said, by God or, more likely, compelled by his poor health, decided to give up living in sin with Pasqua, the mother of his little daughter, she became a nurse for her former lover, looking after him with a submissive devotion certainly made more fervent by her illiteracy, as well as by the hope that her partner would not forget her in his will.[56]

Pasqua, we may infer, simply had no idea that Cappello could have just as easily escaped from this sin by secretly marrying her. More accomplished women, such as Falier's Hortensia, may well have known of such an option, but at a time when sensitivity to family honor was still exceedingly strong within the patriciate, perhaps they dared not even as much as raise the subject with their partners. Of course, it should not be assumed that toward the end of the Republic women were no longer ready to spend their lives at men's sides in such obscure and subdued ways. But more and more women, nobles as well as commoners, preferred to try to arrange secret or clandestine marriages with their patrician lovers, who for their part lent themselves willingly to this resolution. They were, after all, often youths whom the cultural climate of the Enlightenment had made eager to assert their right to a freely chosen love, encouraging them as well to rebel against their fathers' authority and the conventions of society. Though most of these acts of rebellion were doomed to failure, girls so compromised were less willing than before to have the matter settled by accepting the veil or by marriage to some amenable stranger. Among them were women of character such as Teresa Vedova, who in the second half of the eighteenth century fought hard, albeit in vain, to have her marriage to Vettore Pisani di Girolamo dal Banco, by whom she had had a child, ratified by state and church authorities.[57]

A marriage not in conformity with rules, without the interference of families, was apparently the only way open to young people of high rank longing for a love match, and, as we have seen, it was very risky. On this matter, the age of Enlightenment had brought no significant innovations. It is true that even for patricians it had now become almost the rule to declare their daughters free to follow the way of life to which they felt inclined—as, after all, they had not seldom done in previous times. But apart from the impossibility of verifying to what extent such freedom could actually be exercised, a girl destined to marriage had little or no say in the choice of her husband. On the contrary, she was generally completely dependent on the approval of her parents or their executors. In 1554 Hieronymo Regazzola, a notary at the Avogaria, expected his only daughter, seven-year-old Symphorosa, if she was still unmarried at the time of his death, to accept as her husband whomever her mother and elder brother designated for her, "with that dowry they will give you, which I am sure shall be suitable to our condition and means."[58] Most cittadino and patrician fathers, and mothers as well, followed this pattern to the end of the Republic. In 1776 Barbara Contarini Querini obliged her daughter Alba to marry Lorenzo Morosini di Zorzi. Ten years later, in spite of his own very unconventional past behavior, Piero Marcello di Piero forced his daughter Maria into a marriage she abhorred. Indeed, if the eighteenth century witnessed a decrease in forced claustrations, it is not clear that the number of forced marriages decreased. What freedom of choice may have been granted was nonetheless granted within the boundaries of the patriciate.[59] In this class arranged marriages were more or less the rule, as such unions were not meant to satisfy the sentimental needs of individuals but, rather, to fulfil a duty toward the family. A marriage could be considered "happy," and a couple well matched, insofar as husband and wife cooperated in pursuing this aim.[60] But in this matter too it would be inappropriate to generalize. Wills do indeed suggest that marriages blessed by a tender affection, sometimes surprisingly close to the modern concept of love, may have been as frequent as those made bitter by mutual indifference or even hatred.[61]

A noblewoman whose real, violent passion for her husband was frustrated and embittered by his cold-heartedness and shameless infidelity was Fiorenza Cappello Grimani, the lady who had fought against her little daughter's claustration. When cohabitation with Antonio Grimani proved impossible, Fiorenza eventually left him, seeking refuge in her parents' house. She died soon afterwards, leaving her husband to face the terrible charge of having caused her death with his harsh, unfeeling behavior to her. We are left to wonder whether, had she lived, she would have asked for a separation. Certainly such an option was available to wives who could prove their husbands' cruelty, though in Fiorenza's time "it was probably more difficult for a noblewoman than a commoner to dissolve the marriage."[62] Since divorce was inadmissible in a Catholic state, the "dissolution of marriage" needed to be understood either as a separation, which did not grant the partners the right to a legitimate second union, or as a declaration by church authorities that the marriage was invalid, that is, nonexistent.[63] The novelty of the eighteenth century is that the number of instances of both forms of dissolution of marriage increased remarkably within the patriciate, mainly in the last decades of the Republic, to the point that in 1782 the Council of Ten became concerned and six years later issued a law aimed at regulating dissolutions.[64] Remarkably, it was mostly women who took the initiative of applying for a "divorce," in many cases putting forward the argument of "lack of free consent."[65] It is no less remarkable that their aim was not always simply to break off a marriage that had grown unendurable or, in those cases when they could be granted a religious annulment, to make official their relationship with some longtime lover. Some ladies simply wished to rid themselves of all ties and lead as free a life as possible.[66] Their lives were much freer than the sort of life married women could lead even in a patrician society as tolerant as that of late-eighteenth-century Venice, where Caterina Dolfin and Contarina Barbarigo, to cite two well-known examples, initiated their affairs with Andrea Tron and Andrea Memmo long before their marriages were annulled.[67]

Venetian noblewomen's practice of adultery cannot, of course, be considered a novelty encouraged by the uninhibited climate of the Enlightenment.

Such cases are documented in former times as well, though rarely, owing also to the stricter control exercised over women by family and society.[68] But only in the eighteenth century did these sorts of irregular situations recur with frequency and meet with relative indulgence from society. This state of things is undoubtedly indicative of a waning of self-awareness among patrician families, which was at the time a widespread but not a global phenomenon. In confirmation of this one could quote some instances in wills of a close identification of patrician or cittadino wives with their husbands' lineages.[69] A similar attitude is reflected in the stern testamentary instructions of noblewomen who warned their sons or grandsons whom family strategies had excluded from marriage not to disobey and get married "without the necessity of safeguarding the lineage, but out of mere personal satisfaction and whim."[70] They urged them not to commit themselves, that is, to marriages that were not necessary for the survival of families and possibly—if they were rich—even harmful to their interests, since such marriages often led to a subdivision of the family estate.[71] This does not mean, of course, that this age lacked instances of the "greater flexibility in their family and kinship orientation" that Stanley Chojnacki has observed in the wills of fifteenth-century patrician women, who were especially generous to daughters, granddaughters, nieces, and other female relatives.[72] Such flexibility was, indeed, a constant factor in the behavior of Venetian testatrices; evidence for it can be found to the end of the Republic.

Since the Middle Ages Venetian laws had granted women ample freedom of action.[73] In everyday life, however, it was not always easy for them to vindicate their rights. But in the seventeenth and eighteenth centuries women's independence may have enjoyed greater respect, for we find fewer examples from these centuries than from the sixteenth of women complaining of having been forced to make their wills according to the wishes of their male natal or marital kin. On the other hand, married women of all social classes who practiced that virtue which was the peculiar ornament of their sex—"prudence," which meant being wise managers and good housekeepers, always mindful of the well-being of their spouses, their children, and any other relative who needed care—still exercised the "power of love" that Chojnacki saw as typical of patrician marriage since the fourteenth century.[74] From noblemen to cittadini—a class that, from this and other points of view, aimed more and more at modeling its way of life on that of patricians—to popolani, down to the lowest craftsman, countless husbands expressed esteem and a sincere though perhaps not always warm fondness for their wives. Moreover, they showed great appreciation for their spouses' financial contributions to the family's well-being. Besides designating them in their wills "donna e madonna," with a right to the usufruct of the property and full authority over their children, husbands often left their wives their full dowries. Like the boatman Zuanne Barotto, who owed to his wife's dowry everything in their house and his own gondola as well, they did not hesitate under these circumstances to acknowledge that their wives' dowries and their good management of family property had been the financial salvation of their household; and they did not fail to remind their children of this everlasting debt of gratitude to their mother.[75]

It was mainly husbands who belonged to the upper classes who urged their wives, or rather insistently begged them, not to ask for the restitution of their dowries and to keep living in widowhood together with their offspring. The many children of Tommaso Morosini di Andrea, for instance, would be "ruined" should their mother, Agnesina, ask for the payment of her dowry once she was widowed; the whole property of Girolamo Molin di Bernardo could not repay the dowry of his wife Cornelia Formento, to whom most of the house furniture belonged as well, and for this their three daughters were obligated to esteem and obey their mother. The sons of Zuane Badoer di Giustinian were urged to be obedient to their mother Marietta "so that she may not have any reason for getting married, or having her dowry paid, which would greatly damage them and our whole house," and Marietta was entreated to be patient and forbearing in light of the boys' young age and "youthful ardor."[76] Nonetheless, even when a wife brought a rich dowry, her power could be much weaker if her husband was well off and his feeling for his wife was no more than lukewarm, as the conflictual relationship between Fiorenza Cappello and Antonio Grimani makes clear.[77]

Among the lower classes, the dowry could consist of the woman's work or whatever earnings she had been able to put aside. The nature of such work activities is seldom specified in wills. When it is, or when it is possible for us to guess, we see that in very many cases it was service, sometimes even abroad.[78] But it is known that Venetian women were active in many sectors of manufacture, especially textiles, and of trade, especially retail. They could be admitted to membership in the guilds, though apparently without any hope of rising to high ranks. It is also known that women's salaries were usually lower than men's.[79] Some women were schoolteachers or governesses (such, I believe, was the office of the "mistra de le pute" mentioned in many noblewomen's wills).[80] This was the most "intellectual" among professions in which ordinary women could make a living. At the same time, few women of letters had other means of subsistence than their literary production. And painting—which had made

Ottavia Robusti, "Tintoretta," renowned in the seventeenth century and Rosalba Carriera famous in the eighteenth—was considered a craft. Beginning in the sixteenth century women could make a name for themselves by pursuing a musical career. This was sometimes the case with the *figlie del coro,* orphan girls trained to play and sing in the four *ospedali grandi* of Venice. For some this became a real profession, and they spent their whole lives in the institution, in later years as teachers to younger inmates.[81] When opera became popular there was a great demand for *virtuose* (professional singers)—in the sixteenth century often identified, or identifiable, as courtesans—who could thus acquire wealth and fame. The same can be said of actresses once female roles on the stage began to be played by women.[82] Some, like the highly gifted and accomplished Vincenza Armani or Isabella Canali Andreini, could win everyone's favor "for their intelligence and culture as well as their acting abilities," thus embodying a new public role that may well have awakened the self-awareness of their female contemporaries.[83]

What is striking about many female wills of the seventeenth and eighteenth centuries is the pride women took in declaring that everything they owned or everything they had brought their husbands as dowries was the fruit of their own work and that they were not in the least obliged to account for it. Thanks to their earnings, some of these working women were enabled—and obliged at the same time—to play a patriarchal role, dowering daughters, sisters, and nieces, sometimes supporting their whole family, including their own husbands. For example, Antonia, the daughter of the joiner Biasio, a single woman, brought up two orphaned nieces; she married one off and in her will declared the other the sole heir to the property she had acquired through her work. Similarly, Prudentia Pellicciòli, widow of Lorenzo Grigis, could thank, not her son, but herself and four of her daughters—who worked as schoolmistresses—if she succeeded in marrying off her other daughter, Santa. Madalena Talassi, who had received no dowry from her father or from any of his relatives and had been left a penniless widow by the shoemaker Vicenzo Carocher, had slaved in order to bring up her two surviving children, eventually succeeding in getting her daughter married with a dowry of 350 ducats.[84] In fact, Venetian sources do not offer many examples of widows forsaken or exploited by relatives, as far too often happened to unmarried women. No doubt there were such cases; certainly not all resourceless widows had such loving brothers as Regina Balbi, sister of the haberdasher Zaccaria, who had dowered her at the time of her first marriage, helped her at the time of her second marriage, and given her shelter in his house, maintaining her, in her widowhood. But it is much more common to meet mettlesome and enterprising widows, ready to undergo all sorts of hardships to make a living rather than appeal to their relatives for support.[85]

Some women did leave bequests to their daughters or granddaughters in which they explained that the girls' brothers, "being men," could easily earn their living, thus implying that such an opportunity was beyond the reach of girls.[86] Other women, however, took care to state that their daughters had been able to put something aside thanks to their industriousness and warned their sons not to lay hands on their sisters' honest profits. In theory, for girls and women of the higher classes work was conceivable only as an elegant pastime.[87] Nonetheless, it is noteworthy that these young working women did not always belong to the lowest strata of society.[88] Even noblewomen, though no doubt only those belonging to families of limited means, sometimes worked for a salary.[89]

Witchcraft—which was never the object of mass persecutions in Venice that it was elsewhere in Italy and in the Venetian territory itself—could also be considered a career option, often coupled with petty prostitution.[90] Although the life story of Veronica Franco, who in 1580 was accused of various crimes, including sorcery, shows that courtesans too—*courtesan* being the epithet of the so-called *meretrix honesta,* one who distinguished herself from the common prostitute by her good manners and refined education—could be liable to this charge. Prostitution, a phenomenon that won Venice a wide fame (or notoriety) for sexual freedom in early modern Europe, was a profession usually taken up out of need, in many cases just another consequence of dowry inflation, although some courtesans, like Veronica Franco, did have a husband. Veronica was keenly conscious of the economic and social grounds of prostitution. Strongly disapproving of those mothers who, like her own, initiated their daughters into this trade, she advised daughters to resort to public institutions such as the Zitelle, which received girls imperiled by being both beautiful and poor, and the Convertite. In 1577 she urged the foundation of a new establishment for women who did not meet the requirements for admission to either of the two existing ones. Indeed, it was for this purpose that the Pia Casa del Soccorso was founded in that same year.[91]

In the seventeenth and eighteenth centuries both witchcraft and prostitution often were practiced by two or more women living under the same roof. Another remarkable aspect of feminine behavior in this period was the increased frequency of documented cases of fellowship or "sisterhood," though mostly of a quite harmless and often commendable character. In 1719, for instance, two eighty-year-old friends who since their youth had been living together as sisters, sharing the profits of their work, dictated with the same words two wills declaring each other sole heir.[92] Frequent and strong expressions of fondness for women in no way related to them can be also found in many wills of married and well-off ladies; but this increase in "sisterly" friendship and solidarity must have been a great support particularly for the most vulnerable women—those who were single and destitute—and thus must have helped to make lay spinsterhood a more acceptable and safer option than it had been in the past. Institutions such as Ca' di Dio or Pietà saw the growth of warm relationships between inmates, the older ones sometimes adopting the younger as *figlie d'anima* (spiritual daughters).[93] Women could, therefore, seek and find emotional, spiritual, and financial support beyond their family circle, and without a male presence if necessary.

Besides forming friendships among their peers, Venetian women actively practiced patronage toward lower-class persons, especially if they belonged to their own sex. Over the centuries, no significant changes can be remarked in the picture outlined for the fourteenth century by Dennis Romano.[94] For noblewomen, participating in the management and sometimes even in the foundation of charitable institutions was undoubtedly one of the most fulfilling forms of patronage since it enabled their charity to reach far beyond the boundaries of the traditional realms of women, house and parish.[95] Within the private sphere, ladies would show special concern for deserving female servants, especially if they had worked in the household for a long time. Mistresses very often settled on them a life annuity or, in the case of unmarried or widowed servants, provided for them to be sheltered and supported by their heirs for their whole lifetime, even when they were no longer able to work. Nor were the servants' daughters, nieces, or granddaughters forgotten. Servants, in their turn, often expressed their thankfulness to good masters, naming them their executors and often leaving them legacies, which might include valuables. This behavior too had deep roots in Venetian society.[96] Bonds between masters and servants were at times made even stronger by the widespread custom of well-off families' taking on young people without means of support and bringing them up under their roofs in an ill-defined position between that of an adopted child and that of a servant.[97] Besides being generous to their masters and to their own relatives, if they had any, women servants imitated their mistresses in practicing patronage if they had the means for it, benefiting their colleagues or some needy women of the neighborhood.

Servants and, generally speaking, all lower-class women without families of their own found great solace and assurance in belonging to the "artificial family" formed by a *scuola*—a *scuola piccola,* of course, since women were denied membership in the *scuole grandi.*[98] Seventeenth- and eighteenth-century wills prove the strong attachment women felt for these institutions, to the point that they sought affiliation to more than one of them or even left directions for their posthumous enrollment.[99] But on the whole in Venetian society, at least until the partial changes brought by the circulation of the doctrines of the Enlightenment, "the individual found identity as part of a group . . . rather than as an independent being."[100] This explains why patrician women too relied on the scuole, from a spiritual if not from a material point of view. In 1721 a noblewoman demanded that the three scuole to which she belonged be informed of her death in good time so that masses would be said for her soul even if her husband and sons were too busy with their service to the state.[101]

These forms of devotions inevitably raise questions about the piety and the spiritual life of Venetian women in the final three centuries of the Republic, a subject that is closely connected to the issue of the cultural training of women. As we have seen, in the sixteenth and seventeenth centuries it was mostly a very elementary and conventional training, based mainly on prayer books and devotional literature—books which, as wills show, owners usually cherished for a lifetime. Fathers and husbands approved of this reading, which helped strengthen their womenfolk in those "passive" virtues recommended to the female sex by preachers and treatise writers.[102] No one, incidentally, seemed to think it a contradiction that women were expected to practice such virtues within dwellings frequently embellished with pictures depicting the likes of Judith or Delilah, Cleopatra or Semiramis or other far from passive heroines of the past, or such unruly daughters as Bianca Cappello.[103] It is significant also that not only skill in reading and writing but a taste for them as well could often be found among prostitutes, women who, as we know, usually also mastered magic—a double "power over words," which made them awful figures, endowed with a "power in the world and over men" that was openly subversive of the traditional, submissive image of the female role.[104]

In the sixteenth century submission was required of women also by men who belonged to that small but pugnacious minority of Venetian sympathizers for Protestantism, who, like their Catholic counterparts or even more, expected their wives and daughters to conform to their religious opinions.[105] In such cases they might be disappointed, since Catholic women were often ready to react against men's pretensions and to refuse to have their consciences controlled by them; confessors, made strong by an authority that in matters of faith was above that of husbands and fathers, turned out to be invaluable allies in these battles. Although we do not know of contrary cases, that is, of heterodox women openly opposing their Catholic husbands, we do know of heretical couples in which the female partner appears to have been the leader. Such were the cases of Zuanne, a silk weaver, and his wife, Franceschina (who did most of her proselytizing in the company of other women), and of Francesco, a tailor, and his wife, Caterina.[106] Whereas on the Venetian mainland, in Istria, or in other Italian states women of all classes, including not a few noblewomen, were actively involved in the propagation of new religious ideas, in Venice such activities seem to have been limited to popolano women.[107] The religious position of women of high rank, and especially of the patriciate, appears to have been much less definite and generally marked by conventionality: religion continued to be a means of self-effacement, rather than of self-assertion, for women.

For the seventeenth century, documented cases of Venetian women espousing Protestant doctrines are extremely rare, limited mainly to women of foreign origin. More widespread are cases of women, who might also be from the lower classes and of limited education, falling under the spell of a body of ideas, at the time highly fashionable, known as libertinism. In some cases this was the consequence of a state of despondency that led them to deny the omnipotence of God; in other cases it was an excuse for leading a life free from moral restrictions.[108] But the most frequent instances of religious deviance among women are offered by those magical-superstitious practices that often were among a prostitute's professional skills, though they were by no means limited to this sphere. Another crime that flourished in the seventeenth century and that, like magic, enabled its perpetrators to acquire a form of power was the pretense of holiness. In the Venetian territory it was mostly the prerogative of lay and unmarried women who had little education and were of humble social position, who nevertheless—like Cecilia Ferrazzi, heroine of a case that was much talked about in and outside Venice—knew how to find devotees and supporters among high-ranking persons and churchmen, by whom they succeeded in having themselves acknowledged and venerated as "living saints," thus sidestepping the church hierarchy, which after the Council of Trent had tried to enforce strict order on such a delicate matter as discernment of holiness.[109]

Most Venetian women, like their male counterparts, kept faith with the city's age-old Catholic tradition. Seventeenth- and early-eighteenth-century Catholicism, though, was marked by a certain uneasiness and anguish, by a fear of death and the terror of the afterlife, and therefore it easily degenerated into superstition. Objects invested with some sort of power by the church, such as holy oil or water, blessed candles, and consecrated hosts, were much coveted by women practicing magic, especially love magic. Prayers too could serve this purpose, and it was no accident that one of the most popular heavenly intercessors to whom votaries—both men and, even more, women—turned in order to receive help was the miracle worker Saint Anthony.[110] The Madonna, halfway between a powerful patroness and a close friend or relative, was honored by women, who offered or bequeathed their best clothes and most precious jewels as gifts to her statues.

Far from opposing it, the political authorities encouraged popular piety, but they kept an eye on its manifestations, ready to intervene, sometimes harshly, whenever devotion led to dissent, even if implicit, against the government's political choices.[111] The noblewoman Arcanzola da Ponte learned this lesson well when, in spite of her patrician blood and advanced age, she was condemned in early 1607 to spend nearly a month in a "dark prison" for expressing too much affection for the Jesuits and probably for being too outspoken in criticizing the Venetian resistance to the Holy See during the interdict crisis of 1607.[112] In cases like Arcanzola's or that of a woman whose will made plain her wish that her beloved Jesuits might soon return to Venice, we can recognize instances of those very rare occasions in which Venetian women felt themselves driven to pass some sort of critical judgment on the government's decisions.[113] Another, quite exceptional case is the bitterly sarcastic dedication "to the Most Serene Venetian Republic" that opens Arcangela Tarabotti's *Inferno monacale*.[114] These isolated episodes of female dissent, not against a husband or father, but against the collectivity of husbands and fathers that constituted the government of the Serenissima, certainly originated not from a direct female involvement in political questions—for which we can find clues only in the following century—but, rather, from the shared existential experiences these women personally endured.[115] Women could not profess full loyalty to a state that, in the name of its own interests, did not hesitate to deprive them arbitrarily of basic freedoms, such as the choice of one's spiritual director or of one's state of life, thus violating the very dictates of Catholicism and jeopardizing not only the worldly happiness but even the everlasting salvation of its female subjects.

The religious indifference, or at least the weaker religious passion, and sometimes the religious unconventionality of the eighteenth century would lead women to defy the state's authorities in other fields in incomparably more open and more straightforward ways.[116] The most innovative forms of that female assertiveness, of which the century would offer so many instances, were no longer in the traditional language of religion, whether orthodox or hetero-dox, or of magic but in the quite modern language of feelings, inclinations, and personal tastes. The lives of such strong personalities as Caterina Dolfin or Caterina Sagredo and her daughter Contarina Barbarigo illustrate that in this period Venetian noblewomen opposed the government establishment not only by openly challenging it in their personal lives (their liaisons) but even more by their unconventional cultural choices and their irrepressible wanderlust—a re-versal of the time-honored Venetian custom that closely connected a woman's good reputation with her living a secluded life.[117]

Limited, as it was, to circles that were socially, economically, or culturally privileged, this new type of self-confident woman was uninhibited in claiming for herself the right to make her own choices. She valued authenticity above the conventions of her society. In her magazine *La donna galante ed erudita,* published from 1786 to 1788, Gioseffa Cornoldi Caminer, though unable, or unwilling, to offer her readers really innovative proposals concerning the role of women in society, was resolute in condemning such bad habits as inactivity, frivolity, and opportunistic exhibitions of weakness on the part of women.[118] Such views now at least occasionally found sensitive interpreters among repre-sentatives of the male sex, which had been the target of so much criticism and complaint. This included Giovanni Antonio Dolfin, Caterina's much beloved father, who had cultivated his daughter's love for culture. Above all, however, he had trained her to build for herself what most fathers and husbands before him, and certainly not a few in his own time, would have thought a quality most dreaded in a woman: an independent mind.

NOTES

1. Bartolomeo Cecchetti, "La donna nel medioevo a Venezia," *Archivio Veneto* 31 (1886): 33–69, 307–49.

2. Pompeo Molmenti, *La storia di Venezia nella vita privata: Dalle origini alla caduta della Repubblica,* 3 vols., 7th ed. (1927–29; reprint, Trieste, 1973); the one-volume first edition was published in Turin in 1880.

3. Stanley Chojnacki, "Patrician Women in Early Renaissance Venice," *Studies in the Renaissance* 21 (1974): 176–203.

4. On literate and learned women, see Emilio Zanette, *Suor Arcangela monaca del Seicento veneziano* (Venice, 1960); Francesco L. Maschietto, *Elena Lucrezia Cornaro Piscopia (1646–1684), prima donna laureata nel mondo* (Padua, 1978); Ginevra Conti Odo-risio, *Donna e società nel Seicento: Lucrezia Marinelli e Arcangela Tarabotti* (Rome, 1979);

Patricia H. Labalme, "Venetian Women on Women: Three Early Modern Feminists," *Archivio Veneto*, 5th ser., 117 (1981): 81–109; Giorgio Busetto, "Copio (Coppio, Copia, Coppia) Sara (Sarra)," in *Dizionario biografico degli italiani*, vol. 28 (Rome, 1983), 582–84; Adriana Chemello, "La donna, il modello, l'immaginario: Moderata Fonte e Lucrezia Marinella," in *Nel cerchio della luna: Figure di donna in alcuni testi del XVI secolo*, ed. Marina Zancan (Venice, 1983), 95–170; idem, "Gioco e dissimulazione in Moderata Fonte," introduction to Moderata Fonte, *Il merito delle donne: Ove chiaramente si scuopre quanto siano elle degne e più perfette degli uomini*, ed. Adriana Chemello (Milan, 1988), ix–lxiii; Arcangela Tarabotti, *L' "Inferno monacale" di Arcangela Tarabotti*, ed. Francesca Medioli (Turin, 1990); Margaret L. King, *Women of the Renaissance* (Chicago, 1991), 198–201 on Cassandra Fedele, 194–218 for an overall survey on women of letters in the fourteenth- to sixteenth-century Veneto; Margaret F. Rosenthal, *The Honest Courtesan: Veronica Franco, Citizen and Writer in Sixteenth-Century Venice* (Chicago, 1992); Letizia Panizza, introduction to *Che le donne siano della spezie degli uomini*, by Arcangela Tarabotti (London, 1994), vii–xxx; Virginia Cox, "The Single Self: Feminist Thought and the Marriage Market in Early Modern Venice," *Renaissance Quarterly* 48 (1995): 513–81; Franco Pignatti, "Fedele (Fedeli), Cassandra," in *Dizionario biografico degli italiani*, vol. 45 (Rome, 1995), 566–68; Satya Datta, "La presenza di una coscienza femminista nella Venezia dei primi secoli dell'età moderna," *Studi Veneziani*, n.s., 32 (1996): 105–35; and Sandra Olivieri Secchi, "Libelli contro e a favore della donna a Venezia e in Romagna fra Rinascimento e barocco," in *Il libro in Romagna: Produzione, commercio e consumo dalla fine del secolo XV all'età contemporanea. Convegno di studi (Cesena, 23–25 marzo 1995)*, ed. Lorenzo Baldacchini and Anna Manfron (Florence, 1998), 285–325.

5. In the sixteenth century, for example, neither Marina Moro di Marc'Antonio nor Anzola Tagliapietra, second wife and daughter of Francesco Tagliapietra di Girolamo *dottor*, was able to make her signature (ASV, Avogaria di Comun, Contratti di Nozze, reg. 153/14, fol. 104v, 4 July 1584; reg. 155/16, fol. 162v, May 1574). Witness to Francesco's versatile cultural interests is borne by, together with other sources, his father's will (ASV, Notarile, Testamenti, busta 938, no. 455, 25 Feb. 1534). On female literacy, see Paul F. Grendler, *Schooling in Renaissance Italy: Literacy and Learning, 1300–1600* (Baltimore, 1989), 87–102; Ottavia Niccoli, *Introduzione a Rinascimento al femminile* (Bari, 1991), xv–xvii; Martine Sonnet, "A Daughter to Educate," in *A History of Women in the West*, ed. Georges Duby and Michelle Perot, vol. 3, *Renaissance and Enlightenment Paradoxes*, ed. Natalie Davis and Arlette Farge, trans. Arthur Goldhammer (Cambridge, Mass., 1992–94), esp. 128–31; Federica Ambrosini, " 'De mia man propia': Donna, scrittura e prassi testamentaria nella Venezia del Cinquecento," in *Non uno itinere: Studi storici offerti dagli allievi a Federico Seneca* (Venice, 1993), 33–54; Giovanna Paolin, *Lettere familiari della nobildonna veneziana Fiorenza Capello Grimani, 1592–1605* (Trieste, 1996), 6–8; Sandra Olivieri Secchi, " 'Quando mio padre suonava l'arpicordo . . .': Note sulla famiglia e il sentimento della famiglia nel Dominio veneziano e a Venezia tra Cinque e Seicento," in *Musica, scienza e idee nella Serenissima durante il Seicento: Atti del Convegno Internazionale di Studi, Venezia—Palazzo Giustinian Lolin, 13–15 dicembre 1993*, ed. Francesco Passadore and Franco Rossi (Venice, 1996), 13–41, esp. 30 and 33. On the custom

of placing daughters in convents, see Volker Hunecke, *Il patriziato veneziano alla fine della Repubblica, 1646–1797: Demografia, famiglia, ménage* (Rome, 1997), 357–60.

6. For example, Camilla Girardi, a *popolana,* was able to use a pen, certainly very incorrectly but assuredly enough to make it clear that "not a handkerchief" of her property should go to her husband Piero, guilty of having squandered her dowry, starved and beaten her, "given himself a good time with his whores, for which I will never never forgive him," and obliged her, two years earlier, to make her will according to his own interest (ASV, Notarile, Testamenti, busta 12, no. 45). Camilla's will was presented to the notary Antonio Alcherio on 15 May 1574. On cases such as Camilla's, see Ambrosini, "De mia man propia."

7. This widespread opinion concerning the edifying quality of devotional books found a spokesman in Lodovico Dolce (see Chemello, "La donna, il modello, l'immaginario," 100), although for Dolce such readings were preparatory to the Bible, the only means to reach that knowledge of Christ on which religion is founded and consequently the only religious book any Christian, man or woman, could not do without (see Ludovico Dolce, *Dialogo di messer Lodovico Dolce della institution delle donne* [Venice, 1560], 17r–19v).

8. See Federica Ambrosini, "Libri e lettrici in terra veneta nel sec. 16: Echi erasmiani e inclinazioni eterodosse," in *Erasmo, Venezia e la cultura padana nel '500: Atti del 19 Convegno Internationale di Studi Storici, Rovigo, 8–9 maggio, 1993,* ed. Achille Olivieri (Rovigo, 1995), 81. For this and for many other subjects dealt with in this essay, see also idem, "Penombre femminili," in *Storia di Venezia: Dalle origini alla caduta della Serenissima,* vol. 7, *Venezia barocca,* ed. Gino Benzoni and Gaetano Cozzi (Rome, 1997), 301–23. In the late sixteenth century, according to documentary evidence, very few ladies owned libraries, and extremely poor libraries at that (see Marino Zorzi, "La circolazione del libro a Venezia nel Cinquecento: Biblioteche private e pubbliche," *Ateneo Veneto* 170 [1990]: 121, 170, 171).

9. See, e.g., Giovanni Nicolò Doglioni, "Vita della Sig.ra Modesta Pozza nominata Moderata Fonte," in Fonte, *Il merito delle donne,* 9; and Dolce, *Dialogo,* 13r–17r. On the Erasmian point of view, see Ambrosini, "Libri e lettrici," 75.

10. Giovanni Niccolò Bandiera, *Trattato degli studj delle donne, in due parti diviso: Opera d'un accademico intronato, dedicata a Sua Eccellenza la N. D. Procuratessa Lisabetta Cornara Foscarini,* 2 vols. (Venice, 1740); on the advantage of women's learning, see esp. vol. 1, and on the fashion of Gallicizing, see 2:39–44. On Bandiera, see Giuliano Catoni, "Bandiera, Giovanni Niccola (G. Niccolò)," in *Dizionario biografico degli italiani,* vol. 5 (Rome, 1963), 686–88. On this and other such eighteenth-century treatises, see Bruno Brunelli, "La cultura della donna veneziana nel Settecento," *Archivio Veneto,* 5th ser., 62 (1932): 45–46; and Bruno Capaci, "Il ritratto allo specchio: Poesie di Caterina Dolfin Tron," *Studi Veneziani,* n.s., 25 (1993): 242–43.

11. ASV, Notarile, Testamenti, busta 1123, no. 18, 4 January 1739 *mv* (codicil of Antonio Altobello di Agustin).

12. See Madile Gambier, "Dolfin, Caterina," in *Dizionario biografico degli italiani,* vol. 40 (Rome, 1991), 465–69; Piero Del Negro, " 'Amato da tutta la Veneta Nobiltà':

Pietro Longhi e il patriziato veneziano," in *Pietro Longhi*, ed. Adriano Mariuz, Giuseppe Pavanello, and Giandomenico Romanelli (Milan, 1993), 232–33; and Bruno Capaci, "Il tavolino della dama: Lettere e letture di Caterina Dolfin Tron," *Studi Veneziani*, n.s., 31 (1996): 191–228.

13. In 1723 Camilla Giraffi Gervasoni appointed the noblewoman Elena Tiepolo, a nun in San Lorenzo who had always helped her in managing her business and also lent her money, to supervise her executor (ASV, Notarile, Testamenti, busta 315, no. 33, 5 Oct. 1723). For the significance of Venetian women's economic power in family and society since the Middle Ages, see Chojnacki, "Patrician Women in Early Renaissance Venice," 197–200.

14. Francesca Medioli, "Chiavi di lettura. 1. Arcangela Tarabotti e le monacazioni forzate," in Tarabotti, *L' "Inferno monacale" di Arcangela Tarabotti*, 111–35.

15. Stanley Chojnacki, "La posizione della donna a Venezia nel Cinquecento," in *Tiziano e Venezia: Convegno internazionale di studi, Venezia 1976* (Vicenza, 1980), 65–70; Cox, "The Single Self," 551–56.

16. On monastic life and forced claustration in early modern Venice, see Giovanna Paolin, *Lo spazio del silenzio: Monacazioni forzate, clausura e proposte di vita religiosa femminile nell'età moderna* (Pordenone, 1996).

17. See Paolin, *Lettere familiari*, esp. 56–60 (letters between Fiorenza and her aunt Laura Sanudo, who shared her niece's feelings, Mar. 1605); Fiorenza's dislike for the religious life is confirmed by her three wills (76–80). For the blandishments with which nuns tried to allure little girls, see Tarabotti, *L' "Inferno monacale" di Arcangela Tarabotti*, 31–32. Another mother who tried to oppose her daughter's claustration seems to have been the wife of Gabriel Emo di Piero (see his will in ASV, Notarile, Testamenti, busta 65, no. 123, 15 Oct. 1647, 4 Apr. and 4 Sept. 1649).

18. Hunecke, *Il patriziato veneziano*, 383.

19. Some ladies tried to extend their liberality even further: Cecilia Marendella, widow of Baldissera dal Cortivo, a cittadina, openly regretted being unable to bequeath a thousand ducats to each of her young female relatives in order to prevent their claustration (ASV, Notarile, Testamenti, busta 533, no. 323, 4 Dec. 1582).

20. See Hunecke, *Il patriziato veneziano*, 154–57.

21. Cox, "The Single Self," 544.

22. Ibid., 548–50.

23. See, e.g., ASV, Notarile, Testamenti, busta 1261, no. 852, 24 September 1573 (will of Polo Correr di Zanfrancesco); busta 1280, no. 48, 21 May 1688 (will of Cecilia Corner Bragadin); busta 1281, no. 146, 14 June 1705 (will of Marco Giustinian di Antonio); busta 1064, no. 52, 17 May 1721 (will of Cattarina Brevin Biave); and busta 315, no. 128, 11 September 1752 (will of Nicolò Panciera).

24. Gabriella Zarri, "Dalla profezia alla disciplina (1450–1650)," in *Donne e fede: Santità e vita religiosa in Italia*, ed. Lucetta Scaraffia and Gabriella Zarri (Bari, 1994), 213–15; Cox, "The Single Self," esp. 543–51 and 559–69. For the suspicion inevitably aroused by unmarried lay women, see King, *Women of the Renaissance*, 29–31; and Paolin, *Lo spazio del silenzio*, 18–19.

25. See, e.g., ASV, Notarile, Testamenti, busta 655, no. 532, 12 August 1554 (will of

Maria Donà di Alvise di Francesco); and busta 1256, no. 74, 7 January 1587 *mv* (will of Andrea Marcello di Alvise). Both Maria Donà and Paola Marcello, Andrea's sister, were former Augustinian nuns; Maria had left the monastery of Santa Caterina in 1549, and Paola had fled the monastery of Santa Lucia in 1551.

26. Ibid., busta 685, nos. 1297, 1352, 25 August 1586.

27. Cox, "The Single Self," 543–44; see also Guido Ruggiero, *The Boundaries of Eros: Sex Crime and Sexuality in Renaissance Venice* (New York, 1985), esp. 162–63. The percentage of unwilling nuns to be found in Venetian monasteries was probably rather low in the fifteenth century (Donald E. Queller and Thomas F. Madden, "Father of the Bride: Fathers, Daughters, and Dowries in Late Medieval and Early Renaissance Venice," *Renaissance Quarterly* 46 [1993]: 707–9) and in the fourteenth century as well (Dennis Romano, *Patricians and Popolani: The Social Foundations of the Venetian Renaissance State* [Baltimore, 1987], 54–55).

28. ASV, Notarile, Testamenti, busta 1254, no. 986, 22 July 1553 (will of Tarsia Bembo, bequeathing Elena four hundred ducats for marriage, two hundred for entering a convent); busta 1259, no. 616, 25 July 1576 (will of Lorenzo Bembo); busta 1246, no. 690, 29 July 1598 (will of Tommaso Morosini, stating that should more daughters be born, they would be provided for exactly as Marietta and Laura were).

29. In 1285 Maria, wife of Ranieri Migliani, thought it feasible for one of her daughters to "stare in mundo sine marito" (see Fernanda Sorelli, "La società," in *Storia di Venezia,* vol. 2, *L'età del comune,* ed. Giorgio Cracco and Gherardo Ortalli [Rome, 1995], 532).

30. ASV, Cancelleria Inferiore, Miscellanea Notai Diversi, Testamenti, busta 29, no. 2944, 23 March 1525 (will of Zuane Barozzi); ASV, Notarile, Testamenti, busta 1261, no. 852, 21 September 1573 (will of Polo Correr; both Franceschina and Contarina could even marry if they wished).

31. For female tertiaries, see Paolin, *Lo spazio del silenzio,* 43–45, 89–95, 109–12; for the use of the term *dimesse* in a broad sense, see Cox, "The Single Self," 548.

32. ASV, Notarile, Testamenti, busta 382, no. 24, 20 October 1609. In 1584 the printer Giovanni Giolito had drawn attention to the problem of women who, though called to celibacy, were nevertheless unable to enter a convent for lack of a dowry (see Cox, "The Single Self," 546–47).

33. ASV, Notarile, Testamenti, busta 303, no. 373, 19 October 1603 (will of Zuanne Balbi di Zuanne); busta 315, no. 129, 8 October 1749 (will of Nicoletto Grassi, owner of a boatyard). See also Hunecke, *Il patriziato veneziano,* 157.

34. ASV, Notarile, Testamenti, busta 800, register of wills published in 1730–48, fols. 363r–366r, 11 June 1746. Angela's family did not belong to the patriciate.

35. Such had been the choice of Leonora's wealthy maiden aunt in Moderata Fonte's *Il merito delle donne* (see Cox, "The Single Self," 568). On Vittoria Basadonna, see Orazio Vecchiato, "Giudici, patrizi, servitori in un 'giallo' della Venezia settecentesca: L'assassinio della nobildonna Vittoria Basadonna," *Studi Veneziani,* n.s., 8 [1984]: 221–90.

36. On the Ca' di Dio, see Franca Semi, *Gli "ospizi" di Venezia* (Venice, 1983), 87–95.

37. On Contarina Trevisan, see ASV, Notarile, Testamenti, busta 596, fols. 196r–205v, 1 April 1733–8 December 1736 (will of Polo Trevisan di David, exhibiting verbal violence by the embittered patrician, at that time more than eighty years old, against his daughter and daughter-in-law). On Caterina Pasqualigo, see Luca De Biase, *Amore di stato: Venezia, Settecento* (Palermo, 1992), 82.

38. Brian Pullan, *Rich and Poor in Renaissance Venice: The Social Institutions of a Catholic State, to 1620* (Oxford, 1971), 386–87; Cox, "The Single Self," 545–46.

39. ASV, Notarile, Testamenti, busta 324, no. 383, 2 August 1611.

40. Marina Rimondo di Hieronimo, wife of Antonio Pizzamano, before her marriage bore a daughter, Elena, by Vettor Gradenigo; Daria da Molin di Zan Alvise, wife of Maffio Dolfin, mentioned her "natural" daughter Paula in her will (ibid., busta 605, no. 155, 31 Oct. 1556, and busta 296, no. 182, 23 July 1565; apparently, neither husband belonged to the patriciate).

41. See also ASV, Avogaria di Comun, Processi di Nobiltà, busta 351/69, fasc. Tagliapietra, no. 2, 1591 (inquiry about the upbringing of Lucrezia, the natural daughter of patrician Domenego Bembo di Francesco and the wife of another patrician, Jacomo Tagliapietra di Zuanne); ASV, Notarile, Testamenti, busta 265, no. 56, 10 May 1686 (will of Elena Gionzi); and Cecilia Ferrazzi, *Autobiography of an Aspiring Saint, 1609–1664,* ed. and trans. Anne Jacobson Schutte (Chicago, 1996), 31–32. See also Giuseppe Trebbi, "La società veneziana," in *Storia di Venezia,* vol. 6, *Dal Rinascimento al Barocco,* ed. Gaetano Cozzi and Paolo Prodi (Rome, 1994), 157.

42. Gaspare De Caro, "Bianca Capello, Granduchessa di Toscana," in *Dizionario biografico degli italiani,* vol. 10 (Rome, 1968), 15–16. On this occasion the Senate of Venice declared Bianca an "adopted daughter" of the Republic, as it had done in the case of Caterina Corner, queen of Cyprus, in the previous century.

43. Pier Cesare Ioly Zorattini, ed., *Processi del S. Uffizio di Venezia contro ebrei e giudaizzanti, I, 1548–1560* (Florence, 1980), esp. 302–6.

44. In the early sixteenth century Dionora Tiepolo di Mattio, the mother of two daughters, was forced into claustration by her brother (Ambrosini, "De mia man propia," 45–46). Suordamor Zorzi di Mattio, an orphan, could rely only on her two sisters to care for the baby she was expecting by an unnamed man (ASV, Notarile, Testamenti, busta 710, no. 157, 19 Apr. 1561); see also Trebbi, "La società veneziana," 158.

45. Lucrezia Orio di Piero, pregnant by Piero Malipiero, by whom she had already had a daughter, was in such a state of mind when she dictated her will in the parlor of the convent of San Maffio di Murano (ASV, Notarile, Testamenti, busta 195, no. 708, 20 May 1554).

46. Ibid., busta 444, no. 128, 8 December 1597. Perhaps an illegitimate child herself, Sylvia, who styled herself, atypically, as the "daughter of the clarissima madonna Marina Morosini, widow of the late clarissimo signor Francesco Moresini," bequeathed a thousand ducats to "Selvagio, my son, called Fedrigo," whose father is not mentioned. Sylvia's mother, who was to inherit the bulk of her daughter's property, was probably Marina Bon di Nicolò, married in 1550 to Francesco Morosini di Bortolo dalla Sbarra (ASV, Marco Barbaro, "Arbori de' patritii veneti," vol. 5, p. 381; ASV, Giuseppe Giomo, "Matrimoni patrizi per nome di donna," indice 82 ter 1, 146). On

the Convertite, see Pullan, *Rich and Poor in Renaissance Venice*, 377–79; and Guido Ruggiero, *Binding Passions. Tales of Magic, Marriage, and Power at the End of the Renaissance* (New York, 1993), 52–53. No patrician women were to be found among the inmates of the Convertite. For the social aspect of Venetian female monasteries, see Volker Hunecke, "Kindbett oder Kloster: Lebenswege venezianischer Patrizierinnen im 17. und 18. Jahrhundert," *Geschichte und Gesellschaft* 18 (1992): 452–53.

47. ASV, Senato, Terra, reg. 32, fol. 125v, 21 February 1542 mv.

48. Before and even for some time after Trent, consummation of marriage was customary after the mutual promise between bride and groom (see Daniela Lombardi, "Fidanzamenti e matrimoni dal Concilio di Trento alle riforme settecentesche," in *Storia del matrimonio*, ed. Michela De Giorgio and Christiane Klapisch-Zuber [Bari, 1996], 215–27; for abuses in Venice, see Gaetano Cozzi, "Padri, figli e matrimoni clandestini," in *I vincoli familiari in Italia: Dal secolo XI al secolo XX*, ed. A. Manoukian [Bologna, 1983], 195–213, esp. 199–201, and Alfredo Viggiano, "Giustizia, disciplina e ordine pubblico," in *Storia di Venezia*, 6:847–48; for the late Middle Ages, see Ruggiero, *Boundaries of Eros*, esp. 16–69).

49. In his will, a nonpatrician merchant who had had an affair with a woman of noble or cittadino family left his two natural sons in the charge of his brother and his mother, stating that they should be treated as if they had been born of a legitimate marriage, but did not spend one word for their mother, the "magnifica madonna Isabella Contarini" (ASV, Notarile, Testamenti, busta 534, no. 735, 24 Feb. 1593 mv [will of Matthio Robazza]).

50. The quotation is from Alexander Cowan, "Patricians and Partners in Early Modern Venice," in *Medieval and Renaissance Venice: Studies in Honor of Donald E. Queller*, ed. Ellen E. Kittel and Thomas F. Madden (Urbana, 1999); see also Gabriele Martini, "La donna veneziana del '600 tra sessualità legittima ed illegittima: Alcune riflessioni sul concubinato," *Atti dell'Istituto Veneto di Scienze, Lettere ed Arti* 145 (1987): 301–39. Both Lucrezia Tagliapietra and her mother, Bettina Avanzago, the partner of Domenego Bembo ("of noble blood" and "a gentlewoman"), were highly esteemed by all those who knew them (see n. 41 above).

51. The patrician Marc'Antonio Loredan di Tommaso declared that whether "she be or be not" his wife, his partner, Anzola, should be considered his "dear wife"; and even though no religious marriage had taken place between the lawyer Aurelio Pocobello and the noblewoman Isabetta de Mezzo, he insisted that according to his conscience she was really his wife (ASV, Notarile, Testamenti, busta 126, no. 648, 17 Dec. 1552; ASV, Sant'Uffizio, Processi, busta 36, fasc. "Pocobello Aurelio," 1573).

52. In this way one Chiaretta Pantalea, for instance, had gained credit enough to be deemed worthy of becoming the wife of Scipion Donà di Giulio (see the patrician's will in ASV, Notarile, Testamenti, busta 161, no. 452, 19 Jan. 1612 mv). The marriage was a secret one; Scipion died legally unmarried (ASV, Marco Barbaro, "Arbori de' patritii veneti," vol. 3, p. 327. The quotation in the text is from Cowan, "Patricians and Partners in Early Modern Venice," 13).

53. On this increase in the number of secret and clandestine marriages within the patriciate, see Cozzi, "Padri, figli e matrimoni clandestini"; De Biase, *Amore di stato*,

31–40, 48–51; and Hunecke, *Il patriziato veneziano,* esp. 130–46. On the changes in the traditional pattern of the patrician family, see Renzo Derosas, "La crisi del patriziato come crisi del sistema familiare: I Foscarini ai Carmini nel secondo Settecento," in *Studi veneti offerti a Gaetano Cozzi* (Venice, 1992), 309–31.

54. Hunecke, *Il patriziato veneziano,* 167–69.

55. Alvise had not married Gratiosa "because of difficulties which now I cannot relate"; Francesco had taken the virginity of Hortensia, a lady "of good condition and fame," under a promise of marriage, which he was afterwards held from keeping by the respect he owed "to the blessed soul of my father, and to my own reputation" (ASV, Notarile, Testamenti, busta 784, no. 54, 14 Aug. 1579; busta 293, no. 41, 5 Nov. 1587).

56. Ibid., busta 1152, no. 404, 1 March 1598. Though he had no idea of marrying her, Lorenzo did indeed provide for Pasqua as if she were to be his widow, declaring her his executrix and "donna e madonna," with a right to the usufruct of his little property.

57. In 1758 Vettore and Teresa were united in a sort of clandestine marriage that in 1760 the patriarch's court definitely denied to be valid; as late as 1773 Teresa tried to prevent Vettore's marriage to a noblewoman. The most detailed account of the story can be found in Giuseppe Gullino, *I Pisani dal banco e moretta: Storia di due famiglie veneziane in età moderna e delle loro vicende patrimoniali tra 1705 e 1836* (Rome, 1984), 7–14.

58. ASV, Notarile, Testamenti, busta 1210, no. 615, 1 March 1554.

59. Hunecke, *Il patriziato veneziano,* 162–64. On Alba Querini, whose husband's name was actually Zorzi III Lorenzo, cf. Giomo, "Matrimoni patrizi per nome di donna," indice 82 ter 2, 279; and on Maria Marcello, see De Biase, *Amore di stato,* 70–72, 90–92, which deals with several other cases of young patricians of both sexes forced into marriage.

60. See Hunecke, *Il patriziato veneziano,* 164.

61. So "great" was the love between Lorenzo Sanudo di Francesco and his wife, Elena Pasqualigo, that they could not bear to spend "half a day far apart from each other"; according to all their relatives, what Loredana Marcello felt for her husband, Doge Alvise Mocenigo, was "not an ordinary, but rather an excessive, a most extraordinary love"; and Pisana Bembo was thankful for the long years she had spent with her husband, Zuanne Dolfin, whom she hoped would not die before her (ASV, Notarile, Testamenti, busta 1259, no. 628, 1 Sept. 1568 [will of Lorenzo Sanudo]; busta 1256, no. 12, 10 Nov. 1574 [codicil to will of Alvise Mocenigo]; busta 800, reg. for the years 1730–48, fol. 283v [will of Pisana Bembo Dolfin, presented to notary Giovanni Garzoni Paulini on 14 June 1715]. On Zuanne—properly, Daniel III Zuanne—di Daniel II Andrea Dolfin, of the San Pantalon branch, see Gino Benzoni, "Dolfin, Daniele," in *Dizionario biografico degli italiani,* 40:473–79). See also King, *Women of the Renaissance,* 36–37.

62. Joanne M. Ferraro, "The Power to Decide: Battered Wives in Early Modern Venice," *Renaissance Quarterly* 48 (1995): 492–512.

63. Oscar di Simplicio, *Peccato penitenza perdono: Siena, 1575–1800: La formazione della coscienza nell'Italia moderna* (Milan, 1994), 316–26.

64. Gaetano Cozzi, "Note e documenti sulla questione del 'divorzio' a Venezia (1782–1788)," *Annali dell'Istituto Storico Italo-Germanico in Trento* 7 (1981): 275–360.

65. Ibid., 309, 327, 357; Gambier, "Dolfin, Caterina," 466; De Biase, *Amore di stato,* 47–48, 72–73, 87–88; Hunecke, *Il patriziato veneziano,* 163, 190, 378–79.

66. Such was the case with Maria Marcello and Anna Bon, for example (see De Biase, *Amore di stato,* 74–75, 83–84).

67. Gambier, "Dolfin, Caterina," 465–66; Gian Franco Torcellan, "Barbarigo, Contarina," in *Dizionario biografico degli italiani,* vol. 6 (Rome, 1964), 61. See also De Biase, *Amore di stato,* 82–83; and Derosas, "La crisi del patriziato," 325.

68. For fourteenth- and fifteenth-century cases see Ruggiero, *Boundaries of Eros,* 55–56, 58–59, 62–63, 67–68. For the seventeenth century, see Martini, "La donna veneziana," 338.

69. See, e.g., ASV, Notarile, Testamenti, busta 315, no. 107, 11 April 1736 (will of Laura Pasqualigo, wife of Zaccaria Vendramin di Francesco dai Carmini), and no. 144, 19 February 1731 *mv* (will of Sebastian Steffani, whose wife, Cornelia Cavalli, had agreed that her entire dowry, 6,000 ducats, should be incorporated in his *fideicommissum*); and busta 1123, no. 50, 3 October 1754 (will of Chiara Valmarana, widow of Michiel Pisani di Ottavian da Santa Marina).

70. Ibid., busta 1123, no. 50, 3 October 1754 (will of Chiara Valmarana Pisani).

71. Hunecke, *Il patriziato veneziano,* esp. 194–96, 236–50. Many of these marriages were not registered at the Avogaria di Comun.

72. Stanley Chojnacki, " 'The Most Serious Duty': Motherhood, Gender, and Patrician Culture in Renaissance Venice," in *Refiguring Women: Perspectives on Gender and the Italian Renaissance,* ed. Marilyn Miegel and Juliana Schiesari (Ithaca, 1991), 144.

73. See Sorelli, "La società," 530.

74. Stanley Chojnacki, "The Power of Love: Wives and Husbands in Late Medieval Venice," in *Women and Power in the Middle Ages,* ed. Mary Erler and Maryanne Kowaleski (Athens, Ga., 1988), 126–48. For sixteenth-century instances of the "power of love" see Olivieri Secchi, "Quando mio padre suonava l'arpicordo," 35–39.

75. ASV, Notarile, Testamenti, busta 596, fols. 38r–39v, 14 December 1720.

76. Ibid., busta 1246, no. 690, 29 July 1598 (Tommaso Morosini); busta 1139, no. 148, 1 March 1642 (Girolamo Molin); busta 167, no. 177, 1 April 1670 (Zuane Badoer). On widows and their dowries see also Trebbi, "La società veneziana," 159–61.

77. See Paolin, *Lettere familiari*; and idem, *Lo spazio del silenzio,* 17, 148.

78. See ASV, Notarile, Testamenti, busta 315, no. 99, 8 April 1722: Zanetta Cuco, wife of Francesco Granelli, had been a servant "in Vienna, in Venice, and elsewhere."

79. See Richard T. Rapp, *Industry and Economic Decline in Seventeenth-Century Venice* (Cambridge, Mass., 1976), 27–29; Richard Mackenney, *Tradesmen and Traders: The World of the Guilds in Venice and Europe, c. 1250–c. 1650* (Totowa, N.J., 1987), 23, 88; idem, "The Guilds of Venice: State and Society in the *Longue Durée,*" *Studi Veneziani,* n.s., 34 (1997): 15–43 (on women, see 39–41); Dennis Romano, *Housecraft and Statecraft: Domestic Service in Renaissance Venice, 1400–1600* (Baltimore, 1996); Angela Groppi, "Lavoro e proprietà delle donne in età moderna," in *Il lavoro delle donne,* ed. Angela Groppi (Bari, 1996), 119–63; and Simona Laudani, "Mestieri di donne, mestieri di uomini: Le corporazioni in età moderna," ibid., 183–205.

80. See Gherardo Ortalli, *Scuole, maestri e istruzione di base tra Medioevo e Rinascimento: Il caso veneziano* (Vicenza, 1993), 69–70.

81. Ambrosini, "Penombre femminili," 311, 320.

82. Marinella Laini, *Vita musicale a Venezia durante la Repubblica: Istituzioni e mecenatismo* (Venice, 1993), 78–132; Beth L. Glixon, "Private Lives of Public Women: Prima Donnas in Mid-Seventeenth-Century Venice," *Music and Letters* 76 (1995): 509–31.

83. Labalme, "Venetian Women on Women," 106–9. On the two actresses see Ada Zapperi, "Armani, Vincenza," and Liliana Pannella, "Canali, Isabella," in *Dizionario biografico degli italiani,* vols. 4 (Rome, 1962), 221, and 17 (Rome, 1974), 704–5, respectively.

84. The wills of Antonia, Prudentia Grigis, and Madalena Carocher are in ASV, Notarile, Testamenti, busta 9, no. 29, 15 July 1660; busta 673, no. 264, 7 May 1692; and busta 596, fols. 117r–118v, 6 December 1727, respectively. See also ibid., busta 800, undated register, fols. 17r–19v, 12 May 1710 (will of Laura Caponi, widow Scarsini), and fols. 342r–343v, 10 May 1726 (will of Giacomina Colledan, "nicknamed hatter"); busta 596, fols. 26r–27v, 22 March 1718 (will of Camilla Zanardi, wife of Antonio Moro); busta 315, no. 99, 8 April 1722, and no. 127, 28 March 1727 (wills of Zanetta Cuco Granelli and Maria Castellan Meneguzi, both servants); and busta 1123, no. 8, 12 October 1738 (will of Anna Bolderini, probably a single mother).

85. For Regina Balbi, see ibid., busta 596, fols. 78r–79v, 20 August 1725. In Tuscany a young widow could be doomed to carry out servile works in her parents' house; for a 1686 case, see Giulia Calvi, *Il contratto morale: Madri e figli nella Toscana moderna* (Bari, 1994), 197–98.

86. See ASV, Notarile, Testamenti, busta 314, no. 44, 25 August 1580 (will of Isabetta, widow of Matthio de Fondris, a dyer); busta 314, no. 135, 5 April 1581 (will of Stella Dall'Acqua, widow of Vassili di Cesari); busta 1123, no. 42, 10 September 1734 (will of Cattarina Nordio, widow Lizzardi). See also the will of Eleonora Scafani, 4 May 1785, in Ernesto Garino, "Insidie familiari: Il retroscena della successione testamentaria a Venezia alla fine del XVIII secolo," in *Stato società e giustizia nella Repubblica veneta (sec. XV–XVIII),* ed. Gaetano Cozzi, vol. 2 (Rome, 1985), 314–15.

87. See King, *Women of the Renaissance,* 79–80; and Datta, "La presenza di una coscienza femminista," 115, 129.

88. ASV, Notarile, Testamenti, busta 140, no. 71, 10 August 1682 (will of Elena Fondra, widow of Paulo Nardani); see also busta 840, no. 6, 12 July 1612 (will of the cittadino Alessandro Cegia, directions regarding his niece Panthasilea).

89. Between 1470 and 1570 noblewomen were to be found among the silk winders active in Venice (Luca Molà, "Le donne nell'industria serica veneziana del Rinascimento" [paper presented at the conference "Dal baco al drappo; La seta in Italia tra Medioevo e Seicento," Venice, 13–15 November 1997]).

90. Sally Scully, "Marriage or a Career? Witchcraft As an Alternative in Seventeenth-Century Venice," *Journal of Social History* 28 (1995): 857–76. See also Ruth Martin, *Witchcraft and the Inquisition in Venice, 1550–1650* (Oxford, 1989); Ruggiero, *Binding Passions; Le cortigiane di Venezia dal Trecento al Settecento,* exh. cat. (Milan,

1990), esp. Madile Gambier, "La piccola prostituzione tra Sei e Settecento," 37–39; and Anne Jacobson Schutte, "Donne, inquisizione e pietà," in *La chiesa di Venezia nel Seicento,* ed. Bruno Bertoli (Venice, 1992), 235–51.

91. On prostitution in early modern Venice see Rosenthal, *The Honest Courtesan;* Paul Larivaille, *La vita quotidiana delle cortigiane nell'Italia del Rinascimento: A Roma e Venezia nei secoli XV e XVI* (Milan, 1989); and Ruggiero, *Binding Passions,* 24–56. On the Zitelle and the Soccorso, see Pullan, *Rich and Poor in Renaissance Venice,* 383–93.

92. ASV, Notarile, Testamenti, busta 596, fols. 30r–33v, 20 April 1719 (wills of Zanetta Tosoni and Cattarina Briatti). According to Chojnacki, "Patrician Women in Early Renaissance Venice," 181, bequests by women to friends were "rare exceptions" in the fifteenth century, and the same could be said for the sixteenth century (one late instance is offered by the will of the noblewoman Diana Lion Zane, who appointed as one of her executors her "dearest friend, whom I hold as a sister," Lodovica Milan [ASV, Notarile, Testamenti, busta 841, no. 271, 20 Nov. 1596]).

93. Some instances of such bonds of friendships and affection can be found in ASV, Notarile, Testamenti, such as busta 187, no. 354, 14 April 1679 (will of Laura Babini, *quondam* Giovanni Maria); busta 800, undated register, fols. 345v–347v, 26 March 1720 (will of Cattarina, widow Zambelli); busta 800, reg. for the years 1730–48, fols. 49v–51r, 1 October 1728 (will of Laura Grimani, *quondam* Giulio); and busta 800, 1730–1748, fols. 184v–185r, 24 September 1737 (will of Diamante Contarini Zorzi). On hospices, see Semi, *Gli "ospizi" di Venezia;* and Bernard Aikema and Dulcia Meijers, eds., *Nel regno dei poveri: Arte e storia dei grandi ospedali veneziani in età moderna, 1474–1797* (Venice, 1989).

94. Romano, *Patricians and Popolani,* 131–40. For a more general survey of this subject, see Lucia Ferrante, Maura Palazzi, and Gianna Pomata, eds., *Ragnatele di rapporti: Patronage e reti di relazione nella storia delle donne* (Turin, 1988).

95. See Pullan, *Rich and Poor in Renaissance Venice,* 385–86, 393–94.

96. Romano, *Housecraft and Statecraft,* 198–200, 204.

97. Anna Girardi was about four years old when she joined the household of Lucrezia Bernardi Righi as a servant; her mistress had always been so kind to her that Anna made her her executrix and heir (ASV, Notarile, Testamenti, busta 1123, no. 3, 7 Feb. 1713 *mv.* See also Romano, *Housecraft and Statecraft,* 99–100).

98. Brian Pullan, "Natura e carattere delle scuole," in *Le scuole di Venezia,* ed. Terisio Pignatti (Milan, 1981), 9–26.

99. ASV, Notarile, Testamenti, busta 840, no. 65, 21 March 1578 (will of Andriana Ascarelli Balbi).

100. Mackenney, *Tradesmen and Traders,* 51.

101. ASV, Notarile, Testamenti, busta 596, fols. 48r–49v, 20 November 1721 (will of Fontana Boldù, wife of Polo Trevisan di David, about whom see n. 37 above). On the central role of death and the cult of the dead in eighteenth-century popular devotion as practiced in Venetian parishes and scuole, see Antonio Niero, "Spiritualità dotta e popolare," in *La chiesa di Venezia nel Settecento,* ed. Bruno Bertoli (Venice, 1993), 127–57, 139–40.

102. King, *Women of the Renaissance,* 40–41.

103. See Francine Daenens, "Superiore perché inferiore: Il paradosso della superiorità della donna in alcuni trattati italiani del Cinquecento," in *Trasgressione tragica e norma domestica: Esemplari di tipologie femminili della letteratura europea*, ed. Vanna Gentili (Rome, 1983), 12. Pieces of information about paintings and their owners are to be found in ASV, Giudici di Petizion, Inventari. See also Cesare A. Levi, *Le collezioni veneziane d'arte e d'antichità dal secolo XIV ai nostri giorni*, vol. 2 (Venice, 1900); and Simona Savini Branca, *Il collezionismo veneziano nel '600* (Florence, 1965).

104. Ruggiero, *Binding Passions*, 44.

105. King, *Women of the Renaissance*, 37–38.

106. John Martin, "Out of the Shadow: Heretical and Catholic Women in Renaissance Venice," *Journal of Family History* 10 (1985): 21–33.

107. Susanna Peyronel Rambaldi, "Per una storia delle donne nella Riforma," introduction to *Donne della Riforma in Germania, in Italia e in Francia*, by Roland H. Bainton (Turin, 1992), 9–45. But William Monter, "Women and the Italian Inquisition," in *Women in the Middle Ages and the Renaissance: Literary and Historical Perspectives*, ed. Mary Beth Rose (Syracuse, N.Y., 1986), 76, remarks that everywhere in Italy "women comprised fewer than 5 per cent of suspected Protestants."

108. In 1625 Aurora Clario Gemma, the widow of a Venetian heretic who had settled in Cracow, was denounced, together with her second husband, Marco de Domo, as a "Lutheran" (ASV, Sant'Uffizio, busta 80, fasc. "De Domo Marco—Gemma Aurora"). Anzola Civran did not believe in hell, did not care for her soul, and led a disreputable life (ibid., busta 103, fasc. "Fugarola Lodovico," 1646). Faustina Cortesi had felt tempted by atheism; Venetian ladies given to irreligiousness, sacrilegious practices, and sorceries appear in Pellegrina Donà's written confession (ibid., busta 103, fasc. "Caravagio Salvatore," 1647). Lucrezia Millander, the Venetian widow of a German Protestant, herself a devout Calvinist, had to abjure in 1681 (ibid., busta 122, fasc. "15 februarii 1680. Contra Lucretiam Collosini Milander de Venetiis. De Heresi Calvinistarum Reformatorum. Expedita 1681"). The German-born Anna Maria Desmit, a Lutheran turned Catholic, was denounced to the Venetian Holy Office as a heretic (ibid., busta 126, fasc. "Fontanato Gio. Batta," 1692). These and other cases are discussed in Federica Ambrosini, "Between Heresy and Free Thought, between the Mediterranean and the North: Heterodox Women in 17th Century Venice," in *Mediterranean Urban Culture, 1400–1700*, ed. Alexander Cowan (Exeter, Eng., forthcoming). See also Giovanni Scarabello, "Paure, superstizioni, infamie," in *Storia della cultura veneta*, ed. Girolamo Arnaldi and Manlio Pastore Stocchi, 6 vols. (Vicenza, 1976–86), 4, pt. 2: 360–61.

109. See, among other works, Fulvio Tomizza, *Heavenly Supper: The Story of Maria Janis*, trans. Anne Jacobson Schutte (Chicago, 1991); Ferrazzi, *Autobiography of an Aspiring Saint;* Gabriella Zarri, ed., *Finzione e santità tra medioevo ed età moderna* (Turin, 1991); Schutte, "Donne, inquisizione e pietà," 245–48; Adriano Prosperi, *Tribunali della coscienza: Inquisitori, confessori, missionari* (Turin, 1996), 431–64.

110. On 23 April 1684 Laura Noris Piceni, a widow, had a popular Latin rhyme exalting Saint Anthony's powers transcribed in her will as a guarantee of its authenticity

(ASV, Notarile, Testamenti, busta 167, no. 232); in former times biblical verses or regular prayers had usually served this purpose. See also Ruggiero, *Binding Passion,* 88–107.

111. Alberto Vecchi, *Correnti religiose nel Sei-Settecento veneto* (Venice, 1962), 52–63; Scarabello, "Paure, superstizioni, infamie," esp. 357–59.

112. ASV, Consiglio dei Dieci, Criminali, reg. 23, fols. 89v–90v, and reg. 24, fols. 2r, 8r–v; ASV, Consiglio dei Dieci, Minute, filze 35, 36, various writings, esp. one of 16 March 1607 by Arcanzola da Ponte in filza 36. Notwithstanding the reticence of these sources, there can be little doubt about the reason for the imprisonment of this seventy-four-year-old lady, a paragon of piety and a granddaughter of Doge Nicolò da Ponte.

113. ASV, Notarile, Testamenti, busta 840, no. 233, 23 June 1608 (will of Cattarina Mocenigo Vendramin).

114. Tarabotti, *L' "Inferno monacale" di Arcangela Tarabotti,* 27.

115. Alba Querini supported her relative Angelo's demands for reform (De Biase, *Amore di stato,* 90).

116. Caterina Dolfin Tron professed a strong anticlericalism and mocked the credulity of her contemporaries (Capaci, "Il tavolino della dama," 205–6). Cecilia Grimani Sagredo and her daughter Caterina Sagredo Barbarigo were the owners of heterodox books, such a number of them in Caterina's case that she can be suspected of being prompted by something deeper than mere curiosity (Del Negro, "Amato da tutta la Veneta Nobiltà," 233). Labalme, "Venetian Women on Women," 109, refers to an eighteenth-century Venetian manuscript containing, among all sorts of miscellaneous data about Venetian women, a statement that in the past women had been admitted to the priesthood.

117. On the connection between a woman's reputation and the secluded life in the Renaissance, see Dennis Romano, "Gender and the Urban Geography of Renaissance Venice," *Journal of Social History* 23 (1989), esp. 343, 347–48.

118. Gioseffa Cornoldi Caminer, *La donna galante ed erudita: Giornale dedicato al bel sesso,* ed. Cesare de Michelis (Venice, 1983), e.g., 196, 251; see also Madile Gambier, "Destini di donna nel Settecento veneziano," ibid., 313–28.

14

Slave Redemption in Venice, 1585–1797

ROBERT C. DAVIS

Much like Peter Burke's chapter earlier in this volume, this contribution by Robert C. Davis places Venice in a larger context, in this case the history of the Mediterranean world in the early modern period. As is well known—from Shakespeare's Merchant of Venice above all—Venetian ships ran significant risks at sea. What is new here is Davis's emphasis on the danger Venetians confronted of being enslaved by Barbary and other Muslim pirates in the seventeenth and eighteenth centuries. Davis highlights the now virtually forgotten story of the large-scale institutional aspects of the taking of slaves by both Christian and Muslim powers throughout the Mediterranean in the early modern period. Not surprisingly, Venice recognized this threat as both an economic and a religious one since the capture of both Venetians and those in its service not only robbed the Republic of valuable human resources but also resulted in many forced conversions to Islam. The second aspect of this story that Davis illuminates is the way a number of typically Venetian institutions acted to help ransom the slaves. Ever since the publication of Brian Pullan's now classic study Rich and Poor in Renaissance Venice, historians and other scholars of Venetian history have recognized the central role that a wide variety of Venetian institutions, from parishes and confraternities to monasteries and friaries, played in the shaping of Venetian culture. Here Davis grafts his study onto our growing knowledge of these institutions and demonstrates how throughout the early modern period both the church and the Venetian government called upon them in recurrent efforts to raise funds for the ransoming of enslaved Venetians. The interplay of these domestic institutions against the backdrop of both the fear and the reality of enslavement played a significant role in shaping Venetian identity in the early modern period.

SLAVE REDEMPTION on the level of an organized state enterprise began only rather late in the history of Venice, if only because Mediterranean slavery itself did not become a serious problem for the Republic until the early modern era. During the Middle Ages, even as Venetians had routinely dealt in small numbers of slaves from Slavic lands and Africa, so they sometimes ended up as slaves themselves, captured in war or in mercantile rivalries with their Mediterranean competitors—Arabs, Turks, the Uskoks of Dalmatia, occasionally even the Genoese.[1] There are numerous accounts of Venetians taken in this manner from at least the fourteenth century and into the early sixteenth. But slaving of this sort amounted to little more than the casual opportunism of passing marauders compared with the large-scale, institutionalized form it assumed with the rise and consolidation of the Habsburg and Ottoman Empires. In the centuries-long Christian-Muslim jihad that ensued, on both sides piracy and slaving were turned into the policy instruments of state since enslaving soldiers and sailors taken in battle or scooping up ordinary civilians in corsair raids not only deprived the enemy of thousands of useful, productive citizens but also provided serviceable labor and a valuable source of income through ransoming. By the end of the sixteenth century slave-hunting corsair galleys roamed throughout the Mediterranean, seeking their human booty from Catalonia to Egypt. Men and women, Turks and Moors, Jews and Catholics, Protestants and Orthodox—all were potential victims, to be seized and eventually herded into the slave pens of Constantinople, Algiers, Tunis, Tripoli, Malta, Naples, or Livorno and to be resold as galley oarsmen, agricultural laborers, or house slaves.

Italy, lying midway between the two empires but (after the 1550s) heavily associated with Habsburg Spain, was, as "the eye of Christendom," especially vulnerable to the slaving wars that followed. The peninsula was politically fragmented, the coasts for the most part without fortifications, and territorial defense forces were weak and dispersed. Corsair slave-taking there rapidly burgeoned into a full-scale industry, with disastrous effects, apparent at the time and for centuries to come, in "the wretched beaches, the abandoned islands, the huts [reduced] to ashes, the fishermen in flight, and the [slaving ships] . . . loitering past on the sea."[2] The opportunistic nature of medieval slave-taking in the Mediterranean had produced correspondingly improvised responses in Italy when it came to ransoming those who were taken captive. Families that had the means paid to free their own members, usually through the mediation of an Italian or Jewish merchant operating where their relative was held. In Venice, it was not uncommon for the Senate to use state connections and sometimes funds to free Venetian citizens, especially noble commanders of the Republic's naval forces.[3] The explosion of slave-taking after the

1520s made it obvious to governments throughout the Italian peninsula, however, that more permanent state structures were needed if there was to be any
hope of raising the necessary funds both to locate and to ransom an ever-
increasing number of enslaved citizens. The first such magistracy, the Real Casa
Santa della Redentione de' Cattivi, was set up by the Neapolitan viceroy in
1548; it was followed in fairly short order by other cities and states throughout
Italy: Rome in 1581, Bologna in 1584, Palermo in 1596, Genoa in 1597, and
Malta in 1607.[4]

Venice and its mainland territories were comparatively remote from the
principal concentrations of Islamic power. Nonetheless, because of extensive
trading connections, the Republic's sailors and merchants were increasingly
caught up in the wave of corsair activity carried on by the Muslim pirates based
on the Barbary Coast, the Dalmatian islands, and around the mouth of the
Adriatic. Venice's founding of its own ransoming magistracy in 1586 can thus
be tied to this same general trend toward the bureaucratizing of slave ransoming that prevailed throughout Italy. In this as in so many other state approaches
to social needs, however, the Venetians would manage to extract multiple
services, political and cultural as well as merely bureaucratic, from the same
institution.[5]

The initial stimulus for setting up a ransoming office in Venice was fairly
straightforward. Early in 1586 the Republic's *bailo* in Constantinople alerted
the Venetian Senate that the sultan was willing to sell back a number of enslaved Venetians, mostly prisoners of war from the previous decades of hostilities. Considering this primarily a work of charity (those who could have
afforded to do so would, after all, have long since ransomed themselves), the
Senate responded by turning the job over to its magistracy most practiced in
charitable fund-raising. This was the Provveditori sopra Ospedali e Luoghi Pii,
a board of three nobles instituted only twenty years earlier to oversee Venice's
many benevolent foundations, hospitals, and hospices. The Senate instructed
the provveditori to work with the patriarch of Venice to seek the necessary
alms in the usual ways. These consisted, first, in their having the patriarch order
preachers in the city to include a special plea for contributions in three of the
six successive Sunday sermons they customarily gave for the Lenten cycle. The
provveditori were also instructed to see that special lockable collection boxes
were made and placed in each of Venice's churches with a sign attached that
read, "For the Recovery of the Poor Slaves."[6]

The Senate must have soon realized that the city of Venice alone would not
be capable of generating sufficient alms to free "the great number of said poor

slaves who find themselves in the hands of the Turks." Barely a year after its first enabling legislation, the Senate decided to cast its alms-gathering net more widely and ordered Venice's *rettori* on the *terraferma* to carry out similar quests in subsequent Lenten cycles with the help of local bishops and vicars and by "deputizing . . . a person fit and faithful, who will employ in such pious and holy work the greatest possible diligence." Less than two years later the Senate put the provveditori in charge of the whole operation, giving them control over the money thus raised both "in this City and in the rest of our State." Their staff was expanded to include a bookkeeper and a *fante*. At the same time, the Senate also pledged its own contribution, "to assist work so pious and religious": fifty ducats each Christmas and Easter would be debited to that effect from the state's "ordinary charities."[7]

Despite the Senate's apparent confidence in them, the provveditori soon found that when it came to the complex business of ransoming slaves, they faced problems of an altogether different order than simply administering pious foundations in the city of Venice. First was the sheer magnitude of the task, made much greater by the Senate's expressed determination to redeem not only actual Venetian subjects, whether from the city, the terraferma, or the *stato da mar* in Greece and on the Dalmatian coast, but "also [those who are] not subjects, but who are taken [while] in our service." Assiduous searching by the provveditori in the first years after their authority was broadened and made permanent turned up "more than 2,500 of these, found in miserable captivity": merchants, sailors, shipbuilders, fishermen, and others from all over the Venetian empire enslaved in Muslim cities from Persia to Morocco, though concentrated for the most part in Constantinople, Albania, and the Barbary Coast.[8] The difficulties involved in accurately identifying men and women so far from home, often after years if not decades of slavery, were daunting even for a bureaucracy as relatively sophisticated as Venice's, but there were other complicating factors as well. Many of the enslaved were Greek Orthodox, which meant that they could not be ransomed with funds raised in Catholic churches. Others possessed no proof of their identity, though they were more than willing to claim Venetian citizenship if that could gain their freedom. Still others were Venetian deserters or convicts who had escaped from the Republic's own galleys and fallen through misadventure into Turkish hands; these presented the provveditori with the thorny question whether leaving such men to their ironically just punishment as slaves of the Turks outweighed any claims for redemption they might have on their homeland.[9]

Equally troublesome was the challenge of raising money on what turned out to be a grand scale. Within just a few decades of its inception the provveditori found that the Republic's ransoming operation had run seriously into debt: by 1620 the members were lamenting that, "beyond the good sum of money already paid out . . . for the liberation of slaves, the amount previously promised [for others] by [our] predecessors adds up to around 40,000 ducats . . . [and] every day [we are] forced to make new promises to other slaves."[10] Passive alms gathering, in the form of the locked *casselle* placed in the city's churches, had not proven particularly successful. Parishioners tended to leave behind coins that were either foreign or so clipped that the mint refused to accept them; in any case, vandalism, theft, and neglect soon reduced the number of boxes that were providing any regular income: out of only sixteen when records began to be kept in 1596 just four were still operating in 1612, bringing in a miserable eleven ducats a year.[11] Lenten preachers seem to have put more energy into organizing active solicitation, increasing the number of churches included in their exhortations from 23 in 1596 to about 40 by the 1620s; the alms they brought in increased accordingly, though even in the best years the total barely exceeded three hundred ducats. Further afield, fund-raising efforts were still more difficult to manage. Not long after the provveditori had taken control of the operation, tales began to come in from the provinces of the "swindles that are committed by wicked people who, with stolen or false Licenses, pretend to be Collectors for them [the rettori], stealing in Our State the alms destined to this so pious work." And yet, when rettori actually did collect donations in their provinces, it seemed that they then might well find excuses to "covert them to other uses." Even the Senate itself was not too reliable in keeping up its share of the burden: the state's annual Christmas and Easter donations, which in any case were "just sufficient for the liberation of one [slave] only," were often decades in arrears.[12]

In fact the provveditori rarely put up the entire ransom for a slave in these early years, when the Turks of Constantinople or the Barbary cities were demanding 200–300 ducats for each captive. Instead, once they had agreed on the validity of a slave's claims, they issued him or her *mandati,* essentially state checks for the slave's use, in sums of one hundred, or fifty, or even as little as ten ducats. The provveditori evidently expected that "with the foundation of that promise" the slave's kin would be able to come up with the rest, either from their own pockets—"squeezed from the substance of [his] poor family"—or "from the promises of all the usual places," mainly such charities as the fishermen's confraternity of San Nicolò, or the shipbuilders' various brotherhoods. Not altogether surprisingly, such piecemeal collection of ransoming funds was not always successful, and the provveditori once had to admit that "rarely do [the slaves] find a quantity that is sufficient for their liberation, which causes many of them to end their days in those miseries [of slavery]."[13]

Even more daunting than the raising of donations was the actual business of ransoming the slaves. If the provveditori sought to help individual captives by sending their mandati directly to particular slaves, as much as half of the bill's value was wasted by the inflated exchange (the *grosso cambio*) that prevailed in the Barbary ports.[14] Negotiating to purchase and set free large blocks of slaves (as was done by the Spanish and French) was especially difficult in Barbary cities, where, unlike in Constantinople, the Venetians did not maintain a permanent consul until the late eighteenth century. The endless hostilities between Venice, Algiers, and Tunis usually made it far too risky to carry the ransom funds to those cities, but in any case, once slave owners got word that ransomers had arrived in their city with actual cash in hand, they inevitably raised their asking prices. Much the same happened when the provveditori tried to make their payments through the consuls of other nations, since the intervention of another government's representative on behalf of a Venetian slave often accomplished little beyond raising his master's cupidity.[15] As a result, the provveditori were generally compelled to make their payments at one remove, through merchant houses in Marseilles or, more likely, Livorno that had offices in one of the Barbary cities. But with the actual negotiations thereby entrusted "now to merchants, to foreign Consuls, now to Protestants, and finally even [to] Jews," the provveditori could effectively lose control of the money they had so laboriously raised. Not only did these "heretical and Jewish" agents expect their own commission (usually 11–14 percent, the so-called *cambio marittimo*), "making for themselves a true trafficking in these poor Christian Slaves," but the Turks also typically attached to the original asking price their own *aggiunti,* commissions, duties, payoffs, and bribes that could raise the initial ransom price (the so-called *prima compra,* or *primo costo*) by 20–30 percent.[16] Bargaining was almost impossible unless slave owners were in particular financial difficulty: as often as not, any attempts to argue down the cost were met with an immediate increase in the original asking price. As if that were not enough, the largest local slave owners might insist that, along with the slaves they had come to redeem, the ransomers also had to buy a certain number of *aguaitas,* old and worn-out slaves from other nations, and pay top ducat for the privilege.[17]

Despite their magnitude, such difficulties, along with many others, never discouraged the Senate or the provveditori to the point of abandoning their determination to ransom as many enslaved Venetians as possible. They continued their efforts right up to the last days of the Republic, always seeking to cast their net of redemption as widely and as efficiently as possible. The motives behind such extraordinary (and often very costly) exertions were seldom spelled out explicitly either in the generally prosaic minutes and memoranda of the provveditori or in the formulaic pronouncements of the Senate. Nevertheless, some guiding principles do emerge from the documentation of the two-hundred-year life of the enterprise.

In terms of hard-headed public policy, ransoming certain categories of slaves was only common sense. The Senate's continual restating of its determination to buy back "our subjects and also [those] not subjects but taken in our service" must be seen against the background of the Republic's fairly stagnant population and sluggish economy over the last two centuries of its existence. Protecting and profiting from what was left of Venice's once impressive *imperio da mar* required an active maritime and shipbuilding sector, whether to serve in such protracted land campaigns as the Candia or Morea wars or to help reignite the city's Levantine trade, as happened in the later eighteenth century.[18] But if the Senate was going to persuade Venetians of all classes to maintain their seafaring traditions and to continue attracting enough sailors from the terraferma, Dalmatia, and foreign lands to keep Venice's ships fully manned, it had to make a visible and public commitment to protecting these men from the very likely possibility of enslavement, "that horror of which especially Seafarers could well conceive, in having to risk themselves so often to [life at] Sea."[19]

It is difficult to say how much confidence the Senate's promises may have given these sailors since many of them, even those who had already been enslaved, evidently felt that they had little choice but to go back to sea regardless of the risks. A sailor had few options for different work in a declining Venice, and rather than endure unemployment that could leave him "devoid of everything . . . not even having a beggar's outfit," he fatalistically had to admit that "if there came to me the opportunity to procure myself some position on a ship, I would accept it . . . or rather, I am forced to work at this same occupation, not knowing any other."[20] The situation was somewhat different for Venice's shipbuilders. These men—shipwrights, caulkers, makers of masts, pulleys, and guncarriages—were guaranteed by law and tradition a position with regular pay in Venice's Arsenal. As a condition of their work, however, most of them also had to serve as ship carpenters in the Venetian fleet; many others signed on with merchant ships when they were young to augment their pay and gain experience.[21] Trained in their crafts by the state, these men were one of Venice's most precious human resources. Unfortunately, their skills also made them highly prized in the Barbary states, where good shipbuilders were always in short supply. Those with the bad luck to be taken while serving at sea were then "forced and compelled to work at making seaworthy the [corsairing] *bertoni* and at making *galeotte* and *bergantini;* they are held at high prices, on a thousand thalers or a thousand scudi each, and some Masters will not let theirs go for any money."[22]

The Republic's shipbuilders, as well as many of its maritime elite—"the non-commissioned officers, the masters, bosuns, ships scribes, and barbers"— could thus easily disappear into the Barbary Coast world for years, their ransoms of a thousand or more scudi too high for anyone in Venice to pay. One particularly celebrated shipwright, Giacomo Colombin, who had the special misfortune of not only "knowing how to build *galeotte* and *bregantini* [but also] having in his head the model of the *galere grosse* [Venice's own military great galley] . . . and also knowing the Moorish language," was so desirable to his masters that he spent thirty-one years enslaved in Algiers; in the end he only got out by stealing a boat and escaping.[23] Getting back the likes of Colombin and other skilled workers was important policy for the Venetians in these decades of continual warfare, as they sought to husband their own human resources while denying them to the enemy on the Barbary Coast, "who holds them dear": many of the Senate's and the provveditori's efforts over the next two centuries would focus on retrieving men such as these, sometimes regardless of the price. On the other hand, the Senate's continual refrain about ransoming "those taken while in Our service" also carried another, implicit message to those Venetian subjects who might consider taking their employment in the service of some other state—Spain, France, the Empire, or any of Venice's various Italian neighbors. If these men happened to fall into the hands of the Turks while working for some foreigner, they most certainly could *not* expect the Senate or the provveditori to expend any great efforts to buy them their freedom.[24]

At the same time, much more than simple raison d'ètat lay behind Venice's efforts to ransom its subjects. Thanks, somewhat ironically, to the slowly improved communications between the two sides of the Mediterranean, Venetians of all classes could hear much more about the sufferings of "those poor unhappy slaves, deprived of everything." Occasional but very graphic letters arrived from enslaved relatives pleading desperately for money, begging "with tears of blood" not to be forgotten, attesting to "continual mistreatment," "constant beatings and torments," and "sleeping on the naked ground."[25] Reports also circulated about conditions in the Barbary Coast cities—from foreign consuls, neutral or Jewish merchants, ransoming agents, and missionaries and in the form of an entirely new literary genre devoted specifically to the topic, the captivity accounts of ex-slaves.[26]

Such accounts helped make plain to Venetians and others in Christian Europe just how extensive a problem they faced. Some of their information may have been purely conjectural, of course, but when Emanuel d'Aranda wrote in the 1640s that in the state of Algiers alone "the miseries of Slavery have consum'd the lives of six hundred thousand Christians, since the year 1536," the huge figure may have seemed believable to many readers simply because the impact of slave-taking on Christian society had increased so markedly over the previous century. In part this had to do with significant shifts in the political world during these years. As the great Ottoman-Habsburg rivalry wound down, the locus of Muslim-Christian conflict had moved by about 1580 to the smaller, more nimble client states of the two empires, in particular to the corsairing fleets of Algiers, Tunis, Tripoli, the Knights of Malta, and the Knights of Santo Stefano, based in Livorno.[27] The human prey of these marauders were less likely to be the professional soldiers and sailors who had figured so centrally in the conflicts of the previous century and more often those who had a genuine economic and emotional importance for their home societies—merchants and their passengers, fishermen, women, children, and priests. In the accounts they produced of the Barbary Coast, returning captives and ransoming priests stressed the presence of these ordinary folk even as they stressed the huge numbers of all slaves in the cities they had seen.[28] Algiers was said to be fairly flooded with slaves, upwards of 30,000 or 40,000 at any given time, representing perhaps a quarter to a third of the local population. Tunis, Tripoli, and the major cities of the kingdom of Morocco typically had 5,000–15,000 slaves each, and thousands more were held in squalid anonymity in smaller towns and on isolated plantations *(massarie)* from the Straits of Gibraltar to the port of Suez.[29]

Moreover, these accounts produced a fairly grisly picture of the slaves' lot, especially when they were written by the many missionaries and priests who dedicated themselves to the business of ransoming and who almost inevitably emphasized the worst aspects of enslavement in the hopes of soliciting the pity (and the donations) of their audience. Yet even the dragoman Giovanni Battista Salvago, who wrote a fairly straightforward and balanced report about the state of Algiers and its slaves to Doge Giovanni Cornaro in 1625, asserting that "all in all, [the slave] who works at being profitable for his master does not come off badly," went on to stress how dismal the slaves' lot was: "deprived of sweet liberty, far from the fatherland, relatives, friends, and Christian customs, [living] at the whim of someone who for nothing can beat them and with [such] beatings make them die miserably."[30]

Certainly the life of a Christian slave in Barbary was perilous, a stark reality that the hope of eventual ransom did not make any more secure. To better break them for the work they were expected to do (but also, it seems, out of sheer hostility) corsairs set out systematically to demoralize and dehumanize their captives, who were "immediately all stripped of their clothing, left naked," "chained foure and foure . . . forceablie and most violentlie shaven, head and beard" and "each given only an overshirt and a pair of drawers of rough cloth."[31] The main labor expected from male slaves—women were almost all sent to the harem of the local ruler[32]—was rowing the corsair galleys, which every year made two or three month-long voyages covering the breadth of the Mediterranean and out into the Atlantic in search of new booty and slaves. When not out at sea, chained to their oars, slaves in most Barbary ports were locked down in enormous, public prisons known as *bagnos*. To earn their keep, they were sent out to daily hard labor about the city and its surrounding countryside: hauling stone, cutting timber, working in nearby plantations, or digging in salt mines.[33]

Such hardships took a terrible toll even on such relatively hardy souls as sailors and fishermen. During the second half of the seventeenth century 20 percent of the slaves brought into Tripoli each year died, a figure that evidently ran much higher there and elsewhere when the captives were villagers taken on coastal raids since they were mostly too young or feeble to have run away during the sack.[34] Many slaves died almost immediately from "bad treatment and the effects of the psychological shock," beaten by their masters "when[ever] their devilish choller rose"; others slowly starved on a diet of water and "a single, six-ounce piece of half-cooked bread daily, made of rotten grain that even the dogs themselves would not eat." In such weakened condition they had little hope of surviving the diseases that were endemic in North Africa, especially the plague, which "makes them die miserably, decimating and diminishing [them] every third or fourth year."[35]

The Venetian Senate was well aware of the toll that slavery took on its subjects; indeed, by the mid-eighteenth century information was being sent from the Barbary Coast on which and how many Venetians were dying in the slave hospitals there every year.[36] Such high mortality was often given as a reason to hurry with ransoming efforts, just as it was recommended to "redeem as soon as possible the oldest ones, who are bad off for not being able to eat that bread that is usually given out by the Turks; otherwise they will die within a short time."[37] Haste was also necessary because of the possibility that a slave would be sold and resold until he was eventually lost in the vastness of the Islamic world. Corsairs operating out of the Albanian port of Dulcigno (modern-day Ulcinj, in southern Montenegro), a sort of way station in the Mediterranean slave trade, would often threaten their Venetian and Italian captives "that they would sell them in Barbaria if the ransom does not arrive quickly." Certainly it was the lot of many slaves to be sold, often several times. Others—sometimes hundreds at once—would be shipped off across the Mediterranean as gifts, to another local ruler or to the sultan in Constantinople.[38] And if the written pleas of slaves, terrified of being "sold in Barbaria," were not enough, a Dolcignotto slave owner might bring his captives right into Venice, forcing them to beg for their own ransom from the Venetians themselves.[39]

Another motive to move quickly in ransoming was the fear that captives might give in to their despair, their hardship, and the blandishments of their masters and convert to Islam. The Barbary ports were full of such *rinnegati:* d'Aranda claimed that in Algiers "there are Renegadoes of all Christian Nations and in my time [the 1640s] I found above three thousand *French.* . . . [and] the 12,000 soldiers, which are the regular forces . . . are most of them Renegadoes, dissolute persons, without Religion or Conscience." It was widely believed in Venice and elsewhere in Europe that Muslim masters worked tirelessly to turn their slaves away from the Christian faith.[40] Even if this is doubtful—as d'Aranda noted, "the Moors having them in their power, would not suffer them to change their Religion, because a Christian slave is worth much more than a Renegado; for the former are employ'd to row in the Gallies, and the latter are not"—there still existed a pervasive anxiety throughout Christendom about the subversive attractions of Islam, a collective horror that expressed itself through many different strands of conscious and unconscious dread.[41] Traitors to their religion, rinnegati were also feared as traitors to Christianity's other fundamental social elements, the family and the state. Many corsair raids on the coasts of Italy, Spain, or Dalmatia were believed to have been led by rinnegati, who willingly "pilated the Turke to the place where they were borne, and beene instruments in the captivating of their owne fathers and mothers and all their Lineage, taking their part of the price for which their Parents were sold in the Market." And if a certain sympathy was expressed for female slaves who, locked away in the harem, abjured their religion to stay with their children, born of their master and raised as Muslims, men who converted received no such compassion. Those who embraced Islam were seen as weakened yet also intrinsically corrupt, having chosen a creed tailor-made to free them of the strictures of Christianity in order to "wallow in depravity." It was a Faustian bargain that rinnegati sealed with the sexually highly charged and symbolic act of adult circumcision before giving themselves over to a life that was "incorrigibly flagitious . . . commit[ting] Sodomie with all creatures, and tollerat[ing] all vices."[42]

For Venetians, as for all Catholics, the abandonment of the Christian faith represented a kind of voluntary eternal death, a horrific fate, the terror of which, ironically enough, many slaves seem to have known well how to exploit in letters and petitions that included the threat, however oblique, that "reduced to desperation," they might "rush into the diabolic resolution to abjure the true faith."[43] In Christendom, losses to apostasy were typically treated as casualties as much as was physical death—missionaries in Barbary struggled in their hospitals to prevent both—and should be taken into account when evaluating how Venetians perceived the depredations of slavery on their fellow citizens. Thus in 1628, when calculating the losses among 250 Dalmatian villagers enslaved as a group three years earlier, the Senate noted that, "having many of them lost their lives, others changed faith, and some women immured [i.e., in harems], in those places hardly more than seventy can be found there in a state of being able to be freed."[44] Viewed in this way, as it clearly was by the Venetians, the casualty rate of slaves such as these amounted to more than 70 percent in only three years of captivity.

There were thus many political, emotional, and religious incentives for the Senate and the provveditori to maximize the Republic's ransoming activities. This they proceeded to do throughout the course of the seventeenth and into the eighteenth century, in part by continually extending the instruments of alms collection to take in as many sources as possible "so that donations could be made by the devoted with greater ease and in greater quantity." The provveditori ordered periodic reviews of the condition and accessibility of the locked casselle, mounting a determined drive to make sure that there was one in each parish and conventual church in the city and on the terraferma. By the 1780s no fewer than eighty-nine of Venice's own churches had such a box. The provveditori also decided to pursue more active forms of alms gathering, beyond the traditional three Lenten collections at the parish level. They ordered that abbots preach the Lenten collection in their monasteries and also that a special solicitation be made "throughout the year in all the churches during the parish masses." Moreover, they arranged with each parish nonzolo (beadle) that he would not only take care of his church's fixed cassella but also make a collection "around the parish, once a week, with fervor," in which he would presumably approach and appeal directly to the parishioners to make their contributions.[45]

The fund-raising net was also cast wider by enlisting ever more individuals to carry out direct appeals. In 1619 the alms-collecting obligations imposed on Venice's rettori of the terraferma were extended to the *rettori da mar*, the governors of Venetian overseas territories in Istria, Dalmatia, the Ionian Islands, and Crete.[46] Also at about this time the Senate and the provveditori approved the foundation of a *scuola piccola*, a confraternity that would dedicate itself especially to the ransoming of slaves. Attached to the church of Santa Maria Formosa, the Scuola of the Santissima Trinità was designed to provide a focal point for Venetians of all classes who were concerned about the fate of their enslaved fellow citizens, offering them a chance to contribute their alms and energies "to benefit the souls of and to help the poor and unhappy slaves"; it was soon joined by other affiliate *scuole* both in Venice and in its subject territories.[47]

Another route employed for fund-raising sought to blend the secular and the sacred in a single act of solicitation. Venice's notaries were ordered to importune their clients on behalf of the state, with instructions that when drawing up a will they should remind the testator to "remember the poor slaves" in his or her bequest. The Senate first proposed this policy in its enabling legislation of 1588, although in the beginning it does not seem to have been widely followed, perhaps because of the difficulties in enforcing it. In a series of edicts over the course of the seventeenth century the provveditori sought to resurrect this requirement and used ever stricter forms of surveillance to make sure that it was obeyed, culminating in 1675 with an order to the city's notaries that they write into the actual texts of the wills and codicils that they had specifically mentioned this charitable duty to their clients. Moreover, under pain of a 200-ducat fine each notary, directly after the testator had died and his or her will had been opened, was to bring to the provveditori "a copy of those legacies that were left for the aforesaid pious work." The provveditori even went after those notaries who had already joined their clients in the grave, demanding that their *protocolli* from the previous twenty years be brought in so that they could make sure that the heirs of the deceased or the notary himself had not concealed or made off with bequests intended for "the poor slaves."[48]

Just as the provveditori moved to crack down on notaries seeking in one way or another to evade the role imposed upon them as fund-raisers for the state, they also tried to bring wayward rettori out in the provinces to heel.

These aristocratic provincial governors were, of course, somewhat less amenable to pressure in such matters than were the city's middle-class notaries, so, for example, the provveditori had to content themselves with ordering that each newly commissioned rettore send his chancellor to their office rather than come himself. There the chancellor was to pick up the little booklet *(quinternetto)* of instructions they had had printed up, containing that rettore's various obligations for collecting alms in his province. Once a rettore was actually ensconced in his governor's palace in Bergamo, Udine, Corfu, or some other remote spot, the provveditori had even less influence over him, although they did try to enlist local bishops and abbots to keep up the pressure so that he would continue seeking contributions. A rettore was somewhat more vulnerable when his term of office ended, however, since he then returned to Venice in hopes of winning a new appointment. The provveditori therefore ordered the Segretarie alle Voci, that noble board responsible for placing nominations for office before the Senate, to deny to any former rettore his right to stand for a new position *(andare a capello,* as it was called) unless he could give some evidence of having faithfully followed their instructions and brought back actual donations collected during his time abroad.[49] To further prod the rettore along, the provveditori, with the support of the Senate, eventually created a network of supervisors over the existing collection agents, known as the *succolletori,* "who have the precise mission to act, promote, coordinate . . . and correspond as much as is necessary in this matter, both in Venice and outside the State." By the 1760s there were no fewer than forty-four of these at work in the *dominante,* the terraferma, and the imperio da mar.[50]

All this effort definitely made a difference in terms of contributions brought into the city from outside. Averaging around 220 ducats per year during the first two decades in which the provveditori kept records, this income from the *reggimenti* had increased by about a third seventy years later. By the 1780s, with 47 succolletori and 39 rettori and *pubblici rappresentanti* assiduously searching out alms from Adria to Zante, it would multiply nearly five times more, to an average of 1,600 ducats a year.[51] Income from the casselle in churches showed a similar improvement, becoming both greater and more consistent: in the period 1596–1625 the average annual collection was a mere 7 ducats per box, but by the decade 1686–95 this figure had grown to 39 ducats, nearly a century later the take for the single year 1780 was 248 ducats.[52] In the same way, charitable bequests also began to inch up as responsive testators, prodded by their notaries, continuously left their small sums behind "for the poor slaves."[53] By the later eighteenth century new sources of income had also begun to have a significant impact. A dozen or more major legacies by Venetian and foreign nobles in the form of invested funds reliably produced several thousand ducats a year. The confraternity of the Santissima Trinità, a regular contributor, was joined by the Scuola Grande of San Rocco, as well as by the Procuratie di Supra and di Ultra, two of the state's primary boards for investment and property management. Even the public lottery gave a share of its income for the redemption of slaves.[54] Ultimately, it might be said, private and "public" contributions were roughly balanced as sources of funds for the Republic's slave-ransoming enterprise.

But the steady increases in income that such bureaucratic and fiscal efforts produced were never quite enough. Throughout the later seventeenth century and into the eighteenth the provveditori's ransoming operation demanded ever more money even as the actual number of slaves held in Constantinople and on the Barbary Coast began to decline sharply. Clearly, this was in part due to the provveditori's ever greater efficiency in locating enslaved Venetians and arranging for their ransom. Whereas for much of the seventeenth century it was poor information about who was actually enslaved as much as lack of funds that left many slaves "to end their days in those miseries [of slavery]," by the mid-eighteenth century the provveditori's agents throughout Islamic lands were much more active and successful both at seeking out slaves and at negotiating for their eventual ransom and release.[55] Their efforts at rooting out even the most remote and forgotten captives meant that the provveditori kept on bringing back roughly the same number of slaves in the 1780s as they had a century earlier even as the actual number of Christians slaves held by Muslims generally dropped throughout the Mediterranean.[56] These slaves were much more expensive to ransom than they had been in the past, moreover, since the prices that masters were demanding for their property began to register sharp increases from the last decades of the seventeenth century. Although those who busied themselves with the business of ransoming often complained about how "these Barbarians have exorbitantly raised the prices," ransom inflation also appears to have been a case of ever more money chasing ever fewer slaves. The ransom typically demanded for lower-class captives, such as sailors, fishermen, or "ordinary soldiers," grew from a few hundred ducats in the mid-seventeenth century to an average of nearly 900 ducats by the 1760s. For workers "who have some skills" the price could easily top 1,100 ducats, while for ship captains and anyone "of quality" the asking price might be 3,000–10,000 ducats.[57]

Faced with a financial burden that seemed to only increase over time, the Venetian Senate was thus more than willing to listen when, in the 1720s, it was approached by the city's seafaring professionals with a plea that it turn the ransoming end of the process over to the Discalced Trinitarians. The Order of the Holy Trinity, founded in 1197 by Giovanni di Matha and Felice di Valois, had always distinguished itself as pursuing only a single mission, "holding as its [sole] Justification the ransoming of slaves." In the centuries following the Crusades it had played a vital role in arranging prisoner exchanges and ransoming Christian knights who had fallen into Muslim hands.[58] Along with the slaving business itself, the Trinitarians had flourished during the Habsburg-Ottoman conflict, and by the seventeenth century they were well established as the primary ransoming agents for all the Habsburg lands, from Spain to Hungary, as well as for Poland and to a lesser degree France. In what appears to have been something of a concerted pitch to take over slave ransoming throughout Italy—they launched a similar effort in Rome at about the same time—the Trinitarians offered Venice the benefit of not only their long experience but also their ability to carry on slave redemption in volume (the so-called *redenzione generale*). Just the previous year, as the documents they provided made clear, they had in fact arranged for the liberation of no fewer than 790 slaves at a single stroke.[59]

Evidently impressed, the Senate proceeded to give the Trinitarians an abandoned monastery on the island of Pellestrina and commissioned them to carry out some of their "prodigious redemptions" on behalf of the Republic's enslaved citizens, which the order promptly did in Constantinople (1727) and Tripoli (1730).[60] Thereafter, with only an interlude of a decade or so during the 1730s and 1740s, the Trinitarians remained Venice's chief ransom negotiators until the fall of the Republic in 1797. It may seem curious that after going their own way for nearly a century and a half Venetians decided to turn an activity so sensitively and self-consciously linked to their own social order over to an outside organization. (Indeed, when the Trinitarians were temporarily expelled from Venice in 1736 it was precisely because of a dispute over whether Venice or Turin, where the order's mother house in Italy was located, had ultimate control over the Pellestrina monastery.) Actually, the Senate only gave the Trinitarians responsibility over the negotiation and paying of ransom, the aspect of the redemption process that in the past the provveditori had been forced to cede for the most part to outside agents ("heretics and Jews"). Perhaps too by the mid-eighteenth century the Venetians realized that their own once vaunted skills as negotiators with the Muslim world were not as sharp as they had once been: how else to explain their blunder in 1764, when in trying to put themselves in the good graces of the dey of Algiers they sent that Muslim ruler five hogsheads of wine?[61]

Certainly the Trinitarians made an excellent case for taking over Venice's ransom negotiations with the Muslim states. Not only did they shower the Senate with printed up *cataloghi* enumerating the great redemptions they had previously carried out for other states but they also provided handy lists that allowed the senators to compare the prices paid by the order and by the provveditori's other agents for slaves of the same class and category. In these they demonstrated that while through their "Mercanti e Corrispondenti" the Venetians were paying an average of nearly 1,000 ducats per slave, the Trinitarians had been freeing captives for Milan, Germany, and Turin for a mere 315 ducats apiece on average.[62] By being on the spot for the negotiations and enjoying the direct protection of local rulers, the fathers could bring their ransoming funds with them, avoiding the need to charge the Venetians the 14 percent cambio marittimo exacted by those "who make a living out of this." Dealing in bulk slaves for many nations, the Trinitarians were wise to all the tricks that slaves owners used to increase ransoms, and they had a few of their own as well:

> It is our custom . . . to take sick slaves into our hospital, [and] with such opportunity we take in also those who are not sick, [but] who have, with some small coins that they have paid to the Guardian of the Bagno, entrusted themselves to our care; it being necessary [for] this that they should have some sort of illness, we call the physician of the King and, by showing him a certain sum of money, have him recognize the slave [as] sick, and he speaks to the King his master, making him believe of the danger of his [slave's] death, such that one arranges with advantage [the slave's] ransom, and it is contrived with a small sum [of money].[63]

Yet, in taking over ransom negotiations for the Venetians, the Trinitarians left their stamp on more than just the redemption activities in Constantinople and the Barbary Coast. As part of the ransoming process, beginning with their first "prodigious redemption" of 1727, they also introduced to Venice a custom that they had long since perfected—the triumphal procession of ransomed slaves. It is somewhat odd that Venice of all places, a city renowned for its fondness of grand processions, apparently never considered staging one for its returning slaves, especially since the Trinitarians and the other great ransoming order, the Mercedarians, had been doing it for years in capital cities around Catholic Europe. Part of the reason may have been that previously the provveditori had typically ransomed many small groups rather than occasional grand masses of slaves; those that they liberated often apparently never came to Venice on their way home in any case, choosing to pass up the opportunity to visit the capital and return directly to their native towns in the terraferma, Dalmatia, or Greece. On the other hand, although no one seems to have said so at the time, the Venetian nobles who customarily were in charge of staging such affairs may have been unclear just how to build a ceremonial occasion around such wretched (even if redeemed) fellow citizens. After all, Venetian processions usually were designed to bring honor to local elites, the Venetian Church, and above all the Republic itself; the idea of placing at the center of one of its solemn rituals a handful of simple fishermen and sailors, many of whom were not even from Venice, must have struck many as novel at the least. Certainly the Senate hesitated a bit when it came to organizing the first slave procession in 1727 and asked the Trinitarians for some background on how ransoming celebrations were conducted elsewhere. Such information one of the fathers obligingly supplied, with brief descriptions of how these things were done in Rome, Madrid, Cartagena, Livorno, Turin, and Vienna.[64]

The centerpiece of these Trinitarian processions was usually the presentation, or passing in review, of the returned slaves, led by the fathers, before the prince whose subjects they were and whose efforts had supposedly been behind their liberation.[65] For the Trinitarians leading the procession this must have seemed only appropriate, as a recognition of their own vital role in the ransoming process. Such a presentation would also seem to have underscored the reestablishment, with what amounted to a display of fealty, of the prince's rightful rule over subjects whose civil status had been suspended for years or even decades. At the same time, when they passed before the eyes of their legitimate ruler, the ex-slaves could acknowledge to themselves that, unlike so many of their old comrades, they had not chosen the moral and civil annihilation of the life of the rinnegato but had returned intact to live within the proper hierarchies of church and state that delineated life in their homeland.

Interestingly, in the matter of these slave processions, as in so much else, the Venetian Senate decided to go its own way. Not only was the presentation of the ex-slaves to the doge of Venice not to be the central focus of the celebration but the doge himself was eliminated from the affair altogether. The procession, it is true, did pass by sites with strong associations to ducal authority, from its inauguration in the convent church of San Zaccaria to the ritual turn about the Piazza San Marco (the *girata della Piazza*) and the brief passage through the "ducal basilica of San Marco."[66] Plotting such a ceremonial course may well have had more to do with the exigencies of making a good procession than with even an unconscious nod toward ducal authority, however: when the ex-slaves had to be ferried from their quarantine on the Lazzaretto to the Riva degli Schiavoni, San Zaccaria was "the Church appropriate and handy for the beginnings of [such a] grand function"; staging a girata della Piazza was likewise a natural decision if the planners wished "to render the Procession more visible."[67]

The key authority figure in the Venetian version of the slave procession was instead the patriarch of the city, who waited under a baldachin in the church of San Zaccaria to receive the ex-slaves and to "authenticate the merit of this holy work with the majesty of his personal presence."[68] Waiting with him and his canons were Venetian noblemen, appropriate in number to the returning slaves, each seated on his own upholstered chair.[69] The ex-slaves were escorted in by representatives of the several groups that had played the primary role in freeing them: the five Trinitarian fathers who had done the actual ransoming in Algiers and Tripoli, a Jesuit priest who had seen to the freed slaves' religious instruction and reeducation during their time of quarantine, and the state's representatives in the affair, the fante and two of the three provveditori of the Magistrato sopra Ospedali e Luoghi Pii.[70] After a "simple mass" the presentation proper was carried out: the head Trinitarian father, designated as the "procurator of the slaves," with the assistance of two cappe nere (black-hooded confreres), carried to the patriarch and the provveditori two "grand basins" of silver, which held the folio-size printed cataloghi containing the name, age, origin, length of enslavement, and final price paid for each slave. These were accepted by the patriarch and passed around so that the provveditori and each of the nobles received a copy. Then the ex-slaves themselves were presented to the patriarch, "who, at their pious obedience, in the humble awe and gratitude of his abducted subjects, recognized the old sheep from his flock."

This act of recognition and reconciliation by the patriarch and assembled nobility was then made manifest ceremonially, in a procession that stressed in visual terms the reintegration of the returnees into the Venetian world. The Venetian slave procession can be seen as an act of shared, communal worship, a kind of mass writ large enough to include the entire populace, a series of ritual observances in which city streets served as church aisles, entire churches served as altars, and the concluding meal of thanksgiving, a kind of communion service. As with the mass itself, the intention was that Venetians would witness and participate in a miracle. The Trinitarians promised that even as their own order "was born from a prodigy out of the sky," so Venice would witness "new prodigies of Redemption"; the miraculous, redemptive power that was to be celebrated here was both civic and religious in its inspiration.[71]

Led by a company of soldiers "with their military instruments," the processional line was designed to set out the story of the redemptive process. First came the various scuole that had solicited funds to free the slaves, led by the scuola of the Santissima Trinità, each with its "officers, hooded confreres, standards [*segnali*], staffs, torches, and a chorus of priests."[72] Then followed the Trinitarian fathers who had arranged the specific redemption, accompanied by "two enormous placards [*soleri*]," one depicting for onlookers the mystical vision of the order's founder and the other showing the imagined scene of two of the fathers negotiating the ransom, "in a port in Barbary."[73] After the Trinitarians came what was essentially the heart and focus of the procession, a tableau of reconciliation and reacceptance of the "abducted subjects" by those who in their various ways incarnated the Venetian polity. First walked the patriarch, who, preceded by his canons carrying the sacred implements of his cathedral, escorted the first among the ex-slaves; in 1764 this was the ninety-nine-year-old Giovanni Sveggiadanna, also known as "Grandpa," who had been in captivity for sixty-five years. Then came the state's representatives, the provveditori and their fante. each with an ex-slave on his right hand.[74] Then came those who embodied the active citizenry of the Republic, the senators and aristocrats of Venice, each with his own slave and each carrying a two-pound candle. The procession was finally closed by the officers of the scuola of the Santissima Trinità, whose presence at the end of the line implied both the end of one redemptive cycle and the beginning of another.

After making a turn around the Piazza and Basilica of San Marco, most of Venice's slave processions then proceeded through the Clock Tower, the Torre dell'Orologio, and up the Mercerie to the monastic church of San Salvador. Here a high mass and Te Deum were sung, and the patriarch read a homily for the occasion to the assembled company, the nobles seated on their upholstered armchairs, the slaves on stools. These positions were strikingly reversed, however, for the final event of the celebration, which took place in the refectory of San Salvador: "The slaves with the Trinitarian fathers having been assigned and seated each in his respective place at table, there entered in the Refectory his Most Excellent and Reverend Lord [Patriarch] . . . then the Most Excellent Magistrates sopra Ospedali and Luoghi Pii, and the rest of the Nobility . . . and solemnly making the benediction of the meal, the Most Reverend Patriarch began and with him, divided up between all the Tables, there followed all the noblemen to serve the slaves until the end of the meal."[75]

According to one admiring account, such a demonstrative reversal of status roles "rendered tangible and practical that grand act of evangelic moderation and humility that [Jesus] was pleased to repeat . . . in attending more to those whom he served if they were poor." The example of the state's ministers and its leading citizens so demonstratively catering to the needs of these *miserabili* and the send-off *donativo* they gave to each ex-slave were explicitly intended to evoke among Venetians of all classes similar charitable impulses: "to greater stimulate their pious zeal to assist in such Holy Work, with all those most generous expenditures that will be suggested to them by their own piety." Slave processions were, after all, consciously staged with the intention of prompting a new flood of alms from the faithful.[76] At the same time, the provveditori, known for their unsentimental commitment to the bottom line,[77] could hardly have been unaware that such elaborate spectacles were very likely to cost more than they could ever bring in: when all the labor and the outlay for wax, paint, canvas, flowers, music, gunpowder, and so forth, were added up, an extravaganza like the procession of January 1764 cost more than 2,500 ducats, probably five to ten times what those who circulated in the crowd could expect to collect.[78]

Yet even if they were losing propositions financially, once the slave processions were introduced in the city, the Venetian Senate and Council of Ten continued to license them with little restraint. No fewer than eight such events, for anywhere from forty on down to just four slaves, are recorded for the years 1740–61 alone. From the time of the Trinitarians' first great redemption in 1727 until the fall of the Republic seventy years later processions were very likely held at the rate of about one every three or four years.[79] At one point the Trinitarians felt they had to warn the Venetians not to overdo such processions but to stage them only every ten years or so "because bringing with them some expense, they would in such a way damage the Ransomings."[80]

Ultimately, of course, those who ruled Venice turned out to be less concerned with balancing the books than the Trinitarian fathers if only because, whatever expenses these processions incurred, they served Venice as much more than simple fund-raising events. Most patently, they reminded those who had enslaved relatives and those in the audience, Venetians and foreigners alike, that the state was still both willing and able to protect its subjects from a very real social scourge. Clearly such reminding and reassuring was at some level necessary, for there are ample indications that the disconsolate relatives of lost sailors and shipbuilders could easily become desperate enough to pay the charlatans and soothsayers about the city to find out whether their husbands or sons "were alive or dead or had abjured [*s'è fatto Turco*]."[81] A response to the doubts of the fearful, the slave procession was designed, through its "external signs"— the pomp and self-confidence, the unified front presented by clerics and citizens, the "roofs, windows, and terraces . . . stuffed with watching People," and the physical presentation of the liberated themselves—"to render universally plain the fruits of the Public Munificence and Paternal Protection and of the voluntary contributions of individuals in having obtained such a copious Redemption."[82]

In this sense such processions were true spectacles of public power, staged by carefully orchestrated performers for an audience that included everyone from "the foreign Ambassadors and Ambassadoresses of the Crowns [of Europe]" to "the inferior orders of people [who] occupied the roofs and ridgepoles." Thus, it is not altogether surprising that the Venetian authorities staged these affairs far more frequently than the prudent Trinitarians would have counseled. Venice of the 1700s was hardly a great power, so there would have been few occasions for the great victory parades of two centuries earlier. Even the ancient cycle of religious processions, predicated as it was on Venice's privileged relationship with the sacred, had begun to ring somewhat hollow with the decline of the Republic and the ossification of its government and ruling classes.[83] Slave processions still made civic and spiritual sense in Republican Venice's last century, however. They not only celebrated something that the government still seemed able to do well but also broadcast important messages both to the visiting public and to the Venetians themselves in the final decades before the collapse of their ancient society. In making much of these ex-slaves, ritually rebonding them to those in the top ranks of the city, Venice stressed that there continued to exist, even in such miserabili as these, a national identity, a spirit of Venetianness that had persisted and survived sometimes for years in appalling conditions of degradation, dehumanization, and spiritual temptation. It was because of their staunchness, and because of the alacrity of the provveditori and the Trinitarian fathers who managed to intervene in the slave markets of Barbary and the Levant to set a price for their liberty, that these men and women had never become true slaves, debased and robbed of all social moorings except those they received from their masters. Instead, the Venetian state, with the help of the Trinitarians, reinserted itself between master and slave and, by reclaiming its subjects from their bondage, effectively converted them from actual slaves to mere captives (cattivi), or citizens temporarily held by an enemy power.

In this sense redeeming their fellow citizens redeemed all Venetians, and not just through performing another worthy act of pious charity. Rather, the process demonstrated—as the processions proclaimed and commemorated— that Venetians as a national community maintained an identity and a cohesion that raised them above the level of those black Africans who could be permanently uprooted and transported to the American plantations or those other European Christians who, abandoned by their homeland, their faith, and their comrades, had ended up losing their lives, their hopes, and their souls in Barbary.[84]

This proclamation of the Venetian national spirit was joined with ritual demonstrations of solidarity among Venetians. The charity of patriarch, nobles, and confreres provided exemplary and embracing inspiration, and it was noted with approval how each assigned noble patron formed ties with his protegee that extended beyond the temporal confines of the ceremony itself, as "every slave found in his Gentleman an individual protector *(protettore)* who, with alms, with jobs, [and] with advice facilitated his future status."[85]

Just as slave processions were about much more than simply raising funds for the next ransoming expedition, so the entire mission of the provveditori can be seen as going beyond just a form of state-managed mendicancy bent on generating more cash. For all the "minute attention" they might show for soliciting and collecting "many small contributions" from ordinary individuals throughout Venice and its dominions, the provveditori apparently never expected such petty donations to amount to much more than half of what was needed.[86] In Venice as elsewhere in Italy, the remainder of the ransoming monies still had to come from the state itself and from other large charitable sources—the Procuratori di Ultra e di Supra, the "public charities," various scuole, and the income generated from the invested legacies of a few wealthy nobles.[87] But the act of giving, even if it never actually brought in the sums that were needed, still had a tremendously salutary effect on individual citizens as well as on the entire polity, the more so because those who were enslaved were especially deserving objects of such generosity: "If Charity is the best of Knowledge, and if one must fix one's gaze on the infirm first before [doing so] on the strong, who would not say that in any other work of piety [there] could be discovered more clearly [Charity's] excellence than in the Ransom of the faithful Slaves?"[88]

Conscious of the value that slave redemption had in promoting and diffusing a sense of Christian community among Venetians, the provveditori seem to have been determined to push their program right into the center of Venetian life. They constantly and persistently reminded Venetians of all classes, whether or not they were personally touched by the scourge of slavery, of the sufferings of their enslaved fellow citizens and their own obligations to participate in their redemption. The particular occupational groups that the provveditori had targeted for their ongoing campaign were forever prodded to honor their own special duties, to the extent that each was required to have "affixed in a conspicuous place" the magistrate's pronouncements and instructions: parish priests in their sacristies, notaries on their writing desks, and the rettori in the office of their chancellor.[89] For such men a continual awareness of their professional obligations toward freeing slaves was enforced by real penalties, but during the last century of the Republic all Venetians were constantly reminded of their own social and moral responsibilities. Appeals for alms to ransom slaves became as familiar to Venetian ears as the cadences of the sermons into which they were woven each week. The parish nonzolo, circulating and importuning with his cassella labeled "to help the poor slaves," must have been as common a sight about the neighborhood as any beggar or charlatan; hardly less frequent would have been the regular appearances, throughout the city, of the cappe nere of the ransoming scuole and confraternities. Even the peasants and share-croppers out in Istria, Friuli, and the Veneto were continually approached with pleas to give "wheat, rye, scraps, wine, thread, cloth, linen, and cash."[90]

To the modern observer, numbed with pitches and appeals from an infinite number of charities and businesses, such endless importunings might seem merely intrusive, and so they may have become to many Venetians. At the same time, it seems to have been hoped that such ransoming efforts would in fact redeem both the slaves themselves and the entire Venetian society: "In this they will follow the example left to them by Our Lord Jesus Christ, who with the effusion of all his most Precious Blood redeemed Humanity from the Infernal Enemy, [so] we with part of our wealth, we will undertake to free our Brothers from the barbarous slavery of the Infidels, and show ourselves in a certain way as true examples of the Savior [*Salvatore*]." From the continual ritual appeals that periodically culminated in sumptuous processions there hopefully would emerge a true realization of brotherhood, the sort of single, holy, and fraternal community that would be so avidly sought after later in the eighteenth century.[91] And in slave processions, where the bond that connected redeemer and redeemed was made manifest, this seemed to some at least actually to be the case: "Everyone rushed to admire" its positive, redemptive effects on Venice's own class-bound society, where "with Charity, with Humility, with Faith, and with the other Christian Virtues the Nobility, the Splendor, the Wealth, and the Magnificence . . . [were] worked into evangelic harmony."[92]

IT IS WELL KNOWN that the Ottoman and Barbary Coast societies had a profound role in shaping Venetian culture. Despite the endless wars between their home states, Turkish and Venetian merchants kept up a steady contact between the two worlds, ensuring that interest in Turkish life and politics remained high among Venetians of all classes. Turkish themes were important in Venetian political thought and in literature, and many Venetians dressed themselves or their gondoliers *al turco* and furnished their houses with Turkish carpets, silks, lamps, and other furnishings.[93] Even the less attractive side of the Turkish-Venetian exchange, that of enslavement and forced labor, could clearly also be converted by Venetians into valuable cultural capital. How profoundly formative this slavery was in the Venetian cultural world has yet to be fully explored, although it persistently turns up in many forms, for example, in opera productions of the seventeenth and eighteenth centuries, in which Turkish or Moorish slave drivers recur as stock villains.[94] Carnival was especially full of slave imagery, sometimes of Turks and sometimes of Christians, and during the festival of the Ascension (the *festa della Sensa*) even the city's prostitutes apparently parodied one of the most unsettling practices of the Barbary Coast slavers, setting up a slave market right in the Piazza San Marco to sell their own daughters to the highest bidder.[95] Within the limitations of this study it has only been possible to trace some of Venice's more "official" cultural constructions in this realm: those taken in an institutional context, realized by the Provveditori sopra Ospedali e Luoghi Pii. Even within the relatively rigid framework of the state's alms-gathering apparatus and its slave processions, however, the rich ritual elaborations of which Venetians were capable become evident. The extent to which the scourge of slavery and the disturbing constant of the *poveri schiavi nelle mani dei Turchi* gave shape to Venetian culture on other levels, secular and religious, elite and popular, still remains to be seen.

NOTES

1. Charles Verlinden, "Le recrutement des esclaves à Venise aux XIVe et XVe siècles," *Bulletin de l'Institut Historique Belge de Rome* 39 (1968): 83–202; Iris Origo, "The Domestic Enemy: The Eastern Slaves in Tuscany in the Fourteenth and Fifteenth Centuries," *Speculum* 30 (1955): 321–66.

2. A. Guglielmotti, *Storia della marina pontificia,* 10 vols. (Rome, 1886–93), 3:191; Francis Knight, *A Relation of Seaven Yeares Slaverie under the Turks of Argeire* (London, 1640), 19.

3. Museo Civico Correr (MCC), Ms. Gradenigo, busta 171, fols. 144–65.

4. Salvatore Bono, *I corsari barbareschi* (Rome, 1964), 283, 286, 300, 308–9; Archivio Segreto Vaticano (ASVat), Arciconfraternita del Gonfalone (Gonfalone), busta 8, fols. 579–82, busta 1140, fols. 3–5. On corresponding attempts by Islamic states of

North Africa to protect their own enslaved subjects, see Salvatore Bono, "Schiavi maghrebini in Italia e cristiani nel Maghreb: Proteste e attestazioni per la 'reciprocità' del trattamento," *Africa* 49 (1994): 331–51.

5. On the Venetian Arsenal in this regard, see Robert C. Davis, "Venetian Shipbuilders and the Fountain of Wine," *Past and Present*, no. 156 (1997): 55–86.

6. Archivio di Stato, Venice (ASV), Provveditori sopra Ospedali e Luoghi Pii (OLP), busta 99, Senato, Parte, 12 February 1585 *mv;* ASV, Senato, Parte, reg. 45, 20 October 1565.

7. ASV, OLP, busta 98, Parti et ordini concernenti alla liberatione de' poveri schiavi, 19 February 1586 *mv;* 3 June 1588. The rettori were Venice's provincial governors. The 19 February order was sent to the rettori in "Vicenza, Verona, Bressa, Crema, Bergamo, Padoa, Rovigo, Treviso, Udine, Chioza, Feltre, Lendenara, Bassan, Portogruer, Cividal di Bellun, Cividal di Friul, Conegliano, Salò, et Cologna."

8. Ibid., 3 June 1588.

9. On Venetian Greeks, see ibid., 2 January 1619; and ASV, Senato, Terra, filza 1202, 4 February 1695. On escaped *galleoti* and military deserters, see ASV, OLP, busta 98, 14 May 1764, 13 April 1765, and busta 102, fol. 206.

10. ASV, OLP, busta 98, Parti et ordini, 2 January 1619 *mv.*

11. ASV, OLP, busta 103, Zornal Primo, 4 February 1595–20 December 1625.

12. ASV, OLP, busta 98, Parti et ordini, 15 February 1614, 6 June 1630, 28 May 1722, and busta 99, Senato, Parte, 16 May 1671; ASV, Senato, Terra, filza 1202, 4 February 1695.

13. For the mandati of 1595–1625, see ASV, OLP, busta 103, Zornal Primo; for other sources of funds, see ASV, Collegio, Risposte di Dentro, filza 34, 19 October 1643, and filza 93, 16 January 1680 *mv.* On the ransoming efforts of occupational confraternities, see ASV, OLP, busta 98, Senato, Parti, 8 March 1628, 16 May 1671, 23 August 1724, 5 May 1765.

14. Giovanni Battista Salvago, *Relazione al doge di Venezia sulle Reggenze di Algeri e Tunisi del Dragomanno Gio. Battista Salvago (1625),* ed. Alberto Sacerdoti (Padua, 1937), 95.

15. ASV, OLP, busta 98, 2 March 1762, letter of fra Carlo di S. Agonio: "The ransoming of slaves . . . is made more difficult . . . when they are sought out by Crown Consuls, who, as persons representing the authority of Princes, give just motive to those Barbary [Turks] to increase the price and to seek considerable sums for them."

16. Ibid. On *aggiunti,* see ASV, Collegio, Risposte di Dentro, filza 34, 19 October 1643; for their application in Algiers, see ASV, Senato, Rettori, filza 308, 13 May 1762, fol. C, from which the following is taken:

Primo costo	3000
Per la Dogana [the Dey's council], 10%	300
Per il Caffetan [adviser to the Dey]	15
Per Scrivan e Dragoman [translator] del Dey	8⅓
Per il Chiassy [Commander of the Guard]	2
Per il Dritto del Bagno	17

Al Capitanio e Guardie del Porto	7⅓
Per Sansaria a 1%	30
Per le scritture in Cancellaria	2
Per la Patente	1
Per il loro passaggio e nutrimento sino a Livorno	10
	Piastre 3392½
Per cambio Maritimo e provig.ri a 14%	475
	Piastre 3867½

17. ASV, OLP, busta 98, 21 August 1764, letter of fra Ambrogio di S. Agostino.

18. Frederic C. Lane, in *Venice: A Maritime Republic* (Baltimore, 1973), 424–25, stressed the shift in the Venetian economy after 1630 from the city's once potent industrial base back to widespread commercial activity in the Levant.

19. ASV, Senato, Rettori, filza 308. The Senate's repeatedly stressing its obligations contrasts with the reluctance of other governments to ransom nonsubjects even when taken in their service. For the Papal States in this regard, see ASVat, Gonfalone, busta 1139, fols. 46, 229; for the Duchy of Savoy, see ASV, OLP, busta 102, "Relazione del tempo in cui furono introdotti in Torino li Religiosi detti della SS Trinità, con quali condizioni ricevuti."

20. ASV, OLP, busta 103, "1792, Carte pel riscatto di 50 schiavi liberati in Tunisi," nos. 16, 17, 41, 44; Alberto Tenenti, *Piracy and the Decline of Venice, 1580–1615* (Berkeley, 1967).

21. On Venice's state shipbuilders and their various obligations and activities, see Robert C. Davis, *Shipbuilders of the Venetian Arsenal: Workers and Workplace in the Pre-industrial City* (Baltimore, 1991), esp. chs. 1 and 5.

22. Salvago, *Relazione al doge*, 91. See also, ASV, Collegio, Risposte di Dentro, filza 19, 20 December 1628, where the Venetian shipwright Annibal Ricciadei wrote in his petition to the Collegio: "Fate chose that I should be bought by the son of Usuman Dey, king of Tunisia, to whom I was revealed as being skilled in the craft of shipwright (which they hold in great esteem), and it was my lot to be forced by barbarous tyranny to work and build diverse ships and galleys to his satisfaction, with the result that I merited being chosen as the head shipwright of his workforce, but this, by him reckoned as an honor, rendered me eternally his slave, such that I could never (for any amount of gold) hope for my liberation."

23. The story of Giacomo Colombin is detailed in ASV, Senato, Mar, filza 286, 20 September 1633; the quotation is from Salvago, *Relazione al doge*, 91, 96.

24. Thus, the plea of the enslaved ship master Giuseppe Mazzocati, who was unable to receive aid from Rome because he had been born in Venice and was unable to receive aid from Venice because he had grown up, married, and worked in Rimini, which was in papal territory—"just for this he has not been able to get a thing from the Venetian State" (ASVat, Gonfalone, busta 1144, fol. 539). For a Venetian notary convicted of fraud and sent to the galleys, from which he later bribed his way free only to be taken in turn by Turkish corsairs and enslaved for good in Algiers, see Emanuel

d'Aranda, *The History of Algiers and Its Slavery, with Remarkable Particularities of Africa,* trans. John Davies (London, 1666), 129–30.

25. ASV, OLP, busta 99, Terminazioni, 23 January 1701 *mv,* and busta 103, "Carte pel riscatto," no. 43; ASVat, Gonfalone, busta 1139, fols. 73, 80, and busta 1144, fols. 108, 552.

26. The French had a consul at Tunis at least from 1574, and at Algiers by 1579 (Fernand Braudel, *The Mediterranean and the Mediterranean World in the Age of Philip II,* vol. 2 [New York, 1976], 888). For the first contacts made by ransoming missionaries and for references to merchants operating out of Livorno and Marseilles who maintained connections with and visited the Barbary Coast cities in the 1580s, see Salvatore Bono, "La missione dei Cappuccini ad Algeri per il riscatto degli schiavi cristiani del 1585," *Collectanea Franciscana* 25 (1955): 149–63, 279–304; and ASVat, Gonfalone, busta 1144, fols. 7–19, 74. According to Lucetta Scaraffia, *Rinnegati: Per una storia dell'identità sociale* (Bari, 1993), 29–31, the prototypical captivity narrative can be traced to Miguel de Cervantes, who wrote fictionalized and biographical accounts of his own enslavement experience in *Los Baños de Argel, El trato de Argel,* and *Don Quixote* itself. Some near contemporary English enslavement narratives may well have been produced outside of Cervantes's influence, however. See, e.g., Thomas Saunders, *A true discription and breefe discourse, of a most lamentable voiage, made latelie to Tripolie in Barbarie, in a ship named the "Iesus"* (London, 1587); Edward Webbe, *His Trauailes* (1590; reprint, London, 1868); and Richard Haselton, *Strange and Wonderful Things* (London, 1595).

27. D'Aranda, *History of Algiers and Its Slavery,* 106–7. It was, as Braudel put it, "one form of war . . . replacing another" (*The Mediterranean and the Mediterranean World,* 890–91).

28. In his study of one such slave population, those liberated in three Mercedarian ransoming expeditions to Algiers in the 1660s, Claude Larquié found that of the 221 slaves whose occupation was listed, more than 52 percent had been sailors or fishermen; 19 percent, common soldiers; 15 percent, officers or administrators; 8 percent, in the church; and 8 percent, peasants. Of 757 Christians ransomed about 7 percent were women ("Le rachet des chrétiens en terre d'Islam au XVIIe siècle [1660–1665]," *Bibliothèque de la Revue d'Histoire Diplomatique* 94 [1980]: 297–351).

29. Federico Cresti, "Quelques réflexions sur la population et la structure sociale d'Alger à la periode Turque (XVIe–XIXe siècles)," *Les Cahiers de Tunisie* 34 (1986): 151–64; Lucette Valensi, "Esclaves chrétiens et esclaves noirs à Tunis au XVIIIe siècle," in *Annales: Économies, Sociétés, Civilisations* 22 (1967): 1277; Jean Pignon, "L'Esclavage en Tunisie de 1590 a 1620," in *Les Cahiers de Tunisie* 24 (1976): 145–65; Vittorio Salvadorini, "Traffici con i paesi islamici e schiavi a Livorno nel XVII secolo: Problemi e suggestioni," *Atti del Convegno, "Livorno e il Mediterraneo nell'età medicea"* (Livorno, 1978), 206–25; Michel Fontenay, "Le Maghreb barbaresque et l'esclavage méditerranéen aux XVIème–XVIIème siècles," *Les Cahiers de Tunisie* 43 (1991): 7–43. On slaves held outside the main population centers on the Barbary Coast, see ASVat, Collegio di Propaganda Fide, Scritture Riferite nei Congressi, Barbaria, busta 1 (1638–82), fols. 165–66, 251, 323–25, 478.

30. When saying that slaves might do well for themselves, Salvago may well have had in mind Giacomo Colombin, noted above, whom Salvago mentioned in his report. During his thirty-one years as a slave shipwright in Algiers, Colombin rose to be head shipbuilder of the city's arsenal, with a villa and servants of his own (Salvago, *Relazione al doge,* 92, 96).

31. Saunders, *A true discription,* 6, 10; Francesco di San Lorenzo, *Breve relatione, del calamitoso stato, crudeltà, e bestiali attioni, con le quali son trattati da' barbari li cristiani fatti schiavi, e tutto quello, ch'è passato nel viaggio della redentione de' fedeli di Christo nella città di Tunisi l'anno 1653* (Roma, 1654), 10.

32. "The women [who] are made slaves, if they are beautiful and virgin, for the most part [the Turks] transgress; the weathered and old stay in the houses of the master and serve the mistresses" (Salvago, *Relazione al doge,* 94).

33. ASVat, Collegio di Propaganda Fide, Scritture Riferite nei Congressi, Barbaria, busta 1, fols. 323–25, 428; d'Aranda, *History of Algiers and Its Slavery,* 14–15, 18; William Okeley, *Ebenezer: or, a Small Monument of Great Mercy* (London, 1675).

34. Thus, Salvago writes that "in Algiers there have been brought 96 poor things from Perasto [a Dalmatian port belonging to Venice]: of them a third are dead from sufferings and the plague; in Tunis [were brought] 156, and a quarter of them are lost" (*Relazione al doge,* 96).

35. Fontenay, "Le Maghreb barbaresque," 22; Saunders, *A true discription,* 10; Francesco di San Lorenzo, *Breve relatione,* 15–16; François Dan, *Histoire de la Barbarie et des corsaires* (Paris, 1649), 334–69; Salvago, *Relazione al doge,* 94.

36. In both Algiers and Tunis, about two a year died in slave hospitals in 1720–64 (ASV, OLP, busta 99, Senato, Parte, 10 January 1764 *mv,* and busta 101, "Memorie alla materia del Riscatto," fol. 15).

37. ASVat, Gonfalone, busta 1144, fol. 588.

38. Ibid., fol. 115; ASV, OLP, busta 98, Summario de' Decreti, 30 November 1765; ASVat, Collegio di Propaganda Fide, Scritture Riferite nei Congressi, Barbaria, busta 1, fols. 259–60, and busta 6 (1741–60), fols. 207–16.

39. Such instances, which were admittedly termed "rare and extraordinary cases," nevertheless happened more than once, providing a "scandalous example" to the Venetians, who evidently respected property rights even when it meant having their own fellow citizens paraded "with a chain at the neck" right before them (ASV, OLP, busta 99, Terminazioni, 7 June 1721, 2 Aug. 1723).

40. See, e.g., Alfonso Dominici, *Trattato delle Miserie, che patiscono i Fedeli Christiani Schiavi de' Barbari, & dell'Indulgenze che i Sommi Pontefici han concesse per il Riscatto di quelli* (Rome, 1647), 27–29.

41. D'Aranda, *History of Algiers and Its Slavery,* 128; Dan, *Histoire de la Barbarie,* 370–85. The modern-day literature on the *rinnegati* is broad. Some of the more recent works on which this chapter draws are Bartolomé Bennassar, "Les chrétiens convertis à l'Islam: 'Renégats' et leur intégration aux XVIe–XVIIe siècles," *Les Cahiers de Tunisie* 46 (1991): 45–53; Bartolomé Bennassar and Lucile Bennassar, *Les chrétiens d'Allah: L'Histoire extraordinaire des renégats, XVIe–XVIIe siècles* (Paris, 1989); Scaraffia, *Rinnegati;* and Lucia Rostagno, *Mi faccio turco: Esperienze ed immagini dell'Islam nell'Italia moderna* (Rome, 1983).

42. Knight, *A Relation of Seaven Yeares Slaverie,* 18, 50; d'Aranda, *History of Algiers and Its Slavery,* 132.

43. ASV, OLP, busta 102, Missive et Risponsive, fol. 206, 18 September 1771.

44. ASV, OLP, busta 98: Senato, Parti et ordini, 8 March 1628.

45. The Provveditori stipulated that the *cerche* be carried out "every Sunday and on the Saint's day of each respective church." So that they would be "more greatly animated," the nonzoli would he paid for their efforts: 6 soldi on each lira collected, or 30 percent (see ASV, OLP, busta 98, Stampe, 19 Feb. 1694 *mv;* busta 99, Terminazioni, 11 June 1693, 21 Aug. 1721; busta 101, Terminazioni, 5 Sept. 1759, 8 Feb. 1775 *mv,* and the filza from 1780, on casselle).

46. Ibid., busta 98, 2 January 1619 *mv.*

47. The Santissima Trinità apparently sent small mandati to slaves directly on its own (see ASV, OLP, busta 99, Capitolari, 18 Sept. 1604; 15 July 1684). Other foundations concerned with aiding slaves, usually set up through pious bequests, were located in the parish churches of San Fantin (called the "scuola di San Gaetano") and San Stae, and there was an affiliate confraternity of the Santissima Trinità in Chioggia (ibid., busta 99, Terminazioni, 27 Mar. 1675, 17 Feb. 1692 *mv,* and busta 103, "Processione schiavi"; "Modo con cui sarà formata la Processione," fols. 6–8).

48. Ibid., busta 98, Parti et ordini, 3 June 1588, 4 February 1695 *mv,* and busta 99, Terminazioni, 11 April 1608, 8 February 1622 *mv,* 14 August 1669, 19 April 1675, 15 January 1675 *mv.*

49. Alternatively, the rettore could present the Segretarie with a waiver excusing him as long as it was signed by two of the three provveditori (ibid., busta 98, Parti et ordini, 29 July 1630, 6 Mar. 1664, 4 Feb. 1695 *mv*).

50. On the succolletori, see ibid., busta 99, Decreti, terminazioni, ed altri per cerche, n.d., and busta 101, Terminazioni, 5 September 1759, 11 September 1762.

51. See ibid., busta 101, Terminazioni, of March 1789. The provveditori tracked the success of their succulletori program, noting a rise of income *da terra* and *da mar* as follows: 1750–59, 9,893 ducats; 1770–79, 12,967 ducats; and 1780–89, 15,967 ducats (this latter figure "despite the misfortune of the plague in Dalmazia, [for which] in good part the sources for this act of charity have dried up in those regions"). See also ibid., busta 98, Parti et ordini, Senato, Terra, filza 1202, 4 February 1695 *mv,* "Restretto del danaro entrata in Cassa," and busta 103, Zornal Primo.

52. Ibid., busta 98, Parti et ordini, Senato, Terra, filza 1202, 4 February 1695 *mv,* "Restretto del danaro entrata in Cassa"; busta 100, 13 August 1780; and busta 103, Zornal Primo. Income from the Lenten preachings did not show any such improvement, however, despite the provveditori's considerable efforts, which included sending one of their own and their fante around to all the churches in Venice "the day after" the final appeal (on the fifth Sunday of Lent): from an average of 176 ducats annually in 1596–1625 the take actually declined, down to 132 ducats a year in 1686–95 and just 100 ducats in 1763. See ibid., also busta 98, Senato, Parte, 14 May 1764, fol. 10, and busta 114, 8 July 1735.

53. See ibid., busta 101, "Legati per liberation Schiavi," a small account book that lists ca. 250 such bequests for the years 1631–73, ranging from 1 to 300 ducats, with the

total per year averaging about 145 ducats. A sampling of just over half of the testators of these bequests (131) reveals that legacies were not particularly concentrated by residence but came from all over Venice (46 parishes plus Murano), that nobles made up about 10 percent of the total, that women, both noble and common, were responsible for just over 40 percent of the legacies, and that three contributors were Jews, who left a combined total of 270 ducats.

54. Ibid., busta 98, Senato, Parte, 14 May 1764, fol. 10, and busta 114, 8 July 1735.

55. Thus, Venice's agent in Durazzo once passed along to the provveditori the mere rumor of a *"Ceffaloniotto* [i.e., a man from Ceffalonia, and a Venetian subject] deserter . . . held by a certain Agà Nudarini with such jealousy [that] his surname cannot be discovered." For this and similar tales from Cattaro, Tunis, and Constantinople, see ibid., busta 98, Terminazioni, 26 January 1763 *mv*, and busta 102, fols. 9, 21, 207, 208.

56. In Algiers, for example, the estimated number of Christian slaves dropped from as many as 40,000 in the 1680s down to 800–2,000 a century later; in Tunis the figure went from 10,000 to 12,000 at the end of the seventeenth century to fewer than 2,000 in the 1780s (see Cresti, "Quelques réflexions," 158–61; and Valensi, "Esclaves chrétiens," 1276–78).

57. ASV, OLP, busta 98, Senato, Rettori, filza 308, 13 May 1762, fol. 3, and busta 103, "Interrogatorii, 1764–1771," 24 October 1764; ASVat, Gonfalone, busta 1163, 19 September 1722. Jean Mathiex saw a tenfold increase in the prices demanded in Algiers between 1690 and 1790 ("Trafic et prix de l'homme en Méditerranée aux XVIIe et XVIIIe siècles," *Annales: Économies, Sociétés, Civilisation* 9 [1954]: 157–64).

58. ASV, OLP, busta 98, Parti et ordini, 20 September 1720. Those making the plea for the Trinitarians identified themselves as the "Capi di Piazza e Capi di Parcenevoli."

59. Paul Deslandres, *L'Ordre des Trinitaires pour le rachet des captifs* (Paris, 1903), esp. 318–441. For efforts of the Trinitarians to become more active in the Papal States, see ASVat, Gonfalone, busta 1186, fols. 541–44. On the redenzione generale, see ASV, OLP, busta 102, Missive e Risponsive, 2 November 1765; and Dominici, *Trattato delle Miserie,* 38–40.

60. ASV, OLP, busta 103, Terminazioni, 7 May 1727; MCC, Ms. Gradenigo, busta 171, fols. 165–67.

61. As Father Ambrogio di Sant'Agostino complained to the Senate, "The gifts that Father Ignazio brought [from the Venetians] are useless since one cannot present wine to the Turks." The Algerians, predictably enough, were very offended, having been offered "that which was not the gift for a Prince" (ASV, OLP, busta 98, letter of 21 Aug. 1764).

62. The Trinitarians also produced cross-class comparisons, demonstrating the differences between the prices they and the Venetians were paying for "ordinary" slaves as well as for slaves of quality, such as priests, physicians, ship captains, secretaries *(scrivani da nave),* etc. For all the lists and explanatory comments, see ibid., Senato, Rettori, filza 308, 13 May 1762.

63. Ibid., Senato, Parte, 2 March 1762.

64. For the Trinitarian account of how such processions were staged in these cities, see ibid., busta 103, "Processione schiavi," filza 2, fols. 2–3. See also the processions

described in Francesco Valesio, *Diario di Roma,* ed. Gaetana Scano (Milan, 1977), vol. 1, bk. 2, 12 August 1701; vol. 4, bk. 8, 3 June 1724; vol. 5, bk. 9, 21 June 1729; for an earlier account of a Trinitarian procession in Paris, see Dan, *Histoire de la Barbarie,* 60–62.

65. By contrast, the Mercedarians, who staged multiple processions of those they had ransomed, in various cities in Spain, Portugal, or France, seem to have focused more attention on the ex-slaves themselves, often dressing them in rags they had worn as slaves and even occasionally chaining them together again (Larquié, "Le rachet des chrétiens," 336, 348–49; Braudel, *The Mediterranean and the Mediterranean World,* 888).

66. For the close association of San Zaccaria with the Venetian doge, see Muir, *Civic Ritual,* 221–23; on the girata della Piazza held for newly elected doges, see Davis, *Shipbuilders of the Venetian Arsenal,* 164–67; and ASV, OLP, busta 103, "Processione schiavi," filza 1 ("Descrizione della pubblica Presentazione degli Schiavi Veneti riscattati in Algeri e Tunis dall'Ecc.mo Magistrato Sopra Spedali e Luoghi Pii per opera dei Rd. Padri Trinitari, coll'Ordini della Solenne Processione istituita nello Sbarco degli Schiavi medesmi il giorno 15 Gennaro 1765 nella Città Dominante di Venezia").

67. In fact, because the 1727 procession was held in mid-May, it was impossible to have the girata since the piazza was filled with merchants' booths for the festa della Sensa (see ASV, OLP, busta 103, filza 2, fols. 6–8; and MCC, Ms. Gradenigo busta 171, fol. 176).

68. The most exhaustive description of a Venetian slave procession, and the one on which the following is largely based, is that of 15 January 1764 *mv.* Accounts of the processions of 1727, 1753, and 1792, which are also extensive, indicate that the arrangements for 1764 were fairly typical of those throughout the eighteenth century (ASV, OLP, busta 100, Terminazioni, 11 Jan. 1764 *mv;* busta 103, "Processioni schiavi," filza 1, filza 2, fols. 2–16, filza 4, "1792, Carte pel Riscatto di 50 Schiavi liberati in Tunisi," fols. 18–23. MCC, Ms. Gradenigo, busta 171, fols. 160–78). In 1764 the presiding patriarch was Giovanni Bragadin.

69. The corps of nobles comprised those who were "protectors" of the scuola of the Santissima Trinità and enough senators to make the nobles' number equal to the number of the ex-slaves (ASV, OLP, busta 103, "Processioni schiavi," filza 1).

70. Ibid. In 1764, the two provveditori were the secretary and the treasurer.

71. ASV, OLP, busta 98, Parti et ordini, Senato, Parti, 20 September 1721.

72. The representatives of the scuole had been waiting in the campo of San Zaccaria during the presentation ceremony inside the church (ibid., busta 100, Terminazioni, "Ordine de tenersi").

73. The relevant vision of San Giovanni di Matha—of Christ (or in some versions, an angel) freeing a black slave and a white slave of their chains simultaneously—appears in all Trinitarian representations. The same scene figures prominently in published accounts of the order's ransoming missions and in cataloghi. These particular soleri cost well over 200 ducats to make and paint, and there was the additional expense of the porters to carry them (ibid., busta 103, "Processioni schiavi," fols. 1, 35, and "Nota delle Spese occorse per la Processione").

74. For the Venetian tradition of processionally pairing nobles with pilgrims about

to depart for the Holy Land, see Margaret Newett, *Canon Pietro Casola's Pilgrimage to Jerusalem in the Year 1494* (Manchester, 1907), 113, 153. According to Newett, after the pilgrim trade declined in the sixteenth century, senators continued to be paired off on such occasions, "each . . . with a poor man on his right hand as a sign of humility."

75. ASV, OLP, busta 103, "Processioni schiavi," filza 1.

76. MCC, Ms. Gradenigo, busta 171, fol. 169. Typically, two to three ducats were given to each ex-slave (ASV, OLP, busta 98, Summario de' Decreti, Senato, Parte, 10 May 1727, 13 Apr. 1765; busta 99, Terminazioni, 17 Feb. 1692 *mv;* busta 100, Terminazioni, 31 May 1765; busta 103, "Processioni schiavi," filze 1 and 2, fol. 2).

77. When first setting them up as a permanent board, in 1565, the Senate noted approvingly how well and quickly the provveditori, though still just an ad hoc body, had moved to restore the city's many charitable foundations to financial health and in particular how skillfully they had reasserted state control over those that had been "usurped and . . . with trickery cadged by the Apostolic See" (ASV, Senato, Terra, reg. 45, 20 Oct. 1565).

78. The costs for the procession of 1764 included 150 ducats for printing up the cataloghi, which were integral to the ceremony. By way of comparison, it cost three Trinitarian fathers less than 500 ducats to travel to Algiers and Tunis, bring the slaves back, and feed them while they were aboard ship and in quarantine. Outlays for other slave processions were similar: an apparently partial list of expenses for 1792 amounts to around 1,400 ducats, a third of which went to pay for the military escort. As an indication of the discrepancies between the cost of staging processions and what they might bring in through alms, the scuola of the Santissima Trinità spent 260 ducats between 1748 to 1762 on seven "processioni per schiavi riscatti" and took in on those same seven occasions only 64 ducats in contributions (ASV, OLP, busta 98, Summario de' Decreti, Senato, Parte, 17 Dec. 1792; busta 100, Terminazioni, 15 Jan. and 1 Feb. 1764 *mv;* busta 103, "1792, Carte pel Riscatto," fols. 21–23; busta 104, "1762, Bilanzo, Scoso e Spese").

79. Processions for fewer slaves were obviously staged on a more modest scale than those of 1727 and 1764; typically they were managed entirely by the scuola of the Santissima Trinità and its allied confraternities and likely followed a processional route that led from the Riva degli Schiavoni to San Zaccaria to the scuola's headquarters at Santa Maria Formosa (MCC, Ms. Gradenigo, busta 171, fols. 147–69).

80. ASV, OLP, busta 102, Missive et Risponsive, n.d., "Relazione del tempo in cui furono introdotti in Torino li Religiosi detti della SS Trinità."

81. Davis, *Shipbuilders of the Venetian Arsenal,* 113–14.

82. ASV, OLP, busta 100, Terminazioni, 11 January 1764 *mv.*

83. Muir, *Civic Ritual,* 212–50; Davis, "Venetian Shipbuilders and the Fountain of Wine," 80–86.

84. Interestingly, in the heyday of Barbary Coast slavery one nationality that was particularly likely to slide into a degraded state and to lack moral or financial connections with home was the English: "In fine, all of the nations made some shift to live, save only the *English,* who it seems are not so shiftfull as others, and it seems also they have no great kindness one for another. The winter I was in the Bath [*bagno*], I observ'd there

died about twenty of them out of pure want. Nor are they much esteem'd by the *Turks*" (d'Aranda, *History of Algiers and Its Slavery,* 157).

85. ASV, OLP, busta 103, "Processione schiavi," filza 1.

86. Ibid., busta 99, Terminazioni, [after 1735], addressed to the Capi dei Dieci.

87. For a breakdown of the income employed by the confraternity of the Santissima Trinità, see ibid., busta 114, filza titled "Schiavi Riscattati da primo Maggio 1748 sin tutto Luglio 1762 dalla Scuola della SS. Trinità in S. Maria Formosa." Cf. the sources of ransoming funds collected in the Papal States (ASVat, Gonfalone, busta 8, filza 60).

88. Dominici, *Trattato delle Miserie,* 13.

89. ASV, OLP, busta 98, Parti et ordini, 19 April 1675; ASV, Senato, Terra, filza 1202, 4 February 1695.

90. ASV, OLP, busta 98, Stampe.

91. For a similar exaltation, though on a much more radical level, of *fraternité* as the spirit force behind another longed-for "transparency" between citizens of a unified community, see Lynn Hunt, *Politics, Culture, and Class in the French Revolution* (Berkeley, 1984), esp. 19–51.

92. MCC, Ms. Gradenigo, busta 171, fol. 168.

93. Antonio Carile, "La crudele tirannide: Archetipi politici e religiosi dell'immaginario turchesco da Bisanzio a Venezia"; Massimo Villa, "Gentile e la politica del 'sembiante' a Stambul"; and Giovanni Curatola, "Tessuti e artigianato turco nel mercato veneziano," all in *Venezia e i Turchi* (Milan, 1985), 70–85, 160–85, and 186–209, respectively.

94. Paolo Preto, "Il mito del Turco nella letteratura veneziana," in ibid., 134–43; Irene Alm, "Dances from the 'Four Corners of the Earth': Exocitism in Seventeenth-Century Venetian Opera," in *Musica Franca: Essays in Honor of Frank A. D'Accone,* ed. I. Alm, A. McLamore, and C. Reardon (Stuyvesant, N.Y., 1996), 233–57.

95. Jean du Mont, *A New Voyage to the Levant* (London, 1696), 401–3. See also Stefania Bertelli, *Il Carnevale di Venezia nel Settecento* (Rome, 1992), esp. 11–28; the Venetian Carnival also generally culminated with the famed *volo del Turco,* in which a appropriately costumed Venetian would ascend a tight rope (sometimes on a horse) from the Bacino di San Marco up to the top of the Campanile (*Venezia e i Turchi,* 94, 269; ASV, Collegio, Risposte di Centro, filza 93, 14 Mar. 1680).

IV

After the Fall

15

The Creation of Venetian Historiography

CLAUDIO POVOLO

With the collapse of Venice in 1797 the fate of the Republic passed from the hands of politicians to those of historians—from actuality to memory. In this essay Claudio Povolo examines the first century after the fall of the Republic, when historians contested the meanings of the past and its significance for the future of Italy. Many would have been happy to rehearse a myth of Venice, highlighting the beneficent rule of the aristocrats and the complacency of the subject territories. But they were prevented from doing so by the publication in 1819 of Pierre Daru's Histoire de la République de Venise, *a work that bore in on Venetian conceptions of sovereignty and ended up highlighting some of the defining contradictions in the structure of the Venetian territorial state. As a result, nineteenth-century Venetian historians, even when defending the Republic, were forced to grapple directly with such issues as the inability of the Venetian aristocracy either to impose its will on its subject territories or to co-opt its subjects by offering them citizenship in the Venetian state. However, the opportunity to examine these issues was soon buried under the mountain of mythologizing scholarship based on the documentary riches of the Venetian archives. Paradoxically, in a final transformation, during the Fascist era Venice became the model for a strong and unified Italy. Povolo thus offers a highly nuanced history of the invention of modern historical writing on Venice and reveals the degree to which memories of the Republic served the interests of both nationalists and the bourgeoisie as they sought to forge a new Italian state.*

PIERRE ANTOINE NOËL DARU'S *Histoire de la République de Venise* appeared in 1819. The book enjoyed immediate success and was reprinted and translated many times.[1] Daru's work fit perfectly within a French tradition that early on had identified the Venetian Republic as a decadent political system run by an oligarchic ruling class.[2] Yet Daru's text went beyond earlier historiographical traditions, at once mordant and ideologically committed, to attain a decidedly novel level of interpretation, one rich in comparative perspectives.

In writing his *Histoire* Pierre Daru was able to use documents that had reached Paris after being misplaced during the French and Austrian dominations of northern Italy.[3] This documentation was little known before 1819, and even though it was partly apocryphal (as in the case of the infamous *Capitulary of the State Inquisitors*),[4] it enabled him to highlight certain characteristics and contradictions of Venice's power structure. But the author's personality played an even more decisive role in shaping the *Histoire*. This son of a secretary in the intendancy of Languedoc had enjoyed a rapid and brilliant career in the French army, rising to *commissaire-ordonnateur* in 1799. A close collaborator of Napoleon, he was nominated *commissaire en chef* of the army and supervisor of the emperor's military cabinet in 1805.[5] Daru was thus a highly placed functionary, a member of the governing system in a hierarchical and centralized state structure—a position that doubtless helped him to single out institutional peculiarities in the history of the Republic of Venice. Even if from some perspectives these peculiarities seemed to be obsolete branches of an organism unable to keep up with the times or to regenerate itself, Venice nevertheless represented a highly original model of statehood. Though Daru was fascinated, even seduced, by the proven political and governmental skills of the Venetian ruling class, he also unveiled that class's inner contradictions and guiding principles, which he viewed as the basic causes of the ancient Republic's dissolution.

BEYOND THE MYTH AND THE ANTIMYTH

Daru's account clearly reflected a conception of the state and its sovereign authority that had received its fullest and most important expression in France but had also prevailed, with slightly different tones and modes, all over the Continent. This conception had created perceptibly different social and institutional situations from those holding sway in common-law countries.[6]

Mirjan Damaška, an American scholar of European origin, dedicated a substantial, detailed volume to a comparison of the juridical structures still prevalent on the European continent today with those in effect in the Anglo-Saxon world. *The Faces of Justice and State Authority* makes it clear that in continental Europe power structures whose legitimacy was based on a form of an active state developed. By "active state" Damaška means a state that overshadows society and tends to impose well-defined programs through its hierarchically organized institutions (from center to periphery). By contrast, in the Anglo-Saxon world the formation of a reactive state, with an egalitarian, not hierarchical, power structure, led to institutions aimed at maintaining extant equilibria and, in the judicial field, at settling disputes.[7]

Although historians have greatly diversified their approaches to the study of the state in Italy (both modern and premodern), it remains true that Italy's regional states were quite unlike Europe's major monarchies.[8] In the sixteenth, seventeenth, and eighteenth centuries Italian states had a tenaciously articulated social structure and, as a result, a remarkable distribution of power, not yet markedly dominated by the center. Moreover, compared with the other Italian states, the Republic of Venice, especially with regard to the administrative and judicial machinery, was strikingly unique. Overall, in the rest of Italy hierarchical, professional bureaucratic structures were asserting themselves, most notably in the administration of justice. Venice's peculiarities appeared still more conspicuous in the nineteenth century, with the advent of new bourgeois state forms and the unification of Italy.

Thus, the nineteenth-century historiography on Venice reflected, through its particular approach, a social and *cultural* organization that was clearly ill at ease with the then prevalent political and institutional realities. But the defining characteristics of the defunct Republic were seen through a prism colored by *memory*. This memory was rich in symbols and meanings that, paradoxically, impaired the comprehension of the basic social and institutional reality that had for so long held together the vast territory between the Venetian lagoon and the Lombard provinces of Brescia and Bergamo.

Scholars of the salient episodes in the historiography of the Republic of Venice have underlined the patent links between this historiography and the times that produced it. Moreover, they have highlighted how the history of the Republic has been conceived, from the early nineteenth century until very recently, along two main interpretive lines characterized by their mythical and antimythical components.[9] Enclosed within myth and antimyth are ideological constructs endowed with symbols that have a multiplicity of meanings. However varied and complex the formulation of these constructs is, it is tied both to the specific structure of the state (and of the organization of power it represents) and to the particular idea held by whoever wants to interpret this structure.

Yet the mythical and antimythical elements in Venetian historiography derive ultimately from the specific institutional identity of the Serenissima. Aristocratic power in Venice was decentralized, and the city jealously guarded political rights characterized by pragmatism and conservatism; such power could hardly be compared to the types of authority that took root in other

European and even other Italian states. Because of its very nature, Venice's aristocracy was unable to exploit bureaucratic or hierarchical structures to connect center and periphery and to advance families seeking social betterment. Therefore, the aristocracy of Venice had to rule by maintaining a political and institutional separation between the dominant metropolis and its subject dominions. Between the sixteenth and seventeenth centuries the Venetian government employed diverse tools to assert the predominance of the center, something that also happened in other areas. However, this did not alter the basic organization of the state, and, above all, this always prevented Venice from overcoming the political divide that had characterized center-periphery relations in the Republic from the beginning.[10]

Government was based on a conception of sovereignty that boiled down to the rights of Venice's *aristocrats,* without a more totalizing vision of statehood, one able to create interchange between the several parts of the dominions—a characteristic of the state that Daru, as a high-ranking aristocrat, was ideally situated to identify. Governing was left to magistracies in Venice, which carried out strategies of penetration and rule that were invariably pragmatic and informal, never calling into question ancient constitutional arrangements. In particular, Venice never employed a hierarchical administrative structure of the sort that favored monarchical power and the formation of a political elite of diverse social and geographical origins.[11]

Essential to this original governmental arrangement was the publicization of the political role of Venice and the subject regions' autonomy, as well as of the loyalty to the Serenissima of the subject populations, particularly the rural ones.[12] The Venetian government also relied on a culture that had great influence on the subject societies; this was a culture of extreme micromanagement on a municipal level and of profound separation of the subject centers from the dominant metropolis. A further, vital component of this culture was the inability of the people to conceive of the successive state organs except through the important, indeed essential, mediation of the church.[13] Both these structures and the underlying cultural attitudes had great influence on later reinterpretations of the Republic's history. Reinterpretation involved a more or less direct confrontation with the new state structures but also reflected how much the Veneto derived culturally from Venice's age-old domination.

Before the meandering process of reworking memory and historiographical reinterpretation could recover from the shock of the fall of Venice and begin again in earnest, the *Histoire* of the state official Pierre Daru appeared, as unexpected as a bolt of lightning from a clear sky.

As is well known, an early mythical celebration of Venice as a "mixed state" whose perfect constitution mirrored the harmony of its ruling class came to be questioned in writings that took a decidedly critical stance and uncovered the deep fractures within the Venetian patriciate.[14] This new historiography had a quick and wide dissemination in both published and manuscript forms. The most important texts in this critical strain were the *Opinione . . . come debba governarsi internamente et esternamente la Repubblica Venetiana* (Opinion . . . on how the interior and exterior affairs of the Venetian Republic should be regulated), a work first published in 1681 and falsely attributed to Paolo Sarpi, and the *Relatione sulla organizzazione politica della Repubblica di Venezia* (Relation on the political organization of the Republic of Venice), incorrectly attributed to the emperor's ambassador Francesco della Torre.[15]

These works enunciated a quintessentially Venetian political discourse, directed at the ruling patriciate. They could not therefore replicate the polemical spirit of a state official like Daru, whose analysis drew on a radically different institutional perspective.[16] For him the nature of the Venetian state, one of the most recurrent themes in the historiographical dialectic of myth and antimyth, was merely "a controversy of words."[17] Nevertheless, Daru drew on the antimythical tradition to underline the deep divisions within the patriciate of Venice:

> The number of noblemen had reached twelve hundred; though they were constitutionally equal, in practice they were ranked as powerful nobles or nobles of feeble authority. This government proceeded relentlessly toward oligarchy from the time of its foundation. Status envy led to a conventional if not legal classification. . . . The inequality of wealth eclipsed the equality of rights and enabled the privileged to create dependent relations within the equestrian order that were wholly contrary to the spirit of the constitution. . . . There were scarcely sixty members of the patriciate who enjoyed some affluence, and hardly a quarter lived comfortably; the rest lived in indigence.[18]

Daru's critique of the Venetian expansion into the *terraferma* developed out of his concept of sovereignty. Drawing on some remarks made by Machiavelli, he did not hesitate to define this expansion as a grave error, one that deeply modified the earlier structures of the state. For Daru, a republic seeking expansion should have furnished itself with citizens, not subjects. As he noted in his comparison of the Venetian constitution with that of Rome, "Unlike most states, even monarchies, Venice had no citizens; the nobles were not citizens because they ruled; the populace could not be citizens, for they lacked the right to involve themselves in the affairs of the state."[19] The difficulties Venice experienced after the fifteenth century derived basically from the very form of Venice's identity:

> It is characteristic of sovereignty that the larger it is, the less one desires to have it. In monarchies, even despotic ones, the sovereign is only a magistrate. This magistrate is so eminent, his burden so heavy, that one forgets that it was fate that made him monarch, for his own personal advantage: one sees that he never has pleasure, that he is obliged to live a separate life, that he is, so to speak, a creature outside nature.
>
> This is not the case in small states, above all in those where sovereignty is divided. The smaller the fragment of authority, the more accessible it is to vulgar ambitions. When we see those with authority resemble us in their pleasures and seek to increase them by petty means, or to reserve to themselves some advantages, or to rejoice in our humiliation and to glory in their own greatness, we ask ourselves why, by what right, until when will they be our masters.[20]

Moreover, Daru saw in the absence of the sacrality that always characterized great monarchies the intrinsic weakness of the Republic.[21] Nor did he stop at describing the contradiction implicit in an aristocratic power structure:

> The subjects of Venice's lordship must have compared their fate with that of the citizens of other republics. Long superior to almost all peoples, for the others lived in the abject conditions of feudalism, they were now reduced to envying not just free men but even the inhabitants of monarchies.
>
> In a monarchy the monarch is the source of power, but he is compelled to delegate its execution. On the other hand, in aristocracies there is nothing left for the subjects to do but pay and obey.
>
> That is why some philosophers have maintained that the best aristocracy is the one most closely resembling democracy.[22]

For this French historian the specific nature of Venice's power (or the inability of the ruling class to change it) had been one of the main causes of the Republic's decline and fall. Hence, in tackling a topic only marginal to the antimyth writers, Daru finely portrayed the profound institutional gap between Venice and its dominions. On the terraferma, he observed, all subjects were considered equal and were equally excluded from power by the Venetian oligarchy. If there were slight differences in the condition of some cities of the terraferma, such as Bergamo and Brescia, whose treatment was more paternal, this was due to their strategic location on the state's borders. Daru noted that beyond all constitutional niceties, the basic problem was the distribution of power. The aristocracy of the mainland territories was excluded from power, and its unease and inner turmoil were easy to see:

> The nobles of the mainland had to pay homage to the Venetian aristocracy; this was because of justified suspicion that these nobles were dissatisfied with their political insignificance. Thus the government established a system to maintain divisions between families and to destroy the more powerful nobles. The government thought its interests lay in perpetuating hatred, and therefore it tolerated crimes that manifested and cemented private grudges. Normally such crimes were commissioned to those disreputable men called *bravi,* whom the rich, the timid, and vindictive women kept in their pay. This profession was encouraged by the sale of pardons.[23]

These were not offhand observations. They employed rhetoric outside the stereotypical rhetoric of the antimyth to penetrate the specific nature of the organization of power in the Republic of Venice. Daru perfectly understood the institutional blockage of Venice and the inability of the ruling class to move beyond or around it. His understanding is clear from an important passage he dedicated to the complex pyramid of patron-client relations, whose apex Venetian patricians occupied:

> A chain of old ties created by the inequality of power among the citizens of Venice had established a protector in the patriciate for each of the lesser families. This protector exercised the influence and functions of patronage for his clients. The provincial nobles may have thought they could affect independence, dispensing with this mark of respect; but like the people, they chose a patron. Since no client would dare to address his patron without having established some type of credit beforehand, this custom greatly favored the oligarchy.[24]

APRÈS L'HISTOIRE

Pierre Daru's book was received with deep irritation in Venice. Only twenty years had elapsed since the fall of the Republic, and many of its leading figures were still alive.[25] Moreover, this French work was the first to identify so lucidly the deeper causes of the decline and fall of the Venetian state.[26] It proved easy enough to point out errors in a work that relied on apocryphal sources, like the fake *Capitulary of the State Inquisitors,* or on the ambiguous texts of the antimythical tradition, like the *Opinione* falsely attributed to friar Paolo Sarpi. Yet Daru's historical analysis touched a nerve. It pitilessly sliced through a drama whose last act, already written, had not yet been absorbed and whose outline still lacked definition.

It was no fluke that an abbot, Giannantonio Moschini, and a patrician, Domenico Tiepolo, promptly set about trying to persuade Daru to emend his work, removing the many mistakes they had handily discovered in it and also correcting his interpretation, which too often cast Venice in a negative light.[27] In 1828 Tiepolo published his *Discorsi sulla storia veneta,* a two-volume work whose subtitle, *Corrections of Some Errors Discovered in the Venetian History of Monsieur Daru,* took direct aim at his French adversary.[28] Tiepolo sought to defend the role of the Venetian aristocracy and the Republic's image. He therefore dealt principally with the remote past and ignored the social and institutional transformations of the first decades of the nineteenth century.[29] Yet his work undoubtedly contains some interesting approaches to the Venetian past. Daru's harsh critique had shattered Venice's conservative cultural world, compelling Venetian intellectuals to confront tangled issues that even the antimythical literature had treated only tangentially.

Even if he could not undermine Daru's main criticisms, in his *Discorsi* Tiepolo could not avoid at least some of the questions raised by Daru's polemic. Actually, Tiepolo's objections, convoluted and unorganized as they were, confirmed many of the French historian's assertions. For example, Tiepolo vigorously rejected what Daru had to say about the oligarchic nature of power in Venice and about the deep transformations this occasioned for the city's constitution; instead he stressed the controlling influence of the Great Council.[30] But when discussing the patronage of the Venetian patricians over the lesser folk, Tiepolo denied that the titles *protector* and *client* existed in Venice; at the same time, he offered a splendid anthropological explanation of this social system. Thus Tiepolo indirectly confirmed Daru's essential accuracy with regard to some basic characteristics of the Venetian power structure:

> On the contrary, those citizens who, on account of cohabitation or some other factor, entered into relations with a nobleman called themselves his lovers [*amorevoli*], a title that excludes dependence. There was no obligation attached to assistance by the nobles save the natural gratitude of people who receive favors to those who provide them. Nor were the nobles obliged to support or protect those who turned to them beyond the point to which their particular benevolence to the individual, or the justice of his cause, led them. Nobles derived no influence or honor from the relation, for, far from being able to deploy pomp or use those who were somehow their dependents, to have clients would have been a mark of distinction offensive to the aristocratic sense of equality. Hence, for nobles it was only a nuisance to give friendly aid to the affairs of people who were in this relationship with them.
>
> The same held true for relations of Venetian nobles with nobles from the

provincial or subject cities. No one would have made use of the title of protector in public deeds.[31]

Tiepolo used some of Daru's explicit statements regarding revealing moments of popular support for the Republic to discuss the delicate issue raised by the Frenchman: the gap between Venice's aristocracy and all other subjects. But this Venetian patrician could not grasp the complex question of sovereignty. Citing the works of Sandi and Tentori, Tiepolo merely depicted the formal characteristics of Venice's institutions, stressing the independence of the local ruling classes:

> All cities and provinces of the Venetian state were ruled according to agreements and conditions stipulated when they were incorporated into the Venetian state . . . ; not just major cities, capitals to their provinces, but even many minor places and corporations within the provinces, obtained regular statutes first and later their own governing councils, which elected officials to administer, in some cases, all justice. Thus the duty of inspectors sent by the government was only to exercise the rights of sovereignty, to preside over the execution of the law and the proper functioning of civic administration, and, in most cases, to function as appellate judges.[32]

Daru's work followed lines of interpretation that were highly unusual in the Venetian intellectuals' milieu. It reawakened interest in themes and issues that perhaps could not have been ignored much longer even by a historiographical tradition bent on reasserting the myth of the Republic.[33] Beginning in the late 1840s, Venetian historians, particularly Giuseppe Cappelletti and Samuele Romanin, attempted syntheses that reserved ample attention for the wise government of the Republic and the ideal continuities with the social and cultural undercurrents leading first to the uprisings of 1848 and then to Italian unification.[34] But at the same time, some of the more modern historical issues delineated in the 1820s and 1830s were taken up by some of the most careful and acute minds of Venice's intelligentsia.

THE ''WEAK'' MYTH

Agostino Sagredo was an intellectual of patrician origins, but he was fully aware both of the recent political and social transformations and of the indispensable role the upper middle class now had in all institutions. He stepped into the complex historiographical debate by writing a "Storia civile e politica" to introduce two prestigious volumes entitled *Venezia e le sue lagune* (Venice and its lagoons), which was presented at the ninth congress of Italian scientists, held in Venice in 1847.[35] Sagredo was basically outside of the polemic that had marked earlier contributions to the debate, and he was unwilling to reread Venice's history from a nostalgic point of view. Still, he was one of those historians who reinterpreted the myth of Venice, however critically, however willing to take current events into account:

> The Venetians' interior policies were always mild: as few taxes on the subjects as possible; government as much as possible through aristocratic institutions; with abuses (inevitable in human affairs) equitably distributed; and justice equal for all. Considering the times and the moral level of other nations, these policies were unequaled in solidity and in the good they did to the governed, as well as to the government. . . . Considering that in the later situation of our peninsula the Republican government became an aristocratic oligarchy, one with good laws establishing hereditary equality among nobles, and that this guaranteed Venice its political independence for so many centuries, and saved it from intestine dissension and domestic tyranny, no one will be able to curse Venice's government. Later changes took place smoothly, and ancient institutions were always respected. History, soaring above human passions to conquer the centuries, will demonstrate to our fellow Venetians that they should not hate the Republic because its institutions were aristocratic instead of democratic, for the latter are closer to domestic tyranny and foreign rule. As to the opinions of foreigners, they should not concern us much, for they are often unfair and not disinterested about our affairs.[36]

Agostino Sagredo stripped the myth of its usual rhetorical ornaments and dressed it in his lucid critical analysis. But in this analysis the Venetian aristocracy—largely, obviously, because of current affairs—was credited with a historical role and function. Looking beyond the aristocrats' human foibles, this role placed the Venetian patriciate above all other classes and ascribed to it a type of social and cultural superiority. Sagredo acknowledged the deep social divisions within the aristocracy, but he also stressed the institutional homogeneity of this group, at whose head lay the Council of Ten and the State Inquisitors, exclusive preserves of the oligarchs, and at whose base were representative assemblies such as the Great Council.[37] He perspicaciously noted that, appearances to the contrary, this constitutional arrangement changed radically over time:

> Rich nobles, middling and poor ones, had equal rights in the Great Council, the true sovereign in the Republic. Seldom did poor nobles enter the Senate, to which (in theory and practice) the Great Council delegated executive authority and the right to declare war, make peace, form alliances, and regulate finances. The poor noble seldom entered those magistracies with control over the Senate or those who guarded the security of the state. Poor nobles seldom sat on the Councils of Forty. Major offices went to rich nobles, medium-level ones to

nobles of medium fortunes. Nonetheless, in the Great Council all voted equally and the rich and middling nobles depended on the votes of the poor nobles to obtain their offices. So they had to respect and mollify them, providing for their needs . . . as a result many magistracies that had grown obsolete were preserved.[38]

In this lucid analysis the myth of the Venetian Republic gains potency from being examined with all its blemishes. Daru's almost sacrilegious polemic is certainly behind Sagredo's "Storia." But it fails to trouble a historical vision in which the leitmotif is the political, almost ethical superiority of a ruling class that has both the burden and the glory of leading the Republic. This is manifest, for example, in Sagredo's treatment of Venetian patron-client relations:

> Along with other Roman institutions, patronage and clientage reached Venice. There are examples in the earliest chronicles. It never subsided, and no middling or lesser man lacked a patron, who protected him from anyone who sought to do him wrong. The Council of Ten was the great patron of the people, and we could cite cases of violence done against the populace by the nobles that were mercilessly punished. Nobles treated the people fraternally. It was a vital part of an aristocrat's education, once he reached adulthood, to learn to treat the populace fraternally. Venetian aristocrats were quite unlike those nobles who, in imitation of the Spaniards, believed the people to be made of a different clay than Adam was.[39]

The mottling in Sagredo's characterization of the mythic past both defines his approach and makes his work more credible. His chiaroscuro history is far more effective than the nostalgic and openly defensive approach with which earlier Venetian writers had opposed Daru's *Histoire*. But Sagredo's nuanced tone could scarcely be maintained in discussing an issue the Frenchman had identified as all-important, namely, the prickly question of sovereignty and the organization of the state. With his customary clear-sightedness, Sagredo pinpointed the primary cause of Venice's decadence in the state's failure to fuse its components together. He was aware of the mistakes and inertia of the Venetian ruling class:

> The Venetian nobles made a huge mistake by refusing to touch up (if we may use the term) the aristocracy by summoning into the ruling class the richest and most illustrious of citizens and subjects. They would have attained thereby two useful goals: growth and power for the ruling class, and the harmonization of interests of the provinces and the capital city. Those who judge the past by contemporary standards always err, and thus it is wrong to think that the Venetian aristocracy should have summoned the subject peoples to participate in rule as so many representative governments do today. Given the existence of a hereditary aristocracy, the only way to maintain its vigor was to allow the best subjects to enter the government while at the same time perpetuating the privileges of the ruling class.

This promotion should not have been sold for cash, but granted as a reward for useful services rendered, to encourage sacrifices for the Fatherland.[40]

Sagredo views the state's failure to fuse its parts together as a sign of the extreme weakness afflicting the Republic in its later centuries. Just as there were no general and uniform laws throughout the Venetian dominions, so too myriad different laws, customs, and administrative bodies existed.[41]

Subjects did not participate in sovereignty, which was an exclusive prerogative of the patricians of Venice; but, as Sagredo states, rather like Renzo's cousin from Bergamo in Manzoni's *I promessi sposi,* it never occurred to them to complain about this. Instead, it was the mainland aristocracy that chafed at the bit. Nor was this surprising:

> In absolutist governments, everything emanates from the highest authority, which showers honors, privileges, and favors on the nobility. In return, rather than taking offense at having to obey the lord of all, nobles are honored to be able to provide even private services to him. Through these very services the highest authority excludes other subjects from these private services and entrusts his person to the nobles alone. Thereby he makes providing the services desirable. In representative governments, when the subject nobility forms a state organ with the same weight as the rest of the nation, whether it is a personal or hereditary nobility, it does not feel disdain for the office of head of state or for representing the nation of which it is an integral part. But an aristocracy that is subject to another, whose status is reduced to vain titles, cannot love the dominant aristocracy and would prefer the rule of a monarch.[42]

Behind Sagredo's analysis one can discern the critical comment made by Daru, who, in particular, had tackled the whole notion of sovereignty, the exclusive monopoly of Venice's patriciate. If Sagredo understood the accuracy of Daru's critique, he proved unable to identify its basis. Once more he preferred to touch upon one of the classic themes of the myth of Venice:

> The Venetian nobles made a great mistake, fomenting resentment against themselves by their haughty behavior and clear demonstrations that they considered provincial nobles mere subjects to whom they preferred the subject populace. As we have said, if they had gradually absorbed the nobles into the dominant aristocracy, if they had carried out a reasonable fusion of ruling classes, they would not have been detested, and none would have rejoiced over the Republic's destruction. The people of Verona, Brescia, and Bergamo proved by their actions during Venice's dying moments that the mainland's subject populace loved Venice's government.[43]

Because he could not bring himself to confront squarely the concept of sovereignty, a concept whose complexities he understood so well, Sagredo did not push his analysis to the limit. Tackling sovereignty would have involved debating the merits of the institutional structure of the Venetian state and the rights of its ruling class. In the final analysis, it was better to recycle the old myths of paternalism, good government, and the loyalty and attachment of the subject peoples to the Serenissima, for thereby the ideal continuity with the present was confirmed. He evidently chose to ignore the fact that the very components of this myth had a justification, as well as some real roots, in Venice's power structure.

THE CELEBRATORY MYTH

Perhaps the most interesting phase in Venetian history writing of the nineteenth century ended with Agostino Sagredo and his panoramic sketch in *Venezia e le sue lagune*. Though marked by a strong sense of nostalgia and the desire to re-evoke past glory, Venetian historiography also manifested a real vocation for critical re-examination and for historical introspection. Then, with Samuele Romanin's *Storia documentata di Venezia* (Documented history of Venice) the historical myth of the Republic entered a new phase. In this new historiography documentary zeal and celebration of good government left little room for research directed at identifying the key components of Venice's sovereignty and state structure. For Romanin, the defining attributes of the Venetian state were peace and concord, the latter of which was justified by the ample autonomies enjoyed by the subject cities:

> Every sign of modern representation existed, each city governed its own affairs autonomously, the countryside could express its opinions too, there was no lack of strict vigilance over the correct functioning of institutions. Only a few more steps were needed to excise abuses and broaden national representation and admit provincial nobles to the offices of the Republic; this would have made their dependence seem lighter and given them an occupation and would have been a very beneficial reform for the Republic.[44]

Romanin's *Lezioni di storia veneta* (Lessons of Venetian history), written slightly later, expresses the mythical reading of the Republic's history at its most intense. Romanin viewed the inevitable grumblings and even riots not as the fault of Venice's ruling class but rather as an inescapable consequence of the autonomies and rights that, regrettably, Venice granted its subjects:

> Of course the dominated peoples were not always overjoyed, nor without poverty, violence, abuses, and suffering. This was especially on account of the counts and lords to whom, upon the conquest or annexation of their cities, Venice

granted the maintenance of their privileges or customs, more properly called abuses. But the general population loved the Venetian government because they knew it did everything possible to find solace and solutions for their ills, because they knew it did not squeeze the provinces to enrich the metropolis, which, on the contrary, bore a heavier fiscal burden since it enjoyed more privileges. . . . The subject populations measured their government by contemporary standards and evaluated it with common sense, never imagining a future when learned writers and famed lawyers would fault the Venetian administration for not introducing into its judiciary systems several centuries earlier the rights that the nineteenth century expects.[45]

In 1855 the patrician Girolamo Dandolo's *La caduta della Repubblica di Venezia* (The fall of the Republic of Venice) appeared.[46] It originated as a polemical response to the bitter and unreasonable pages written by Fabio Mutinelli, who had portrayed the Republic in its last centuries as decrepit, soft, and mummified. But more precisely, it was a late fruit of the cultural climate of the preceding decades, when a historiography concerned with some political and institutional aspects of the Venetian state had developed.[47] In fact, in his book Dandolo squarely confronted the political problems of sovereignty and the unity of the Republic. In particular, in commenting on and critiquing Scipione Maffei's *Consiglio politico* (Political advice), Dandolo held that the root cause of the Republic's crisis was the failure to enlist the support of the ruling classes of the subject areas.[48] While evincing perplexity in the face of the Veronese marquis's proposal, the Venetian patrician advanced a quite unpersuasive thesis. This thesis nevertheless reveals how he had comprehended the specific and different nature of the Venetian state. According to Dandolo, every town council on the Venetian mainland and in the maritime dominions should have been allowed to elect representatives who "in perpetuity" would enjoy the right of participating in the supreme council of the Republic:

> The Great Council would have been strengthened by a considerable but not overwhelming number of votes. Through these representatives of the provinces, the union with the metropolis would have grown ever tighter, while the interest of the provincial nobles in maintaining the government would have efficiently contributed to a more vigorous and free government. . . . Yet this would not have enabled Venice to perpetuate its governmental form. . . . However, a new age of generous and enlightened reforms would have begun, and Venice would have been better prepared for the shock of new opinions from beyond the Alps. Surely the Republic would have vanished anyway, but probably later than it did. And this spontaneous movement from a tighter to a looser aristocracy might have proved a means of transition toward monarchy, the only way to preserve national independence.[49]

Italy's unification left Venetian historiographers divided but still tending to dust off the old myth of the Republic, even if in their writings this myth was modernized and based on a positivist cult of the historical document.[50]

Thus, along with the historiographical myth, what might be called the "archival" myth arose. As the Venetian State Archive became more accessible and easier to use, the ancient and vast documentation produced by Venice's magistracies served to accelerate the reevaluation of the past by historians who aimed at organizing a cult of the city's memory.[51] This historiography neglected investigation of the origins, the institutional uniqueness, and especially the political characteristics that, together with a long domination of vast and heterogeneous territories, gave rise to Venice's original and contradictory concept of sovereignty, issues that, as we have seen, had been present in the works of Sagredo and Dandolo.

Despite the variety of scholars active in this period and the huge scholarship lavished upon a few major Venetian institutions, the written history of the Republic retained some of its fundamental traits. These traits betrayed certain cultural attributes that still reflected long-term social and anthropological tendencies in Venice.[52] History written by the intellectual elite of upper-middle-class extraction tended to focus upon the historical and cultural specificities of the metropolis; history produced by mainlanders of more modest background was anchored to an extreme, fragmented localism.[53] Debate on the intrinsic reality of the Venetian state was almost nonexistent.[54] Instead, the urge to give new mythical luster to the historical function of the Republic was very strong,[55] even though, in this vision of the past, cultural links still binding the Veneto's society at the deepest level to long centuries of Venetian rule were not taken into account.[56]

THE STRONG MYTH

Within a historiography crushed by the narrowness of the myth of Venice, Vincenzo Marchesi is a figure of some relevance. In the last decade of the nineteenth century he became involved in a bitter polemic with Pompeo Molmenti, the standard-bearer of the army of historians seeking to celebrate the glories of the ancient Republic.[57] Marchesi seems to sail smoothly through the shallows of the historiographical myth, but actually his analysis never deals with intrinsic political or cultural characteristics of the Serenissima. Instead Marchesi heads for horizons ominous with new, unsettling interpretations of past history.

Marchesi's short but dense piece entitled "Le origini e le cause storiche della rovina della Repubblica veneta" (The origins and historical causes of the wreck of the Republic of Venice) confronts some issues pertaining to the organization of the Venetian state. It does so in some especially noteworthy passages. According to Marchesi, Italian political history was marked by the persistence of elements that had prevented the formation of a unified state:

> This is the main distinction between European history in general and Italian history in particular. With us, the fragmentation of power and the prevalence of individual and local interests have eclipsed general and national interests. On the other side of the Alps, by contrast, we find the concentration of power and the subordination of the privileges of corporations and cities to a loftier end, to a higher authority that gradually dons so much majesty as to become inaccessible to the populace and even to the proud barons who for so long had kept it silent and impotent.[58]

Venice had perceived the profound transformations as they took place and had initiated a determined expansion into the mainland in the fifteenth century. But she had been unable to rejuvenate her institutions:

> Venice erred in behaving like Italy's other major powers, that is, in treating the conquered cities as subjects while leaving them their ancient constitutions and autonomies. The Republic contented itself with making of the cities friendly subjects but never allowed them to participate in its life, or never shared power with them. Whence it happened that particular interests always prevailed over general ones, so the state lacked unity and strength.[59]

This analysis did not depend on a true understanding of the specific structure of the Republic's institutional organization or of the power relations within Venice's ruling class and between it and the subjects of the dominions. Nevertheless, Marchesi did recognize that the fate of the Serenissima had depended increasingly on the rapid expansion within Europe of states with a different type of organization:

> The Republic of Saint Mark insanely believed that it could defy the new times from the security of its lagoons and that it could use the same systems that had worked so well in the Middle Ages (but proved fatal in modern times) to keep its wealth, power, and fearsome reputation. All of this holds true, more or less, for each of Italy's states, with the sole exception of Piedmont. This small state understood, at least in part, the transformation of old Europe and sought and wanted to be needed, convinced as it was that any state in whose existence neighboring states had no interest was destined, sooner or later, to be erased from the map.[60]

As is evident, a concrete treatment of sovereignty is left in the background by design. Nor is this surprising in light of Marchesi's concluding arguments:

> Venice suffered much in this period, paying excessively for its past glory and mistakes; now, at last, reunited with the great Italian Fatherland, Venice strives to make up for lost time and to be worthy of its sister cities. Even today, if Venice wants, it has a very lofty role, that is, to become the greatest merchant and military port in the Adriatic Sea, to erect new and magnificent buildings, and to send its vessels to remote shores with the Italian tricolor flag hoisted alongside the emblem of Saint Mark.[61]

This is a different inflection of the myth. Building on reflections about the historical causes of the Republic's decline and fall, Marchesi's explicit wish is for new, more incisive interventions by the state and its ruling class. Here we are far removed from the self-critical version of the myth that we saw in Sagredo's writings. Much like Marchesi, a few decades later Antonio Battistella attributed the decadence of the Republic to the absence of the kind of solidity only a strong state could ensure. In his *La repubblica di Venezia* Battistella wrote:

> For Venice waited with great cunning and patience to assemble its dominions, but when it had managed to do so, it proved unable to unify them or to give them the rational, solid unity that, to a greater or lesser extent, other European states achieved. If there is an apparent external resemblance between Venice and other early modern states, there is also great dissimilarity. For Venice, unification went little beyond external appearances; unification was only territorial, for the state remained Venice alone. . . .
>
> There was no uniformity in the enfeebled, overprotected municipal governments. Feudal leftovers persisted, unreconcilable, in strident contrast with the reformed municipal constitutions. All this confused and hybrid jumble of dissimilar things generated a certain indeterminateness in executing government and consequently weakened it.[62]

For a few decades the upper middle class had favored a historiography that indulged certain traditional themes in the myth of Venice. This had imparted legitimacy to the adoption of a specifically Venetian identity and had served to claim a larger role for this class's political representation. But now the upper middle class had endowed itself with new interpretive frameworks within which the evocation of the ancient Republic became a tool for affirming the pressing need for new power structures in which, evidently, the bourgeois felt completely integrated.

The new outlook is enunciated in what can surely be considered the first systematic study of Venetian institutions. In the introduction to his *Costituzione di Venezia dopo la serrata del Maggior Consiglio* (Constitution of Venice after the closing of the General Council), first published in 1931, Giuseppe Maranini has no doubts. He declares that "to study the political institutions of a great Italian state, of the greatest and purest heir to Rome, in terms of the grandiosity and vigor of its political conceptions, is no sterile task for bookworms. It is rather a vibrant investigation, pertinent to the resolution of the gravest political problems. In the evolution of the Venetian State we can detect some fundamental laws of life and of political development, shared by every time and place."[63] The Venetian state was an expression of a great aristocracy. Even if this class underwent some decline in the last centuries, it still had no equals:

> Venice's aristocracy had an uncompromising awareness of the nature of its state. When it became necessary, with prudent industry the aristocrats proclaimed and defended their state's principles, transforming an unwitting, spontaneous creation of historical accident into a self-aware, thoughtful manifestation of the human will. It was thanks to this that the Republic of Venice did not follow the fate of all other Italian communes. Venice's aristocracy not only avoided domestic tyrannies but also eluded foreign domination. It carried out governmental activity of admirable and formidable complexity, preserving the sea empire, building a new dominion on the mainland, asserting itself as a global power, tenaciously resisting the severest reverses.[64]

This, then, is a conception in which the state is identified concretely with the role and function of the ruling class. Paradoxically, this notion appears in a historical interpretation that, despite—indeed beyond—the "decadence," reappropriated some of the most traditional elements of the myth of Venice. Yet this interpretation also abandoned those nineteenth-century readings of the uniqueness of Venetian sovereignty and of the innermost workings of the power structure that shaped Venice's physiognomy as well as its contradictions.

The new historiography accomplished what can be considered the ultimate interpretive paradox of the myth. The proud, even vainglorious search for a strong, compact model state with valid institutions ended up discovering it in the history of a Republic that only a century earlier had aroused quite opposite reactions. Through this paradox the Republic of Venice, an institutional structure whose very makeup singled it out as the antithesis of statehood, rose to mythical status as an exemplar for the new political scenarios of unified Italy.

Translation by Paolo Squatriti

NOTES

1. Pierre Antoine Noël Daru, *Histoire de la République de Venise,* 7 vols. (Paris, 1819); a second edition appeared in Paris in 1821. All citations are from the 1819 edition. Daru's history was translated into German in 1824, and after another Parisian printing (1826) an Italian version appeared: *Storia della Repubblica di Venezia,* trans. Bianchi Giovini, 11 vols. (Capolago, 1837–38). Two further French editions followed, in 1853 and 1907. See G. Luciani, "Un complément inédit à l'*Histoire de la République de Venise* de Daru: La correspondence avec l'abbé Moschini," *Revue des études italiennes* 6 (1959): 110.

2. A. N. Amelot de la Houssaie, *Histoire du gouvernement de Venise* (1676; reprint, Amsterdam, 1714); H. de Saint-Didier, *La ville et la République de Venise* (1680; reprint, Amsterdam, 1697); C. Freschot, *Nouvelle rélation de la ville et la République de Venise* (Utrecht, 1709); M. A. Laugier, *Histoire de la République de Venise depuis sa fondation jusqu'à présent,* 12 vols. (Paris, 1758–68). On these works see Piero Del Negro, "Forme ed istituzioni del discorso politico veneziano," in *Storia della cultura veneta,* ed. Girolamo Arnaldi and Manlio Pastore Stocchi, 6 vols. (Vicenza, 1976–86), 4, pt. 2: 418–22; and Luciani, "Un complément inédit," 108–9.

3. Luciani, "Un complément inédit," 105; Claudio Povolo, *Il romanziere e l'archivista: Da un processo veneziano del '600 all'anonimo manoscritto dei Promessi Sposi* (Venice, 1993), 99–100.

4. On this document, the "falso *capitolare* degli inquisitori di stato," see Povolo, *Il romanziere e l'archivista,* 102–6.

5. Luciani, "Un complément inédit," 111–13.

6. As R. C. Van Caenegem noted in *Judges, Legislators, and Professors: Chapters in European Legal History* (Cambridge, 1987), 114, "Right through the early Middle Ages and up to the mid-twelfth century English and continental law belonged recognisably to one legal family, Germanic and feudal in substance and procedure. . . . A century later the landscape had changed: Roman law and Roman-canonical procedure were transforming life in many parts of the Continent (and others were to follow), whereas in England a native law, common to the whole kingdom, that was—and remained— free from the substance and procedure of the new continental fashion, had arisen."

7. Mirjan R. Damaška, *The Faces of Justice and State Authority* (New Haven, 1986). Damaška identifies two different conceptions of the functions of the state, which he connects to the administration of justice: "One solution is to see these views as embodying two contrary inclinations, each rarely strong enough totally to displace the other: the one is to have government manage the lives of people and steer society; the other is to have government maintain the social equilibrium and merely provide a framework for social self-management and individual self-definition"(11). See also Van Caenegem, *Judges, Legislators, and Professors,* on the differences between common-law and civil-law systems.

8. On the complexity of this historiography, see Giorgio Chittolini, Anthony

Molho, and Pierangelo Schiera, eds., *Origini dello stato: Processi di formazione statale in Italia fra medioevo ed età moderna* (Bologna, 1994). For Schiera, Italy offers "an ideal test-case" for studying the beginnings and difficulties of new states, especially in places where highly particularistic and autonomous institutional systems existed. The essays in this volume analyze specific cases, comparing them with general pictures. But the crucial issue for *ancien régime* states, that is, the deeper connections between dominant and dominated centers, does not seem to have been tackled. These connections provided an ineluctible mechanism of social ascent for families and lineage groups through administrations and bureaucracies that tended to be hierarchical. In societies whose rankings depended on status and honor such distinctions dictated the degree of osmosis that was possible between center and periphery and determined the effective strengthening of ruling elites. For an English version of this work, see Julius Kirshner, ed., *The Origins of the State in Italy, 1300–1600* (Chicago, 1995), which, however, does not include the comments of the respondents at the conference upon which the Italian edition was based.

9. Luciani, "Un complément inédit," 10–48; M. Canella, "Appunti e spunti sulla storiografia veneziana dell'Ottocento," *Archivio Veneto* 106 (1976): 72–115; James Grubb, "When Myths Lose Power: Four Decades of Venetian Historiography," *Journal of Modern History* 58 (1986): 43–94; G. Benzoni, "La storiografia," in Arnaldi and Stocchi, *Storia della cultura veneta,* 6:597–623; as well as John Martin and Dennis Romano's introduction to this volume.

10. The undeniably predominant center was never integrated with the peripheral societies, which often had large cities within them whose identity was thereby squashed. Tighter patron-client bonds with Venice's patricians substituted for the integration and ascent in the power structure of the powerful families of the mainland (a process of integration rendered impossible by the absence of a real court) (Claudio Povolo, *L'intrigo dell'onore: Poteri ed istituzioni nella Repubblica di Venezia tra Cinque e Seicento* [Verona, 1997]). According to some, the distinction between the constitutional level, dominated by the center, and the administrative level, with reciprocal concessions between center and periphery, began to prevail among Italy's states in the early seventeenth century. Yet this distinction is misleading if one considers the real concentration (or distribution) of power that took place through the potential for ascent, from periphery to center, of parental and lineage groups (L. Mannori, *Il sovrano tutore: Pluralismo istituzionale e accentramento amministrativo nel principato dei Medici [secoli XVI–XVIII]* [Milan, 1994]). Beyond their appointed functions, hierarchically arranged administrative and judicial machineries moved power toward the center, depriving local societies of their vitality. Wherever this proved impossible, as in the Republic of Venice, the dominant center asserted itself, while the vigor of the municipalities was preserved.

This sketch of the general political and institutional characteristics of Venice does not seek to rob specific contexts of meaning or simplify the messy processes that made their histories. Rather, it seeks to highlight the *cultural* structures that imprinted themselves on the social fabric and to a certain extent influenced institutional arrangements far more than the formal legal structure.

11. See José Antonio Maravall, *Estado moderno y mentalidad social (siglos XV a XVII)* (Madrid, 1972).

12. The authority of the dominant center depended on the maintenance of the ancient institutions and exploitation of the heated conflicts between town and country or those between social groups. The supposition of loyalty on the part of the subject populations arose from the policies of a government in an institutional impasse that Venice's patricians could not or would not overcome. Such propagandistic elements are fully formed in nineteenth-century historiography, especially where Venice's institutions or society are examined (ignoring the fact that this city-state had quickly become a territorial state, however exceptional).

13. In his examination of the salient characteristics of society in the Veneto, Silvio Lanaro speaks of the "genealogy of a model" in *Storia d'Italia: Le regioni dall'Unità ad oggi: Il Veneto,* ed. Lanaro [Turin, 1984], 5–96). If we can speak of a model at all, we must locate its origins in cultural and anthropological structures whose early modern vitality depended on a highly original political system that had a deep impact on later times. *Culture* here reflects a range of meanings and symbols that interact with the social system. As an interpretive tool, the distinction between culture and social system avoids "the simplistic view of the functional role of religion in society which sees that role merely as structure-conserving, and [substitutes] for it a more complex conception of the relations between religious belief and practice and secular social life" (Clifford Geertz, "Ritual and Social Change: A Javanese Example," in *The Interpretation of Cultures* [New York, 1973], 146). The extreme legalism of the Republic was balanced (or even explained) by the tenuous sacrality of the doge, a "first among equals" who could not embody the human and divine, the sacred and the profane, as happened in monarchical states.

14. On the myth of Venice, see F. Gaeta, "L'idea di Venezia," in Arnaldi and Stocchi, *Storia della cultura veneta,* 3, pt. 3: 565–641; and idem, "Venezia da 'stato misto' ad aristocrazia 'esemplare,'" in ibid., 4, pt. 2: 937–94.

15. *Opinione del Padre Paolo Servita, consultor di stato, come debba governarsi internamente ed esternamente la Repubblica venetiana, per haver il perpetuo dominio* (Venice, 1680); G. Bacco, ed., *Relatione sulla organizzazione politica della Repubblica di Venezia al cadere del secolo decimosettimo* (Vicenza, 1856). On the antimyth, see Piero Del Negro, "Forme ed istituzioni," 411–20; and idem, "Proposte illuminate e conservazione nel dibattito sulla teoria e la prassi dello stato," in Arnaldi and Stocchi, *Storia della cultura veneta,* 5, pt. 2: 123–45.

16. Still, the *Histoire* offers several positive evaluations of the organization of the Venetian magistracies: "In republics the frequency of elections makes for a stormy society; in Venice, where every office was temporary, with the exceptions of the doge's, the grand chancellor's, and the procurators', this problem never arose, for elections were slow, immutable, silent, and the offices so brief as to confer little importance on those who held them. The need for votes imposed on the ambitious quite humble and placid behavior" (5:476–77).

17. Ibid., 5:433.

18. Ibid., 5:455, 462, 464. Bianchi Giovini, irritated by these comments, repeatedly objected in his edition of the *Histoire* that Venice's aristocracy had only become oligarchic in the seventeenth century (Daru, *Storia,* 9:283, 291).

19. *Histoire,* 5:546–47.

20. Ibid., 4:160. Daru recognizes the achievement of the ruling class in securing for the population a period of stability and peace. But "rich and at ease in possession of power, the rulers of Venice had a single goal, namely, to preserve this leisure, even at the expense of their self-respect. They might have updated their republic and kept up with the times if they had considered Holland's example and, by sagacious, slow modifications of their constitution, elevated their subjects to the dignity of citizenship. . . . But on the contrary, aristocratic pride, lacking any sense of purpose in its haughty indolence, became obsessed with petty privileges and, prevailing everywhere, soon was obliged to bend under the iron yoke imposed by the oligarchy" (4:162–63).

21. Daru's comments on Venice's ecclesiastical policies are likewise noteworthy: "They were no less zealous in containing the priestly powerlust. Venice's rich and numerous clergy always remained as it should be everywhere, respected and subordinate. Public liturgies were carried out regularly and with great splendor. Thirty-seven bishops, archbishops, and patriarchs made up the higher clergy. As long as the Republic remained strong, it retained the right to name the subjects upon whom the pope could confer the bishoprics. . . . In early times the doge told the bishop, even as he handed him the staff and ring, 'Receive this bishopric from God and Saint Mark.' When the disasters of the War of Cambrai reduced the Republic to obedience to the Holy See, it relented on this. The papal court appropriated the right of nomination for most bishoprics, leaving a quarter for the government to name; but all offices always had to go to Venetians. All clerics, from patriarch to the lowliest monk, answered to the Council of Ten. Finally, no clergyman, regardless of origins, could hold governmental posts; their relatives were barred from offices holding jurisdiction over ecclesiastical affairs, and in the Senate, the Great Council, and other state assemblies, whenever a matter of interest to the papacy was debated, all those with dealings with Rome or relatives in the church were required to abstain" (ibid., 4:168–75). These observations, which missed some of the complexity in the role of the doge, nonetheless moved beyond a simple legalistic view of church-state relations; after 1850, especially with the rediscovery of Paolo Sarpi, Daru's evaluation became quite popular.

22. Ibid., 4:161–62. Bianchi Giovini noted that "this would be true of current times, when even absolute monarchies (I mean the great ones, for some of the small ones are still infected by the vice of aristocratic privilege) have adopted arrangements that are vastly preferable to the late Venetian anarchy on the mainland. But before the great revolution, this was not so, and the Republic's subjects never manifested any jealousy for other peoples in even more straightened circumstances than their own." Actually, as we shall see, Daru referred to the aristocrats of the mainland, who could have climbed in rank through a hierarchical state structure. From his later arguments relating to the intrinsic nature of the Venetian state it is clear that Bianchi Giovini misunderstood the essence of Daru's insights: "Because of these complicated forms, of the constant overlapping of magistracies and tribunals, it was impossible in Venice for

an excessive concentration of power to form, as the author wrongly supposes; so the reasons for Venice's decadence must be sought elsewhere" (Daru, *Storia*, 6:88–89).

23. Daru, *Histoire*, 5:480–81. The connection between aristocratic feud and brigandage and the prevalence of *bravi*, incidentally, was only feebly dealt with later by Besta and Molmenti in their monographs.

24. Ibid., 5:480. See also 497–506 for interesting comments on further limits to the doges' power, and the remarks in vol. 4 on religious policies.

25. See Povolo, *Il romanziere e l'archivista*, 102–13, for early reactions to the *Histoire*.

26. The former patrician Carlo Antonio Marin's *Storia civile e politica del commercio dei Veneziani* (Venice, 1808) is noteworthy. Marin analyzed the crisis of Venice as an outcome of the city's persistent metropolitan bias, which lasted even through "the prosperity of the states of the terraferma and overseas" on account of economic policies directed at maintaining Venice's preeminence. But Marin still defended his class's political privileges and the Serenissima's constitution (see Canella, "Appunti e spunti," 76–81).

27. On Moschini, see Luciani, "Un complément inédit," 121ff.; on Tiepolo, see Canella, "Appunti e spunti," 81–82. Moschini, who was the librarian at the patriarchal seminary in Venice, began a translation of Daru's book. He soon gave up because of the government's opposition. Both of these Venetian historians corresponded frequently with Daru; the Daru-Tiepolo correspondence is in an appendix to the 1953 edition of the *Histoire*, which also contains a biography of the author (see p. 81). Tiepolo's notes on Daru's *Histoire* appear in a much-abbreviated translation of this work into Italian: *Storia della Republica di Venezia di P. Daru . . . con note e osservazioni*, trans. Bianchi Giovini (Capolago, 1832). Giovini was also the editor of the complete Italian edition of Daru: *Storia della Republica di Venezia*, 11 vols. (Capolago, 1832–34) (see Luciani, "Un complément inédit," 119).

28. Giovanni Domenico Tiepolo, *Discorsi sulla storia veneta, cioè rettificazioni di alcuni equivoci riscontrati nella storia di Venezia del sig. Daru* (Udine, 1828). Tiepolo's two volumes were divided into six "rectifications" on themes he considered important to an understanding of Venice's political makeup.

29. See Canella, "Appunti e spunti," 82.

30. Daru maintained that oligarchy was consolidated by the exclusion of indebted nobles from office, with the result that they were easily influenced by the more powerful members of their class. Despite inevitable abuses, according to Tiepolo, Venice's political system had continued to control and balance affairs, for it conveyed "to all members of the Major Council, and to other bodies that distributed office, the right to veto those elected to office while in debt . . . so this law did not create dependent relations inimical to the constitution but strengthened it by preventing abuse of those occasional inequalities that no state can avoid" (*Discorsi*, 196–97).

31. Ibid., 193–95. Tiepolo confirmed that patron-client relations tended to function outside institutional channels: "The choice of these figures Daru calls protectors depended not on their reputation for power or on the wealth of the noble but on the coincidence of having carried out a service to him or on the noble's having favored an individual or group while in office. Officeholding was so brief that this tie of patronage

was widespread in all the classes Daru treats, and it could not therefore favor oligarchy, as indeed Daru himself confesses despite himself" (195).

32. Ibid., 381, 383. Tiepolo did not treat the issue of aristocratic feuding, which Daru had raised, connecting it to banditry laws. "Such laws [regarding *bravi*, bearing weapons, and brigands] prove clearly enough that even if, on account of the spirit of the times and influences from the barbaric past, the custom of using these hired hands to get what one wanted was widespread in Venice, the government did not tolerate and indeed tried to eradicate such practices. Nor is it remarkable that the government's efforts have only been successful in recent years, since no law has ever instantly changed the customs of a people" (ibid., 377–78).

33. A significant example is the introduction to Bianchi Giovini's translation of Daru's history, where the mythic vision of the Republic serves to mitigate the French historian's assertions: "One advantage held by Venice's aristocracy over all others was that the people never hated it. Venetian aristocrats grew great by providing benefits to the populace and treating it kindly. The government always kept this in mind, and the more so when the patricians came to hold all authority. No other government was so solicitous toward the people, both of the metropolis and of the provinces, even with regard to popular entertainments. It is not power that is distasteful but how it is used. Knowing this, the Venetian aristocracy burdened itself with duties, rules, regulations, and never appropriated a privilege that would harm the public treasury or offend the honor of the populace. . . . They committed grave mistakes in their odd colonial system and by not admitting the mainland nobles, or those from the Dalmatian islands, to a part of the rights Venetian nobles held. But here too there is room for argument; benefits, but also ills, might have arisen from these policies" (Daru, *Storia,* 1:12–17). The harsh rebuttals to many of Daru's claims betray the searing impact his history had in Venice. In his introduction to volume 4, Bianchi Giovini stressed that the errors in Daru's *Histoire* were far more numerous than those Tiepolo had listed and proved the Frenchman's "strong bias against Venice." Moreover, "since he owed everything to Napoleon, his work sought to preempt posterity's judgment on the unjust, indeed perfidious treatment reserved for Venice by that conqueror" (Daru, *Storia,* 6:vi).

34. During one of the habitual commemorative reunions held at the University of Venice toward the end of the nineteenth century the lecturer commented that Venetian history written between 1830 and 1846 had "the noble aim of establishing truth, clouded by the calumny of foreigners" (see G. Brognoligo, "La cultura veneta," in *La Critica* 20 [1922]: 206. Brognoligo observes that this leitmotif of nineteenth-century historiography "is the strongest and most tenacious, and only through it can one pass from loving truth out of love for one's misrepresented homeland to loving truth out of love of truth, which then degenerates into love of the document alone"). See also G. Cappelletti, *Storia della Repubblica di Venezia,* 13 vols. (Venice, 1848–55); and Samuele Romanin, *Storia documentata di Venezia,* 10 vols. (Venice, 1853–61). On these works, see Canella, "Appunti e spunti," 91–104; Benzoni, "La storiografia," 604–5; and Brognoligo, "La cultura veneta," 207–8. These latter works treat the most significant historians of Venice, including E. A. Cicogna, all of whom were vital to the recovery of the Republic's memory.

35. A. Sagredo, "Storia civile e politica," in *Venezia e le sue lagune,* 2 vols. (Venice, 1847). On Sagredo, see Canella, "Appunti e spunti," 85–90; and Benzoni, "La storiografia," 603–4.

36. Sagredo, "Storia civile e politica," 1:129–30.

37. Ibid., 1:112–13.

38. Ibid., 1:127–28.

39. Ibid., 1:188.

40. Ibid., 1:113.

41. According to Sagredo, "We have seen with what rules the Venetians dealt with the subject populations, how they preserved their laws, institutions, and customs, the customs that speak to a man's heart and say, you are not a stranger in your country. Whether generous or expedient, this conservatism was not useful for fusing the state together, and uniform laws would have been better, since rulers and the ruled had been born in the same country and, however divided in dialects, they all spoke the beautiful soft language of 'sí.' We noted how Venetian nobles ruled every city and territory, while lesser places were ruled by locals, and that cities, territories, even villages all had their own governments with ambassadors in Venice to defend their interests. The privileges of subjects were protected by the Council of Ten. Taxes were trifling, and the balance sheet of Venice's finances proves that Venetian nobles paid more than their own subjects" (ibid., 1:193). Daniele Manin's "Giurisprudenza veneta," also in vol. 1 of *Venezia e le sue lagune,* deals with legal issues; see esp. 1:288–89 for echoes of Sagredo's prose.

42. The subject nobility had privileges and authority but not "dominion." Sagredo divided this nobility into two categories. "The first was made up of families illustrious for their antiquity, many having come to Italy with the German emperors, who gave them fiefs and jurisdiction. They were the holders of castles and lands who sought citizenship in the *comuni* and then occasioned their destruction. The second group was made up of rich bourgeois whose money or merit incorporated them into the provincial nobility and who soon forgot their origins. Both shared a dislike for Venice's nobility, and when the *podestà,* a Venetian noble, presided over their councils, or they had to court the *podestà,* they felt the burden of their inferior status" ("Storia civile e politica," 1:194–95). Manzoni's novel *I promessi sposi (The Betrothed)* was first published in Lugano in 1825–27.

43. Ibid., 1:195.

44. Romanin, *Storia documentata di Venezia,* 8:263. In ibid., 6:348, he writes that "the citizens were very happy, their government touched their purses little and its taxes existed more in theory than in reality. . . . If they looked around, they could easily console themselves, seeing the sad conditions of other states, their vicious intestine wars . . . they must have blessed a government that had no need of troops to keep the peace."

45. Samuele Romanin, *Lezioni di storia veneta,* 2 vols. (Florence, 1875), 161–63.

46. Girolamo Dandolo, *La caduta della Repubblica di Venezia ed i suoi ultimi cinquant'anni* (Venice, 1855).

47. See F. Mutinelli, *Memorie storiche degli ultimi cinquant'anni della Repubblica veneta* (Venice, 1854), vi.

48. Scipione Maffei, *Consiglio finora inedito presentato al governo veneto nell'anno 1736* (Venice, 1737). Maffei had proposed that Venetian noble status be extended to the elites of the cities and countryside of the terraferma in order that they might be represented in the institutions of the dominante. On Maffei, see Piero Del Negro, "Proposte illuminate e conservazione nel dibattito sulla teoria e la prassi dello stato," in Arnaldi and Stocchi, *Storia della cultura veneta*, 5, pt. 2: 135–37.

49. Dandolo, *La caduta della Repubblica di Venezia*, 631–33.

50. An example of this cult is the introduction to the first issue of *Archivio Veneto* (1871) by Adolfo Bartoli and Rinaldo Fulin. Citing Romanin's work and praising "the great supply of documents," they insisted that the history of the Republic still needed rewriting, despite the mass of scholarship on a vast number of topics: "For just as we said there is no place on earth so rich as ours in histories, so we must add that in no other place have so many errors been written, fabricated, and published as in our country" (v–vi).

Italian unification tended to strengthen the trend in historiography (already discernible in Romanin) toward interpreting the Venetian Republic as a federal state. The attraction of this reading lay in its legitimation of the role of a ruling middle class that was well positioned within a new, highly centralized state. On this phase, see U. Pototschnig, *L'unificazione amministrativa nelle provincie venete* (Venice, 1967), which describes the opposition of the Veneto's most prominent bourgeois to the imposition of Piedmontese administration as of 1866. See also M. Isnenghi, "La cultura," in *Venezia*, ed. E. Franzina (Bari, 1986), 381–482, noting that "authors, patrons, and audience mutually stimulate and reassure each other amidst the ruins of a past that, in the pettiness of the present, seems great and legendary" (399); See Lanaro, "Geneaologia di un modello"; and G. L. Fonatana, "Patria veneta e stato italiano dopo l'Unità: Problemi di identità e di integrazione," in Arnaldi and Stocchi, *Storia della cultura veneta*, 6:553–96.

51. See Brognoligo, "La cultura veneta," 209ff.

52. These cultural traits could only in part be understood and manipulated by an upper-middle-class elite that was nevertheless condemned to interact with them; and they could only in part be sapped of their vitality by new institutional structures able, despite appearances, to mediate and compromise. Interestingly, the Correnti Commission, formed to oversee the imposition of the new administration in 1866, noted that "with regard to the towns of the Veneto, we should not ignore how they enjoyed ample autonomies under Venice. This autonomy was regulated by statutes that they themselves voted on and Venice approved. Old traditions did not languish, and the inhabitants remained more accustomed than those elsewhere to take care not only of community interests but also of charity and church property, which they considered communal property. In the highland villages it is easy to find complete municipal archives stretching back to the fifteenth century. In applying the law code promulgated after 1815, the influence of these ancient customs was felt. Thus, though *identical in external form,* the local administration was a bit different from that in the old Lombard provinces" (quoted in Pototschnig, *L'unificazione amministrativa*, 27, emphasis added).

53. See, e.g., Enrico Besta, *Il senato veneziano (origine, costituzione, attribuzioni e riti),*

in Miscellanea di storia veneta, 2d ser., vol. 5 (Venice, 1899): 5–6; and Emilio Morpurgo, "Le inchieste della Repubblica di Venezia," *Archivio di Statistica* 3 (1879), esp. 5–
7. On historical studies in the Veneto, see Benzoni, "La storiografia," 612ff. It is
pertinent that the Republic's image remains foggy in the volumes of the *Grande il-
lustrazione del Lombardo Veneto,* ed. Cesare Cantù (1858–62). The exception is Francesco Antonio Bocchi, "Il Polesine di Rovigo" (5:2–160). Bocchi contrasted the "mild
and paternal government" of the Republic with "today's centralization" (5:111). With
Solomonic even-handedness Augusto Meneghini traced the history of Padua under the
Republic, stating that "the Lion's government was neither better nor worse than its
contemporaries, and, like all governments, it can be praised or chastised according to
one's point of view or according to which facts one cites or omits" (4:141). Carlo
Berlinghieri wrote similarly of Verona, citing Venice's mild rule and adding, "Nevertheless, there was no blind obedience to the ruler; desires and needs were aired and
expressed, and Maffei early on dared write about the reform of the Republic" (4:290).
From Venice, E. Morpurgo noted, significantly, that "the too puny assemblies of
provincial nobles contributed to Venice's decadence. . . . in the history books, however,
we find no word of this and other facts except where they shed more light directly on
Venice. The subject populations are left to oblivion; it is almost as if they did not live
their lives, did not rule themselves with institutions worthy of memory, did not leave
any trace in the historical record" ("Le rappresentanze delle popolazioni venete di
Terraferma presso il governo della Dominante," *Atti dell'Istituto Veneto di Scienze, Lettere
ed Arti* 4 [1878]: 869–70).

54. See C. Manfroni, "Gli studi storici in Venezia dal Romanin ad oggi," *Nuovo
Archivio Veneto* 8 (1909): 352–72. Manfroni noted the importance of German scholarship in the development of "good scientific methodology." He also remarked that it
seemed that "light has not yet been shed on the real relations, especially economic and
moral, between Venice and the terraferma cities." Actually, some significant elements
of the myth deeply influenced German historiography, which was almost exclusively
concerned with Venice's political discourse and the institutional arrangement of the
metropolis's magistracies. On one of the best-known exponents of the German school,
see Leopold von Ranke, *Venezia nel Cinquecento con un saggio introduttivo di Ugo Tucci,*
trans. Ingeborg Zapperi Walter (Rome, 1974), 3–69.

55. In both the quality and the quantity of their production Pompeo Molmenti and
Bartolomeo Cecchetti stand out from the crowd. Cecchetti wrote *La repubblica di
Venezia e la corte di Roma* (Venice, 1874), which reveals all too clearly the connections
between the Holy See and the Serenissima. He also wrote *Di alcuni dubbi sulla storia di
Venezia* (Venice, 1888). Molmenti wrote numerous tracts. See, e.g., the collection *I
nemici di Venezia* (Bologna, 1924), where, among other things, his 1894 speech to the
assembled Deputation of the Veneto is published: "It was oligarchy, certainly unloved
in our days, government by optimates, that is, a great anomaly amidst such normal
things as government by all and government by one alone, oligarchy that saved Venetian independence. This happened at a time when elsewhere in Italy free popular
government had retreated before dictators who, using charm or torture, seized the
throne" (344). On Molmenti's political career see M. Donaglio, "Il difensore di Vene-

zia: Pompeo Molmenti fra idolatria del passato e pragmatismo politico," *Venetica* 13 (1996): 45–72.

56. Emilio Morpurgo gives perfect expression to such attitudes. He was one of the most representative Venetian historians of the late nineteenth century. His description of the paternalistic attitude of the *rentier*, so much a part of the Veneto's culture, is interesting but very much upside-down: "One must not think that the patrician, the landowner, stood by, aloof from the people, nurturing, through a haughty demeanor such as the Spaniards affected, the universal rage that was so justified in other areas. On the contrary, there were friendly sharings between patricians and rustics; even in our day the name 'excellency,' used to greet the landlord, has not disappeared from the rural vernacular; most nobles firmly followed the type of moderate customs that made a doge say, 'When we left our lands we received with all due solemnity even village headmen'" (Morpurgo, *Saggi statistici ed economici sul Veneto* [Padua, 1868], 104). On Morpurgo, see Silvio Lanaro, "Una regione in patria," in Lanaro, *Storia d'Italia,* 442–46.

Eugenio Musatti, author of another general history after Romanin's, gave the myth of a Republic arranged along federal lines its highest expression. For him, Venice respected local institutions, and this attitude gained relevance especially in comparison with the situation in other European nations: "If all this served to strengthen the affection of the *subjects* for the lordship of Venice, it was not enough to satisfy those who longed for innovation. Among these were those Venetian aristocrats who wanted to accelerate the most adventuresome reforms to the Republic's constitution, even at cost of the Republic's life. The French monarchy's situation was not dissimilar, on account of the depraved customs of the upper classes and the desperate condition of public finances. But whereas feudalism never managed to penetrate Venice, and the equality of all before the law received sanction, in France the nobles and clergy, who owned two thirds of the land, were exempt from taxes" (Musatti, *Storia di un lembo di terra ossia Venezia e i Veneziani* [Padua, 1886], cols. 1480–81).

57. In his treatise *Le relazioni dei luogotenenti della Patria del Friuli al Senato veneziano* (Udine, 1893) Marchesi highlighted the decadence of the Republic in its last centuries. Molmenti retorted harshly in his "Il dominio veneto nel Friuli," *Nuovo Archivio Veneto* 6 (1893): 87–110. Marchesi, in turn, replied with "Il dominio veneto nel Friuli (risposta al prof. Pompeo Molmenti)," *Atto dell'Accademia di Udine* 1–2 (1893–94): 7–26. Marchesi was an important exponent of the Friulian cultural circles that produced much history in the second half of the nineteenth century. Some of their historiographical output was highly critical of Venetian domination and sought to reaffirm the myth of the Patriarchate of Aquileia (see Brognoligo, "La cultura veneta," 155–59, on Friuli's literary circles).

58. V. Marchesi, "Le origini e le cause storiche della rovina della Repubblica veneta," *Ateneo Veneto* 13 (1889): 266–67.

59. Ibid., 267–68.

60. Ibid., 272.

61. Ibid., 273.

62. Antonio Battistella, *La repubblica di Venezia ne' suoi undici secoli di storia* (Venice,

1921), 797, 801. But Battistella maintained that the inevitable decline never undermined the Republic's reforming tradition (see esp. 566; on Battistella and his patrons, see Isnenghi, "La cultura," 425–26, and Lanaro, "Genealogia di un modello," 13–14).

63. G. Maranini, *La costituzione di Venezia,* vol. 2 (1931; reprint, Florence, 1974), 21.

64. Ibid., 30.

Index

Abrami family, 76–77
absolutism, 199, 218, 242
Accetto, Torquato, 186
Acton, John, Lord, 395
Adriatic Sea, 90, 174, 187, 189, 456, 507; and "Spanish" conspiracy, 194, 198
Africa, 19, 455, 476
Agnadello, battle of (1509), 27, 44, 106n1, 143, 168, 169, 265, 322; and republicanism, 137, 138, 140, 141, 146, 147, 149, 150, 151; and terraferma, 148, 152, 159
Agostini family, 349, 351
agriculture, 12, 20, 50, 223
Al-Aziz, Abd, 401
Albania, 151, 457, 464
Alberti, Leon Battista, 318, 398, 399, 409
Alberto family, 289n50
Aldus Manutius, 399, 400, 401
Aleppo, 392
Alexandria, 392
Algiers, 469, 481n26; slaves in, 455, 459, 461, 462, 464, 472, 481n28, 482nn30,36, 484n56
Altino, 42, 49
Amadi family, 344, 351, 355
ambassadors, 170, 174–78, 188–89, 196, 312, 313; information from, 393–94
Ambrosini, Federica, 18, 19, 21, 390, 420–53
Americas, 188, 191, 389, 403, 407; discovery of, 390, 402, 405
Amiana Islands, 52
Amsterdam, 390, 400, 405
Anabaptists, 396
Ancona, 90
Andreini, Isabella Canali, 435
Andreozzi, Giovanni, 247
Antoniano, Silvio, 318
Antwerp, 390, 400, 405

Apulia, 173, 178; war in, 170, 171, 172
Aquileia, 49, 155, 518n57
Arabic language, 389, 401
Arabs, 455
Arborsani, Benedetto, 355
Arborsani family, 344, 349, 350, 351–52, 355, 362nn70,75
architecture, 22, 24, 26, 27, 399, 409–10
archives, Venetian, 394, 395, 505
Aretino, Pietro, 398
Arimondo family, 273, 289n50, 291n74
Ariosto, Ludovico, 402
Aristotle, 15, 94, 138, 141, 147, 301, 304
Armani, Vincenza, 435
Armenian language, 407
Armenians, 21
Arrivabene, Andrea, 396, 401
Arsenal, the, 18, 48, 408, 460
art: and doge, 10, 23, 93–95, 107, 111; and historiography, 9, 22, 27; in noble palaces, 309–10; publications on, 399; and social history, 16, 17; and Venetian identity, 25–26; women in, 434–35. See also opera; patronage, artistic
Arteaga, Stefano, 249
artisans, 16, 141, 340; homes of, 309, 319; loyalty to Venice of, 138, 151, 159; and other classes, 67, 348; and sumptuary laws, 320, 321; of terraferma, 150, 151
Ascension. See Sensa
Assarino, Luca, 408
Athens, 140
Auditori Novi, 146
Auduino, Nicolò, 77
Augustinians, 46
Austria, 17, 172, 192, 492. See also Habsburg empire
Averroes, 401
Avicenna, 401

Avogadori (avogaria) di comun, 75, 146, 158, 327, 377, 430; and citizenship, 343, 344, 346–50, 353, 354; and registration of nobles, 267–79, 280–82, 286n27, 290n62
Avogadro, Giambattista Birago, 407
avvisi (newsletters), 397

Badoer, Agnesina, 379
Badoer, Angelo, 394
Badoer, Gianalvise, 281
Badoer, Girolamo di Giacomo, 379
Badoer, Zuane di Giustinian, 434
Badoer family, 46, 82, 291n74
Bagdad, 392
Balbi, Gasparo, 392, 403
Balbi, Regina, 435
Balbi family, 289n50, 291n74
Balla d'Oro (Barbarella), 32n49, 286nn28,30, 288n44, 379
ballet, 222, 224, 225, 248, 249, 256n58
Bandiera, Giovanni Nicolò, 422, 423
baptism, 100, 102, 131n40, 352; registration of, 271–74, 288n43
baptisteries, 99–102, 111, 113, 115, 116, 131n40
Barbarella. See *Balla d'Oro*
Barbarigo, Caterina Sagredo, 441, 453n116
Barbarigo, Contarina, 432, 441
Barbaro, Daniele, 394
Barbaro, Marco, 69–70, 76, 83, 359n42
Barbary Coast: and slave trade, 454, 456–59, 461–63, 468, 470; and Venetian culture, 477–78
Barcelona, Treaty of (1529), 175
Bardi, Girolamo, 399, 408
Bareggi, Claudia, 390
Barezzi, Barezzo, 402
Baron, Hans, 5, 161n10
Barotto, Zuanne, 434
Barozzi, Pietro, 77
Barozzi, Zuanne di Giacomo, 426, 427
Barozzi family, 278, 279, 280, 291n74
Basadonna, Vittoria di Alvise, 428
Basilikon Doron, 199
Bastille, the, 251n6, 255n46
Battistella, Antonio, 507, 519n62
Bedmar, Marquis of (Don Alonso de la Cueva): report by, 393; and "Spanish" conspiracy, 187, 189, 192, 194–98, 202, 203, 208, 394
Bellegno family, 291n74
Bellini, Gentile, 333n53
Bellini, Giovanni, 1, 122, 123

Bembo, Alvise di Gaspare, 430
Bembo, Lorenzo di Andrea, 426
Bembo, Piero, 426
Bembo, Pietro, 321, 403
Bembo family, 291n74
Benedictines, 46
Benefido di Cristo, 396
Berengo, Marino, 6, 11
Bergamo, 219, 397, 493; Venetian control of, 142, 145, 151, 496, 502
Bey, Janus, 177
Bianchi, Francesco, 247, 248
Bianco, Andrea, 392
Bisaccioni, Maiolino, 407
Bistort, Giulio, 324
Boccaccio, Giovanni, 398
bocche di leone, 395
Bocco, Marino, 81
Bodin, Jean, 340
Boldù, Cipriano di Nicolò, 310
Boldù family, 273
Bollani, Maffeo, 278
Bologna, 90, 397, 398, 456
Bologna, Treaty of (1530), 23, 168–84
Bomberg, Daniel, 391, 401
Bonfadio, Gilio, 405
Bonifacio, Balthasar, 395
Bortali family, 407
Boscán, Juan, 402
Boschini, Marco, 408
Botero, Giovanni, 187, 340, 393, 399
Bouleaux, Charles, 194
Bouleaux, Jean, 194
bourgeoisie, 221–22, 339, 491, 493, 507, 515n42; and opera, 227, 247
Bouwsma, William James, 5, 6, 9, 186, 190, 207
Bracciolini, Poggio, 298, 340
Bragadin, Alvise, 401
Bragadin family, 276, 277, 291n72, 292n87
Braudel, Fernand, 6, 390
bravi, 497, 513n23, 514n32
Brenta River, 49, 50, 64n53
Brescia, 12, 219, 360n47, 493, 496, 502; Venetian control of, 142, 151
Brindisi, siege of, 176
Brown, Horatio, 194, 202
Brown, Patricia Fortini, 14, 17, 19, 23, 24, 295–338
Bruni, Leonardo, 161n10
Brusasorci, Domenico, 371
Bruslart, Nicolas, 196
Brusoni, Girolamo, 407

Brussels, 397, 406
Buia, commune of, 154–58
Burckhardt, Jacob, 15
bureaucracy, 144, 250, 493, 510n8; and *citta-dini*, 16, 339; ecclesiastical, 11; and environment, 49, 56; and ransoming of slaves, 456, 468; and Venetian state, 13, 143, 494 *See also* public office
Burke, Peter, 23, 389–419, 454
Burma, 389, 392
Buzzacarini, Fina, 131n40
Byron, George Gordon, Lord, 4, 208
Byzantine empire, 2, 4, 90, 129n29, 190, 400; Venetian traditions from, 6, 95, 103

cabala, 391
Ca' di Dio, 428, 437
Cadore, 151
calendar, French revolutionary, 223, 249, 254n33
Callergi, Zacharias, 400
Camaino, Tino di, 133n51
Cambio, Arnolfo di, 133n51
Cambrai, League of, 151, 168; War of (1508–17), 11, 138, 139, 153, 154, 169, 265, 282, 317, 340, 512n21
Cambrai, Peace of, 175, 176
Caminer, Gioseffa Cornoldi, 441
Canaletto, 25
canals, 46, 48, 51–52, 54; Grand Canal, 46, 52, 252n19
Candia war, 460
Capello, Domenico di Nicolò, 309, 314, 316
capitalism, 2, 5, 19, 20
Cappelletti, Giuseppe, 499
Cappello, Bianca di Bartolomeo, 429, 438
Cappello, Fiorenza, 424, 432, 434
Cappello, Lorenzo di Silvan, 430
Carafa, Gian Pietro, 370
Caravia, Alessandro, 24
Carinthia, 157
Carlo Emmanuele I (duke of Savoy), 187
Carmelites, 46
Carnia, 151
Carnival season, 218, 222, 225, 257n71, 478
Carocher, Vicenzo, 435
Carpaccio, Vittore, 58n2, 312, 313, 316
Carrara, Francesco il Vecchio da, 344
Carrara, Marsilio da, 110, 111
Carriera, Rosalba, 435
Cartagena, 471
Carthage, 174
Casola, Padre Pietro, 296, 306, 308, 327

Cassiodorus, 39, 41, 43
Castanheda, Lopes de, 403
Castiglione, Baldassare, 398, 399
Catholicism, 439–40, 465; in England, 191, 198–99, 200. *See also* the Church
Cavalli, Marino, 397
Cavazza family, 351
Cavos, Alberto, 224, 225
Cecchetti, Bartolomeo, 421, 517n55
censorship, 223, 394–95
Cervantes, Miguel de, 402, 481n26
Cervelli, Innocenzo, 265
Cervia, 172, 175, 176, 177, 183n57
Cessi, Roberto, 67, 73, 77–78
Ceylon, 389, 392
chancellors, 75; grand, 89, 93, 111, 342, 344, 354, 395
chancery, 90–91, 124n6, 341–45, 352, 353, 354. *See also* bureaucracy
charitable institutions, 18, 24, 339, 437, 486n77; and ransoming of slaves, 456–57, 465–66, 467, 474, 476. See also *scuole; scuole grandi; scuole piccole*
Charles V (Holy Roman Emperor), 177, 181n15, 397, 402; and wars of Italy, 171, 172, 174–80
Chiarelli, Lamberto, 196
China, 1, 403
Chioggia, War of (1379–81), 72, 77, 80, 267, 345
Chittolini, Giorgio, 12
Chojnacka, Monica, 18
Chojnacki, Stanley, 10, 17, 69, 263–94, 339, 351, 433; on women, 18, 21, 22, 268–80
Christ: and doge, 95, 97, 102; images of, 107, 113, 115; and Venice, 103–4, 126n16
Christianity, 41–42, 218, 223; and Islam, 455, 462. *See also* the Church
Church, the, 6, 22, 23, 46, 217, 319, 321; as art patron, 24, 386n41; patriarch of, 472–73, 476; and ransoming of slaves, 454, 456, 457, 458, 465–66, 467, 471; and slave processions, 471, 472; and Venetian state, 11, 60n16, 486n77, 494, 512n21
Cicero, 142
Cicogna, Emmanuele A., 100, 366, 514n34
Ciera family, 351
Cigna-Santi, Vittorio Amadeo, 235
Cimarosa, Domenico, 224
citizenship, 346–50, 353, 495–96; for foreigners, 21, 82–83, 145, 343, 344, 354, 355; and nobility, 496, 512n20; in *terraferma*, 137, 163n22, 491

cittadini, 18, 19, 22, 92, 163n22, 316; and arts, 24, 247; and Council of Ten, 342, 343, 344, 357n15; elite, 339–64; in government, 16, 91, 339, 342, 344, 354; and Great Council, 343, 344, 345, 346, 348, 349, 363n89; homes of, 312, 319; marriages of, 270, 278, 287n34, 349, 350–52, 354; and nobility, 83–84, 278, 287n34, 298–99, 345–46, 348–52, 354; occupations of, 339, 342, 344, 345, 346, 352, 358n27, 363nn79,89; and *popolo,* 339, 348, 350, 356; serrata of, 352, 356; and sumptuary laws, 327, 329; in *terraferma,* 159, 357n15; wealthy, 295, 345, 350, 355; women, 287n34, 350–52, 433
cittadini originari, 299, 340–46, 352, 354, 355, 357n15, 363n89
class structure: and houses, 317–19; institutionalization of conflict in, 140, 158, 159; and slaves, 460, 484n62; and sumptuary laws, 295, 319; and wealth, 298
Clement IV, Pope, 128n22
Clement V, Pope, 82
Clement VII, Pope, 169, 171, 172, 175, 176, 177
clientalism. *See* patron-client relations
clothing, 320, 321, 322, 326, 327–29, 423
Clovis (king of France), 102, 103
coats of arms (*stemme*), 316–17, 355, 380
Cognac, League of, 170, 171, 175
Collegio, 170, 173, 288n45, 325, 344; and doge, 171, 172; and *terraferma,* 146, 147, 149; and wars of Italy, 174, 175, 176
Colluraffi, Antonio, 304
Colombin, Giacomo, 461, 482n30
colonies, Venetian, 10, 20, 68, 90, 457, 466, 467. *See also terraferma*
Columbus, Christopher, 403
commemorative medals, 91, 92
commerce. *See* trade
Committee of Public Instruction, 223, 224, 225, 226, 229, 254n36, 259n83
commoners. See *popolo*
communes, 12, 143, 145, 152–58
Commynes, Philippe de, 20, 340
Compagnia dei corrieri, 391
compagnie della calza, 263–64, 274, 320, 322, 324
concordia, 297
concubinage, 429–30
Coniglio, Giuseppe, 196
Conservatori ed Esecutori alle Leggi, 344
Constantinople, 89, 181n16; and ransoming of slaves, 455, 456, 457, 458, 459, 464, 468, 469, 470; and Venice, 25, 68, 85n14, 95
constitution, Venetian, 1, 3, 140, 179, 180,

513n26; changes to, 5, 69, 159, 169, 518n56; and doge, 10, 89; and Great Council, 78, 498; and nobility, 269, 495, 513n30; and *Serrata,* 68, 263, 508
constitutions, 223, 506
Contarini, Ambrogio, 403
Contarini, Elisabetta, 106
Contarini, Gasparo, 16, 148, 160n7, 181n16, 265, 404, 408; on *cittadini,* 339–40, 347; *De magistratibus et republica Venetorum* of, 15, 23, 140, 147, 168, 178–80, 282, 283, 299, 339, 340; and dowry law, 282–84, 293n107; on nobility, 299–300, 301; as Venetian ambassador, 170, 174–78
Contarini, Jacopo, Doge, 69
Contarini, Marcantonio, 172
Contarini, Marino, 24
Contarini, Niccolò, Doge, 395
Contarini, Piero, 193
Conti, Nicolò, 392
convents, 420, 422; as art patrons, 24, 386n41; forced entry into, 423–24, 425–26, 431; noblewomen in, 270, 287nn33,36
Convertite, the, 436
Corbett, Julian, 194
Corfu, 1, 176
Cornaro, Giovanni, Doge, 462
Corner, Caterina, 446n42
Corner, Cateruzza, 373, 374, 375, 380, 381
Corner, Giorgio, 388n55
Corner, Giovanni di Giorgio, 381
Corner, Giovanni Francesco, 174
Corner, Marco, 49, 50, 51, 52
Corner, Nicolò, 227
Corner, Zorzi, 24, 373, 374
Corner family, 371, 380, 381
Correnti Commission, 516n52
Correr, Lorenzo, 315
Correr, Polo di Zuanfrancesco, 427
Cortés, Hernando, 403
Coryat, Thomas, 297, 308, 327, 329
Council of Lyons (1245), 82
Council of Ten, 3, 4, 11, 147, 179, 512n21; antielectioneering laws of, 263–64, 269, 272; and Buia, 158; and *cittadini,* 342, 343, 344, 357n15; and La Fenice opera house, 221; and information, 393, 394, 397; and marriage, 432; members of, 309; and nobility, 269–71, 274, 275, 277, 278, 280, 281, 283, 290n62, 300, 347, 500, 501, 515n41; and publishing, 395, 401, 403; and Querini-Tiepolo conspiracy, 92; and slave processions, 474; and sumptuary laws, 324

Council of Trent, 439, 447n48; and Tridentine reforms, 365, 369, 370, 371, 381, 430
Counter Reformation, 5, 186, 368–69, 371, 377, 405
Cox, Virginia, 424
Cozzi, Gaetano, 5, 6, 11, 12, 173, 197, 205, 265
Cracco, Giorgio, 67, 77, 78, 348
Crasso, Niccolò, 340, 371
Crema, 194, 200, 203, 204, 206
Crescenzi, Victor, 266
Crespi family, 362n77
Crete, 1, 76, 77, 466
Croat language, 389, 401
Crouzet-Pavan, Elisabeth, 10, 39–64, 266
Crucifixion mosaic (San Marco), 111–12, 113, 114
Crusades, 89–90, 190
culture: and historiography, 13, 18, 22, 505; Muslim, 477–78; and social structure, 16, 510n10, 511n13; Venetian, 22, 23, 25, 26, 389, 390, 477–78, 494
currency, 90, 129n29; religious imagery on, 94, 95, 97, 99
Cyprus, 1, 188–89, 393

da Canal, Martino, 97, 109, 126n16
da Canal family, 289n50, 290n66, 291n74
da Colonna family, 347
d'Alemagna, Giovanni, 379
da Lezze, Donado di Michael, 310
Dall'Agata, Michele, 222
Dalmatia, 1, 151, 460; and ransoming of slaves, 457, 466, 471; and slave trade, 456, 464, 465
d'Alviano, Bartolomeo, 138
Damascus, 393
Damaška, Mirjan, 492
Dandolo, Andrea, Doge (1342–54), 70, 71, 76, 89, 93–136; and art, 93–95; education of, 93, 110; images of, 112, 114, 117; tomb of, 112–14, 116, 117
Dandolo, Bernardo, 379
Dandolo, Elisabetta, 379
Dandolo, Enrico, 102, 129n29
Dandolo, Francesco, Doge (1329–39), 104–7, 109, 110
Dandolo, Giovanni, Doge (1280–89), 73, 79–80, 81, 98, 99
Dandolo, Girolamo, 504, 505
Dandolo, Marco, 176
Dandolo, Marino, 81

Dandolo, Tommaso, 75, 80
Dandolo family, 77, 79, 81, 82, 105
da Ponte, Arcanzola, 440
da Ponte, Niccolò, Doge (1578–85), 176
d'Aranda, Emanuel, 462, 464
Dardani, Barnaba, 344
Dardani family, 349
Dario, Giovanni, 24, 342
Daru, Pierre Antoine Noël, 3, 491, 494, 495–99, 501, 502
Davidson, Nicholas S., 7
Davis, Robert C., 21, 26, 454–87
death, 225, 451n101
de' Barbari, Jacopo, 57n1, 110, 112, 392
de la Vega, Garcilaso, 402
Delicado, Francisco, 402
de Liques, David, 200
Della Casa, Giovanni, 405
Della Scala, Cangrande, 76
Del Negro, Piero, 11
democracy, 15, 179, 496; in French propaganda, 226, 229, 230, 232, 233; and opera, 246, 249, 250
Denmark, 406
de' Pitati, Bonifacio, 371
Dese River, 52
d'Hilliers, Baraguey, 230
Diacono, Giovanni, 41
Diodati, Giovanni, 200–201, 202, 204
diplomats, 392–93. See also ambassadors
disease, 49–50, 52, 53, 463; plague, 47, 173
doge, 13, 15, 179, 232, 379, 394, 471; and art, 10, 23, 93–95, 107, 111; and Christ, 95, 97, 102; and Church of San Marco, 93–95, 97, 111; and Collegio, 171, 172; Council of, 73, 74, 77, 80; and electoral system, 72, 74, 75; and marriage contracts, 282–83, 293n107; and nobility, 78, 274, 300, 347; and religious imagery, 93–98; role of, 4, 10, 512n21; sacrality of, 89–136, 511n13; and St. Mark, 93–94, 97–98, 99, 117–22, 123; and sumptuary laws, 319, 321, 329; tombs of, 95–97
Doglio, Maria Luisa, 187
Doglioni, Giovanni Niccolo, 409
Dolce, Ludovico, 398, 443n7
Dolfin, Caterina, 423, 432, 441, 453n116
Dolfin, Gabriele, 86n45
Dolfin, Giovanni Antonio, 441
Dolfin family, 306, 308
Domenichi, Ludovico, 398, 399
dominante, 6, 8, 20, 40, 169, 467
Dominicans, 46, 128n22, 129n27

dominio, 6, 8. See also *terraferma*
Domzalski, Oliver Thomas, 11
Donà, Cecilia, 379
Donà, Leonardo, Doge, 89, 199, 207, 397; as ambassador, 188–89; and Interdict Crisis, 186, 187–88; and reason of state, 190, 191
Donà, Maria di Zuanne, 425
Donà, Marina, 379
Donato, Leonardo, 199
Doni, Anton Francesco, 306, 307
Doria, Andrea, 174
Dorigo, W., 64n52
dowries, 308, 350, 380, 434, 435; inflation in, 269–70, 279, 423, 426, 436; limits on, 274, 281, 282–84, 293n107, 362n73; sizes of, 287n33, 288n40, 375
Ducal Council, 73, 74, 77, 80
Dulcigno (Albania), 464
Duodo, Nicolò, 312

Easter, 93, 97
East Indies, 403
economy: capitalism in, 2, 5, 19, 20; and citizenship, 82–83; and class, 295, 298, 345, 350, 355; decline of, 78, 90, 169, 221; and dowry inflation, 269–70, 279, 423, 426, 436; historiography of, 6, 19–20; industrial, 1, 12, 19, 20, 480n18; and information, 390, 391, 392, 394, 404; and nobility, 169, 266–69, 300, 301, 319, 347–48, 495, 500–501, 513nn26,31; and power, 300, 327; and ransoming of slaves, 460, 462; and sumptuary laws, 301, 321, 325, 329; of *terraferma*, 144–45, 148–53, 513n26; Venice's domination of, 149–53; and war, 173, 177, 180n7; and women, 420, 424, 428, 433–34. See also publishing; textile industry; trade
Egnazio, Giovanni Battista, 61n21
Egypt, 405
electoral system, 72–77, 79, 140, 141, 353, 511n16; and election campaigning, 263–64, 269, 272; franchise in, 3, 264
elites: citizen, 339–64; and wealth, 295–338. See also nobility
elites, provincial: bourgeoisie as, 515n42; citizenship for, 137, 163n22, 491, 501, 502, 503; economy of, 144–45, 148–53, 513n26; and peasants, 150; rebellion of, 142, 148–49, 159; social mobility of, 512n22; and taxes, 515nn41,44; and Venetian government, 138, 139, 141, 143, 144, 156, 504, 516n48, 517nn53,54; and Vene-

tian nobility, 147, 497, 506, 510n10, 514n33, 515n41
Emo, Lunardo, 171
England, 138, 139, 141, 485n67, 509n6; Catholicism in, 191, 198–99, 200; publishing in, 399; and Spain, 188, 206, 207
Enlightenment, the, 3, 6, 12, 431; and women, 420, 423, 432, 438
environment, 1–2; and myth of Venice, 39–64; as threat, 49–53, 56; and Venetian state, 10–11, 13
Erasmus, Desiderius, 422
Este family, 76
ethnic minorities, 8, 24
Euripedes, 398
event, and historical structure, 218–20, 251n6
Exclusion Crisis, 192

factionalism, 26, 77–83, 144, 163n21, 353–54, 394
Falier, Francesco di Marc'Antonio, 430
families: as art patrons, 23, 24–25, 365–88; commoner, 277–78; conflict between, 77, 497; homes of, 304–8, 316–17; and marriage, 273–74, 275, 277, 432; noble, 67, 68, 433; provincial, 143, 149–50, 510n10; and ransoming of slaves, 455, 464; roles within, 22; social mobility of, 510n8; and state, 144, 190, 225–26, 359n43; and wealth, 20, 298; and women, 420, 433
Fascism, 491
Fasoli, Gina, 8, 9
Febvre, Lucien, 405
Fedele, Cassandra, 422
Federici, Cesare, 392, 403
Feldman, Martha, 14, 17, 26, 217–60
La Fenice opera house, 217, 218–19; class hierarchy in, 220–23; in French occupation, 227, 228, 233, 247, 250; *Mitridate* in, 242, 243, 246; reopening of, 224–25; Society of, 219, 221, 222, 247, 251n9, 253n25
Ferrara, 67, 76, 82, 177, 379; publishing in, 395, 398; war with, 138, 321
Ferraro, Joanne, 18
Ferrazzi, Cecilia, 439
Ferro, Marco, 340
festivals: Carnival season, 218, 222, 225, 257n71, 478; as propaganda, 219–20, 223–50; *Sensa*, 97, 129n27, 222, 224–29, 257n71, 478, 485n67
feudalism, 155–56, 496, 518n56
feuding, 12, 13, 163n21, 514n32

Fieschi, Gianluigi, 208
Filarete, Antonio Averlino, 318
Finlay, Robert, 265
Fino, Pietro da, 405
Fiore, Jacobello del, 58n2
Florence, 15, 131n40, 154, 271, 340, 399; and
    America, 402; art patronage in, 24, 379;
    Ordinances of Justice in, 67; republicanism
    in, 5, 6, 67, 137, 140, 141; and Venice, 9,
    21, 25, 76, 169; wars of, 173, 175
Fonte, Moderata, 425
foreigners, 18, 20–21, 62n34, 351, 404, 405;
    citizenship for, 21, 82–83, 145, 343, 344,
    345, 354; in public office, 76, 353; in pub-
    lishing, 400–402
Formento, Cornelia, 434
Foscari, Elena, 379
Foscari, Francesco, Doge (1423–57), 71, 89,
    120, 122, 379
Foscarini, Antonio, 394
Foscarini, Marco, 160n7
Foscolo, Ugo, 249
Fracastoro, Girolamo, 403
France, 150, 218; historiography in, 340, 491–
    92; kingship in, 102, 103, 115, 518n56;
    occupation of Venice by, 135n75, 219–20,
    223–50; and ransoming of slaves, 459, 461,
    464, 469, 481n26, 485n65; revolutionary
    calendar of, 223, 249, 254n33; revolution
    in, 141, 223, 229, 248; and "Spanish" con-
    spiracy, 192, 195, 196, 198, 201, 205, 206;
    Venetian alliance with, 95, 171, 172; wars
    of, 138, 140, 170, 174, 175, 177, 219
Francis I (king of France), 171, 174, 175
Franciscans, 46, 104, 106, 133n57
Franco, Veronica, 1, 436
Frari, Church of the, 365, 377
Frederick II (Holy Roman Emperor), 82
Frederick of the Palatinate, 193
French language, 423
Freschi, David, 355
Freschi, Zaccaria, 342
Freschi family, 355
Frescobaldi, Lionardo di Niccolò, 308
Friuli, 13, 143, 145, 149, 477, 518n57; and
    Buia, 154, 155, 156, 157; elites of, 12,
    360n47; peasants of, 18, 151, 152–53, 158,
    165n47; Turks in, 156, 172, 182n24; and
    Venice, 137, 142, 151

Gabriel, Cecilia di Bertucci, 429
Gaeta, Franco, 8, 9
Gaismair, Michael, 153

Galileo, 406
Gara, Giovanni di, 401
Gardano family, 399
Garzoni, Tommaso, 300–301
Garzoni, Vincenzo di Alvise, 385n23
Garzoni family, 277, 349
Gastaldi, Giacomo, 392
Gattinara (Charles V's chancellor), 178
gender, 19, 21–22. See also women
Genoa, 24, 90, 100, 144, 208, 390, 397; and
    slave trade, 455, 456; war with, 73, 79
George of Neydeck, bishop of Trent, 150
Germans, 21, 296
Germany, 153, 400, 406, 470; and provincial
    elites, 150, 152; and "Spanish" conspiracy,
    193, 201; and terraferma, 148, 149, 156, 157;
    and Venice, 138, 140, 205, 517n54. See also
    Habsburg empire
Gerulaitis, Leonardas, 390
Ghibellines, 79, 82
Giannotti, Donato, 72, 140, 265, 340, 343
Giberti, Gian Matteo, 377
Ginzburg, Carlo, 18
Giolito, Gabriele, 405
Giolito, Giovanni, 398, 402, 445n32
giovani, the, 186, 188; and "Spanish" conspir-
    acy, 190, 197, 199, 207
Giovini, Bianchi, 512nn18,22, 514n33
Giovio, Paolo, 394, 399, 402, 403, 404
Girard, René, 255n51
Giudecca Nuova, 47
Giuliano, Andrea, 407
Giustinian, Agnesina, 379
Giustinian, Bernardo, 41–42, 70, 71
Giustinian, Marco Antonio, 401
Giustinian, Zorzi, 199–200
Giustinian family, 381
Giustizieri Vecchi, 18, 69
Gleason, Elisabeth G., 16, 23, 168–84, 282
Gobbo di Rialto, 396
Goldthwaite, Richard, 296, 316
gondoliers, 329, 434
Gonzaga, Lodovico, 76
government: absolutism in, 191, 199, 218,
    242; aristocracy as form of, 15, 179, 496;
    communal, 143, 153, 154; indirect, 144,
    146; mixed, 140, 141, 495; republican, 9–
    10, 137–67, 223, 258n77; sacrality in, 94,
    115; of terraferma, 145–46, 149. See also
    monarchy; oligarchy
government, Venetian: art patronage of, 23–
    24, 25; cittadini in, 16, 91, 339, 342, 344,
    354; control of private sphere by, 270, 274,

government, Venetian (cont.)
283–84, 298; decentralization of, 144, 493;
as diarchy, 10, 143–44, 146, 149; and
environment, 10–11, 13, 50–51, 56–57;
and expansion of Venice, 46–47, 48; hierarchy in, 15–16; historiography of, 4, 9–
15; iconography of, 93–98, 383n13; and
papacy, 5, 6, 183n57, 189, 199–200, 201,
369, 512n21; and provincial elites, 138,
139, 141, 143, 144, 156, 504, 516n48,
517nn53,54; provisional, 223, 229, 233; and
ransoming of slaves, 454, 455–61, 464, 471,
474–75, 476; reforms of, 34n65, 69, 265,
282; and ritual, 25–26; sacrality in, 115,
123, 190–91; secretiveness of, 2–3, 5, 15,
185, 393–95; and terraferma, 147, 494,
511n12, 516n48; unanimitas in, 16, 147,
297, 365; and women, 440–41. See also
bureaucracy; electoral system; nobility;
public office; and particular branches
governors, provincial, 146, 149, 467
Gozze, Nicolò Vito di, 304
Gozzi, Gasparo, 408
Gradenigo, Bartolomeo, Doge (1339–42),
107–11
Gradenigo, Pietro (18th c.), 91
Gradenigo, Pietro, Doge (1289–1311), 81, 82,
91, 92; and enlargement of Great Council,
68, 70, 71, 72, 76, 78, 79, 80, 83
Gradenigo family, 77, 81
Granada, Luis de, 402, 405
Grand Canal, 46, 52, 252n19
grand chancellors, 89, 93, 111, 342, 344, 354,
395
Granzini, Alessandro, 196
Great Council (Maggior Consiglio), 13, 15,
179, 500–501; age requirement for, 75,
269; and cittadini, 343, 344, 345, 346, 348,
349, 363n89; election to, 72–77, 79; eligibility for, 68–70, 263, 267–80, 283, 347,
350, 352, 353, 363nn79,89; enlargement of,
68, 70–72, 76, 78–80, 83, 504; factionalism
in, 77–83; on legitimacy, 86n45, 377; and
nobility, 16, 299, 513n30; and popolo, 69–
72, 76, 79; and secrecy, 394, 404; and
"Spanish" conspiracy, 194, 203, 204; and
sumptuary laws, 319, 321, 325; and Venetian constitution, 78, 169, 498. See also the
Serrata
Greece, 457, 471
Greek language, 389, 407
Greeks, 21, 291n80, 400
Grendler, Paul, 390

Grevembroch, Jan, 91, 92, 117, 118, 121, 122
Grigis, Lorenzo, 435
Grigoropoulos, Janos, 400
Grimani, Antonio di Zuanne, 424, 432, 434
Grimani, Marcantonio, 371, 373, 388n52
Grimani, Virginia Chigi, 227, 254n36
Gritti, Alvise, 172
Gritti, Andrea (governor of Monopoli), 173
Gritti, Andrea, Doge (1523–38), 64n61, 89,
171, 174, 177, 181n20, 292n87; reforms of,
179, 282, 283, 284
Gritti, Bernardo, 428
Grubb, James S., 7, 8, 18, 19, 145, 163n22,
287n34, 291n80, 339–64
Guazzo, Marco, 399
Guelfs, 79, 82
Guevara, Antonio de, 402
Guicciardini, Francesco, 140, 168–69, 175,
399
guilds, 18, 20, 21, 24, 67, 69; and Venetian
government, 79, 190; women in, 434
Guisconi, Anselmo, 408
Gunpowder Plot (1605), 191, 199, 200
Guzzetti, Linda, 18

Habsburg empire: and Milan, 171, 172; and
Ottoman empire, 462, 469; and ransoming
of slaves, 455, 461; and Venice, 17, 140,
168–80, 192, 201, 204, 205, 248
Hakluyt, Richard, 403
Hale, John, 17, 390
Haskell, Francis, 24
Hebrew language, 389, 401, 405
Henry VII (Holy Roman Emperor), 133n51
heresy, 24, 390, 396, 405, 406, 439
Hetepolonios, Dominikos, 400
Hohenstaufen family, 82
Holy League, 188
Holy Roman empire, 82, 189. See also
Charles V
homes, 304–19; and class structure, 317–19;
color in, 315–16; furnishings of, 308–11,
315, 317, 321, 324; gardens of, 311–12;
order in, 314–15; and sumptuary laws, 321,
322, 325, 326
Hook, Judith, 183n57
Hormuz, 392
Houssaie, Amelot de la, 397
humanism, 91, 94, 110, 124n6; and reason of
state, 187, 209; and republicanism, 6, 137,
142; and unanimitas, 147, 148, 365
Humfrey, Peter, 16, 23, 24, 365–88
Hunecke, Volker, 11

Hungary, 90, 172, 342, 469
hydrology, 44–54, 56–57

illegitimacy: of *cittadini*, 343, 344, 352, 355; and Great Council, 86n45, 377; and nobility, 76–77, 268–80, 284, 377, 379, 381; and shared surnames, 346; and women, 278–80, 281, 284, 290n67, 428, 429
immigrants. *See* foreigners
India, 1, 14, 389, 392, 403, 408
Infelise, Mario, 404
information, 389–419; censoring of, 394–95; commercialization of, 396–99; historiography of, 390–91; involution of, 404–9; on non-European world, 402–4; secrecy of, 185, 391–96; and spying, 393–94
Inquisition, 199, 396, 405
Inquisitori di Stato, 196, 223, 394
Interdict Crisis (1606–7), 5, 6, 141, 161n10, 440; and "Spanish" conspiracy, 185–86, 187, 200, 201, 202
Islam, conversions to, 454, 464–65, 476. *See also* Muslims
Istanbul, 390, 392, 400, 406. *See also* Constantinople
Istria, 1, 466, 477
Italy: historiography of, 9–10, 493, 510n8, 516n50; and ransoming of slaves, 455, 464, 469; and Spain, 171, 174; and "Spanish" conspiracy, 193; unification of, 4, 232, 491, 493, 499, 505, 507, 508, 516n50; and Venice, 1, 3, 205, 508; wars of, 168, 171, 172, 174–80
Ivanovich, Cristoforo, 408

James I (king of England), 191, 193, 199, 200
James II (king of England), 191, 207
Jardine, Lisa, 296
Jenson, Nicolas, 398, 400
Jerusalem, 25
Jesuits, 202, 440, 472
Jews, 8, 21, 173, 389, 401, 405, 429; and ransoming of slaves, 455, 459, 462, 469, 484n53
John XXIII, Pope, 131n40
Joseph, Father, 206
Judaism, 348, 391
Justinian's Code, 156

King, Margaret, 16, 147
Kirke, Percy, 207
Kissling, Hans, 391, 404

Knapton, Michael, 197
Knights (*cavalieri*), 329, 344
Knights of Malta, 462
Knights of Santo Stefano, 462
Koran, 401
Kretschmayr, Heinrich, 195

Labia family, 24
land, 20, 62n33, 152
Lane, Frederic C., 5, 18; on *Serrata*, 67, 70, 71, 75, 77, 78–79, 83
Lanteri, Giacomo, 304, 305, 318
Larquié, Claude, 481n28
Las Casas, Bartolomé de, 407
Latini, Brunetto, 143
Latin language, 389
laws (*statuti*): antielectioneering, 263–64, 269, 272; on citizenship, 341–42, 343, 354; communal, 156, 158; on dowries, 282–84, 293n107; on illegitimacy, 377, 379; inheritance, 304; of *Libro d'Oro*, 271–72, 273–75, 283; on nobility, 144, 286n30, 288n40, 300, 350; and ransoming of slaves, 466; and republicanism, 143. *See also* sumptuary laws
legal system: and Buia, 155–58; and clergy, 186; and common law, 154; and litigation, 154, 155–58, 159, 160n4; and notaries, 154, 158; and peasants, 138, 142; reforms of, 179; and republicanism, 138, 139, 153, 156, 158, 159; and Roman law, 143, 144, 146, 154, 509n6; and social status, 16, 19; in *terraferma*, 143, 144, 146–47, 502
legitimacy, political, 56, 57, 147, 287n37
Legrenzi, Angelo, 408
Lepanto, battle of, 188
Lerma, fall of, 198
Levi, Eugenia, 204
libertinism, 420, 439
Libro d'Argento, 353
Libro d'Oro, 75, 76, 221, 353, 395; burning of, 232; laws of, 271–72, 273–75, 283; surnames in, 346
Lippomano, Bortholamio di Thomà, 425
literacy, 153–54; of women, 420, 421–23, 430, 438
literature, 16, 94, 115, 422, 478; captivity accounts, 462–63; in diverse languages, 389, 401, 405, 407, 423. *See also* publishing
Livorno, 248, 455, 459, 462, 471
Lombard invasion, 41, 59n8
Lombardy, 171, 173, 174
Longo, Tommaso, 77
Longo family, 289n54

Loredan, Alvise di Lorenzo, 427
Loredan, Leonardo, Doge (1501–21), 122,
123, 169, 317
Loredan, Marco, 135n73
Loredan family, 276, 278, 291n72
lottery, 32n49, 173, 286nn28,30, 288n44, 379,
468
Lowry, Martin, 390
Lucca, 21, 344, 345, 355
Luther, Martin, 153, 396
Luzio, Alessandro, 197
Lyon, 400, 406

Machiavelli, Niccolò, 137, 140, 160n7, 495;
on class conflict, 158–59; on nobility, 298–
99, 300; publication of, 405, 406; on the
state, 9–10, 186; on terraferma, 138, 148,
150; on Venice, 3, 168, 340
Mackenney, Richard, 3, 24, 185–216, 266,
361n63
Madre Giovanna, 391, 405
Madrid, 196, 390, 471
Maffei, Scipione, 504
Magellan, Ferdinand, 392
Maggior Consiglio. See Great Council
magic, 22, 26, 391, 439–40, 441
magistracies, 18, 47, 54, 56, 69, 500, 511n16
Magistrato alle Pompe, 325, 326–27
Malamocco, 14, 63n50
Malipiero, Domenico, 265, 375
Malipiero, Gasparo, 293n107
Malipiero, Simeone, 379
Malipiero, Ursia, 379
Malipiero, Zuanne di Vettor, 428
Malombra, Riccardo, 93
Malta, 455, 456, 462
Manenti, Alvise, 342
Manetti, Giannozzo, 396
Mansueti, Giovanni, 316
Mantegna, Andrea, 136n78
Mantua, 197, 206, 219, 341, 379; and Venice,
76, 138
Manucci, Nicolao, 408
Manzoni, Alessandro, 4, 502
maps, 57n1, 58n4, 310, 392, 395, 399
Maranini, Giuseppe, 347, 508
Marcello, Piero di Piero, 431
Marchesi, Vincenzo, 505–7
Marin, Carlo Antonio, 513n26
marriage: of cittadini, 270, 278, 287n34, 349,
350–52, 354; and concubinage, 429–30;
consummation of, 447n48; contracts of,
282–83, 293n107; and definition of

nobility, 268–80, 275–77; dissolution of,
432; and family, 273–74, 275, 277, 432;
forced, 431; limits on number of, 423;
model of, 314–15; of nobility, 76–77, 263,
264–65, 430, 431–32; of nobility and cittadini, 349, 350–52, 354; of nobility and
popolo, 277–78, 350, 362n73; registration
of, 263, 270–71, 274, 300, 346, 350, 353;
secret, 430–31; and sumptuary laws, 319,
320, 322–23; and third Serrata, 267; and
women, 420, 423, 429–32, 447n48. See also
dowries
Marseilles, 459
Martin, John, 1–35, 390
Martire d'Anghiera, Pietro, 403
Masser, Lunardo, 392
Matha, San Giovanni di, 469, 485n73
Mathieu, Pierre, 407
Mauro, Antonio, 256n60, 259nn79,82
Mauro, Fra, of Murano, 392
Maximilian I (Holy Roman Emperor), 157
McNeill, William, 390, 404, 405
Medici, Cosimo I de', 429
Medici family, 140
Medina, Pedro, 402
Memmo, Andrea, 432
Memmo, Giovanni Maria, 305, 307, 311, 314,
318–19
Memmo, Michele, 317
Mendoza, Diego Hurtado de, 402
Mendoza, Gonzalez de, 403
Merano, Articles of (Landesordnung), 153
Mercedarians, 470, 481n28, 485n65
merchants, 16, 67, 405; citizenship of, 82–83,
343; and Great Council, 78, 83; and infor-
mation, 392, 393, 403, 404, 477; and ran-
soming of slaves, 459, 462, 481n26; and
sumptuary laws, 319, 327; and terraferma,
144–45
Merlini, Martino, 151
Merores, Margarete, 74
Mestre, 138
mezzadria, 152
Micanzio, Fulgenzio, 190
Middle East, 1, 19
Milan, 177, 206, 219, 301, 392, 470; arts in,
248, 379; and Habsburg empire, 171, 172;
publishing in, 397, 402
Milledonne, Antonio, 340
Minadoi, G. T., 403
Minucci, Minuccio, 204
Miselli, Giuseppe, 406
missionaries, 462, 465, 481n26

Mocenigo, Alvise, 176, 293nn100,107
Mocenigo, Andrea, 394
Mocenigo, Tommaso, 42
Molin, Nicolò, 199
Molin di Bernardo, Girolamo, 434
Molmenti, Pompeo, 14, 308–9, 421, 505
monarchy, 15, 141, 149, 179, 496, 504,
   512n22; French, 102, 103, 114–15, 518n56
monasteries, 24, 173. *See also* convents
Montemayor, Jorge de, 402
Morea war, 460
Mornay, Philippe du Plessis, 200–201
Morocco, 462
Morosini, Andrea, 395
Morosini, Domenico, 265, 283, 284
Morosini, Francesco, 174
Morosini, Marcantonio, 288n40
Morosini, Marino, Doge (1249–53), 97
Morosini, Paolo, 408
Morosini, Sylvia, 429
Morosini, Tommaso di Andrea, 426, 434
Morosini di Zorzi, Lorenzo, 431
Morosini family, 81, 276, 291n71, 292nn88,89
Morpurgo, Emilio, 518n56
Moschini, Giannantonio, 498
Mozart, Wolfgang Amadeus, 235
Muir, Edward, 12–13, 25–26, 168, 265
murazzi (sea walls), 53, 54
Musatti, Eugenio, 518n56
music, 3, 9, 16, 22, 399; and myth of Venice,
   25–26
Muslims, 454, 455, 462, 468, 470, 477–78
Musurus, Marcus, 400
Mutinelli, Fabio, 504
Muzio, Girolamo, 301
myth, 217, 247, 248, 249
myth of Venice, 2–10, 246; and antimyth, 2–
   9, 27, 188, 207, 209, 492–94, 495, 497,
   498; celebratory, 503–5; and *De magistratibus,* 168, 178–80; doge in, 90; and
   environment, 39–64; and equality of
   nobility, 297–98; founding, 14, 41–42, 43,
   44, 135n67; and French occupation, 230–
   32, 248–49; historiography of, 8–9, 491,
   499, 507, 508; Musatti on, 518n56; and
   music, 25–26; and oligarchy, 231–32;
   Sagredo on, 503, 507; Sarpi on, 187–88,
   209; and *Serrata,* 68, 84n2, 249; and "Spanish" conspiracy, 189, 191; strong, 505–8;
   "weak," 499–503

Nani, Battista, 395, 408
Naples, 172, 175, 206, 398; nobility of, 300–

301, 302; and ransoming of slaves, 455, 456;
   Real Casa Santa della Redentione de' Cat-
   tivi, 456; and "Spanish" conspiracy, 185,
   189, 194, 195, 196, 198
Napoleon Bonaparte, 3, 13, 14, 16, 492,
   514n33; conquest of Venice by, 1, 7, 217,
   219, 223, 228, 247
Nasolini, Sebastiano, 233
Navagero, Andrea, 403
Navagero, Bernardo, 397
Neff, Mary, 339, 342
Nenna, Giovambattista, 300
Netherlands, 139, 188, 205, 399, 406, 512n20
newspapers, 397, 404, 407, 408
New World. *See* Americas
nobiles (nobles), 68, 304, 339
nobility: abuses by, 6, 7, 14; and Charles V,
   170, 174, 176, 178, 181n15; and citizenship,
   496, 512n20; and *cittadini,* 83–84, 278,
   287n34, 298–99, 345–46, 348, 349, 350–
   52, 354; clothing of, 303, 327, 328; and
   constitution, 269, 495, 513n30; Contarini
   on, 299–300, 301; and Council of Ten,
   269–71, 274, 275, 277, 278, 280, 281,
   283, 290n62, 300, 347, 500, 501, 515n41;
   decline of, 221, 251n12, 268, 286n27; definition of, 17–18, 67–88, 72, 83, 263–94;
   298–304, 365; divisions within, 26, 77–83,
   92, 331n26, 353–54, 500; and doge, 78,
   274, 300, 347; economic status of, 169,
   266–69, 300, 301, 319, 327, 329, 347–48,
   495, 500–501, 513nn26,31; and electoral
   system, 74–77, 264; equality within, 297–
   98, 319, 329, 495; families of, 67, 68,
   359n43, 433; and French occupation, 223–
   33, 247–50; and Great Council, 16, 299,
   513n30; historiography of, 10, 26, 493–94,
   498–99, 501, 503, 508; homes of, 252n19,
   304–19; identity of, 295, 304, 316–19; and
   illegitimacy, 76–77, 268–80, 284, 377, 379,
   381; laws on, 144, 286n30, 288n40, 300,
   350; lifestyles of, 295–338; marriages of,
   76–77, 263, 264–65, 268–80, 349, 350–52,
   354, 362n73, 430, 431–32; as oligarchy,
   512nn18,20, 513n30, 514n31; and opera,
   217–23, 250, 253n31; and *popolo,* 69, 83,
   268, 269, 270, 514n33, 518n56; population
   figures for, 16, 268–70; and provincial
   elites, 147, 497, 506, 510n10, 514n33,
   515n41; in public office, 11, 55, 268, 269,
   301; and ransoming of slaves, 455, 471,
   472–73, 476, 484n53; registration of, 80,
   263, 271–75, 300, 347, 353; and the state,

nobility (cont.)
  15, 179, 267, 271, 493–94, 508; and sumptuary laws, 295, 319–29; and terraferma,
  147, 159, 491, 496–97; and trade, 145, 268,
  299, 300–301, 304, 305, 310; and women,
  268–80, 421–22, 428, 429, 436, 439
notaries, 153–54, 271, 308, 422; of Buia,
  155–58; cittadini as, 344, 345, 346, 352,
  358n27; and ransoming of slaves, 466, 467,
  477
novi homines (new men), 73, 74, 76, 79, 80

occultism, 22, 26, 391, 439–40, 441
Oderzo, 42, 49
oligarchy: historiography of, 491, 495, 496–
  97, 498, 500, 517n55; in Italian city states,
  164n38, 298; and myth of Venice, 231–32;
  nobility as, 512nn18,20, 513n30, 514n31;
  in printing industry, 398; in terraferma, 11,
  149, 150; and theater, 217–18, 219, 223,
  224, 225, 226, 242; Venice as, 153, 169, 179
opera, 26, 217–60, 435, 478; death onstage in,
  225; as propaganda, 219–20, 223–50
opera seria, 217–18, 222, 249, 253n31; at La
  Fenice, 218, 220, 227, 228, 233, 247
Ortalli, Gherardo, 68
Orthodox Church, 102, 457
Osoppo, fortress of, 155–56, 157, 158
ospedali grandi, 25
Ossuna, Pietro Giron di (viceroy of Naples),
  187, 189, 192–98, 202, 204, 208
Ottoman empire, 401, 407; and Habsburg
  empire, 462, 469; information from, 389,
  392, 393, 395, 403–4; and Venetian culture,
  477–78. See also Turks
Otway, Thomas, 191–92, 195, 207, 208,
  212n25

Padovano, 151
Padua, 67, 131n40, 145, 150, 153, 399,
  517n53; Annunciation in, 110, 134n67; and
  control of rivers, 61n19, 64n54; university
  in, 1, 93, 144, 422; and Venice, 42, 76, 110,
  142, 148, 149; war with, 73, 79
Paganinis, Paganino, 401
paganism, 218, 234
Paine, Thomas, 223
Palazzo Barbarigo, 311, 317, 318
Palazzo Capello, 317, 318
Palazzo Corner-Spinelli, 305, 306
Palazzo Ducale, 117–22, 396
Palazzo Salviati, 312
Palermo, 456

Palladio, Andrea, 1, 305, 314, 399, 409, 410
Pallavicino, Ferrante, 406
Palma Giovane, 376, 377
Palmanova, 158
Palma Vecchio, 379
Palumbo-Fossati, Isabella, 309, 315
papacy, 82, 172, 186, 188; Venetian relations
  with, 5, 6, 183n57, 189, 199–200, 201, 342,
  369, 512n21. See also Interdict Crisis
Parenzo family, 401
Paris, 398, 399, 402, 403
parishes, 24, 25
Paruta, Paolo, 188, 301, 340, 347, 408
Pasqualigo, Caterina, 428
patronage, artistic, 16–17, 23–26, 225, 365–
  88; historiography of, 23–25, 89; of religious institutions, 23, 24, 386n41; and
  social status, 19, 24–25; of women, 23, 365,
  366, 379–80, 381, 420
patron-client relations, 144, 156, 272, 510n10;
  historiography of, 12, 13, 163n21, 497,
  498–99, 501, 513n31; and women, 350,
  437
Paul V, Pope, 185, 200
Pavia, battle of, 171
peasants: of Buia, 155; of Friuli, 18, 151, 152–
  53, 158, 165n47; historiography of, 12, 18,
  26; and legal system, 138, 142; loyalty to
  Venice of, 138, 141, 142, 152, 159; revolts
  by, 150, 151, 153, 158, 165n47
Pellegrini, Vincenzo, 371, 373
Pellestrina, 469
Pelliccioli, Prudentia, 435
Peloponnesian War, 140
Penn, William, 191
Perna, Pietro, 396
Persia, 389, 393, 403
Pesaro, Francesco, 290n63
Pesaro, Girolamo, 172, 173, 176
Pesaro family, 24, 133n50
Peschiera, 150
Petrarch, 2, 93, 398
Petrucci, Ottaviano dei, 399
Philip II (king of Spain), 188–89, 393
Philip III (king of Spain), 198, 206
Pia Casa del Soccorso, 436
Piave River, 50, 63n39, 64n52
Piazza San Marco, 471, 473, 485n67
Piccolomini, Alessandro, 304, 314
Piedmont, 506
Pietà, the, 437
Pigafetta, Antonio, 392
Pincus, Debra, 10, 89–136

Pinelli, Antonio, 395, 407
Piovego, 47
pirates, 454–55
Pirenne, Henri, 405
Pisa, 90
Pisani, Marino, 77
Pisani, Vettore di Girolamo del Banco, 431
Piscopia, Elena Lucrezia Corner, 422
Pivati, Gianfrancesco, 406
pizzochere, 420, 426, 427
Pocock, J.G.A., 140, 141
Podocataro, Livio, 377, 378
Poland, 139, 406, 469
Pole, Reginald, 370
Polesine, 151
poligrafi, 390, 398, 399, 402, 406–7
politia (refinement, politeness), 297–98, 308, 309, 316
Polo, Marco, 1, 403, 408
Polybius, 15, 138, 140, 398
Popish Plot, 192
popolo, 15, 18, 80, 477; and citizenship, 145, 496; and *cittadini,* 339, 348, 350, 356; families of, 277–78; and Great Council, 69–72, 76, 79; marriages of, 277–78, 350, 362n73; and nobility, 69, 81, 83, 268, 269, 270, 277–78, 350, 362n73, 514n33, 518n56; noble, 348–49; theater for, 224, 226–29, 233; wealthy, 300, 319; women of, 433, 439
popolo grande, 267
populares veteres (distinguished commoners), 68
population: of Buia, 154, 166n57; censuses of, 395; and environment, 55–56; of nobility, 16, 268–70; Venetian, 1, 47, 52, 460
Portugal, 14, 19, 485n65
postal system, 391–92, 406
Postel, Guillaume, 391, 405
Poveri Vergognosi, 428
Povolo, Claudio, 3, 4, 8, 12, 217, 491–519
power, 12, 114, 117, 129n29, 143, 186, 220; economic, 300, 327; hierarchical, 492–93; historiography of, 10, 497, 506
praedestinatio, 14, 42, 93, 110, 122, 126n16
Preto, Paolo, 197, 202, 390
Price, Lake, 305, 306, 311, 312, 317, 318
priests, 156, 353
printing, 1, 389, 398. *See also* publishing
Priuli, Girolamo, 21, 44, 169, 212n31, 265, 340, 349
Priuli, Lorenzo, 332n35, 386n35
Priuli, Maria, 281
Priuli family, 289n50, 291n74

private and public spheres, 12, 190–91, 209, 292n96, 305; government control of, 270, 274, 283–84, 298; and information, 391, 396; and sumptuary laws, 319, 322, 327
propaganda, 219–20, 223–50
property rights, 20, 186, 271
prostitution, 436, 439
Protestantism, 156, 200–201, 438, 439
provveditori di comun, 82, 344
Provveditori sopra Ospedali e Luoghi Pii, 456–60, 461, 465–76, 478
public office, 277, 294n110, 320, 327, 398; *cittadini* in, 339–42, 344, 352, 353–54, 355, 356; and nobility, 268, 269, 301. *See also* bureaucracy
public sphere. *See* private and public spheres
publishing, 23, 389–419; and book trade, 396, 401, 402, 405; decline and revival of, 404–5, 406; and heretical books, 396, 405; of historical works, 399, 412–13; languages used in, 389, 401, 405, 407, 423; plagiarism in, 398, 403
Pullan, Brian, 22, 24, 339, 342, 348, 454

Quarantia, 267, 274, 347, 500; and electoral system, 72, 73, 74, 75, 77, 80
Quarantia Civile, 157, 158
Quarantia Criminale, 344
Quartari family, 350, 355
Queller, Donald, 268
Querini, Barbara Contarini, 431
Querini, Girolamo, 280
Querini, Lise, 366, 373, 374, 377, 380, 388n54
Querini family, 77, 82, 278, 279
Querini-Tiepolo conspiracy (1310), 4, 71, 76, 80, 81, 83; and doge, 91, 92; in opera, 226, 227

Raby, Julian, 390
Racine, Jean, 256n61
Ramberti, Benedetto, 403–4
Ramusio, Giovanni Battista, 403
Ranke, Leopold von, 4, 195, 340, 395
Raulich, Italo, 196
Ravagnani, Benintendi, 93
Ravenna, 49, 95, 172, 175, 176, 177, 183n57
reason of state, 187–88, 189, 190, 191, 207, 209, 461; and "Spanish" conspiracy, 196, 198
reform: governmental, 34n65, 69, 179, 265, 282–84; Tridentine, 365, 369, 370, 371, 381, 430

Reformation, 396
Regazzola, Hieronymo, 431
Reggio, 248
regional state, 12, 13, 20, 144, 493
Regnault, Nicholas, 194, 195, 207
relazioni, 393, 397
religion, 19, 23, 186, 190, 191, 511n13; and
  women, 438–40, 441, 443n7. *See also* the
  Church; heresy; *and particular religions*
Renaissance, the, 4, 6, 90; republicanism in, 5,
  13, 137–67; Venetian nobility in, 263–94;
  women in, 420–53
republicanism, 9–10, 15, 25–26, 137–67, 170,
  187; exportability of, 144; in Florence, 5, 6,
  67, 137, 140, 141; and legal system, 138,
  139, 143, 153, 156, 158, 159; in opera, 223,
  258n77; Venetian, 3, 4–5, 9, 12–13, 67,
  149
res publica, 142–43, 145–46, 153, 158, 159;
  Buia as, 155, 156
revolution, 247, 257n67; of 1688 (England),
  191; American, 141; French, 141, 223, 229,
  248; in opera, 248, 250
Rialto, the, 14, 45, 48, 57n1, 144, 230, 396
Ricci, Giuseppe, 407
Ricci, Sebastiano, 383n11
Richelieu, Cardinal, 186
Ricoeur, Paul, 8, 280
Ridolfi, Carlo, 375
Rizzardi, Costantino, 156, 157
Rizzardi, Simone, 156
Rizzardi family, 156
Robusti, Ottavia ("Tintoretta"), 435
Roe, Sir Thomas, 206
Romanin, Samuele, 4, 195, 499, 503
Roman law, 144, 146, 154, 509n6
Romano, Dennis, 1–35, 266, 267, 437
Rome (Italy), 171, 248, 400, 402, 495; infor-
  mation in, 390, 397; myth of, 249; in opera,
  242, 243, 246, 247, 258n77; and ransoming
  of slaves, 456, 469, 471; and Venice, 25,
  138, 392, 394, 397
Rome, ancient, 14, 145, 508; and republican-
  ism, 140, 141, 142
Ronsaggio, Luigi, 403
Rosand, Ellen, 25
Rösch, Gerhard, 10, 17, 67–88, 263, 265
Rousseau, Jean-Jacques, 3, 25, 223
Rubertis, Achille de, 196
Ruggiero, Guido, 26, 94, 266, 270
Ruscelli, Girolamo, 398, 399
Ruskin, John, 4
Rycaut, Paul, 408

Sabbadino, Cristoforo, 63n38
Sabbadino, Paolo, 62n38
Sabellico, Marcantonio, 72, 156, 339, 340
sacrality: of government, 94, 115, 123, 190–
  91, 496; of ruler, 89–136, 114–15, 511n13
Sadoleto, Jacopo, 370
Sagredo, Agostino, 499–503, 505, 507
Sagredo, Caterina, 441, 453n116
Sagredo, Cecilia Grimani, 453n116
Sagredo, Giovanni, 407
Sagundino family, 350
Saint-Didier, Alexandre Toussaint Limojan
  de, 395
Saint-Réal, abbé de, 192, 195, 208
saints, 368; "living," 391, 405, 439; name, 375,
  381
Salomone, Castellano, bishop, 134n64
Salvago, Giovanni Battista, 462
Sambo, Piero, 64n53
Sandei, Francesco, 352
Sandi, Vettor, 340, 499
San Francesco della Vigna, church of, 369,
  379, 381
San Giorgio, church of (Braida, Verona),
  368–69
San Giovanni Evangelista, chapel of (San
  Marco), 113
San Marco, church of, 23, 112, 129n31, 370;
  Baptistery of, 99–102, 111, 113, 115, 116;
  and doge, 93–95, 97, 111; procurators of,
  89, 98, 99, 113, 130n32, 341, 343; tombs
  in, 99–102, 107–11
Sanmicheli, Michele, 380
San Nicolò, estuary of, 51
San Sebastiano, church of, 23, 365–88
Sansovino, Francesco: on doge, 91, 98; on
  foreigners, 21; on palaces, 296–97, 308,
  309, 316, 317, 329; publications of, 397,
  398, 399, 404, 408, 409, 413–14
Sansovino, Jacopo, 296, 377, 378, 382n2,
  385n23
Santa Maria Formosa, church of, 466
Santa Maria Gloriosa dei Frari, church of,
  104, 106, 107, 132n50
Sant'Elena, church of, 379
Santi Giovanni e Paolo, church of, 95, 96
Santissima Trinità, confraternity of, 468, 473,
  483n47, 485n69, 486nn78,79
Santo Spirito in Isola, church of, 370
Sanudo, Marino, 264, 265, 309, 390, 394, 396;
  on aftermath of Agnadello, 138, 149, 150;
  on *cittadini,* 340, 349, 360n47; map of, 310;
  on nobility, 85n22, 274, 286n30, 288n40;

on palaces, 308, 327; on wars of Italy, 173, 175, 182n24
San Zaccaria, church of, 379
Sardella, Pierre, 390
Saros, Nikolaos, 400
Sarpi, Paolo, 1, 6, 406, 495, 512n21; and myth of Venice, 187–88, 209; in public office, 190–91; and "Spanish" conspiracy, 185, 198, 200, 201, 202–7
Sassoferrato, Bartolo di, 298
Savorgnan, Antonio, 164n32
Savorgnan, Girolamo, 156, 157, 158, 163n22
Savorgnan family, 12, 155, 156
Savoy, 196
Scarabello, Giovanni, 11, 197, 270
Schiavo, Domenico, 80
Schiavone, Andrea, 371, 373, 388n52
Schiller, Friedrich, 208
Schio, 146
Schipa, Michelangelo, 198
Scott, James C., 160n4
Scrovegni, Enrico, 76
scuole (confraternities), 24, 341, 343, 345, 361n63; and ransoming of slaves, 458, 468, 473, 476–77, 483n47
scuole grandi, 24, 35n73, 163n22, 190, 340, 379; and *cittadini,* 342, 345, 346, 348, 354
scuole piccole, 24, 438, 466
Second Genoese War (1294–99), 70, 82
Senate, 15, 179, 205, 300, 500, 512n21; on citizenship, 354; and electoral system, 72, 73; and information, 393, 395, 404, 405, 406, 408; and marriage, 281, 282–83; and nobility, 269, 270, 274, 283, 298; and ransoming of slaves, 455–60, 461, 463, 465–71, 474; and "Spanish" conspiracy, 196, 197; and sumptuary laws, 320, 322, 323, 324, 325, 326, 327; and wars of Italy, 170, 171, 174, 175, 176; and women, 429, 446n42
Sensa (feast of Christ's Ascension), 97, 129n27, 257n71, 478, 485n67; operas at, 222, 224–29
Serbia, 102
serfdom, 149, 152
Serrata, the (Closing of the Great Council), 16, 17, 27, 67–88; and *cittadini,* 344, 346, 352, 353; and constitution, 68, 263, 508; and doge, 89, 90; and electoral system, 72–77; historiography of, 263, 266; and myth of Venice, 68, 84n2, 249; and nobility, 221, 267, 271, 298; and noble commoners, 348; in opera, 217, 226, 227, 254n33; and

Querini-Tiepolo conspiracy, 81; second, 69, 266, 269, 271, 272, 347; and social structure, 263, 265; third, 69, 263–94, 274
Sertor, Gaetano, 247, 248, 258n77
servants, 18, 297, 301, 305, 318, 350, 437; and sumptuary laws, 320, 321, 323, 326, 329
Seville, 400
Sewell, William H., Jr., 220
sexuality, 22, 26, 420, 428–29, 432–33, 465
Seyssel, Claude de, 340
Sforza, Ascanio, 341
Sforza, Francesco (duke of Milan), 172, 177
Shakespeare, William, 186, 205, 208, 454
Shaw, George Bernard, 209
shipbuilding industry, 460–61
Sidney, Viscount, 207
Sile River, 50, 52, 64n52
Sinding-Larsen, Staale, 8
slaves, 271, 350; prices of, 458–59, 461, 468; processions of, 470–76, 477, 478; ransoming of, 21, 454–87; and sumptuary laws, 320, 323
Slavonic, Old Church, 389, 401, 410–11
Slavs, 21
social status, 16, 20, 24–25, 278
social structure, 78; and gender, 22, 278; hierarchy in, 15–16, 220–23, 331n26, 492–93, 494, 510n8; historiography of, 15–22, 89, 339–41; mobility within, 9, 17–18, 19, 21; and opera, 220–23, 233; and *Serrata,* 263, 265. See also *cittadini;* nobility; *popolo*
Sografi, Antonio Simeone, 224, 225–26, 227, 233, 247, 249, 254nn33,36, 259n79; and *Mitridate,* 234, 235, 241, 244, 246
Solis, Antonio de, 407
Soranzo, Alvise, 374, 380
Soranzo, Angela di Alvise, 427–28
Soranzo, Benetto, 428
Soranzo, Francesco, 374, 375, 379, 381
Soranzo, Giovanni (d. 1500), 366, 374, 375
Soranzo, Giovanni (d. 1558), 373, 374, 375, 388n54
Soranzo, Giovanni, Doge (1312–28), 99–102, 104
Soranzo, Jacopo, 374, 381, 387n51
Soranzo, Lazzaro, 395
Soranzo, Pietro, 374, 375, 380, 381
Soranzo, Remigio, 308
Soranzo, Vettor, 173, 374
Soranzo family, 16, 366, 371, 373–75, 379–81, 387n43
sovereignty, 495–96, 499, 501–5, 507, 508

Spain, 170, 393, 401; "black legend" of, 188;
and England, 188, 206, 207; and Italy, 171,
174; and ransoming of slaves, 455, 459, 461,
464, 469, 485n65; and "Spanish" conspir-
acy, 192–98, 200, 201, 204, 205, 209; and
Turks, 188, 206; and Venice, 138, 177,
188–89, 394, 402
"Spanish" conspiracy of 1618, 185–216
Spanish language, 389, 412
Speladi, Bartolomeo, 350
Speladi, Zuan, 350
Speladi family, 355
Spinelli, Gasparo, 194
St. Andrew, 113
St. Anthony, 440
St. Bartholomew, 107, 109
St. Elizabeth of Portugal, 106, 133n57
St. Francis, 106
St. John the Baptist, 100, 102
St. Mark, 14, 42, 103–4, 126n16, 134n62; and
doge, 93–94, 97–98, 99, 117–22, 123; lion
of, 58n2, 117, 118, 119, 120, 122, 149, 150,
160; on tombs, 107, 109
St. Sebastian, 368, 369, 370
state, the, 509n7; active vs. reactive, 492–93;
European, 209; and family, 190, 225–26; in
Italy, 493; modern, 143, 144; nature of,
186–87, 188, 191; regional, 12, 13, 20, 144,
493; Venetian, 4, 281, 494
stato da mar, 10, 457, 466, 467
stato di terra, 60n18
Suleiman the Magnificent, Sultan, 172, 174
Sumatra, 392
sumptuary laws, 19, 220, 259n83, 295, 319–
29
surnames, 345–46, 348, 351
Sweden, 406
Syria, 392, 405

Tafuri, Manfredo, 26, 27, 184n69, 265, 282
Talassi, Madalena, 435
Talier, Angelo, 230, 231
Tarabotti, Arcangela, 423, 424, 440
Tasso, Torquato, 401
Tasso family, 392
taxes, 173, 264, 515nn41,44, 518n56; of cit-
tadini, 353, 355; and sumptuary laws, 322,
323
Taylor, Charles, 281
Teatro Civico, 227, 247, 260n83
Teatro La Fenice. See La Fenice opera house
Teatro San Giovanni Grisostomo, 219, 227–
28, 254n36

Teatro San Luca, 219
Teatro San Samuele, 248, 258nn73,77
technology, 48, 52, 53–54, 55
tenancy, 151–52
terraferma: after Agnadello, 138, 147–48, 168,
169; autonomy of, 506, 516n52; citizenship
in, 137, 163n22, 491; cittadini in, 159,
357n15; conquest of, 40, 45, 50, 53, 148,
506; economy of, 144–45, 148–53,
513n26; historiography of, 8, 10, 11, 13,
20, 60n18, 494–97, 503, 510nn8,10,
511n12; legal system in, 143, 144, 146–47,
154, 502; loss of, 147–48, 219; and myth of
Venice, 42–44; oligarchy in, 11, 149, 150;
and ransoming of slaves, 457, 460, 465–66,
467, 471; and republicanism, 137, 141–42.
See also elites, provincial
textile industry, 1, 337n107, 345, 434
theater: commercial, 217–18; for popolo, 224,
226–29, 233; as propaganda, 219–20, 223–
50. See also opera
Thirty Years' War, 185, 193, 201
Tiberius II (Byzantine emperor), 97
Tiepolo, Baiamonte, 77, 81, 92. See also
Querini-Tiepolo conspiracy
Tiepolo, Domenico, 498–99
Tiepolo, Jacomo, 71
Tiepolo, Jacopo, Doge (1229–49), 81, 95, 96
Tiepolo, Lorenzo, 81, 100, 397
Tiepolo family, 77, 81, 82
Tintoretto, 381, 387n51
Titian, 2, 107, 311, 365, 370, 371, 372, 377,
379
Toledo, Don Pedro de (governor of Milan),
192, 193
Torcello, 52
Tories, 191
Torlioni, Fra Bernardo, 367, 370, 375, 377
Torre, Francesco della, 495
Torresano, Andrea, 401
trade: book, 396, 401, 402, 405; cittadini in,
339, 342; and environment, 40, 50, 54; and
information, 391, 404; and nobility, 5, 268,
281–82, 299, 300–301, 304, 305, 310;
regional, 20, 408; slave, 456–63, 464, 468,
470, 481n26; and Venetian citizenship, 82–
83; Venice as center of, 19, 43, 149, 151,
152, 404; wealth from, 1, 297, 319, 329;
women in, 434
traghetti, 24
Trebbi, Giuseppe, 339
Trelawny, Charles, 207
Trevigiano, 151

Trevisan, Contarina, 428
Trevisan, Nicolò, 70, 71
Trevisan family, 276, 277, 278, 279, 291nn71,73
Treviso, 42, 76, 134n64, 142, 360n47
Trevor-Roper, Hugh, 197
Tridentine reforms. *See* Council of Trent
Trieste, 226, 234
Trinitarians (Order of the Holy Trinity), 469–78; and slave processions, 472–73, 474, 475
Tripoli, 455, 462, 463, 469, 472
Tron, Andrea, 432
Tron, Antonio, 288n40
Tron, Caterina Dolfin, 423, 432, 441, 453n116
Tron, Hieronimo, 174
Tron, Luca, 290n63
Tübingen, 401
Tunis, 455, 459, 462, 482n36, 484n56
Turin, 397, 469, 470, 471
Turks, 174, 400, 405; in Friuli, 156, 172, 182n24; information on, 392, 394, 398, 403–4, 409; and slave trade, 455, 457, 458, 461, 464; and Spain, 188, 206; and Venice, 14, 21, 60n18, 157, 177, 342, 477–78. *See also* Ottoman empire
Turloni family, 350
Tuscany, 298
Tyrrhenian Sea, 174

Udine, 151, 156, 157, 172
Ulloa, Alfonso de, 402
Ulvioni, Paolo, 404
unanimitas, 16, 147, 297, 365
United Provinces, 201
Uskoks, 187, 193, 204, 455

vagabonds, 8, 18
Vailà, battle of, 160n1. *See also* Agnadello, battle of
Valgrisi, Vincenzo, 396, 398, 400, 405, 408
Valier, Agostino, 424, 427
Valle, Pietro della, 403, 407
Valois, Felice di, 469
Valtelline, the, 205, 206
Vasari, Giorgio, 25, 380, 381, 388n52
Vavassore, Giovanni Andrea, 392
Vecellio, Cesare, 301, 302, 303, 328
venezianità, 23, 25
Veneziano, Paolo, 107
Venice: economic hegemony of, 19, 149–53, 404; exceptionalism of, 2, 23, 25; expansion of, 44–48, 137; guides to, 408–

9; historiography of, 1–35, 491–519; iconography of, 40–41, 183n51; isolation of, 42–43, 44; Napoleon's conquest of, 1, 7, 217, 219, 223; political history of, 9–15; *praedestinatio,* 14, 42, 93, 110, 122, 126n16; rise and fall of, 13–14, 23, 27, 496, 497; stability of, 15, 21, 339. *See also* myth of Venice
Venice, Peace of (1177), 189
Venier family, 273, 277, 289n50, 291n74
Ventura, Angelo, 6, 7, 11, 12, 34n65, 137, 159, 267
Ventura, Comin, 397
Verona, 145, 150, 154, 219, 502; painters from, 370–71, 380; and Venice, 76, 142, 149
Verona, Raffaello da, 371
Veronese, Benedetto, 388n55
Veronese, Paolo Caliari, 23, 365–88
Vespucci, Amerigo, 403
Vicenza, 145–46, 150, 397; opera in, 226, 234; and Venice, 12, 142, 149
vicini, 62n33
Vico family, 348
Vienna, 172, 406, 471
Viganò, Onorato, 222
Viggiano, Alfredo, 146
Vinciguerra, Antonio, 342, 350
violence: popular, 26; sacrificial, 231–32, 255n51
Virgin Mary, 190, 440; images of, 106–7, 109, 369–70, 383n13; and Venice, 103–4, 255n45
Viroli, Maurizio, 187, 191, 207, 209
virtù (fame, virtue), 140, 298, 355
Visconti, Giangaleazzo (duke of Milan), 141, 161n10
Vitruvius, 394, 399, 409, 410
Vittoria, Alessandro, 371
Vitturi, Giovanni, 173
Vitturi family, 273, 291n74
Vivarini, Antonio, 379
Vlastos, Nicholas, 400
Voltaire, 192
von Speyer, Johan, 400
Vrins, Francesco, 310, 311

War of the League of Cambrai. *See under* Cambrai, League of
Weber, Max, 143, 144, 158
wills: holograph, 421, 422; and ransoming of slaves, 466, 467, 476, 484n53; of women, 433, 435, 436, 452n110

witchcraft, 18, 26, 436. *See also* magic
women, 420–53; as art patrons, 23, 365, 366,
373–80, 381, 420; as *cittadini,* 145, 287n34,
350–52, 433; and definition of nobility,
263, 268–80; economic rights of, 271,
293n99; economic roles of, 25, 420, 424,
428, 433–36; historiography of, 8, 16, 18,
421; household roles of, 305, 314–15; and
illegitimacy, 278–80, 281, 284, 290n67,
428, 429; as lay spinsters, 424–28; lower-
class, 421, 433, 437–38, 439; noble, 268–
80, 287nn33,36, 421–22, 428, 429, 436,
439; political roles of, 82, 148, 264; and
ransoming of slaves, 484n53; and religion,
438–40, 441, 443n7; sexuality of, 428–29;
432–33; as slaves, 463, 481n28, 482n32; and
sumptuary laws, 319, 321, 322, 323, 326,
327; in theater, 242, 260n83; in third *Serrata,* 270–80; wills of, 433, 435, 436,
452n110
Wootton, David, 191, 192, 205
workers, 8, 16, 20, 26. *See also* artisans
Wotton, Sir Henry, 199, 200

Xenophon, 304, 334n71, 398

Zambler, Amelia, 196
Zane family, 291n74
Zannini, Andrea, 339
Zara, 90
Zardon, Antonio, 256n59
Zen, Carlo, 350
Zeno, Caterino, 403
Zeno, Ranieri, Doge (1253–68), 97, 126n16,
129n27
Zeno family, 278
Zenos, Demetrios, 400
Zero River, 52
Ziani, Pietro, 81
Ziani family, 81
Zingarelli, Nicola, 233, 235, 239–45
Zitelle, the, 436
Zonca, Giovanni, 405
Zorzi, Francesco, 391
Zorzi, Marino, Doge, 92
Zulian family, 291n74

The Library of Congress has cataloged the hardcover edition of this book as follows:

Venice reconsidered : the history and civilization of an Italian city-
state, 1297-1797 / edited by John Martin and Dennis Romano.
        p.   cm.
Includes bibliographical references and index.
ISBN 0-8018-6312-0 (alk. paper)
1. Venice (Italy)—Civilization—To 1797. 2. City-states—Italy—
Civilization. I. Martin, John, 1951–   II. Romano, Dennis, 1951–
DG675.6.V39 2000
945´.31—dc21   00-021349

ISBN 0-8018-7308-8 (pbk.)